Money, Banking, and the Economy

A Monetarist View

Money, Banking, and the Economy
A Monetarist View

BARRY N. SIEGEL
University of Oregon

ACADEMIC PRESS
A Subsidiary of Harcourt Brace Jovanovich
New York   London
Paris   San Diego   San Francisco   São Paulo
Sydney   Tokyo   Toronto

Academic Press, Inc.
111 Fifth Avenue
New York, New York 10003

United Kingdom Edition published by
Academic Press, Inc. (London) Ltd.
24/28 Oval Road, London NW1 7DX

ISBN: 0-12-641420-3

Printed in the United States of America

To My Wife Jetta

Contents

Preface   *xiii*

1
Problems of a Money Economy

1.1 The Functions of Money and Economic Efficiency   *3*
1.2 Money and Economic Instability   *12*
     Summary   *22*
     Discussion Questions   *22*
     Important Terms and Concepts   *23*
     Additional Readings   *23*

2
The United States Money Stock: Changing Definitions

2.1 The U.S. Money Stock—Old and New Definitions   *25*
2.2 Which Definition of Money Is Best?   *35*
     Summary   *39*
     Discussion Questions   *40*
     Important Terms and Concepts   *40*
     Additional Readings   *41*

3
Financial Markets and Financial Institutions

3.1 Types of Financial Markets   *43*
3.2 Some Detail on Financial Intermediaries   *51*
3.3 Federal and Federally Sponsored Credit Agencies   *55*
3.4 Financial Instruments   *57*
     Summary   *68*
     Discussion Questions   *69*
     Important Terms and Concepts   *70*
     Additional Readings   *70*

4
The Banking Business: Fundamentals

4.1 Commercial Banks as Firms 73
4.2 Time and Savings Deposits; Borrowing and Bank Capital 86
4.3 Bank Assets 93
Summary 97
Discussion Questions 98
Important Terms and Concepts 98
Additional Readings 98

5
Bank Operations, Regulation, and Structure

5.1 Running a Bank 101
5.2 Bank Regulation 113
5.3 The Structure of the U.S. Banking Industry 118
Summary 125
Discussion Questions 125
Important Terms and Concepts 126
Additional Readings 126

6
The Money Supply Process

6.1 An M-1 Money Supply Model 129
6.2 Shifts in the Money Multipliers 142
6.3 Analysis of Monetary Changes, 1960–1978 144
Summary 146
Discussion Questions 146
Important Terms and Concepts 147
Additional Readings 147

7
Organization and Control of the Federal Reserve System

7.1 Organization of the Federal Reserve System 149
7.2 Independence of the Federal Reserve System 158
7.3 The Fed's Declining Membership 160
7.4 The Monetary Control Act of 1980 161
Summary 164
Discussion Questions 164

Important Terms and Concepts *165*
Additional Readings *165*

8
The Federal Reserve System as a
Central Bank
8.1 The Fed's Balance Sheet *167*
8.2 Member Bank Reserve Equation *173*
8.3 The Monetary Base as a Policy Target *177*
Summary *180*
Discussion Questions *180*
Important Terms and Concepts *181*
Additional Readings *181*

9
The Instruments of Monetary
Policy
9.1 Open Market Operations *183*
9.2 The Discount Mechanism *187*
9.3 Reserve Requirements as a Policy Instrument *194*
9.4 Selective Instruments of Monetary Policy *197*
9.5 Moral Suasion *205*
Summary *205*
Discussion Questions *206*
Important Terms and Concepts *206*
Additional Readings *207*

10
The Strategy of Monetary Policy
10.1 An Outline of the Strategy Problem *209*
10.2 Past Monetary Policy Strategies *217*
10.3 Recent Strategies of Monetary Policy *224*
Summary *232*
Discussion Questions *233*
Important Terms and Concepts *233*
Additional Readings *233*

11
Say's Principle and Monetary
Equilibrium
11.1 Demand, Supply, and the Concept of Market
Equilibrium: A Review *237*

11.2 Say's Principle *241*

11.3 Monetary Equilibrium and Disequilibrium *245*

11.4 Income Equilibrium and Monetary Equilibrium *249*

11.5 Equilibrium Income and Full Employment *252*

Summary *253*

Discussion Questions *254*

Important Terms and Concepts *254*

Additional Readings *255*

12
Money and the Theory of Money Income

12.1 The Quantity Theory of Money *257*

12.2 The Demand for Money *262*

12.3 A Monetary Theory of Money Income *270*

Summary *280*

Discussion Questions *282*

Important Terms and Concepts *283*

Additional Readings *283*

13
The Rate of Interest and the Theory of Income

13.1 Say's Principle and the Bond Market *288*

13.2 The Theory of Interest *291*

13.3 A Monetary Theory of Income *307*

Summary *311*

Appendix: The Term Structure of Interest Rates *312*

Discussion Questions *315*

Important Terms and Concepts *316*

Additional Readings *316*

14
The Federal Budget and the Economy

14.1 Methods of Financing Government Spending *319*

14.2 Effects of a Pure Fiscal Policy on Money Income *322*

14.3 Fiscal Policy Financed with Changes in the Money Supply *33t*

14.4 Empirical Evidence on Fiscal Policy *340*

Summary *341*

Discussion Questions *342*

Important Terms and Concepts *343*

Additional Readings *343*

15

Transmission Mechanism of Monetary Influences on Income

15.1 How Monetary Shocks Affect Nominal Income *346*

15.2 The Effects of Monetary Shocks on Output and Prices *354*

Summary *364*

Discussion Questions *365*

Important Terms and Concepts *366*

Additional Readings *366*

16

Money and Business Cycles: The U.S. Experience

16.1 Monetary and Nonmonetary Theories of the Business Cycle *369*

16.2 Behavior of Money Supply over the Business Cycle *374*

16.3 Cyclical Changes in the Cambridge *k* (or the Income Velocity of Money) *381*

16.4 A "Neoclassical" Supply-side Monetary Model *385*

Summary *387*

Discussion Questions *390*

Important Terms and Concepts *390*

Additional Readings *390*

17

Inflation: Cause and Effects

17.1 The Problem and Its Causes *393*

17.2 Some Myths of Inflation *404*

17.3 Effects of Inflation on Households and Business *411*

17.4 Inflationary Redistributions of Wealth and Income *417*

17.5 Effects of Inflation on Resource Allocation *422*

Summary *423*

Discussion Questions *425*

Important Terms and Concepts *426*

Additional Readings *426*

18

Inflation and Unemployment: The Stagflation Problem

18.1 The Natural Unemployment Rate Hypothesis *430*

18.2 Expectations-augmented Phillips Curves and the Accelerationist Hypothesis *436*

Summary *447*

Discussion Questions *448*

Important Terms and Concepts *448*

Additional Readings *449*

19
Money, the Balance of Payments, and Exchange Rates

19.1 Money and the Balance of Payments under Fixed Exchange Rates *451*

19.2 Flexible Exchange Rates and the Purchasing Power Parity Theory *466*

19.3 World Inflation *475*

Summary *477*

Discussion Questions *479*

Important Terms and Concepts *480*

Additional Readings *480*

20
New Views on Stabilization Policies

20.1 Brief Review of Empirical Evidence on Policy Activism *484*

20.2 The Credibility Effect, the German Hyperinflation, and the Fed *493*

20.3 Incomes Policies *495*

20.4 Can Democracy Tame Inflation? *497*

Summary *506*

Discussion Questions *508*

Important Terms and Concepts *508*

Additional Readings *508*

Glossary *511*

Index *533*

Preface

Readers are warned that they will find no IS–LM diagrams in this book. Instead, they will find a systematic development of a model of nominal income based upon the Cambridge equation and the loanable funds theory of interest. They will also find an application of that model to the business cycle, to inflation and stagflation, to the balance of payments and foreign exchange rates, and to monetary and fiscal policy theories.

The major innovation of this book is its systematic "monetarist" approach. The approach is a blend of the pre-Keynesian quantity theory, the tradition represented by D.H. Robertson, and the modern monetarist school, represented by Milton Friedman and his followers. Although some space is devoted to the question of monetary versus nonmonetary theories of the business cycle, very little attention is paid to the monetarist–Keynesian debate. This by now stale conflict was reduced by Franco Modigliani in 1977 to a discussion over the value of activist stabilization policies.[1] In 1980, stabilization policies themselves were "officially"—but probably temporarily—laid to rest by the Joint Economic Committee of Congress and the International Monetary Fund.[2]

As a teacher, I have found that an eclectic approach to monetary theory more often confuses than enlightens the typical undergraduate student. In addition, it frequently leads to rather academic discussions of doctrinal history that are more important to the instructor than the student. Students expect and want a theory that helps them understand and evaluate events and policies of their own time. In my opinion, the monetarist framework is most appropriate for that purpose. Keynesian economics, as J.R. Hicks once said, is depression economics. When it came to inflation, Keynes himself was more of a monetarist than a Keynesian.[3]

Except for its monetarist emphasis, the book is conventional. Any money and banking text worth its salt must equip students with knowledge of the language and institutions of the field. Thus the first half of the book is taken up with the concept of money (Chapter 1); the new and

---

[1]Franco Modigliani, "The Monetarist Controversy, or, Should We Forsake Stabilization Policies," *American Economic Review*, Vol. 67, No. 2, March 1977, pp. 1–19.

[2]*The 1980 Midyear Review of the Economy: The Recession and the Recovery* (Washington, D.C.: Joint Economic Committee, U.S. Congress, August 1980), Chapter II; and the International Monetary Fund, *Finance and Development*, September 1980, pp. 9–10.

[3]For substantiation of this point, see Thomas M. Humphrey, "Keynes on Inflation," Federal Reserve Bank of Richmond, *Economic Review*, Vol. 67, No. 1, January/February 1981, pp. 3–13.

old definitions of the things that serve as money (Chapter 2); the structure and institutions of financial markets and financial instruments (Chapter 3); banks, banking markets, and banking regulations (Chapters 4 and 5); the money supply process (Chapter 6); the structure and functions of the Federal Reserve System (Chapters 7, 8, and 9); and an analysis of the problem of implementing monetary policy (Chapter 10). The book is as up-to-date as possible on important banking and financial legislation—including a discussion of the Monetary Control Act of 1980—and the practices of the monetary authorities. In these times of rapid change, however, a six-month lag in publication can render parts of the manuscript obsolete. Today, competence in teaching money and banking requires daily perusal of such publications as *The Wall Street Journal*.

The middle sections of the book are devoted to a development of the monetary theory of income. Chapter 11 discusses the Clower–Leijonhufvud idea of Say's Principle, a concept that is essential for understanding the intimate connection between the idea of monetary equilibrium and income equilibrium. But attainment of income or monetary equilibrium in an economy requires application of the Fundamental Proposition of Monetary Theory, which, according to J.M. Keynes and Milton Friedman, asserts that movements in income and/or prices are required to bring into equality the aggregate demand for and the existing stock of money. This proposition is the cornerstone of the quantity theory of money as described by the equation of exchange or the Cambridge equation (Chapter 12).

A complete monetary model of nominal income requires a theory of interest. Chapter 13 develops such a theory through the loanable funds approach and then integrates the theory of interest into the theory of income through the agency of a two-equation model that simultaneously determines the rate of interest and nominal income. The model is then extended (Chapter 14) to include the effects of fiscal policy on these two variables.

Chapters 15 and 16 draw upon the work of Milton Friedman and Anna Schwartz, Michael Darby and Robert Barro to develop the connection between money and business cycles. This "frontier stuff" is a natural framework for breaking down the theory of nominal income into a theory of real output and a theory of price level fluctuations. Moreover, it sets the stage for Chapters 17 and 18, which provide rather extensive treatments of inflation and stagflation. The discussion in these chapters keys on the crucial role of inflationary expectations—adaptive and rational—in explaining the links between monetary changes, changes in output, and changes in prices.

The last two chapters are also close to the frontiers of macroeconomic thought. Chapter 19 features a monetarist model of the balance of payments and exchange rates, and Chapter 20 provides a monetarist–public choice perspective upon the efficacy of monetary and fiscal policies. Readers will note that the author lets off a little ideological steam in this chapter.

Readers who wish a more detailed guide to this book are urged to consult the table of contents and especially the chapter preview outlines.

I wish to thank a number of people who have kindly read and criticized portions of the manuscript. These include, first, students in my money and banking classes, many of whom were subjected to the first 14 chapters in test runs. I also want to thank my colleagues, Robert Campbell, Richard Davis, Henry Goldstein, Michael A. Groves, and Stephen Haynes for their encouragement and comments upon various parts of the book. Richard Sandell (Mercy College), Conrad Caligaris (Northeastern University), John Marcis (Kansas State University), Allen Sanderson (Princeton University), and Susan Woodward (UCLA) were most helpful in reviewing the manuscript for the publisher.

Finally, I want to thank my wife, Jetta. Without her untiring and good natured (and sometimes not so good natured) help, this book would have taken at least one more year to write. She typed the bulk of the manuscript and provided invaluable editorial comment. I drew heavily upon credit built up from 29 years of marriage.

BARRY N. SIEGEL

Eugene, Oregon

Money, Banking, and the Economy
A Monetarist View

Problems of a Money Economy

1

O U T L I N E

The Functions of Money and Economic Efficiency
Direct and Indirect Exchange
Benefits of Indirect Exchange through Money
Money as a Standard of Value (Unit of Account)
Money as a Store of Value
Money as a Standard for Deferred Payment
Money and Capital Formation
Money and Economic Instability
Say's Law, Say's Principle, and "Generalized Overproduction"
Monetary Sources of the Business Cycle
The Role of Credit in Business Fluctuations

Money is a social institution that brings great benefits to people by permitting efficient exchanges of goods and services. But when money is mishandled by the powers that be, it is a source of inflation and unemployment. It would be good to have a monetary system that generates only benefits; but that is probably not possible. Why this is so will be an important part of the story told in this book. Before we proceed with that story, however, we must spend some time discussing the functions of money and, particularly, the benefits that accrue to society from its use.

1.1
The functions of money and economic efficiency

Lenin is said to have once declared that the best way to kill off a capitalist society is to debauch its currency. How right he was! But he should have gone on to say that *any* society that depends upon the division of labor and exchange between productive parties would be severely retarded if its monetary system were destroyed. Money is a social institution that transcends the categories of socialism and capitalism. It is an institution that any society pretending to sophistication and complexity must sooner or later adopt. Money greatly reduces the costs of market exchange, and it provides a basis for rational economic calculations. Moreover, economic growth, which depends on technological change and capital formation, is significantly enhanced by its presence.

All these good things are difficult to demonstrate with facts. For that reason, the benefits associated with a well-functioning monetary system may go unappreciated by people who live within such a system. Even so, we can develop such an appreciation by comparing the operations of a money-exchange economy with systems of exchange that do not use money. In so doing, we can also develop an understanding of the basic functions of a monetary system.

1.1.1
Direct and indirect exchange

People produce and consume goods and services, but they seldom consume what they produce. In a barter economy, everybody specializes in the production of specific items they think other people want, and they trade for whatever they need. If they are lucky, they always find someone with whom to trade. For example, the butcher acquires through trade bread, butter, shirts, beer, shoes, trousers, and all other things he needs to satisfy his wants. The same is true of the tailor, the baker, the cobbler, the dairyman, and all the rest of the people in the economy.

Unfortunately, a market economy based upon voluntary exchange cannot function effectively by barter alone. Barter is the *direct* exchange of goods between two people who find the exchange mutually advantageous. It is always possible to find someone to trade with, but it is not always possible to trade in a manner that leaves everyone better off.

This point is easily demonstrated with an example of a minimal exchange economy—one with three traders (Al, Bob, and Carol) and three goods (apples, berries, and cherries).[1] Suppose we initially endow Al with berries, Bob with cherries, and Carol with apples. Suppose also that the preferences of the three individuals are quite different than the way we have distributed the three goods to them, as indicated in the following table (where *a* stands for apples, *b* for berries, *c* for cherries, and > for "preferred to"):

Individual	Preferences	Initial Endowments
Al	$a > b > c$	b
Bob	$b > c > a$	c
Carol	$c > a > b$	a

Al prefers apples to berries, and berries to cherries. He would like to improve on his initial position by trading his endowment of berries for apples, but he cannot. Bob would gladly give him cherries for his berries, but Al would refuse, since that would put him in a position he regards as less desirable than his initial position. Carol would refuse to trade with Al because she would have to give up apples for berries, and that would put *her* in a less preferred position.

And so it goes with the other individuals. Each has the means to achieve a preferred position, but none can reach it through direct trade. That being the case, each person must remain in a less preferred position, consuming what he or she has, with the forbidden fruit just out of reach.

The example is rigged to make barter impossible. The real world actually contains many opportunities for improvement through direct exchange. Nonetheless, as the number of traders and commodities multiply, the situations in which barter is impossible also increase. At some point, it pays society to drop barter and adopt a different system of exchange.

You guessed it. An economy needs money. But before we introduce

---

[1]This example was inspired by J. Huston McCulloch in *Money and Inflation* (New York: Academic Press, 1975), Chapter 1.

money it is helpful first to discuss *indirect exchange*. Indirect exchange gives people options that barter exchange excludes.

To demonstrate, let Carol trade her apples for Al's berries. As the table shows, if she stops with this trade, she worsens her situation, since she actually prefers apples to berries. But, Carol is now in a position to trade with Bob, since she can now exchange the berries she has acquired through trade for the cherries held by Bob. This second exchange puts Carol in her most preferred position; moreover, as a result of her enterprise, Al and Bob end up in their preferred positions: Al has his apples and Bob has his berries.

Our example proves that a lack of mutual coincidence of wants between traders need not so impair exchange as to prevent the efficient allocation of resources in an economy. Indirect exchange permits people to increase their productivity by specializing in the production of goods and services for which their talents, education, and endowments best suit them. They can then trade their surplus products for surplus products produced by others. In so doing, they not only end up with *more goods,* but they also have, what is from their point of view, a *better assortment of goods.*

1.1.2
Benefits of indirect exchange through money

Indirect exchange as we have pictured it has definite drawbacks. These drawbacks, which barter shares, include relatively high transactions costs and relatively high storage costs. In our example, these costs were submerged. Carol was willing to acquire berries for further trade because she *knew* Bob liked berries better than cherries or apples. She did not have to spend time and effort searching for a buyer, and she did not have to suffer spoilage and other storage costs. In the real world, these costs always exist. When they are very high, direct and indirect exchange with non-monetary commodities is burdensome. For that reason, people sooner or later try to reduce their exchange costs. The best way they have found so far is through the invention of money.

Money is an object that people, through market activity, law, and custom have agreed to use as a standard trading commodity—a *medium of exchange.* Some societies adopt regular commodities to use as money, such as gold, silver, copper, and cigarettes (as in prisoner-of-war camps); others use objects with less intrinsic value, such as paper currency and bank deposits. But, whatever its form, everywhere it is used money helps to reduce substantially the transactions and storage costs associated with the process of exchange. Money is so effective in doing this that, except for a few primitive tribes, all societies use it.

Exchange in nonmonetary economies generates high transactions costs. In a barter economy, people must spend time and effort searching for exchange opportunities that simultaneously satisfy their wants and the wants of their trading partners—situations in which there is a *mutual coincidence of wants*. Such situations are relatively uncommon, and the cost of finding them is not only high, but for many individuals who wish to consume a large variety of goods the cost is probably prohibitive. The situation is not much better in economies practicing indirect exchange with nonmonetary commodities, since possession of trading goods for which there is no widespread demand still leaves individuals with high transactions costs. They must still find others who have what they want and want what they have. Failing that, they must exchange their goods for others more pleasing to their potential trading partners, and the extra transactions must impose upon them additional expenditures of time and effort.

Since money is an object that all people accept in exchange for goods they have to sell, its use eliminates the extra transactions costs imposed by barter and by indirect exchange with nonmonetary commodities. Transactions costs still remain—sellers and buyers must still seek out each other—but they are substantially less. The time and effort saved by money represent additional opportunities to produce or to have more leisure. In either event, people are better off, and the nice thing about it is that the benefits accrue to *everyone*. Money is one of those social contrivances that benefits both the rich and the poor.

In nonmonetary economies, people must maintain relatively large stocks of various commodities for the purpose of reducing the number of trading ventures they make and for the purpose of having on hand the right goods to trade when they do embark on such ventures. Both of these purposes serve to reduce transactions costs, but only by raising storage costs. Commodity stocks must be maintained, and they are subject to spoilage. In addition, capital invested in such stocks cannot be employed elsewhere, and the individual who makes such an investment gives up opportunities to profit from his capital by using it in other ways. For these reasons, people are under pressure to economize on commodity stocks. They will not allow them to grow to the point where the extra storage costs outweigh the savings in transactions costs.

Introducing money into an economy helps to lower costs of storage. Since use of money substantially lowers transactions costs, people no longer must accept high storage costs in order to reduce the transactions costs imposed by exchange carried out with nonmonetary commodities. As a result, in a money economy they carry much smaller stocks of goods, and the stocks they do carry are more directly related to their specialized production and consumption needs. Costs associated with maintenance of stocks and spoilage are less, and the capital released from investment in the stocks is available for alternative productive employment. Again, the social contrivance of money enriches just about everyone.

1.1.3
Money as a standard of value
(unit of account)

Once a society has adopted a medium of exchange, it usually adopts it as its *standard (measure) of value*. This use is also frequently called the *unit of account* function in the literature of money.

These fancy terms refer to the fact that in a money economy it is usually the custom to quote prices in terms of the medium of exchange. In the United States, for example, each good or service is usually sold for a given number of dollars, and the price of each good or service is normally *stated* in terms of dollars. In principle, money need not perform this function. Sellers could, for example, quote their prices in terms of bushels of wheat, but sell their goods for dollars. But in order to calculate the number of dollars they should receive for their goods, sellers would also have to know the dollar price of wheat. This cumbersome procedure would be especially awkward if each seller decided to use a different commodity as his standard of value. For that reason, people in the United States and all other countries normally use their medium of exchange as their standard of value.[2]

Using money as a standard of value gives rise to using it as a unit of account. Income statements and balance sheets are used by businesspeople and individuals to calculate profit and net worth. It would be impossible to calculate either one without some sort of unit of account. For example, profits (or losses) represent the difference between receipts and expenditures. In order to make the necessary calculations, a firm must express each sale and each purchase in terms of some common unit. As above, it could express its transactions in terms of a commodity like wheat, but it is much more convenient to use the monetary standard. That way, whoever reads the income statement will be able to understand it better and to compare it with other income statements calculated in the same unit.

If you still need to be convinced of the convenience of having a common standard of value, consider the following argument. In a barter or semi-barter economy, each good is priced in terms of every other good. For example, if there are 100 commodities to be traded, then each good has 99 different prices, one for each of the other goods for which it can be traded (assuming that a single price is established in the market for each commodity). Thus, a pound of apples may trade for 2 pounds of

---

[2]At times, people actually do use a standard of value that differs from their medium of exchange. In England, for example, prices are often quoted in terms of an ancient but no longer existing monetary unit called the guinea, which is worth 1.05 English pounds. American tourists abroad frequently insist on having prices quoted to them in terms of dollars even when they are using foreign currencies to make their purchases.

cherries, 3 pounds of berries, 1 pound of nuts, and so forth, up to the 99th other good.

Altogether, there are 100 goods, each with 99 different prices; but that does not mean there are 9,900 different relative prices. Each time a price is established for one good in terms of another, the other good automatically has its price established in terms of the first. For example, when 1 pound of apples costs 2 pounds of cherries, 1 pound of cherries automatically costs 1/2 pound of apples. Hence, instead of 100×99, there are $100 \times 99/2$, or 4,950 different prices in the economy.

As the number of goods to be exchanged in a barter economy grows, the number of prices to be established also grows, but much faster. For example, an economy with 1000 goods to be traded has $1,000 \times 999/2$, or 499,500 separate prices. In general, an economy with n different goods has $n(n-1)/2$ different prices.

Adoption of the money unit as a common standard of value substantially reduces the amount of price information traders must acquire in order to do their work. Instead of $n(n-1)/2$ different relative prices, they need cope with only n different money prices.

In a modern economy, n different money prices is still a considerable number (something in the millions), but once a trader knows any two money prices, he also knows the rate of exchange between the commodities in question (when apples cost 50¢ a pound, and oranges cost 25¢ a pound, 1 pound of apples trades for 2 pounds of oranges). That being the case, an economy that uses its monetary unit as a common standard of value gives its participants a device that substantially reduces the amount of information needed to perform exchanges and to evaluate the results of its economic activities. Since acquisition of price information is a costly activity, requiring time and effort, the reduced need for information also releases resources that people can use in other ways.

1.1.4
Money as a store of value

Money is also an asset people hold in order to preserve purchasing power for the future, that is, as a *store of value*.

Since there is almost always some lapse of time between the receipt of money and subsequent outlays, the medium of exchange function automatically gives rise to the use of money as a short-run store of value. Nonetheless, there appear to be considerable sums held by individuals and businesses for purposes unconnected with immediate transactions. The U.S. money stock (defined as currency and demand deposits) in 1980 was about one-sixth of gross national product, which is equivalent to about 8.5 weeks or 2 months worth of gross national income. Recently, Paul S. Anderson estimated that in the United States, the average currency holdings by adults are equivalent to about 7 percent, or 3.6 weeks worth of personal income.[3] Much of this cash seems to be concentrated in very large holdings of perhaps $5,000, $10,000, or more by a minority of individuals. Since few people need such large cash holdings for transactions, there must be some other motive, such as use of money in illegal transactions in drugs and other smuggled items, or for tax evasion. However, after a careful review of the problem, Anderson could only conclude that the large currency holdings represent ordinary liquid savings by individuals who distrust banks or who prefer to keep their wealth a secret.

Holding money as a store of value is costly. Currency and demand deposits do not earn interest, and inflation takes its toll on their purchasing power. Thus, despite the benefits, real or imagined, which money confers on its holders, people also hold other assets as stores of value. These assets include time and savings deposits; shares in savings and loan associations and credit unions; short-term and long-term bonds issued by private and public bodies; equity shares in corporations; real assets such as land, diamonds, and houses; and so forth. Each of these alternative assets has its merits and demerits as a store of value in comparison to money. Some earn interest, and others are more inflation proof.

The most *liquid* of all, however, is the medium of exchange. Money is the perfect liquid asset. It can be exchanged for other assets with virtually no effort or cost. Its value does not fluctuate in terms of the unit of account because it *is* the unit of account. Inferior liquidity detracts from other assets as stores of value. Forced sales of real and marketable financial assets for funds to use in transactions may bring the seller less than the assets are "really" worth. For many people, time and effort are required to convert savings deposits or shares in nonbank financial institutions into money, though recent changes in regulations and in electronic fund transfer techniques have greatly improved their liquidity.[4]

Thus, though money has certain drawbacks as a store of value, its superior liquidity is a feature prized by enough people to cause it to be held in sometimes substantial amounts.

Occasionally, the public attempts big shifts into or out of money holdings. When it does, it causes sharp fluctuations in the prices of other

---

[3]Paul S. Anderson, "Currency in Use and In Hoards," *Federal Reserve Bank of Boston New England Economic Review,* March/April 1977, pp. 21–30. In Switzerland (1970) currency holdings were 19.6 percent of national income! See J. S. Cramers and G. M. Reekers, "Money Demand by Sector," *Journal of Monetary Economics,* Vol. 2, No. 1, January 1976, pp. 99–112.

[4]In many banks, funds can be transferred from savings to checking deposits by phone or by prearrangement in case of overdrawn accounts. Commercial banks and savings banks are now permitted to offer interest earning deposits from which depositors can transfer funds to third parties by written order—in effect, by check. These are called negotiable order of withdrawal (NOW) accounts.

assets. Massive attempts to shift into money are often accompanied by large sales of stocks and bonds, which cause their prices to fall. Similarly, when people try to move out of money, they often move into stocks and bonds, causing their prices to rise. As discussed below, the sharp fluctuations in the prices of nonmonetary assets are frequently communicated to the rest of the economy, causing disruptions in production and employment. Thus, the store of value function of money is highly significant for the understanding of business fluctuations in a money economy.

1.1.5
Money as a standard for deferred payment

Once a society has adopted money as a standard of value, it also tends to use it as a means of expressing debt obligations, that is, as a *standard for deferred payment*. The importance of this function becomes obvious once you think of the alternatives. Suppose you wish to borrow money from a bank to build a house. The bank expects you to return the money, with interest, over a series of years. Suppose, however, you are a subsistence farmer with no money income with which to pay your debts. So you tell the banker that you will pay him back with bushels of wheat, pigs, chickens, milk, and the like. To accommodate you, the banker would have to accept a great deal of extra work and uncertainty. To reduce the possibility of fraud or misunderstanding, the loan contract would have to be carefully written in order to specify the quantity and quality of the items you would be obligated to pay him. Moreover, he would not be able to estimate his profits from the loan unless he could forecast accurately the future prices of the items for each payment date, clearly a difficult task, even with the services of a professional economist. Thus, the banker is likely either to insist upon a very high premium to make the loan, or to insist that you obligate yourself in terms of money. If you were to refuse these terms, you probably would not get your loan.

An inflationary environment promotes the breakdown of money as a standard for deferred payments. The reason is not simply that a rise in the price level lowers the purchasing power of monetary units. If every individual could accurately forecast future prices, then future prices would automatically be taken into account in loan and other contracts. Lenders would insist on higher interest rates, workers would insist on an acceleration of money wage rates, firms would raise their prices in anticipation of higher costs, and so on. Borrowers and buyers, expecting higher money incomes, would agree to the higher money payments.

But, when people cannot accurately forecast inflation, as is true most of the time, they must find alternative means to protect themselves against the loss in purchasing power of the loans and other future money payments for which they are making present contracts. One method is to adjust payments for changes in the cost of living as measured by changes in the consumer price index or some other mutually agreed upon measure of the rate of inflation. The term for this practice is *indexation*.

Once contracts are "indexed" to reduce the risk of loss of purchasing power of money payments, money ceases to perform its function as a standard for deferred payments. It is no longer the dollar that is promised, but the *indexed* dollar. Although indexing is practiced in many countries, few use it extensively. The most thoroughly indexed country today is Brazil, which by government decree indexes wages, loan contracts, pensions, and its foreign exchange rate. Indexing loans is relatively rare in the United States, but indexation of wages, rental contracts, and pensions (for example, social security benefits) is becoming more common.[5] There is not yet a massive movement away from the use of money per se as a standard for deferred payments, but if inflation persists, the movement into indexed money will undoubtedly grow.

1.1.6
Money and capital formation

Money is an essential ingredient for the efficient operation of capital markets. Capital markets transmit funds from savers to investors. Savers are people who spend less than they earn in order to increase their consumption in the future (or to leave money to their heirs). Investors are people who see future profit opportunities in expanding or creating new enterprises and who are willing to take the risk of investing in them. Investors frequently lack sufficient resources to carry out their plans; hence, they must supplement their own savings by borrowing from or selling an interest in their enterprises to the main body of savers.

In barter economies, the transfer of resources from savers to investors is particularly awkward. As discussed above, few people would agree to execute loan contracts expressed in terms of individual commodities. Money economies do a much better job. Money is generalized purchasing power, and its use greatly facilitates the stating and carrying out of the terms of payment specified in debt contracts. If people had to express and meet payment of their debts with particular commodities or services, the incidence of fraud and bad faith would greatly increase, and the willingness of savers to advance loans to investors would be much reduced. Moreover, since money and claims to money would not be available as a store of value, savers would be forced to set aside most of their savings in the form of stocks of various commodities, with all the attendant storage

---

[5]An interesting discussion on indexation is found in "The Concept of Indexation in the History of Economic Thought," by T. M. Humphrey in the *Federal Reserve Bank of Richmond Economic Review*, Vol. 60, No. 5, November/December 1974, pp. 3–16. In the same issue is a useful piece by James Tucker and Warren Weber, "Indexation as a Response to Inflation: An Examination," pp. 17–21. See also "The Case For and Against Indexation: An Attempt at Perspective," *Federal Reserve Bank of St. Louis Review*, Vol. 56, No. 10, October 1974, p. 2.

costs. Thus, money not only produces social benefits in its medium of exchange and other functions, but it also enhances capital formation by facilitating the transfer of resources from the providers to the users of productive capital. Altogether, it is hard to imagine how modern societies could have evolved without it.

1.2
Money and economic instability

Having recognized the benefits of money, it is time to acknowledge its costs. Fluctuations in the growth rate of the money stock, or substantial changes in its rate of turnover, can cause a great deal of trouble. Inflationary booms, for example, are usually accompanied by acceleration of the growth rate of the money supply and by a speeding up of its rate of use. Economic contractions, which bring with them widespread declines in production and employment, frequently follow or accompany decreases in the growth rate of the money stock and a slowing of its rate of use.

In fact, over the last 100 years all major and minor contractions in economic activity have been preceded or accompanied by reductions in the rate of growth of the money supply. The great depression of the 1930s, which began late in 1929, followed over a year of zero monetary growth; by the time it touched bottom in 1933, the money stock had declined by over one-third of its 1929 level.[6] As for inflation, there never has been a prolonged period of rising prices that has not been accompanied by a rising flood of money. To quote Milton Friedman, the leading authority on the subject:

> There is perhaps no empirical regularity among economic phenomena that is based on so much evidence for so wide a range of circumstances as the connection between substantial changes in the stock of money and in the level of prices. To the best of my knowledge, there is no instance in which a substantial change in the stock of money per unit of output has occurred without a substantial change in the level of prices in the same direction. Conversely, I know of no instance in which there has been substantial change in the level of prices without a substantial change in the stock of money per unit of output in the same direction. And instances in which prices and the stock of money

---

[6]Documentation for these remarks can be found in Milton Friedman and Anna J. Schwartz, *A Monetary History of the United States, 1867–1960* (Princeton, N.J.: Princeton University Press for the National Bureau of Economic Research, 1963), pp. 299 ff., and in M. Friedman and A. J. Schwartz, "Money and Business Cycles," in M. Friedman, ed., *The Optimum Quantity of Money and Other Essays* (Chicago: Aldine, 1969), pp. 189–235.

have moved together are recorded for many centuries of history, for countries in every part of the globe, and for a wide diversity of monetary arrangements.[7]

These matters are discussed at greater length in Chapters 12, 15, 16, 17, and 18. For now, take it on faith that the empirical relationships between money and business fluctuations and between money and inflation are well established. Few economists would dispute the evidence. What is at dispute is the cause-and-effect interpretation given to the facts. Milton Friedman and other members of the so-called *monetarist school* of macroeconomics believe that fluctuations in and excessive rates of growth of the money supply are the proximate *causes* of the business cycle and of inflation. Other thinkers, including some, but not all, followers of the *Keynesian school*[8] argue the reverse: Fluctuations in the money supply are the *effect,* not the cause, of forces that produce the business cycle and inflation.

The chart reproduced in Figure 1.1 gives an example of the evidence many economists use to show the relationship between monetary movements and economic fluctuations. Monetary movements are traced by a lagged two-quarter rate of change of M-1B, expressed in real terms. M-1B is a definition of money discussed in Chapter 2. Real money is the money supply corrected for changes in prices, as measured by a price index for gross national product (the so-called GNP implicit deflator). The higher the price level as measured by the index, the less a real dollar will buy of a unit of gross national product. Real gross national product is the nominal (money) value of national product "deflated" by the price index.

Figure 1.1 shows that changes in real output are typically preceded by changes in the real money supply. Although this correlation is consistent with the theory that variations in the money supply are the causes of fluctuations in real output, it does not actually prove the case. It is quite possible that the forces that caused gross national product to fluctuate are also responsible for the fluctuations in the real money supply. Statistical correlations rarely prove causation; they merely support the possibility. Only when a correlation is consistent with a well-defined theory can we begin to speak of causal relationships, and even then only with a measure of caution.

Again, these matters are discussed more thoroughly in Chapters 15 and 16. In the meantime, it is possible to give a brief theoretical demon-

---

[7]"The Supply of Money and Changes in Prices and Output," in M. Friedman, ed., *The Optimum Quantity of Money,* pp. 172–73.

[8]John Maynard Keynes was the noted English economist who revolutionized macroeconomic theory in 1936 with the publication of his book, *The General Theory of Employment, Interest and Money* (New York: Harcourt, Brace and Company).

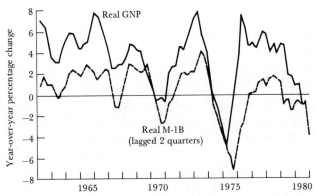

Figure 1.1 *Real money (M-1B) and real output: growth rates. (Source: Adrian W. Throop,* Money in the Economy *(Federal Reserve Bank of San Francisco, August 1980).)*

stration of how money misbehavior *can* cause fluctuations in the economy and lead to inflation. To do so, it is convenient to start with two fundamental ideas: Say's Law and Say's Principle.

1.2.1
Say's Law, Say's Principle, and
"generalized overproduction"

Say's Law is named after a nineteenth century French economist, J. B. Say. It was upheld by many classical economists, such as James Mill, John Stuart Mill, and David Ricardo. Malthus, Marx, and a number of other nineteenth century writers ridiculed it. In our century it has been rejected by Keynes and most of his followers.[9] Some recent writers have shown a renewed appreciation of the idea and have started a movement to rehabilitate it on the grounds that it is fundamental to an understanding of how a money-using market economy works.[10]

Say's Law of Markets (its full title) asserts that in a market economy there cannot be a *general* oversupply of goods and services, because in such an economy "supply creates its own demand." If true, the law also implies that a general deficiency of demand for goods and services cannot be the source of economic depression and unemployment. But, because business cycle experience since the nineteenth century appears to contra-

---

[9]A good review of the literature is found in Thomas Sowell, *Say's Law* (Princeton, N.J.: Princeton University Press, 1972).

[10]W. H. Hutt, *A Rehabilitation of Say's Law* (Athens, Ohio: Ohio University Press, 1974); Robert Clower and Axel Leijonhufvud, "Say's Principle, What It Means and What It Doesn't Mean," *Intermountain Economic Review,* Vol. IV, No. 2, Fall 1973, pp. 1–16.

dict Say's Law, it is important to examine it more closely before accepting it.

Say's Law is valid for barter and semi-barter economies, but not for money economies. In the former, producers either keep what they make, or offer their products in direct exchange for goods and services produced by others. Thus, to "supply" a good in a nonmonetary economy is automatically to "demand" the good itself or a commodity produced by someone else. Goods and services supplied to the market *constitute* (are) the demand for other goods and services. Economic demands are not simply wishes or desires. *Effective demands* must be backed up by purchasing power; otherwise sellers would not respond to them. In nonmonetary economies commodities are the purchasing power for commodities.

Understood in this way, Say's Law is an important truism. It does not assert that each and every good must find a market. Suppliers of a particular good may be exerting demand for commodities that are not available at acceptable prices. But such a situation is a symptom of excess supply in a particular market, not (net) excess supply for the economy as a whole. Goods that are oversupplied are matched by goods that are undersupplied (overdemanded); in the aggregate, there is no excess supply. Instead, there is an improper composition of production. The situation is corrected by a fall in the price of the oversupplied good, and by a rise in the prices of the undersupplied goods, not by an increase in aggregate demand for all goods.

Now, look at Say's Law in the context of a *money economy*. People in a money economy trade goods for money and use the money they acquire to buy other goods. They rarely trade goods for goods. In a money economy, therefore, the effective demand for goods and services takes the form of an *effective money demand*. If for some reason people prefer to hold instead of spend the money they earn, they may break the link between the supply and demand for goods and services that arises naturally in a barter economy.

This point requires amplification. A person selling $1,000 worth of goods or services for $1,000 in cash can use the money to buy $1,000 worth of goods or services or hoard it. Hoarding means adding money to existing cash balances; money earned, so to speak, is spent on itself, not upon goods or services produced by other people.

Thus, unlike a barter economy in which the sale of a good automatically constitutes the demand for other goods or services, sales in a money economy may result in the build-up of the cash balances of a particular group of individuals, instead of the demand for products produced by others. And, unlike a barter economy, the failure of people in a money economy to buy one set of goods and services does not necessarily mean they are trying to buy another set. That is, the problem may not necessarily be one of imbalance between the supply and demand for different products or services; instead, it may be a failure of effective demand in an aggregative sense. The excess supply in the affected industries may not be matched by excess demand in other industries.

Classical economists called the above situation a condition of *general overproduction*. They believed that such a condition will arise whenever, on balance, people in the economy as a whole desire to add money to their cash balances in excess of the amount of money that may exist in the economy. In Section 11.3 we define this condition as an aggregate excess demand for money. When it occurs, people, on balance, are trying to acquire additional cash by increasing their sales and reducing their purchases of goods and services. The effect on the economy is either to drive prices and wages down, or to reduce the quantities of goods and services purchased at prevailing prices. This lowers money incomes and further reduces the demand for goods and services. Thus a generalized excess demand for money leads directly to a slumping economy, in which prices weaken, production falls, and unemployment increases.

When in a money economy there is (on balance) a zero excess supply of (or demand for) goods in general, there is also (on balance) a condition of zero excess demand for (or supply of) money. This is an implication of a version of Say's Law that was seen by J. S. Mill in 1829 (in an essay entitled, "Of the Influence of Consumption on Production"),[11] but which is now called Say's Principle.[12] Say's Principle is based on the idea that in a money economy equilibrium in the markets for goods and services implies equilibrium between the demand for money and its existing supply. That is because, in a market equilibrium, every offer to sell something at a given price implies a corresponding desire by the buyer to reduce cash balances by an equal amount. When, at prevailing prices, the offers to sell goods and services equal the offers to buy, there is not only equilibrium in the markets for goods and services, but also equilibrium in the "market for money." That is, a zero excess supply or demand for goods and services in general implies a zero excess demand for money, and vice versa. A zero excess demand for money implies that sellers of goods and services desire to add to their cash balances at the same rate that buyers desire to reduce theirs, so that equality of sales and purchases of commodities implies that, *in the aggregate,* people are satisfied with the existing stock of money. They desire neither more nor less.

One implication of Say's Principle is, as described above, that an economy-wide excess demand for money is accompanied by a general reduction of prices, production, and employment. Another implication is that an excess *supply* of money creates an inflationary tendency—a situation in which excess demand for goods and services is driving up prices

---

[11]Reprinted in Henry Hazlitt, ed., *The Critics of Keynesian Economics* (New Rochelle, New York: Arlington House, 1977), pp. 23–45.

[12]Discussed in more detail in Chapter 11.

and wages. When there is large-scale unemployment, as in the 1930s, the tendency is weak, since an excess demand for goods and services is likely to raise production and employment more than prices and wages. As full employment is approached, an excess supply of money has stronger effects upon prices and wages than upon production and employment. As a general rule, therefore, we can say that an excess supply of money implies an *expansionary* condition for the economy in general, but whether or not it also implies an *inflationary* condition depends in part upon the state of employment.

1.2.2
Monetary sources of
the business cycle

There is no question that nonmonetary events can cause fluctuations in income and employment. In ancient times, drought, plagues, and pestilence were frequent sources of economic decline, and benign turns of the weather created good crops and economic prosperity. Today such events are capable of affecting even the most advanced countries. In addition, there are heavy, man-made shocks such as the quadrupling of oil prices in 1974 by OPEC countries (which, according to some experts, reduced economically efficient productive capacity in the United States by 5 percent). Nonetheless, Say's Principle should remind us that money-using economies may fluctuate for reasons quite unconnected with the assaults of nature and organized men.

To illustrate, imagine a situation in which there is relatively full employment and in which the money supply is growing at roughly the same rate as is the output of goods and services in the economy. In such a situation, there would be little tendency for the price level to rise or to fall, since the demand for money for transactions needs would be growing at about the same rate as the growth of output and employment, and these needs would be met by the postulated growth in the money supply.

Now, suppose for some reason the monetary authorities decide to stop the money stock from growing. This act could force the economy into a recession, or even a depression. The reason is that if the economy were to continue to grow, people's monetary needs would also continue to grow. The combination of a growing money demand and a nongrowing money supply would cause a condition of general excess demand for money to occur. The excess demand for money would lead people to reduce their demands for commodities, which would cause a condition of excess supply of goods and services to appear. An excess supply of goods and services signifies that producers cannot find markets for their products at current prices. They would, therefore, be led to restrict outputs and perhaps to cut prices and wages.

The uncertain conditions may also lead people to increase their desire to hold money as a hedge against future trouble. Such an act would reinforce the excess demand for money and would depress the economy even more.

Economic revivals are frequently preceded by increases in the growth rate of the money supply. Say's Principle explains why. Prolongation of an accelerated growth rate of the money stock eventually raises the stock above the amount people wish to hold in their cash balances. Once that happens, an excess supply of money and a corresponding excess demand for commodities emerges. With unemployed productive capacity, and a labor force anxious for jobs, the stage is set for producers to respond by increasing their outputs with only minimal increases in prices and wages. Provided the growth of the money stock continues to exceed the rise in the public's demand for money (which accompanies the growing volume of business to be transacted), the revival will continue, perhaps becoming a boom. Once that happens, inflation of wage rates and commodity prices may dominate output and employment growth, setting the stage for a new contraction in the economy. The contraction is not inevitable, since the monetary authorities may seek to prolong the boom by accelerating the growth of the money supply. More commonly, however, they try to fight off further inflation, and in so doing they reduce the money supply growth rate. If overdone, the action of the authorities can create an excess demand for money and force the economy into another recession.

1.2.3
The role of credit in business fluctuations

A money economy is also a credit economy. Variations in the growth rate of the money supply commonly coincide with similar variations in the rate of growth of bank credit. This may not be surprising, since (as we will discuss in Chapters 5 and 6) bank deposits to a large extent come into being as a result of extensions of bank credit. Nonetheless, even nonbank credit rises and falls over the business cycle. Thus a monetary economy may fluctuate not only because of the variations in the rate of growth of the money supply, but also because of variations in the rate of growth of both bank and nonbank credit.[13]

Nonbank credit is borrowing and lending taking place outside the banking system. It takes three major forms: (a) direct loans, (b) indirect loans through nonbank financial intermediaries, and (c) trade credit.

Direct loans consist of loans made by one private party to another (for example, when your profligate brother-in-law hits you up for a loan) and loans made through organized stock and bond markets. Technically

---

[13]For the post-war period, see J. A. Cacy and Mary Hamblen, "Trends and Cycles in Credit Market Borrowing," *Federal Reserve Bank of Kansas Monthly Review*, March 1974, pp. 3–12.

speaking, purchase of stock in a corporation does not represent a loan, as does purchase of a corporate bond. But, from our present viewing angle, which is directed to sources of change in the effective demand for goods and services, purchases of stocks have the same effect as purchases of bonds.

A direct loan represents the transfer of money from one party to another. The purchasing power of the lender is temporarily reduced while that of the borrower is increased. Since, in making the loan, the lender may be reducing his demand for goods and services, the increased demand by the borrower may not represent a net increase in the demand for goods and services in the economy, in which case the loan will not cause an acceleration of economic activity. But, the lender may have been keeping a store of idle cash balances. If he uses these balances to make the loan, the borrower receives purchasing power that was not previously being exercised. In this event, the effective demand for goods and services is raised (assuming the borrower does not hold the cash idle), and economic activity is stimulated.

An economy stimulated by an increase in direct lending can also be depressed by a decrease in such lending. The latter occurs when lenders refrain from renewing or making new loans and instead try to build up their stores of cash. Thus, both ups and downs in the economy need not be rigidly linked to changes in the growth rate of the money *supply;* changes in the *demand* for money can also set off vibrations in the markets for goods and services.

Indirect loans through nonbank financial intermediaries have the same general effect on the economy as do direct loans. These intermediaries include savings and loan associations, mutual savings banks, credit unions, insurance companies, mutual investment funds, and pension funds. When people invest money in the intermediaries, the latter usually lend almost all of it, setting aside only a small amount for meeting unanticipated outlays. As with direct lending, the loans people make indirectly through the intermediaries may come from money they had been lending in a direct fashion, or from income previously used for their own spending. In this event, there is no net increase in purchasing power in the economy. However, if people place previously idle cash balances with the intermediaries, new effective money demand is created, just as it is in the case of direct lending that is financed by reductions in cash balances. Similarly, when people take their money out of intermediaries and place it in idle balances, there is a shrinkage in the effective demand for goods and services.

Although nonbank financial intermediaries do not necessarily prevent fluctuations in the economy, they may moderate them. People who wish to increase their holdings of liquid assets by selling off stocks and bonds may put their money into nonbank intermediaries instead of holding it idle. Since intermediaries lend almost all the money placed with them, the expansion in their loans will offset most, if not all, the decline in private lending. Thus, the presence of nonbank financial intermediaries may help to cure fluctuations in the economy brought about by changes in the demand for money. In so doing, of course, they rechannel loanable funds from one sector to another. The sector receiving loans will expand, while the sector losing funds will contract. So things are not made rosy for everyone. But, this is a better situation than one in which everyone is made worse off by massive attempts on the part of the public to increase its holdings of idle money balances.

Trade credit arises out of direct sales on credit. The buyer of the goods does not give cash to the seller; instead, he signs a note promising to pay the seller for the goods at a specific date or series of dates in the future. Thus, money does not change hands at the time of the sale, but only later when the note is paid off by the buyer.

Transactions involving trade credit occur at both the wholesale and retail level. Businesspeople frequently employ it when they purchase goods and services from each other, and they often extend it to consumers when the latter purchase home appliances, furniture, and clothing. Credit card purchases and department store purchases based upon installment credit are examples of the use of trade credit by consumers.

During any given period of time, buyers are paying off their notes and new notes are coming into existence as a result of new credit purchases. Thus, the mere presence of trade credit does not signify instability of effective demand for goods and services. At times, however, new extensions of trade credit will exceed extinguishments, and vice versa. These *net* changes in the volume of outstanding trade credit signify changes in the effective demand for goods. Such changes in the effective demand can either provoke, or, as is more common, reinforce fluctuations in the economy.

Figure 1.2 shows how variations in the rate of growth of credit in the economy are related to the fluctuations of the economy. Each recession in the 1952–1978 period was preceded by a decline in the growth rate of private debt, though the declines were clearly more pronounced for the household than the business sector. Federal government debt growth rates did not share this pattern; instead, they rose during recessions. As with Figure 1.1, relating variations in the growth rate of money to economic fluctuations, Figure 1.2 does not prove causation. In fact, because of the magnitude of bank credit, much of the variation in total credit may simply be a reflection of the growth rate in the money supply. Undoubtedly, however, some of the fluctuations also reflect shifts in the demand for money.

In brief, the element of credit loosens the relationship between variations in the rate of growth of the money supply and fluctuations in the economy. It does so because it provides a source of the effective demand for goods and services additional to the stock of money. For that reason,

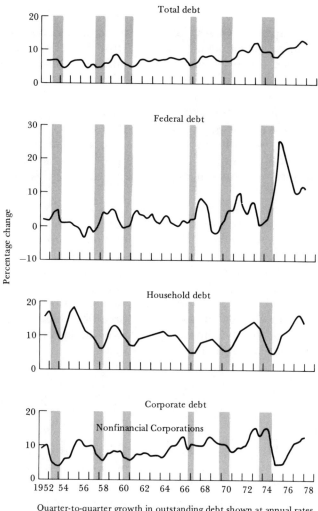

Quarter-to-quarter growth in outstanding debt shown at annual rates,
seasonally adjusted. Total debt includes liabilities of state-and-local
governments, foreign borrowers and noncorporate nonfinancial
businesses, in addition to federal, household, and corporate debt. All
figures represent Federal Reserve flow-of-funds concept of "credit-
market debt." Data smoothed by 1-2-1 three-quarter moving averages.

Figure 1.2 *Credit and the business cycle—rates of debt growth, 1952–1978. (Source:*
Citibank Monthly Letter, *June 1978.)*

we cannot analyze the workings of a money economy by concentrating
sole attention upon the factors affecting the supply and demand for
money. Our inquiry, of necessity, must take into account the presence of
financial markets, of financial intermediaries, and of people's behavior respecting the use of credit.

SUMMARY

This chapter discusses the chief merits and demerits of a money-using economy. Nonmonetary economies use barter or semi-barter systems of exchange. These systems are economically inefficient since they maximize the transactions, storage, and information costs that accompany exchange. As a result, too many resources are tied up in trading activities, and too few are in activities that involve the production of goods and services. As a universally accepted medium of exchange, a measure of value, and a standard for deferred payments, money helps to reduce substantially these costs. In addition, it provides a basis for an expanded flow of savings into investment, which in turn enhances the growth process in the economy.

The chief drawback of money is that it can and frequently does become a major source of economy-wide fluctuations in production, employment, and prices. It is also the major source of long-term inflation. Most of these problems arise from changes in the growth rate of the money supply that differ from the growth rate of the demand for money. However, since goods and services are also effectively demanded as a result of variations in the extension of nonbank credit, economic fluctuations can also emanate or be reinforced by changes in the use of credit. Because of this, it is important to study the institutions of credit as well as the institutions of money.

DISCUSSION QUESTIONS

1. Thinking over the functions of money, is it true (as Lenin is said to have said) that the best way to wreck a capitalist system is to debauch its currency?

2. Compare the level of transactions costs that would occur under (a) direct exchange (barter), (b) indirect exchange without money, and (c) indirect exchange with money.

3. Why does the use of money lead to a greater division of labor and to a more efficient consumption?

4. Compare the number of prices people would have to know in a barter economy containing 2,000 different commodities with a money economy that also contains 2,000 different (nonmonetary) commodities.

5. What prevents people from reducing their money holdings to zero during inflationary times?

6. Does inflation destroy money as a standard for deferred payments?

7. How would the absence of money affect the form and volume of capital formation in society?

8. A noted American economist of the early 1900s once said that the business cycle is a "dance of the dollar." The monetarist school would agree. Explain.

9. Distinguish between money and credit.

10. Many older writers thought that Say's Law implied the impossibility of an aggregate level of overproduction (i.e., a "general glut") of goods and services. Why would such a belief be true for a barter economy, but not for a money economy?

IMPORTANT TERMS AND CONCEPTS

- ☐ barter
- ☐ credit
- ☐ demand deposits
- ☐ effective demand
- ☐ excess demand for (supply of) money
- ☐ indexation
- ☐ indirect exchange
- ☐ Keynesian school of macroeconomics
- ☐ liquidity

- ☐ money
- ☐ medium of exchange
- ☐ monetarist school of macroeconomics
- ☐ Say's Law
- ☐ Say's Principle
- ☐ standard for deferred payment
- ☐ standard of value
- ☐ store of value
- ☐ transactions costs
- ☐ unit of account

ADDITIONAL READINGS

The superiority of money over barter economies is nicely treated in Robert Clower (editor), *Readings in Monetary Theory* (Baltimore: Penguin, 1969), "Introduction," pp. 7–16. In the same book are two other articles that bear on the topics of Chapter 1. The first, an ancient piece by W. Stanley Jevons, "Barter," gives an excellent treatment of the usefulness of money as a medium of exchange. The second piece, by Leland B. Yeager, is called "The Essential Properties of the Medium of Exchange." This article is somewhat difficult for beginning students, but it provides an excellent foundation for modern monetary theory and the role of money in economic fluctuations.

The United States Money Stock: Changing Definitions

O U T L I N E

The U.S. Money Stock—Old and New Definitions
Pre-1980 Definitions of Money
Currency Component of the Money Stock
Post-1979 Definitions of Money
Which Definition of Money Is Best?
A Priori Definitions of Money
The Empirical Definition of Money

Economists define money theoretically and empirically. The theoretical definition emphasizes money's functions as a medium of exchange, measure of value, standard for deferred payment, and liquid store of value. The empirical definition focuses on the objects that actually perform the money functions. The theoretical definition is good for all societies that use money. But the empirical definition changes over time and space.

The things that serve as money in a particular country may change over time. In early U.S. history, domestically minted coins circulated alongside foreign coins as money. Bank notes issued by private state banks competed with notes issued by the government sponsored First and Second Banks of the United States. In the latter part of the nineteenth century, bank deposits displaced bank notes as the most important form of bank-created money. Now, most paper money in circulation is issued by the Federal Reserve System. As we will discuss in this chapter, our generation is evolving even more exotic monetary forms.

During colonial times, money frequently took the form of wampum, beaver skins, and tobacco. In world history, gold, silver, cattle, cowry shells, cigarettes, and a large number of other items have also served as money. Our present monetary system, which features currency, coin, checking accounts, and other relatively new monetary forms, would look very strange to people of antiquity. In fact, it may soon begin to look strange to us! Our system is in a state of flux; the computer, electronic gadgets, changes in the law, and numerous financial innovations have made possible new systems of payment, many of which are likely to survive and grow. For that reason, it is difficult to define and measure the money stock with precision.

Until quite recently, economists worked primarily with two or three relatively simple empirical definitions of the money stock—M-1, M-2, and M-3 (defined in Section 2.1.1). Since most monetary theory and empirical research in modern times has been carried out within the framework of these concepts, we use the first part of Section 2.1 to discuss them. The discussion will illustrate the many difficulties that plague attempts to define money precisely. In the last part of Section 2.1, however, we take up a set of new definitions of the money stock released by the Federal Reserve System in January 1980. The new definitions bring into the fold of money a number of new liquid assets that came into importance in the 1970s.

2.1
The U.S. money stock—old and new definitions

Economists have always had trouble agreeing on the proper empirical definition of money. Why this is so is discussed in Section 2.2. For the moment, we can say that the lack of consensus arises from differences in opinion over the importance of the medium of exchange function as opposed to the store of value function of money. The pre-1980 definitions of money illustrate how these differences resulted in publication by the Federal Reserve System of time series representing several different monetary concepts. The different monetary concepts frequently go under the name of monetary aggregates. Data on the pre-1980 monetary aggregates were published monthly in the *Federal Reserve Bulletin* and released weekly for publication in such periodicals as the *Wall Street Journal*, *Barron's, Business Week,* and the financial section of the *New York Times.* The post-1979 monetary aggregates are also reported in these periodicals.

2.1.1
Pre-1980 definitions of money

The various pre-1980 monetary aggregates are defined on the right-hand side of Table 2.1. The M-1 money stock is most closely related to the medium of exchange function of money. M-1 includes currency and coin in the hands of the nonbank public and demand deposits due (owned by) the nonbank public. It *excludes* (a) currency and coin held by the U.S. Treasury, the Federal Reserve banks, and all commercial banks; (b) deposits due to the U.S. government and all commercial banks; and (c) "cash items in the process of collection" (CIPC).

Currency and coin held by the Treasury and commercial banks are excluded from M-1 because they are not in circulation and, therefore, cannot affect the spending behavior of the public. The same thing is true of commercial bank deposits due the U.S. government (called tax and loan accounts) and other commercial banks. The U.S. government's own spending is dictated by congressional budgetary decisions; it is not limited by its holdings of liquid assets, especially since in the final analysis it can borrow or create any money it needs to finance its budgetary deficits. CPICs represent checks in the process of being cleared. People have written checks on their deposits; recipients of the checks have deposited them in their banks; but the paying banks have not yet been notified. As a result, they have not deducted the money from their customers' accounts. To avoid double counting of demand deposits that are simultaneously shown on the books of two banks, CIPCs must be deducted from total commercial bank demand deposits due to the nonbank private sector in order to arrive at the demand deposit component of M-1.

M-2 is equal to M-1 plus savings and time deposits in commercial banks. It excludes large negotiable certificates of deposit (CDs) issued in denominations of $100,000 or more by large banks. CDs are money market debt instruments that resemble short-term securities issued by nonbank firms. CDs are bought and sold in active markets; but, since other marketable short-term securities are not included in the money supply, many analysts believe that CDs should also be excluded.

M-3 is M-2 plus deposits or shares in the so-called thrift institutions—

savings and loan associations (S&Ls), mutual savings banks (MSBs), and credit unions. Deposits or shares in these institutions closely resemble passbook savings deposits or fixed-value certificates of deposit issued by commercial banks; for this reason, some analysts prefer to include them in the definition of the money supply.

The next two definitions of the money supply are designed to satisfy those who may doubt the logic of excluding large CDs from the money stock. M-4 is M-2 plus the large CDs and M-5 is M-3 plus the CDs. Relatively few economists use M-4 and M-5 in analyzing monetary movements.

As noted in Table 2.1, there are vast quantitative differences between the various money supply concepts. In November 1979, M-1 was $383 billion; M-2 was $945 billion, and M-3 was $1,610 billion. Large CDs raised M-4 and M-5 by another $96 billion.

These differences would not disturb analysts if they were consistent. Unfortunately, however, the various pre-1980 measures did not move in exact parallel fashion over time, as illustrated by the eleven-year sample in Figure 2.1. Except for occasional short periods, M-1, M-2, and M-3 usually moved in the same direction, but the *rates* at which they moved differed quite substantially. Economists were thus left with the difficult problem of selecting the "best" definition of money to use to analyze the economy.

2.1.2
Currency component of the money stock

Each definition of money includes currency and coin in circulation outside the holdings of the Treasury, the Federal Reserve banks, and commercial banks. Fifty or sixty years ago, most economists identified the money supply with the currency in circulation, treating deposits as money substitutes. The modern explosion of money supply definitions, therefore, represents a radical departure from past practices.

Nonetheless, currency and coin (which we will simply refer to as "currency" when speaking of them as a component of the money stock) do represent a significant fraction of the money stock. In November 1979, the currency component was $107 billion, which was 28 percent of the M-1 money supply of that month.

The bulk of the currency component consists of Federal Reserve notes, issued (of course) by the Federal Reserve banks. (Look in your purse or wallet for samples.) The Federal Reserve System was organized as the United States central bank in 1913. One of the main functions of a central bank is the issuing of currency. In the United States, however, currency issued by the Federal Reserve banks has competed with currency issued by the Treasury—silver certificates, United States notes ("greenbacks")—and with currency issued by federally chartered, but private, national banks, which, under the Currency Act of 1863 and the National Bank Act of 1864 were authorized to issue national bank notes. These forms of currency, along with Federal Reserve *bank* notes (which differ from Federal Reserve notes and which were designed to replace national bank notes) are in the process of being retired from circulation.

Table 2.1 *New and Old Monetary Aggregate Definitions*

	The New Monetary Aggregates	Amount in billions of dollars, November 1979		The Old Monetary Aggregates	Amount in billions of dollars, November 1979
M-1A	Currency	106.6	M-1	Currency	106.6
	Demand deposits[1]	265.5		Demand deposits[2]	276.0
M-1B	M-1A	372.2			
	NOW and ATS account balances, credit union share draft balances, demand deposits at mutual savings banks	115.7			
M-2	M-1B	387.9	M-2	M-1	382.6
	Overnight RPs issued by commercial banks[3]	20.3		Savings deposits at commercial banks	210.6
	Overnight Eurodollar deposits at Caribbean branches of U.S. banks held by U.S. nonbank residents	3.2		Time deposits at commercial banks[4]	352.1
	Money market mutual fund shares	40.4			
	Savings deposits at all depository institutions	420.0			
	Small time deposits at all depository institutions[5]	640.8			
	M-2 consolidation component[6]	−2.7			
M-3	M-2	1510.0	M-3	M-2	945.3
	Large time deposits at all depository institutions[7]	219.5		Savings and time deposits at thrift institutions	664.2
	Term RPs issued by commercial banks	21.5			
	Term RPs issued by savings and loan associations	8.2			
					1609.5

Table 2.1   *(continued)*

	The New Monetary Aggregates	Amount in billions of dollars, November 1979		The Old Monetary Aggregates	Amount in billions of dollars, November 1979
			M-4	M-2	945.3
				Large negotiable time deposits at all depository institutions	95.9
					1041.2
			M-5	M-3	1609.5
				Large negotiable deposits at all depository institutions	95.9
					1705.4
L	M-3	1759.1			
	Other Eurodollars of U.S. nonbank residents	34.5			
	Bankers acceptances	27.6			
	Commercial paper	97.1			
	Savings bonds	80.0			
	Liquid Treasury obligations[8]	125.4			
		2123.8			

[1]Equals demand deposits at all commercial banks other than those due to domestic commercial banks and the U.S. government, less cash items in the process of collection and Federal Reserve float, less demand deposits due to foreign commercial banks and official institutions.

[2]Equals demand deposits at all commercial banks other than those due to domestic commercial banks and the U.S. government, less cash items in the process of collection and Federal Reserve float, plus foreign demand balances at Federal Reserve Banks.

[3]Estimated as 51 percent of all commercial bank RPs with the nonbank public and net of RPs held by money market mutual funds.

[4]Time certificates of deposit other than negotiable time certificates issued in denomination of $100,000 or more.

[5]Time deposits issued in denominations of less than $100.000.

[6]Consists of demand deposits included in M-1B that are held by thrift institutions and are estimated to be used for servicing their savings and small time deposits included in the new M-2 measure.

[7]Negotiable and nonnegotiable time certificates of deposit issued in denominations of $100,000 or more.

[8]Consists of Treasury bills with an original maturity of one year or less plus Treasury notes and bonds which mature within 18 months.

Source: Neil G. Berkman, "Some Comments on the New Monetary Aggregates," *Federal Reserve Bank of Boston New England Economic Review,* March/April 1980, p. 47.

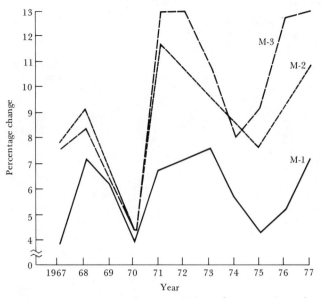

Figure 2.1 *Percentage change over time of M-1, M-2, and M-3. (Source: Federal Reserve Bank of St. Louis.)*

Since less than $1 billion remain in circulation, they no longer effectively compete with Federal Reserve notes as the main form of currency.

Coins are minted and issued by the Treasury. Their value as money exceeds the value of the metal that they contain. Coins account for about $10 billion of the U.S. money stock. From time to time, the market values of the metals in coins rise so high that people find it profitable to hoard them or to melt them down to sell the metal. The Treasury has reduced the content of fractional coins in the United States in recent years to counter the negative effect on coin circulation brought about by the rise in the price of silver during the 1960s.[1]

Public demands, not the policies of the authorities, determine the currency component of the money supply. Individuals who want currency or coin simply cash checks with their banks. Banks buy currency and coin from the Fed with deposits they have at the Federal Reserve banks. The Federal Reserve banks get the currency and coin they sell from the Bureau of Engraving and Printing and from the Mint—the U.S. government's money factories. Since commercial banks and Federal Re-

---

[1]An informative booklet about U.S. currency and coins was published in 1972 by the Federal Reserve Bank of Atlanta under the title, *Fundamental Facts About United States Money*. See also, Colin and Rosemary Campbell, *An Introduction to Money and Banking 4th edition* (Hinsdale, Ill.: Dryden Press, 1981), Chapter 3.

serve banks always stand ready to honor depositors' demands for cash, the currency component of the money supply is completely determined by the demands of the nonbank public.

2.1.3
Post-1979 definitions of money

The February, 1980 issue of the *Federal Reserve Bulletin* began publication of a new set of monetary aggregates. The new money definitions, which replace the old, emerged from a long process of research within the Federal Reserve System and discussions between economists in the Fed and the outside academic and professional community. The need for new definitions arose from a series of changes in the law and in practices of the financial community that introduced new types of payments instruments and liquid stores of value. Table 2.2 catalogues the major developments that led to the new monetary aggregates.

Pre-1980 definitions of money were in part guided by the principle that considerable differences exist between deposits issued by commercial banks and deposits issued by thrift institutions. As a result, the definitions excluded from M-1 checkable thrift institution deposits (interest-bearing NOW accounts in savings and loan associations, demand deposits in mutual savings banks, and share drafts in credit unions.) Also, the M-2 aggregate excluded time and savings deposits in thrifts.

The new definitions of money (Table 2.1 and Figure 2.2) recognize the increasing similarity of bank and thrift institution deposits brought about by numerous regulatory and institutional changes during the decade of the 1970s. Thus the Fed now has two M-1s—M-1A and M-1B. M-1A is the same as the old M-1, except that it excludes certain foreign commercial bank deposits that were included in the old M-1 aggregate. M-1B adds to M-1A checkable and other transferable deposits issued by all depository institutions. It includes automatic transfer from savings to checking deposits (ATS) accounts, authorized by the Fed in 1978 and by Congress in the Depository Institutions Deregulation and Monetary Control Act of 1980 (hereafter called the "Monetary Control Act of 1980"). The new M-2 and M-3 broad definitions also measure money by type of deposit, rather than by institution of origin; thus they treat time and savings deposits of the same type in the same way, even though they may be offered by different types of depository institutions.

In addition to authorizing ATS accounts, which provide for preauthorized automatic transfers of savings to checking accounts (in case of overdrafts) in banks and thrifts, regulatory changes now permit telephone transfers to checking accounts of bank customers' savings balances, point-of-sale (POS) automated teller terminals permitting remote savings deposit withdrawals from savings and loan associations, and nonfederal government and business savings deposits similar to those owned by individuals.

Table 2.2 *Selected Developments Affecting the Nature of the Monetary Aggregates*

Development	Date First Introduced	Deposit Liability	New Monetary Aggregate Containing Deposit Liability
Preauthorized transfers	9/70	Savings balances at S&Ls and commercial banks	M-2
NOW accounts	6/72	Savings balances at MSBs, S&Ls, and commercial banks	M-1B
2½ year, 4-year, 6-year, and 8-year time deposits	1/70, 7/73 12/74, 6/78, respectively	Time deposits at MSBs, S&Ls, and commercial banks	M-2, M-3
Substantial penalty on early withdrawal of time deposits	7/73	Time deposits at commercial banks, S&Ls, and MSBs	M-2, M-3
Point-of-sale terminals (POS) permitting remote withdrawals of deposits from savings	1/74	Savings balances at S&Ls	M-2
Credit union share drafts	10/74	Regular share accounts at federal credit unions	M-1B
Savings accounts from domestic governments and businesses	11/74, 11/75, respectively	Savings balances at commercial banks	M-2
Telephone transfers	4/75	Savings balances at commercial banks	M-2
Demand deposits at thrifts	5/76	Deposits of MSBs and S&Ls	M-1B
6-month money market certificates	6/78	Time deposits at S&Ls, MSBs, and commercial banks	M-2
Automatic transfer services (ATS)	11/78	Savings balances at commercial banks and thrifts having transactions balances	M-1B

Source: Thomas D. Simpson, "A Proposal for Redefining the Monetary Aggregates," *Federal Reserve Bulletin*, Vol. 65, No. 1, January 1979, p. 15.

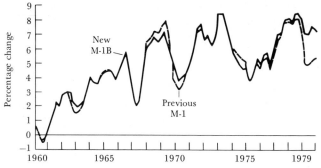

M-1A = Currency
    + Adjusted demand deposits at commercial banks
    − Demand deposits of foreign commercial banks and official institutions

M-1B = M-1A
    + Other checkable deposits (includes NOW accounts, ATS accounts, share
       draft balances at credit unions, demand deposits at thrift institutions)

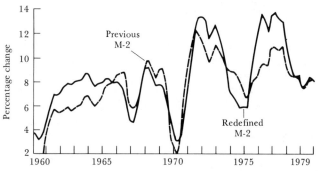

M-2 = M-1B
    + Savings deposits at commercial banks
    + Savings deposits at all other depository institutions
    + Small denomination (less than $100,000) time deposits at commercial banks
    + Small denomination time deposits at all other depository institutions
    + Money market mutual fund shares
    + Overnight repurchase agreements (RP's) issued by commercial banks
    + Overnight Eurodollar deposits at Caribbean branches of U.S. commercial banks
    − M-2 consolidation component

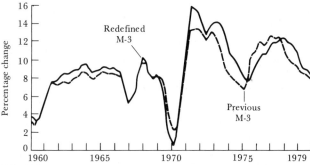

M-3 = M-2
    + Large denomination ($100,000 and over) time deposits at commercial banks
    + Large denomination time deposits at all other depository institutions
    + Term RP's issued by commercial banks
    + Term RP's issued by savings and loans
  Note: Data are year-to-year percentage changes

Figure 2.2 *New and old monetary aggregates definitions. (Source:* Federal Reserve Bank of San Francisco Weekly Letter, *February 29, 1980.)*

The significance of the new changes is that the lines between transactions deposits and savings and many types of time deposits are becoming increasingly blurred. The ATS accounts and other innovations mentioned above reduce the cost of using savings and time deposits as transactions balances and increases the incentives to use them as such.

In addition to adding together similar deposits at commercial banks and thrifts, the new M-2 monetary aggregate includes shares in money market mutual funds, overnight repurchase agreements (RPs) issued by commercial banks, and overnight Eurodollar deposits at Caribbean branches of U.S. commercial banks. These latter items represent financial innovations that sprang up during the 1970s. Money market mutual funds pool savings from large numbers of people and invest them in U.S. Treasury bills, large CDs, or other short-term securities. They pay interest to their depositors based upon earnings from their investment portfolios; in addition, they permit withdrawal of funds on demand and even grant check-writing privileges (in minimum denominations). Thus deposits in money market mutual funds have the characteristics of both transaction balances and short-term savings deposits and compete for the public's favor with deposits offered by banks and thrift institutions.

Repurchase agreements are a sophisticated device used by large corporations or state and local governments to increase yields from their demand deposits or low-interest-bearing savings accounts. Using this device, a bank sells a customer a security out of its portfolio and agrees to buy it back at an agreed price at a specified future date (perhaps the next day). "Eurodollar" deposits arise when a firm arranges to have its excess demand deposit balance transferred to a dollar-denominated deposit at an offshore subsidiary of a U.S. bank near the end of a business day for repatriation the next day or at some convenient date in the near future. Both RPs and Eurodollars earn more interest for businesses or governments than can be earned by holding transactions deposits in domestic U.S. banks; yet, like demand deposits or savings and time deposits, these devices give holders ready money when they need it. At the end of 1979, Caribbean Eurodollar deposits reached $3.5 billion and total commercial bank RPs exceeded $40 billion, up from less than $15 billion in 1975.

The new M-2 is designed to measure the stock of transactions balances plus close substitutes for transactions balances held by the public. For that reason, savings deposits (which ordinarily do not require written notice of withdrawal), small denomination time deposits, money market mutual fund shares, and overnight RPs and Eurodollars are added to M-1B to calculate the new M-2. The new M-3, however, is close in purpose to the old M-4 or M-5: in addition to the new M-2, it contains large CDs and term RPs issued by banks and savings and loan associations. The new M-3 is, therefore, a measure that embraces more clearly both the medium of exchange and liquid store of value functions of money.

Finally, the Fed has defined a very broad new aggregate, called L— for liquid assets. It is constructed by adding to the new M-3 longer term

Eurodollars held by U.S. nonbank residents, various kinds of short-term bonds and U.S. Teasury bills, and short-term Treasury bonds and notes destined to mature in less than 18 months. L is not shown in Figure 2.2, but it is a very large aggregate, totalling $2.1 billion at the end of 1979, which is only 15 percent less than the $2.5 trillion fourth-quarter GNP of that year. L is probably better interpreted as a measure of total short-term liquidity in the economy than as a broad monetary aggregate, such as the new M-3.

2.2
Which definition of money is best?

Since the time series representing the various monetary aggregates do not move in a parallel fashion, the proper definition of money would seem to be a high priority item for monetary analysts. But, despite a debate that extends centuries back into time, and despite the new definitions of money, considerable disagreement still prevails over what collection of assets ought to be designated by the word "money."

The problem is to translate an abstract theoretical concept into concrete, real-world terms. What objects, for example, serve as the medium of exchange? Again, what objects best correspond to the notion of liquid assets as used in monetary theory? Unless these questions are satisfactorily answered, our ability to use monetary theory as a device for interpreting events in the real world can be severely restricted. As discussed in Chapter 1, changes in the money stock and changes in the demand for money alter the aggregate effective demand for goods and services. It would be nice to have an empirical definition of money that allows us to correlate real world changes in effective demand with monetary events.

Attempts to define the real world money stock fall into two categories: (a) the a priori, or theoretical approach; and (b) the empirical approach.

2.2.1
A priori definitions of money

Some monetary theorists stress the medium of exchange function of money, while others think that an understanding of the role of money in the economy requires emphasis on its use as a liquid store of value. Accordingly, the first group prefers something like the M-1 definitions, while the second prefers one or more of the broader concepts.

Unfortunately, not all items in M-1A or M-1B give equal service as a medium of exchange. Currency, for example, is more universally accepted in payment for goods and services than are personal checks. But checks are better when payments must be made through the mails, or when large sums of money are involved. Moreover, large denominations are inferior media of exchange, since few people can make change for a

$1,000, $5,000, or $10,000 bill offered in exchange for a small purchase.

The old distinction between savings and demand deposits is now very weak. Demand deposits are transferable from one owner to another by written order (by check), and banks will give, without delay, currency to their demand depositors. These features give demand deposits their status as media of exchange. Savings deposits differ from demand deposits in that they are ordinarily not transferable by written order; nor are they technically available for encashment without a written 30 day notice. But banks usually ignore the 30 days notice requirement, which brings savings deposits closer to demand deposits in terms of their economic functions. Moreover, the changes in banking regulations permitting banks and thrift institutions to pay utility and other regularly occurring bills from customers' savings accounts, and allowing banks to transfer money automatically or by phone from savings deposits to demand deposits have further blurred the line between demand and time deposits.

The difficulty of drawing the line between various items to be included in the M-1s and other monetary aggregates throws light upon the ambiguities involved in defining money solely in terms of its medium of exchange function. Milton Friedman and Anna J. Schwartz have argued that this approach begs the question of whether the *essential* feature of money is its use as a medium of exchange.[2]

In a money economy, as distinct from a barter economy, acts of purchase are separated from acts of sale. To be sure, separation of these acts cannot be accomplished without a generally accepted medium of exchange, but it is also true that during the interval of time between a sale and a purchase there must be some liquid asset—some *temporary abode of purchasing power,* to use one of Friedman's favorite phrases—to serve sellers before they turn into buyers. This feature of money is also one of its essential functions. An object that cannot serve as a temporary abode of purchasing power probably cannot serve as a medium of exchange.

But therein lies the problem. The asset that serves as a temporary abode of purchasing power need not also serve as a medium of exchange. As we have seen, savings deposits in banks and thrift institutions are very good temporary abodes. In descending order, so are time deposits (with fixed near-term maturity dates) in both banks and thrifts, U.S. Government savings bonds such as Series E and H varieties, U.S. Treasury bills, and short-term bonds issued by big firms. To be sure, most of these items are held for more than a few weeks or months; but so are the M-1s. As indicated in Chapter 1, currency and demand deposits in the hands of the public average many weeks worth of GNP.

Thus it is impossible to classify assets held by individuals and businesses solely in terms of their medium of exchange function or their temporary store of value function. For this reason, Friedman, Schwartz, and

---

[2]The following discussion is drawn from their *Monetary Statistics of the United States* (New York: National Bureau of Economic Research, 1970), pp. 106–111.

many other authors[3] accept a broader definition of money. In their empirical work, Friedman and Schwartz used the old M-2 concept; other authors with similar persuasions have used the old M-3 or even broader concepts. But, whatever concept is used, if we accept the Friedman–Schwartz arguments, no a priori theoretical reason forces us to accept one definition over the other. Since many assets serve as liquid, temporary abodes of purchasing power, many are eligible for inclusion in a broader definition of money. No convincing theoretical basis exists for drawing a line between one set of assets and another.

2.2.2
The empirical definition of money

It thus appears that a priori reasoning alone cannot give us a unique empirical definition of the money stock. Perhaps we should not be surprised. It may well be that no issue of principle is involved, and that no single definition of money need be best.

The problem is how to choose an empirical counterpart to an abstract theoretical concept. The real world is a lot messier and more changeable than the simple world we usually assume for the purpose of developing theories of the relationship between changes in the money supply and changes in the effective demand for goods and services. This being so, many economists are prepared to follow the advice of Friedman and Schwartz when they argue:

> the test is strictly pragmatic: which counterpart is most useful in making predictions about observable phenomena on the basis of the theory one accepts? The answer may well vary with time and place and may differ according to the phenomena to be predicted and also according to the theory accepted. Any answer is necessarily tentative and subject to change as further evidence accumulates.[4]

This pragmatic approach was recently endorsed by the prestigious Bach Committee in its report to the Federal Reserve System.[5]

---

[3]Including J.M. Keynes. See the *General Theory*, p. 167, n. 1, where Keynes argues that, depending on the problem at hand, money can be defined to include all bank deposits and even Treasury bills.

[4]M. Friedman and A.J. Schwartz, *Monetary Statistics of the United States*, p. 1.

[5]Advisory Committee on Monetary Statistics, *Improving the Monetary Aggregates* (Board of Governors, Federal Reserve System, June 1976), p. 7. "In conducting monetary policy, the Federal Reserve should use . . . that monetary total (aggregate), or totals, through which it can most reliably affect the behavior of its ultimate objectives—the price level, employment, output, and the like. Which total or totals best satisfy that requirement depends in turn upon (1) how accurately the total can be measured; (2) how precisely . . . the Fed can control the total; and (3) how closely and reliably changes in the total are related to the ultimate policy objectives."

Well then, what *is* the evidence? As might be expected it is mixed. Most of the studies of the question have used the strength of the relationship between the levels and changes in gross national product and various definitions of money as a criterion for selecting the best definition of money. This led Milton Friedman and David Meiselman to accept the old M-2 definition in 1963, Richard H. Timberlake, Jr. and James Fortson to accept old M-1 in 1967, and George G. Kaufman to accept a concept close to old M-3 in 1969.[6] In 1974, Frederick C. Schadrack, a Federal Reserve economist, concluded that there is "little support for the view that money should be defined narrowly (as M-1)" and that on the basis of the strength of the money–gross national product relationship, stability of the relationship over time, and predictive accuracy, M-2 is the best measure of money. Having said this, however, Schadrack hastened to add that the "superiority of M-2 is not overwhelming . . . and additional data are needed to determine conclusively which definition of money is most closely related to GNP."[7]

The jury is also out on the new monetary aggregates. On the whole, they perform slightly better than the old aggregates in standard empirical applications. Nonetheless, they are not all equal in different applications. M-1B and the M-2 are better than the old monetary aggregates in studies that try to measure the long-run demand for money, though new M-2 is better than M-1B. For quarter-to-quarter movements in money demand, however, M-1B and the new M-3 are about as reliable as the old definitions. Studies that link changes in gross national product to changes in the money supply give the nod to new M-2 as being a more reliable predictor than old M-2 and old M-3; but M-1B and new M-3 are only marginally better than old M-1 or old M-4 and M-5 in "explaining" GNP.[8]

So, even the empirical approach has not settled the definitional issue. Where does that leave the student? Exactly in the same place as the expert. When applying the money concept to the real world, he must make do with several competing definitions of money. He will be comforted by the fact that the various monetary aggregates generally move in the same

---

[6]M. Friedman and D. Meiselman, "The Relative Stability of Monetary Velocity and the Investment Multiplier in the United States, 1897–1958," in *Commission on Money and Credit, Stabilization Policies* (Englewood Cliffs, N.J.: Prentice-Hall, 1963), pp. 165–268; R.H. Timberlake and J. Fortson, "Time Deposits in the Definition of Money," *American Economic Review,* Vol. 57, No. 1 (March 1967), pp. 190–194; Kaufman, "More on an Empirical Definition of Money," *American Economic Review,* Vol. 59, No. 1 (March 1969), pp. 78–87; See review of these and other studies in M. Friedman and A.J. Schwartz, *Monetary Statistics of the United States,* pp. 178–188.

[7]"An Empirical Approach to the Definition of Money," in *Federal Reserve Bank of New York Monetary Aggregates and Monetary Policy,* October 1974, p. 39. Of course, Schadrack's M-1 and M-2 are the pre-1980 definitions of money.

[8]The conclusions in this paragraph are drawn from Neil G. Berkman, "Some Comments on the New Monetary Aggregates," *Federal Reserve Bank of Boston New England Economic Review,* March/April 1980, pp. 45–63.

direction, so that if he wishes to have a broad indicator of monetary changes, he might feel free to use any or all of the three major measures. But, before making up his mind, he should consider situations in which the measures move in opposite directions. He may then have to choose. In so doing, it would be well for him to recall two of the criteria mentioned by the Bach Committee (see footnote 5): (1) the ability of the monetary authorities to control the aggregate; and (2) how closely and reliably changes in the aggregate are related to ultimate policy objectives. As we shall see, the Fed probably has more power to influence total commercial bank deposits than it does just demand deposits. Recent changes in the law will, in the near future, give it direct controls over deposits in thrift institutions as well. These facts seem to argue in favor of using the new M-2 definition of money.[9] But, as the spirit of the above discussion indicates, we should not be rigid about this choice. At times, M-1A, M-1B, new M-3, or some other monetary aggregate, to be defined in the future, may be more useful for the problem at hand. It is important to keep an open mind.

SUMMARY

Money can be defined theoretically in terms of its functions as a medium of exchange, measure of value, standard for deferred payment, and liquid store of value. But the empirical definition must focus upon what serves as money. This definition must, of necessity, vary over time and space, since the things that function as money differ in different places and times.

The main pre-1980 definitions of money included M-1 (bank demand deposits and currency), M-2 (M-1 plus bank savings and small time deposits), and M-3 (M-2 plus thrift institution savings and small time deposits). The new definitions of money recognize many legal and other changes in bank practices and broaden the narrow definition of money to include all transactions deposits in all depository institutions, as with M-1B. The new M-2 and new M-3 also differ substantially from the old M-2 and old M-3, including items such as money market mutual funds shares, repurchase agreements, and Eurodollar deposits.

The proper definition of money eludes economists. The a priori or theoretical approach is unable to segregate assets according to the medium of exchange and store of value functions, which overlap in different monetary assets. The empirical approach, which tries to define money

---

[9]Money market mutual fund shares, however are not covered by the changes in the law; hence new M-2 may not be totally subject to Federal Reserve policies. Straws in the wind, perhaps, are the brief controls placed on the funds during the spring and early summer of 1980, when the Fed imposed a broad range of direct control measures on the financial system in order to break an extraordinary leap in the inflation rate during that period. Also, at this writing (May 1981) proposed legislation in being considered to impose reserve requirements on money market fund liabilities.

according to which aggregate best correlates with general economic activity, is also unable to isolate a single definition that is good for all times and places. As a result, economists and policy makers must exercise considerable judgement in deciding upon which definition to use for the purpose at hand.

DISCUSSION QUESTIONS

1. What is the reason U.S. government deposits in banks are excluded from the definition of money? Should the same considerations apply to state and local government deposits?

2. Since the principal function of money is to serve as a medium of exchange, why don't economists limit the definition of money to currency, coin, checkable, and other transferable deposits?

3. Are all stores of value money?

4. What type of money is strictly a medium of exchange, and not a store of value?

5. Compare the a priori or theoretical definition of money to the empirical definition.

6. Some monetary theorists argue that the definition of money ought to include short-term government bonds, such as 90-day U.S. Treasury bills and cashable assets, such as cash surrender values of life insurance companies. Do you agree?

7. What are the principle differences between the old (pre-1980) definitions of money and the new?

IMPORTANT TERMS AND CONCEPTS

- ☐ automatic transfer from savings (ATS) accounts
- ☐ cash items in the process of collection (CIPC)
- ☐ certificates of deposit (CDs)
- ☐ currency and coin
- ☐ Eurodollars
- ☐ Federal Reserve notes
- ☐ M-1
- ☐ M-1A
- ☐ M-1B
- ☐ M-2
- ☐ M-3
- ☐ national bank notes
- ☐ negotiable order of withdrawal (NOW) accounts
- ☐ repurchase agreements (RPs) at commercial banks
- ☐ tax and loan accounts

ADDITIONAL
READINGS

The whole problem of defining money empirically is interestingly presented in Milton Friedman and Anna J. Schwartz, *Monetary Statistics of the United States* (New York: National Bureau of Economic Research, 1970). The Fed's deliberations on defining the new monetary aggregates are discussed in the *Advisory Committee on Monetary Statistics, Improving the Monetary Aggregates* (Washington, D.C.: Board of Governors of the Federal Reserve System, June 1976) and in two articles in the *Federal Reserve Bulletin:* Thomas D. Simpson, "A Proposal for Redefining the Monetary Aggregates," Vol. 65, No. 1, January 1979, p. 13 and Thomas D. Simpson "The Redefined Monetary Aggregates," Vol. 66, No. 2, February 1980, p. 97. A good discussion for students is in Carl M. Gambs, "Money, a Changing Concept in a Changing World," *Federal Reserve Bank of Kansas Monthly Review,* January 1977, pp. 3–12.

Financial Markets and Financial Institutions

3

O U T L I N E

Types of Financial Markets
Direct and Indirect Finance
Are Financial Markets Necessary?
Why Financial Intermediaries?
Some Detail on Financial Intermediaries
Federal and Federally Sponsored Credit Agencies
Financial Instruments
Bonds
Purchasing Power Loans, Variable Interest Rate Loans, and Shared Appreciation Mortgages:
Defenses Against Inflation
Common Stocks
Capital Markets and Money Markets
Interest Rates and Security Prices

Much of the action in a modern money-using economy takes place in its financial markets. These markets consist of a cluster of institutions that have as their principle function the transmission of funds from savers and lenders to business, consumer, and government borrowers. The cluster includes the stock and bond markets; financial intermediaries, such as banks and thrift institutions; a number of highly specialized firms, such as stock brokers and bond dealers, investment bankers, pension funds, investment companies, and insurance companies; and governmental agencies, such as the Federal Reserve System, the U.S. Treasury, and federal lending agencies.

The people who work in the financial markets are not participating in a sideshow. As of the middle of 1980, 5.2 million people were employed by the financial sector. That is more than the number of workers in the whole agricultural sector and about the same number employed by the transportation system and the public utilities.[1] Even more impressive is the dollar value of the work they do: In 1979 financial markets made it possible for borrowers to raise $395 billion.[2]

Since the gross national product in 1979 was $2,365 billion, the financial markets moved the equivalent of one-sixth of the GNP from households and other primary borrowers in the business, consuming, and government sectors.

A broad overview of the structure and functions of the financial system is necessary for an understanding of how a money-using economy works. To this end, the balance of this chapter is given over to a schematic portrayal of financial markets, a description of their most important institutions, and a discussion of the major vehicles (financial instruments) they use to carry on their work.

3.1
Types of financial markets

The main job of financial markets is the transmission of loanable funds and financial capital from surplus income units to deficit spenders. Surplus income units are individuals and organizations whose current inflows of money income exceed their current money outlays. Deficit spenders are units whose current outlays exceed their current inflows of money.

In the absence of borrowing and lending and of changes in the money supply, much of the existing stock of money would gradually shift into the hands of surplus income units and out of the hands of deficit spenders. Over time, a drift of cash into the money hoards of surplus in-

---

[1] *Federal Reserve Bulletin*, July 1980, Vol. 66, No. 7, p. A47.
[2] See the "Flow of Fund Accounts," *ibid.*, p. A44.

come units might be damaging to the economy, since the build-up of money hoards could provoke a drop in the effective demand for goods and services.

It is, therefore, a fortunate thing that surplus income units have a strong motive to lend or invest cash they do not wish to use and that deficit spenders are quite willing to borrow or accept financial capital from them. The motives are not complicated. Surplus spending units want to spread their spending over time and, therefore, desire to accumulate financial assets in order to fulfill their plans for future outlays. They prefer to lend or to buy stocks because that gives them assets that have positive financial yields, as opposed to the zero or low yield that comes from holdings of the medium of exchange. Deficit spenders have various motives for wanting to borrow or acquire investment capital for current spending. Businesspeople think they can make profitable investments; consumers want to buy homes, automobiles, furniture, and appliances, and governments, for reasons that lie deep in the political system (see Section 20.4), cannot seem to help spending more than they take in (state and local governments frequently have budgetary surpluses, but the federal government rarely does).

Thus the existence of surplus and deficit spending units sets the stage for the development of financial markets. Although the main job of all these markets is to transmit funds between surplus and deficit units, their evolution has been characterized by a high degree of differentiation. Not all lenders want the same kinds of financial assets, and not all borrowers are willing to make the same kinds of commitments. For that reason, the financial system contains a number of different markets, each with its own characteristic features. Before we examine these features, however, it is necessary to have an overview of the financial system. To this end, we first turn to a study of the basic paths by which funds flow from surplus income to deficit spending units.

3.1.1
Direct and indirect finance

Figure 3.1 is almost self-explanatory. Even so, we should identify some of the actors and explain some of the terminology in the diagram. The principle actors are the groups that make up the surplus income and deficit spending units. Notice that each sector—household, nonfinancial business, government, and foreign—shows up as both a lender and a borrower. Within each sector there are individual units that either specialize in lending or borrowing or do both. For example, many households may go into debt, say for a new house or car, while at the same time putting money into a bank or buying a stock or a bond. The same is true of many, if not most, individual members of the other sectors. Probe any balance sheet, public or private, and you will most likely find both earning assets

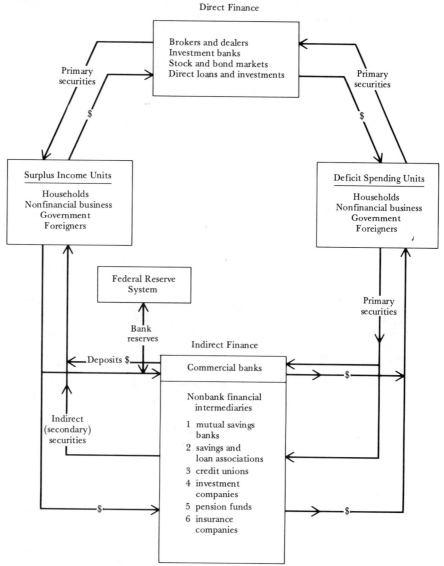

Figure 3.1 *Financial institutions.*

and liabilities; commonly, the earning assets include interest earning deposits or shares in financial intermediaries, stocks, bonds, and so forth.

The flow of loanable funds originating with the surplus income units divides into two streams, one direct and one indirect. Each of these streams ultimately reaches the deficit spenders; but, as the diagram shows, the channels through which they flow are quite different. Most of the direct financial flow goes into the hands of brokers and dealers in the stock and bond markets. A *broker* is an agent who acts for people who wish to buy or sell securities. *Brokers* do not buy and sell securities for their own accounts; but, working through the stock exchanges or through their widespread networks of contacts, they find buyers for sellers and sellers for buyers. In return for their services, they charge fees to their customers.

Dealers buy and sell securities for their own accounts. They are wholesalers who make their livings from spreads between the buying and selling prices of securities. Their incomes depend both upon the volume of securities they buy and sell and upon their ability to guess right about the price spreads. Needless to say, it can be a risky business. Perhaps that is why many dealers double as brokers. The latter may occasionally suffer from a lack of customers, but at least they do not bear the risks of taking speculative positions.

In the United States there are a number of securities markets. The New York Stock Exchange and the American Stock Exchange carry a number of listed stocks that are bought and sold by brokers and dealers who have seats of their own, or connections with others who have seats, on the exchanges. There is also the over-the-counter market, which deals mainly with securities not listed on the other two exchanges and which operates through brokers and dealers scattered throughout the country. Security trading in the New York and American Stock Exchanges takes place on their floors.

Firms desiring to float new issues of stocks or bonds frequently employ the services of *investment bankers*. Investment bankers are an adventurous breed. They are specialized firms or banks that have capital, access to short-term credit, sales forces, and above all, expert knowledge about the state of the security markets and the sources of loanable funds. This unique combination of attributes enables them to go to companies wishing to issue large blocks of securities and to offer to underwrite or to sell the securities for them. When they underwrite issues, they actually buy the whole block at a fixed price, hoping to use their connections and market knowledge to "retail" the securities at favorable prices. Typically, a number of investment bankers will compete individually or in syndicates for the privilege of underwriting the security issues of well-known and respected companies. When the companies are less well known, the investment banker will operate mainly as a broker, promising his "best effort" for a fee.

Funds do not only move through formal market channels. As Figure 3.1 indicates, surplus income units also lend and invest directly. Since much of this activity is done on a face-to-face basis, it is not captured by official statistical compilations. For that reason, we don't know how much of it takes place. However, compared to the flows captured in the data relating to formal markets, it cannot be very much. It mostly consists of loans between friends and family members and of personal credit advanced to small businesses.

The stock and trade of formal markets consists of marketable *primary securities* issued by deficit spending units. The function of the markets, of course, is to bring buyers of these securities into contact with sellers. Generally speaking, the security markets are among the most competitive and active of all markets. It is relatively cheap for security buyers to enter the markets, although it is more difficult for sellers to do so. There are thousands of companies and governmental units (federal, state, and local) that sell new issues in the markets every year.

Deficit spenders who cannot market their debts directly must go to bank and nonbank financial intermediaries for their capital. There they will find less competition for their debts; but, if their prospects are good and if they are known to be honest and trustworthy, they will frequently find more than one willing lender, particularly if they can pay competitive interest rates.

Financial intermediaries are the heart of the system of *indirect financial markets*. The intermediaries collect funds for relending from surplus income units by selling them various kinds of *indirect* or *secondary securities* (to use the lingo of the finance field). Indirect securities consist of deposits in commercial banks and in mutual savings banks, shares and deposits in savings and loan associations and in credit unions, shares in investment companies, rights in pension funds, and policy rights in insurance companies.

From a formal point of view, a share in a thrift institution is an ownership claim on the institution, while a deposit is a debt instrument; however, from a practical point of view, they are the same. Both are fixed value claims that are honored by the institutions in exactly the same way. A savings and loan association or a credit union will cash a share as readily as a bank will cash a savings deposit.

Investment companies typically collect money from surplus income units by selling them shares. The funds so acquired are invested in marketable stocks and bonds of business firms or government units. Investment companies pay dividends to share holders out of the interest, dividends, and capital gains earned by their investments. The market values of the shares in the investment companies fluctuate with the market values of the stocks and bonds they own.

Pension funds and insurance companies collect monies from their members and clients in the form of regular contributions or premiums. The funds are usually reinvested in marketable stocks and bonds, though insurance companies, in particular, invest considerable sums in mortgages and real estate.

Although most loanable funds are provided by surplus spending units, a small but highly significant sum comes in the form of new money created by the Federal Reserve System. As indicated in Figure 3.1, this money ultimately ends up as additions to the reserves of the banking system. As such, it provides the banks with the wherewithal to expand their loans to, and investments in, the private sector and their purchases of securities issued by federal, state, and local governments. In the process of expanding its loans and investments, the banking system creates new deposits and thereby expands the money supply. For this reason, the interaction between the Fed and the banking system is a very important topic. We shall discuss it in great detail in Chapters 6, 7, 8, 9, and 10.

3.1.2
Are financial markets necessary?

It is possible to imagine a system in which lenders and borrowers seek each other out by knocking on doors, using the telephone, advertising in newspapers, working through mutual acquaintances, and so forth. But, clearly, such a system would be very inefficient. The costs of search would be high for both borrowers and lenders, and systematic information on the credit-worthiness of borrowers would be expensive to acquire. Lenders would be forced to conduct most of their business at the local level, lending only to friends or local businessmen with good reputations, even though trustworthy businesses in other parts of the country might need capital and might be willing to pay handsomely for the privilege of borrowing it. Moreover, the lack of organized markets would destroy the liquidity of financial assets: To avoid locking up their funds in long term commitments, lenders would tend to restrict their loans to short periods of time.

Organized financial markets provide clear advantages over do-it-yourself lending and borrowing. Companies that pass muster with the Securities and Exchange Commission and that abide by the rules of the organized stock exchanges can list their securities for sale with them. Attached to the market are firms of brokers and dealers who provide or buy research services giving current information and opinions about the financial health of borrowing firms. Individual investors can also subscribe to these services, or perhaps reply upon information given in the financial press.

Over the years, the rules and the customs of the security markets have resulted in a high level of honest trading and dealing. Though frauds certainly occur, they are relatively rare, considering the volume of business done every year.

Finally, a major advantage of organized markets is the competitive environment they establish for lenders and borrowers. This environment helps lenders get the highest yields on funds consistent with the risk and terms under which they wish to commit their funds. Borrowers, not being confined to local sources, are in a position to acquire funds at the lowest interest rates available in the markets for their risk categories.

The markets are national and even international in their scope, and the information on the prospects and capabilities of borrowers generated by expert researchers and informed opinion leaders is available to most market participants. The leading participants, the major traders and investment companies, tend to establish the going prices for the securities issued by the various borrowers. When expert opinion judges a particular stock or a bond to be overpriced relative to the alternatives available in the market, traders tend to shy away from it, causing its price to fall. The firms issuing the securities get less money for each security issued, and, as a result, their costs of borrowing increase. When expert opinion judges a stock or a bond to be underpriced, traders increase their demand for the security, raising its price, which lowers the cost of borrowing for the issuing firm.

Thus, except for random movements, the prices of various securities, and by implication, their yields,[3] are, to a large extent, governed by the best and most informed opinion in the market. To be sure, this opinion is often wrong, and in any event it is rarely uniform; but, it is likely to be far better than the information available to the ordinary lender, whose ability and resources severely limit the information he can collect on his own. If he is willing to accept the inevitable risk that goes along with investments in marketable stocks and bonds, he is at least assured that their prices will reflect the most up-to-date information about the prospects of the borrowers to whom he is committing his savings.

3.1.3
Why financial intermediaries?

Many people prefer to place their funds with financial intermediaries rather than to invest in securities sold through the stock and bond markets. They do so even when the financial return they receive from indirect claims is less than the yields they can get from holding primary securities. Why?

One part of the answer is the liquidity provided by deposits and shares in banks, thrift institutions and some of the mutual investment companies, such as the money market funds. It is much easier, and far less costly, to convert to cash assets invested in these forms than it is to sell stocks or bonds through brokers or dealers. The smaller risk of investing in intermediary liabilities compared to the risk of investing in portfolios of primary securities is another part of the answer.

There are two kinds of risk people want to avoid: default (sometimes called credit) risk and market risk. Default risk arises when a company or some other borrower is unable to repay all or part of a loan. Market risk comes from the fluctuations in market prices of stocks and bonds. People may be forced to sell their stocks and bonds at prices below those at which they bought.

---

[3]Roughly speaking, "yields" are the periodic earnings investors get from holding stocks and bonds, expressed as a percentage of their purchase prices. We will discuss this concept in greater detail in Section 3.4.5.

Individuals with large financial resources can find ways to reduce both types of risk. By spreading their resources among the securities issued by many borrowers, they may stabilize the total value of their investments, provided that the prices of the individual securities they buy do not always fluctuate in the same direction and to the same degree. For example, from a risk-avoidance point of view, it is better to invest in two $50 stocks whose prices typically fluctuate by equal amounts in opposite directions than it is to purchase a single $100 stock whose price fluctuates by twice the amount of either of the $50 stocks. In addition, combining in one portfolio stocks and bonds with both stable and volatile characteristics reduces the overall volatility of the value of a portfolio.

Making many loans instead of just a few also reduces default risk. For example, if every loan carries a 10 percent chance of default, regardless of its size, then the chance of loss of a portfolio of two independent loans is only 1 percent (10 percent of 10 percent). The chance of loss of three loans is .1 percent, of four loans .01 percent, and so forth.

Risk spreading by means of enlarging the variety of loans and investments is time consuming and costly in terms of the effort and expense of searching out borrowers and of acquiring information about their prospects and trustworthiness. That is why people, many with substantial wealth, frequently prefer to put some or all of their financial investments into the hands of a financial intermediary. The financial yields from investments in indirect claims may not be as high as those derived from direct investments, but the effective returns, after taking into account search and information costs, may actually be higher. In addition, most intermediaries provide lenders with assets that have superior liquidity, stable value, and relatively little default risk.

What gives financial intermediaries their superiority as lenders? It is not the genius of those who operate them. Their superiority comes from size and experience. By collecting driblets of funds from large numbers of surplus income units, intermediaries can create large portfolios out of small ones. They can afford to spread the costs of acquiring information on prospective borrowers and of diversifying investments in order to reduce both default risk and market risk. Frequent contact with borrowers gives them expertise in appraising loan opportunities. In addition, their very existence attracts borrowers who, because they wish to economize costs that arise in connection with direct borrowing, are willing to pay intermediaries higher interest rates than they would pay by borrowing through channels of direct finance. Moreover, many borrowers are too small and too little known to sell their debts on organized security markets.

Thus, the justification for financial intermediaries comes from increasing the liquidity of lenders and from the cost and risk reduction that accompany their operations. If they did not provide such benefits to lenders and borrowers, they would go out of business. For that reason, it is absurd to argue, as do many well-intentioned but uninformed reformers, that banks and other financial institutions are parasites upon the body of the productive sector of the economy. The people who work for financial intermediaries earn their keep. Provided that financial markets stay open to competition, we have more to gain than to lose from their activities. That is not to say we should leave them alone. Financial history is replete with instances of fraud and deceit that have led to financial and economic collapses.[4] Some regulation is in the best interest of both the financial sector and the economy at large. But regulation is not abolition. The problem for social policy in this area is to maximize the benefits that lenders, borrowers, and the economy in general derive from well-functioning capital and money markets, while, at the same time, minimizing the dangers arising from defects in the system.

3.2
Some detail on financial intermediaries

Financial intermediaries best known to the public include commercial banks, thrift institutions, life insurance companies, investment funds, and pension funds. All of these intermediaries have grown very rapidly in the post–World War II era. Table 3.1 documents this growth for banks, thrift institutions, and life insurance companies.

Notice how uneven are the growth rates between the various kinds of intermediaries. These uneven rates reflect the differences in the kinds of business conducted by the various intermediaries and differences in the degree and kinds of regulations to which they are subjected by federal and state governments. These differences are reflected in the modes of operation of the various intermediaries and the kinds of assets and liabilities they acquire.

Figure 3.2 summarizes the asset structures of banks, thrift institutions, and life insurance companies. Commercial banks are by far the most diversified of all financial intermediaries. By law they are empowered to acquire securities issued by federal, state, and local governments, commercial paper (a form of short-term bond issued by large corporations), corporate bonds (but not stocks), mortgages secured by both private residences and commercial property, business loans, and consumer loans. We shall discuss the commercial banking business in much greater detail in Chapters 4 and 5.

Traditionally, savings and loan associations acquired most of their

---

[4]Examples abound. See Charles Mackay, *Extraordinary Popular Delusions and the Madness of Crowds* (New York: Noonday Press of Farrar, Straus and Giroux, 1932, 22nd printing, 1974) and Cedric B. Cowing, *Populists, Plungers, and Progressives* (Princeton, N.J.: Princeton University Press, 1965).

Table 3.1 *Assets of Selected Financial Institutions, 1950 and 1979*

Sector	Assets (billions of dollars)		Average Rate of Change, 1950–1979 (percent)
	1950	1979	
Commercial banks	171	1351	7.4
Savings and loan associations	17	579	12.0
Life insurance companies	64	432	6.5
Mutual savings banks	22	163	7.1
Credit unions	1	66	15.5

Source: *1976 Statistical Abstract of the United States* (Washington, D.C.: U.S. Dept. of Commerce, 1976), Section 16. *Federal Reserve Bulletin,* Vol. 66, No. 7, July 1980, A17 and A27.

funds by issuing fixed-value shares and certificates of deposit to savers. But the Consumer Checking Account Equity Act of 1980, which is Title III of the Depository Institutions Deregulation and Monetary Control Act of 1980, authorized these institutions (as well as all other depository institutions) to offer interest-bearing NOW accounts to individuals and nonprofit religious, philanthropic, charitable, or educational institutions. Previously, these accounts were available to savings and loan associations only in the northeast part of the country; they are now available nationally.

The 1980 law also amended the old Homeowners Loan Act to allow savings and loan associations to go beyond their main territory of mortgage loans to homebuyers; they may now invest up to 20 percent of their assets in consumer loans, commercial paper, and corporate debt securities. They may also invest in shares or certificates of open-end investment companies registered with the Securities and Exchange Commission, provided the companies' portfolios are restricted to investments that the savings and loan associations may make directly. The same amendment authorized the associations to offer credit-card services and to exercise trust and fiduciary powers (which allow them to manage estates and property of widows, orphans, and others who for some reason cannot manage their own).

The changes in the law clearly blur the line between savings and loan associations and commercial banks. As the years pass, the competition between the two types of institutions will undoubtedly increase. At present, the competition is already formidable. There are approximately 5,000 associations throughout the United States, as compared with about 15,000 commercial banks. Savings and loan associations are chartered by both the federal government and by individual states. All federally chartered associations (about one-third of the total) must belong to and be regulated by the Federal Home Loan Bank Board (FHLBB). State associations can

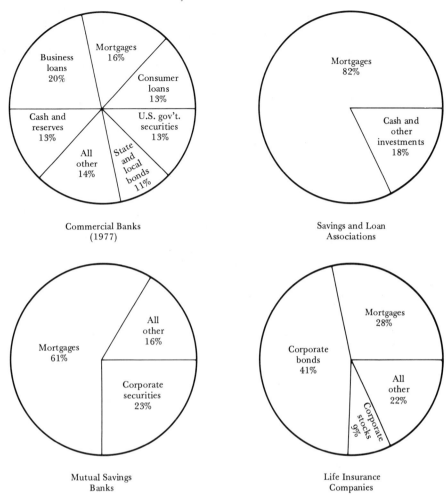

Figure 3.2 *Assets of selected financial intermediaries, 1979. (Source:* Federal Reserve Bulletin.*)*

join if they wish, and most do. Over four-fifths of all S&Ls belong. Among the benefits of membership is the privilege of borrowing from the Board when private saving flows into the associations begin to dry up or turn into outflows. The FHLBB loans help to stabilize Savings and Loan mortgage loans. Finally, the 1980 law authorizes the FHLBB to set up a check-clearing system for member associations.

Mutual savings banks are state-chartered organizations. They are concentrated primarily in the New England and Middle Atlantic States. They can, but are not required to, join the Federal Reserve System. Almost all of their funds come from savings deposits, though the 1980 law permits them to issue NOW accounts and regular checking accounts. The bulk of their assets are invested in home mortgages and high-grade corporate securities, though the law now allows them to invest up to 5 percent of their assets in commercial, corporate, and business loans within 75 miles of their offices. In most states in which mutual savings banks exist, the laws specify quite clearly the assets to which they must restrict themselves.

Life insurance companies sell both risk protection and income to their policy holders. Many families, especially young ones, cannot build estates through normal savings and investment channels, but still need the protection estates provide family members in the event of loss of life of the head of the household. Life insurance is designed to provide this protection. In addition, it frequently carries a savings component, so that the premiums paid by policy holders often have both an insurance and a savings element. Unlike savings accounts and certificates of deposit in banks and thrift institutions, life insurance policies provide relatively little liquidity for policy holders, except, perhaps, for the accumulated cash value of their policies or policy loans they can get from the companies. Except for emergencies, people rarely turn to their insurance policies for funds.

Steady and predictable premium inflows plus the statistical predictability of their liabilities enable life insurance companies to anticipate their cash inflows and outflows. This, plus the permissiveness of the law, gives them the ability to plan and to diversify their assets into stocks, bonds, mortgages, real estate investments, and other loans. As a result, their asset structures are more complicated than the structures of the savings banks.

Other important intermediaries include credit unions, pension plans, and investment companies (mutual funds). Credit unions are chartered either under the federal government, in which case they are regulated by the Bureau of Federal Credit Unions, or under state governments. Individual credit unions are organized around affinity groups, such as employees of a firm, a school district, or a government agency. They collect most of their money by selling shares (some of which are checkable interest-bearing "share draft" accounts) to their members. Loans are restricted to members, taking the form primarily of automobile, furniture, appliance, and personal loans, although changes in the regulations governing their activities have, in recent years, enabled them to make real estate loans as well.

Pension funds take regular contributions from employers and invest them mainly in stocks and bonds for the purpose of providing workers with annuities during their retirement years. Investment companies appeal to small savers and others who are unable or do not desire to invest directly in stocks and bonds themselves. They offer both diversification and expertise to their customers. Since the values of their liabilities fluctuate with the market value of their assets, investment companies are not as good as banks or thrift institutions as a source of liquidity for savers. Nonetheless, they are very popular. At the end of 1979, assets of mutual investment funds amounted to $49 billion compared to $66 billion for credit unions.

3.3
Federal and federally sponsored credit agencies

A number of federal and federally sponsored lending agencies are active financial intermediaries. The most active are in the fields of agricultural and housing finance. The principal agricultural credit agencies supervised by the Farm Credit Administration include the Banks for Cooperatives, Federal Intermediate Credit Banks, and the Federal Land Banks. The agencies supplying mortgage credit include organizations such as the Federal Home Loan Banks, the Federal National Mortgage Association (FNMA, or "Fannie Mae"), and the Government National Mortgage Association (GNMA, or "Ginnie Mae").

The federal government originally subsidized these agencies, but now they are mostly owned by their borrowers. Since they are not subject to state usury laws, which put ceilings on interest rates, and since they pay no federal income taxes, these institutions have a competitive advantage over private lenders. They get much of their lending capital by issuing securities that, while not carrying the guarantees of U.S. Treasury bonds, are regarded as virtually free of risk by investors. As a result, they are highly prized by banks and other institutions, which treat them on a par with Treasury securities. The interest rates they carry are only slightly higher than Treasury obligations, which, along with their other advantages, allow them to lend to their customers more cheaply than private intermediaries.

Among the three major farm credit agencies, farmers can find money for crop, equipment, storage, and even mortgage loans. At the end of 1980, the agencies had about $60 billion of outstanding debt. They lend primarily to farm coops and credit associations that, in turn, make loans to farmers.

The Federal National Mortgage Association (Fannie Mae) is a major force in the housing field. At the end of 1980, it had over $50 billion of debt outstanding, which is about 27 percent of all the debt owned by federal credit agencies at that time. Fannie Mae's main function is to provide a secondary market for mortgage loans guaranteed by the Federal Housing Administration and by the Veterans Administration, which it buys from banks, thrift institutions, and other lenders who, when in need of funds, may desire to liquidate some of their own mortgage investments.

The twelve Federal Home Loan Banks are lenders to savings and loan associations. As such, they also provide support for the mortgage market. However, instead of buying mortgages with the funds they acquire from selling their securities, the Home Loan Banks simply make direct loans to savings and loan associations. The latter seek such loans in time of stress, when shortages of deposit funds put pressure upon them to reduce their real estate loans. In December 1980, the Federal Home Loan Banks had outstanding debt of over $35 billion, or about 70 percent of the amount outstanding from Fannie Mae.

The Government National Mortgage Association (Ginnie Mae) is a wholly-owned government corporation within the Department of Housing and Urban Development. It has several functions. One is to use funds borrowed from the Treasury to buy mortgages from private lenders at favorable prices in order to help government-favored kinds of housing; it then resells them to Fannie Mae at the market price, taking a loss. Ginnie Mae also raises funds for housing by issuing securities backed by pools of mortgages held by Fannie Mae and other federal housing lending agencies. One important program of the GNMA involves "pass-through securities." Under this program, principal and interest payments collected on mortgages in specified pools are "passed through" to holders of GNMA guaranteed certificates, after deduction of servicing and guarantee fees. The certificates are issued against specified mortgage pools of Federal Housing Administration and Veterans Administration guaranteed mortgages.[5]

An important, but little known, federal lending agency that began operation in 1974 is the Federal Finance Bank (FFB). The FFB makes loans from funds borrowed from the U.S. Treasury and the public. It does not, in turn, make direct loans to the public; instead, it lends money to so-called on-budget federal agencies that, in turn, lend money to the private sector. Among the FFB clients are the Commodity Credit Corporation, the Veterans Administration, the Small Business Administration, the Tennessee Valley Authority, the Farmer's Home Administration, the Rural Electrification Administration, and (close to home for students) the Student Loan Marketing Association. In 1980, the FFB had over $75 billion of loans outstanding.[6]

Figure 3.3 details the trends of federal credit from 1971 to the level

[5]Further details on the GNMA are in *First Boston Corporation Handbook of Securities of United States Government and Federal Agencies,* 27th edition (New York: 1976), pp. 98–102.

[6]These loans are financed with debt issued by the FFB, *not* by the U.S. Treasury. The activities of the bank are, therefore, "off-budget," even though it makes loans to "on-budget" agencies. For a discussion of off-budget financing, see "The Sugar Daddy of Federal Credit," *Citibank Monthly Economic Letter,* June 1980.

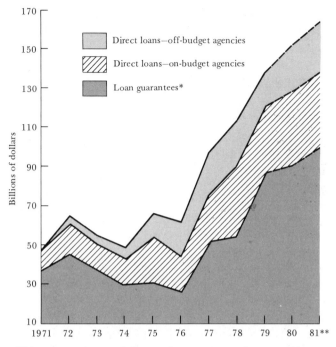

Billions of dollars

Direct loans—off-budget agencies

Direct loans—on-budget agencies

Loan guarantees*

1971 72 73 74 75 76 77 78 79 80 81**

*Primary guarantees: excludes secondary guarantees and guaranteed loans
acquired by on-and-off-budget agencies.
**Projected

Figure 3.3 *Federal credit: how it soared in the 1970s. (Source: Office of Management and Budget,* Special Analysis on Credit, Fiscal Years 1973–1981.*)*

projected for 1981 by the Office of Management and Budget. Clearly, the large loan programs of federal agencies must have an enormous impact on the allocation of investment resources and the level and distribution of wealth in the country.

3.4
Financial instruments

Financial instruments arise in the course of borrowing and lending. They are contracts specifying the terms borrowers agree to meet when repaying their loans. Financial instruments are frequently bought and sold in financial markets, though for many there are no active markets, and for some, like the U.S. government savings bonds, the terms of the contract preclude sale to third parties.

Individual financial instruments differ in many ways. Even so, each of them contains provisions specifying the number, timing, and magnitude of the payments to be made to the lender.

These three characteristics give rise to a large number of possible differences between financial instruments. Payments may be regular or irregular, be stretched over very long periods or compressed into very short ones, and be large or small. In the case of common stocks, payments may be highly uncertain, contingent only upon the ability and willingness of the firm to declare dividends.

3.4.1
Bonds[7]

The most common finance instrument is a bond. A bond is traditionally a *fixed income security*—a contract specifying the amount of each payment and the number of payments to be made. There are many types of bonds, with different types of payments, different terms to maturity, and different provisions for the security of the bond holder. It is not appropriate here to provide a complete catalog of bond types; but, it is useful to note some of the characteristics of the major types.

Term to Maturity The period that must elapse before final payment is due on a bond is called the term to maturity. There is an enormous variation between bond types in this respect. At one extreme is a security, issued by some governments, called a *consol,* or *perpetuity.* Consols never mature; the issuer simply promises to pay owners an annual sum of money forever. Only when the issuer buys back the bond can the debt be extinguished.

Most bonds have definite terms to maturity. It is customary to designate bonds redeemable after 10 years as long-term bonds; those that mature within a 3–10 year period are regarded as intermediate-term bonds; and those with less than 3 years to run, as short-term instruments. The shortest term bonds are redeemable on demand by the holder. Call money loans made by banks to stock brokers are examples of this category.

As we shall see, classification of bonds by term to maturity is important because the prices of short-term bonds are more stable in the face of changing short-term interest rates than are the prices of long-term bonds in the face of changing long-term interest rates.

Credit Risk Bonds differ as to credit risk and the provision of security for the bond holder. Companies with good management and good earnings prospects are less likely to default in whole or part on their interest

---

[7]For a more extensive treatment of bonds see the excellent discussion in Helen O'Bannon, David Bond, and Ronald Shearer, *Money and Banking: Theory, Policy and Institutions* (Harper & Row, 1975), pp. 32–43.

and principal payments than are companies with weak managements and poor-to-middling prospects. For the latter, life is unfair; they must pay bond holders higher interest rates and provide them with stronger security.

Provision for security takes many forms. *Mortgage Bonds* are backed by real estate. Bonds backed by the general assets and earning power of the debtor, and not by any specific asset, are called *debentures,* although when they are short term they are most likely to be referred to as *promissory notes,* or just plain *notes.* Some bonds require provision for *sinking funds*—money required to be put aside every year by the debtor for eventual retirement of the issue. Finally, some bonds call for gradual payment of principal at various times during the term of the loan, as do the *serial bonds* issued by many municipal governments.

Payments Stream   Most bonds call for periodic equal payments of interest plus a balloon payment at maturity. The periodic interest payments (usually semi-annual) are called *coupon payments,* and the balloon payment is known variously as the *face value, par value,* or the *redemption value* of the bond. Most corporate bonds are issued with face values of $1,000, though there are many that carry other values. The market value of a bond may be higher or lower than its face value. A person buying a bond for more than its face value must be prepared to accept the face value if he holds the bond to maturity.

Not all bonds carry coupons. Treasury bills promise only a payment of the face value at maturity. Treasury bills are usually issued in denominations of $10,000 for periods of three months (actually, 91 days) to one year, though the three-month bill is the most popular among investors. Since Treasury bills are free of credit risk and are highly liquid, they play an important role in the financial system. We shall have frequent occasion to refer to them.

Marketability   Unless forbidden by the terms of their sale, most bonds can be sold or transferred to third parties. But that does not mean that they are marketable. To be marketable, a bond must be saleable to a third party on short notice at a reasonably predictable price. Such can be true only of bonds for which there is a broad and active secondhand market, such as that for U.S. government bonds and high quality corporate bonds. The fact that a firm can issue and directly sell bonds to particular primary lenders does not necessarily imply that the bonds have a good secondary market. If they do not, the issuer may have to give lenders higher coupon interest than is justified on the basis of credit risk. Generally speaking, bonds issued by small firms with little reputation are less marketable than bonds issued by large and well-known firms.

3.4.2
Purchasing power loans, variable interest rate loans, and shared appreciation mortgages: defenses against inflation

Inflation undermines the purchasing power of money and fixed income securities. Lenders who anticipate inflation frequently demand higher coupon interest rates in order to compensate them for the deterioration in the purchasing power of the redemption value of the bonds they hold. But it is almost impossible to make accurate predictions of the rate of inflation, particularly over long periods of time. For that reason, lenders frequently seek to protect themselves against the ravages to their capital imposed by unanticipated inflation.

One device is the purchasing power loan. The terms of such loans require changes in the redemption value of the loan according to changes in the price level as measured by the consumer price index or some other index. Thus a lender and borrower might agree that at the end of, say, a 10-year loan, the sum of money to be repaid will be the original sum lent multiplied by the percentage change in the consumer price index that has occurred during the period. If the lender sells the bond before maturity, the price of the bond would include any change in the purchasing power of money that has occurred from the date of the loan to the date of the sale. Purchasing power loans are common in Israel, Brazil, Argentina, and other countries with long inflationary experiences.

A second device is the variable interest rate loan. As will be discussed in Chapter 13, during inflationary periods lenders and borrowers typically adjust rates on loans in accordance with expected inflation. As a result, a rise in inflation frequently leads to a rise in interest rates beyond the rates that would be charged during periods of lower inflation. The variable interest rate loan is a relatively long-term loan that adjusts interest payments as they come due over the term of the loan in accordance with current changes in short-term interest rates. These loans eliminate the need for borrowers and lenders to predict future interest rates. However, they protect lenders against inflation only to the extent that short-term interest rates adjust rapidly to changes in the current inflation rate.

Commercial banks frequently issue variable interest rate loans to business customers. The interest payments on the loans are tied to some index of interest rates, as agreed to by the borrower and the bank. The index may include rates on commercial paper, the prime rate of interest (the rate charged large prime bank customers by large banks), or some other rates.

The variable interest rate loan may be thought of as a series of short-term loans automatically terminated and renewed at new interest rates under conditions specified in the loan contract. Alternatively, they may be thought of as term loans with variable income streams to the lender, one of the features of common stocks.

Another example of this kind of security is the variable interest rate mortgage offered by many banks and thrift institutions. The terms of these mortgages vary from state to state and lender to lender, though Fannie Mae and the FHLBB are attempting to establish a standard instrument in the mortgage market. Variable rate mortgages (also called adjustable-rate mortgages) permit lenders to adjust the interest rate on mortgage loans up or down by ½ to 1 percentage point a year—usually with a limit of 5 percentage points change over the life of the loans—in response to changes in market interest rates on mortgages. In some cases, lenders write loans that dispense completely with the limits on interest rate changes. In 1981, a regulatory ruling by the FHLBB authorized S&Ls to issue variable rate mortgages.

Another interesting development, not yet widely adopted, is the "shared appreciation mortgage" (SAM), proposed by the FHLBB and actually put into practice by a few lenders.[8] SAMs commit homebuyers to share the increased profits inflation has made possible from the sales of their homes. In return, the lenders reduce interest rates below the going market rate. For example, if the shared equity is one-third of the appreciated value of the house, the interest charged by the lender is two-thirds of the market rate.

Although these new loan instruments have in common the attempt of lenders to protect themselves from rising and variable trends in interest rates and inflation, they are technically quite different. The variable rate loan retains the fixed redemption value and duration of the loan, while allowing the coupon return to fluctuate over the life of the instrument. The shared appreciation mortgage retains the coupon return, but permits the redemption value to increase with the price of the home bought with the borrowed money. In addition, the loan terminates when the home is sold before the term of the contract is over.

3.4.3
Common stocks

Common stocks are financial instruments, but they differ from most bonds in several important respects. They are issued without maturity dates, and they carry no promise of a fixed schedule of payments. Instead, stockholders are entitled only to their *pro rata* share of dividends as may be declared from time to time by the directors of the corporations in which they hold their stocks. The dividends usually vary with the profits

---

[8]See "When Lenders Share Homebuyer Equity," *Business Week*, October 13, 1980.

made by the company, but the directors may choose to retain all or part of the profits for expanding the capital base of the firm.

Holders of common stock own residual rights to the assets of their firms. If the company fails, the bondholders and other debtors must be paid off first. What is left belongs to the stockholders.

Since the profits of a firm may vary from time to time, so too will the dividend payments and the earnings that are retained to build the asset base of the firm. For that reason, common stocks are regarded as *variable income securities*. Like most bonds, variable income securities fluctuate in price as interest rates change. Unlike most bonds, however, the prices of common stocks also fluctuate in response to the expectations of traders respecting the size and variability of the future income streams of the issuing firms. Since bonds do not ordinarily carry variable income streams, such expectations affect their prices only when the market perceives a linkage between a firm's credit worthiness and its earning prospects.

Although the common stock is the best known variable income instrument, there are others. An example is the *preferred stock*. Preferred stocks have no dates of maturity, although the issuing corporations have the option of retiring them on specified terms. Owners of preferred stock have prior claims on dividends, up to a specified maximum rate, before dividends can be paid to holders of common stock. Some preferred stocks are *participating*, in the sense that after a minimum dividend has been paid to common stockholders the preferred stockholders share in any additional dividends declared by the directors. Thus, for some classes of preferred stockholders, what they are promised is a minimum, not a maximum, return.

Enough has now been said to convey the idea that an almost infinite variety of financial instruments can exist, each differing from the other in terms of maturity and in frequency and size of payments. This being the case, it should not be surprising that financial markets have evolved instruments designed to appeal to the specific preferences of many different borrowers and lenders. It should also be understood that as conditions change, so too will the various types of instruments bought and sold in the markets. That such has been the case is clear to anyone who has studied financial history.

3.4.4
Capital markets and money markets

Financial analysts frequently make a distinction between the capital market and the money market. The capital market deals in stocks and bonds and other loans with more than a one-year duration. By contrast, the money market deals in loans of less than one year.

This distinction is somewhat arbitrary, but it does make some sense. Firms draw on capital markets for investments in fixed capital (plant and equipment), while the money market is frequently utilized by borrowers who are temporarily illiquid and who are in need of immediate funds. Since short-term interest rates frequently change, and since each new issue of debt entails transactions costs, it is risky and costly for firms to borrow short for long-term needs. Except during unusual periods, when capital markets are clogged with borrowers, most firms do not draw upon the money market for the financing of plant and equipment.

Major borrowers in the capital markets include nonfinancial, and to some extent financial businesses, the U.S. government, U.S. government credit agencies, state and local governments, households who wish mortgage finance, and consumers. Major lenders are individuals who wish to have income-earning financial assets, life insurance companies, pension funds, investment companies (who act as individuals), thrift institutions, and commercial banks. Generally speaking, financial intermediaries with long-term liabilities are interested in lending long. Those with short-term liabilities (for example, commercial bank demand deposits) prefer to match their liabilities with short-term assets.

Major money market instruments include U.S. government Treasury bills, negotiable bank CDs, commercial paper,[9] and bankers' acceptances (defined in Section 4.2.3). About $570 billion of Treasury bills were outstanding in mid-1980. Treasury bills were introduced in 1929. Since they are free of default risk, and since there is a large and active secondary market in them, they are an almost perfect vehicle for short-term investment. Large negotiable CDs of major banks (minimum denomination $100,000) are next in importance. Introduced in 1961, they carry a bit more risk than Treasury bills, but since there is a large and active market for them, they too are highly liquid. They are a favorite vehicle for corporate treasurers with temporary surpluses of funds to invest.

Commercial paper is issued by major nonfinancial firms and finance companies. Yields on commercial paper are a bit higher than those on Treasury bills, but, like CDs, an active market makes such paper a favorite short-term investment vehicle for corporate treasurers. Bankers' acceptances, which arise to a large extent in international trade dealings, are another important money market instrument. Table 3.2 shows the major market securities outstanding in mid-1980.

Another active money market, not indicated in the table, is the "federal funds market." Federal funds are surplus reserves of banks lent to other banks with reserve deficiencies, usually on an overnight basis. Although the general public is not directly involved, the federal funds market plays a major role in the conduct of monetary policy. We shall discuss it in more detail in Section 4.2.2.

---

[9]Commercial paper consists of marketable short-term unsecured promissory notes issued by businesses in denominations of $100,000 or more, usually with maturities of 60 days or less.

Table 3.2 *Major Money Market Securities Outstanding (Mid-1980)*

Instrument	Amount Outstanding (billions of dollars)
U.S. Treasury bills	570
Large negotiable bank CDs	228
Commercial paper	124
Bankers' acceptances	54

Source: Federal Reserve Bulletin, September 1980.

3.4.5
Interest rates and security prices

Generally speaking, long-term bonds and corporate equities fluctuate more in price than do short-term bonds. This is partly due to differences in credit risks as judged by market participants, but it is also due to the purely technical fact that given changes in market interest rates have a stronger impact upon long-term security prices than they do upon short-term security prices. A brief discussion of the technical relationships between interest rates and stocks and bonds is a necessary background to an understanding of this point.

As we have seen, a bond is a debt instrument issued by a borrower stating the terms upon which he is willing to repay the lender. The terms typically include the date of maturity, the redemption value of the bond at maturity, the so-called coupon rate of interest, and the frequency of coupon payments.

For example, consider a 10-year $1,000 bond that carries a 10 percent coupon. At the end of 10 years, the borrower promises to pay the holder of the bond $1,000. In the meantime, he pays the holder $100 per year; that is, the coupon written on the face of the bond.

An important distinction must be made between the coupon rate of interest and the market interest rate, or yield. Bonds that are bought and sold in organized markets frequently carry prices above or below their redemption values. A bond bought for less than its face value and held to maturity, earns more than the coupon rate of interest. Similarly, a bond bought for more than the face value earns less than the coupon rate. For example, suppose that an individual purchases the 10-year, 10 percent coupon bond for $900 instead of for its redemption value of $1,000. If she holds it to maturity, she gets $100 per year plus an additional $100 in capital appreciation. The $100 of appreciation of the bond from $900 to $1,000 over the 10-year period is equivalent to about 1 percent per year. As a result, the effective *yield,* or the *market rate of interest* earned on the bond, is 11 percent, instead of the 10 percent coupon.

As the example indicates, the market price of a fixed-income bond varies inversely with its yield, and vice versa. When the market rate of interest on the bond rises, that is a sign that its price has fallen. When the yield of the bond falls, its price has risen. The relationship is, in fact, quite mechanical; as such, it can be easily understood with a small refresher on the mathematics of investment.

Suppose a person invests V dollars at an interest rate of $100r$ percent in a financial instrument that promises to pay him C_1 dollars at the end of the year. He can look upon C_1 dollars as an accumulation of V dollars at the interest rate $100r$ percent:

$$V(1+r)=C_1 \tag{3.1}$$

If he knows both V and r, it will be easy for him to calculate the sum of money C_1 he will get at the end of one year (that is, if $V=\$100$ and $r=.05$, $C_1=\$105$). He may, however, already know C_1. If so, he may want to know how much to pay for it—he may wish to find V. To do so, he merely uses the known values of C_1 and r and Equation (3.2), which is derived from Equation (3.1):

$$V=\frac{C_1}{1+r} \tag{3.2}$$

Equation (3.2) is the basic expression for calculating the *present value* of a single future payment to occur after one year. The present value of an investment is a sum of money that, if invested at an interest rate of $100r$ percent, will yield a given future payment, such as C_1. A sum of money left to accumulate for two years is[10]

$$V(1+r)\,(1+r)=C_2 \tag{3.3}$$

so that the present value of a known sum C_2 is

$$V=\frac{C_2}{(1+r)^2} \tag{3.4}$$

Suppose that we now consider investing a sum of money V to yield a *series* of coupon payments (identified by C) over n years. Part of that sum will accumulate at interest for one year, to yield C_1; another part will accumulate for two years to yield C_2; and so forth. A final part will accumulate to the redemption value of the loan at maturity M. Adding up, the present value of the series of future payments $C_1, C_2, C_3, \ldots, C_n, M$ is

$$V=\frac{C_1}{(1+r)}+\frac{C_2}{(1+r)^2}+\frac{C_3}{(1+r)^3}+\cdots+\frac{C_n}{(1+r)^n}+\frac{M}{(1+r)^n} \tag{3.5}$$

---

[10]The formulas and examples given here assume that current and future annual interest rates are equal. Clearly, this need not be true. Nevertheless, the assumption simplifies the presentation.

Equation (3.5) can be applied to determine the price of a bond. Suppose a person desires to invest in a bond whose annual coupon is $100 and whose redemption value at the end of five years is $1,000. If the interest rate on bonds of equal risk and equal term to maturity is 8 percent, the individual will pay no more than $1,079.84 for the bond, which, as indicated by the following calculation, is the present value of its coupons plus the present value of its redemption value:

$$V = \frac{\$100}{(1.08)} + \frac{\$100}{(1.08)^2} + \frac{\$100}{(1.08)^3} + \frac{\$100}{(1.08)^4} + \frac{\$100}{(1.08)^5} + \frac{\$1,000}{(1.08)^5}$$

$$= \$92.59 + \$85.73 + \$79.38 + \$73.58 + \$68.06 + \$680.58 + \$1.079.84$$

The price of a bond will fluctuate inversely with the market rate of interest. It is also true, however, that changes in long-term interest rates provoke larger changes in the prices of long-term bonds more than changes in short-term rates affect the prices of short-term bonds.

To illustrate, assume that the market rate of interest on five-year bonds jumps from 8 percent to 10 percent. The five-year bond in the above example will fall in price to $1,000, a drop of $79.84. Suppose, however, that the bond had only one year to maturity. In that event, its present value at an 8 percent one-year interest rate would have been $1,018.84:

$$V = \frac{\$1,000 + \$100}{(1.08)} = \$1,018.84$$

A rise in the one-year interest rate to 10 percent would reduce the price of the bond to $1,000, a drop of only $18.84.

The closer a bond is to redemption, the less its price is affected by changes in the rate of interest. A 2-percentage point change in the market rate of interest would barely touch the price of a bond with one day remaining before redemption.

Since prices of short-term bonds respond less sharply to changes in interest rates than do prices of long-term bonds, they are less risky forms of investment for people who wish to invest for short periods. But, if a person has no need to redeem his bond before it matures, he can disregard the risk arising from fluctuations in the rate of interest.[11] Insurance companies and pension funds are institutions whose liabilities must be paid at relatively remote dates. For that reason, they can invest in long-term bonds without regard to interest rate risks. But banks and other lenders, some of whose own liabilities are short term in nature, expose

[11]Unless, of course, inflation risk is high, in which case, he should try to make a purchasing power or variable interest rate loan.

themselves to such a risk unless they match their short-term liabilities with investments in short-term bonds.

Before leaving this topic, we should briefly comment on the relationship between interest rates and the prices of Treasury bills and the prices of common stocks. As indicated above, Treasury bills are almost perfectly secure short-term bonds that carry no coupons. Instead, they promise single payment at maturity. The yield on Treasury bills is, therefore, determined solely by the relationship between their market prices and their redemption values. Suppose, for example, that a 91-day $10,000 bill is sold to an investor for $9,781.40. If the investor holds the bill to maturity, he will receive $218.60 in interest, which is equivalent to an annual rate of interest of 8.96 percent.[12]

The factors affecting common stock prices are best discussed in terms of Equation (3.5). As we have seen, a common stock is a variable income security without a redemption date; its present value cannot be calculated from knowledge of market interest rates and the coupon rate of interest. A common stock investor must instead combine a forecast of future streams of per share earnings of the company with her knowledge of market interest rates to arrive at an *estimate* of the present value of the stock. If the stock is selling above her estimate of its present value, she will not buy it; if it is selling for less, she will try to buy it. Bids for and offers of a common stock should bring its price in line with the price set by informed opinion.

An important school of financial writers argues that stock markets are efficient. An efficient market is one in which stock prices always reflect the (frequently divergent) opinions of well-informed investors and investment analysts. That is to say, in an efficient market, the price of the stock of any particular company will reflect the best and most up-to-date information concerning the company, its competitors, and the general conditions in its industry.

If this theory is correct, profits from continuous speculation in common stocks are likely to be sparse. Information reaching the ordinary investor is likely to have already reached and been acted upon by the experts. Only investors with inside information, unavailable to the experts, are likely to beat them.

Nothing in the efficient markets theory precludes speculative profits on individual investments. New information affecting the fortunes of a company always comes along. But such information can be negative as well as positive. For that reason, it is frequently a matter of luck that

---

[12]The formula for determining the equivalent of the annual coupon rate of interest on a 91-day Treasury bill is $r = [(10,000 - P)/P]\ (365/91)$ where P is its market price and r is the rate of interest.

investors make money from changes in stock prices. The efficient markets theory implies that *systematic* profits from speculative activity are highly unlikely.

SUMMARY

Financial markets exist to transfer funds from surplus income units to deficit spending units. Direct finance takes place when lenders and investors transact their business through stock and bond markets. Institutions in these markets include stock exchanges, bond and stock dealers and brokers, investment analysts, and investment bankers. The objects exchanged in the markets are money and stocks and bonds issued by primary borrowers.

Indirect finance operates through banks, thrift institutions, mutual investment companies, insurance companies, and pension funds. Banks and thrift institutions issue fixed value deposits and shares to lenders and use the funds so pooled to lend to primary borrowers. Other intermediaries also issue liabilities on themselves in order to attract funds for lending to or investing in obligations of primary borrowers.

Financial markets greatly reduce the risks and costs of borrowing and lending. Depository institutions' shares and deposits offer surplus income units safe and liquid assets. They also have the size and expertise that allow them to reduce and spread the costs and risks of lending. In so doing, they raise the return, net of risk, most lenders can get on their portfolio investments; they also provide great conveniences for borrowers who have limited access to finance in the organized security markets.

Numerous government finance agencies exist to assist, guarantee, or subsidize borrowers in the farm sector, homeowners, students, small businesses, and so forth. Some of the agencies are part of regular on-budget departments of government; others were organized by the government, but have been spun off the budget and operate with funds borrowed in the open market. Fannie Mae is a good example of this type of off-budget agency.

Financial instruments consist of bonds and stocks. Bonds are usually fixed-income securities that specify coupon interest, frequency of payment, duration of the loan, and redemption value. Some are marketable; some are not. Some bonds carry variable interest rates tied to changes in other interest rates. A new bond-type is the shared appreciation mortgage. Common stocks are securities with variable income streams and no specific duration.

The prices of marketable financial instruments are determined in the security markets. Lenders' appraisals of the soundness of borrowers interact with borrowers' abilities to carry out promises of income streams and redemption values attached to the securities they issue. The prices lenders are willing to pay for securities reflect the present values of the securities they are considering. The present values of the securities are the discounted streams of returns promised or expected from the borrowers. The discount rates used to calculate the present values are rates of return on similar securities. Long-term bonds are more sensitive to interest rate changes than short-term bonds. Uncertain income streams make stock prices more variable than long-term bond prices. In general, the prices of securities sold in security exchanges represent the best judgments of expert investors, taking into account the latest information at their disposal. Fluctuations in security prices come from new information, previously unanticipated by security investors.

With these three chapters as a background, we can now probe more deeply into the details of the banking system. As indicated above, commercial banks are not only major financial intermediaries, with contacts in virtually all parts of the financial system, but they also provide through their operations the major part of the money supply. As such, banks are the principle vehicle through which the monetary authorities attempt to regulate the volume of effective demand in the economy. Understanding the workings of the banking system is a prerequisite to understanding the operation of monetary policy.

DISCUSSION QUESTIONS

1. Why do people put their money into banks or thrift institutions instead of lending it directly at higher interest rates?

2. If you have $10,000 to invest, why might it be better to put the money into five different bonds yielding an average of 11 percent per year rather than one bond yielding 12 percent a year?

3. Why is it that even very well-informed investors are unlikely to make abnormally high profits from frequent trading on stock and bond markets?

4. What has happened to make thrift institutions more like commercial banks?

5. Pension funds and insurance companies are not depository institutions, yet we still call them financial intermediaries. Why?

6. Distinguish between credit risk and market risk.

7. How has inflation affected the form of financial instruments?

8. Assuming an interest rate of 10 percent a year, calculate the present value of (a) a 90-day $10,000 Treasury bill, (b) a 5-year bond with annual coupons of $120 and a redemption value of $1,000 at maturity, and (c) a perpetuity yielding $120 per year. Recalculate with an inter-

est rate of 12 percent per year. Compare what has happened to the present values of each.

IMPORTANT TERMS AND CONCEPTS

- ☐ bonds
- ☐ broker
- ☐ capital market
- ☐ commercial banks
- ☐ commercial paper
- ☐ common stocks
- ☐ dealers
- ☐ default (credit) risk
- ☐ direct and indirect finance
- ☐ efficient market
- ☐ federal funds
- ☐ financial intermediaries

- ☐ investment bankers
- ☐ investment (mutual) companies
- ☐ market risk
- ☐ money markets
- ☐ mutual savings banks
- ☐ present value of a bond
- ☐ primary and secondary (indirect) securities
- ☐ savings and loan associations
- ☐ surplus (deficit) income units
- ☐ Treasury bills

ADDITIONAL READINGS

The theory of financial markets is nicely discussed by John G. Gurley in "Financial Intermediaries in the Saving–Investment Process," *Proceedings of the 1959 Conference on Saving and Residential Financing* (U.S. Saving and Loan League, 1959). A good primer on the subject is Dorothy Nichols' *Two Faces of Debt* (Federal Reserve Bank of Chicago, 1968). A historical treatment is in Edward Ettin, "The Development of American Financial Intermediaries," *Quarterly Review of Economics and Business,* Vol. 3, No. 2, Summer 1963, pp. 51–69.

Burton Malkiel's *Random Walk Down Wall Street* (New York: W. W. Norton, 1975) is an entertaining and valuable introduction to the securities markets. A good textbook treatment of the subject is Morris Mendelson and Sidney Robbins, *Investment Analysis and Security Markets* (New York: Basic Books, 1976). The theory of prices of securities is treated in Richard Brealey, *An Introduction to Risk and Return from Common Stocks* (Cambridge, Mass.: The M.I.T. Press, 1969).

A good brief survey of thrifts and other intermediaries is by Doris E. Harless, *Nonbank Financial Institutions* (Federal Reserve Bank of Richmond, 4th edition, 1979). A text that stresses theoretical aspects of financial intermediation is by Paul P. Smith, *Money and Financial Intermediation* (Englewood Cliffs, N.J.: Prentice-Hall, 1978).

An excellent guide to federal credit programs and market instruments is the *Handbook of Securities of the U.S. Government and Federal Credit Agencies* (New York: First Boston Corporation, published biennially). On the same subject, see the standard (but somewhat old) treatment in Commission on Money and Credit, *Federal Credit Agencies* (Englewood Cliffs, N.J.: Prentice-Hall, 1963).

The Banking Business: Fundamentals

O U T L I N E

Commercial Banks as Firms
Balance Sheets
Setting Up a Bank
Deposit and Clearing Operations
Bank Reserves and Reserve Requirements
Bank Lending and Deposit Creation
Time and Savings Deposits; Borrowing and Bank Capital
Bank Time and Savings Deposits
The Discount Window, Federal Funds, and Other Borrowed Money
Bankers' Acceptances
Capital Accounts
Bank Assets
Investments
Bank Loans

A commercial bank is a firm (usually a corporation chartered by a state or the federal government) whose business it is to receive demand deposits and pay customers' checks drawn upon them, to receive time deposits and pay interest upon them, to make loans to business and consumer borrowers, to invest in government and privately issued securities, to collect checks for customers' credit transactions, to certify depositors' checks, and to issue cashiers' checks.

Many commercial banks do more. Some issue credit cards, manage payrolls for business customers, pay bills for household customers, underwrite security issues, operate trust departments for investments of wealthy individuals, buy and sell foreign currencies, and so forth. In short, many banks are so-called "department stores of finance."

Most of these activities are not peculiar to commercial banking. Other financial institutions also engage in them. But commercial banks are peculiar in the degree to which they specialize in the acceptance and creation of demand deposits. No other financial institution has such a large proportion of its deposits subject to withdrawal or transfer immediately upon receipt of an order by a customer. That being so, commercial bank deposits serve as media of exchange to a far greater extent than do the deposit liabilities of any other financial intermediary.

The demand deposit function of commercial banks has long made them a special object of control and regulation by the monetary authorities. Banks must keep reserves as dictated by the authorities and submit to a variety of regulations designed to make them sound financial institutions. Few other industries are so thoroughly regulated.

The monetary nature of demand deposits makes commercial banks a favorite object of study by monetary economists. These economists believe that interactions between the supply and demand for money are a major source of variations in prices, production, and employment in modern industrial economies. For that reason, they must study the business of commercial banking. The information gleaned helps them understand the forces that underlie fluctuations in the economy at large.

4.1
Commercial banks as firms

The term "commercial banks" arises from the ideas of nineteenth century theorists. These theorists believed that banks should confine their leading to short-term loans for commercial purposes, such as loans to farmers to harvest their crops and inventory loans to merchants and manufacturers. They believed loans of this sort to be self-liquidating because the goods pledged as collateral[1] against them would, upon sale in the near future,

---

[1]Collateral is *specific* property a borrower pledges as security for repayment of a loan.

make money available to repay the loans. This doctrine, variously identified as the *commercial loan theory* or the *real bills doctrine,* was popular in both the United States and in Great Britain.

The doctrine made sense in at least one respect: Because demand deposits are a major source of funds to the individual bank, and because these deposits are subject to immediate loss on written order of a customer who wishes to withdraw money or to write a check payable to someone not a depositor in the bank, the individual bank must maintain a *liquid position.* A bank has a liquid position if it has at its disposal cash, or ready access to cash, sufficient to meet unexpected demands by depositors. If a bank makes long-term loans, it freezes its assets in a form that reduces its liquid position. Short-term loans, properly staggered, usually assure a bank that each day or week a number of loans will be repaid, making funds available in the event demand depositors should impose an extraordinary drain upon its resources.

Banks no longer adhere rigorously to the commercial loan theory. They now lend to consumers, make long-term loans, and offer business loans unsecured by inventories or other forms of collateral. Even so, the concept embodied in the term "commercial banks" reminds us of the special problems faced by an institution having a principal liability subject to payment on demand. These problems explain a good deal of the behavior of commercial bankers.

4.1.1
Balance sheets

A step-by-step description of the setting up and operation of a bank is the best way to describe its peculiarities as a business institution. For this purpose, we must first discuss an essential tool of the monetary economist's trade—the balance sheet.

The financial position of an economic unit is described by the money values of its assets, liabilities, and net worth. Assets are the things the unit owns. Liabilities are its debts. The net worth of the unit is calculated by subtracting its liabilities from its assets. Because liabilities represent outside claims on assets, net worth stands for the unit's residual claims on its assets. If it were to liquidate assets and pay off its debtors, it would be left with cash equal to its net worth.

These considerations allow us to put a unit's assets, liabilities, and net worth into an algebraic identity:

$$\text{assets } (A) = \text{liabilities } (L) + \text{net worth } (NW)$$

This identity is also described by a balance sheet, such as the one given here for a hypothetical family:

Jones Family Financial Position
(Dec. 31, 1978)

A		L+NW	
Cash	$ 1,000	Mortgage	$ 40,000
Stocks and bonds	10,000	Other debts	2,000
House	50,000	Net worth	41,000
Furniture	15,000		
Car	5,000		
Clothing, etc.	2,000		
Total	$ 83,000	Total	$ 83,000

Several properties of the balance sheet are worth emphasizing:

1. All items are recorded as of a given date.

2. Total assets must always equal the sum of liabilities and net worth. This property arises from the description of net worth as the economic unit's residual claims on its assets.

3. Use of one asset to purchase another changes the *composition* of assets, but leaves the *total value* of assets and net worth unchanged. Thus, the net worth and total assets of the Jones family would be unchanged if it used $500 of its cash to buy a dining room table.

4. Assets purchased on credit increase assets and liabilities equally, leaving net worth unchanged.

5. Use of an asset to pay off debt reduces assets and liabilities equally, leaving net worth unchanged.

6. An increase in net worth can occur in four ways: (a) saving, (b) endowment, (c) capital gains, and (d) stealing. Saving occurs when an economic unit decides to use a portion of its income to purchase an asset or to reduce its debts. An endowment is a gift from some other unit. A capital gain is an increase in the market value of the assets held by the unit. An example would be an increase in the market value of the Jones family home. Stealing speaks for itself.

7. A decrease in net worth can also occur in four ways: (a) consumption, (b) gifts, (c) capital losses, and (d) theft losses. Consumption represents the deterioration or depletion of assets. Unless an economic unit replaces consumption with fresh saving, its net worth will decline. Decreases in net worth by way of gifts of assets to outside units, by way of reductions in market value of assets, or by way of losses through theft are self-explanatory.

An important implication of these principles is that no single item on a balance sheet can change without alteration of another. Using the balance sheet to record changes in the economic status of a unit requires a *double entry accounting system*. Changes in any asset category must be accompanied by an opposite change in another asset category or an equal change in liabilities or in net worth. The same is true of changes in terms on the right side of the balance sheet. This property of balance sheet accounting helps to make it an important tool for analyzing the effects of the actions of banks and of the monetary authorities.

4.1.2
Setting up a bank

To go into the banking business, it is necessary to form a corporation, to obtain sufficient capital, and to acquire a charter.

Banks need capital to purchase buildings, equipment, and supplies and to invest in earning assets. They also need capital as a cushion to pay off their creditors should the need arise. A bank acquires capital by selling shares and by accumulating a surplus in excess of those shares—first, by charging share holders a premium for their purchases of capital stock and, second, by retaining profits not distributed to share holders in the form of dividends. In an accounting sense, the capital recorded on a bank's balance sheet is its net worth.

Banks obtain charters from state banking supervisors or from the Comptroller of the Currency, an official of the U.S. Treasury with the responsibility of administering national banks under the National Banking Act of 1863. A bank can apply for a charter under either kind of authority, but it cannot get a charter from both. At the end of 1979, there were about 4,600 national banks and more than 10,000 state banks chartered by 50 different state banking departments.

A bank cannot acquire a charter without satisfying minimum capital requirements laid down by the chartering authorities. The requirements differ between the authorities, but in general they depend upon the size of the community in which the bank wishes to operate. In all cases, the authorities require capital to be fully paid in cash before permitting a bank to open its doors for business.

Now, let us trace through the opening of a new bank and watch its progress as it develops its operations. After obtaining a charter and selling $5 million worth of stock, the bank's balance sheet would look like this:

A		L + NW	
Cash	$5,000,000	Capital stock and surplus	$5,000,000

One of the bank's decisions may be to join the Federal Reserve System. If it has a federal charter, it must belong to the System. If it has a state charter, it has a choice. If our bank joins, it becomes a *member bank* of the System. Before passage of the 1980 Monetary Control Act, only member banks had to satisfy the reserve requirements and other regulations of the System. Privileges of membership included the ability to borrow from the local Federal Reserve bank and use of the System's check clearing and wire facilities. Now, all banks are subject to reserve requirement regulations of the Fed and have privileges similar to those of members.

The initial steps in opening a bank include the purchase of a building, equipment, and supplies; investing a portion of its cash in earning assets; and, in preparation for conducting its deposit business, placing a portion of its cash on reserve at the regional Federal Reserve bank. Each of these acts affects the bank's balance sheet on the asset side.

To show the changes prior to displaying the revised balance sheet we employ what is known in the trade as a T-account. The T-account is a record of the financial transactions of a bank. Information recorded on the T-account is posted on the balance sheet in order to show how the transactions have transformed the composition of the bank's assets, liabilities, and net worth.

Suppose the bank puts $1 million into a building and supplies. The T-account would record this act as follows:

A		L+NW
Cash	− $1,000,000	
Buildings and supplies	+ $1,000,000	

Next, record a $3 million investment in government bonds and a shift of $800 thousand of cash to the bank's deposit at the Fed:

A		L+NW
Cash	− $3,800,000	
Deposit at Fed	+ $ 800,000	
Government bonds	+ $3,000,000	

Notice that all of the changes are recorded on the asset side of the balance sheet. The net worth of the bank is as yet untouched—its ownership position remains intact. Even so, the new balance sheet has a decidedly different look. It now shows the bank as a going concern, ready for business, and already earning interest for its stock holders:

A		L + NW	
Cash	$ 200,000	Capital	$5,000,000
Deposit at Fed	800,000		
Government bonds	3,000,000		
Buildings and supplies	1,000,000		
	$5,000,000		

4.1.3
Deposit and clearing operations

The next step is to attract demand deposits. Demand deposits expand a bank's power to lend or to invest in securities. Except for interest-bearing NOW accounts issued to individuals and nonprofit organizations, the law currently prohibits payment of interest on demand deposits. Thus, dollars a bank attracts and holds in the form of demand deposits contribute much to its profits. Although the contribution is diminished somewhat by the requirement, legal as well as self-imposed, to hold a fraction of deposits as reserves—vault cash (currency and coin in the vault or till) or deposits in the Fed—the lure of profits leads banks to desire large numbers of demand deposit customers.

Suppose our bank attracts $10 million of demand deposits. Most, if not all, such deposits would be in the form of checks the new customers have written on deposits in banks they are deserting. The initial entries in our bank's books would be:

A		L + NW	
Cash items in the process of collection	+$10,000,000	Demand deposits	+$10,000,000

Note, our bank does not yet have the additional cash. It must first *collect* the funds from the other banks. It usually does so by forwarding the checks drawn upon them to the local Federal Reserve bank. The Fed then adds $10 million to our bank's deposits and subtracts $10 million from the deposits of the other banks. The transactions look like this:

Our Bank

A		L+NW
Cash items in the process of collection	−$10,000,000	
Deposits at Fed	+$10,000,000	

Other Banks

A		L+NW	
Deposits at Fed	−$10,000,000	Demand deposits	−$10,000,000

Federal Reserve Bank

A	L+NW	
	Deposits of our bank	+$10,000,000
	Deposits of other banks	−$10,000,000

The check clearing system provided by the Fed is a major convenience. Before the advent of the Federal Reserve System, banks leaned heavily upon clearing house systems of their own. Even today there are a number of such clearing houses located in various cities. Banks daily receive checks drawn upon other banks, and the other banks receive checks drawn upon them. By establishing and working through clearing houses, banks avoid the need to present checks directly to the individual banks upon which they have been drawn. Instead, they send the checks to their clearing houses and receive credit for their total value.

For each bank, the clearing house figures out the balance of payments. When checks drawn against a bank exceed in value the checks it receives, the clearing house requests payment from the bank. When checks a bank receives and presents to the clearing house exceed the value of the ones drawn against it, it gets paid by the clearing house. At the end of each day, after all the smoke has cleared, each bank will have either increased or decreased its position with the clearing house; as a result, it will have either gained or lost cash assets. Taking all banks together, the *net* payments into and out of the clearing house must total zero, because the sums received by banks having positive clearings must match the sums paid out by banks having negative clearings.

The Federal Reserve System is the major clearing house for member banks. Nonmember banks occasionally keep deposits in the Fed for clearing purposes, but they mainly work through larger *correspondent banks.*[2] Correspondent banks are usually members of the Federal Reserve System. State banking laws frequently permit state chartered banks to count deposits in other banks as part of their required reserves. These deposits, in turn, are sought by correspondent banks because they increase their lending power. In return, the correspondent banks use their connections with the Fed to collect and disburse moneys for the nonmember banks.

The Federal Reserve System's clearing facilities are especially useful for banks collecting and disbursing funds to and from different parts of the country. There are 12 Federal Reserve districts, each with its own Federal Reserve bank. There is also an Inter-District Settlement Fund. After receiving checks drawn on banks in other districts, a bank sends them to its own district Federal Reserve bank, receiving in return a credit to its Federal Reserve deposit. The district Federal Reserve bank then sends the check through the Inter-District Settlement Fund for clearing. When a district Federal Reserve bank receives more checks than it sends, its balance at the Fund increases. When clearings go against it, its balance declines.

4.1.4
Bank reserves and reserve requirements

After accepting the $10 million of demand deposits and placing the new cash in its account at the Fed, our bank's balance sheet looks like this:

A		L+NW	
Reserves*	$11,000,000	Demand deposits	$10,000,000
Government bonds	3,000,000	Capital	5,000,000
Buildings and supplies	1,000,000		
	$15,000,000		$15,000,000

*Reserves are cash assets—vault cash plus deposits at the Fed.

Note that "vault cash and deposits at the Fed" have been replaced with the more generic term, "reserves." Banks keep reserves for several purposes. The first is to pay out currency and coin to demand deposit

---

[2]Correspondent banks hold deposits from other banks, providing check collections and other services in exchange. The 1980 Monetary Control Act extends Federal Reserve System clearing privileges to nonmember banks, for a price. Depending on relative costs, nonmember banks may choose to remain with correspondents, or work through the Fed.

customers who wish to cash checks. If vault cash runs out, banks simply ask the Fed for more, in which case their deposits with the Fed are reduced by an equal amount. The second use of reserves is to make payments to other banks that have received checks drawn upon them by their depositors. Reserves in the form of deposits at the Fed are best for this purpose.

Finally, banks *must* keep some reserves to satisfy requirements laid down by the Federal Reserve System. Required reserves for national banks were first instituted by the National Bank Act of 1863. The concept was carried over to the Federal Reserve Act of 1913, which applied reserve requirements to all member banks, including state member banks as well as national banks. The Banking Act of 1935 gave the Federal Reserve Board power to vary the reserve requirements over a substantial range. Before the 1980 Monetary Control Act, the law permitted the Fed to establish reserve requirements within the following limits for individual banks:

Between 3 and 10 percent of savings and time deposits.

Between 7 and 14 percent of net demand deposits of banks with deposits up to $400 million.

Between 10 and 22 percent of net demand deposits[3] of so-called reserve city banks—banks having $400 million or more in deposits. (Reserve city banks used to be defined as banks located in cities having reserve banks or branches.)

The 1980 Monetary Control Act has changed all this. It set an initial reserve requirement of 3 percent against transaction deposits (demand deposits, NOW accounts, ATS accounts, etc.) of $25 million or less in all depository institutions (banks and thrift institutions, members and nonmembers of the Fed). For transactions accounts exceeding $25 million, it set an initial reserve requirement of 12 percent, but authorized the Federal Reserve Board to change it within a range of 8 to 14 percent. As of December 31, 1981, the Board was required to raise the $25 million break-point for transactions balances of individual banks by 80 percent of the percentage increase in total transactions balances of all depository institutions.

The 1980 law also spoke to reserve requirements on *nonpersonal* time deposits. Each depository institution is required to maintain between 0 and 9 percent reserves against such deposits, as determined by the Fed.

The law provided for an eight-year phase-in of reserve requirements

---

[3]Net demand deposits of a bank are its gross deposits minus cash items in the process of collection and demand balances due from other domestic banks. For a review of reserve requirements history, see "Member Bank Reserve Requirements—Heritage From History," *Federal Reserve Bank of Chicago Business Conditions,* June 1972, pp. 2–18.

for nonmember depository institutions. It also permitted nonmember banks to hold deposits in correspondent banks that are members of the Fed, provided that the correspondents pass through the reserves to the Fed. Nonbank depository institutions may keep reserves at correspondent institutions holding deposits at the Federal Home Loan Bank Board (S & Ls) or the National Credit Union Central Liquid Facility (credit unions), provided, again, that the reserves are passed through to the Fed. As under the old law, vault cash is an acceptable form of reserves.[4]

An interesting implication of the law is that it cuts across reserve requirements in nonmember state banks. These requirements, which differ from state to state, were put in place in order to assure depositors of the liquidity of the institutions they do business with. Accordingly, state imposed required reserves need not take the form of cash. Instead, many states permit reserves to be held in the form of deposits at correspondent banks (not necessarily passed through to the Fed) and short-term securities, such as U.S. Treasury bills.

Required reserves for banks and thrifts do not increase their liquidity. They are there for a different purpose—monetary control. The Fed attempts to limit the total reserves available to the banking system. The reserve requirements of banks limit the total volume of deposits they can have with their available reserves. Thus, using its powers to manipulate both available reserves and reserve requirements, the Fed influences the size of the deposit portion of the money supply.

4.1.5
Bank lending and deposit creation

When a bank's total reserves exceed its required reserves, it has *excess reserves*. Assume that the Fed's reserve requirement policies lead our hypothetical bank to have a 15 percent average reserve requirement against its demand deposits. This requirement, plus its $10 million of demand deposits, implies a required reserve total of $1.5 million. The bank's total reserves are $11 million; its excess reserves are, therefore, $9.5 million.

This large sum of money is available for a variety of uses. The bank could keep it idle, but that would not be very smart. To be sure, the bank loses some of its reserves every day from cash withdrawals and from checks drawn on its deposits and placed with other banks. But it also gains reserves from cash deposits and from checks drawn on other banks that have come into the possession of its deposit customers. On most days, the bank will lose a little and gain a little. If its average cash holdings are

---

[4]The details of the law are given in Charles R. McNeill and Denis M. Rechter, "The Depository Institutions Deregulation and Monetary Control Act of 1980," *Federal Reserve Bulletin*, Vol. 66, No. 6, June 1980, pp. 444–453.

large in relation to its probable net deposit losses, its excess reserves are too large. The bank should, therefore, exchange its surplus reserves for income producing loans and securities. In that way, it can increase its profits.

If our bank lends $9 million of its $9.5 million in excess reserves, its T-account will show the transactions as follows:

A		L +NW	
Loans	+ $9,000,000	Demand deposits	+ $9,000,000

Pay close attention to the way the bank makes its loans. It does not, as would you or I, lend money by reducing its cash assets. *Instead, it simply creates $9 million in new demand deposits.* It does so by crediting the deposit accounts of the borrowers with the new money. In exchange, it receives promissory notes totaling $9 million. In effect, the new deposits it creates are backed by its loan customers' promises to pay. Economists refer to this process as one that *monetizes debt.*

Individual bankers frequently deny that their loan operations monetize debt. From their point of view, they are simply lending money they have received from depositors, or money they have borrowed. They believe they are simply lending the excess reserves generated by such transactions.

But, from the point of view of the whole banking system, every dollar of excess reserves creates an opportunity for banks to expand the total deposits of the system. And any expansion in total deposits represents an increase in the money supply as it is defined by economists and the monetary authorities.

Thus, the $9 million of loan-backed new deposits credited to the deposit accounts of our bank's borrowers is available for their spending. The $10 million of deposits already in the bank is similarly available for spending, since nothing has happened to reduce their amount. The logic is inescapable: By making loans equal to $9 million, our bank has increased the deposit portion of the money supply by an equal amount. Unless and until the bank reduces its loans, the money supply will continue to be $9 million larger than before.

When borrowers spend the new deposits, the checks drawn on them frequently fall into the hands of other banks. The other banks present the checks to their clearing houses or to the Federal Reserve banks for clearing. If our bank loses $9 million in reserves in this manner, its T-account and that of other banks will read as follows:

Our Bank

A		L + NW	
Reserves	− $9,000,000	Demand deposits	− $9,000,000

Other Banks

A		L + NW	
Reserves	+ $9,000,000	Demand deposits	+ $9,000,000

Notice, the $9 million of new deposits did not disappear when they were spent. Instead, they appeared at other banks. This confirms the conclusion that banks increase the deposit portion of the money supply when they use excess reserves to increase loans.

At times, bank loans may also increase the currency portion of the money supply. Recall that the money supply is defined as currency and deposits *owned by the nonbank public*. Bank reserves, including vault cash, are not part of the money supply. But, if borrowers decide to take payment on their loans in cash rather than in deposits, the bank's reserves are automatically transformed into money, as the term is officially defined.

As an example of this transformation, assume that our bank lends $500 thousand to a group of borrowers who demand cash, not deposits, in return for the promissory notes they give to the bank. The bank's T-account, and that of the nonbank public (of which the borrowers are a part), would record the transactions as follows:

Our Bank

A		L + NW	
Reserves	− $500,000		
Loans	+ $500,000		

Nonbank Public

A		L + NW	
Currency	+ $500,000	Bank debt	+ $500,000

After making its loans, losing the deposits it created to other banks, and losing currency to the nonbank public, our bank's balance sheet looks like this:

A		L+NW	
Reserves	$1,500,000	Demand deposits	$10,000,000
Loans	9,500,000	Capital	5,000,000
Government bonds	3,000,000		
Buildings and supplies	1,000,000		
	$15,000,000		$15,000,000

The bank has just enough reserves to meet the 15 percent reserve requirement laid down by the Fed. This is no accident. Had it lent out more than the original $9.5 million in excess reserves, it would have run the risk of losing more than $9.5 million to other banks and to customers demanding cash. In that event, its reserves would have fallen below $1.5 million, which would have been insufficient to meet the 15 percent reserve requirement against its original $10 million of deposits. Such a failure would have forced it to reduce loans or to borrow in order to restore its reserves to the required level. Otherwise, it would have faced a fine by the Fed.

A bank attempts to protect itself against reserve deficiencies by confining its lending and investing to an amount equal to or less than its excess reserves. Its deposits come to it in two forms. The first are *primary deposits*, which come into being when customers place currency or checks written on other banks into their deposit accounts. The second are *derivative deposits*, which are the demand deposits the bank itself creates in its loan and securities investment activities. Primary deposits are relatively stable, because regular demand deposit customers are continually adding to, as well as drawing down, their deposits. The reserves needed to meet requirements against primary deposits are, therefore, relatively predictable, and the excess reserves they generate can be lent out with little fear.

Derivative deposits are another matter. Borrowers rarely wish to keep them idle. Instead, they generally use them immediately to make payments to their suppliers or creditors. In that event, the bank is likely to lose all or most of these deposits (including the excess reserves upon which they are based) to other banks. When the bank lends more than its excess reserves, it runs the risk of creating a reserve deficiency. In that event, it will be penalized by the Fed, be forced to reduce its loans and investments, or be forced to borrow.

When a bank follows the rule of lending an amount equal to or less than its excess reserves, it can be fairly sure that its reserve losses will not dip deeply into its required reserves. That is because most of the deposits on its books at any moment are likely to be primary deposits. Derivative deposits created by recent loans will have mostly been checked away. So the rule of confining lending to excess reserves is the bank's major device for minimizing costs and embarrassments arising out of reserve deficiencies.

4.2
Time and savings deposits;
borrowing and bank capital

The basic nature of the banking business is described by the material in the previous sections of this chapter. We now examine the business in more detail by looking at other sources of funds and the nature of bank assets. In this section, we shall study time and savings deposits, different sources of bank borrowing, and the structure of capital accounts. Section 4.3 deals with bank investments and bank loans. In studying both of these sections, keep in mind the total structure of bank assets and liabilities as illustrated in the following balance sheet, which is a condensed version of the composite balance of the U.S. commercial banking system.

U.S. Commercial Banks—Assets and Liabilities
June 30, 1978
(Billions of Dollars)

A		L+NW	
Currency and coin	12.0	Demand deposits	374.7
Reserves with Fed	29.6	Time deposits	365.0
Deposits in other banks	56.0	Savings deposits	226.0
Cash items in process of collection	69.3	Federal funds purchased and securites sold under repurchase agreements	93.2
Securities held	262.3	Other liabilities	54.8
Federal funds sold and securites resale agreements	48.6	Bankers' acceptances outstanding	17.1
Other loans (net)	650.2	Capital	83.7
Other assets	86.5		
Total	1,214.5	Total	1,214.5

Source: *Federal Reserve Bulletin*, Vol. 65, No. 2, February 1979, A 18. Figures here are summaries of much greater detail in original; hence, they contain small rounding errors.

4.2.1
Bank time and savings deposits

Although demand deposits are a major source of bank funds, time and savings deposits are even more so. On June 30, 1978, for example, time and savings deposits in commercial banks in the U.S. were $591 billion as compared to $375 billion of demand deposits.

Savings and time deposits, as noted in Chapter 2, come in various forms. Savings, or passbook accounts mostly belong to individuals, although a change in regulations in 1975 authorized commercial banks to make them available to business firms in amounts up to $150 thousand per customer per bank. Deposits and withdrawals of savings in this form can be made at any time, although banks may technically require 30 days notice prior to withdrawal. The automatic transfer of savings to checking account service (ATS), authorized by the Fed in 1978, substantially improved the liquidity of savings deposits—in effect, converting them into interest-bearing demand deposits.

Consumer-type time certificates of deposit have specified denominations and fixed terms to maturity at fixed interest rates. Most mature within four years, though regulations now permit banks to issue consumer time certificates with much longer maturities. Savings and loan associations issue similar certificates of deposit. All are subject to stiff interest penalties if redeemed before maturity.

Large certificates of deposit—frequently called CDs—have minimum denominations of $25 thousand, but are usually issued in denominations of $1 million. Although these deposits have fixed terms to maturity, ranging from 1 to 18 months, most of the large CDs issued are negotiable— they can be sold to third parties. There is a very lively CD market, and large firms or wealthy individuals invest heavily in them when they have temporary surplus funds. Small investors have indirect access to CDs when they purchase shares in money market funds, which use pooled funds of small savers to purchase CDs and other large denomination short-term securities. A bank fixes its CD interest rate at the time it sells certificates to initial depositors. However, because the prices of CDs in the secondary market vary, the effective yield to secondary investors may differ from the yield original holders get when they hold them to maturity.

Payment of interest to holders of savings and time deposits makes them less profitable for banks than demand deposits. Even so, there are compensations. Reserve requirements against savings and time deposits are much less than the requirements against demand deposits. In addition, they turn over far less frequently, and to a large degree the turnover is predictable. That is because time certificates of deposit are dated, and customers cannot convert them to cash before redemption dates without incurring interest penalties. Passbook savings accounts are held by household and business customers because they do not plan to use the funds immediately, so it is to their advantage to hold the funds in an interest-earning form.

Payment of daily interest on passbook savings and the advent of ATS accounts have eroded some of the advantages to banks of savings deposits, but the prospect of putting such funds to profitable uses continues to make them attractive.

In 1933, Congress gave the Federal Reserve System power to set interest-rate ceilings on savings and time deposits. The Fed exercises this power under *Regulation Q*. In 1966, Congress extended the regulation to thrift institutions.

In recent years, Regulation Q has become an important instrument of monetary policy. In addition, it has become highly controversial, because it interferes with banks' freedom to manipulate deposit rates in order to attract and maintain savings deposits.[5] In times of rising interest rates on Treasury bills and other short-term market interest rates, people have tended to pull their money out of time and savings deposits in order to reinvest them in other securities. This process is frequently identified by economists with the awkward word, *disintermediation*.

To counter disintermediation, the Federal Reserve in 1978 authorized banks to issue six-month floating rate *money market certificates*. These certificates, which are issued in minimum denominations of $10,000, carry ceiling rates tied to the average interest paid by the U.S. Treasury at its weekly auction of six-month Treasury bills. Regulatory authorities also permit thrift institutions to issue such certificates.

Experience with money market certificates indicates that they are a mixed blessing to banks and other depository institutions. As might be expected, they were an instant hit with households. Their total mounted rapidly as interest rates rose in 1978 and the years that followed. Instead of buying Treasury bills and other short-term securities, savers bought the certificates. From zero in 1978, the amount outstanding in banks rose to over $90 billion by the end of 1979. Even more were issued by thrift institutions.

So disintermediation became less of a problem. Nonetheless, the high interest rates that emerged in those years created a severe earnings problem for banks and thrift institutions. Many loans on their books, particularly mortgage loans, had been made at lower interest rates. The escalating interest costs of money market certificates made many of these loans unprofitable. The inability of banks and thrifts to turn over the loans at higher interest rates severely reduced the overall profitability of their operations.

The T-account treatment of savings and time deposits is straightfor-

---

[5]The 1980 Monetary Control Act requires elimination of Regulation Q over a six-year period. See Section 7.4.

ward: Assuming the reserve requirement against such deposits averages 5 percent, a $1 million inflow of time deposits increases the excess reserves of a bank by $950 thousand. If the bank lends these reserves, and the derivative demand deposits thus created are checked away, we can show the results of the new time and savings inflow as follows:

	A		L + NW	
Reserves	+ $ 50,000		Time and savings deposits	+ $1,000,000
Loans	+ $950,000			

4.2.2
The discount window, federal funds, and other borrowed money

Although deposits are the main source of loanable funds for banks, they also borrow funds. A minor, but very important, source of borrowed funds is the Federal Reserve System. Banks with reserve deficiencies must somehow remove them in order to satisfy their local Federal Reserve banks. To aid banks in such embarrasing situations, every Federal Reserve bank maintains a "discount window"—a loan facility administered by a vice-president of the bank. Banks can use this facility to borrow on a short-term basis, during which time the Fed expects them to get their affairs in order.

The interest rate the Fed charges banks that borrow is called the *discount rate*. The discount rate is not a penalty rate, because it is usually lower than the interest rates banks get from their own loans and security investments. Even so, the Fed discourages continuous borrowing by member banks. If a bank overuses the discount window, it may get a warning letter from its local Federal Reserve bank, or even a refusal of a loan.

Banks also borrow in the *federal funds market*. The term "federal funds" has two meanings. The first refers to interbank lending of funds banks have on deposit with the Federal Reserve System. For many years, banks with reserve deficiencies have borrowed reserves owned by banks with excess reserves. That helps them to avoid trips to the Fed's discount window. Federal funds loans are typically made on an overnight basis in denominations of at least $1 million at an interest rate set in the federal funds market. Federal funds acquired by a bank are free of reserve requirements, so the total sum borrowed is available for use. Federal funds loans are effected by an order to the Fed from the lending bank to transfer immediately part of its reserve balance to the borrowing bank.

Many large banks almost continuously make loans and investments beyond their excess reserves and use steady borrowing of federal funds to make up resulting reserve deficiencies. These borrowings are made easy by the existence of a large number of banks that possess federal funds and that are in contact with brokers who act as intermediaries. Information on the price and availability of federal funds comes through telephone contact, and banks use the Fed's wire system to transfer reserves between lenders and borrowers in different districts.

Federal funds are immediately available funds that come to a bank without a reserve requirement. For that reason, the term has in recent years come to be applied to all such funds, even those not resulting from loan transfers of reserves between banks.

In addition to borrowing from other commercial banks, Federal Reserve regulations permit banks to borrow immediately available reserve free funds from federal agencies, savings and loan associations, mutual savings banks, domestic agencies and branches of foreign banks, and, to a limited extent, government security dealers.

Market terminology has recognized these regulations, and a federal funds loan has now taken on a second meaning—an overnight (and sometimes longer) loan, not just between two commercial banks, but also between two institutions from which banks may borrow free of required reserves. For example, a bank may borrow federal funds from a savings and loan association, and the latter may borrow federal funds from a security dealer. More important, a bank may also lend immediately available reserve funds to its correspondent bank. Traditionally, correspondent balances earned no interest, but now many small banks accumulate large balances with their correspondents and lend them the funds not needed for check clearing or other purposes. In such cases, banks do not use the Federal Reserve wire service to transfer reserve balances. Instead, bookkeeping entries by the lending and borrowing banks reflect the fact that a noninterest-bearing correspondent demand balance has been converted into a federal funds loan.

Another class of transactions generating immediately available funds for a commercial bank is the *repurchase agreement* (RP), sometimes referred to as a "repo" or "buy back." We discussed RPs in Section 2.1.3. An RP occurs when a bank sells a depositor, perhaps a nonfinancial corporation, a security it promises to repurchase the next day. The funds released by such a transaction are free of reserve requirements; hence they are very close to federal funds loans in the senses defined above.

None of the methods of borrowing discussed to this point requires a bank to hold reserves against the liability created by the loan. Even so, the methods vary in terms of their effects upon a bank's balance sheet. For example, a bank borrowing directly from its local Federal Reserve bank receives a credit to its reserve account equal to the size of the loan. Its liabilities and cash assets go up by an equal amount, and because no new deposits are created by the transaction, none of the new reserves contributes to an increase in required reserves—all are available to support the bank's loans and security investments.

A federal funds loan between banks transfers excess reserves from the lending to the borrowing bank. Like funds borrowed from the Fed, excess reserves borrowed from another bank are fully available for loans and investments. But a transfer of excess reserves between banks does not increase the total reserves of the banking system, as does a loan from the Fed to the bank. Instead, the existing reserves in the banking system are put to more intensive use. Thus, both types of loans lead to the same thing—an enlargement of the volume of bank credit and bank deposits of the whole banking system.

Funds borrowed by a bank from a nonbank financial intermediary, such as a savings and loan association, do not generate an equal amount of excess reserves. Suppose, for example, that an S&L has $1 million on deposit with a bank and that, because it does not plan to use the deposit until the next day, it makes a $1 million overnight loan to the bank. The transaction would look like this (assuming a 15 percent reserve requirement):

Bank

A		L + NW	
Required reserves	− $150,000	S&L demand deposit	− $1,000,000
Excess reserves	+ $150,000	Loan from S&L	+ $1,000,000

The transaction releases the reserves *required* against the S&L bank deposit, but it does not release an amount equal to the loan, as in the case of a federal funds loan between two banks.

Because a repurchase agreement is essentially an overnight loan between a depositor and a bank, the balance-sheet interpretation is similar to the one given the S&L loan—an RP also releases required reserves in an amount equal to a fraction of the reduction in demand deposits.

Two other sources of short-term funds for banks are Eurodollars (first discussed in Section 2.1.3) and holding companies.

Eurodollars are dollar-denominated deposits in foreign banks or in overseas subsidiaries of U.S. banks. These deposits obligate overseas banks to pay dollars to holders. When interest rates in Europe exceed rates in the United States, holders of deposits in U.S. domestic banks frequently switch their money abroad. As a result, the foreign banks acquire ownership of deposits in the domestic banks.

When domestic banks are short of reserves, they frequently borrow deposits from their overseas subsidiaries or from foreign-owned Eurodollar banks. Such loans cancel overseas bank deposits in the domestic banks and free required reserves for domestic bank loans.

In 1969, the Fed began to apply reserve requirements to bank borrowings from Eurodollar banks. Although these requirements were smaller than the ones levied against the demand deposits released by the loans, the regulation had the effect of reducing the volume of such borrowings.

Most large banks are owned by holding companies. Before the late 1960s holding companies were used by banks to bring a number of separately chartered banks within their own and other states into a single organization. In 1956 Congress passed the Bank Holding Company Act in order to curb the growth of bank holding companies—the motive was to prevent monopolization of the banking business through the device of holding companies.

But banks could still put themselves under *one-bank holding companies*. These companies engage in a variety of nonbank activities in addition to owning a single bank. In the inflationary environment of the late 1960s, the Fed was using Regulation Q to hold down time deposit interest rates in order to make it difficult for banks to sell CDs. A number of banks organized themselves under one-bank holding companies in order to open up another source of borrowed money. Holding companies are able to borrow money in the commercial paper market. By relending money borrowed in this fashion to their bank subsidiaries, holding companies help them to acquire reserve free funds not subject to Regulation Q. The Fed gave this end run the same treatment it gave bank borrowings in the Eurodollar market. In 1970 it required banks to hold reserves against funds channeled to them out of funds raised in the commercial paper market by their holding companies.

4.2.3
Bankers' acceptances

Another important liability item appearing on the balance sheets of a typical bank is the *banker's acceptance*. Acceptances are one of the oldest financial instruments connected with the banking business. They are jointly created by banks and their business customers, particularly when the latter are engaged in international transactions. A firm without immediate funds to pay for goods it wants to buy draws up an order for a commercial bank to pay. If the firm has good local credit standing, it may convince its bank to guarantee or "accept" the order to pay, in which case it becomes a banker's acceptance. With the bank substituting its own credit standing for that of its customer, the foreign seller of the goods is happy to receive payment in this form. The bank's guarantee allows it to sell the acceptance in the money market and to get its money immediately.

A bank rarely loses money on acceptances; moreover, they are a good source of income because they enable the bank to extract a fee for the service from its business customers. Also, in making its commitment the bank is not directly involving its own funds, which remain free for other loans. In periods of tight money, when funds are particularly difficult to acquire, banks are especially pleased to increase their acceptance business.

4.2.4
Capital accounts

Before we leave the right-hand side of the balance sheet, we should say a word about banks' capital accounts. The accounts consist of stock (par value), surplus, undivided profits, and special reserve accounts. Capital stock is created when a bank issues new stock. When the sales proceeds exceed the par value of the stock, surplus is created. Surplus also changes when the bank's directors vote to transfer funds into the account from undistributed profits instead of retaining them for subsequent distribution to stockholders in the form of dividends. The directors also transfer undistributed profits into a special reserve account to cover losses on bad loans and investments. This act does not involve a special transfer or segregation of funds, but is primarily a device to remove a portion of undivided profits from stockholders' claims to profits.

It is important to note that banks do not actually tuck away cash to match their capital accounts. Capital accounts are simply a measure of the bank's net worth or the claims of its owners to the assets the bank holds in all forms. If the bank wishes to pay off its stockholders, or to increase its dividends, it can draw upon any of its assets. That is, it can acquire the necessary funds by reducing cash, by selling securities, or by reducing loans.

Although all banks acquire their initial funds from capital stock, subsequent increases in loanable funds come mainly from expansion of deposits. Over the last 20 years, bank capital has averaged only about 7 percent of total sources of funds for the U.S. banking system.

4.3
Bank assets

The asset side of a bank's balance sheet also says much about the nature of its business. Generally speaking, assets break down into three major categories—cash, loans, and investments. Cash assets consist of vault cash, reserves with the Fed, balances with other banks, and cash items in the process of collection. Since we have already discussed these items, we shall not give them further attention here, except to say that cash is not the only thing a bank can use to make quick adjustments to a sudden onset of reserve losses. Sales of short-term securities, federal funds loans, and access to the Fed's discount window perform a similar function.

4.3.1
Investments

Bank investments consist of holdings of marketable notes and bonds, mostly U.S. government securities issued by the Treasury or by other U.S. government agencies, and obligations issued by state and local governments. In 1978, for example, U.S. banks held $138 billion of U.S. government Treasury and agency issues and $117 billion of state and local obligations. All other security holdings amounted to a mere $6 billion.

Why do banks invest so much in U.S. government securities? First, U.S. government securities are safe; unlike private securities, there is no default risk attached to them—the money creation and tax powers of the federal government guarantee payment of interest and repayment of principal. Second, there is a wide market for government securities, and banks in need of quick infusions of funds can get them from low-cost quick sales to any of a number of government bond dealers who, in turn, have access to a broad set of potential buyers. Third, banks must have collateral in the form of U.S. government bonds to hold against loans from the Fed and against government deposits, as required by law and regulations. Last, but not least, banks earn interest on their holdings of U.S. government securities.

Interest earnings, together with superior liquidity and safety, make U.S. government bonds a favorite vehicle for bank investments. Even so, banks that are not careful can still lose money on such investments. They must balance their portfolios between long- and short-term bonds. As discussed in Chapter 3, long-term bonds tend to fluctuate more in price in response to interest rate changes than do short-term bonds. A bank that overloads its portfolio with long-term bonds risks selling them at a loss during periods of financial tightness. It is precisely in such periods that interest rates shoot up and depositors start to withdraw their money in large sums.

Banks can, to some extent, avoid losses on long-term bonds by borrowing in the federal funds market, by issuing more CDs, or by borrowing from the Fed. Because these devices may, in some circumstances, be too expensive, it is good strategy for a bank to buy short-term Treasury securities. Although these securities frequently carry lower interest rates than do long-term bonds, their prices do not fluctuate much in response to changes in interest rates, which reduces the risk of capital losses on their sale.

To stay reasonably liquid, therefore, banks frequently hold short-term bonds in their investment portfolios. This practice is so common that bankers regard short-term investments as *secondary reserves*. The Fed does not recognize such reserves; but, from the point of view of the individual bank, price stability and a ready market make short-term U.S. government securities almost as good as the reserves the Fed does recognize.

Bank investments in state and local bonds are a major source of bank income. These investments are unusually attractive because interest income earned from them is exempt from federal taxes.

The tax incentive is powerful. Corporate income taxes go up to 46 percent of net income. A 6 percent state and local bond has a yield equivalent to an 11.1 percent taxable security for a bank in the 46 percent tax bracket.[6]

Despite their profitability, state and local securities do pose a problem for banks. The market for such securities is far more limited than is the market for U.S. government bonds. Moreover, the risk is often much higher. State and local governments frequently twist local bankers' arms to force them to buy local bond issues, particularly when national markets are not being receptive to their issues. A case in point is New York City, which in 1975 was on the verge of defaulting on its bonds. Several of the large banks in the city were for a time unable to collect on their holdings of the city's securities, and they were unable to sell them to anyone else. Although New York's financial problems continue, a solution of sorts has been worked out with a promise by the federal government to guarantee a portion of New York's debt. Even so, this case provides dramatic evidence that investments in state and local securities can be far more risky than many other types of investments.

Bank investments in nongovernment securities are minimal. Bank regulatory agencies do not favor such investments. In fact, the law does not permit banks to buy common stock as investments. Only their trust departments, which manage portfolios of nonbank customers, are permitted to buy common stock. Such investments do not appear on banks' balance sheets.

4.3.2
Bank loans

Over one half of all bank assets consist of loans to business and household customers. Loans are distinguishable from bond investments in two main ways. First, most loans are not negotiable instruments. As a result, they are less liquid than security investments, in the sense that they cannot be sold for cash in an active market.

A second distinction is that a loan is initiated by the borrower. A bank cannot drag a customer off the street and force him to borrow money. In contrast, a bank's security holdings are the result of its own initiatives. When it wants to buy a bond, it simply places an order through an appropriate broker or dealer. The importance of this distinction is that banks need not wait for borrowers to request loans in order to elim-

---

[6]Let r be the yield on a taxable bond and r' be the yield on a tax-free state and local bond. If the tax rate is t, then the after-tax yield on a taxable bond equals the yield on the tax free bond when $r(1-t)=r'$. To compete with a 6 percent tax-free bond, a taxable bond must therefore yield 11.1 percent to a bank in the 46 percent tax bracket: $r=6/.54=11.1$.

inate their excess reserves; they can always invest in short- or long-term bonds.

Commercial and industrial customers borrow from banks for a variety of reasons. Short-term loans provide them with funds to meet payrolls, to stock up on inventories in anticipation of heavy sales, to overcome a temporary shortage of cash needed to repay loans, and so forth. Firms that are good customers of a particular bank frequently acquire *lines of credit*—predetermined amounts the bank is willing to lend them on demand, without going through the formal loan application process. A credit line appears on a bank's balance sheet only when the line is used.

Most short-term loans mature within a year; long-term loans, which firms may use to finance plant and equipment, have durations of 1 to 10 years.

Almost 30 percent of bank loans are mortgage loans, mainly for residential construction. These loans are typically long-lived, running from 10 to 30 years, though the high variability of interest rates in recent years have reduced their maturity to 5–10 years in many cases. In the past, residential mortgage loans were risky, even when secured by property. The Federal Housing Administration now has programs to underwrite and insure a large volume of real estate loans of many types. The programs have virtually removed default risk for lenders. In addition, the secondary market in mortgages, developed in conjunction with Fannie Mae and other federal credit agencies, has increased significantly the liquidity of mortgage loans.

Loans to consumers are the third most important loan category. Although some of these loans are of the single payment type, most are installment loans that borrowers repay over a period of time in small chunks. On June 30, 1978, loans to individuals by all commercial banks were $154 billion, while installment loans were $214 billion. Banks make installment loans for a variety of purposes—auto purchases, home repair and modernization, credit card plans, mobile home purchases, furniture and appliance purchases, and so forth.

Banks today are a major source of consumer credit. Before World War II, they supplied very little credit to consumers, preferring instead to concentrate upon business lending. But, since that war they have found consumer lending to be a very profitable and stable source of business, and they have developed a variety of techniques to handle it—the credit card is one obvious example.

Other important parts of the loan business include federal funds loans to other bankers, loans to finance companies, loans to security brokers and dealers, loans to individuals for the purpose of purchasing or carrying securities, and loans to other depository institutions.

Security loans to individuals are to some extent regulated by the Federal Reserve System. These loans are designed to cover the difference between the purchase price of the securities and the money actually paid for them by the buyers. Security loans, therefore, permit the buyers to speculate with borrowed money. Because such speculation can lead to instability in the stock market, Congress in 1935 authorized the Fed to regulate the maximum credit margin—credit as percentage of the value of a stock at the time of the extension of credit—for stocks purchased by traders and private individuals.

SUMMARY

This chapter provides an overview of the business of banking. Banks have evolved from simple depository institutions into complex organizations with many functions. Their distinctive feature is the checking (demand) deposit function. No other financial institution has such a large proportion of its liabilities subject to sudden call on demand.

Demand deposits in a bank originate with primary deposits of customers and as derivatives of bank lending and investing. Derivative deposits are created when banks make loans and buy securities in order to reduce excess reserves to a minimum. In so doing, banks exchange nonearning assets for earning assets and raise their profits.

The amount of demand deposits banks can have outstanding is legally limited by reserve requirements imposed by the Federal Reserve System authorities. The Fed requires member banks to hold reserves in the form of vault cash or Federal Reserve bank deposits. State banks may satisfy most of their reserve requirements with security holdings or with deposits in other banks that, under the 1980 Monetary Control Act, must pass through required reserves to the Fed.

Other sources of bank funds include time and savings deposits, federal funds loans and repurchase agreements, loans from the Federal Reserve banks, Eurodollars, bank holding companies, and equity capital. Time and savings deposits are less volatile than demand deposits; but, when interest rates are changing rapidly, large inflows or outflows of time and savings deposits occur. Most borrowed money is also short term in nature, and banks that use a lot of it must constantly seek to renew their loans, particularly in the federal funds market. The Federal Reserve banks frown upon continuous borrowing by banks.

Bank assets consist mainly of loans and investments. Investments are mostly in U.S. government and state and local government securities. Aside from earning income, securities frequently act as secondary reserves for a bank. Banks lend money to a wide range of business and household customers. In this respect, they differ from other financial intermediaries, which specialize more in one or another form of lending, such as housing or consumer loans. Even so, banks are a mainstay of the business community, which depends heavily upon short-term bank loans to finance inventories, payrolls, and other expenses.

1. How do commercial banks differ from other depository institutions?
2. How can a bank improve its liquid position?
3. Which of the following transactions affects a bank's net worth?
   (a) Receipt of a new deposit
   (b) Purchase of a new building
   (c) Payment of dividends to stockholders
   (d) Sale of a bond
4. Why do banks hold reserves?
5. Distinguish between a primary deposit and a derivative deposit.
6. How can a debt be "monetized"?
7. What is the significance of the presence of excess reserves on a bank's balance sheet?
8. What are the two meanings of federal funds?
9. Compare the role of loans and investments in banks' asset positions.

IMPORTANT TERMS AND CONCEPTS

☐ balance sheet
☐ banker's acceptance
☐ bank capital
☐ bank holding companies
☐ capital accounts
☐ clearing house
☐ commercial loan theory
☐ Comptroller of the Currency
☐ correspondent banks
☐ derivative deposits
☐ discount rate
☐ disintermediation
☐ excess reserves
☐ federal funds market
☐ Federal Reserve System

☐ investments (bank)
☐ line of credit
☐ liquid positions of banks
☐ Monetary Control Act of 1980
☐ monetization of debt
☐ money market certificates
☐ net worth
☐ primary deposits
☐ Regulation Q
☐ required reserves
☐ reserves
☐ savings deposits
☐ T-account
☐ time deposits

ADDITIONAL READINGS

The classic work on early banking theory is Lloyd Mints, *A History of Banking Theory* (Chicago: University of Chicago Press, 1945). A popular treatment of recent trends in American banking is Martin Mayer, *The*

Bankers (New York: Weybright and Talley, 1974). A collection of useful articles on federal funds, CDs, repurchase agreements', bankers' acceptances, the Eurodollar market, and other topics dealing with bank assets and liabilities is the *Federal Reserve Bank of Richmond Instruments of the Money Market* (1977). Other useful works dealing with important items on the balance sheets are Charles Lucas, Marcos Jones, and Thom Thurston, "Federal Funds and Repurchase Agreements," *Federal Reserve Bank of New York Quarterly Review*, Summer 1977; *First Boston Corporation Handbook of the Securities of the United States Government and Federal Agencies and Related Money Market Instruments* (New York: published biennially), and *Twentieth Century Fund Task Force on the Municipal Bond Market: Building a Broader Bond Market* (New York: McGraw- Hill, 1976). The topic of reserves requirements is treated in "Member Bank Reserve Requirements—Heritage From History," *Federal Reserve Bank of Chicago Business Conditions*, June 1972. Finally, a set of fine articles on various topics affecting bank operations is in Thomas Havrilesky and John Boorman, *Current Perspectives in Banking* (Arlington Heights, Illinois: AHM Publishing, 1976).

Bank Operations, Regulation, and Structure

OUTLINE

Running a Bank
Analyzing Bank Profits
Managing a Bank's Portfolio
Liability Management
Bank Regulation
Brief History of U.S. Banking
The Regulatory Authorities
The FDIC, Deposit Insurance, and Bank Failures
The Structure of the U.S. Banking Industry
Branch Banking
Regulating Foreign Banks
Bank Mergers
Bank Holding Companies
Bank Competition with Other Lenders

We take up three interrelated topics in this chapter. The first is bank operations, or how banks survive and perhaps prosper in their peculiar line of business. The second is bank regulation, or how the laws and regulatory authorities shape and limit banks in their pursuit of profits. The third topic, market structure, has to do with the degree of competition in the banking business.

5.1
Running a bank

A bank that means to stay in business must earn a competitive rate of return for its stockholders. A competitive rate of return is a yield on capital at least equal to the yield the bank's owners could get by investing in another business with equivalent risk. Stockholders can accept a few bad years, but if the good years do not bring a sufficiently high return, they will take their capital elsewhere, and the bank must close its doors.

Banks earn profits by maintaining a spread between the cost of the funds they acquire from deposits and from borrowing and the returns they get from lending, investing, and servicing their customers. This spread pays the wages and salaries of bank employees and covers other costs of operations.

When the returns exceed the costs, the bank earns a profit. Part of the profit goes to the tax collectors, and the rest is distributed as dividends to stockholders or is put into one of the capital accounts.

If making profits were merely a matter of finding borrowers who are willing to pay high interest rates, a banker's life would be relatively easy. He would be concerned mainly with keeping his costs down and finding depositors. But that is no way to run a bank. The world is filled with untrustworthy people who like to play with borrowed money and who are willing to pay high interest rates to get the chance. For that reason, a banker must take care. Otherwise, he might bring disaster upon his institution.

Trouble for a banker comes in two forms: insolvency and illiquidity. An insolvent bank is one whose assets have so deteriorated in value that its capital is no longer sufficient to pay off its debtors and depositors. An insolvent bank has a negative net worth—its liabilities exceed its assets. It is also a failed bank, and the regulatory authorities will put it into receivership and either liquidate its assets or sell them to another bank.

Illiquidity means the inability of an institution to honor on short notice with cash claims against it. Because a large portion of a bank's liabilities are demand deposits and other short-term claims, and a small portion of its assets are cash or secondary reserves in the form of short-term securities, it is in the nature of banks to be relatively illiquid. For that reason, they must pay close attention to their liquid positions. Failure to make prompt payments to claimants can initiate dangerous rumors about their soundness, which might lead depositors to withdraw funds on a massive scale. To guard against such eventualities, bankers must balance the maturity structure of their assets and liabilities in ways that give them maneuverability in the short run.

In the long run, a bank that stays liquid and solvent is a healthy bank. But, in the short run, there is a clash between profitability and both solvency and liquidity. Risky loans usually carry the highest yields, but too many risky loans may lead to insolvency. Long-term loans and investments usually have higher interest rates than do short-term loans and investments, but stretching out the average maturity of assets jeopardizes liquidity. On the liability side, long-term time deposits reduce the frequency of claims upon the bank's cash resources, but the increase in liquidity thus obtained must be bought by paying depositors higher interest rates.

The day-to-day task of the banker is to search for an optimal collection of assets and liabilities. A perfectly sound and liquid bank is usually not a very profitable one. Indeed, complete solvency and liquidity is found by holding only cash. But cash is a sterile asset. It yields peace of mind, but no money profits for the stockholders. At the other extreme, a bank that acquires the riskiest and longest term assets available may for a time make huge profits, but each day it invites a collapse. The same would be true of a bank that built its loan portfolio primarily with overnight funds. A sudden and sharp increase in the cost of these funds would convert profitable loans into losers.

Somewhere in between is the proverbial golden mean—a structure of assets and liabilities that gives bank stockholders a competitive rate of return and adequate protection for their capital.

5.1.1
Analyzing bank profits

It is convenient to analyze the factors affecting bank profitability with ratios of bank profits (net income) to bank capital and bank assets. Statistics suitable for this type of analysis are published by the Federal Reserve System and the Federal Deposit Insurance Corporation. Table 5.1 gives an abstract of these statistics—called operating or income ratios—for member banks in 1977. Figure 5.1 gives a history of the ratios since 1920.

Consider the following profit identity:

$$\frac{\text{net income}}{\text{capital}} = \frac{\text{net income/assets}}{\text{capital/assets}} = \frac{\text{net return on assets}}{\text{capital–asset ratio}}$$

Net income is the after-tax profit of a bank, computed by subtracting all operating expenses from operating revenues. Capital is owner's equity, including all surplus accounts. Assets are total assets—cash, loans, investments, and physical property.

Table 5.1   *Selected Member Bank Income Ratios, 1977*

I	Percent of Assets	
	Operating revenue	6.620
	Operating expenses	5.790
	Income before taxes	.830
	Taxes to assets	.210
	Net income after taxes	.620
	Capital–asset ratio	.061
	Net income as percent of capital	10.160
II	Percent of Operating Revenue	
	Loan interest and fees	65.32
	Securities	14.89
	Other	19.79
III	Percent of Operating Expenses	
	Salaries, wages, benefits	17.58
	Interest on deposits	43.06
	Interest on borrowed money	1.55
	Provision for loan losses	3.73
	Other	21.59
	Taxes and security losses	12.49
IV	Selected Rates of Return (Percents)	
	U.S. Treasury securities	6.34
	U.S. government agency issues	6.54
	State and local obligations	4.65
	Loans	7.92
V	Selected Assets as a Percent of Total	
	Loans	57
	Securities	17
	Cash	20

Source: Annual Statistical Digest, 1973–1977, Board of Governors of the Federal Reserve System, 1978, p. 300.

In 1977, net income averaged 10.2 percent of capital for all member banks. As the formula implies, this net income was affected by three major factors: earnings on assets, expenses, and the capital–asset ratio. The latter is especially important. A bank's capital is essential to its operation, since it provides a cushion out of which depositors and creditors are paid if the bank gets into trouble. A bank must *leverage* its capital in order to earn significant profits. Leveraging means acquisition of deposits and borrowed money to expand loans and investments. The margins between the returns on earning assets and the costs of deposits and borrowed funds provide the earnings a bank needs to pay its bills and to satisfy its stockholders. The more deposits and credit a bank can attract per dollar of its capital, the greater will be its ability to expand its net earnings per unit of capital (recall the bank balance sheet identity: assets = deposits + borrowing + capital). The capital–asset ratio, therefore, acts as a measure of the degree of leveraging. The smaller the ratio, the higher the degree of leveraging, and vice versa.

Table 5.1 reveals the importance of leveraging. Had the member banks not leveraged in 1977, they probably would not have earned a return on capital of much more than 4 to 6 percent, after taxes and expenses. That is because they were earning about 8 percent on their loans and 6.5 percent on their best security investments. Stockholders could have done better by investing their capital directly in the security markets. Instead, they were attracted to the banks because each dollar of bank capital multiplied net earnings per dollar of assets by 16.4 (the reciprocal of the capital–asset ratio of .061). Thus, even though member bank net income as a percent of assets in 1977 was only .62, net income as a percent of capital was 10.2. A 10.2 percent return was higher than most stockholders could have received had they tried to lend their money directly to business, consumers, and government borrowers.

Bank loans provide banks with their highest returns. In 1977, for example, rates of return on bank loans were 7.92 percent as compared to 6.34 and 6.54 from U.S. government securities and 4.65 percent (tax free) from state and local bonds. It is, therefore, not surprising that the banks put 57 percent of their assets into loans and that, as a result, 65 percent of their operating revenues came from them.

Things were not always this way. In 1950, for example, loans were

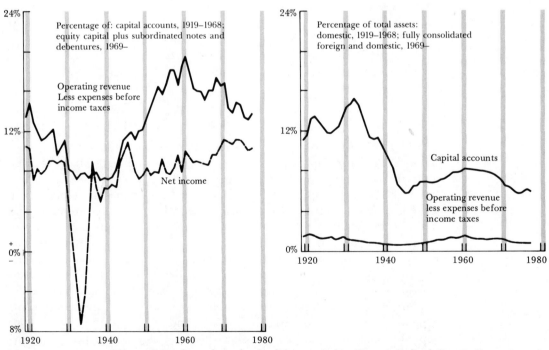

Figure 5.1 *Annual member bank income ratios. (Source: Federal Reserve System.)*

29 percent of bank assets and 50 percent of their operating revenue came from them. In the years since 1950, loans have steadily increased in importance as both assets and sources of revenues.

The prime rate   Finding good loan customers is not necessarily an easy task. Banks prefer to lend at high interest rates to high-quality borrowers. The best prospects for loans have good credit ratings and are able to play one lender against another. Most large corporations, for example, can borrow at the *prime interest rate*. The prime rate is the interest rate major banks charge to their best corporate customers. The major banks usually set their prime rates to exceed Treasury bill rates and the commercial paper rate. In past years they changed the prime rate infrequently. In recent years, however, they have changed it more often and have, as a result, caused its fluctuations to match much more closely changes in the commercial paper rate, as is shown in Figure 5.2.

The prime rate is important to all bankers and all loan customers. Generally speaking, it is the rate large and small banks use as a benchmark for lending to all customers. Interest rates on loans to consumers and to small businesses will generally equal the prime rate *plus* an adjustment to take into account extra risk, term to maturity, and local credit conditions. For that reason, the prime rate of interest is a key rate in

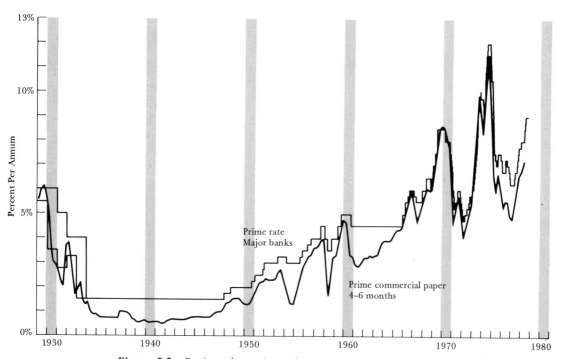

Figure 5.2   *Business borrowing: Short-term interest rates (prime rate, effective date of change; prime paper, quarterly averages). (Source: Federal Reserve System.)*

transmitting the effects of general changes in market rates of interest to individual borrowers at the local level. Changes in Treasury bill rates cause similar fluctuations in commercial paper rates. Changes in these money market rates provoke major banks to change the prime rate, and the latter is then transmitted throughout the country to rates charged loan customers, large and small, by banks that are large and small.

Compensating balances   The profitability of bank loans is also affected by the practice of imposing compensating balances upon customers. Compensating balances are deposits banks require their loan customers to keep with them as a condition for making the loans. For example, a business firm that borrows $100,000 from a bank might be required to keep $15,000 on deposit with the bank. Since such deposits have the character of primary deposits, they increase the capacity of the lending bank to further increase its loans.

Compensating balances may or may not raise the effective cost of loans to borrowers. All firms must maintain working balances in a bank to pay their bills. If compensating balance requirements do not exceed their working balance requirements, then borrowers are no worse off. They do suffer, however, if the compensating balance requirements exceed their working balance needs. In that event, they cannot make full use of the money they have borrowed, but they must still pay interest to the bank on the total sum.

Deposit costs   As Table 5.1 shows, the major expense facing a bank is deposit interest. A bank with a large proportion of its deposits in savings deposits, time certificates, or NOW accounts usually pays more in deposit interest than a bank that emphasizes demand deposits. Even so, demand deposits are not all gravy. Because they turn over more rapidly than do time deposits, they entail greater clerical, computer, and operating expenses. For that reason, substituting a dollar of demand deposits for a dollar of time deposits does not reduce bank operating expenses by an amount equal to deposit interest.

Nonetheless, banks in the post–World War II period have greatly expanded their time deposit business. In 1950, time deposits in member banks were 24 percent of total deposits. In 1977, the corresponding figure was 66 percent. This increase, plus the extensive rise in deposit interest rates, raised the interest cost of deposits as a portion of total operating expenses from 8.3 percent in 1950 to the 43 percent figure in 1977 as shown in Table 5.1.[1]

It is clearly difficult to neatly summarize all the factors that determine the profitability of a bank. The profit identity given here merely

---

[1]Post–World War II banking data is available in the *Board of Governors of the Federal Reserve System Banking and Monetary Statistics* (1976) and in its *Annual Statistical Digest.*

provides a framework for such an analysis. Because this is not a book about bank operations, we cannot provide a complete statement of the problem here. We can say, however, that the return a bank provides to its stockholders depends critically on the ability of management to provide maximum leverage consistent with safe operations. In addition, it depends upon the ability of the bank's officers to provide a balanced portfolio of loans and investments—one that maximizes returns to assets consistent with maintaining solvency and liquidity for the institution.

5.1.2
Managing a bank's portfolio

A bank's financial assets consist of cash, loans, and security investments. Cash assets consist of required and excess reserves. Most banks today carry a tiny amount of excess reserves. At the enc of 1977, for example, member banks taken together had less than $200 million in excess reserves, while their total reserves were over $36 billion.

The major portfolio decision for a bank is the division of earning assets between loans and investments. For some banks this decision is not altogether freely made, because state, local, and federal governments require their deposits in private banks to be collateralized with U.S. government securities. But many banks desire to hold even more government bonds. As indicated in Chapter 4, U.S. government bonds are highly liquid and, as a result, are in effect interest-bearing secondary reserves. The major question facing a bank is how much loan income it should sacrifice for the liquidity and superior maneuverability provided by a good stock of U.S. government securities.

The answer clearly depends in part upon the availability of safe and profitable loan opportunities. When the demand for loans is high, banks shift funds out of securities into higher yielding loans. In so doing, they sacrifice liquidity and perhaps increase the overall riskiness of their asset positions. But, if the increased demand for loans means a growing spread between loan interest rates and yields on securities, bankers may feel that the extra profit makes deterioration of quality in their balance sheet worthwhile.

That bankers do, in fact, behave this way has been confirmed by economic research. Banks usually increase their loan assets at a rapid rate during economic booms, and reduce their rate of acquisition of marketable securities. During periods of slump, they reduce the rate of growth of their loan assets and increase their rate of acquisition of securities. Figure 5.3 demonstrates this behavior for the 1970–1978 period, which had two periods of slump in 1970 and 1974–1975, and two of rapid economic growth in 1970–1973 and 1975–1978.

The long-term trends in the various components of bank portfolios are documented in the Table 5.2, which records the changes that have taken place in the asset compositions of all U.S. commercial banks in the

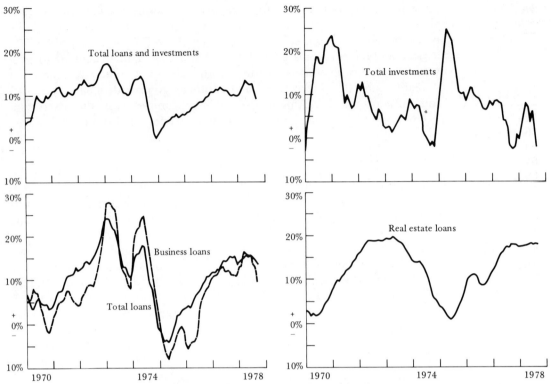

Figure 5.3 *Growth of commercial bank loans and investments, seasonally adjusted annual rate of change, six-month moving averages, centered. (Source: Board of Governors of the Federal Reserve System.)*

period 1952–1975. Note that loans in all categories, commercial and industrial (C&I), real estate, and consumer (individuals), rose as a proportion of earning assets. At the same time, investments in U.S. government securities fell steadily to less than one-fourth their share of assets at the beginning of the period. This drop was offset in part by the rise in holdings of state and local government securities and federal agency issues.

Overall, the impression given by the table is that the U.S. commercial banking system has become decidedly less liquid than it was in the early 1950s. In addition, the system is now exposed to more default risk. It has replaced a large portion of its secondary reserves with loans and with investments in state and local obligations. Neither of these categories of assets is as marketable as are U.S. government bonds; nor are they as safe. The taxing and money creation powers of the U.S. government make its obligations safer than any other security. Each dollar shifted out of U.S. securities into private sector loans or state and local securities exposes the banking system to additional risk.

An appreciation of the role of loans in banking cannot stop with a simple recording of changes in ratios of loans to total assets. In the past,

Table 5.2 *Secular Changes in the Composition of Bank Credit Outstanding: Percentage of Total Loans and Investments, 1952–1975*

	Loans[1]					Investments			
	Total	C&I	Real Estate	To Individuals	Other	Total	U.S. Treasury	S&L Government	Other[2]
1952–1955[3]	46.3	18.8	11.7	9.7	6.2	53.6	42.6	7.6	2.6
1956–1959	54.6	22.1	13.7	11.6	7.2	45.4	34.2	8.4	2.1
1960–1963	59.1	21.0	14.6	13.2	10.2	40.9	28.6	10.0	1.8
1964–1967	65.4	23.6	16.3	14.8	10.8	34.5	19.2	13.0	2.4
1968–1971	67.3	25.2	16.6	15.1	10.4	32.7	13.9	15.3	3.5
1972–1975	70.0	24.8	18.0	15.0	12.3	30.0	9.8	14.9	5.4

[1]Equals "other loans" in *Federal Reserve Bulletin*, that is, excludes federal funds sold and securities purchased under agreements to resell.

[2]Consists mostly of securities issued by federal agencies.

[3]Averages of semi-annual call data over each four-year period.

Source: Jack Beebe, "A Perspective on Liability Management Bank Risk," *Federal Reserve Bank of San Francisco Economic Review*, Winter, 1977.

bankers regarded loans as liquid assets. They emphasized short-term business loans that customers either paid off or renewed within a year. A properly staggered portfolio of such loans provided banks with a continuous incoming stream of uncommitted funds over which they could exercise control. Under such conditions, a large loan portfolio was not, for individual banks, necessarily a fact that severely curtailed their liquidity. Their main job was to see to it that the loans were made to sound businesses, that the loans were well secured with collateral and that the total loan portfolio was spread among a number of borrowers in different lines of business. The latter condition—diversification of the loan portfolio—was necessary to reduce the riskiness of the overall asset structure. Loans concentrated on particular individuals or on a number of individuals facing the same kinds of business risks do not serve that end.

Today, the loan business is quite different. Banks now conduct a lively business in consumer and real estate lending. These loans are frequently medium or long term in nature. Business loans, too, are for longer periods. "Term loans" (to be contrasted with "short-term loans") can run on for years—five to eight years in initial maturity is considered in some quarters to be an intermediate term loan! The terms of repayment are negotiated at the time the loan is taken out. Some agreements call for installment payments, but others allow for lump sum payments at the end of the period. Some loans call for fixed interest rates, but today many are so-called *floating rate loans*, with the agreement calling for the interest rate to change with changing market rates.

Business term loans, real estate loans, and long-term consumer loans lock up bank assets and reduce bank liquidity, causing serious problems for banks whose deposits or deposit costs are subject to wide fluctuations. Agreements by borrowers to repay bankers on an installment basis help to restore some of the lost liquidity, but the overall effect of having more term loans, as opposed to short-term loans or U.S. government securities, is to reduce bank liquidity.

Some observers[2] have argued that the growth in long-term lending has deprived many U.S. banks of the ability to maintain the overall quality of their assets and has thus contributed to a decline in the soundness of the banking system. The problem is particularly serious if the long-term loans are large. In the 1970s many large banks made huge loans to real estate investment trusts, third world governments, and large corporations. Then came the OPEC oil embargo and the quadrupling of world oil prices. This event, accompanied by a severe recession in 1974–1975, caused great and continuing difficulties for precarious third world governments, for a number of domestic real estate investment trusts, and many domestic corporations. But the banks, having made very large term loans to these troubled borrowers, were not in a position to call in all the loans or to demand adherence to repayment schedules. To do so might have caused financial collapse for many of their customers. The collapse would, in turn, have forced the banks to write down their loan assets and to recognize the losses in their capital accounts. Instead of taking such a drastic step, many banks simply renegotiated loans with their troubled customers, stretched out their repayment schedules and, in some cases, moderated interest rates.

Thus term loans can tie a bank to the fortunes of its customers. In contrast, short-term loans permit a bank to reassess the soundness of a decision to extend credit to a particular individual, firm, or government. But banks have been led into the term loan business because of a desire to accomodate borrowers' demands. Borrowers who demand such credit are not in a position to repay loans each year. They want long- or intermediate-term loans to finance long- or intermediate-term projects—projects that will not bear fruit for several years. They do not want to "borrow short" in order to "invest long." To do so would expose them to the risk of not having funds when they need them, or to the risk of having to pay interest rates that, when their projects were being planned, would have caused them to decide against the investments. A term loan at agreed upon interest rates protects them against these risks. Because term borrowers have been willing to pay good interest rates to banks, the latter have been enticed into the business, away from their more traditional concentration on short-term loans.

---

[2]See, for example, Paul M. Holman, "Changes in the Composition of Bank Assets and Liabilities" in Thomas Havrilesky and John Boorman, *Current Perspectives in Banking* (Arlington Heights, Ill.: AHM Publishing, 1976).

5.1.3
Liability management

In the past, bankers by and large accepted the deposit structure their customers gave them and adapted their assets to fit that structure. Their traditional concern was asset, or portfolio management, not liability management. The past 20 years have seen great changes in this attitude. Bankers are now just as keen to manage their liabilities as in the past they were to manage their assets.

It all began when bankers discovered the negotiable certificate of deposit—the CD—in 1961. Previously, time certificates could not be sold by their owners to third parties in an organized market. In 1961, a dealer-operated secondary market came into being. The market gave bankers an opportunity to sell certificates with denominations of $100,000 or more to large firms, charitable organizations, other domestic financial institutions, foreign banks, and state and local governments. These organizations frequently have spare cash to invest on a temporary basis; they are especially attracted by the opportunity to buy CDs that can be disposed of in a secondary market. Starting from zero in 1960, CDs now account for about 10 percent of all sources of funds for the banking system.

The CD was the first of several developments that gave banks a way of raising loanable funds on a national scale. It showed bankers that they need not passively wait for customers to bring them deposits. They now have a set of instruments that enable them to go after money. Instead of dividing a predetermined total of deposits among meritorious borrowers, they can expand their resources and satisfy a larger number of borrowers. The only catch is that they must be willing to pay the price the market demands for loanable funds. If other financial intermediaries, governmental and business borrowers, are paying higher rates for short-term money, so must they.

The CD is the most important of a whole class of liabilities that have come to be labeled as *purchased funds*. Other types of purchased funds include federal funds and securities sold under repurchase agreements, Eurodollars, and subordinated debentures (a type of general obligation bond used on a long-term basis). The concept has even been extended to NOW accounts and to certificates of deposit sold to consumers—the so-called money market certificates, which are six-month obligations having minimum denominations of $10,000 and carrying interest rates comparable to, and varying with, Treasury bill interest rates. All of these instruments have brought banks into head-on competition for funds with other major money market borrowers.

Thus, the tradition of "accepting deposits" and "managing assets" has given way to a state of affairs in which banks must now manage both liabilities and assets. Indeed, for some banks, the reverse of the traditional responsibilities may now be the case. High-cost liabilities have forced them into making bank loans a very high fraction of total assets. And, although they would like to keep most of their loans short, their loan customers frequently demand term loans.

It is much more difficult for a bank to appeal for loan business on a national basis than it is for it to appeal for purchased money on a national basis. Thus, desires of local business and consumer borrowers may dominate the term structure of a bank's assets. If it is forced to accept the asset portfolios dictated by the market, the bank has no alternative other than to manage its liabilities, since the term structure of deposits and borrowed money can, to a degree, be changed by purchasing funds on the national money and capital markets. Adapting liabilities to assets, rather than assets to liabilities, is now the primary concern of many banks.[3]

Liability management has many implications for the health of individual banks, the structure of competition in the banking and financial sectors of the economy, and the effectiveness of monetary policies pursued by the Federal Reserve System. We shall discuss these implications at several points in the balance of the book. Most relevant here is the impact on the health of individual banks.

Unfortunately, there is no clear concensus on this issue. Taken by itself, the ability of a bank to compete for funds in national markets gives it the power to stabilize its overall level of funding. A bank that is willing to pay the price can offset deposit losses with purchased money. In effect, it can buy liquidity on a national market.

But the expensiveness of such liquidity has forced banks to reduce secondary reserves and increase loans, reducing liquidity on the asset side. Another consequence is an increase in the riskiness of the banking business. Term loans are much more exposed to default risk than are government bonds. Moreover, the profitability of such loans is severely impaired if the cost of funds banks use to sustain them rises rapidly. Loan losses deplete bank capital and increase risks for depositors and others who have sold funds to the banks.

The pluses and minuses of liability management make it difficult to come to an overall assessment of its impact upon the health of the banking system. In addition, bank portfolio management policies continue to evolve. For example, banks are expanding the use of floating interest rate loans to offset the risk of fluctuating interest rates on their deposits and borrowed funds. Even so, some observers have come to believe that the banking system in the period since World War II has become more exposed to economic and financial market risks.[4]

---

[3]This is the theme of Professor Paul S. Nadler, an authority in the banking field. See his *Commercial Banking in the Economy*, 3rd edition (New York: Random House, 1979), pp. 146–147.

[4]Widely fluctuating interest rates in 1979–1981 created a near crisis for banks and especially thrift institutions. Forced to pay high deposit rates, many institutions were "technically insolvent" in 1981. See Sanford Rose, "Dark Days Ahead for Banks," *Fortune*, June 30, 1980, pp. 86–90 for a discussion of this problem.

5.2
Bank regulation

Banking is one of the most regulated industries in the American economy. The high degree of regulation is due in part to the traditional American distrust of "Wall Street." More important, the deposits of the banking system constitute the major fraction of the United States money supply. An unsound banking system cannot be the basis for a stable money supply, a proposition that received dramatic confirmation in the early 1930s when a collapse of the banking system was accompanied by a 34 percent drop in the (old) M2 money supply.

The laws under which bank regulatory agencies work have three major stated purposes: protection of depositors and stockholders against fraud and mismanagement by bank operating personnel; protection of depositors and, ultimately, the whole economy against events that might produce a failure or collapse of the whole banking system; and the regulation of bank competition.

The regulatory field is split up between several authorities: state banking commissioners, the Comptroller of the Currency, the Federal Deposit Insurance Corporation, and the Federal Reserve System. States and, especially, the federal government have given these agencies a highly complicated set of laws to work with. Each agency has its own specialty in the regulatory field. Even so, there is considerable overlap in their duties, and this overlap has given rise to both competition and cooperation between them.

In this section, we shall explore the composition of the U.S. banking system. The structure of the system has been shaped by the unique character of American politics and history. The banking system that has emerged is one that poses special problems for the banking and monetary authorities. It is a system that is difficult to regulate and difficult to understand. But it is the only banking system we have, and the authorities must make do with it as best they can.

5.2.1
Brief history of U.S. banking

America's dual banking system—part national and part state—was a long time coming. Most banks in our early history were chartered by state governments. In 1791, Congress chartered the First Bank of the United States. It was designed to be both a commercial bank and a fiscal agent of the government. Its principal liability was currency convertible into specie (coined money). The bank had eight branches. It was not very popular with the common man, who thought it to be the forerunner of financial monopoly. It refused to accept notes of state banks that it suspected were not redeemable in specie. This behavior earned it the enmity of many state banks that were thereby prevented from expanding loans based upon currency creation. For this and other reasons, opposition to the bank grew so much that in 1811 Congress refused to renew its charter.

The Second Bank of the United States was chartered in 1816. Its functions were similar to those of the first. So too, was its history. Growing resentment of its powers and the enmity of President Andrew Jackson led to its demise in 1836. The field was left open to the state banks, which flourished in great numbers on charters issued by state legislatures and by state banking authorities.

One result of the luxuriant growth of state banks was a vast array of bank notes issued by the individual banks in the various states. State banking authorities could not keep up with the growth, despite various attempts by banks in New England and legislatures in New York, Louisiana, Ohio, and elsewhere to regulate banking and discourage unsound practices. Many banks in this period failed, and many note holders were stuck with currency they could not redeem for specie or exchange for banknotes of more responsible institutions.

The National Banking Acts of 1863 and 1864 set up a national banking system with a uniform currency backed by U.S. government bonds purchased by federally chartered banks. The acts also set up reserve requirements limiting the ability of national banks to expand deposits, and they created the Comptroller of the Currency, whose job it is to approve charters and to see to it that national banks obey the laws and regulations handed down by Congress and the Comptroller's office.

In 1865, Congress passed a law placing a 10 percent tax on state bank notes. Within a few years, the law wiped out a number of state banks and destroyed state bank notes in circulation. State banks were down, but not out. The action of Congress came at the time deposit banking was on the rise. The growth in the use of checking and other deposits saved the state banking system. Indeed, many banks preferred state to federal charters because of low reserve requirements, greater leniency of many state bank regulators, and lower capital requirements.

Congress created the Federal Reserve System in 1913. After one and a quarter centuries of existence, the United States had a full-fledged central bank. Widespread hostility to such a bank had been based upon fear of concentration of financial power. But a number of serious business contractions, capped by the sharp setback and financial panic of 1907, finally convinced the Congress that something had to be done.

The national banking system's power to create currency was damaged by the limited availability of government bonds. When banks throughout the country found themselves in need of extra currency to satisfy their customers, they tended to draw upon their deposits with large correspondent banks in the cities and the major money market centers in New York and Chicago. The latter, unable to print more currency, sold off earning assets and called in loans. Banks that could not get currency shut their doors and refused to redeem deposits. Panic ensued, with masses of depositors descending on banks, and banks trying to get cash by selling off securities. Interest rates shot up and bankruptcies multiplied.

The Federal Reserve Act of 1913 authorized the Federal Reserve banks to issue Federal Reserve notes to needy member banks. The latter could get the notes by exchanging reserves for them or by borrowing from the Fed through the discount window. The loans from the Fed were collateralized with short-term paper arising out of member bank business loans. Thus, the Federal Reserve Act set in place a mechanism that made bank loans into semi-liquid assets. Instead of closing their doors in the event of a depositors' run on their resources, the banks could go to the Fed for necessary currency. During World War I, the discount facility was open to bankers desiring to use U.S. government bonds as collateral for their Federal Reserve loans. As a result of these reforms, the country had an "elastic" currency—a currency no longer limited by the supply of U.S. bonds in the hands of national banks.

Even the Fed could not prevent bank failures. In the 1920s and, especially the early 1930s, a very large number of banks went under. The reasons for these failures are too complex to discuss here; however, the underlying cause of many of them was depositors' loss of confidence in the banks' abilities to maintain convertibility of deposits into currency. The Fed was not an unlimited source of loans to the member banks; besides, many state chartered banks did not belong to the Fed. Also, because of a decline in loans during the depression, member banks ran out of eligible short-term loan paper to use as collateral at the Fed's discount window. As a result, many banks fell before the onslaught of currency-hungry depositors.

Congress' answer to the problem of bank failures was the establishment in 1934 of the Federal Deposit Insurance Corporation and the strengthening of the powers of the Federal Reserve System in 1935. Establishment of the FDIC was particularly important. Congress authorized it to offer deposit insurance to state banks. The law required member banks to have insurance. Today, the deposit liabilities of mutual savings banks, savings and loan associations, and credit unions are insured by federal agencies.

5.2.2
The regulatory authorities

In 1979 there were approximately 4,600 national banks and 10,000 state banks in the country. Almost all state banks are insured by the FDIC, but not all belong to the Federal Reserve System. In 1979, only 1,000 of the 10,000 state banks were member banks. Except for the few nonmember state banks that are not insured by the FDIC, most banks are subject to the regulations of more than one agency. National banks are under the Comptroller of the Currency, the Federal Reserve System, and the Federal Deposit Insurance Corporation. Insured state member banks are subject to the regulations of the Fed, FDIC, and state banking commissioners. Nonmember insured state banks are fortunate in having only two supervising agencies.

The regulators do not make life for banks as hectic as it would seem. In some respects, they split up their duties. For example, in bank examinations—the auditing of banks' books and operations to verify conformance with regulations and sound management principles—the regulatory authorities have agreed upon a division of labor. The Comptroller examines national banks, the Fed examines member state banks, and state authorities and the FDIC examine insured nonmember state banks. The various agencies accept each others' reports.

Relations between the regulatory authorities are frequently strained. In the 1960s, for example, the Comptroller sought to liberalize the working environment of the national banks by supporting their desire to underwrite municipal revenue bonds (prohibited by a 1930s law) and by ruling that they could establish subsidiaries to engage in bank-related functions. The Fed opposed these proposals. Relations between the Comptroller and the FDIC also became strained in this period.

Conflicts between agencies charged with regulating the same entities should perhaps be expected. Agencies differ in interpretation of the same statutes and have different personalities in charge of making decisions. The problem lies in the existence of conflicting jurisdictions, not in the personalities of the people who run the agencies. For that reason, numerous proposals have been made by individuals and prestigious commissions to consolidate federal regulation into one agency. To date, no proposal has won the day. There is no agreement over which agency—the Fed, the Comptroller, or the FDIC—should take over.

5.2.3
The FDIC, deposit insurance, and bank failures

Believe it or not, in 1921 there were 31,000 banks in the United States. It has never been the same since. By 1929, the number had dropped to 25,500. Then came the Great Depression. So many banks failed that when the economy touched bottom in 1933, only 14,800 banks remained alive—many barely breathing. In 1933 alone, 4,000 banks failed.

In those days, there was no federal agency charged with insuring deposits. The bank failures destroyed many fortunes, large and small. Jittery depositors descended upon strong and weak banks alike; many of the strong could not meet their demands. Federal deposit insurance calmed depositors and reduced their pressures on the banking system. In 1934, the year the FDIC was established, bank failures fell to 62; in 1942, there were 23. Since then, it has averaged less than 6 per year.

Most financial economists consider establishment of federal deposit insurance the most important piece of banking legislation since the creation of the Federal Reserve System. Professor Milton Friedman, a leading monetary historian, says it is *more* important; all those bank failures in the 1920s and 1930s took place under the nose of the Fed, which either could not, or would not, try to stop them.

Deposit insurance currently applies to the first $100,000 of each deposit in each bank (prior to the 1980 Monetary Control Act it was $40,000). Demand and time deposits qualify for insurance. Deposits in excess of $100,000 do not have insurance. Holders of the large certificates of deposit exceeding $100,000 are insured up to $100,000; the remaining money is uninsured. That is the main reason why the sale of CDs is concentrated in large prestigious banks.

Should a bank fail, the FDIC has two choices. In one approach, it can pay off the depositors up to $100,000 and liquidate the bank's assets to pay off the rest. The depositors must then stand in line with the rest of the bank's creditors. In recent years, depositors of liquidated failed banks have received an average of 90 cents for each dollar of deposits. The record since 1934 is impressive—99 percent of depositors of closed banks have been paid in full.

Using a second approach, the FDIC frequently merges failed banks with healthy ones. With this so-called "assumption method," the agency saves 100 percent of the deposit money, since the acquiring bank assumes the deposits of the failed bank.

The FDIC gets its operating money from an assessment fee of $\frac{1}{12}$ of 1 percent of *all* deposits of insured banks. In recent years, however, legislation has provided for credits against current assessments from past payments by individual banks. The effective assessment rate in 1976 was $\frac{1}{27}$ of 1 percent of deposits. The FDIC has over $7 billion in assets. It is also authorized to borrow $3 billion more if needed. So far, it has never used its borrowing authority; its income has been more than adequate to pay expenses and losses incurred as a result of failed insured banks.

The FDIC is important to both depositors and the banking system. Bank runs by frightened depositors may not wholly be a thing of the past, but they are clearly now a very rare event. Moreover, the FDIC has probably toned up the whole business of banking.[5] As the chief insurer of the system, it has a clear interest in sound banking practices. Its examiners comb through the books of almost 8,000 banks. When they report unsafe or shady practices, the FDIC pressures the offending banks to mend their ways. Banks that do not respond face termination of insurance. Few are willing to ignore continued warnings. In the first 35 years of its existence, the FDIC initiated termination proceedings only 198 times.

---

[5]Except, perhaps, for lulling depositors into complacency so that they are no longer watchdogs of their banks.

5.3
The structure of the U.S. banking industry

In most countries, a few major banks dominate the industry. Great Britain, France, and Germany each have 4; Canada, a smaller country, has 10. The banks are in each case very large. They operate nationwide through systems of branch offices

The situation in the United States is totally different. Instead of a few banks, we have a very large number—almost 15,000 at the end of 1979! No single bank in the United States has branches throughout the country. In fact, branch banking is not permitted in many individual states. So, although there are a fair number of very large banks in the United States[6], no single bank or small group of banks dominates the banking industry on a national scale.

5.3.1
Branch banking

Over half the banks in the United States are unit banks—banks with just one office. Fifteen states allow only unit banks to operate. Sixteen permit limited branching, and nineteen allow statewide branching. To be classified as a branch, a banking office must accept deposits as well as make loans. A number of large banks have loan offices outside the cities containing their head offices, but these are not classified as branch banks by the banking authorities. Currently, there are over 30,000 branch offices in the United States—more than double the number of banks.

State laws govern the degree of branching allowed for both state banks and national banks. Federal law does not permit the Comptroller to authorize a national bank to set up branches in a state if the law of the state does not permit branches for state chartered banks. If a state permits limited or statewide branching for state banks, the Comptroller can authorize national banks in the state to have equivalent privileges.

To set up a branch, a bank must make application to a state banking authority, if it is a state bank, or to the Comptroller of the Currency, if it is a national bank. These authorities will not permit the branch to be established unless the bank proves there is a "need" for a new banking office in the area. An additional consideration is the idea of market power. If authorities think that a new branch will impair local bank competition, they will deny the application.

State laws that limit or prohibit branching are in large measure a response to political pressure from small rural banks that fear competition

---

[6]At the end of 1978, there were 160 billion-dollar banks (measured in deposits). The largest was Bank of America, with $78.8 billion of deposits. Citicorp was second with $61.1 billion, and third was Chase Manhattan with $48.5 billion. See "Annual Scorecard of Banks," *Business Week*, April 23, 1979.

from larger more efficient banks. Many of these banks would not survive the introduction of competition from branches of large banks into their communities. Even so, branch banks are not always more efficient than unit banks. Studies on this matter are not conclusive, particularly when they compare branch and unit banks of similar size with similar mixes of services.[7]

The effect of branching laws on the degree of market (concentration) is also unclear. Concentration is frequently measured by the percentage of statewide deposits held by the three largest banking organizations. In 1976, the percentage averaged 61.5 in statewide branching states, 30.3 in limited branching states, and 27.5 in unit banking states. But these averages cover up a considerable degree of overlap between categories. For example, concentration ranged between 34.6 and 86.8 percent in statewide branching states and between 9.0 and 51.6 percent in unit banking states. In limited branching states the range was 17.8 to 45.7 percent.[8]

At times the competitive process may be enhanced rather than reduced by the presence of branching, particularly when state banking laws shelter stodgy, high-cost small banks from the competition of larger banks that might, if the law would permit, open branches nearby. On the other hand, competition may not improve when the large banks simply take over and make branches out of the smaller banks without introducing new practices. Still, in the states that permit branching, even the *threat* of competition from larger banks can have a healthy influence upon the practices and efficiency of smaller banks.

The public is more concerned with the prices and availability of bank services than it is with the degree of concentration of the banking business. In this regard, branch banks are clearly not inferior to unit banks. The weight of the evidence indicates that branch banking provides more bank offices in towns and metropolitan areas with 7,700 people or more than does unit banking. In smaller towns and villages, the two systems are about equal. But, when it comes to pricing of services, most studies indicate that branch banks charge less for business loans, mortgage loans, and consumer installment loans than do unit banks. The latter, however, tend to give higher time deposit interest rates and to levy lower service charges for demand deposits.

Branch banking has frequently been criticized for siphoning funds away from residential and rural areas for the purpose of making loans to large business borrowers at bankers' home offices. It is a little difficult to confront this issue. It may seem inequitable for communities to lose funds they have saved, but there is no inherent reason why funds gathered in

---

[7]For a survey of cost studies, see Larry Mote, "The Perennial Issue: Branch Banking," *Federal Reserve Bank of Chicago Business Conditions*, February 1974, pp. 3–23.

[8]Statement by Phillip E. Coldwell, Member Board of Governors, Federal Reserve System, before the Committee on Banking, Housing, and Urban Affairs, U.S. Senate, March 7, 1978, reprinted in the *Federal Reserve Bulletin*, March 1978, p. 179.

a local community should stay in the same community. Allocative efficiency is served when limited resources are put to their highest valued uses. If large corporate customers are willing to pay higher interest rates for loans than, say, local merchants, then capital should flow to the large corporate customers. That is because the willingness of a firm to pay higher interest rates is a sign that it has higher valued use for the funds. The social productivity of capital would be severely reduced if public policy dictated that capital funds may be used only in the localities in which they are collected.

The economic argument of allocative efficiency does not necessarily appeal to everyone. Many may still prefer funds collected locally to remain in uses nearby. Such people may be both pleased and surprised to find out that branching does not necessarily channel funds to the big cities and to big borrowers. Branch banks tend to have higher loan-to-deposit ratios than unit banks. Also, while there is a definite tendency for some branches to be primarily deposit-gathering offices, others tend to be loan-issuing offices. Moreover, branches outside the communities of home offices show no signs of being drained of deposits in the aggregate. Thus, banks with systems of branches do redistribute loanable funds, but a community away from the head office is just as likely to receive an inflow as it is an outflow of funds. The main determinant of the direction of flow, presumably, is the availability and relative profitability of loan opportunities.[9]

5.3.2
Regulating foreign banks[10]

Growth and penetration of foreign banks in the United States led Congress to pass the International Banking Act of 1978. The Act for the first time brought foreign banks under a *national* regulatory policy. Previously, foreign banks operated principally under regulations of states in which they are chartered.

The problems raised by the invasion of foreign banks can be illustrated by a few facts. First, they have become a major force. In 1972, there were only 52 foreign banks with assets of $18 billion. In the middle of 1979, their number reached 300, and their assets grew to more than $140 billion—about 10 percent of the assets of all banks in the United States. In San Francisco, New York, and Los Angeles, foreign banks in that year actually held 32 percent of all bank assets and did 38 percent of all commercial lending.

---

[9]The last four paragraphs draw heavily on Mote, pp. 9–22.

[10]Material in this section is based on Hang-Sheng Cheng, "Regulating Foreign Banks," *Federal Reserve Bank of San Francisco Weekly Letter*, November 17, 1978.

Second, the lack of a national policy gave foreign banks an opportunity to operate full-line branches across state lines, something forbidden to domestic banks under the McFadden Act. At the time of passage of the International Banking Act in 1978, there were 123 foreign banks operating with branches in two or more states. The Barclay Group (British), for example, operated banks in New York, San Francisco, Boston, and Chicago. American banks also operate across state lines, but the offices are not full-fledged branches; instead, they are specialized "loan production offices" (scouting business for the head offices) or agencies engaged in nonbank financial business—leasing, mortgage banking, credit-related insurance, and consumer financing. Under the Edge Act, domestic banks can also establish corporations in various states for the purpose of financing international trade, but full-fledged out-of-state branches, which accept deposits and disburse loans, are illegal.[11]

Third, foreign banks, almost all of which are in the $1 billion plus category, were not subject to Federal Reserve reserve requirements. In this respect they had considerable competitive advantage over large U.S. banks, most of which were members of the Federal Reserve System.

The International Banking Act cleans up some of these inequities, but many remain. Each foreign bank must now select a home state; branching across state lines depends on the state's permission. Although these new branches may have a full line of services, they can accept deposits only from nonresidents or from activities related to international trade financing. Even so, existing branches owned by foreign banks in operation in 1978 can continue their out-of-state branches and even establish new ones for the purpose of making loans, a privilege denied domestic banks.

Another provision of the law equalizes the reserve requirements for large foreign banks and domestic banks. If the parent foreign bank has worldwide assets of $1 billion or more, the foreign bank in the United States must adhere to the Fed's reserve requirements. Moreover, they will have access to the Fed's discount window and other services on terms equivalent to those faced by home banks.

Although this aspect of the law equalizes competitive conditions for most foreign and state chartered domestic banks, it does not do so for subsidiaries of foreign banks, which are excluded from the law, and

---

[11]Considerable pressure is building to permit U.S. banks to have interstate branches. The International Banking Act of 1978 carried a provision instructing the Fed to permit Edge Corporations set up in separate states by a single bank to operate as full branches, provided that a certain percentage of their business is international. Congress also used the Act to instruct President Carter to review the McFadden Act and report back to Congress in 1980. When he did, he recommended against interstate branching. Instead, he suggested easing the "Douglas Amendment" to the 1956 Bank Holding Act to permit out-of-state banks to acquire local banks.

which in 1978 accounted for about one-fifth of all foreign owned bank assets in the United States. Many of these subsidiaries are larger than $1 billion in assets. Morever, this loophole in the law invites new foreign banks to adopt this form of operation in the United States.

Clearly, the last has not been heard of this matter of foreign banks. The remaining inequities will undoubtedly lead to further changes in the law, some of which may give branching and other privileges possessed by foreign banks to domestic banks. If so, we may soon see the repeal of the 1927 McFadden Act and a radical reshaping of the structure of banking markets across the country.

5.3.3
Bank mergers

A bank that wants to get larger can either set up a new branch or take over another bank. A takeover is a *merger*. Mergers reduce the number of banks and increase concentration in the industry.

A rash of mergers in the 1950s led Congress to pass the Bank Merger Act of 1960. The Act gives federal regulatory authorities power to approve mergers. In Solomon-like fashion, it divides the responsibility: The Comptroller approves mergers initiated by national banks, the Federal Reserve System approves merger actions by state member banks, and the FDIC deals with merger plans of insured nonmember banks. The law requires the agencies to disapprove mergers they consider damaging to competition and that they believe do not serve the needs or convenience of the local communities.

As might be expected, the agencies have developed different interpretations of the standards to be used to judge the impact on competition of proposed mergers. In addition, the agencies have differed over the importance of competition over other factors that may make a merger desirable. For example, a merger may save a badly managed and failing bank, even though it may at the same time reduce competition in a geographical area.

The U.S. Justice Department has disagreed with some agency merger decisions. A major example is the Philadelphia National Bank case of 1963, in which the Supreme Court agreed with the Justice Department that the merger of the Philadelphia National Bank with the Girard Trust Corn Exchange Bank was a violation of the antitrust laws.

The Bank Merger Act of 1966 advised the agencies to adopt common standards for the purpose of approving mergers that might, in the vague language of the law, "substantially lessen competition." It also gave the Justice Department power to challenge agency merger approvals in the courts, provided that it files an action within 30 days of the approvals.

Thus, bank mergers are subject to several layers of authority—the regulatory agencies, the Justice Department, and the federal courts.

5.3.4
Bank holding companies

Many banks belong to parent corporations called *holding companies*. A holding company may own several banks or just one bank. Holding companies are not subject to the same legal restrictions affecting banks. Historically, bankers created holding companies to enable banks to expand where branching was not allowed—across state lines, for example. In 1956 Congress enacted a law designed to limit the growth of multibank holding companies and to prevent expansion to their business into some nonbank activities. The act did not apply to one-bank holding companies, which in 1970 came under regulation with the passage of amendments to the 1956 law.

In 1955 there were 50 registered bank holding companies controlling 417 banks and 7.5 percent of total U.S. commercial bank deposits. Twenty years later, at the end of 1976, there were 1,802 holding companies controlling 3,791 banks and 66 percent of all commercial bank deposits. One-bank holding companies were by far the most important, accounting for 1,504 of the 1,802 companies.

The explosive growth of bank holding companies was due to several factors. In the 1960s, for example, vigorous administration of Regulation Q by the banking authorities weakened the ability of banks to compete for time deposits and sent them on a search for ways to acquire additional loanable funds. At hand was the one-bank holding company device. Banks put themselves under newly organized holding companies in order to utilize the latters' powers to acquire loanable funds through the issuance of commercial paper.

Another important reason for holding company growth is the power it gives banks to expand into other lines of commerce. The law permits bank holding companies to open subsidiary firms whose business is related to banking. In this way, banks have been able to get into the insurance business, accounting services, computer leasing, data processing, investment advising, loan servicing, and so forth.

Holding companies must register with the Federal Reserve System. Formation of a new holding company is subject to the approval of the Federal Reserve Board. Before gaining approval, a company must satisfy the Board that it has sound management, good prospects, ability to fill needs and provide conveniences for the communities it serves, and that it will not contribute to the deterioration of competition. Thus, holding companies are subject to much the same kind of regulation that is applied to branch banking and to branch mergers.

5.3.5
Bank competition with other lenders

In the past, banks had few competitors in the lending business. Today they have many. For that reason, it is misleading to express the degree of concentration in the banking field solely in terms of bank concentration ratios. In almost every market area, banks face competition from savings and loan associations, credit unions, mutual savings banks, finance companies, insurance companies, and other intermediaries. Even nonbank corporations are beginning to take part of the business. An example is Armco, the nation's sixth largest steelmaker, which has created a subsidiary, Armco Credit Corporation, to offer small and medium size industrial companies working capital financing, secured intermediate-term loans, and revolving credit.[12]

Competition exists in every field. Thrift institutions battle banks for savers' money and are every day becoming more competitive in the demand deposit field with instruments such as NOW accounts and share drafts. Money market funds pay small savers short-term interest rates that compete with rates on CDs and Treasury bills. They also offer them checking account privileges and redemption of shares via wire and telephone.[13]

In the lending area, savings and loan associations, as a group, lend more to consumers than do commercial banks as a group. The same is true of mutual savings banks, credit unions, finance companies, and other major lenders taken as a group.[14] Although it is true that most business firms rely upon banks for short-term and other loans, many have other alternatives. Major corporations, for example, have been making increasing use of the commercial paper market.

The increased competition between financial intermediaries is putting pressure on the regulatory authorities and Congress to change regulations and laws respecting the allowable activities of the various institutions. Although many changes have already occurred in the deposit area, changes of similar magnitude are yet to occur in the lending area. On the liabilities side of their balance sheets, thrift institutions are beginning to resemble commercial banks more and more. On the asset side, they are still largely restricted to traditional areas—mostly housing loans for savings and loan associations and mutual savings banks, and consumer loans for credit unions.

---

[12]"A Steelmaker Pushes Into Lending," *Business Week*, March 5, 1979.

[13]For an interesting discussion of the new demand deposit substitutes, see Martin Mayer, "Merrill Lynch Quacks Like a Bank," *Fortune*, October 20, 1980.

[14]See "Consumer Banking: Why Everybody Wants a Piece of the Business," *Business Week*, April 23, 1979.

Even so, the direction of change is clear. S&Ls may now issue credit cards and invest up to 20 percent of their assets in consumer loans, commercial paper, and corporate debt securities; credit unions can now make mortgage loans. Many observers think it is only a matter of time before Congress and the regulatory authorities remove more of the restrictions from nonbank financial intermediary lending, in which case they might in the future closely resemble commercial banks.

SUMMARY

Banks are much like other businesses, because to survive and prosper they must earn competitive rates of return on their stockholders' investments. To do that they must wisely manage their asset portfolios while, at the same time, attract loanable funds through a variety of techniques. At all times they must pay heed to their liquid positions and maintain solvency.

The fortunes of the banking system are deeply entwined with the fortunes of the economy as a whole. An unsound banking system can wreck the whole economy, which is a major reason the industry has over the years been subjected to increasing government oversight and control. The first halting steps of federal regulation came with the First and Second Banks of the United States. Then came state regulation, the National Banking Acts, The Federal Reserve Act, and the legislation of the 1930s setting up the FDIC and strengthening the powers of the Federal Reserve System. This legislation has been joined by other, the purpose of which is to mold and control the pattern of competition in banking markets. The latest is the 1980 Monetary Control Act. The result is an industry that, perhaps more than any other, has its activities shaped by the regulatory authorities.

DISCUSSION QUESTIONS

1. Discuss the role of leveraging in increasing banks' net earnings per unit of capital.

2. What other measures can a bank use to increase its net earnings per unit of capital?

3. Why do banks stop short of making loans and investments that might maximize returns on earning assets?

4. What is the relationship between the prime rate and the commercial paper rate?

5. Why have commercial banks increased the loan proportion of their earning assets over the last 25 years?

6. What are the risks to banks and other intermediaries that must "borrow short" and "lend long"?

7. Why is the Federal Deposit Insurance Corporation considered to be such an important agency?

8. Discuss the pros and cons of branch banking.

IMPORTANT TERMS AND CONCEPTS

- [ ] Bank Merger Act of 1960
- [ ] branch banking
- [ ] compensating balances
- [ ] Federal Deposit Insurance Corporation
- [ ] illiquidity
- [ ] International Banking Act of 1978
- [ ] leveraging

- [ ] liabilities management
- [ ] National Bank Acts of 1863 and 1864
- [ ] portfolio
- [ ] prime interest rate
- [ ] secondary reserves
- [ ] solvency
- [ ] term loans

ADDITIONAL READINGS

Bank management is a complex subject. For three overviews, see Edward W. Reed, Richard V. Cotter, Edward K. Gill, and Richard K. Smith, *Commercial Banking* (Englewood Cliffs, N.J.: Prentice-Hall, 1976); Thomas Havrilesky and John T. Boorman, (editors,) *Current Perspectives in Banking: Operations, Management, and Regulation* (Arlington Heights, Ill.: AHM Publishing, 1976); and Paul S. Nadler, *Commercial Banking in the Economy*, 3rd edition (New York: Random House, 1979). Also useful are J.A. Cacy and Margaret E. Bedford, "Commercial Bank Profitability," *Federal Reserve Bank of Kansas Monthly Review*, September/October, 1972, and E. Kane, "The Three Faces of Liabilities Management," M. Dooley *et al.* (editors), *The Political Economy of Policy Making* (Beverly Hills: Sage Publications, 1979).

Bank regulation is a lively topic. In the 1970s, two major government studies recommended a series of changes. The first was the so-called Hunt Commission, which issued the *President's Commission on Financial Structure and Regulation Report* (Washington, D.C.: U.S. Government Printing Office, 1971). The second was the U.S. Congress, Committee on Banking, Currency, and Housing, *Financial Institutions and the Nation's Economy (FINE): Discussion Principles*, 94th Congress, 1st session, November 1975. Havrilesky and Boorman, cited above, has a useful collection of articles on the subject.

On the subject of banking market structures and competition, see Havrilesky and Boorman, Parts VII and VIII. Also useful is Jack Guttentag and Edward S. Herman, "Banking Structure and Performance," *The Bulletin*, Institute of Finance, New York University, February 1967.

The Money Supply Process

O U T L I N E

An M-1 Money Supply Model
The Monetary Base, Bank Reserves, and the Money Supply
Expansion and Contraction of Demand Deposits
Currency Behavior of the Public and the Money Supply
Time Deposits and Money Supply Theory
M-2 and Other Money Supply Concepts
M-1B and the Other New Monetary Aggregates
Shifts in the Money Multipliers
Analysis of Monetary Changes, 1960–1978

All definitions of money include currency in circulation and some deposit aggregate. The old M-1 definition used demand deposits in commercial banks. The old M-2 definition included all commercial bank deposits except CDs. The newer definitions include deposits and other liability items in nonbank financial intermediaries, such as thrift institutions and money market funds. As time goes on, newer more complicated definitions of money may gradually emerge.

This situation makes it very difficult for the Federal Reserve System and other interested parties to understand the forces that cause one or another of the monetary aggregates to change. Nevertheless, the situation is hardly desperate. Over the years, economists have developed a basic theory of the money supply process that can be expanded to include the more complicated definitions of money, as the latter emerge from the studies and deliberations of official and academic economists. In this chapter we will first illustrate this theory with reference to the old M-1 and M-2 definitions of money, and then show how it can be expanded to include some of the newer definitions.

6.1
An M-1 money supply model

The M-1 money supply consists of currency and coin (which we shorten to just "currency") in circulation and demand deposits held by the nonbank public. Currency in bank vaults or owned by the federal government is not part of M-1; neither are federal government demand deposits in commercial banks. Money supply theory describes the factors that determine the size of the money stock and that settle its division between deposits and currency. The theory incorporates observations about the behaviors of the Federal Reserve System, the commercial banking system, and the nonbank public. All of these entities interact to produce the money stock we observe in the statistics.

6.1.1
The monetary base, bank reserves, and the money supply

Figure 6.1 provides a simple description of the money supply process. The foundation of the money supply is a variable called the *monetary base* (B). Another name for the base is high-powered money. The base consists of the reserves of the banking system (R) and the currency in the hands of the public (C). Thus,

$$B = R + C \qquad (6.1)$$

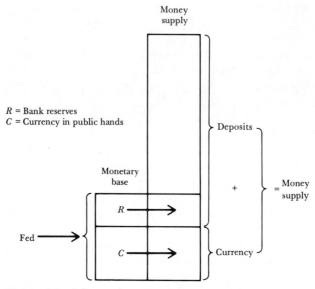

Figure 6.1 *Schema of money creation: (1) Fed creates the monetary base; (2) public decides division of base between currency and reserves; (3) banks, by lending, decide on degree of deposit expansion up to limit; (4) Fed sets limit of deposit expansion through control over reserve requirements.*

The monetary base is the creation of the monetary authorities. Paper money and coins are manufactured by the Bureau of Engraving and the Mint and are put into circulation on demand from banks and individuals through the Federal Reserve System. Some of the currency ends up in bank reserves. The rest goes into the pockets of the nonbank public.

Another part of the base emerges from actions of the Federal Reserve System and the Treasury. An important example of the Federal Reserve base creation is open market purchases of government securities. When the Fed buys securities from nonbank individuals or institutions, it pays with checks drawn upon itself. The individuals or institutions deposit the checks in commercial banks, and the commercial banks send the checks to the Fed. The Fed, on receiving the checks, credits the banks with additional reserves. The new bank reserves represent additional reserves for the banking system as *a whole*—in the chain of transactions no bank loses reserves, but a number gain some.

Another example is the use by the Treasury of its deposits at the Federal Reserve to pay some of the government's bills. The Treasury uses checks drawn on its Fed account to pay private individuals who, in turn, deposit them with their banks. The banks, in turn, send the checks to the Fed and receive reserve credits for their deposits at the Fed. The credits represent additional reserves for the whole banking system.

We shall discuss the sources of the monetary base more thoroughly in Sections 8.2 and 8.3. In the meantime, we make the following assertions: (a) the *size* of the monetary base is under control of the Federal Reserve System and the Treasury, and (b) the *division* of the base between reserves and currency (and coin) depends upon the tastes and preferences of the nonbank public.

The first statement implies the existence of an apparatus of controls managed by the monetary authorities. Such an apparatus does in fact exist and is the subject of much discussion in the following chapters.

The second statement implies that the public can, by changing its mind, shift money into and out of the reserves of the banking system and thereby affect the volume of deposits the banking system can create. Such shifts do in fact occur, and we shall describe them later in this chapter.

The reserves of the banking system support a given amount of deposits. In fact, at any moment the volume of demand deposits is a relatively predictable multiple of the volume of bank reserves. As illustrated by the hypothetical example of Figure 6.1, banking system demand deposits greatly exceed banking system reserves.

We shall discuss the deposit–reserve ratio in great detail in Section 6.1.2. In the meantime, take note of what it means. First, the ratio is governed in part by the behavior of the banking system. Banks can choose either to hold their reserves idle as excess reserves or to lend them out. As discussed in Chapter 4, bank loans based upon excess reserves create derivative deposits that remain outstanding so long as the loan volume is maintained.

Second, the ratio is limited by the legal reserve requirements imposed by the monetary authorities. If the requirement is that reserves must be at least 20 percent of deposits,[1] deposits cannot be larger than five times the volume of reserves possessed by the banking system. If the requirement is 10 percent, deposits can be ten times larger than reserves, and so forth. Thus the deposit–reserve ratio can be less than or equal to the maximum dictated by the reserve requirement, but it cannot be larger.

Third, increases or decreases in the monetary base, or changes in its composition, can have multiple impacts on the money supply. Consider, first, a $1 billion increase in the base. If one-fourth of the increase goes into bank reserves, the latter rise by $250 million, and currency in the hands of the public increases by $750 million. Assuming a deposit–reserve ratio of 5, the deposit portion of the money supply increases by $1.25 billion—$250 million times five. Together, the increase in deposits and currency add $2 billion to the M-1 money supply, which is twice the increase in the monetary base!

Finally, note what happens when the public changes the composition

---

[1] The 20 percent reserve requirement is no longer possible under the 1980 Monetary Control Act. However, it was possible under the old law. We retain it here for purposes of illustrating the theory.

of the base by shifting into currency out of deposits. Let a number of people cash checks and demand currency from the banks—say $1 billion. If the deposit–reserve ratio is 5, as above, the $1 billion of reserve losses by the banks must force a $5 billion loss of deposits. However, because the public now has $1 billion in currency, the money supply is down by a net of $4 billion (−$5 billion in deposit losses + $1 billion in currency gains = $4 billion).

The opposite case of a $1 billion reduction in currency, coupled with a $1 billion increase in reserves, would *raise* the money supply by the $4 billion. Thus, the shifts in the public's desired holdings of currency versus deposits, by affecting the reserves of the banking system, lead to magnified changes in the money supply.

6.1.2
Expansion and contraction of demand deposits

We now take up the reserve–deposit expansion process. In this process, increases in reserves work themselves through the whole banking system to increase its total deposits.

Consider a very simple case. Assume the required reserve–demand deposit ratio of every bank in the system is 20 percent. For every dollar of demand deposits, each bank is required to hold 20 cents as vault cash or as deposits at the Fed.

Next, assume that no bank wishes to hold excess reserves. Each time a bank receives a new deposit, it lends an amount equal to the excess reserves that come with the deposit.

Finally, assume that when a bank makes a loan it credits the demand deposit account of the borrower, who uses the new money to pay bills to people with deposits in another bank. As a result, each time a bank makes a loan, it expects to lose reserves to another bank.

These assumptions suffice to demonstrate the deposit expansion process. Let Bank A receive a new primary deposit of $1,000. If this deposit is to represent an increase in the reserves of the whole banking system, it cannot come from a check drawn on another bank, because Bank A would gain reserves at the expense of the other bank. To avoid this possibility, assume that the $1,000 of extra reserves comes from a customer currency deposit.

A T-account description of the deposit would show the following changes in Bank A's balance sheet:

Bank A

A		L + NW	
Required reserves	+$200	Demand deposits	+$1,000
Excess reserves	+$800		

To increase its profits, Bank A lends $800 to a business customer. It credits the customer's deposit account with $800 and records an $800 increase in its loan assets. The loan customer uses the borrowed money to pay some bills, and his creditors deposit the checks in Bank B. Bank B sends the check to the local Federal Reserve bank, which credits it with $800 in new reserves and deducts $800 from Bank A's reserves.

The transactions appear on the following T-accounts for both banks. (*1.* indicates results of Bank A's loan transactions; *2.* indicates results of the clearing process):

Bank A

A		L + NW	
1. Loans	+$800	*1.* Demand deposits	+$800
2. Fed deposits	−$800	*2.* Demand deposits	−$800

Bank B

A		L + NW	
2. Fed deposits	+$800	*2.* Demand deposits	+$800

As indicated in Table 6.1, Bank A now is left with its new primary deposit of $1,000, an increase in reserves of $200, which satisfies the 20 percent reserve requirement against the $1,000 deposit, and an $800 increase in its earning assets.

Bank B now has the $800 derivative deposit created by Bank A; 80 percent of that deposit, or $640, represents excess reserves. Bank B, like Bank A, abhors excess reserves, so it buys a $640 security from a dealer. The latter spends the money to buy another security, and the seller deposits the check with Bank C. Bank C sends the check to the Fed, which deducts $640 from Bank B's reserve account and adds it to Bank C's account.

As shown in line B of Table 6.1, Bank B is left with $160 in reserves, which is just sufficient to satisfy the 20 percent reserve requirement against the $800 of new deposits left to it as a result of having received a favorable clearing against Bank A. In the meantime, the $640 derivative deposit it created is now a liability of Bank C.

The process now repeats itself. Bank C, with $512 of excess reserves, makes a $512 loan and adds it to the deposit account of the borrower. The latter spends the new money, and it ends up in Bank D (not shown), which now has an opportunity to lend 80 percent of $512.

There is no need to trace the transactions through to the last bank. The process stops once the deposits received by the last bank fail to gen-

Table 6.1 *Results of a $1,000 Increase In Bank Reserves*

Bank	Increase in Reserves	Increase in Earning Assets	Increase in Demand Deposits
A	$200	$800	$1,000
B	+160	+640	+800
C	+128	+512	+640
–	+	+	+
–	+	+	+
–	+	+	+
–	+	+	+
–	+	+	+
Totals	$1,000	$4,000	$5,000

erate enough excess reserves to make it worthwhile for it to increase its loans. At that point the deposit expansion process stops. In our example the stopping point is $5,000 of new deposits.[2]

Bankers frequently deny that they create deposits. From their point of view, they simply lend a portion of any new primary deposits they happen to receive. This is an accurate perception from their *individual points of view*; but, it is not accurate from the point of view of the banking system.

When a loan-created derivative deposit is checked away from an originating bank, the bank is left with its original primary deposit. From *its* point of view, the derivative deposit no longer exists. However, from the standpoint of the system it *does* exist. It resurfaces as a new deposit in *some other bank*. The latter does not know how the deposit first arose. It only knows that it came from a customer and was accompanied by new reserves. The receiving bank, therefore, regards its new deposit as a primary deposit. As a result, it feels free to increase its loans and deposits by an amount equal to its enlarged excess reserves. When the newly created deposits are checked away, the second bank, like the first, may claim that its balance sheet shows no sign of outstanding deposits exceeding those it has received as primary deposits. As with the first bank, such a claim overlooks the fact that the new derivative deposit is lodged in other banks.

Table 6.1 shows that the deposit expansion process stops when the increase in the banking system's reserves is absorbed into required reserves. If any bank has excess reserves, there is still opportunity for further expansion, and the deposit total will continue to rise until the excess reserves are eliminated. From this principle it follows that the degree of

---

[2]In reality, the last bank may keep a few dollars of excess reserves, so that the stopping point may be just short of $5,000. This detail does nothing to compromise the basic principle, which is that, under the assumption of our example, the banking system *is capable* of converting a deposit of $1,000 of new reserves into $5,000 of new demand deposits.

deposit expansion varies inversely with the legal reserve requirement. The lower the reserve requirement, the larger is the deposit total that can arise from a given reserve base. The higher the reserve requirement, the smaller is the deposit total.

More generally, let rd be the ratio of required reserves to outstanding demand deposits. Let R be the total reserves of the banking system and DD be the demand deposit potential of the system. If the system reaches its potential, then all reserves are required:

$$R = (rd)(DD) \tag{6.2}$$

Dividing both sides of this equation by rd, we get

$$DD = R\left(\frac{1}{rd}\right) = \frac{R}{rd}$$

Applying Equation (6.2) to *changes* in bank reserves (ΔR), we derive a formula showing the change in deposit potential for the system:

$$\Delta DD = \frac{\Delta R}{rd} = \Delta R\left(\frac{1}{rd}\right) \tag{6.2a}$$

Apply Equation (6.2a) to the example in this section: In the example, $\Delta R = \$1,000$ and $rd = .2$; therefore, $\Delta DD = \$1,000 \times 5 = \$5,000$. Had rd been .1, ΔDD would have been $\$10,000$, which proves that the change in deposits potential given by any change in the reserves of the banking system is inversely proportional to the reserve requirement ratio.[3]

---

[3] A more formal, dynamic derivation of Equation (6.2a) is as follows: The first bank to receive a currency deposit has its deposits raised by the amount of the new reserves, ΔR. It creates a new deposit equal to $\Delta R(1-rd)$, which, after the clearing process, ends up in another bank. The latter lends out $\Delta R(1-rd)(1-rd) = \Delta R(1-rd)^2$. This loan is a new deposit that appears in a third bank, which loans out and creates new deposits equal to $\Delta R(1-rd)^2(1-rd) = \Delta R(1-rd)^3$. Carrying the series out to n banks we get:

$$\Delta DD = \Delta R + \Delta R(1-rd) + \Delta R(1-rd)^2 + \Delta R(1-rd)^3 + \cdots + \Delta R(1-rd)^n \tag{1}$$

Now multiply (1) by $(1-rd)$ to get:

$$(1-rd)\Delta DD = \Delta R(1-rd) + \Delta R(1-rd)^2 + \Delta R(1-rd)^3 + \cdots + \Delta R(1-rd)^{n+1} \tag{2}$$

Subtract (2) from (1) and divide by $[1-(1-rd)]$:

$$\Delta DD = \frac{\Delta R[1-(1-rd)^{n+1}]}{1-(1-rd)} \tag{3}$$

If n, the number of banks is large, rd being a fraction, Equation (3) reduces to:

$$\Delta DD = \Delta R/rd \tag{4}$$

When the banking system *loses* reserves, there usually ensues a multiple *contraction* of deposits. Suppose that a deposit customer cashes a $1,000 check and demands $1,000 of currency from Bank A. If the bank has no excess reserves, it will have an $800 *reserve deficiency* (assuming a 20 percent reserve requirement). What can it do to make up the deficiency?

The possibilities include (a) sale of securities, (b) calling in loans, (c) refusal to renew maturing loans, (d) borrowing reserves from another bank, or (e) borrowing from the Fed. Borrowing from the Fed restores the lost reserves to the system and prevents deposit contraction. Borrowing reserves from another bank does nothing to increase system-wide reserves, but it may utilize previously idle excess reserves possessed by the lending bank. If so, system-wide deposit contraction will not occur. But, if the Fed is not lending, and if there are insufficient excess reserves in the system to offset the reserve loss, then the banking system must contract earning assets and deposits. That is because none of the possibilities (a) through (c) restores the lost reserves to the system.

As an example of how the deposit contraction process works, let Bank A meet its reserve deficiencies by selling $800 worth of securities to a nonbank private buyer. The latter pays with a check drawn on Bank B. Bank B loses $800 of reserves to Bank A; but, because the reserve requirement is 20 percent, its reserve deficiency is only $640. So, Bank B sells $640 of securities, shifting the burden to Bank C. The latter loses $640 of deposits and reserves, but its reserve deficiency is only $512. It, therefore, sells $512 of securities, causing Bank D to lose reserves and deposits.

So it goes: the *system* loses $1,000 + $800 + $640 + $512 + $\cdots$ + = $5,000 of demand deposits, which is five times the system's reserve loss of $1,000. The *deposit multiplier also works in reverse!*

Some economists argue that deposit contraction and expansion are not symmetrical. To some extent, that is true. No law or rule *forces* banks to increase deposits when they get excess reserves; but, they must reduce deposits when they have a collective reserve deficiency. Even so, the profit motive is powerful. Except for extraordinary circumstances, such as those existing in the uncertain years during and following the Great Depression of the 1930s, most banks keep reserves close to required levels. There are few occasions during which shifts in banks' desires for excess reserves compromise the Federal Reserve System's control over the money supply.

6.1.3
Currency behavior of the public and the money supply

The nonbank public holds its money in the form of currency and demand deposits. Shifts between these money forms can have dramatic effects on the money supply. Money pulled out of deposits lowers bank reserves. Unless the Fed offsets the reserve losses, bank deposits must decline by a multiple of the losses. Conversely, decisions by the public to shift out of currency into deposits raises reserves and leads to a multiple expansion of deposits.

Monetary economists usually link the public's desired holdings of currency to their holdings of deposits. The linking concept is the *currency–deposit ratio*, c. Thus, if currency is C, we have:

$$C = c(DD) \tag{6.3}$$

In December 1979, the currency component of the money supply was \$97.5 billion, and demand deposits were \$264 billion; so that the currency–deposit ratio was .37. Ten years earlier, the ratio was .29 and ten years before that, in 1958, it was .26. Thus, over time, the ratio can change quite a bit. For that reason, it is important to recognize it as a component of our theory of the money supply process.

The way to do it is as follows: Recall Equations (6.1), (6.2), and (6.3), and state Equation (6.4), the definition of money:

$$B = R + C \tag{6.1}$$

$$R = (rd)(DD) \tag{6.2}$$

$$C = c(DD) \tag{6.3}$$

$$\text{M-1} = DD + C \tag{6.4}$$

Substitute Equations (6.2) and (6.3) into (6.1), which allows us to define demand deposits in terms of the monetary base, B:

$$DD = \left(\frac{1}{rd + c} \right) B \tag{6.5}$$

Now, according to Equation (6.3), currency is a fraction, c, of demand deposits. So,

$$C = c(DD) = c \left(\frac{1}{rd + c} \right) B \tag{6.6}$$

Substitute Equations (6.5) and (6.6) into (6.4), and, factoring out B, we get:

$$\text{M-1} = \left(\frac{1 + c}{rd + c} \right) B = (m1)B \tag{6.7}$$

The ratio $(1 + c)/(rd + c) = m1$ is frequently called the *money multiplier*. It multiplies each dollar of the base, which is under the control of the Fed, to produce the money supply. If the multiplier is reasonably stable, the monetary authorities can gain tolerable control over the money supply by adjusting the base up or down.

To understand the importance of the currency–deposit ratio in the money supply process, assume the ratio is 0. Such an assumption carries us back to the example in Section 6.1.2. As newly created deposits are transferred from one bank to another, there is no leakage into currency. That is, the reserves shift from the bank creating the deposits to the bank receiving the deposits with no drainage into the currency holdings of the public. Reserves are, therefore, preserved for further deposit expansion. The money multiplier, in this case, is $1/rd$, and each dollar of new base raises the money supply by $(1/rd)$.

Now, let the currency–deposit ratio be positive, say $c = .25$. Twenty five cents of each dollar of new deposits is now diverted from reserves into currency holdings of the public. Clearly, a given increase in the base must raise the money supply much less than in the previous case, where $c = 0$. The cash drained from the reserves of the banking system cannot be used by it to expand deposits.

In brief, the money multiplier varies inversely with the currency–deposit ratio. In situations where the ratio is rising, as during the last 20 years, the Fed must either lower required reserve ratios or increase the growth rate of the base in order to maintain any given growth rate of the money supply. A falling currency–deposit ratio implies the opposite policies.

6.1.4
Time deposits and money supply
theory

The theme of Section 6.1.3 is that innocent decisions by the public to change its currency holdings have important impacts on the M-1 money supply. The decisions create or destroy bank reserves and cause large secondary movements in demand deposits. In this section we note that similar repercussions come from people's decisions to convert savings or time deposits into demand deposits, or to exchange demand deposits for savings or time deposits.

To illustrate, let Jane Doe convert $1,000 of her demand deposits into a savings deposit. Because savings deposits carry much lower reserve requirements than do demand deposits, the switch creates excess reserves for the banking system—$150 if the savings deposit required reserve ratio is 5 percent and the demand deposit reserve ratio is 20 percent. The new excess reserves are available for loan and deposit expansion.

The example also illustrates a situation in which the money supply and bank credit may move in opposite directions. If all of the $150 of excess reserves created by the initial $1,000 deposit switch goes into demand deposit expansion, the latter will rise by a multiple of five ($1/rd = 1/.2 = 5$) times $150, or $750. The $750 represents new demand deposits created by an equal amount of bank loans or security investments. Putting the $750 of demand deposit *expansion* against the initial $1,000 demand deposit *contraction*, we observe a net demand deposit *loss* of $250. Thus M-1 falls as bank credit rises!

When people switch from savings and time deposits to demand deposits, the M-1 money supply increases and bank credit decreases. The situation is symmetrical with the opposite switch described in the previous paragraph.

Since the early 1950s, people have increasingly favored savings and time deposits over demand deposits. In 1950, for example, savings and time deposits were only 40 percent of demand deposits; in 1980, they were 266 percent of demand deposits! This tremendous change was caused by rising savings and time deposit interest rates and by a series of innovations, such as negotiable CDs, money market certificates, automatic transfer of savings to demand deposit services, and so forth. Ordinary demand deposits, with their zero interest yields, gradually became less and less attractive to depositors.

Integrating savings and time deposit behavior into the base-multiplier theory of the money supply is relatively simple. Let rt be the official required reserve ratio against savings and time deposits, and assume that people wish to hold s cents worth of savings and time deposits (*TD*) for each dollar of demand deposits. These assumptions permit us to rewrite Equation (6.2), the reserve equation, and to add a new equation, (6.3a), to the system from which we derive the base-money multiplier formula. The system now reads as follows:

$$B = R + C \tag{6.1}$$

$$R = (rd)(DD) + (rt)(TD) \tag{6.2a}$$

$$C = c(DD) \tag{6.3}$$

$$TD = s(DD) \tag{6.3a}$$

$$\text{M-1} = DD + C \tag{6.4}$$

Now, substitute Equation (6.3a) into (6.2a) and then substitute the result and Equation (6.3) into (6.1). This allows us to define demand deposits as:

$$DD = \left(\frac{1}{rd + s(rt) + c} \right) B \tag{6.5a}$$

Since currency is a fraction, c, of demand deposits, we can write:

$$C = c(DD) = c\left(\frac{1}{rd + s(rt) + c}\right)B \qquad (6.6a)$$

Putting Equations (6.5a) and (6.6a) into Equation (6.4), and factoring out B, we have a new base-money multiplier formula:

$$\text{M-1} = \left(\frac{1+c}{rd + s(rt) + c}\right)B = m1B \qquad (6.7)$$

The new formula tells the story of the impact of time deposits. As public preference for savings and time deposits (embodied in s) increases, the money multiplier ($m1$) declines, and vice versa, In addition, the very existence of such a preference reduces the multiplier below the value indicated in Equation (6.7). When banking system excess reserves expand, the new deposits created by the system flow into currency and into savings and time deposits. The first flow drains reserves out of the system, and the second locks a portion of them into savings and time deposit required reserves. In both cases, fewer reserves are available as a basis for further demand deposit expansion. The M-1 money multiplier is, therefore, hostage to both the currency and savings–time deposit behavior of the public.

6.1.5
M-2 and other money supply concepts

The M-1 money supply model set forth in Sections 6.1.2–6.1.4 illustrates the basic methodology of most money supply theories. The objective of the methodology is to summarize in the form of a base-money multiplier formula the ways in which decisions of the monetary authorities, the banks, and the public affect the money supply. The formula tells us in rather precise terms how changes in the base, changes in reserve requirements, changes in the public's currency behavior, and changes in its time deposit preferences will alter the M-1 money supply. Because the base-money multiplier approach is so useful, economists usually extend it to other money supply concepts, such as (old) M-2.

(Old) M-2 is M-1 plus commercial bank savings and time deposits other than large certificates. To develop a base-money multiplier formula for M-2 requires a simple extension of the M-1 formula. Repeat Equations (6.3) and (6.3a); then set forth the definition of M-2:

$$C = c(DD) \tag{6.3}$$

$$\text{TD} = s(\text{DD}) \tag{6.3a}$$

$$\text{M-2} = \text{M-1} + TD = DD + C + TD \tag{6.8}$$

Now substitute Equations (6.3) and (6.3a) into (6.8):

$$\text{M-2} = DD + c(DD) + s(DD) = DD(1 + c + s) \tag{6.9}$$

According to Equation (6.5a), $DD = [1/(rd + s(rt) + c)]B$. Substituting this term into Equation (6.9) gives us the base-money multiplier formula for the M-2 money supply:

$$\text{M-2} = \left(\frac{1 + c + s}{rd + s(rt) + c} \right) B = m2B \tag{6.10}$$

The old M-2 money multiplier, $m2$, was larger than the old M-1 multiplier. Both algebra and factual information (Table 6.2) demonstrate this fact.

6.1.6
M-1B and the other new monetary aggregates

Having developed the base-money multiplier formulas for the old definitions of money, it is now but a small step to develop the multipliers for the new definitions of money. We shall not repeat the algebra for this exercise, but simply show how the formulas would look under the simplifying assumption that all transactions deposits in banks and thrift institutions are subject to a single, uniform reserve requirement. Under current regulations, and those to come for thrift institutions under the 1980 Monetary Control Act, deposits are subject to different reserve requirements, depending upon bank or thrift institution size and type of deposit.[4]

Let us first examine the formula for M-1B. Recall that M-1B consists of all transactions deposits in depository institutions, inclusive of interest-bearing share drafts, ATS accounts, and NOW accounts. Assuming a uniform reserve requirement of rd against all transactions accounts, and let-

---

[4]For more complete discussions of the effects of new deposit types on the base-multiplier formulas, see John A. Tatom and Richard W. Lang, "Automatic Transfers and the Money Supply Process," *Federal Reserve Bank of St. Louis Review,* Vol. 61, No. 2, February 1979, pp. 2–10; and Anatol Balbach and David H. Resler, "Eurodollars and the U.S. Money Supply," same *Review,* Vol. 62, No. 6, June/July 1980, pp. 2–12.

Table 6.2

Year	Money Multipliers	
	$m1$	$m2$
1960	3.25	4.83
1965	3.07	5.31
1970	2.98	5.63
1975	2.73	6.03
1978	2.58	6.19

Source: Federal Reserve System data.

ting the interest-bearing accounts be a fraction, n, of noninterest-bearing demand deposits, the M-1B formula reads as follows:

$$\text{M-1B} = \left(\frac{1 + c + n}{rd + n(rd) + s(rt) + c} \right) B \qquad (6.11)$$

The higher order new monetary aggregates are developed in the same way. For example, the new M-2 formula is approximated by the formula in Equation (6.12), where h represents Eurodollar borrowings by domestic banks and p, u, and f, respectively, stand for overnight bank repurchase agreements, money market mutual fund shares, and overnight Eurodollar deposits as fractions of demand deposits:

$$\text{new M-2} = \left(\frac{1 + c + n + s + p + u + f}{rd(1 + n) + s(rt) + h(rh) + c} \right) B \qquad (6.12)$$

Note that, although the definition of new M-2 includes money market mutual fund shares, overnight Eurodollar deposits, and repurchase agreements, the 1980 Monetary Control act does not require reserves against them. However, the law does authorize the Fed to impose reserve requirements *(rh)* against net balances owed by domestic offices to overseas subsidiaries and unrelated depository institutions. For this reason, the money supply does not increase dollar-for-dollar with loans based upon funds acquired from Eurodollar loans.

6.2
Shifts in the money multipliers

As Table 6.2 shows, money multipliers can change greatly over the long run. In the short run, they are usually more stable. The key ratios that affect their values reflect legal reserve requirements and bank and public behaviors, neither of which in the absence of sharp alterations in the legal or economic environment is likely to change very much.

For example, rarely do bankers suddenly take to increasing or decreasing their holdings of excess reserves. If they did, the reserve ratios in the denominators of the money multipliers would shift about, causing the multipliers to do the same. Similarly, individuals usually do not abandon habitual currency or time deposit ratios, without being prodded by changes in the law or in the economic environment.

But, as illustrated in Figure 6.2, absolute rigidity of money multipliers in the short run is not to be expected. For example, people may redistribute deposits away from large to small banks. Because small banks have lower legal reserve requirements than large banks, such a redistribution would lower the weighted average of reserve requirements in the banking system and enlarge the money multipliers. Another illustration is a shift in the ownership of the money supply that favors households over business. Such a shift would increase the aggregate currency–deposit ratio and reduce the money multipliers. Finally, a redistribution of deposits favoring time depositors over demand deposit account customers would lower the M-1B multiplier and raise the M-2 multiplier.

Another important source of deposit-mix change is shifts from private to U.S. Treasury deposits at commercial banks. When the Treasury collects taxes from private firms or individuals, or sells them securities, it frequently holds the proceeds in the form of commercial bank deposits (tax and loan accounts). Even though Treasury deposits are not part of the money supply, banks must hold reserves against them. These reserves are not available to support private deposits. As a result, there is a drop

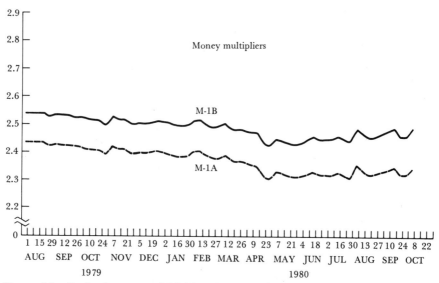

Figure 6.2 *Ratio of money stock M-1A or M-1B to adjusted monetary base. (Source: Federal Reserve Bank of St. Louis.)*

in the money supply. The drop may be interpreted either as a fall in the effective base (because a portion of the base can no longer support the money stock), or as an effective drop in the money multiplier.

Money multipliers are also subject to change from forces that affect economic incentives. These forces can alter the excess reserve behavior of banks and the currency and time deposit behaviors of the public. Examples include reductions in excess reserves held by banks during periods of rising interest rates and high loan demand, larger currency usage by the public in order to escape higher income taxes (currency transactions are less traceable than check transactions), and a drop in savings and time deposit holdings due to an increase in interest rates on Treasury and privately issued securities relative to deposit interest rates.

In brief, the key ratios affecting money multipliers are subject to shifts resulting from changes in the mix of monetary aggregates and from forces affecting economic incentives. In the short run, changes in these ratios usually do not radically change the multipliers, partly because the ratios change in offsetting directions, and partly because behavioral changes of the banks and public are not large. Over long periods, however, the multipliers do change greatly, for it is over such periods that trends in behavior and changes in policies manifest themselves the most.

6.3
Analysis of monetary changes, 1960–1978

Over the years, most of the change in the U.S. money supply, however defined, has come from changes in the monetary base. As we shall see, this fact has great significance for the interpretation of the U.S. business cycle and inflation experience. For now, we need only to illustrate this point for 1960–1978, which encompasses one of the most inflationary periods in our history.

Any change in the money supply decomposes into the change due to variations in the base; variations in the money multiplier, and the interaction between variations in the base and the multiplier.

To see this, define any *new* level of the money stock as its old level plus a change:

$$M + \Delta M = (B + \Delta B)(m + \Delta m) \tag{a}$$

$$M + \Delta M = Bm + \Delta Bm + \Delta mB + \Delta B \Delta m \tag{a'}$$

Subtracting the old level, $M = Bm$, from Equation (a'), we have

$$\Delta M = \Delta Bm + \Delta mB + \Delta B \Delta m \tag{b}$$

Now divide both sides of Equation (b) by $M = Bm$:

$$\frac{\Delta M}{M} = \frac{\Delta Bm}{Bm} + \frac{\Delta mB}{Bm} + \frac{\Delta B \Delta m}{Bm} \qquad (c)$$

$$\frac{\Delta M}{M} = \frac{\Delta B}{B} + \frac{\Delta m}{m} + \frac{\Delta B \Delta m}{Bm} \qquad (c')$$

In Equation (c') $\Delta M/M$ is the proportionate change in the money stock. $(\Delta B)/B$, $(\Delta m)/m$ and $(\Delta B \Delta m)/Bm$ represent changes due to changes in the base, the multiplier, and the interaction between the base and multiplier, respectively.

Relevant data for 1960 and 1978, where old M-1, old M-2, and B are in billions of dollars, are

	1960	1978
M-1	143.5	352.9
M-2	212.6	846.7
B	44.0	136.7
$m1$	3.26	2.58
$m2$	4.83	6.19

Applying these data to Equation (c') we get:

$$\frac{\Delta M}{M} = \frac{\Delta B}{B} + \frac{\Delta m}{m} + \frac{\Delta B \Delta m}{Bm}$$

M-1: 1.46 = 2.11 − .21 − .44

M-2: 2.98 = 2.11 + .28 − .59

In 1960–1978 changes in the monetary base dominated the increase in both money aggregates. M-1 increased by 146 percent and M-2 rose by 298 percent. The rise in the base was 211 percent. Had the money multipliers remained unchanged, both monetary aggregates would have also risen by 211 percent. As things turned out, $m1$ fell and $m2$ rose, so that M-1 increased less than the base, and M-2 more than the base.[5]

---

[5] In the period 1960–1978, the currency deposit ratio, c, rose from .25 to .36, and the time–demand deposit ratio, s, rose from .6 to 1.9. The *weighted average* of reserve–deposit ratios, r, fell from .11 to .05. The drop in r worked to increase both $m1$ and $m2$. The rise in c worked to decrease the multipliers. The divergence trends in $m1$ and $m2$ must, therefore, be explained by the rise in s, which increased $m2$ while decreasing $m1$.

Although the base-money multiplier formulas aid analysis of the factors affecting the money supply, they should be used with caution. They do not, for instance, tell us why the base changes, nor why the key ratios affecting the money multipliers shift about. Answering these questions frequently requires sophisticated and detailed economic and policy analysis. Even so, the formulas do give us a place to start—a place to look for significant clues as to the major sources of change. They bring a sense of order and structure to the study of monetary history and policy.[6]

SUMMARY

All money supply definitions include currency and some deposit aggregate. Money supply theory attempts to isolate the factors affecting each part of the money supply. One factor is the monetary base, the total size of which is strongly influenced by actions of the monetary authorities. Another factor is the division of the base into bank reserves and currency, which depends upon the currency–deposit ratio adopted by the nonbank public. A rise in the ratio drains reserves from the banking system, and a fall in the ratio increases reserves. The deposit portion of the money supply is regulated by the size of the bank reserves, legal minimum reserve–deposit ratios, and the excess reserve behavior of the banking system. Deposits exceed bank reserves to an extent that is inversely related to reserve ratios and bank holdings of excess reserves.

The various factors affecting the money supply are summarized in the form of base-money multiplier formulas, examples of which are given for the old M-1 and M-2 and the M-1B and new M-2 definitions of the money supply. These formulas provide a convenient format for analyzing the factors affecting the money supply.

Applications of the base-money multiplier formulas to recent U.S. experience demonstrate the high empirical significance of the monetary base. The base is largely the product of Federal Reserve System policymaking. For that reason, we now need to turn to a description of the Federal Reserve System and a more detailed discussion of the instruments by which it exercises its power over the money supply.

DISCUSSION QUESTIONS

1. Describe the effects on the M-1B money supply of the following events (hold constant all but the mentioned factors):
   a. An increase in currency holdings of the public

---

[6]A classic study using the base-money multiplier formula is Milton Friedman and Anna J. Schwartz, *Monetary History of the United States, 1867–1960* (New York: National Bureau of Economic Research, 1963).

b. A decrease in the ratio of time to demand deposits desired by the public
c. A rise in time deposit interest rates
d. An increase in excess reserves held by the banking system

2. Why is the M-2 money multiplier larger than the M-1B multiplier?

3. Compare the money multiplier with the deposit multiplier.

4. What would be the effects on the money multiplier of a 100 percent reserve requirement against all deposits?

5. Describe the roles of the banks, the nonbank private sector, and the Federal Reserve System in creating the money supply.

IMPORTANT TERMS AND CONCEPTS

☐ base-multiplier formula   ☐ money multiplier
☐ currency–deposit ratio   ☐ money supply theory
☐ deposit–reserve ratio   ☐ time deposit ratio
☐ monetary base

ADDITIONAL READINGS

A standard reference article to introductory money supply theory is Jerry L. Jordan, "Elements of Money Stock Determination," *Federal Reserve Bank of St. Louis Review* (October, 1969). An advanced treatment is given by Albert E. Burger, *The Money Supply Process* (Belmont, California: Wadsworth Publishing Company, 1971). A useful application of the model to recent experience is in Jane Anderson and Thomas M. Humphrey "Determinants of the Change in the Money Stock: 1960–1970," *Federal Reserve Bank of Richmond Monthly Review* (March 1972). A classic application of the base-money multiplier theory is in Phillip Cagan, *Determinants and Effects of Changes in the Stock of Money, 1875–1960* (New York: National Bureau of Economic Research, 1965). The theory is also a central concept in Milton Friedman and Anna J. Schwartz, *Monetary History of the United States, 1867–1960* (New York: National Bureau of Economic Research, 1963).

Organization and Control of the Federal Reserve System

O U T L I N E

Organization of the Federal Reserve System
Formal Structure of the Federal Reserve System
The Fed's Relations with Congress
Independence of the Federal Reserve System
The Fed's Declining Membership
The Monetary Control Act of 1980

Question: Who runs the country's monetary policies? Answer: The Federal Reserve System? The question mark at the end of the answer is appropriate. The Fed is at the center of policy making, but a system runs nothing; only people do. So, the question should be phrased: Which person or persons run the monetary policies of the country? The answer to this question is not so simple. Power and influence are spread throughout the Federal Reserve System. Moreover, the President and Congress on occasion also lend a hand in policy making. What emerges as monetary policy is the result of a continuous process of consultation, political pressure, and economic analysis, all of which filter through a structure of decision-making bodies, which, in many respects, is unique in the world of central banking.

This chapter surveys the organization of the Federal Reserve System and delineates its major functions. The formal structure of the System includes member banks, district Federal Reserve banks, the Board of Governors, the Federal Open Market Committee (FOMC), and a minor body called the Federal Advisory Council. Congress has given the System a number of monetary and nonmonetary functions and has assigned these responsibilities to different parts of the System.

The President, with the approval of the Senate, appoints the members and the Chairman of the Board of Governors, and the House and the Senate oversee the System's policies. In the last analysis, the Fed is Congress' own creation. The President also has considerable influence, but it is Congress that the System must ultimately satisfy. If it consistently fails to do so, it risks losing its independence.

7.1
Organization of the Federal Reserve System

The present structure of the Federal Reserve System reflects Congress' legislative intent in the original Federal Reserve Act of 1913 and in modifications made in the Banking Acts of 1933 and 1935 and the Monetary Control Act of 1980. The original act placed considerable power in the hands of the district Federal Reserve banks. The district banks were set up to discount commercial paper and to issue currency. They were, and still are, owned by member banks and guided by boards of directors made up of bankers, businessmen, and prominent lay persons. The 1935 Act shifted much power away from the district Reserve banks to the Board of Governors, which underwent a reorganization. The 1980 Act extended Federal Reserve controls to nonmember banks and to thrift institutions. Thus, far from its original state, the Fed is now the most powerful monetary control agency the United States has ever known.[1]

7.1.1
Formal structure of the Federal
Reserve System

Figure 7.1 summarizes the main components of the Federal Reserve System and says something about their powers and relationships.

Member banks   At the base of the system are the member banks. Member banks own district Federal Reserve banks and provide a portion of the membership of their boards of directors. As we have said, all national banks must belong to the System, but state banks need not; in fact, only a minority of state banks have chosen to join. Member banks must subscribe 6 percent of their capital and surplus to stock in their district Federal Reserve banks; in return, they receive a statutorily determined dividend rate of 6 percent.

Member banks have little control over the operations of the Federal Reserve banks. Before the 1980 Monetary Control Act, the main advantages of belonging to the system included use of its check clearing system, free wire transfer of funds through the Fed's nationwide network of wire-transferring facilities, the right to obtain currency from the Fed at no service charge, safekeeping facilities for negotiable securities, and the right to borrow funds at the discount rate.

But the costs of belonging to the System were potentially substantial. Reserves required by the Fed in the form of vault cash or deposits with the district Federal Reserve banks do not earn interest; in contrast, non-member state banks are generally authorized to keep some of their reserves in the form of short-term securities or balances with correspondent banks in return for which they receive some of the same services—for example, access to wire transfer of funds, check clearing, currency and safekeeping services—that member banks received.

Thus, over the years, many smaller banks left the Federal Reserve System, or failed to join. The larger banks that received benefits from Fed services exceeding the costs of membership joined or remained in the System. As interest rates rose in the 1970s, however, the costs of membership began to rise very rapidly, and the decline in membership be-

---

[1]It is a frequently noted irony that Congress rewarded the Fed with more monetary powers just after the System had, from the point of view of many monetary economists, massively failed to deal with the Great Depression, using powers it already possessed. Similarly, the extension of powers contained in the 1980 Act came during a period when the Fed was under attack for failing to deal with an acceleration of inflation.

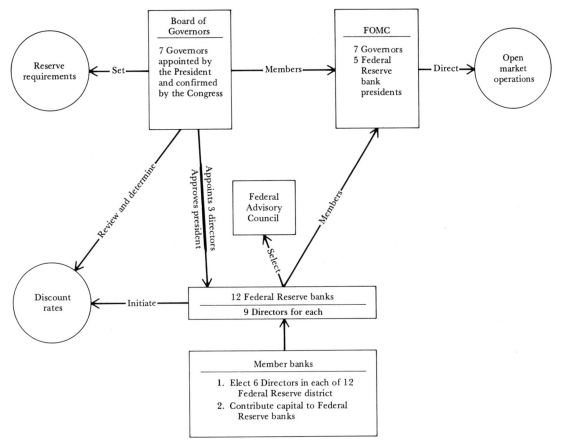

Figure 7.1 *Formal structure of the Federal Reserve System.*

came a more acute problem. We shall address this situation and its relation to the 1980 Monetary Control Act in Sections 7.3 and 7.4.

District Federal Reserve banks   There are 12 Federal Reserve districts, each with its own Federal Reserve bank. The Reserve banks, in turn, have a total of 25 branches. Figure 7.2 is a map of the System.

Each Federal Reserve bank has a nine-member board of directors, six of whom are elected by member banks and three of whom are appointed by the Board of Governors. The directors elected by the member banks include three bankers and three nonbankers, usually business leaders. The Board-appointed and nonbanker directors are called public members. The chairman and deputy chairman of Reserve bank directors are chosen from the public members appointed by the Board of Governors.

Although Reserve bank directors have little power, they are not mere

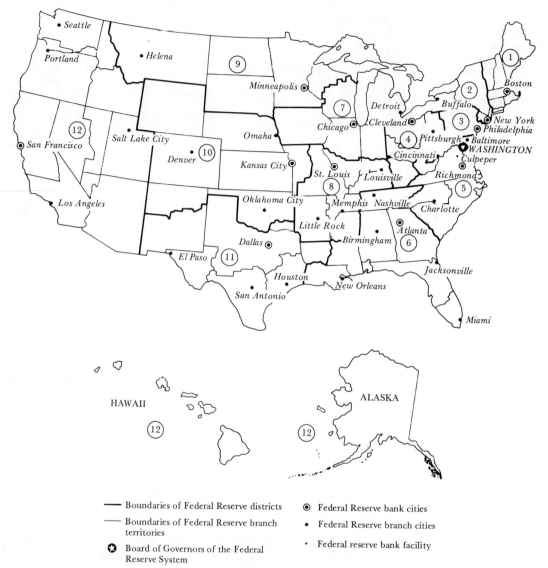

Figure 7.2 *The Federal Reserve System: boundaries of Federal Reserve districts and their branch territories. (Source:* Federal Reserve Bulletin.*)*

ornaments; they appoint the presidents of their Reserve banks. Even though these appointments are subject to the approval of the Board of Governors, the power to initiate the appointments is not an empty one, because Reserve bank presidents sit on the powerful Federal Open Market Committee, in which capacity they are positioned to transmit directors' monetary policy views. Another function of the directors is to establish discount rates Federal Reserve banks charge borrowing banks. As discount rates are subject to "review and final determinations" by the Board of Governors, this power is rather empty. The Board of Governors does not long tolerate different discount rates in different Federal Reserve districts. Finally, directors oversee the day-to-day operations of the banks and provide a channel of communications between the business community and the Federal Reserve banks. Through the latter, they also communicate local views to the Board of Governors and the Federal Open Market Committee.

The Federal Reserve banks have many tasks. They are key links in the chain that forms the national payments system. They provide the currency demanded by commercial banks and the public, and they oversee an important component of the country's check collection and check clearing facilities.

Federal Reserve banks are also fiscal agents for the federal government. In that capacity, they maintain Treasury working balances; safekeep securities commercial banks must keep as collateral against Treasury deposits; sell and service customers for Treasury bonds; and, in the case of the Federal Reserve Bank of New York, act as a transfer agent for official gold transactions with foreign governments and international institutions.

Each Federal Reserve bank maintains a staff to examine member state banks, while delegating examination of national banks to the Comptroller of the Currency to avoid duplication. In addition, although the Board of Governors is charged by law with the task of regulating the structure of the banking system, the task of collecting data for merger and bank holding company applications is shared by Federal Reserve bank research staffs and the staff of the Board of Governors.

Finally, each Federal Reserve bank maintains a research staff. These staffs advise the bank directors and presidents on monetary policy matters. Staff research covers a number of important areas, including monetary and fiscal theory and policy, regional economics, urban economics, international economics, and agricultural economics. New developments in the financial system are frequently first discussed in articles written by Federal Reserve economists in the System's publications. Occasionally, individual banks will adopt particular themes and use their research facilities to push their points of view. An example is the Federal Reserve Bank of St. Louis, which during the 1960s became the leading force for monetarism in the System. In recent years, other Federal Reserve banks, such as San Francisco and Minneapolis, have adopted a similar approach to monetary theory and policy. The work of economists in these banks, as well as in the others, is disseminated through periodical publications—available free of charge to the public—and through papers and memoranda circulated throughout the System. Academic and nonacademic economists from outside the System frequently participate in this work. Thus, the research conducted at the Federal Reserve banks can be, and frequently is, quite influential in changing views and practices concerning monetary policy.

Board of Governors   The Board of Governors is the most powerful body in the System. It consists of seven members, none of whom may be the Secretary of the Treasury or the Comptroller of the Currency. This latter requirement represents a change from the specifications in the original Federal Reserve Act; it is there to enhance the independence of the System.

The manner of appointment also enhances the Board's independence. Each board member has a 14-year term. He or she is appointed by the President and confirmed by Congress. The terms are staggered in such a way that one expires every two years. No governor may repeat an appointment after having completed a full term of office. Governors appointed to fill terms left vacant by board members who have retired early or who have died are eligible for subsequent full-term appointments.

One of the board members is Chairman. He (there has yet to be a she) is appointed by the President, subject to confirmation by the Senate. The appointment begins in the middle of the President's term and is for 4 years, after which time he may be removed as Chairman (but not as a board member), if that is the President's wish. The President permitting, the Chairman may hold a series of 4-year terms until his term as Governor has been fulfilled.

The Chairman has only one vote on the Board of Governors. Even so, he is a most powerful individual. He is the chief administrator of the Board and the chief spokesman for the System before Congress and the public. His views are constantly on display in newspapers and magazines and over radio and television. The stock market has been known to rise and fall in reaction to his (sometimes casual) remarks. As befits such an important person, the Chairman has frequent conferences with the President and other notables. Thus, although the Chairman is equal to other members of the Board when it comes to voting on important policy issues, he is more than equal when it comes to representing the System to the country.

The duties of the Board over which the Chairman presides are many. The major ones include:

Determining reserve requirements for member and nonmember banks and thrift institutions within the limits prescribed by the 1980 Monetary Control Act.

Reviewing and (in effect) determining the discount rates charged by Federal Reserve banks.

Establishing fees for Fed services to banks and thrift institutions.

Establishing ceilings on savings and time deposit interest rates—administering Regulation Q. The 1980 Act provides for a phasing out of the ceilings by 1986.

Evaluating applications for bank mergers and for acquisitions of banks and other firms by holding companies.

Establishing bank supervision and examination policies.

Approving appointments of Federal Reserve bank presidents and appointing three public board members for these banks.

Serving on the Federal Open Market Committee (a most important duty).

Those who wish to follow these and others of the myriad activities of the Board of Governors can do so in the pages of the *Wall Street Journal* and other financial publications. The Board communicates with the public through the *Federal Reserve Bulletin* and through its *Annual Report*, which is a thick document containing much information on System activities and upon legislation affecting financial affairs. Be warned, however, that there is no single source covering all of the Board's activities.

The Federal Open Market Committee (FOMC) Most monetary economists agree that Federal Reserve open-market transactions in United States government bonds are the most important instrument of monetary policy. The purchases and sales of bonds inject and absorb reserves from the banking system; in so doing, they increase and decrease the monetary base. The body within the System that determines open-market policies is the Federal Open Market Committee—the FOMC.

The FOMC evolved out of an informal committee within the Federal Reserve System as it was originally structured. The Banking Act of 1935 made the committee official and defined its composition. The FOMC now has 12 members, 7 of whom are the members of the Board of Governors and 5 of whom are presidents of Federal Reserve banks. The presidents serve one-year terms on a rotating basis; however, because the Federal Reserve Bank of New York conducts open market operations for the System, the president of that bank is a permanent member of the FOMC and serves as its vice-chairman. The Chairman of the Board of Governors is also the chairman of the FOMC.

The FOMC meets in Washington every four weeks, 10 times a year. In attendance are the Committee, the 7 nonvoting Federal Reserve bank presidents, the senior staffs of the Federal Reserve banks, the senior staff of the Board of Governors, and the bank officers in charge of domestic and international security operations (the FOMC is also charged with policies to stabilize the dollar–foreign currencies exchange rates). The staff members brief the FOMC on the state of the economy and the effectiveness of past and current policies. They also provide projections of the economy and recommend changes, if necessary, in current policies. The members then discuss and vote on policies to be followed during the next four weeks.

The policy statement emerging from the vote is a formal directive to the Manager of the Open Market Account, a vice-president of the Federal Reserve Bank of New York. It includes the Committee's evaluations of the economy, a specification of the Committee's policy objectives, and a statement outlining the money market conditions conducive to achieving those objectives. These conditions include the federal funds rate and the growth rate of the money supply.

The directives to the Manager of the Open Market Account are not made public until about one month after the meetings. FOMC sessions deal with operations for the coming month. The Committee is reluctant to broadcast its plans to people who might profit from them and to markets whose reactions to the information might upset policy intentions. This leaves financial analysts and other interested parties with the problem of divining FOMC policies from the open-market actions of the Federal Reserve Bank of New York.

From time to time, conditions in the economy change between FOMC meetings, and there is a need for a change in the policy directive. In that event, a telephone conference is held and, if needed, the Committee votes a change in the directive. Thus, FOMC procedures allow for considerable flexibility in the decision making process.

The Federal Advisory Council   We mention the Federal Advisory Council only out of a sense of completeness. It is a council of 12 members, usually bankers, each of whom is appointed from a different Federal Reserve district. The framers of the original Federal Reserve Act saw this group as a bridge between the Board and the banking community. Although it meets quarterly with the Board, it has no power, and, in the opinion of most students of the System, it has little influence.

7.1.2
The Fed's relations with Congress

If the Fed has any master, it is Congress. Congress created it. Congress oversees its operations. Congress modifies its structure. And, if ever push comes to shove, Congress can destroy it.

Having said all this, however, we can report that the Fed is neither in imminent danger of disappearing nor faced with a serious reduction of its powers. Political and economic pressures have brought forth central banks all over the world. If the Fed did not exist, Congress would probably invent it all over again. Its form and powers might differ, but it would still be recognizable as a central bank.

Federal Reserve Board Governors frequently testify before congressional committees. The House and Senate banking committees are the natural podiums for testimony, primarily because all banking and financial institution legislation is either referred to or originates with these committees. The Joint Economic Committee of Congress is also important. This committee does not deal with legislation, but it operates an ongoing seminar on the country's economic affairs. Its major task is to review and comment upon the annual Economic Report of the President, but it also sponsors studies on numerous topics and holds hearings to get the views of private experts and government officials. Federal Reserve officials contribute frequently to the hearings. Also important are the House and Senate budget committees. These committees are charged by law with recommending overall limitations on government spending and the government's deficit for the coming fiscal year. Because these matters bear upon monetary policy, Federal Reserve officials also testify before these committees.

The Fed has much leeway in establishing and carrying out its policies, and Congress has not always been happy with the way it does its job. Especially critical have been some of the members and even chairmen of the Senate and House banking committees, such as Representatives Wright Patman (deceased) and Henry Reuss and Senator William Proxmire. Usually the critics cannot gather enough support on the committees or in Congress to force the Fed to change its ways. On occasion, however, congressional discontent is widespread enough to cause a significant change in the System's practices. A case in point is Congress' 1975 Concurrent Resolution 133, which stipulated that the Fed must appear periodically before the congressional banking committees to report on the FOMC's plans respecting the ranges of growth or diminution of monetary and credit aggregates for the coming 12 months. As a consequence of this resolution, which has since been made into law with the passage of the 1977 Federal Reserve Reform Act, Board members now appear quarterly, alternately before the House and Senate banking committees. These meetings have done much to force the Fed to quantify its monetary policy targets in terms of growth rates of the money supply and federal funds rates, a practice that was not regularly followed in most of the years of the Fed's existence prior to 1975.

The 1978 Full Employment and Balanced Growth (Humphrey–Hawkins) Act also influences Fed planning. The Act requires the Board of Governors to transmit to Congress, by February 20 and July 20 of each year, written reports concerning the objectives and plans of the Board and the FOMC with respect to the ranges of growth of monetary aggregates for the calendar year during which the report is transmitted; and in the case of the July report, the Fed must state the ranges for the following calendar year as well. The act also requires the Fed to set forth in its report an analysis of the developments affecting the country's economic trends and the relationship of its plans and objectives to the short-term goals set forth in the most recent Economic Report of the President and any short-term goals approved by Congress. In short, the Act holds the Fed's feet to the fire, requiring it to rationalize its actions to Congress as to how and why those actions are consistent or inconsistent with the policies set forth by the other branches of government.

7.2
Independence of the Federal Reserve System

These attempts to increase the Federal Reserve System's accountability to Congress must be seen in the context of historical debate concerning the proper relationship between central banks and governments.

One school of thought believes that a central bank should subordinate its policies to those of the central government, because the latter best reflects the wishes of the people and has the primary responsibility for managing the affairs of the country. Another school of thought believes in "separation of bank and state." They argue that the long-term interests of the country are best served by a stable financial and monetary environment. Central governments conduct wars, carry out public investment programs, and engage in numerous schemes to provide education, welfare, health insurance, and so forth. Government officials and legislators are under constant pressure to expand many of these programs, even when they cannot raise enough tax revenues to finance them. In recent years, central governments in Western countries have also accepted the responsibility for using fiscal policies to attempt to stabilize their economies during periods of economic slump and excessive boom. For these reasons, governments frequently run budgetary deficits—they spend more money than they receive from tax revenues. Having a central bank under their control gives them an easy way of financing the deficits, particularly if they can borrow directly from the central bank. The core of the separation of bank and state argument is that governments should not have the power to direct central banks to finance their deficits. Such a power reduces the need for governments to seek public support for new taxes to expand their activities; popular control is undermined. In addition, power over central banks leads government to finance programs with expansions in the monetary base. Heavy use of this method of finance over long periods can be highly inflationary. Inflation, if out of control, may lead to government regulation and suppression of individual liberties, not to mention economic stagnation. Thus, many of those who argue for an independent central bank, free of control of either the executive or the legislative branch of government, claim to be on the side of popular and limited government.

The degree of independence of central banks varies among countries. In Great Britain, the previously private and semi-independent Bank of England has been nationalized, and its policies are strongly influenced, if not completely determined, by the British Treasury. In most countries, central banks are similarly organized.

In the United States, there appears to be more of a balance of power. There is no organic connection between the Treasury and the Federal Reserve System. They are separate agencies. Congress does not appropriate funds to run the System; it finances itself with interest earned from holdings of U.S. government bonds, bankers acceptances, and loans to banks and thrift institutions. Another safeguard is statutory limitation on the Fed's authority to make direct purchases of U.S. government obligations from the Treasury. The authority is limited and is from time to time renewed by acts of Congress. Other important barriers to congressional or presidential interference with Federal Reserve decision making include the 14-year terms of the Governors and the overlapping of the terms of the Chairman of the Board of Governors with those of the President.

Although the structural safeguards for Federal Reserve System independence are important, we should not conclude that the System is completely free from the influence of the rest of the government, or even from the public at large. There are numerous occasions in its history in which the Fed has subordinated its will to that of the President and of Congress. An example is the willingness of the System to support U.S. bond prices at a high level after World War II. The Treasury feared high interest rates would restore the depressed conditions that prevailed before the war. In addition, the government's huge war debt gave it an incentive to keep interest rates low.

The pegging of interest rates at low levels was highly inflationary; it gave banks and others the opportunity to sell bonds to the Fed without loss, in effect making government bonds the equivalent of interest earning money. Moreover, the Fed was without power to fight inflationary increases in the money supply. To do so would have required it to sell off large blocks of government securities, depressing their prices and raising interest rates.

Power to conduct monetary policy was not restored to the Fed until the inflationary pressures of the Korean war led the Treasury to agree to the famous Accord of March 1951, in which the two agencies announced that they had "reached full accord with respect to debt management and monetary policy" in furthering "their common purpose to assure the successful financing of the government's requirements and, at the same time, to minimize the monetization of the public debt." Many monetary economists hailed the Accord as a release from bondage for monetary policy.

Since the Accord, the Federal Reserve System has had considerable freedom to pursue its policies. But, it lives in a political world, and it is not immune to outside pressures. Political pressures become particularly acute during periods of rapid increases in interest rates, which, for reasons not altogether understandable to many economists, are abhorrent to both the public and politicians, who often appear willing to accept accelerating inflation as the price for keeping interest rates low. Politicians increase the pressures when the Fed, in fighting to keep the money supply from growing too rapidly, fails to prevent an escalation of interest rates. In so doing, they frequently force the System into more expansionary policies than it might otherwise pursue.

Such may have happened during the Carter administration, which in its early years frequently and publicly criticized the Fed for allowing interest rates to rise after the economy had recovered from the 1974–1975 recession. However, in November 1978, President Carter switched his ground, primarily because the country's easy monetary policies had led, at home and abroad, to a collapse of confidence in the government's will to fight inflation. Frightened dollar holders rushed to purchase German marks, Swiss francs, and Japanese yen, pushing the dollar 17 percent below its 1977 foreign currency value. The Fed cooperated with President Carter's policy reversal by sharply increasing the discount rate, by raising the reserve requirement against large CDs, and by announcing its intention to support the dollar with massive sales of borrowed foreign currencies.

In brief, on paper we have an independent central bank. In reality, to paraphrase (an old humorist) Mr. Dooley's comment on the Supreme Court, "The Fed frequently follows the election returns." We return to this subject in Section 20.4.

7.3
The Fed's declining membership

Although the Federal Reserve System has never had a majority of the country's banks as members, it has always had the bulk of the banking system's deposits. In 1965, for example, member banks accounted for 83 percent of all commercial bank deposits. But, the situation was rapidly changing. In the decade ending in 1978, over 550 banks, some of them very large, withdrew from the System, and a majority of the newly formed banks chose not to join. By 1978 only 73 percent of commercial bank deposits were under Federal Reserve control.

Left to continue, the end result of the membership decline would have been a Federal Reserve System composed mainly of large banks and a loss of direct ties to the rest of the banking community. In the view of the Fed, the membership erosion threatened to weaken the nation's financial system by moving more and more of the country's payments and credit transactions outside the safe channels provided by the Federal Reserve, by reducing the number of banks with access to Federal Reserve bank credit facilities, and by spreading around and hence diluting bank regulation and supervision. Finally, and perhaps most important in the Fed's view, was the increasing difficulty of conducting monetary policy in the presence of a system of banks largely outside the Fed's controls over reserve requirements.

Ironically, the Fed's membership problem was indirectly related to its failure to curb inflation. As we shall explain in later chapters, continued and rising inflation leads to higher and rising interest rates. As interest rates rise, the "tax" banks pay to hold nonpaying required reserves also rises. In 1978 the Fed estimated this tax to be $650 million for banks in the System. At the same time, banks were receiving about $420 million in check clearing and other services connected with System membership.[2] Some large banks were probably still making a profit from their association with the System, but many small banks clearly were not.

The membership problem involved a wider group of financial institutions than just nonmember commercial banks. As noted in earlier chapters, nonbank financial intermediaries were expanding their offerings of NOW accounts, share drafts, and other forms of transactions accounts. Transactions accounts are bank demand deposits and ATS accounts plus all similar instruments issued by nonbank intermediaries. The Fed believed that all transactions accounts should be subject to reserve requirements administered by the System. Such a rule would remove the advantage nonmember banks and nonbank financial intermediaries possessed in attracting deposits away from member banks, and would impose the membership tax on nonmembers as well as on members. More important, the rule would substantially increase the leverage of the System over all means of payment.

7.4
The Monetary Control Act of 1980

After a series of proposals made by the Federal Reserve System and other financial authorities, Congress passed the Depository Institutions Deregulation and Monetary Control Act of 1980. Table 7.1 summarizes the major points of the act.

Among other things, the act "solved" the Fed's membership problem. However, instead of requiring membership in the Federal Reserve of all depository institutions, it simply extended monetary control powers of the Fed to nonmember banks and to all thrift institutions. At the same time, it directed the Federal Reserve to extend most of the privileges of membership—access to borrowings from Federal Reserve banks, wire transfer services, currency and safekeeping services, check clearing, and collection and automated clearinghouse services—to nonmember banks and to savings and loan associations, mutual banks, and credit unions. In addition, however, the act directed the Fed to establish a list of fees for these services, to be charged to all institutions choosing to use them.

---

[2]The $650 million figure comes from the *Federal Reserve Bank of San Francisco Weekly Letter,* July 21, 1978. The $420 million figure is from "A Fed Move to End Defections," *Business Week,* July 3, 1978.

Table 7.1 *Depository Institutions Deregulation and Monetary Control Act of 1980**

Permits nationwide NOW accounts	All depository institutions (after December 31, 1980) may offer NOW accounts (interest-earning checking accounts) to individuals and nonprofit organizations. The act also allows banks to provide automatic transfer services from savings to checking accounts, permits S&Ls to use remote service units, and authorizes all federally insured credit unions to offer share draft accounts, effective immediately.
Phases out deposit interest rate ceilings	Congress declares that interest rate ceilings on deposits discourage saving and create inequities for depositors, especially those with modest savings. The act therefore sets up machinery to phase out interest rate ceilings on deposits over a 6-year period.
Eliminates usury ceilings	State usury ceilings on first residential mortgage loans are eliminated (as of March 31, 1980) unless a state adopts a new ceiling before April 1, 1983. Credit unions may increase their loan rate ceiling from 12 percent to 15 percent and may raise the ceiling higher for periods up to 18 months. The act also preempts state usury ceilings on business and agricultural loans above $25,000 and permits an interest rate of not more than 5 percent above the Federal Reserve discount rate, including any surcharge, on 90-day commercial paper. This provision expires on April 1, 1983 or earlier if the state reinstitutes its ceiling.
Increases level of federally insured deposits	The act increases Federal Deposit Insurance at commercial banks, saving banks, S&Ls, and credit unions from $40,000 to $100,000, effective immediately.
Requires reserves on all transactions accounts at depository institutions	The act specifies that any reserve requirement will now be uniformly applied to *all* transactions accounts at *all* depository institutions. Transactions accounts include demand deposits, NOW accounts, telephone transfers, automatic transfers, and share drafts. Specifically, all banks, savings banks, S&Ls, and credit unions will have to maintain reserves in the ratio of 3 percent for that portion of their transactions accounts below $25 million and 12 percent (the Board can vary this between 8 and 14 percent) for the portion above $25 million. They also must maintain reserves of 3 percent (or within a range of 0 to 9 percent) against their nonpersonal time deposits and must report (directly or indirectly) their liabilities to assets to the Federal Reserve. The act provides for an 8 year phase in of reserve requirements for depository institutions which are not Federal Reserve members and a 4-year phase down of previous reserve requirements for member banks.

Table 7.1 *(continued)*

Permits board to impose supplemental reserves	The act permits the Federal Reserve Board, in "extraordinary circumstances," to impose an additional reserve requirement on any depository institution of up to 4 percent of its transactions accounts. If it were imposed, this supplemental reserve would earn interest.
Provides access to discount window	Any depository institution issuing transactions accounts or nonpersonal time deposits will have the same discount and borrowing privilege at the Federal Reserve as member banks, effective immediately.
Establishes fees for fed services	The Federal Reserve is required to establish fees for its services, such as currency and coin services, check clearing and collection, wire transfers, and automated clearing house services. The fees will take effect by October 1, 1981, and the Board must publish a proposed fee schedule by October 1, 1980.
Expands power of thrift institutions	The act authorizes Federal credit unions to make residential real estate loans. It also gives S&Ls greater lending flexibility and higher loan ceilings, expands their investing authority, permits them to issue credit cards, and gives them trust powers.
Simplifies truth in lending disclosures and financial regulations	The act reduces the number of disclosures that must be made under truth in lending (TIL) requirements and eliminates agricultural credit from TIL coverage. It also requires the use of "simple English phrases" to describe key terms in such disclosures, effective March 31, 1982.

*H. R. 4986 was signed into law by President Carter on March 31, 1980. Although the act took effect 6 months later, the various provisions have different effective times, as noted.

Source: *Federal Reserve Bank of Atlanta Economic Review,* Vol. LXV, No. 2, March/April 1980, pp. 4–5.

Thus member and nonmember depository institutions now have essentially the same costs and benefits of belonging to the Federal Reserve System. The major difference is that member banks, through their influences in electing members of district Federal Reserve bank boards of directors, have an indirect influence on monetary policy. It remains to be seen whether many member banks will choose to bear the continued costs of membership—for example, the low 6 percent return on their holdings of Federal Reserve stock and the regulations imposed on national banks by the law and by the Comptroller of the Currency.

SUMMARY

The Federal Reserve System is a creature of Congress, to which it owes its form of organization and its powers. Congress exerts indirect influence upon Fed decisions by means of confirming appointments of the Chairman and the other six members of the Board of Governors, by overseeing its operations, and by holding frequent hearings on the conduct of monetary policy. The President influences the System by making appointments to the Board, by conferring with the Chairman of the Board of Governors, and by making public comments on the System's policies. Even so, the System does have enough independence in making monetary policy decisions to make what ultimately comes out as policy—a brew of political pressure, debate, and study by Congress, the Administration, the Federal Reserve System, and the public.

The formal organization of the System includes member banks, the Federal Reserve banks, the Board of Governors, and the Federal Open Market Committee. The Board is ultimately responsible for discount policy, reserve requirements, Regulation Q, and administering the laws respecting bank mergers and bank holding companies. The Federal Reserve banks hold reserves of member banks, operate the discount facilities, conduct research, and contribute to policy formulation by means of membership of their presidents on the FOMC. The FOMC is responsible for the conduct of open market operations, which makes it the premier monetary policymaking body in the System.

Membership erosion in the System, a serious problem menacing the ability of the Fed to conduct monetary policy, was "solved" by the Depository Institutions Deregulation and Monetary Control Act of 1980, which extended Federal Reserve control powers to nonmember banks and thrift institutions.

DISCUSSION QUESTIONS

1. Just how independent is the Federal Reserve System?

2. Would it be wise to put the Federal Reserve System into the U.S. Treasury department, subservient to the wishes of the President?

3. How has the 1980 Monetary Control Act affected the regulatory environment of the financial system?

4. How much political control over the Fed can be exerted by the executive branch of government? By the legislative branch?

5. Do member banks and the business community have any impact on monetary policy decisions?

6. Which body within the Fed has primary responsibility for the conduct of monetary policy?

7. The Federal Reserve System is the central bank of the United States.

Is it true to say that if the country didn't have a central bank, Congress would have to create one?

IMPORTANT TERMS AND CONCEPTS

- [ ] Accord between the Federal Reserve System and the Treasury
- [ ] Board of Governors of the Federal Reserve System
- [ ] central bank

- [ ] district Federal Reserve banks
- [ ] Federal Open Market Committee (FOMC)
- [ ] Humphrey–Hawkins Act
- [ ] member banks

ADDITIONAL READINGS

The formal organization of the Fed is discussed in detail in *The Federal Reserve System: Purposes and Functions* (Washington D.C.: Board of Governors of the Federal Reserve System, 1974), Chapter 2. An inside view of the Fed is provided by former Board Governor Sherman Maisel in *Managing the Dollar* (New York: Norton, 1973). A thoughtful analysis of the Fed's structure and place in policymaking is Thomas Mayer, "Structure and Operations of the Federal Reserve System," in *Compendium of Papers Prepared for the Financial Institutions and the Nation's Economy Study*, Book II, Committee on Banking, Currency and Housing, 94th Congress, 2nd Session (Washington, D.C.: U.S. Government Printing Office, 1976).

Edward J. Kane discusses some of the newer congressional restraints on the Fed in "How Much Do New Congressional Restraints Lessen Federal Reserve Independence?" *Challenge*, November/December 1975. Discussions of Federal Reserve membership problems and solutions are in the *Federal Reserve Bulletin*, August 1978 (Statements to Congress by Chairman G. William Miller and Governor Phillip E. Coldwell), and in "An Analysis of Federal Reserve Attrition Since 1960," *Federal Reserve Bulletin*, January 1978.

Finally, a disturbing discussion of internal political dissension and possible censorship within the Federal Reserve System is reported in "The Politicization of Research at the Fed," *Business Week*, July 16, 1979. For discussions of the role of internal and external politics in Fed policymaking in a historical context, see Milton Friedman and Anna J. Schwartz, *A Monetary History of the United States, 1867–1960* (Princeton University Press for the National Bureau of Economic Research, 1963). A group of essays on policymaking with an "inside" flavor is in David P. Eastburn, editor, *Men, Money and Policy* (Philadelphia: Federal Reserve Bank of Philadelphia, 1970).

A detailed summary of the provisions of the 1980 Monetary Control Act may be found in the *Federal Reserve Bulletin*, June 1980.

The Federal Reserve System as a Central Bank

O U T L I N E

The Fed's Balance Sheet
Gold Certificates and Special Drawing Rights
Other Federal Reserve Assets
Federal Reserve System Liabilities
Member Bank Reserve Equation
Factors Supplying and Absorbing Member Bank Reserves
Use of the Member Bank Reserve Equation
The Monetary Base as a Policy Target

A central bank is a bankers' bank. It is the central depository for the reserves of the banking system and the major source of new reserves. It is also the agency mainly responsible for issuing a country's currency. The Fed clearly performs these central banking functions.

In this chapter we examine the mechanics of central banking as practiced by the Federal Reserve System. To this end, we first study the System's consolidated balance sheet. We then utilize this information to discuss the sources of bank reserves and of the monetary base.

8.1
The Fed's balance sheet

Table 8.1 reproduces in simplified form the end-of-March 1979 consolidated balance sheet of the Federal Reserve System. The main reason for studying this balance sheet is to learn how the Fed and other agencies, such as the Treasury, affect bank reserves and the monetary base.

Two important components of reserves and of the monetary base are entries on the liabilities side of the Fed's balance sheet. Most of the currency available for bank vault cash and for private nonbank holdings is issued by the Fed as Federal Reserve notes, and a major portion of bank reserves takes the form of deposits at the Federal Reserve banks.

The significance of these items appearing on the Fed's balance sheet is that their variations may be studied as responses to changes in other balance sheet items. Some of the other items are under the influence or actual control of the Fed. As a result, changes in bank reserves and the monetary base are frequently responses to System policy as set by the FOMC and by the Board of Governors. Also influential at times are U.S. Treasury decisions respecting their holdings of Federal Reserve deposits and the issuance of gold certificates and coins. Foreign banks and other depositors,[1] with their small balances, have little influence to exert on bank reserves or the volume of outstanding currency.

8.1.1
Gold certificates and special drawing rights

On March 31, 1979 the Federal Reserve banks owned $11.5 billion of gold certificates and $1.3 billion of Special Drawing Rights (SDRs). Gold certificates are issued by the U.S. Treasury and SDRs come from the International Monetary Fund. Gold certificates represent Treasury-owned gold stored in Fort Knox, Kentucky. Prior to the establishment of the

---

[1]Other depositors include certain international organizations, such as the International Monetary Fund and the United Nations, certain international banking corporations, and a few U.S. government agencies.

Table 8.1 *Federal Reserve System (end-of-March 1979; billions of dollars)*

Assets		Liabilities and Capital Accounts	
Gold certificates and special drawing rights	$12.8	Federal Reserve notes	$100.7
Cash	0.4	Member* bank deposits	31.7
Loans	1.0	U.S. Treasury deposits	5.7
U.S. government and agency securities	118.8	Foreign and other deposits	1.0
Acceptances	0.2	Deferred availability cash items	5.9
Cash items in process of collection	10.3	Other liabilities and capital accounts	4.8
Bank premises and other assets	6.3		
Total Assets	$149.8	Total	$149.8

*As the 1980 Monetary Control Act is phased in, the Fed will also hold nonmember bank and thrift institution deposits as required reserves.

Source: Federal Reserve Bulletin.

Federal Reserve System, most gold certificates were owned and used as reserves by commercial banks. For a long time after the establishment of the System, variations in the volume of certificates continued to exert an influence on bank reserves. They are no longer important; since 1971, the Treasury has substantially reduced its volume of gold purchases and sales.

The mechanics of Treasury gold transactions are easy to understand. The Treasury buys gold with checks drawn on its accounts with the Federal Reserve banks. At the same time, it issues and sells to the Fed new gold certificates. The Fed adds the certificates to its assets and credits the Treasury with an equal amount of money. In the meantime, the check used by the Treasury to purchase gold is deposited in a bank by the gold seller. The bank raises the seller's demand deposits and sends the check to its local Federal Reserve bank to be credited to its reserve account. In this manner, the Treasury "monetizes" the gold it buys. At the same time, the purchase raises the monetary base and expands the potential for further money creation through the multiple expansion of bank deposits.

The following T-account entries describe the various transactions. The items labeled *1.* record the effects of the Treasury's use of its Fed deposit to purchase the gold. The items labeled *2.* show the effects of its sale of a gold certificate on the Fed.

Fed

2. Gold certificates	+$100	*1.* Member bank deposits	+$100
		1. Treasury deposits	−$100
		2. Treasury deposits	+$100

Treasury

1. Gold	+$100	*1.* Gold certificates	+$100

Commercial Bank

1. Fed deposit	+$100	*1.* Gold seller deposit	+$100

A Treasury gold sale to the public reverses the process. The Treasury uses the money so acquired to buy back gold certificates previously sold to the Fed. The transactions reduce bank reserves, diminish gold certificates held by the Fed, and lower private demand deposits in the commercial banking system.

In August 1971, in line with President Nixon's decision to take the United States off the gold exchange standard, the Treasury suspended virtually all buying and selling of gold. Under the gold exchange standard, Treasury purchases and sales of gold helped stabilize the value of the dollar relative to foreign currencies.

Following the Nixon decision, on December 31, 1974 Congress removed a 41-year-old prohibition against private dealings in and holdings of gold, established during the 1933 banking crisis. Since the end of 1974, the Treasury has occasionally sold gold from its hoard in order to support the value of the dollar against foreign currencies.

Special Drawing Rights (SDRs) are issued by the International Monetary Fund (IMF) and allocated to its member countries. SDRs are part of their international reserves; they are used as a means of settlement of debts between central banks. In honor of this financial function, writers call SDRs "paper gold".

The Treasury sends its allocations of SDRs to the Federal Reserve System in exchange for an equal amount of dollars credited to its Exchange Equilization Fund account at the Federal Reserve Bank of New York. The crediting is reflected as an increase in "other deposits," shown on the balance sheet in Table 8.1.

When the Treasury uses SDRs to purchase foreign currencies, it simply buys them back from the Fed and exchanges them for foreign currency with a foreign central bank. It then sells the foreign currency to a foreign exchange dealer, who pays with a dollar check drawn on a commercial bank. When the Treasury deposits the dealer's check in its Exchange Equilization Fund account at the Fed, the Fed deducts the money from the commercial bank's deposit and gives it to the Treasury, *an act that reduces member bank reserves.*

A Treasury decision to acquire SDRs from a foreign central bank increases member bank reserves. The purchase is made with dollars from the Treasury's special Exchange Equilization Fund account at the Fed.

The foreign central bank uses the dollars acquired from the Treasury to buy foreign exchange, or its own currency, from private dealers. The private dealers then increase their dollar deposit balances in U.S. commercial banks, *an act that increases bank reserves.*

Thus, Treasury purchases and sales of SDRs affect member bank reserves in the same way as do Treasury purchases and sales of gold. However, since August 1971, neither item has been of major importance in determining the changes in the monetary base, because the United States and other countries have abandoned attempts to maintain fixed exchange rates.

Still, the world does not have a system of freely floating exchange rates; central banks and treasuries do intervene to prevent wild fluctuations in the rates. It is, therefore, important for students of monetary affairs to realize that sales of gold and SDRs, designed to keep up the international value of the dollar, have the effect of reducing bank reserves and inducing downward pressure on the money supply. Conversely, purchases of gold and SDRs, designed to reduce the value of the dollar, increase bank reserves and generate conditions for expansion of the money supply.

8.1.2
Other Federal Reserve assets

1. *Cash* is a minor item consisting mostly of coin, but also of a small amount of currency issued by the Treasury. Federal Reserve notes issued by one Federal Reserve bank and held by another wash out on the consolidated balance sheet for the System. Fluctuations in Federal Reserve cash holdings cause fluctuations in member bank deposits. For example, when a bank ships coins to the Fed, the latter's cash account goes up and, in payment, it credits the bank with an increase in reserves on deposit.

2. *Loans* go to banks and thrift institutions at the borrowers' initiatives. As indicated in Section 9.2.1, Federal Reserve bank loans to depository institutions are primarily for the purpose of providing temporary credit for banks with reserve deficiencies. Also, in 1973 the Fed established a borrowing privilege for banks that demonstrate a seasonal need for funds and that lack access to national money markets.

    Prolonged access to credit (for more than eight weeks) is available to individual banks only in exceptional circumstances, as when they are faced with a sudden and massive deposit drain, or a sudden rash of loan defaults by their customers. For example, in 1974 the Fed made a temporary loan to the failing Franklin National Bank, the twentieth largest bank in the country, in order to help it ease the effects of its failure on its customers.

A loan to a bank directly increases its reserves, and that of the banking system as a whole, as shown by the following T-account entries.

Fed			
Loans	+$100	Bank deposits	+$100

Bank			
Fed deposits	+$100	Fed loan	+$100

3. *U.S. government and agency securities* enter and leave the Fed's balance sheet as a result of its open market operations. The Federal Reserve Bank of New York conducts these operations for all Federal Reserve banks through their participation in the System Open Market Account.

In conducting its operations, the New York Fed deals mainly with a group of about 25 dealers that specialize in U.S. government and agency securities. The dealers buy and sell the securities from banks, state and local governments, foreigners, and the nonbank public. They have a widespread clientele and are a good focal point for the Fed's own market dealings.

The Fed buys and sells bonds outright and under repurchase agreements. Outright purchases and sales represent permanent shifts in the ownership of the securities. The transactions, therefore, entail permanent injections or withdrawals of reserves into or out of the banking system.

Securities bought and sold under repurchase agreements provide temporary and self-reversing additions or subtractions of reserves, because the agreements contain a promise of the selling party to buy back at a stated time, perhaps in a day or two, the securities it has sold. The Fed frequently uses repurchase agreements when it wants to smooth over temporary fluctuations in bank reserves caused by factors outside its control.

The effects on the balance sheets of the Fed, bond dealers, and the commercial banking system of a $100 million open market purchase are shown in the following T-accounts:

Fed			
Government bonds	+$100	Bank deposits	+$100

| Demand deposits | +$100 | | |
| Government bonds | −$100 | | |

Bank

| Fed deposits | +$100 | Dealer's demand deposits | +$100 |

4. *Acceptances* are a minor Federal Reserve asset. They are bought out-right or held under repurchase agreements. Purchases or sales of acceptances change bank reserves in exactly the same way as transactions in government securities.

5. *Cash items in process of collection* are checks and any other items payable on demand that the Federal Reserve accepts as a cash item (for example, negotiable orders of withdrawal), that have been received by the Fed and, on the date the balance sheet is cast, are in the process of collection. For example, a check drawn on a California bank and paid to a New York bank, which has sent it for a clearing to the New York Fed, is considered a cash item in process of collection until the California bank's reserve balance at the Federal Reserve Bank of San Francisco is reduced.

8.1.3
Federal Reserve System liabilities

Most items on the liabilities side of the Fed's balance sheet speak for themselves. The important thing to remember is that bank deposits at the Federal Reserve banks vary inversely with every other liability. For example, reserves decline when banks purchase Federal Reserve notes from the Fed, and they increase when they sell the notes back. When the Treasury or a foreign bank spends money from its Federal Reserve accounts, the checks it writes typically end up as deposits in some commercial bank, which receives a credit to its reserve account at the Fed. At the same time, the Fed records a reduction in the Treasury or foreign bank deposits.

The oddly labeled *deferred availability cash items* needs special explanation. Recall that a balance sheet must balance. Each time an entry is made, an offsetting entry must be placed on the asset or liability side of the balance sheet. When the Fed first receives a check for collection, it records the event on the asset side under cash items in process of collection and on the liability side under deferred availability cash items. In so doing, it refrains from immediately crediting the reserves of the bank that received the check. Instead, the Fed waits a maximum of two days while the check is in the process of clearing. At the end of that period, it reduces the deferred credit and increases the reserve account of the receiving bank.

An important consequence of this procedure is that the reserves of the receiving bank may be credited *before* the check has cleared the system and the Federal Reserve deposit of the paying bank has been reduced. This possibility exists because the Fed's two-day schedule for shifting money into the receiving banks' reserve account may be too optimistic. Bad weather, airline or other strikes, and other events may slow the check clearing process. When that happens, the Fed's procedure results in automatic loans to the banking system. The loans occur because the receiving banks' reserve accounts are credited before the paying banks' accounts are debited. Until 1980 the loans were free, but the 1980 Monetary Control Act directed the Fed to charge a fee for the service.

These loans have a name—"float." Float equals cash items in process of collection *minus* deferred availability cash items. On occasion, float bulges suddenly to a very large number. For example, during the cold winter of 1979, the daily average of float rose to a peak of $12.9 billion for the week ending February 21, before ending at a $6.6 billion figure for the week ending March 21. As discussed in Section 8.2.2, a major task of the Manager of the Open Market Account is to use purchases and sales of government securities to offset the effects of changes in float on the volume of bank reserves. If he ignores this duty, large random fluctuations in float will cause large random fluctuations in the monetary base and in the money supply.

8.2
Member bank reserve equation[2]

The detailed discussion of Federal Reserve System balance sheet items has an important purpose. Although the balance sheet displays the effects of a number of variables upon bank reserves, it doesn't capture them all. In particular, it doesn't show how the currency behavior of the public affects the bank reserves. The Fed's balance sheet is, therefore, not the best tool for summarizing all of the factors affecting bank reserves. A better tool is a device developed by Federal Reserve economists, called the *member bank reserve equation*.

8.2.1
Factors supplying and absorbing member bank reserves

The member bank reserve equation lists all the factors that supply or add to the volume of member bank reserves, and all the factors that absorb or subtract from reserves (see Figure 8.1). Table 8.2, which is based upon a similar table published regularly in the *Federal Reserve Bulletin*, is an ap-

---

[2]Full implementation of the 1980 Monetary Control Act will eventually make this equation applicable to all depository institutions.

plication of the equation. The bottom line of the table shows member bank reserves at the end of March 1979 to have been $41.5 billion. How did they get that way?

1. The major source of member bank reserves is *Reserve bank credit*, the name given to Federal Reserve assets arising from System purchases of government securities, loans to the banking system, float, and other miscellaneous activities. As indicated in the table, Federal Reserve holdings of securities make up the bulk of Reserve bank credit.

2. The gold stock and SDRs are two additional factors supplying reserves. Almost all gold held by the Treasury is matched by gold certificates held by the Fed. At times, however, the Treasury acquires gold that it does not use as backing for gold certificates. Even so, the member bank reserve equation should record such purchases; it is the purchase of gold, not the issuance of gold certificates, that raises bank reserves. A similar statement holds for Treasury purchases of SDRs.

3. *Treasury currency outstanding* consists primarily of coins issued by the Treasury, but also includes a few hundred million dollars of currencies no longer issued by the Treasury, national banks, or the Fed. Treasury currency outstanding is held by the public, financial institutions, Fed-

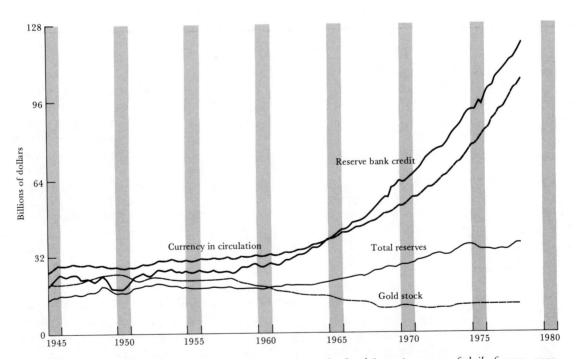

Figure 8.1 *Member banks' reserves and related items (averages of daily figures, quarterly). (Source:* Historical Chart Book *(Washington, D.C.: Board of Governors of the Federal Reserve System), 1978.)*

Table 8.2 *Member Bank Reserve Equation (March 31, 1979; billions of dollars)*

1. Factors supplying reserves (+):	
Reserve bank credit:	
U.S. government and agency securities	$118.7
Loans to member banks	1.0
Float	4.4
Miscellaneous Federal Reserve assets	6.6
Gold stock and SDRs	12.8
Treasury currency outstanding	12.1
Total	155.6
2. *Less* factors absorbing reserves (−):	
Currency in circulation (outside the Fed, the Treasury, and member bank vaults)	102.2
Treasury cash holdings	0.4
Treasury, foreign, and other deposits at Federal Reserve banks	6.7
Other Federal Reserve liabilities and capital	4.8
Total	114.1
3. *Equals* member bank reserves:	
Member bank deposits with Fed	31.7
Member bank vault cash	9.8
Total (*1.* − *2.*)	$41.5

Source: Federal Reserve Bulletin, May 1979, pp. A4 and A5.

eral Reserve banks, and by the Treasury itself. Only part of it shows up as member bank reserves.

4. *Currency in circulation* consists of currency and coin held outside the Treasury, outside the Federal Reserve banks, and outside member banks. Except for the vault cash held by nonmember banks, it is identical with the currency portion of the money supply.[3] Decisions by the public to deposit coins or paper currency (of any kind) in member banks are recorded as decreases in currency in circulation and reductions in member bank reserves. Similarly, recorded increases in currency in circulation denote reductions in member bank reserves.

5. *Treasury cash holdings* also absorb reserves. They consist mainly of coins held by the Treasury in its own vaults.

6. *Treasury, foreign, and other deposits* absorb reserves because they are built up from shifts of deposits out of member banks. An example is a shift of a Treasury deposit from its tax and loan account in a member

---

[3]The Fed's definition of currency in circulation includes member bank currency holdings. The definition given here removes member bank currency holdings in order to make the definition of currency in circulation consistent with the definition of the currency portion of the money supply.

bank. The shift is recorded in the equation as an increase in Treasury deposits at the Federal Reserve and as a decrease in member bank reserves.

7. *Other Federal Reserve liabilities and capital* also absorb reserves. For example, a new member bank typically purchases stock in its Federal Reserve bank by authorizing the Fed to deduct the appropriate sum from its reserve account.

8.2.2
Use of the member bank reserve equation

The long and perhaps tedious explanation of the member bank reserve equation given in the previous section is a necessary prelude to discussion of the difficulties faced by the Fed in conducting its monetary policies. The Fed has complete control over only one item (its securities portfolio) affecting bank reserves. The other items displayed in the reserve equation are under control of the Treasury, foreign banks, member banks, or the nonbank public. Even the weather can play a role, as when a storm interrupts the check clearing process and forces a rise in the float.

In conducting its monetary policies, the Fed frequently uses open market operations to change bank reserves. By changing reserves a given amount in a given direction, it hopes to cause a change in the money supply by an amount consistent with its monetary growth targets. But the reserve equation demonstrates that the good intentions underlying policy actions may be frustrated by actions of parties over whom the Fed has little or no influence. Movements in Treasury deposits, currency in circulation, or float may take reserves in a different direction than the one planned by the Fed. Thus, the Fed must monitor and try to forecast movements in bank reserves originating in factors beyond its control. The member bank reserve equation is an essential tool for this purpose. Without it, the Fed would be unable to make effective use of its open market operations.

There are two categories of open market operations: defensive and dynamic. *Defensive open market operations* are purchases or sales of government securities designed to offset predicted or unexpected changes in bank reserves emanating from influences outside the Fed. They are defensive in the sense that they are designed to protect a given target level of reserves from being upset from the outside influences. Examples of defensive open market operations are purchases of securities designed to offset reserve drains expected from increases in currency in circulation during the Christmas season, and open market sales to offset sudden and unexpected rises in the float.

Dynamic open market operations are designed to increase or decrease bank reserves by a given amount to implement policies set by the FOMC. As a matter of principle, dynamic open market operations differ greatly from defensive operations. Unfortunately, however, outsiders cannot distinguish the two kinds of actions in the statistics produced by the System. Even dynamic actions must take into account the influence on reserves of Treasury and other outside forces. For example, a policy to increase reserves may happen to be implemented by a Treasury decision to reduce its Federal Reserve deposits, in which case the Fed would have no need to execute an open market purchase. To an outside observer, the Fed would appear to be doing nothing; but from the point of view of the System, it would be dynamically pursuing its policy goals.

Perhaps 80 or 90 percent of all open market operations are defensive in nature. The rest are dynamic. Because of the difficulty outsiders have in distinguishing between the two in the data released by the System, most private financial analysts use other information in trying to discover the Fed's policy directions. Other information includes official pronouncements, interest rate (especially federal funds rate) movements, decisions over reserve requirements, and the like.

8.3
The monetary base as a policy target

Bank reserves as a policy target have two drawbacks. The first is that they are directly linked with only a portion of the money supply, bank deposits. If the object of policy is control over the total money supply, it is better to have a policy target that is more directly related to the total, that is, the monetary base.

The second drawback relates to the first. Bank reserves are only part of the monetary base; currency in circulation is the other part. Because the division of the base between reserves and currency depends upon the behavior of the nonbank public, the monetary authorities are unable to exert as much control over reserves as they can over the base taken as a whole.

Many monetary economists recommend that the monetary authorities manipulate their policy instruments to control the monetary base, not member bank reserves. An accounting system for measuring the factors affecting the base is easily derived from the bank reserve equation. Recall that the monetary base equals bank reserves plus currency in circulation. As indicated by Table 8.2, currency in circulation is a factor that absorbs bank reserves. Shifting currency in circulation out of that category into an alliance with member bank reserves creates an equation that gives the *sources and uses of the monetary base*. Table 8.3 illustrates the application of the monetary base equation to the end-of-March 1979 data given in Table 8.2.

An open market purchase gives rise to a change in Reserve bank credit. The rise is usually reflected in an immediate increase in bank deposits and in member bank reserves. Very soon, however, the public may

Table 8.3 *Sources and Uses of the Monetary Base (end-of-March 1979; billions of dollars)*

Sources		Uses	
Reserve bank credit	$130.7	Member bank reserves	41.5
Gold stock and SDRs	12.8	Currency in circulation	102.2
Treasury currency outstanding	12.1		
Minus			
Treasury cash holdings	0.4		
Treasury, foreign, and other deposits	6.7		
Other Fed liabilities	4.8		
Total	$143.7	Total	$143.7

Source: Table 8.2.

convert part of its new deposits into currency. If so, member bank reserves will decline by an equal amount. It is, therefore, more accurate to say that an open market operation permanently changes the monetary base (which includes currency in circulation) rather than bank reserves (which do not).

Unfortunately, such a statement is not totally accurate. An open market operation initially changes *nonborrowed reserves.* Banks may take advantage of the situation to reduce their loans from the Fed, in which case a decline in borrowed reserves would offset the increase in unborrowed reserves. Aside from such repercussions, however, it is still true that an open market operation is more closely related to control over the monetary base than to changes in reserves alone.

Even though the monetary base may be a better policy target than member bank reserves, it is still not completely under control of the Fed. Outside influences such as the float, member bank borrowing and Treasury deposits are capable of throwing it off course. Thus, if the Fed were to use the base as a target, it would still need to use defensive open market operations.

Control over reserves or the base does not guarantee control over the money supply. As demonstrated in Chapter 6, the money multiplier is not absolutely predictable. Complete control over the money supply requires ability of the Fed to forecast outside influences on the monetary base and to predict the behavior of the key ratios affecting the multiplier. Such forecasts require information unavailable to the Fed on a day-to-day, or even month-to-month basis. Over time, however, trends in the factors affecting the base and the money multiplier become more apparent, and control over the money supply becomes more feasible. In assessing the Fed's record on monetary control, therefore, look for six-month or yearly changes in the money supply (for example, Figure 8.2). Weekly or monthly charges have far less meaning.

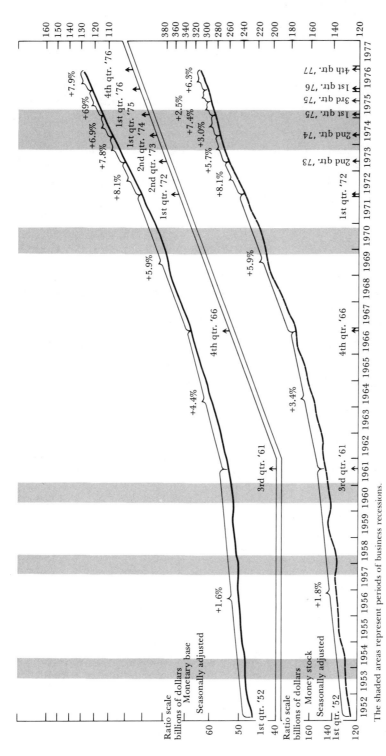

Figure 8.2 *The monetary base and the money supply, 1952–1976. (Source: Richard W. Lang, "The 1975–1976 Federal Deficits and the Credit Market," Federal Reserve Bank of St. Louis Monthly Review, January 1977, p. 4.)*

The shaded areas represent periods of business recessions.

A major goal of Federal Reserve policy is monetary control. The Fed cannot exert such control without first acquiring information on the factors affecting bank reserves. To gather such information, the Fed uses the framework provided by the member bank reserve equation, which details the factors that supply and absorb member bank reserves. Manipulation of the bank reserve equation gives another equation stating the factors affecting the monetary base. Both equations reveal that the Fed directly controls only one of the factors, open market operations. The rest are under the influence of the Treasury, the banks, and the public.

Dynamic open market operations represent attempts by the Fed to move bank reserves or the monetary base by a particular amount in a particular direction. Defensive open market operations represent attempts by the Fed to offset the effects of outside influences on reserves or the base that may upset its plans. Because the outside influences are frequently unpredictable, complete short run control over reserves or the base is impossible. The same is true of the money supply, especially because monetary control also requires predictability of the key ratios affecting the money multiplier. Even so, most monetary economists believe the Fed can, if it wants to, exert control over the money supply on a yearly, or perhaps even a six-month basis.

DISCUSSION QUESTIONS

1. As an exercise, trace through the effects on member bank reserves of the following events (use T-accounts):
   a. Purchase by Treasury of $1 billion of gold from a gold miner
   b. Foreign central bank purchase of U.S. Treasury bond from an American citizen
   c. Open market purchase of bonds by the Federal Reserve System from a bond dealer
   d. An increase of deferred availability cash items at a Federal Reserve bank

2. In your own words, describe float and how it arises. Could the Fed reduce float?

3. Compare the member bank reserve equation with the equation describing the sources and uses of the monetary base. What events can affect bank reserves that cannot affect the monetary base?

4. Compare dynamic open market operations with defensive open market operations. What insight does the comparison reveal when discussing the information contained in the weekly Federal Reserve reports on member bank reserves and the monetary base?

5. Does control over bank reserves or the monetary base give the Fed firm control over the money supply?

IMPORTANT TERMS
AND CONCEPTS

- [ ] currency in circulation
- [ ] defensive open market operations
- [ ] deferred availability cash items
- [ ] dynamic open market operations
- [ ] float
- [ ] gold certificates
- [ ] member bank reserve equation
- [ ] nonborrowed reserves
- [ ] reserve bank credit
- [ ] special drawing rights (SDRs)
- [ ] Treasury cash holdings
- [ ] Treasury currency outstanding
- [ ] Treasury (foreign and other) deposits at Federal Reserve banks

ADDITIONAL
READINGS

Two useful treatments of the Federal Reserve System's balance sheet and the factors affecting bank reserves are Dorothy M. Nichols, *Modern Money Mechanics* (Federal Reserve Bank of Chicago, 1975), and the more detailed *Glossary: Weekly Federal Reserve Statements* (Federal Reserve Bank of New York, 1975), written by David H. Friedman. Both items can be obtained free of charge by dropping a card to the public information departments of the two banks.

The Federal Reserve Bank of St. Louis is especially fond of the monetary base as a target of control. For a good discussion of the base by two of its economists, see Leonall C. Andersen and Jerry L. Jordan, "The Monetary Base: Explanation and Analytical Use," *Federal Reserve Bank of St. Louis Review.*, Vol. 50, No. 8, August 1969.

Robert V. Roosa invented the distinction between defensive and dynamic open market operations in his now out-of-print monograph, *Federal Reserve Operations in the Money and Government Securities Markets* (Federal Reserve Bank of New York, 1956). Copies are available in most university libraries, and perhaps even in a number of public libraries.

The Instruments of Monetary Policy

9

O U T L I N E

Open Market Operations
Effects on Money and Credit Markets
The Manager's Operating Techniques
Open Market Operations and Treasury Financings
The Discount Mechanism
Mechanics of the Discount Mechanism
Lender of Last Resort Function
Discount Rates and the Reluctance Theory
Coordination of Open Market Operations and Discount Rates
The Discount Rate as a Signal and Announcement Effects
Reserve Requirements as a Policy Instrument
Mechanics of Reserve Requirements
Lagged Reserve Requirements and Monetary Policy
Reserve Requirements as a Policy Instrument
Selective Instruments of Monetary Policy
Margin Requirements
Selective Credit Controls—The 1980 Experience
Regulation Q
Moral Suasion

The goal of monetary policy is to establish and maintain monetary and credit conditions consistent with a healthy economy. Federal Reserve authorities believe that a healthy economy is characterized by high employment, a good and sustainable rate of economic growth, price level stability, and a reasonably stable value for the dollar in terms of foreign currencies. The Fed tries to manipulate the money supply and credit conditions to achieve some or all of these goals. The tools it uses to influence monetary and credit conditions are called the instruments of monetary policy.

There are two classes of monetary policy instruments: general and selective. The general instruments of control are reserve requirements, the discount mechanism, and open market operations. The discount mechanism and open market operations influence the total amount of reserve bank credit available to the banking system; the Fed uses them to change bank reserves and the monetary base. Changes in reserve requirements affect the structure and potential volume of bank deposits, money, and commercial bank credit, but leave the monetary base and total reserves the same. Selective tools, which consist of control over margins in the stock market, Regulation Q, and controls over consumer and other kinds of credit (occasionally imposed) are designed to affect the allocation of credit.

9.1
Open market operations

Monetary economists everywhere agree that open market operations are the Fed's primary instrument of monetary policy. It is a tool that permits the monetary authorities to exercise initiative. It also allows them to inject or absorb dollars from the monetary base in large or small amounts at time intervals they find most convenient and to correct mistakes with quick reversals in the direction of operations.

9.1.1
Effects on money and credit markets

As discussed in Section 8.2.2, open market operations give the Fed power to engage in defensive as well as dynamic policies. Defensive operations, in particular, force the Fed to buy and sell securities in relatively large amounts every day, even though the net accumulated impact of the operations upon bank reserves or the monetary base over a week or month may not be large.

Bankers, security traders, and other participants in financial markets have grown accustomed to the continuous nature of open market operations. The policy tool is, therefore, relatively free of announcement effects. Announcement effects are real or imagined policy intentions the money and capital market participants read into Federal Reserve actions. They frequently accompany policy actions carried out with discount rate changes and changes in reserve requirements. Many economists think the effects are undesirable because they may at times lead market participants to responses that blunt or even cancel the intended impact of the policy actions.[1]

Open market purchases of government securities have two effects on money and capital markets. The first, which we have already discussed at great length, is to increase bank reserves, the monetary base, and the money supply. The second is a lowering of interest rates, at least in the short run. The drop in interest rates occurs because in purchasing securities the Fed adds its demand for bonds to those of private individuals, financial institutions, nonfinancial businesses, and other investors. Assuming the Fed's purchases create no announcement effects, the additional demand tends to raise bond prices over those that would otherwise prevail. The rise in bond prices lowers interest rates.

Another force causing interest rates to fall is the excess reserves generated by the open market purchase. In their attempts to eliminate the excess reserves, commercial banks increase their own lending and investing operations, which further lowers interest rates.

Federal Reserve open market sales of securities reduce bank reserves and increase the supply of bonds coming into the market. The reduction in bank reserves forces banks to reduce lending and to sell off some of their security holdings. The effect of the increase in bond supplies is to lower bond prices and raise interest rates, provided, of course, that announcement effects of the Fed's actions do not change the plans of private traders.

For reasons we shall discuss in Section 13.2.4, the interest rate effects of open market operations may be temporary. Still, many economists regard them as the main justification for monetary policy. They believe that low interest rates stimulate the economy and that high interest rates depress it. We discuss the effects of interest rates on the economy in Chapter 13. In the meantime, we note that open market operations give the Fed direct access to money and capital markets, which enhances its power to manipulate market rates of interest.

---

[1] A 1975 court suit to force the FOMC to release immediately its decision was lodged by David Merril, a Georgetown University Law Center student. He claimed that the Freedom of Information Act required immediate disclosure and forbade the one-month delay currently practiced by the FOMC. Although a lower court agreed with Merril, the Supreme Court in 1979 sent the case back for another trial. Immediate disclosure of FOMC decisions would introduce announcement effects into open market operations.

The manager's operating techniques

We have already seen that the Manager of the System Account takes his general instructions from the FOMC. Even so, he has great latitude in deciding how to carry out the instructions. The Manager is clearly better positioned than the FOMC to decide on the amount, timing, and appropriate techniques to use in trading government bonds with security dealers.

The Manager is in constant touch with money and security market conditions. He also receives daily information on bank reserves for the previous day that might influence current reserve positions. In addition, his staff provides him with weekly projections of money and credit aggregates.

The Manager typically uses outright purchases and sales of securities to make permanent changes in bank reserves. For temporary operations, designed to smooth over short-term fluctuations in reserves, he usually employs repurchase agreements or "matched sale-purchase transactions," a device almost identical to repurchase agreements.[2]

Outright purchases and sales of securities are made through an auction process in which all bond dealers in the Fed's panel are canvassed by telephone for offers or bids. In selling, the Manager takes the highest prices bid; in buying, he takes the lowest prices offered.

The Fed prefers to conduct most of its transactions in Treasury bills. Indeed, for an eight-year period beginning in March 1953, the FOMC religiously adhered to a *bills only policy*. The policy was a reaction to the World War II and postwar policy of interest rate pegging, imposed upon the Fed by the Treasury. After the 1951 Federal Reserve–Treasury Accord, the Fed was anxious to avoid any suggestion of interest rate pegging. By confining open market operations to the Treasury bill market, it believed it could avoid interfering with market processes that determine long-term interest rates.

The bills only policy was abandoned in 1961, when the Fed engaged in a maneuver called *Operation Twist*. The purpose of the operation was to help the U.S. balance of payments by raising short-term interest rates, and thus to pull in short-term loan money from abroad, and to help stimulate domestic investment in plant and equipment by lowering long-term

---

[2]In making a repurchase agreement, the Fed buys or sells back securities to dealers at the original price, plus an amount equal to interest at a competitively determined rate, within an agreed period of up to 15 days. In absorbing reserves with a matched sale–purchase agreement, the Fed sells Treasury bills for cash and simultaneously purchases the same issue for delivery back a day or more later. The Fed sets the selling price and takes competitive bids from dealers for the reoffering price.

interest rates. To pursue "twist," the Fed sold short-term securities (to raise short-term interest rates) and bought long-term securities (to lower long-term interest rates).

Operation Twist is an example of the use of open market operations for the purpose of managing the government's debt. *Debt management* is a technique designed to change the maturity composition of government bonds in the hands of the private sector, not to affect its total amount. In so doing, the authorities hope to alter the structure of interest rates, but not their average level. Because debt management open market operations leave the size of the Fed's government bond portfolio unchanged, they do not change the stock of bank reserves or the monetary base.

9.1.3
Open market operations and treasury financings

The Federal government has a large and growing debt. Each week the Treasury must enter the bond markets to raise new money or to offer borrowers securities to replace the ones that are maturing. Only rarely does the Treasury borrow directly from the Fed. Limitations in the law, and a general fear that direct borrowing would open the way to inflationary expansion of the bank reserves, insulate the Fed from official pressure to assist the Treasury in financing the government's deficits.

The Fed ordinarily limits its participation in Treasury refinancing operations to purchasing maturing government securities in its own portfolio. If the Fed did not replace the maturing bonds, the Treasury would have to redeem them by drawing down tax and loan accounts in commercial banks, an action that would shrink bank reserves.

For the most part, therefore, the Treasury must market its debt through the open market. Its marketings include new borrowing issues and refinancing issues designed to replace maturing bonds held by parties other than the Federal Reserve System. Because the Fed ordinarily resists allowing Treasury refinancings to affect the direction of monetary policy, the Treasury usually pays market interest rates.

Occasionally, the Treasury must sell an especially large issue of securities. A concentrated sale of a very large issue may force a sudden and sharp drop in bond prices, especially if the issue contains intermediate or longer term debt, instead of Treasury bills. (Intermediate- and long-term bond markets contain fewer buyers than the short-term market, which is the habitat of Treasury bills.) To avoid such a disturbance, the Fed frequently makes special temporary purchases of government bonds. The purchases inject reserves into the banking system beyond those the Fed would normally allow to meet its monetary policy objectives.

The term "even keel" is used by market participants to describe the periods of time these special injections of funds remain in the banking system. An even keel period may last one to three weeks, during which time the Fed endeavors to prevent sharp changes in market interest rates. Monetary policy during such periods is in a kind of holding pattern, waiting for the Treasury to complete its financing operations. The Fed still has some freedom of maneuver, but it must walk on eggs for fear of letting its normal open market operations jolt the security markets.

Used sparingly, even keeling is a useful adjunct to Treasury debt management. But frequent and large Treasury financings that force the Fed into almost continuous support operations could upset the normal conduct of monetary policy and lead to a partial restoration of interest rate pegging.

9.2
The discount mechanism

The discount mechanism, not open market operations, was the principal tool of monetary policy mentioned in the original Federal Reserve Act. Indeed, open market operations went unrecognized in the law until the Banking Act of 1935, which formally installed the FOMC as a major policymaking body in the System. The Fed in the 1920s had already discovered the value of open market operations as a policy instrument, first using it to help recovery from the 1923–1924 recession. Even so, in the 1920s the discount mechanism was still considered the main tool of monetary policy; open market operations were relegated to a supporting role.

The primacy of discounting in the 1930s arose from the high degree of member banks' dependence upon Federal Reserve borrowing; it averaged about 30 percent of their reserves. Thus, the discount rate was a major cost element in their operations, and the Fed's willingness to lend was an important factor in their portfolio decisions.

Today, the situation is totally different. Borrowed reserves represent a tiny fraction—rarely more than 2 to 3 percent—of total reserves, and individual banks have access to the federal funds market and to the markets for CDs, money market certificates, and other instruments as alternative sources of funds. As a result, the discount mechanism now plays a secondary role, while open market operations carry the primary burden of implementing monetary policy.

9.2.1
Mechanics of the discount
mechanism

Each Federal Reserve bank maintains a discount facility. Although banks have two ways of borrowing—by advances or by discounts—it is customary to refer to both activities as "discounting." An actual discount involves the sale of member bank-endorsed commercial paper arising from their loan business, approved as "eligible paper" by the Federal Reserve bank under rules set forth in the System's regulations. Discounts are now relatively rare; instead, almost all lending is done by means of advances.

Advances are loans to banks backed by collateral acceptable under the law—U.S. government bonds; federal agency obligations; debt guaranteed by the U.S. government or its agencies; "eligible commercial, industrial, and agricultural paper," and other securities deemed satisfactory to the Reserve banks. In practice, most advances are backed by U.S. government securities, primarily because the Fed automatically approves such collateral and because banks already have such securities at the Reserve banks for safekeeping.

The Fed insists that access to the discount window is a privilege, not a right under the law. Moreover, borrowing is usually for short periods; a few days for large banks, and a maximum of two weeks for small banks. Reserve banks scrutinize loan requests for evidence of illegitimate purpose. The main purpose of the privilege is to give banks breathing space when faced with unexpected deposit losses, sudden and unexpected increases in loan demand, and inability to obtain immediate funds from other sources in the money market.

If banks *en masse* were allowed unlimited access to borrowed funds, the Fed might lose control over the monetary base. To keep down excessive borrowings, the Fed studies each application for a loan against the background of a bank's indebtedness relative to its required reserves, the frequency of its borrowing, and any other special factor that might affect its current position. Banks with records of borrowing too much or too often are pressed to repay their debts to the System and to reduce their earning assets.

9.2.2
Lender of last resort function

As pointed out in Section 8.1.2, some small banks are eligible for extended seasonal loans. These loans inject relatively small amounts of additional reserves into the system. More rarely used, but potentially more far-reaching, is the power of the Fed to extend emergency credit to individual large banks or groups of banks facing financial stringency as a result of regional or national developments outside their control. In providing such credit, the Fed performs the traditional role of central banks, that of a *lender of last resort*. As the ultimate provider of liquidity (ready cash) to the economy, it must play such a role in times of emergency; otherwise, widespread panic among distrustful depositors may force a systemwide loss in reserves that even federal deposit insurance may fail to prevent.

An unusual example of Federal Reserve System provision of emergency credit occurred in the summer of 1970, following the collapse of the Penn Central Railroad. The corporation defaulted on its outstanding commercial paper, an event that drove investors away from the paper of a number of other corporations. The latter were forced to use back-up credit lines at their banks, instead of borrowing through normal commercial paper market channels. The extra demand for bank credit overloaded the resources and reserve positions of the banks, which were obliged to honor the sudden demand for credit from the corporations. To prevent the banks from suddenly depriving other customers of loans, the Fed threw open the discount windows of the Reserve banks for emergency borrowing. In addition, it suspended interest rate ceilings under Regulation Q on large short-term CDs.

The 1980 Monetary Control Act authorized the Fed to provide credit to nonmember depository institutions as well as to member banks. In the past the law permitted only emergency credit for nonmember institutions. Although the power was rarely exercised, there were times when deposit drains on nonmember banks, mutual savings banks, and savings and loan institutions caused the Fed to put in place contingency plans for emergency lending.

9.2.3
Discount rates and the reluctance theory

The Fed could prevent banks from borrowing for the purpose of making profits by charging a *penalty rate*. A penalty rate is a discount rate set above the interest rates banks earn on their own investments and loans. A penalty rate would lead banks to borrow from the Fed only when driven to do so by sudden and unexpected reserves losses they have no other way of restoring. Moreover, because the net cost of borrowing would grow with the length of the period of the Fed loan, the banks would desire to make rapid adjustments in their loan and investment portfolios.

Owing to the organization of the banking and financial system in the United States, the Federal Reserve System has never been able (or perhaps willing) to employ a penalty rate discount mechanism. One reason is the very large number of banks scattered throughout the country in regions having different credit conditions and interest rate levels. Another reason is the differences among banks in asset portfolios. The structure of asset yields of banks with high loan–deposit ratios is not the same as the yield-structure of assets in banks with low loan–deposit ratios. Thus, even if the Fed were to charge a discount rate that always exceeded the Treasury bill rate, it would be more of a penalty rate for some banks than it would be for others.[3]

Although the discount facility of the Fed is a profitable source of funds for banks, they do not use it with abandon. In fact, most seem to prefer making reserve adjustments through the more costly federal funds market, or through the use of their secondary reserves of commercial paper and Treasury bills. Why is this so?

One traditional argument, first advanced in the 1920s by Federal Reserve economist Winfield W. Riefler, is that banks do not like to be in debt to the Reserve banks. This idea, which came to be known as the *reluctance theory*, rationalized the seeming unwillingness of banks in the 1920s to borrow uninhibitedly when market interest rates were above the discount rates. Actually, banks seemed anxious to reduce their debts. The Fed discovered that when it injected reserves into the banking system through open market operations, banks used most of their new-found nonborrowed reserves to repay loans from the Reserve banks.

Although there is an element of truth in the reluctance theory, banks are not completely insensitive to changes in the gap between market interest rates and the discount rate. As demonstrated in Figure 9.1, member bank borrowings from Reserve banks go up and down with increases and decreases in the gap between the federal funds rate and the discount rate. Thus, the profit motive does enter into bank decisions to borrow. Moreover, even though the Reserve banks rarely refuse loans to member banks, their constant surveillance over bankers' activities may be one of the key factors restraining them from trying to borrow more.

9.2.4
Coordination of open market operations and discount rates

In the 1920s, the discovery of open market operations led the Fed to develop an interesting theory of credit and monetary control. The theory called for the coordination of open market operations and discount policy.

To illustrate its elements, consider a decision on the part of the System to reduce credit availability and increase interest rates. To implement

---

[3]A discount rate that floats above the federal funds rate would be a penalty rate too, since it would penalize banks that go to the Fed's discount window instead of to federal funds lenders. But this kind of rate system would also penalize unevenly, since many banks are not well positioned to borrow in the federal funds market. Twice in 1980, and again in 1981, the Fed applied a discount rate surcharge to short-term adjustment credit borrowing by institutions with deposits of $500 million or more that had borrowed frequently. The surcharges of 3–4 percentage points were not exactly penalty rates, but they clearly reduced the profitability of borrowing.

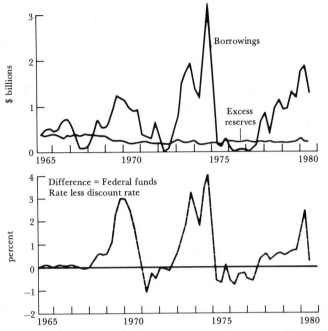

Figure 9.1 *Member bank borrowings and discount rate differential. (Source: Adrian W. Throop,* Money in the Economy *(San Francisco: Federal Reserve Bank of San Francisco), August 1980.)*

the decision, the Fed sells securities from its portfolio, draining reserves from the banking system. Individual banks, unable to distinguish between a temporary and a permanent loss in reserves, are driven to borrow from the Reserve banks, thus offsetting the drop in reserves imposed by the open market operation. According to the reluctance theory, however, banks respond to a deterioration in their *reserve positions*—that is, an increase in their debts to the Fed. Hence, even though the open market operation may leave total reserves unaffected, their increased debt puts the banks under pressure to find funds to repay the Reserve banks. In order to do so, they reduce loans and dispose of secondary reserve assets. These actions reduce the availability of bank credit and increase market rates of interest. To make sure the banks do the right thing, the Reserve banks raise discount rates in a coordinated fashion. (Recall that in the 1920s, power over discount rates resided in the individual Federal Reserve banks.)

A policy of easy money and credit implies a reversal of the above procedure. In this case, open market purchases of securities improve banks' reserve positions by giving them unborrowed reserves. They use the reserves to reduce borrowings from the Reserve banks. The easier positions lead banks to acquire more earning assets, which raises bond prices and lowers interest rates. To reinforce such bank behavior, the Reserve banks lower the discount rate.

Since banks no longer carry large sums of borrowed reserves, the Fed can no longer effectively use the 1920s theory of credit control. Even so, it must still coordinate discount policy with open market policy. The presence of the discount window still makes it possible for banks to frustrate with borrowing open market operations that are designed to drain reserves from the banking system. Similarly, reductions of bank borrowing can reduce reserves while the FOMC is trying to increase them. For that reason, the Fed tends to raise the discount rate when the federal funds rate and other money rates are rising and to lower it when the other rates are falling. These "technical adjustments" in the discount rate (illustrated in Figure 9.2) discourage member bank borrowing behavior that might be perverse from the standpoint of open market policy.

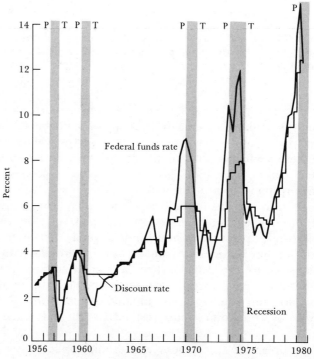

Figure 9.2 *Discount rate and federal funds rate. (Source: Adrian W. Throop,* Money in the Economy *(San Francisco: Federal Reserve Bank of San Francisco), August 1980.)*

The discount rate as a signal and
announcement effects

In the days when discounting was the main policy instrument of central banks, changes in the discount rate had great significance. An increase in the rate acted as a signal to the world that the central bank was tightening money and credit, making reserves more expensive for banks, and forcing them to raise their lending rates. A decrease in the discount rate signalled a policy of ease, and the public came to expect lower interest rates.

Even today, the Fed occasionally uses discount rate changes to signal its policy intentions. A dramatic example is the 1 percentage point jump on November 1, 1978. This unprecedented increase in the rate accompanied a series of other tightening moves; it was designed to convince the world that the Carter Administration was launched upon a serious anti-inflation program.

The use of discount rate changes as signals of Federal Reserve intentions conflicts with their use as a coordinating device with open market operations. The latter requires frequent and small adjustments of the rate—one-quarter to one-half percentage point—in order to prevent wide swings in the incentive to borrow. Thus, even though the discount rate is changed at the discretion of the authorities, it tends to follow rather than to lead other short-term interest rates. Unfortunately, the technical role of the discount rate is not well understood by the press nor by the general public. Each change of the rate is widely publicized and made the subject of much comment. As a result, all rate changes probably produce announcement effects, even though relatively few of them are actually designed to signal the market of changes in Federal Reserve policies.

Several remedies have been proposed by academic and other financial experts. The late Professor Warren Smith of the University of Michigan suggested that the Fed use the English language, instead of discount rate changes, as a device for signaling its intentions. Others have proposed elimination of discretionary Federal Reserve power over the discount rate. Instead, they would tie it to some open market rate, such as the federal funds rate, letting it float up and down with a constant spread. Such a system would eliminate unintended announcement effects of discount rate changes.

The Bank of Canada actually used a tied discount rate from 1956 to 1962. Moreover, in recent years, large American banks have tied their prime interest rates to commercial paper rates and to Treasury bill rates. In addition, interest rates on money market certificates, some savings certificates, some mortgage loans, and a large proportion of bank business loans are tied to one or another set of open market interest rates. Thus, there is plenty of experience with such a system.

Most central bankers dislike tied discount rates because they want to retain discount rate changes as a discretionary tool. They believe that the tool gives them a useful market signaling device. Be that as it may, words do not convince as well as actions; power over discount rates still leaves the authorities with a tool that, when used in certain situations, may endanger the effectiveness of open market operations.[4]

The problems associated with administration of the discount mechanism would disappear if discounting were abolished. This radical proposal has support from some distinguished economists, such as Milton Friedman. Federal Reserve officials oppose it, arguing that discounting is essential for providing banks with reserve adjustment funds and for providing the whole banking system with liquidity in case of emergency.

In reply, it can be argued that if banks could not resort to the discount window for adjustment credit, they would still be able to borrow in the federal funds market, or, failing that, even carry more excess reserves as a form of self-insurance against unexpected losses. As for emergency credit, there are always open market operations, particularly as implemented by repurchase agreements. And, as Friedman has argued, the existence of federal deposit insurance reduces the probability that bank runs will require the Fed to perform as a lender of last resort to the whole banking system.

In recent years the Fed has refined its administration of the discount mechanism. Instead of the sharp and infrequent changes in the discount rate of the past, it now usually uses frequent and relatively small rate changes. This practice reduces announcement effects. And, better controlling the spread between open market interests rates and the discount rate, it also keeps better control over the banks' incentives to borrow.

Still, the presence of the discount facility does give rise to some slippage in monetary policy. Moreover, as we shall see in the Section 9.3.2, the Fed virtually invites banks to use the facility by the manner in which it administers reserve requirements.

9.3
Reserve requirements as a policy instrument

The Banking Act of 1935 gave the Federal Reserve Board power to vary reserve requirements. In accordance with this legislation, the Fed was authorized to set requirements within the range of 7 to 22 percent against demand deposits and 3 to 10 percent against time deposits. As discussed in Section 7.4, the 1980 law authorizes new requirements that will be

---

[4]A remedy for this problem may be a flexibly tied discount rate. Such a rate would ordinarily float with some base rate (say, the Treasury bill rate) with a constant spread. In addition, the Fed could, at its discretion, announce changes in the spread. Market participants would interpret all discount rate changes resulting from announced changes in the spread as signals. However, because all other discount rate changes would be simple reflections of Treasury bill rate changes, they would be free of announcement effects.

gradually extended to all depository institutions. In recent years, for the purpose of applying reserve requirements, the Fed broadened the definition of deposits to include commercial paper issued by bank holding companies or nonbank subsidiaries, when the purpose is to finance credit expansion by affiliated banks. It has also on occasion applied reserve requirements to bank borrowings in the Eurodollar market, to money market mutual funds, and to repurchase agreements.

Under the old law the Fed set reserve requirements by deposit size. Smaller banks had lower reserve requirements. They were favored in this way because the Fed worried that they would leave the System if forced to meet the higher reserve requirements levied upon larger banks. The Fed's services were highly valued by the larger banks; hence, to stay in the system, they were willing to pay the price of higher reserve requirements. Many smaller member banks were not so willing. The 1980 law eliminated the Fed's incentive to manipulate the reserve requirements to favor small banks.

It is important to recall that required reserves do not provide liquidity for banks. Instead, their sole purpose is to give the Fed control over the volume of bank credit and bank deposits. When the Fed changes reserve requirements, it changes the total amount of deposits and earning assets the banks can support with the reserves they have on hand. For that reason, reserve requirements are considered a general policy instrument.

9.3.1
Mechanics of reserve requirements

Member bank reserves must be held in deposits in the Fed or as vault cash. Nonmember depository institutions may hold reserves at correspondent member banks (S&Ls) or at a Federal Home Loan Bank (credit unions) or at the National Credit Union Central Liquidity Facility, provided that such reserves are passed through to the Federal Reserve banks. Required reserves are calculated on a weekly basis. The week runs from each Thursday through the next Wednesday. During any given week, the daily average of required reserves must equal the minimum percentages of average net deposits (gross deposits minus cash items in process of collection and deposits due to domestic banks) held by the banks two weeks earlier. Owing to this system of lagged reserve requirements, a bank or thrift institution planning its reserve balances at the beginning of any accounting week already knows what its prospective daily reserve balances must average in order to satisfy the authorities.

But knowing the reserve target does not mean that bankers always succeed in hitting it. If they aim too high, they may find themselves with an average of excess reserves over the week, in which event they have sacrificed earnings to satisfy the authorities. If they aim too low, however, they may accumulate a reserve deficiency. The law permits a reserve deficiency without fines if a banker makes it up within the week, after carrying over shortfalls into the next statement week (excess reserves can also be carried over one week). However, if the banker still cannot make up the deficiency, he must pay an interest penalty equal to the discount rate plus 2 percentage points.

9.3.2
Lagged reserve requirements and monetary policy

Individual banks frequently have little control over their deposit flows. This lack of control interferes with their ability to meet reserve requirements. When they cannot meet the requirements, they must borrow in the federal funds market, borrow in the Eurodollar market, sell off secondary reserve assets, or even borrow from the Fed.

During the weeks in which the Fed is draining reserves from the banking system through open market sales, many banks are actually driven to the discount window. The system of lagging reserve requirements almost guarantees this behavior. Aggregate required reserves for any particular week are determined by the distribution and size of average deposits two weeks earlier. If open market sales reduce the actual level of aggregate reserves below the given level of required aggregate reserves, some bank or banks inevitably will be caught with deficient reserves. Banks that succeed (through sales of Treasury bills or other secondary reserve assets) in making up their reserve deficiencies will inevitably impose reserve deficiencies on other banks. As in the game of Old Maid, someone will be left holding the bag, and that someone (bank) must go to the Fed's discount window.

9.3.3
Reserve requirements as a policy instrument

A reduction in reserve requirements does not change the dollar amount of reserves in the banking system, but it does increase the amount of excess reserves. In so doing, it increases the deposits the existing reserve base can support. An increase in reserve requirements has the opposite effect; it reduces excess reserves and forces a reduction in the system's deposit potential.

Changes in reserve requirements also change deposit and money multiplers. A reduction in required reserve ratios increases the multipliers, and an increase in the ratios reduces them. Thus, the second effect of changes in reserve requirements is to strengthen or weaken the power of open market operations or bank borrowing to change the money supply.

The Fed uses reserve requirements as a general policy instrument less frequently than it uses open market operations. The latter are equally effective as a general policy instrument, but are far less clumsy. Frequent changes in reserve requirements would greatly complicate forward planning by bank managers and would be inequitable as among banks, whose deposit structures vary widely in terms of size and distribution as between demand and time. In addition, even fairly small changes in reserve requirements, such as one-half of a percentage point, may have fairly large impacts upon excess reserves, in which case open market operations may have to be called upon to mitigate their effects upon deposits and bank credit.

Although reserve requirements are not handy for day-to-day general monetary policy, they are useful for implementing major policy changes. Unlike open market operations, changes in reserve requirements produce announcement effects, which in cases of major policy shifts are desirable signal devices. In addition, changes in reserve requirements instantly affect liquidity and bank costs in every part of the country; in contrast, open market operations first hit the major money market banks, and their full effects must await the spread of the impact to other banks in the system.

A dramatic example of the Fed's use of reserve requirements as a policy tool is its decision on November 1, 1978 to raise reserve requirements on large CDs ($100,000 and over) by 2 percentage points. The occasion was an attempt by the Fed and the Carter Administration to stop the decline in the value of the dollar against foreign currencies. As discussed earlier in this chapter, the reserve requirements change was coupled with a rise in the discount rate of 1 percentage point. The coupling of the two policy instruments was clearly designed to magnify the power of the signal the government was trying to convey to the world about its policies. Up to that point, words had not been enough to convince foreign currency speculators of the Administration's anti-inflation program. The signal may have worked: after the policy announcement, the dollar's fall ceased, and it recovered much of its lost value.[5]

9.4
Selective instruments of monetary policy

Selective instruments of monetary policy include control over stock market margins, controls over consumer and real estate credit, and Regula-

---

[5]For a study of this episode, see Douglas R. Mudd, "Did Discount Rate Changes Affect the Foreign Exchange Value of the Dollar During 1978?" *Federal Reserve Bank of St. Louis Review*, April 1979. Recall from the discussion in Chapter 7 that the Fed and Treasury supplemented the above policy moves with actions designed to increase the capacity of the government to undertake support operations of the dollar in cooperation with other central banks. These actions increased the availability of foreign currencies to be sold for dollars during periods when the dollar was under speculative pressure.

tion Q. In one way or another, each of these instruments is designed to affect the direction or cost of credit flows.

9.4.1
Margin requirements

Under authority given to it by the Securities and Exchange Act of 1934 and subsequent amendments, the Board of Governors regulates margins in the stock and bond markets. The regulations apply to domestic bank credit, credit advanced by brokers and dealers, and credit acquired from abroad for the purpose of buying securities.

The margin on purchase is the difference between the purchase price of the securities and the credit advanced to the buyer. Thus, if a loan of $4,000 is required to be secured by stock having a market value of $10,000, the margin is at least $6,000, or 60 percent of the market value of the stock, and the maximum loan value of the stock is 40 percent. The maximum loan value of a security, therefore, varies inversely with the margin requirement. A rise in the requirement to 65 percent would reduce the loan value to 35 percent and vice versa.

Power over margin requirements was given to the Fed as a response to its unhappy experience in attempting to control the stock market boom, which culminated in the 1929 crash. The boom was fueled in large measure by credit, much of which originated in the banking system. Credit flowing into stock market purchases is not available for commercial or industrial uses. Not having the tools to allocate credit away from securities back into the business sector, the Fed was forced to use its general policy instruments to limit speculative borrowings. In so doing, it substantially slowed the growth of the money supply, an event that aided, if it did not directly cause, the onset of the Great Depression in 1929.

Thus the rationale for control over stock margins lies in the desire of the authorities to limit speculative activity in securities markets without damaging general credit conditions or reducing the rate of growth of monetary aggregates. The Fed recognizes that sharp changes in stock prices can occur without credit-financed speculation. Nevertheless, it feels that by controlling the credit factor it can help limit cumulative rises or declines in the securities prices and thus minimize their potential disruptive effects on the economy.[6]

---

[6]Sharp changes in security prices may precipitate sharp changes in wealth holdings of individuals who own securities. The changes in wealth can bring about changes in individuals' expenditures on goods and services, which in turn may generate fluctuations in total expenditures on goods and services produced in the economy.

9.4.2
Selective credit controls—the 1980
experience[7]

During World War II, Congress gave the Federal Reserve System power to set minimum down payments and maximum periods for consumer installment credit. During the Korean War, Congress extended credit controls to housing. In exercising these controls, the Fed set minimum down payments and maximum loan-to-value ratios on mortgage-financed purchases.

These controls no longer exist. However, in 1969 Congress passed the Credit Control Act, which provides that "whenever the President determines that such action is necessary or appropriate for the purpose of preventing or controlling inflation generated by extension of credit in excessive volume, the President may authorize the Board (of Governors) to regulate and control any and all extensions of credit."

On March 14, 1980, faced with an acceleration of the rate of inflation, President Carter invoked the 1969 Act. Although the Federal Reserve System had claimed over the years that it did not want responsibility for such controls, it moved quickly to apply them in what it called the Special Credit Restraint Program (SCRP). The program was short lived, being partially rescinded on May 22 and fully terminated on July 3 of 1980. Still, the experience is quite instructive. Never before had the monetary authorities tried to impose such a comprehensive set of controls, even during World War II.

The main provisions of SCRP are shown in Table 9.1. Note that the controls were designed to discourage certain kinds of credit—business loans, consumer lending, and "low social priority" items. At the same time, small business loans and loans to farmers and home buyers were to be encouraged. These features of SCRP were typical of direct credit control programs, which in large measure reallocate credit to ends favored by the authorities over those that might emerge from unregulated market forces. Some of the effects of SCRP were quite dramatic. Extensions of consumer installment credit, for example, took a nosedive (Figure 9.3). Credit card usage fell sharply, as did the demand for credit for autos, furniture, and appliances. As for business loans, however, by the time the Fed got around to applying the controls, the economy-wide recession that began in January of 1980 was already pulling down the demand for business credit, so there was no real test of how serious the strains and distortions in business credit markets would have become had the program been continued.

---

[7]This section draws upon the brief, but useful "Looking Back on Credit Controls," *The Morgan Guaranty Survey*, September 1980. Also see A. F. Ehbar, "Why the Fed Doesn't Want Those Credit Controls," *Fortune*, April 21, 1980.

Table 9.1 *SCRP Highlights*

The Fed's March 14 controls program contained these key elements:

• Banks were advised to hold loan growth within the 6 to 9 percent range previously targeted for total bank credit by the Fed.

• Banks were also encouraged to hold back on lending considered to be nonproductive, inflationary, or of low social priority. Included were unsecured consumer lending, financing of corporate takeovers or mergers, and financing of speculative holdings of commodities.

• Lenders were urged to make "special efforts" to maintain credit flows for farmers, home buyers, and small businesses.

• Restraint was advised on certain types of consumer credit, including credit cards, check credit overdraft plans, and unsecured personal loans. The Fed established a special deposit requirement of 15 percent for all lenders on increases in covered types of credit.

• Marginal reserve requirements were increased from 8 to 10 percent on the managed liabilities (large time deposits, Eurodollar borrowings, repurchase agreements against U.S. government and federal agency securities) of large banks.

• Restraint on the amount of credit raised by large nonmember banks was sought through a special deposit requirement of 10 percent on increases in their managed liabilities.

• Rapid expansion of money market mutual funds was to be restrained by a special deposit requirement of 15 percent on increases in their total assets above the level of March 14.

• To discourage the use of the discount window and to speed bank adjustments in response to restraint on bank reserves, a surcharge of 3 percentage points was applied to borrowings by large banks.

Source: *The Morgan Guaranty Survey,* September 1980.

The 1969 Credit Control Act was passed as a "rider" to another bill whose main purpose was the extension of federal powers to set ceilings on interest rates payable on time deposits by depository institutions. It was never subjected to the scrutiny of Congressional hearings before its passage. The broad powers given to the Fed when the Act was finally invoked led many people to favor its repeal. In July 1980, the Senate did just that; but, at this writing, the House has not yet ratified the action of the Senate.

Selective credit controls are frequently justified to control inflation. But inflation visits an economy when there is a general excess demand for goods. During periods of monetary ease, credit diverted away from consumer durables or housing does not necessarily hold down aggregate demand. Credit may still be available to support excessive purchases of business inventories; plant and equipment; and federal, state, and local governmental services.

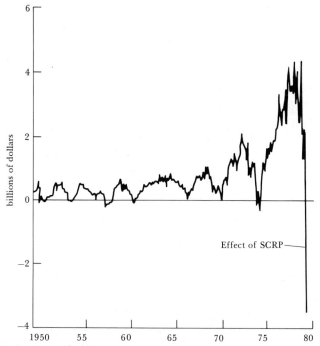

Figure 9.3 *Net change in consumer installment credit. (Source:* The Morgan Guaranty Survey, *September 1980.)*

Thus, the major justification for selective credit controls must be the redirection of credit into government-favored uses, away from uses that, in the absence of government intervention, would be determined by various actors in the market place. Needless to say, the government and participants in many government sponsored programs, such as housing, are usually the chief beneficiaries of credit allocation schemes.[8]

9.4.3
Regulation Q

An important control instrument for many years has been Regulation Q—the Fed's authority to set ceilings on interest rates paid to savings and time deposit customers. Many years of professional economists' criticisms, plus the agitation of small saver groups, like the Grey Panthers, finally led Congress to eliminate the authority of monetary authorities to set de-

---

[8]The Fed does not participate directly in such schemes. Most credit allocation is accomplished with several credit programs, such as those discussed in Chapter 3. Even so, in holding government agency securities in its portfolio, the Fed indirectly supports these programs.

posit interest rate ceilings. The 1980 Depository Institution Deregulation and Monetary Control Act authorized the formation of a committee of financial regulators to phase out Regulation Q over a period of six years after the passage of the act. Nonetheless, since the Regulation has played such an important role in the economic history of the last 25 years, it is still important to discuss it.

Regulation Q was not originally designed as an instrument of credit control. Congress gave it to the Fed in 1933 as a concession to bankers in return for their support of the federal deposit insurance plan, also enacted in 1933. Because the original insurance plan was expensive to the banks, calling for an assessment of one-half percent per dollar of deposits, the banks insisted upon controls that would shelter their deposit costs from competition. To strengthen their argument for control over deposit interest rates, bankers' lobbyists asserted that the massive bank failures of the early 1930s were caused by excessive competition for deposits. Modern research by George Benston and Albert Cox (cited in Additional Readings at the end of this chapter) and others has questioned this thesis.

Responsibility for setting ceiling rates on savings and time deposits in member banks rests with the Board of Governors. Ceiling rates on deposits in nonmember banks and savings banks are set by the Federal Deposit Insurance Corporation; in savings and loan associations they are determined by the Federal Home Loan Bank Board. The agencies set ceiling rates only after consulting among themselves.

In setting the structure of ceiling interest rates, the regulatory agencies pay close attention to the capacity of the banks and thrift institutions to compete for interest bearing deposits. Owing to the structure of their assets, nonbank thrift institutions have in recent years been somewhat disadvantaged in competing for funds. They are loaded with illiquid long-term home mortgages. Thus, when interest rates rise during periods of monetary stringency, the yields on their earning assets lag behind. As a result, sharp increases in their deposit rates cut into their profits, perhaps fatally for some individual institutions.

Because bank assets are much more diversified and generally contain many short-term loans and investments, banks can pay higher deposit rates as interest rates in general rise. To prevent banks from drawing funds away from thrifts during such periods, the regulatory authorities usually set a structure of deposit rates below those banks can afford to pay. In so doing, they hope to hold to a minimum operating losses that might impair the solvency of thrift institutions working at the margin of profitability.

While preserving "equity" among depository institutions, ceiling deposit rates frequently damage the competitive powers of both sets of institutions they are designed to protect. As discussed in Chapter 3, rising interest rates enable issuers of direct debt and money market funds to siphon savers' funds away from depository institutions that are subject to interest rate ceilings. Ironically, money market funds invest heavily in large bank CDs, which, being exempt from Regulation Q, enable at least some small savers to receive competitive rates. (See Figure 9.4.)

The continuation of high short- and long-term interest rates in the inflationary environment of the 1970s has forced the authorities to grant higher ceiling rates for bank and thrift institution deposits. In addition, it has forced them to create a maze of savings alternatives, involving a graduated scale of deposit rates for savings and time certificates of varying maturities, and a floating rate certificate that, after being introduced in 1978 for the first time, permitted depository institutions to compete with U.S. government borrowing via Treasury bills. In 1979, further changes, including floating rate instruments with four-year maturities and interest rates set 1 percentage point below four-year Treasury bonds, were authorized by the regulators.

As we have said, Regulation Q is on its way out. Some observers may wish for an earlier demise than the six-year period provided in the 1980 law. But the thrift industry insists it needs the longer period to adjust to the new competitive environment. Whatever the period, abolishing Regulation Q has entailed changing the laws respecting allowable loans and investments by the thrifts. In the new competitive environment, they cannot be confined mainly to their traditional turf on home mortgages or

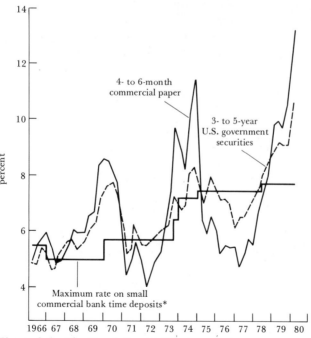

Figure 9.4 *The Regulation Q lid—how market rates geyser above it; selected interest rates, 1966–1979. (Source:* Federal Reserve Bank of Kansas Economic Review, *April 1980.)*

government bonds. Eventually, they may even have access to the full range of opportunities possessed by banks. That is, they may become banks.

The demise of Regulation Q will not be lamented by many economists. The regulation has imposed deadweight costs on the economy as a whole and has redistributed income from small savers to (mainly) home mortgage borrowers. The deadweight costs arise from the methods used by banks and thrift institutions to attract deposits from small savers by means other than raising interest rates, which Regulation Q prohibits. The other methods include gifts, heavy advertising, and the proliferation of branch offices designed to bring in more customers. From 1957 to 1977, the number of commercial banks grew by about 6 percent, while the number of branches quadrupled from about 8,000 to more than 32,000. Although there was undoubtedly a need in this period for additional offices, the disproportionate growth of branches must have been largely the result of a wasteful form of competition for new deposits.[9]

The redistribution of income from low income savers to higher income mortgage borrowers was documented by Ohio State University Professor Edward J. Kane in testimony before the Senate Banking Committee of April 12, 1979. Kane found that 88 percent of the financial wealth of households with $1,000 or less is lodged in rate-regulated financial assets. The percentage is 40 percent for households in the $1,000–$5,000 category, 20 percent for those with wealth of $5,000–$10,000 and, lastly, 5 percent for people in the $50,000 or better category. Studies by economists have shown that the average income of savings depositors is substantially below that of the average mortgage borrower. Since advertising and operating expenses for extra branch offices have kept down profits that depository institutions may have received from the lower interest costs they must pay savers, the major beneficiaries of the rate controls have probably been the mortgage borrowers.

Given the history of Regulation Q, it is a great irony that the banks and thrift institutions have probably not been the major recipients of the benefits of ceiling interest rates on deposits. Instead of making financial institutions better off at the expense of their customers, Regulation Q has primarily been a way of cheating everyone with deadweight losses and of

---

[9]In 1970, Massachusetts' savings banks for the first time became subject to interest rate ceilings. According to a study by Robert Taggart and Geoffrey Woglom, by 1975 the banks were paying depositors an interest rate 1 percentage point lower than they would have paid without regulation. In addition, the banks had 84 extra branches, which cost them $93 million to operate. The findings of Taggart and Woglom are reported in "Savings Bank Reactions to Rate Ceilings and Rising Market Rates," *Federal Reserve Bank of Boston New England Economic Review*, September/October 1978, pp. 17–31. The material in this and the next paragraph is based upon Frank E. Morris, "The Cost of Price Control in Banking," *New England Economic Review*, May/June 1979, pp. 49–54.

redistributing income from poor and low income savers to middle and high income borrowers.

9.5
Moral suasion

Policymakers frequently try to influence banks and other actors in financial markets with "moral suasion," more properly called "open mouth policy." Through speeches, congressional testimony, articles in papers, and so forth, the Chairman of the Board of Governors and other officials of the System try to change the behavior of the financial community.

The open mouth policy rarely works, unless it is backed up by other measures. Nevertheless, moral suasion is a way of giving signals to the market; if it is reinforced by other measures, such as sharp changes in the discount rate or in reserve requirements, it may be a useful supplement to general policy instruments. It must be understood, however, that the monetary authorities cannot by the use of verbal threats or exhortations change the behavior of tens of thousands of banks and other depository institutions, most of which are not members of the Federal Reserve System.

SUMMARY

The Fed has two sets of policy tools: general and selective. The most important general instrument is open market operations, whose virtues include flexibility and the absence of announcement effects.

Discount policy is less important, primarily because borrowed reserves are a small fraction of total reserves. Nevertheless, discount rates must constantly be changed to prevent bank borrowing from interfering with open market operations. Because these changes are often misinterpreted by the public, they are capable of generating undesirable announcement effects. Suggested reforms of the discount mechanism include tying discount rates to Treasury bill or federal fund rates and outright abolition. The Fed resists these proposals because it wishes to retain the ability to signal the market about important policy changes and because it believes banks need the discount window as a source of adjustment credit.

The third policy tool, changes in reserve requirements, is clumsy and seldom used by the authorities. Nevertheless, it is valued as a signalling device and is used to broadcast major policy decisions.

Selective instruments of control include margin requirements, Regulation Q, and direct controls over consumer and business. The major purpose of these tools is to give the Fed power to influence the cost and allocation of credit. Regulation Q is the most controversial selective instrument. Its use has led to disintermediation, redistribution of income between small savers and borrowers, deadweight losses for the economy, and a complicated structure of rates designed to maintain "competitive equity" between commercial banks and thrift institutions. Abolition of Regulation Q has been widely advised by economists; the 1980 Depository Institution Deregulation and Monetary Control Act contains measures to phase it out. An important side effect of elimination of the regulation may be the restructuring of the financial system, eventually giving thrift institutions lending powers similar to those of banks.

DISCUSSION QUESTIONS

1. What are the dangers of "even keeling?" Would Fed failure to even keel pose dangers to the economy?

2. Do high discount rates imply a tight monetary policy? Do low discount rates imply a liberal policy?

3. What would be the effects of eliminating discounting at the Federal Reserve System?

4. Why do economists regard open market operations as the major tool of monetary policy?

5. Which policy instrument is least likely to have announcement effects?

6. What is the relationship between housing starts and the manner in which Regulation Q is administered?

7. Compare monetary policy to debt management policy.

8. Compare the nature and purposes of general money and credit controls to those of selective credit controls.

9. Is there likely to be a correlation between the differential between the federal funds rate and the discount rate on the one hand, and the volume of bank borrowing from the Fed on the other hand? Explain.

10. Should the monetary authorities coordinate policies respecting open market operations and the discount mechanism? If so, how?

11. What is the significance of the term "reserve position?"

IMPORTANT TERMS AND CONCEPTS

- [ ] announcement effects
- [ ] Bills only policy
- [ ] Credit Control Act of 1969
- [ ] debt management
- [ ] discount mechanism
- [ ] even keel policy
- [ ] instruments of monetary policy
- [ ] lagged reserve requirements
- [ ] lender of last resort
- [ ] Manager of the System Account

☐ margin requirements   ☐ penalty rate
☐ moral suasion   ☐ reluctance to borrow theory
☐ open market operations   ☐ reserve position of a bank
☐ Operation Twist   ☐ tied discount rate

ADDITIONAL READINGS

Open market operations are discussed in *The Federal Reserve System: Purpose and Functions* (Washington, D.C.: Board of Governors of the Federal Reserve System, 1974), Chapter 3, and in more detail in Paul Meek, *Open Market Operations* (New York: Federal Reserve Bank of New York, May 1973). A classic article on all the instruments of general control, but especially of the discount mechanism, is Warren Smith, "The Instruments of General Monetary Control," *National Banking Review*, September 1963, since reprinted in many places, including Warren Smith and Ronald Teigen, *Readings in Money, National Income, and Stabilization Policy* (Homewood, Ill.: Richard D. Irwin, 1970). Another useful discussion of instruments of general control is included in a series of short articles published in William N. Cox III, *Some Institutional Aspects of Monetary Policy* (Federal Reserve Bank of Atlanta, October 1974). *Purposes and Functions*, Chapter 4, gives the official Federal Reserve version of the use of discount policies and reserve requirements. See also articles in *Reappraisal of Federal Reserve Discount Mechanism*, Vols. 1, 2, and 3 (Board of Governors of the Federal Reserve System, 1971, 1972, and 1973).

Selective instruments of control are described in *Purposes and Functions*, Chapter 4. On Regulation Q, see also George Kaufman, *Money, the Financial System, and the Economy* (Chicago: Rand McNally College Publishing Company, 1977), pp. 124–130. A summary of the effects of Regulation Q on economic welfare is in Frank E. Morris, "The Cost of Price Control in Banking," *Federal Reserve Bank of Boston New England Economic Review*, May/June 1979, pp. 49–54. Well-known studies questioning the original justification for interest rate ceilings on bank deposits are George Benston, "Interest Rate Payments on Demand Deposits and Bank Investment Behavior," *Journal of Political Economy*, Vol. LXXII, No. 5, October 1964, pp. 431–449, and Albert H. Cox, Jr., "Regulation of Interest on Bank Deposits," *Michigan Business Studies*, Vol. XVIII, No. 4, 1966.

10

The Strategy
of Monetary Policy

O U T L I N E

An Outline of the Strategy Problem
Setting Goals and Intermediate Targets
Operating Targets
Targets and Indicators
Past Monetary Policy Strategies
The Commercial Loan Theory
The Free Reserve Doctrine
Interest Rates as Policy Targets
Recent Strategies of Monetary Policy
The Fed's Procedures for Controlling Monetary Growth
Criticism of the Fed's Monetary Control Procedures in the 1970s
The New Monetary Control Procedures—Post-October 6, 1979

To be effective, authorities must have a strategy for the conduct of monetary policy. A proper strategy defines both means and ends. In the case of monetary policy, the ends are the general goals mentioned at the beginning of Chapter 9—an acceptable rate of growth of real output, low unemployment, reasonable price level stability, and a relatively stable international value of the dollar. The means are the policy instruments and a set of financial or monetary targets.

Unfortunately, monetary policymakers must contend with numerous linkages between manipulation of their instruments and the ultimate effects of the instruments on policy goals. The exact nature of these linkages is only partially understood, and a good deal of research in the Federal Reserve System and among academic economists is devoted to sorting out their relative importance. In the meantime, such knowledge as is possessed by the Fed must be applied to carrying out monetary policy strategies.

A complete strategy of monetary policy would include specification of policy goals, setting policy instruments and targets to achieve the goals, and using a monitoring system to assure the authorities that their actions are working in the desired directions. Much of the time, monetary policy decisions are unaccompanied by a complete strategy in the minds of the authorities. In the past, for example, they frequently ignored some of the critical linkages between instruments and targets and between targets and ultimate policy goals. At other times, they failed to develop effective indicators for monitoring the impact of their policies on the economy. Present practices, while far from perfect, are an improvement over those of the past.

The goal of this chapter is to provide you with a basic understanding of current policy practices. The means for achieving the goal will be (1) a brief description of the strategy problem, (2) a commentary upon past policy strategies, and (3) a brief description of the current policy process.

10.1
An outline of the strategy problem

In this section we shall walk our way through the various parts of the policy strategy problem. The problem is illustrated in Figure 10.1. Although the diagram contains most of the important elements of the problem, it is neither complete nor necessarily representative of what the Fed does all of the time. As we shall see in Section 10.2, it has not always explicitly adhered to a complete strategy.

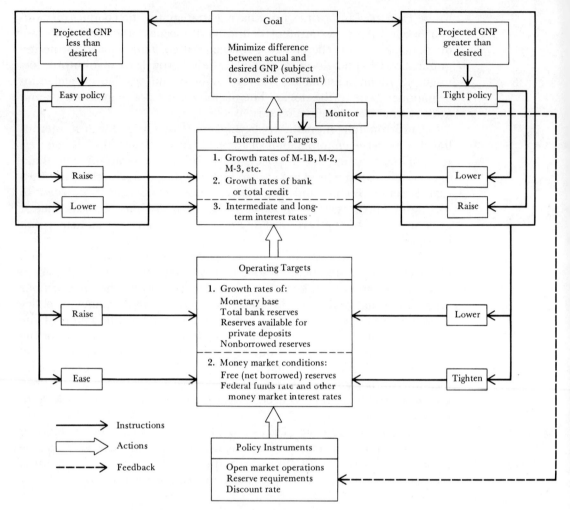

Figure 10.1 *Outline of the strategy problem.*

10.1.1
Setting goals and intermediate targets

You cannot have a strategy without having goals. The goal in Figure 10.1 is minimization of the differences between desired and actual gross national product (GNP). This is not necessarily the only goal the authorities might wish to pursue, but it is sufficiently general to be representative of a broad range of policy strategies.

Projected GNP is the level staff economists at the FOMC meetings forecast to prevail in perhaps a year if current monetary policies continue. Desired GNP is the level that members of the FOMC, with the advice of the staff economists, believe to be consistent with acceptable levels of unemployment and rates of inflation. For example, if GNP projected one year ahead carries with it a projected acceleration of the inflation rate, the FOMC might want a lower GNP than the one projected. Conversely, if the Committee believes the projected GNP may be accompanied by an unacceptable level of unemployment, it may want a higher GNP. A successful strategy is one that at the end of the year minimizes the difference between the GNP actually attained and the one desired by the FOMC.

Notice the goal is to *minimize* the gap between actual and desired GNP, not necessarily to eliminate it. Attempts to eliminate the gap may set in motion forces that interfere with other objectives. For example, if in pursuing a policy to stimulate GNP the Fed causes a drop in the international value of the dollar, the authorities may decide to settle for a GNP lower than the one desired. Conversely, a move to lower the growth rate of GNP may force interest rates to rise much faster than is acceptable to FOMC members or the politicians they listen to. Thus, policy goals are rarely formulated solely to *eliminate* the gap between the actual and desired values for some objective. They are almost always subject to some side constraint, the effect of which is to make their attainment conditional upon salvaging some other end or ends.

The monetary authorities cannot directly manipulate GNP or its component parts. Instead, they must try to attain their ultimate goals by wielding their policy instruments to affect variables that in turn influence the level of GNP. We call these variables *intermediate targets.* They are targets because our theory of monetary and credit policy tells us that it is within the power of the Fed to affect their values and because, by affecting the targets, the authorities believe they can move GNP in the desired direction. The targets are intermediate because they are not ultimate goals, but rather links in the chain that connects manipulation of policy instruments with attainment of the ultimate goals.

Note that Figure 10.1 contains several possible intermediate targets. That is because there is still considerable dispute over which target or targets should be pursued. The disagreements originate in part from different theories economists have concerning the influence of financial and monetary variables on GNP. As noted in Section 1.2, monetarists believe that control over the growth rate of the money supply is the best way to influence effective demand. Keynesians stress credit conditions and interest rates. Thus, although both schools agree that variations in the growth rate of GNP are influenced by variations in effective demand, they disagree over the relative importance of the different target variables. The role of interest rates in determining GNP is discussed in Section 13.3.

Uncertainty over the proper definition of money and interest rates is also a source of disagreement over targets. As indicated in Chapter 2, there is by no means consensus over the definition of money. Moreover, the rapid pace of financial innovation in recent years, with the introduction of NOW accounts, money market funds, ATS accounts, credit union share drafts, bank borrowing from corporate customers via RPs, and so forth, has further clouded the money supply definition issue.

There is also no clear doctrine about interest rate targets. Traditionally, economists have focused upon long-term interest rates as being the most important, but in recent years some analysts have stressed short-term interest rates. In addition, there is the important distinction between real and nominal interest rates. Nominal interest rates are the ones we observe in the market place; but, because their heights are to some extent determined by inflationary expectations of borrowers and lenders, nominal interest rates are not real interest rates. The latter are rates that would prevail in the absence of expected inflation; they are the ones thought to be influential for the investment and savings decisions that Keynesians believe to be critical for effective demand. Unfortunately, we cannot measure real interest rates without first measuring public expectations of inflation, a task that economists have yet to accomplish in a convincing fashion. Moreover, even if they could measure expectations, it is doubtful that the authorities could manipulate real interest rates by setting policy targets in terms of nominal rates. The raising or lowering of a nominal interest rate target may in itself affect expectations and thus change the real rates associated with the higher or lower nominal rates. Perhaps because of these difficulties, the Fed appears more interested in nominal than in real interest rate targets.

Timing is another aspect of the strategy problem. Effective demand does not respond immediately to changes in the growth rate of the money supply or interest rates. Instead, it typically responds with a series of lags spread over many months or even several years. Milton Friedman has argued that the economy responds to changes in the growth rate of the money supply with a highly variable lag of 6 to 18 months, the average falling between 9 and 12 months. Other researchers have argued for shorter or longer lags. In any event, significant lags do exist; hence, to bring actual GNP in line with desired GNP within, say, 12 months, the authorities must change the rate of growth of the money supply within a shorter period, say, 3 to 6 months. Similar statements hold for interest rates as intermediate targets.

10.1.2
Operating targets

Operating targets are variables the Fed tries to manipulate in order to influence the intermediate targets. Monetary aggregates and interest rates are not under the direct control of the Fed. When FOMC members decide to change the growth rates of the monetary aggregates, they instruct the Manager of the Open Market Account to seek "bank reserve and money market conditions that are consistent with the longer run ranges for monetary aggregates" adopted as intermediate targets.[1] Thus, operating targets are links in the chain connecting policy instruments with intermediate targets.

Operating targets consist of two sets of variables. The first set, the so-called *reserve aggregates,* consists of the monetary base, total bank reserves, reserves against private deposits, nonborrowed reserves, and so forth. The second set, the so-called *money market conditions,* consists of free reserves (or net borrowed reserves), the federal funds rate, and other money market interest rates close to Fed control.

There is no settled doctrine as to which of the several reserve aggregates is most useful for hitting growth rate targets for monetary aggregates set forth in FOMC directives. Although the money supply theory set forth in Chapter 6 suggests the monetary base as an operating target, the Fed has never used it. Instead, it has experimented with a variety of bank reserve aggregates. One is total reserves, which consists of borrowed and nonborrowed reserves, held against all deposits, and of excess reserves. Another is reserves available for private deposits, which equal total reserves minus those required against government deposits and deposits at other banks. Still another is nonborrowed reserves, which equal total reserves minus borrowed reserves. Nonborrowed reserves (which the Fed began to use in October 1979) are more directly controllable by the Fed than are total reserves, which include bank borrowings.

Each of these reserve aggregates has its champions in and outside the System. The Federal Reserve Bank of St. Louis has for years supported the monetary base, but other Reserve banks and Board of Governors economists have pushed for one or another of the bank reserve aggregates. Economists outside the Fed are similarly divided. The issue is basically empirical: Which reserve aggregate is most controllable by the authorities?; and, Which is best correlated with the growth of the monetary aggregates that form the intermediate targets? Until these questions are resolved, we cannot expect the Fed to settle permanently on any single reserve aggregate as its major operating target.

Money market conditions refers to the degree of tightness or ease in credit markets and the banking system. Although the concepts of tightness and ease are not easy to define, broadly speaking, they refer to the capacity and disposition of lenders to speed up or slow down the growth rate of credit and to the degree of severity of interest rates and other credit terms lenders demand from borrowers.

Over the years, Federal Reserve authorities have used a variety of in-

---

[1]From the November 21, 1978 "Record of Policy Actions of the FOMC," as reprinted in the *Federal Reserve Bulletin,* Vol. 65, No. 1, January 1979, p. 59.

dices designed to measure money market conditions. One important index, heavily used in the 1950s and 1960s, is *free (or net borrowed) reserves*. Free reserves consist of the excess reserves of member banks minus the reserves they have borrowed from the Reserve banks. Net borrowed reserves are negative free reserves, which arise when borrowed reserves exceed excess reserves. Figure 10.2 traces free and net borrowed reserves for much of the Fed's history.

Other important indices of money market conditions are Treasury bill rates, commercial paper rates, prime bank lending rates, and the federal funds rate. These interest rates are generally quite responsive to dynamic open market operations and changes in reserve requirements. Together with free or net borrowed reserves, which in the short run are similarly responsive, they are highly regarded in some quarters as useful operating targets. The real issue is whether money market conditions are stronger than reserve aggregates as links in the chain that connects use of the policy instruments within intermediate targets.

Sad to report, economists also disagree on this issue. In the 1920s, in the 1950s, and in the 1960s the Federal Reserve policymakers made great use of money market conditions. In the late 1960s, and even more in the 1970s, they paid ever increasing attention to reserve aggregates, although

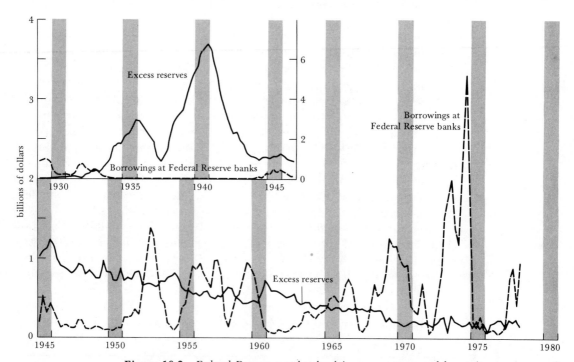

Figure 10.2 *Federal Reserve member banks' excess reserves and borrowings; averages of daily figures, quarterly. (Source: Board of Governors of the Federal Reserve System,* Historical Chart Book, *1978.)*

as we shall see in Section 10.3.1, money market conditions still played an important role in their policy strategies.

Academic economists also disagree on this issue. Monetarists favor the use of reserve aggregates, primarily because they believe reserve aggregates are closely tied to monetary aggregates, their favored intermediate targets. In addition, they feel that concentration on money market conditions too frequently results in loss of control over reserve aggregates and hence over the money supply. Keynesians do not necessarily disagree with monetarists over the importance of controlling reserve aggregates, but they also believe in the importance of money market conditions, primarily because they think that their preferred intermediate targets, interest rates in capital markets, respond to changes in those conditions. For that reason, at least some Keynesians accept loss of control over reserve and monetary aggregates when that control comes into conflict with desired money market conditions.

10.1.3
Targets and indicators

Having set their policy goals and intermediate targets, the monetary authorities must try to influence their intermediate targets in a manner consistent with their overall strategy. To do a good job they must have knowledge of the various linkages in the chain connecting policy instruments with their ultimate goal or goals. In addition, they must take into account the timing relationships connected with the linkages. There is a relatively short lapse of time between changes in the policy instruments and the impacts of those changes on the operating targets. A somewhat longer time period exists between changes in operating targets and changes in intermediate targets. And, as noted above, the longest policy lag occurs between changes in operating targets and their effects on ultimate policy goals.

As we have said, the Fed has imperfect knowledge of the nature of the linkages between instruments and targets and of their timing relationships. It is in the position of a navigator trying to find port with incomplete charts and maps. It has a rather hazy idea of the landmarks and currents needed to guide it safely to its objective, and it cannot distinguish clearly the real from the false signs it sees looming in the fog about its ship. Like the navigator, it needs a good indicator to help it monitor progress toward its goal.

Professor George Kaufman has defined a policy indicator as "a variable that quantifies the relative strength of policy actions on the ultimate objectives of policy."[2] This definition stresses the linkage between policy

---

[2]George Kaufman, *Money, the Financial System, and the Economy* (Chicago: Rand McNally, 1977), pp. 521–522. The discussion in this section draws heavily on Kaufman.

targets and policy goals and the Fed's ability independently to control the targets, but other factors are also involved.

Kaufman scores indicators by how well they conform to several criteria that an ideal indicator should possess. His criteria suggest that a good indicator must:

1. Be an important link in the chain between policy actions and effects on ultimate goals.
2. Be positioned close to Federal Reserve control.
3. Permit frequent, timely, and accurate readings.
4. Be influenced solely by the Fed.

None of the indicators frequently mentioned by writers in the field gets a perfect score in terms of these criteria. Monetary aggregates and intermediate and long-term interest rates are theoretically important determinants of GNP, the ultimate policy goal, but they are not closely positioned for control by the Fed. In addition, interest rates are affected by inflationary expectations and private demand for and supply of credit; hence, they are not under sole control of the Fed. Money market conditions are positioned close to Fed control and permit relatively frequent, timely, and accurate readings, but they are somewhat remote from ultimate goals and are not completely controlled by the authorities. Reserve aggregates can be brought under control within a reasonably short period of time, but they are not the only factors affecting the behavior of monetary aggregates and interest rates in capital markets. Reserve aggregates are also relatively remote links in the chain of variables affecting ultimate policy goals.

As a practical matter, the Fed and other analysts use a variety of indicators. Monetarists tend to use monetary aggregates, mainly because they believe that the Fed can within a 3 to 6 month period control their rates of growth. For quicker readings, they rely upon the monetary base, or the base adjusted for changes in reserve requirements and deposits shifts, because they believe that the money multipliers have a good degree of short-term predictability. Other analysts pay more attention to money market conditions, particularly the federal funds rate and other short-term money rates, although for the longer term thrust of policy they also pay attention to reserve or monetary aggregates and interest rates in capital markets.

The role of indicators is to provide information for the Fed and others on the thrust of its policies. If the indicators suggest that policies are not working, or are not working well enough, the authorities should adjust their instruments to bring their policies back on course. (Note the dotted feedback line in Figure 10.1.) Thus indicators provide a necessary if imperfect device for monitoring and maintaining a given policy strategy. If they are not perfect, that is not the fault of the policymakers. Moreover, they have little choice. If the country has entrusted them with the conduct of monetary policy, they best pursue that task with the aid of policy strategies monitored, if necessary, by imperfect indicators. To do otherwise would be like entrusting our navigator to guiding his ship without any charts or maps.

10.2
Past monetary policy strategies

For most of its history the Federal Reserve System has operated without a complete policy strategy. As we have said, a complete strategy entails setting targets and instruments in conformance with well-defined goals and monitoring the progress of policy with the aid of one or several indicators. Because a truly complete strategy requires full knowledge of the links in the chain between instruments and goals, the Fed has never been in the enviable position of using one, even if it wished to do so. Nevertheless, it was not until the 1960s that the nature of a complete strategy was understood. Until it was, the Fed was unable to place its policy actions within a meaningful framework. So, for most of its history, it conducted its business with an incomplete strategy or no strategy at all.

In this section we shall study three examples of an incomplete strategy from Federal Reserve history: the commercial loan theory, the free reserve doctrine, and interest rate targets.

10.2.1
The commercial loan theory[3]

The Federal Reserve Act was based upon the commercial loan theory. That theory, which, roughly stated, asserts that commercial bank credit should expand and contract with "the needs of trade," could never have led to a development of a complete strategy in the sense discussed in the Section 10.1. On the contrary, it surrendered to the ebb and flow of economic activity the credit provided member banks through the discount windows of the Reserve banks. Manipulating the size of bank reserves with the aid of open market operations was antithetical to its tenets, for that would have given the Fed power to act upon the economy at the initiative of the monetary authorities. As a result, manipulation of policy instruments with the intent of attaining some particular goal was quite

---

[3]Section 10.2.1 draws heavily upon Lester V. Chandler, "Impacts of Theory on Policy: The Early Years of the Federal Reserve," in David P. Eastburn, *Men, Money and Policy* (Federal Reserve Bank of Philadelphia, February 1970), pp. 41–53.

out of keeping with the way the commercial loan theory, and by implication, the original Federal Reserve Act, stated the System should operate.

The act contained many provisions that illustrate its origin in commercial loan ideas. For example, it instructed the System to furnish the country with an elastic currency and to afford means of rediscounting commercial paper. Provision of an elastic currency was as much a credit reform as it was a monetary reform designed to solve the shortage of currency that occurred under the national banking system; for, in addition to solving the currency shortage, it ensured that currency flowing into and out of banks would not interfere with bank credit conditions. Types of commercial paper eligible for discount at the Reserve banks were "notes, drafts, and bills of exchange issued or drawn for agricultural, industrial, or commercial purposes, or the proceeds of which have been used, or are to be used, for such purposes. . . ." Only such paper and federal government securities (privileged exceptions to the general rule) were eligible as collateral for advances. The act specifically excluded "notes, drafts, or bills covering merely investments or issued or drawn for the purpose of carrying or trading in stocks, bonds, or other investment securities, except bonds and notes of the Government of the United States." Additionally, the act encouraged Reserve banks to deal in acceptances, which were regarded as model commercial paper tied to the needs of trade. Finally, it provided that currency issued by the System be backed by gold and eligible commercial paper.

Although the Federal Reserve Act linked Reserve bank credit to commercial paper, it provided virtually no guidance to the System concerning the *amounts* of funds to be issued or withdrawn from the banking system. Absence of such instructions is in complete accord with the commercial loan philosophy embedded in the act, which stressed the need for "elasticity" of Federal Reserve notes and provided that discount rates should "be fixed with a view of accommodating commerce and business."

The congressional father of the Federal Reserve System, Carter Glass, and his closest advisor on banking affairs, H. Parker Willis, were convinced commercial loan theorists. So were many of the officials in the System in its early years. These officials were unhappy with the activist role of the Fed during the 1920s, and in the years before and after the Great Depression they were the main force behind System actions that reduced the rate of growth and then aided the collapse of the money supply. In the late 1920s, for example, their objections to the use of bank credit for the purpose of supporting speculation in real estate and in stock and bond market securities led them to favor policies that not only tightened credit for these activities, but that also reduced its flow into commercial, agricultural, and other business uses.

The failure of the Fed to prevent or even act to prevent the serious collapse in the money supply during the 1929–1933 period owes much to the influence of adherents to the commercial loan theory both within the System and among outside financial experts. Although Irving Fisher and a few other prominent quantity of money theorists advocated large Federal Reserve purchases of government securities, many other respected authorities, such as H. Parker Willis of Columbia, O. M. W. Sprague of Harvard, Benjamin M. Anderson of Chase National Bank, and Edwin Kemmerer of Princeton opposed them. Thus the traditional lender of last resort function of central banking was ignored in favor of a theory that argued that it is not only unnecessary, but it is undesirable to stimulate "artificially" bank credit during periods of economic decline, even if in the course of the decline large numbers of banks crumble and disappear, taking with them the fortunes of millions of depositors.

In fairness to the Fed, monetary and credit control theory in the 1920s and the early 1930s was in a chaotic state. Even so, some of the basic flaws of the commercial loan theory might have been investigated more deeply by its adherents. One flaw was the assertion that confining discount window acceptance to "eligible" commercial paper would guarantee that bank credit would flow only into channels of "trade." No law prevented banks from lending borrowed reserves to stock brokers or real estate speculators. Hence, to concentrate on the *form* of a loan through the discount window, as opposed to the subsequent uses of the money, was to overlook the fact that the Fed could not guarantee retention of the funds within channels that served the "needs of trade."

A second, more important flaw is the procyclical bias inherent in operating the Fed according to the tenets of the commercial loan theory. The theory stressed *accommodation* of business. As such, it ruled out changes in the discount rate for the purpose of regulating the volume of Reserve bank credit through the discount window. As a result, increases in business loan demand from member banks could be easily translated into additional member bank borrowing at given discount rates. The additional borrowing, in turn, would lead to an expansion of the money supply, which would stimulate business activity and additional loan demand. The latter would result in more bank borrowing, additional money growth, additional credit demand, and so forth.

The process could also work in reverse, because a decline in loan demand would be followed by liquidation of member bank debt to the Fed and a reduction in the money supply that would depress the economy and further depress loan demand. Thus strict adherence to the commercial loan theory implied not only credit and monetary accommodation to the "needs of trade," but complete abandonment of any meaningful strategy of monetary policy. It was the acceptance of the commercial loan theory, and the failure to have a policy strategy (whether complete or incomplete) that led the Fed into the fatal errors it made before and during the Great Depression.

10.2.2
The free reserve doctrine

During the 1950s and the early 1960s, Federal Reserve policymakers frequently employed the concept of free reserves. Criticisms by Professors Warren Smith, Milton Friedman, Karl Brunner, Allan Meltzer, and many other prominent monetary economists revealed that, unless used with extreme caution, the concept can be downright damaging to a complete monetary policy strategy.

Free (or net borrowed) reserves are the algebraic difference between member bank excess reserves and member bank borrowing from the Fed. When free reserves are positive, excess reserves exceed borrowed reserves; when they are negative, borrowed reserves exceed excess reserves. Free reserves are affected by a variety of forces: open market operations, member bank borrowing, float, currency in circulation, and so forth. Because daily and weekly variations can be very large, it normally takes 3 to 4 weeks before Federal Reserve economists can judge their direction of change. Over time, however, the primary factor affecting variations in free reserves is member bank borrowing. Using monthly figures, Warren Smith estimated that during 1953–1962 variations in member bank borrowing in one way or another accounted for over 90 percent of the variations in free reserves.

In using free reserves as a policy guide, Federal Reserve officials frequently failed to appreciate three distinct meanings that may be assigned to the concept: (1) its role as a causal link between policy instruments and changes in monetary or credit aggregates, (2) its use as an operating policy target, and (3) its use as a policy indicator.

Free reserves as a causal link in the policy transmission mechanism would be rejected if there were little or no correlation between variations in free reserves and variation in the growth rates of monetary and credit aggregates. Although several critics of the concept have on this basis rejected free reserves as a significant causal variable, the evidence is mixed as to whether free reserves are worse than other conceptions, such as total reserves or reserves available for private deposits. Even so, as Professors Brunner and Meltzer have said, the issue goes beyond the causal significance of free reserves. If free reserves are not in fact causal with respect to changes in the monetary aggregates, then they are useless as policy targets and indicators. But being causal does not necessarily signify that they should be used as an operating target or policy indicator.

To appreciate this point, assume that the FOMC has adopted a monetary growth rate target range of 5–7 percent a year. In pursuit of that target, it instructs the Manager of the Open Market Account to keep free reserves in the range of $1–1.5 billion. To do that, the Manager must purchase government bonds when free reserves fall below $1 billion, and he must sell bonds when they go above $1.5 billion.

The potential incompatability between the free reserve target and the

FOMC's monetary growth target should now be clear. Suppose that market interest rates rise in response to acceleration of bank customer loan demand. If member banks partly meet the increased loan demand by raising their borrowings from the Reserve banks, free reserves may drop below the $1 billion level. If so, the Manager must bring free reserves bank into the target range by accelerating his purchase of government bonds. This action would raise the growth rate of the money supply above the 7 percent limit originally set by the FOMC. A reduction of monetary growth below the target range might result from a drop in market interest rates. The drop in interest rates would lead banks to reduce their borrowings from the Reserve banks and to curtail their own lending. If the resulting rise in free reserves were large, the Manager would sell bonds in the open market, an act that would reduce total reserves and bring free reserves back within the target range. In the meantime, the money growth rate would fall below 5 percent per year, the lower end of the target range set by the FOMC.

Even though free reserves may not function well as an operating target, are they acceptable as a reliable device for monitoring the success of a policy that uses some other target? The answer appears to be no, particularly if we accept Professor Kaufman's list of criteria (mentioned in Section 10.1.3) for an ideal indicator. In the first place, daily or even weekly readings of free reserves are so contaminated by changes in float, currency in circulation, and other factors that they provide little evidence for the independent influence of policy on their level. Second, Federal Reserve actions are only one of a large set of influences upon free reserves. Actions by member banks and the public at large are equally if not more important in determining their level. Finally, they are relatively remote from ultimate policy goals, so that their variations give little evidence of the impact of policy on the economy.

The decline of the free reserve doctrine set in during the 1960s. Its misleading character became particularly apparent during the onset of the 1960 recession. Although the recession started around May 1960, the Fed in March had decided to switch from its previously tight policy stance to one of ease. It continued this policy until June. During that period, interest rates were dropping and net borrowed reserves were falling (that is, free reserves were rising). Unfortunately, total bank reserves and the growth rate of the money supply were also falling. The inconsistent behavior of money growth and free reserves arose from a decline in borrowers' demands for bank credit, which lowered interest rates and led banks to reduce their own borrowings from the Reserve banks. In the meantime, following FOMC instructions, the Manager of the Open Market Account was "mopping up reserves" in order to prevent an easing of bank reserve positions., Needless to say, the mopping up operations caused total reserves and the money supply to decline, contrary to the intentions of the majority of the FOMC members.

Thus, even if free reserves have a causal role in the money supply process, they cannot, without considerable amendment, play a useful role in a complete monetary policy strategy. Fortunately, the need for such a strategy has, among other reasons, forced the Fed to abandon the conception as a centerpiece in its policy deliberations.

10.2.3
Interest rates as policy targets

During much of its history the Fed has adopted interest rates as a major intermediate policy target. Indeed, the purpose of manipulating bank borrowed reserve positions in the 1920s and free reserves in the 1950s and 1960s was to influence money market conditions so as to achieve tight or easy interest rates.

We have already seen that interest rates are not a very good indicator of policy. To repeat the objections: They are to a large extent determined by variations in the supply and demand for loanable funds by business and household lenders and borrowers, and variations in real as opposed to nominal interest rates are not easily measured. Thus interest rates fail to satisfy two very important criteria of an ideal indicator—measurability and dominance of control by the monetary authorities. But failure to meet the standards for a good policy indicator does not necessarily disquality interest rates as an intermediate policy target. What can we say about that?

Interest rates as an intermediate policy target may serve different goals. Balance of payments difficulties, for example, frequently lead monetary authorities to try to raise market interest rates for the purpose of attracting foreign money and of discouraging domestic money from being lent abroad. A recent illustration of this motivation was the decision of the monetary authorities to raise the discount rate by one-half of a percentage point in the aftermath of President Carter's controversial decision in July 1979 to replace a number of his chief cabinet officers, including Treasury Secretary Michael Blumenthal who, at the time, was regarded the world over as a cautious economic conservative. President Carter's decision, together with his announced intention to embark upon an expensive program for energy independence, had caused a sharp drop in the international value of the dollar. Thus, the Fed hoped that it could prevent further damage by announcing the rise in the discount rate.

Perhaps the most frequent reason for using interest rates as targets is to influence the level of business investment and consumer spending on new housing. Low interest rates encourage such expenditures, and high interest rates discourage them. Thus, if variations in investment and housing outlays give rise to variations in effective demand, influence over interest rates may give the Fed a handle on influencing the direction of change of GNP.

To influence interest rates is not actually to determine them. During periods of economic prosperity, high levels of investment and housing demand raise the demand for loans and also increase interest rates. When the economy is in a slump, low levels of capital and housing outlays depress loan demand and interest rates. Thus, to control interest rates, the Fed must use its powers either to supplement or to offset the market forces that determine their levels in the present and immediate future. If, during a boom, its purpose is to remove excessive investment and housing outlays, the Fed will wish to raise interest rates above the levels determined by the supply and demand for loanable funds. Conversely, if during a recession the Fed wants to stimulate business and household capital outlays, it will wish to lower interest rates below the rates determined by market forces.

Unfortunately, the Fed rarely has sufficient knowledge of market forces to permit it to estimate or forecast accurately interest rates that will clear the market for loanable funds. The lack of knowledge hinders efficient use of interest rates as intermediate policy targets.

For example, if in attempting to slow overexpansion of capital spending, the Fed unknowingly sets target interest rates that are too low, an excess demand for loanable funds would force up market interest rates. In attempting to keep the rates on target, the authorities would have to inject additional reserves into the banking system, an act that would raise the rate of growth of the money supply; instead of restraining the growth of spending, it would actually encourage it. Conversely, if in attempting to stimulate capital expenditures the Fed inadvertently sets target interest rates too high, market forces would push the rates down. In that event, the Fed would be obliged to try to raise rates to their target levels, in which case it would actually reduce bank reserves and, hence, the monetary base, an act that would depress, not stimulate, the economy.

Carried to an extreme, using interest rate targets would lead to a return of the commercial loan theory as a basis for monetary policy—that is, the complete abandonment of any strategy for monetary policy. For, suppose that the authorities insisted that policy is always best served by a given interest rate target. Such a target would lead the Manager of the Open Market Account to use his powers to peg long-term interest rates at the desired level with purchases and sales of government securities. Reserves and the money supply would then fall victim to forces in the loanable funds market.

For example, a boom in investment demand might raise market interest rates above the target level. The rise in rates would signal the Manager to buy bonds, which would raise their prices, lower interest rates, and increase the monetary base. Similarly, a fall in investment demand might lower market interest rates below target levels and force the Manager to reduce bond prices and the monetary base by selling securities in the open market. In this manner, therefore, swings in investment demand would be accompanied by swings in the same direction of the growth rate of the money supply. That is, money would be adjusted to "the needs of trade."

We do not suggest that the Fed actually uses a single target set of interest rates. Nevertheless, the converse is also untrue. The Fed in its history has rarely let market forces completely determine interest rates. Instead, it has used its policy instruments to keep their variations within a certain range. Although the range has over time drifted up and down with the state of the economy, there have been instances, such as the 1960 episode mentioned in the Section 10.2.2, when the use of interest rate targets has led to unexpected and perverse movements in reserve and monetary aggregates. Only complete abandonment of interest rates as targets would prevent such recurrent mistakes.

10.3
Recent strategies of monetary policy

Inflation control has dominated monetary policy since the latter part of the 1960s. Because inflation originates in excessive growth of the money stock, controlling the growth of monetary aggregates is a major target of monetary policy. In 1968 such control was recommended by the Joint Economic Committee of Congress. In 1970 Federal Reserve authorities made monetary aggregates equal in importance to interest rates as intermediate targets, even though it publicly expressed doubts over its ability in the short run to control monetary growth. But empirical evidence on the connection between money and inflation and the urging of Congress and a growing number of professional economists gradually strengthened the case for using monetary aggregates as targets. Also, in 1975 Congress directed the Federal Reserve to establish growth targets for monetary aggregates and report back to it at regular intervals. On October 6, 1979 the Fed launched a new procedure designed to emphasize control over the growth of the monetary aggregates.

10.3.1
The Fed's procedures for controlling monetary growth

Although the Fed's procedure for controlling monetary growth during most of the 1970s is too technical for full description here, it is still possible to outline its main elements.

The first step in the procedure was to select a year-long target for monetary growth. The target depended upon the goals set by the authorities for the behavior of the economy in comparison with the forecasts made by the staff economists. Depending upon the direction and degree of divergence between the goals and the forecasts, the policy either raised or lowered the target growth rate for the monetary aggregates. Econometric models constructed by the staff economists helped authorities put numbers on growth rate targets.

The next step was to arrange for growth in reserve aggregates in a manner consistent with the target growth rates of the monetary aggregates. To do this, the Fed followed a surprising procedure. Instead of employing the monetary base–money multiplier formula, it tried to control expansion of the money stock with the federal funds rate.

The procedure can be described as follows: First, employing an econometric model, the staff economists estimated the money growth needed to attain the GNP goal set by the authorities. Next, they estimated a federal funds rate consistent with the money growth target. A low federal funds rate encouraged banks to speed up their lending, and a high rate slowed them down. Thus the "right" federal funds rate permitted bank reserve aggregates and, by implication, monetary aggregates to grow at the targeted rate. Hence, the FOMC, taking its information from technical staff, instructed the Manager of the Open Market Account to conduct the System's purchases and sales of government securities with an eye to holding the federal funds rate within a particular range thought to be consistent with the money growth targets.

Thus during most of the 1970s the FOMC in effect established two targets. The first was a monetary growth target, and the second was a federal funds rate target. The latter was designed to enforce the former. When the federal funds rate wandered above the top figure in the target range, the Manager automatically increased his purchases of securities so as to supply more reserves and bring the federal funds rate back within the target range. If the federal funds rate drifted below the bottom figure in the target range, the Manager absorbed reserves until the rate rose back into the target range.

To correct mistakes, the federal funds rate target range was reset at each monthly meeting of the FOMC. If necessary, more frequent corrections were made with telephone conferences of the Committee.

10.3.2
Criticism of the Fed's monetary control procedure in the 1970s

The Fed's procedure for controlling monetary growth was not particularly successful. The variations in the growth rate of the monetary aggregates in the 1970s were quite large. Although policy shifts in growth targets accounted for some of this variability, much of it came from the control procedure itself.

The problem lay with the ill-understood relationship between the federal funds rate and the growth of the money supply. Unexpected and unmeasured shifts in the demand for member bank loans led to shifts in member banks' demands for federal funds. The shifts in banks' demands for federal funds caused variations in the federal funds rates. If the variations pushed the rates outside the target range set by the FOMC, the Manager of the Open Market Account automatically injected or absorbed reserves until the rate came back within the range. The variations in reserves, in turn, led to growth rates of the money supply that exceeded or fell short of the FOMC's targets.

Each monthly meeting of the FOMC gave it an opportunity to correct the federal funds rate target range. But a mistaken belief that the money growth errors are random could have led the Committee to delay its decision, causing divergence between desired and actual monetary growth rates to continue for another month. Unfortunately, the longer the Committee took to discover and react to errors, the larger were the necessary corrections in the federal funds rate targets in order to return monetary growth rates back to the long-term targets.

As things have turned out, the Fed far more frequently failed to meet its monetary growth targets than it did its federal funds rate targets. In the 47-month period following the first announced targets in 1975, the federal funds rate fell outside its target ranges only 5 times; in the same period, M-1 growth fell outside its target range 23 times, essentially 50 percent of the time.[4] The data presented in Figure 10.3 show the experience for 1978.

Monetary economists give several reasons for this performance. One, as we have said, is the uncertainty surrounding the correct relationship between the federal funds rate and the money supply growth rate. Another, however, is the reluctance of the Federal Reserve to abandon interest rates as an independent target of monetary policy. As stated in Chapter 7, political pressures frequently prevent the FOMC from raising interest rates to levels necessary to tighten monetary growth rates. Moreover, at least until recently, the Fed has often resisted sharp increases in rates for fear of unsettling security markets. Because unsettled money and capital markets can lead to unsettled general economic conditions, the fear may at times be well justified. Even so, if it is carried to an extreme, the authorities risk losing control over growth of the monetary aggregates. That is, the money supply during these periods may respond more to the "needs of trade" than to policy initiatives of the Federal Reserve System.

Distaste for interest rate targets even exists within the System. Lawrence K. Roos, President of the Federal Reserve Bank of St. Louis, made the following statement on May 10, 1979:[5]

---

[4]Lawrence K. Roos, "Monetary Targets—Their Contribution to Policy Formation," *Federal Reserve Bank of St. Louis Review*, May 1979, p. 13.

[5]Ibid., p. 15.

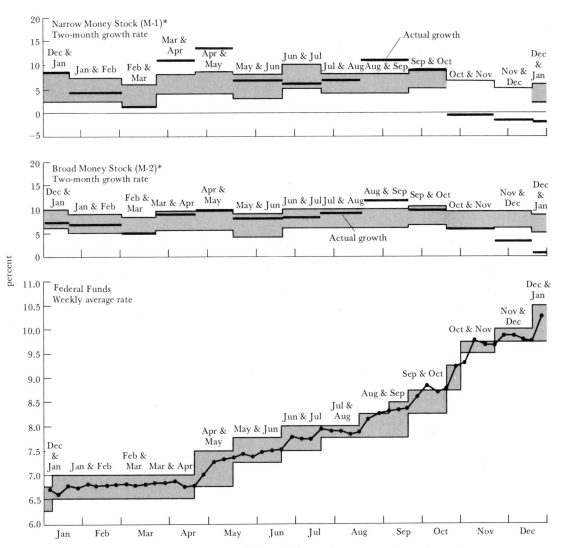

Shaded bands in the upper two charts are the FOMC's specified ranges for money supply growth over the two-month periods indicated. No lower bound was established for M-1 at the October and November meetings. In the bottom chart, the shaded bands are the specified ranges for Federal Funds rate variation. Actual growth rates in the upper two charts are based on data available at the time of the second FOMC meeting after the end of each period.

*Seasonally adjusted annual rates.

Figure 10.3 *FOMC ranges for short-run monetary growth and for the federal funds rate, 1978. (Source:* Federal Reserve Bank of New York Quarterly Review, *Vol. 4, No. 1, Spring 1979, p. 60.)*

Interest rate stabilization as a means of seeking economic stabilization has had its day in court and its results certainly have been less than satisfactory. We are still experiencing persistent and accelerating inflation, and again we face the grim prospect of recession. If we respond as we have in the past, if we persist in repeating past errors, we will have failed in our responsibility as monetary policymakers. We must be prepared to try new methods which offer the potential for success. Targeting on interest rates at the expense of stabilizing the growth of the money supply has brought us the situation we face today. If we feel there is a better way . . . I suggest we move ahead without further delay.

10.3.3
The new monetary control
procedures—Post-October 6, 1979

1979 was a bad year for the FOMC. Using the federal funds rate as an instrument for controlling monetary growth was not working. Even though the Committee was meeting its interest rate targets, it was losing control over the money supply. For most of the year, money growth exceeded the upper range of the targets it set for M-1 and M-2 (see Figure 10.4). At the same time, inflation was accelerating and the dollar was plunging on international money markets. Foreigners were threatening massive sales of their dollar assets, and foreign central banks were warning American officials of the possibility of a major collapse of the dollar. In early October, this concern was communicated to Federal Reserve Chairman Paul Volcker at an International Monetary Fund meeting in Belgrade. Volker rushed home; at an emergency meeting on Saturday, October 6, the Fed decided to put in place a set of new open market procedures, emphasizing control over the money supply, and deemphasizing control over interest rates.

To implement the new procedure, the FOMC made two decisions. The first was to widen dramatically the tolerance range for fluctuations in the federal funds rate. The second was to instruct the manager of the open market desk to use total bank reserves as an operating target for monetary control. The first decision immediately set in motion wide fluctuations in the federal funds rate and other interest rates (see Figures 10.4 and 10.5). The second decision caused the manager to focus attention on nonborrowed bank reserves as a means of acquiring control over total reserves. Since currency movements and bank borrowing from the Fed influences the level of total reserves, the Fed must try to control reserves by means of controlling nonborrowed reserves. That this is a difficult task can be seen by reviewing Table 10.1, which is an excerpt from a staff paper released by the Board of Governors on January 31, 1980, clarifying its new monetary policy procedures.

The jury is still out on the value of the new procedures. As shown in Figure 10.5, the Fed was unable to keep money growing within its target

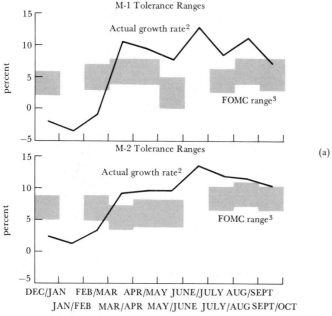

(a)

Note: After the October 6, 1979 FOMC meeting, the FOMC no longer specified tolerance ranges for M-1 and M-2 in the same manner. See table 1.

[1]During the January-February and June-July periods, ranges for M-1 and M-2 were not specified by the FOMC.
[2]Actual growth rate data are revised as of January 10, 1980.
[3]The shaded areas represent two-month ranges adopted by the Committee at each regularly scheduled meeting.

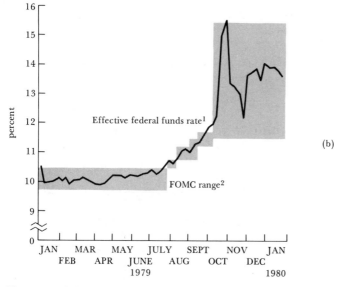

(b)

[1]Weekly averages of effective daily rates.
[2]At each meeting during 1979, the FOMC established a range for the federal funds rate. These ranges are indicated for the first full week during which they were in effect.

Figure 10.4 *FOMC ranges for short-run monetary aggregates and the federal funds rate, 1979. (Source: Richard W. Lang, "The FOMC in 1979: Introducing Reserve Targeting,"* Federal Reserve Bank of St. Louis Review, *Vol. 62, No. 3, March 1980, pp. 2–25.)*

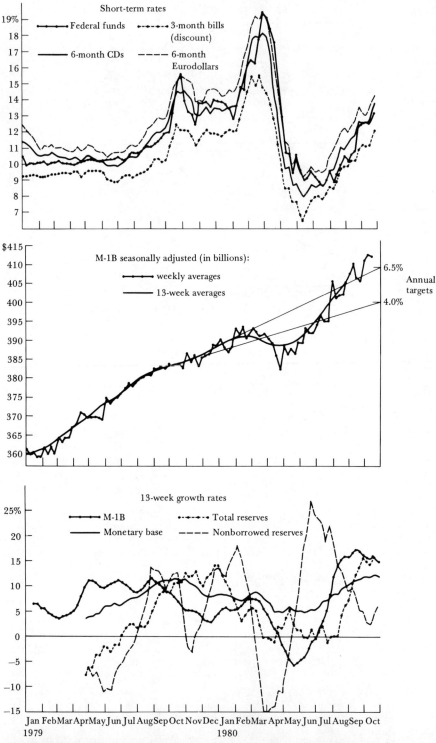

Figure 10.5 *Interest rates, money growth, and changes in reserve aggregates, 1979 and 1980.* (*Source:* The Morgan Bank, Weekly Money Market Bulletin.)

Table 10.1 *Excerpts from "The New Federal Reserve Technical Procedures for Controlling Money"*

(1) The policy process first involves a decision by the FOMC on the rate of increase in money it wishes to achieve . . . .

(2) After the objective for money supply growth is set, reserve paths expected to achieve such growth are established for a family of reserve measures. These measures consist of total reserves, the monetary base (essentially total reserves of member banks plus currency in circulation), and nonborrowed reserves. Establishment of the paths involves projecting how much of the targeted money growth is likely to take the form of currency, of deposits at nonmember institutions, and of deposits at member institutions (taking account of differential reserve requirements by size of demand deposits and between the demand and time and savings deposit components of M-2). Moreover, estimates are made of reserves likely to be absorbed by expansion in other bank liabilities subject to reserve requirements, such as large CDs, at a pace that appears consistent with money supply objectives and also takes account of tolerable changes in bank credit. . . . [E]stimates are also made of the amount of excess reserves banks are likely to hold.

(3) The projected mix of currency and demand deposits, given the reserve requirements for deposits and banks' excess reserves, yields an estimate of the increase in total reserves and the monetary base consistent with FOMC monetary targets. The amount of nonborrowed reserves—that is total reserves less member bank borrowing—is obtained by initially assuming a level of borrowing near that prevailing in the most recent period. . . .

(4) Initial paths established for the family of reserve measures over, say, a 3-month period are then translated into reserve levels covering shorter periods between meetings. . . .

(5) Total reserves provide the basis for deposits and thereby are more closely related to the aggregates than nonborrowed reserves. *Thus total reserves represent the principal overall reserve objective.* However, only nonborrowed reserves are directly under control through open market operations, though they can be adjusted in response to changes in bank demand for reserves obtained through borrowing at the discount window. [*Emphasis* added.]

(6) Because nonborrowed reserves are more closely under control of the System Account Manager for open market operations (though subject to a small range of error because of the behavior of non-controlled factors affecting reserves, such as float), he would initially aim at a nonborrowed reserve target (seasonally unadjusted for operating purposes) established for the operating period between meetings. To understand how this would lead to control of total reserves and money supply, suppose that the demand for money ran stronger than was being targeted—as it did in early October of last year. The increased demand for money and also for bank reserves to support the money would in the first instance be accompanied by more intensive efforts on the part of banks to obtain reserves in the federal funds market, thereby tending to bid up the federal funds rate, and by increased borrowing at the Federal Reserve discount window. As a result of the latter, total reserves and the monetary base would for a while run stronger than targeted. Whether total reserves tend to remain above target for any sustained period depends in part on the nature of the bulge in reserve demand—whether or not it was transitory, for example—and in part on the degree to which emerging market conditions reflect or induce adjustments on the part of banks and the public. These responses on the part of banks, for example, could include sales of securities to the public (thereby extinguishing deposits) and changes in lending policies.

(7) Should total reserves be showing sustained strength, closer control over them could be obtained by lowering the nonborrowed reserve path (to attempt to offset the expansion in member bank borrowing) and/or by raising the discount rate. A rise in the discount rate would, for any given supply of nonborrowed reserves, initially tend to raise market interest rates, thereby working to speed up the adjustment process of the public and banks and encouraging a more prompt move back to the path for total reserves and the monetary base. Thus, whether adjustments are made in the nonborrowed path—the only path that can be controlled directly through open market operations—and/or in the discount rate depends in part on emerging behavior by banks and the public. Under present circumstances, however, both the timing of market response to a rise in money and reserve demand, and the ability to control total reserves in the short run within close tolerance limits, are influenced by the two-week lag between bank deposits and required reserves behind these deposits.

(8) Other intermeeting adjustments can be made to the reserve paths as a family. These may be needed when it becomes clear that the multiplier relationship between reserves and money has varied from expectations. . . . Given the naturally large week-to-week fluctuations in factors affecting the reserve multiplier, deviation from expectations in one direction over a period of several weeks would be needed before it would be clear that a change in trend has taken place.

Source: Richard W. Lang, "The FOMC in 1979: Introducing Reserve Targeting," Federal Reserve Bank of St. Louis Review, *March 1980.*

range for the first year following the October 6, 1979 policy revolution. Not only did interest rates fluctuate widely throughout the period, but monetary aggregates were frequently well outside the target ranges set in the fall of 1979. The failure to keep on target was to some extent caused by complications set in motion by changes in the definition of money that took place in January 1980. But, as the bottom panel of Figure 10.5 shows, the FOMC must take a good part of the blame. In attempting to deal with the recession and accompanying inflationary forces, it caused wide gyrations to occur in the bank reserves and in the monetary base. Had it set a steadier course for reserves and the base, the growth rate of the money supply would also have been steadier.

SUMMARY

Monetary policy strategies must be designed with explicitly stated goals, intermediate targets, and operating targets. Implementation of a strategy requires manipulation of policy instruments to hit operating targets that, in turn, affect the intermediate targets that change the ultimate goal variables. In addition to targets, a useful strategy must contain a method for monitoring its effects on the economy. The monitoring is accomplished with a set of policy indicators.

Monetary policy goals typically include stabilization of prices, low unemployment, satisfactory economic growth rates and stability of the international value of the dollar. Intermediate targets include monetary aggregates, credit aggregates, or capital market interest rates.

Operating targets consist of various reserve or bank reserve aggregates and money market conditions, such as free reserves, the federal funds rate, and the Treasury bill rate.

Federal Reserve policies have frequently been implemented without the aid or even an understanding of the nature of a policy strategy. The Federal Reserve Act contained a built-in bias in favor of the commercial loan theory, a doctrine that preached passive accommodation of bank credit to the "needs of trade" and that dominated much of the authorities' thinking during the early years of the System. The free reserve doctrine employed in the 1950s and the 1960s is an example of the Fed's confusion over the use of variables as targets and indicators. The System's use of interest rate targets frequently conflicts with the use of monetary aggregates as targets.

In the 1970s, the Fed raised monetary aggregates to equal position with interest rates as intermediate targets. It tried to control the growth of monetary aggregates with the aid of federal funds rate targets. In so doing, it frequently accepted monetary changes outside its target range. The reason may be that interest rates ranked above monetary aggregates as intermediate targets. In any event, this policy control procedure failed to keep money growth in the target ranges. On October 6, 1979, the

FOMC substantially widened the tolerance limits for the federal funds rate and installed a policy procedure emphasizing control over nonborrowed reserves as a method for controlling the growth rate of the money supply.

DISCUSSION QUESTIONS

1. Why is it important for the Fed to have a monetary policy strategy?

2. How does a complete monetary policy strategy differ from an incomplete strategy?

3. What is wrong with the commercial loan theory as a basis for monetary policy?

4. What is wrong with using interest rates as operating or intermediate targets of monetary policy?

5. Does it make sense for the Fed to use both interest rates and money growth rates as targets of monetary policy?

6. Can a variable be both a target and indicator of monetary policy? Can it be one without being the other?

7. What are the properties of good monetary policy indicators?

8. Why did the Fed change its monetary control procedures on October 6, 1979? What difference did the change make in 1980? In 1981? (Do a little research.)

IMPORTANT TERMS AND CONCEPTS

☐ commercial loan theory
☐ free (or net borrowed) reserves
☐ free reserves doctrine
☐ indicator of monetry policy
☐ intermediate policy targets
☐ monetry control procedures

☐ money market conditions
☐ operating policy targets
☐ policy goals
☐ strategy of monetary policy
☐ tight money (versus easy money)

ADDITIONAL READINGS

Early and influential articles on the strategy of monetary policy are Thomas R. Saving, "Monetary Policy Targets and Indicators," *Journal of Political Economy,* Vol. 75, No. 4, Part II, August 1967, pp. 446–456, and

Jack M. Guttentag, "The Strategy of Open Market Operations," *Quarterly Journal of Economics,* Vol. 80, No. 1, February 1966. A somewhat more accessible piece is Albert E. Burger, "The Implementation Problem of Monetary Policy," *Federal Reserve Bank of St. Louis Review,* Vol. 53, No. 3, March 1971, pp. 20–30.

The Free Reserve Doctrine has been widely discussed. A well-known critique is Karl Brunner and Allan H. Meltzer, *The Federal Reserve's Attachment to the Free Reserves Concept* (U.S. Congress, House Committee on Banking and Currency, Subcommittee on Domestic Finance, 88th Congress, 2nd session, 1964). Also well-known, but a bit technical in its central chapters, is A. J. Meigs, *Free Reserves and the Money Supply* (Chicago: University of Chicago Press, 1962). An article originating within the Fed is "The Significance and Limitations of Free Reserves," *Federal Reserve Bank of New York Monthly Review,* November 1958, pp. 12–26.

On the general theme of targets and indicators, see the articles in Karl Brunner and Allan H. Meltzer, *Targets and Indicators of Monetary Policy* (San Francisco: Chandler Publishing, 1967).

The Federal Reserve Bank of Boston has held two conferences on controlling monetary aggregates. The bank has published the papers in *Controlling Monetary Aggregates* (1969) and *Controlling Monetary Aggregates II: The Implementation* (1972).

A useful description of the Fed's pre-October 6, 1979 policy process is Raymond E. Lombra and Raymond G. Torto, "The Strategy of Monetary Policy," *Federal Reserve Bank of Richmond Monthly Review,* Vol. 61, September/October 1975, pp. 3–14. Sharp criticism of the policy procedures is in Lawrence K. Roos, "Monetary Targets—Their Contribution to Policy Formation," *Federal Reserve Bank of St. Louis Review,* Vol. 61, No. 5, May 1979, pp. 12–15. This article is a reprint of a talk before the Conference on Monetary Targets, The City University, London, England, May 10, 1979. A historical treatment is in Peter M. Keir and Henry C. Wallich, "The Role of Operating Guides in U.S. Monetary Policy: A Historical Review," *Federal Reserve Bulletin,* Vol. 15, No. 9, September 1979, pp. 679–691. A useful discussion of the events leading up to the shift in policy procedures and a description of the new procedures is in Richard W. Lang, "The FOMC in 1979: Introducing Reserve Targeting," *Federal Reserve Bank of St. Louis Review,* Vol. 62, No. 3, March 1980, pp. 2–25. Targeting monetary growth is now an exercise engaged in by central banks in England, Germany, Japan, and elsewhere.

Say's Principle and Monetary Equilibrium

O U T L I N E

Demand, Supply, and the Concept of Market Equilibrium: A Review
Demand and Supply
Market Equilibrium
Say's Principle
Say's Principle Illustrated at the Individual Transactor Level
Say's Principle at the Aggregate Level
Some Implications of the Aggregate Version of Say's Principle
Monetary Equilibrium and Disequilibrium
Monetary Equilibrium: Individual and Aggregate
Monetary Equilibrium and Equilibrium in the Market for Nonmonetary Goods and Services
Income Equilibrium and Monetary Equilibrium
Money Income
Say's Principle and Equilibrium Money Income
Equilibrium Income and Full Employment

This chapter is an introduction to monetary theory. It introduces and discusses the connection between two important ideas: monetary equilibrium and Say's Principle. Monetary equilibrium occurs when the total or aggregate demand for money by people in the economy equals the existing stock of money made available by the joint actions of the Federal Reserve and the banking system. Realization of monetary equilibrium requires the presence of forces that also produce an equilibrium between the aggregate supply and aggregate demand for goods and services in the economy. Forces that disturb the equilibrium between the demand for and stock of money can also disturb the equilibrium between the aggregate demand for and supply of goods and services. We will discuss these forces in detail in Chapters 13, 14, 15, and 16.

Say's Principle is the essential idea that connects monetary equilibrium or disequilibrium with equilibrium or disequilibrium in the markets for goods and services. As such, it helps to show how monetary impulses or shocks work their way through the economy to impose changes in money prices or the level of output and employment. For that reason, it is a most important idea for the understanding of business cycles and the problem of inflation, subjects that will occupy much of the remainder of this book.

11.1
Demand, supply, and the concept
of market equilibrium: a review

This section contains a review of the concepts of market demand, market supply, and market equilibrium. Readers with a good foundation in these subjects may wish to pass on immediately to the next section on Say's Principle. If you believe your grasp of these concepts is weak, you should read this section, since the material in the balance of the chapter will have little meaning if you don't understand it.

11.1.1
Demand and supply

Demand and supply are terms that have reference to an exchange economy. An exchange economy is one in which people specializing in the production of goods or services satisfy their wants by selling the results of their efforts for goods or services produced by others. The demand for any particular good has two aspects: (1) the wish for the good by one or many buyers and (2) an offer or offers of equivalents in exchange. In a barter economy, the equivalents come in the form of other goods or services. In a money economy, the equivalents take the form of units of the medium of exchange.

Looked at in this way, the supply of any good or service is simply the reciprocal of the demand for other goods, including money. Sellers desiring goods owned or produced by others offer to exchange various amounts of their own goods for money or for the goods of others. Thus, given the motive to exchange, every expression of market supply must be accompanied by an offer to buy.

Economists formalize the notions of demand and supply with *schedules* representing the various quantities of goods or services that traders plan to buy or sell at different market prices. Figure 11.1 illustrates this idea with a demand schedule for bread, showing the amount of bread buyers would plan to buy at various prices. The demand curve slopes downward, in obedience to the *law of demand*, the famous principle that states that the cheaper a good, the more of it people will plan to buy. A good becomes cheaper as it falls in price relative to the prices of other goods a buyer might wish to buy instead. Hence, the price of bread, shown on the vertical axis of the figure, should be considered a *relative price*; as it goes up or down, the implicit assumption is that the prices of all other goods are being held constant.

The amount of a good supplied to the market also depends on the prevailing market price. The higher the relative price of bread, for example, the more incentive bakers have to produce, and the more bread they bring to the market. The upward sloping curve in Figure 11.1 illustrates this principle.

Each point on a demand or supply curve reflects the *planned behavior* of buyers or sellers. For example, when faced with the prevailing market price p_2, buyers plan to purchase Q_1 loaves of bread; sellers plan to sell Q_3 loaves. At a lower market price, say p_1, buyers increase planned purchases to Q_4 and sellers reduce planned sales to Q_2.

So, as the prevailing market price varies, so too do the planned market responses of buyers and sellers. The responses are made after traders

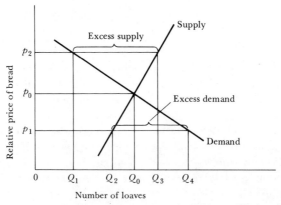

Figure 11.1 *Supply, demand, and market equilibrium for bread.*

have consulted their resources and opportunities and have come to conclusions about the best courses of action to follow. Each time the market price changes, opportunities facing different traders either improve or deteriorate, depending upon whether the price has gone up or down, and upon whether the trader is a buyer or seller. Supply and demand curve diagrams are simple devices designed to show expected reactions of traders faced with different market prices.

Excess supply and *excess demand* are terms that summarize the net result of planned sales and purchases by market participants. When the prevailing price of a good brings forth an excess of planned sales over planned purchases, an excess supply of the good exists. In Figure 11.1, an excess supply of bread equal to $Q_3 - Q_1$ is the market response to a price of p_2. An excess demand emerges when planned purchases exceed planned sales at a given price—for example, $Q_4 - Q_2$ at price p_1. (Sometimes economists refer to a condition of excess supply as a negative excess demand.) The excess demand for a good is zero when the market price is such that planned purchases and planned sales are equal, as at p_0 in Figure 11.1. At that price, buyers and sellers plan to buy or sell the same quantity of the good, Q_0.

11.1.2
Market equilibrium

Market equilibrium is a situation in which the prevailing price of a good brings the supply and demand for the good into equality. In Figure 11.1, p_0 is the price that produces an equilibrium level of trade, Q_0. In such a situation, the excess demand for the good is zero—traders' planned purchases and planned sales of the good are equal. But there are other, less mechanical meanings to the equilibrium concept.

In making their plans, market participants must take into account the expected price of the product, the prices of other products, and general economic conditions. In competitive markets, such as the one depicted in Figure 11.1, traders have no control over these conditions; they control only their own resources. In attempting to carry out their planned purchases or sales, they may discover that market conditions have unexpectedly changed or that for some reason they have not properly assessed market opportunities. When that happens, transactions that actually occur at prevailing prices will reflect only partial fulfillment of planned purchases or sales.

Viewing the problem in this way gives us an important behavioral interpretation of market equilibrium. A market is in equilibrium when traders' actual purchases and sales of a product equal their planned purchases and sales at the prevailing market price. It is a situation in which the expectations of both buyers and sellers concerning the conditions in the market have been realized. As a result, no trader is disappointed; each has made his or her plans, and each has successfully carried them out. Assuming no change in tastes, preferences, resources, or expectations, the equilibrium will continue, since market participants will have no motives to change their plans.

The concept of market disequilibrium immediately follows from the behavioral interpretation of equilibrium. Disequilibrium occurs when the plans of one or more market participants are unfulfilled—when one or more traders are disappointed. For example, when the prevailing price (p_2 in Figure 11.1) brings forth an excess supply of a good ($Q_3 - Q_1$), one or more producers have clearly miscalculated the chance of selling all the goods brought to the market. Buyers will take only a fraction of the quantity offered for sale; the rest must either be stored in unsold stocks, or if perishable, be thrown away. Another option is to mark down the price to recover at least part of the cost of production. Persistence of an excess supply condition eventually teaches suppliers to mark down prices of new production, in which case some high cost producers must withdraw from the market because the lower price does not cover their marginal costs.

A market condition of excess demand has opposite effects. At the prevailing price (p_1 in Figure 11.1) sellers cannot cover the cost of providing all (Q_4) of the good demanded by buyers. The latter are disappointed; they cannot buy all they would like at the prevailing price. Producers must have higher prices before they are willing to undertake additional production at the higher marginal cost. Assuming that market conditions remain stable, output and prices will eventually rise, diminishing the gap between planned purchases and sales.

Thus market price is an important device for coordinating the plans of buyers and sellers. Variations in the price lead traders to expand or contract their purchases and sales in the direction of market equilibrium. The equilibrium is characterized by (1) equality between planned and realized purchases and sales of the good and (2) the absence of disappointed expectations on the part of buyers and sellers, which is an implication of (1). If for some reason (say government controls) market prices cannot adjust to the pressures generated by an excess demand or supply condition, the market will fail to coordinate the plans of buyers and sellers. The result will either be the accumulation of surpluses by sellers (when price is fixed above its equilibrium level) or the presence of shortages (when price is set below the equilibrium level). Persistent surpluses or shortages are sure signs of lack of market coordination.

Temporary surpluses and shortages can emerge when market conditions unexpectedly change. For example, an unexpected increase in the money supply that puts more cash into the hands of bread buyers may shift the demand curve for bread to the right. If so, p_0 and Q_0 can no longer describe the equilibrium price and quantity in the bread market. Although the shift of the curve is not shown in Figure 11.1, it is easy to imagine that the initial effect of the increase in demand is to create an excess demand at p_0. Bread buyers, with their new found extra wealth, will at first be unable to satisfy their planned expansion of bread consumption. But rising price will eventually encourage more production, in which case the price and quantity of bread bought and sold will eventually rise to higher equilibrium levels.

11.2
Say's Principle

The above dissertation on supply, demand, and market equilibrium was a necessary prelude to a discussion of Say's Principle. This principle permits us to go beyond the treatment of a single market to show the logical links between all markets. Analysis of these linkages is essential to an understanding of monetary theory. Say's Principle is a relatively simple, straightforward idea. It represents but a minor extension of the concepts used in analyzing the economics of a single market. Moreover, it gives us a basis for a consistent analysis of most of the important issues that arise in connection with the effects of changes in the money supply on the overall performance of the economy.[1]

11.2.1
Say's Principle illustrated at the individual transactor level

Say's Principle has reference to an exchange economy. In such an economy any individual trader must purchase a good by giving up an equivalent good in exchange. In a money economy, the usual equivalent is the medium of exchange. In a barter economy, the equivalent is some other good or set of goods. But, in either case, *the individual trader must plan his exchanges in such a manner that the net value of all his planned trades is zero.* This is what is meant by Say's Principle.

Stated in more familiar terms, Say's Principle says no more than that at the time transactors are planning to purchase a set of goods, they must at the same time be planning to acquire the means to pay for the goods. A transactor's budgetary plan must simultaneously consider his sources as well as his uses of funds.

The implications of Say's Principle are best developed with a modest reformulation of this point. Suppose that there *n* different marketable goods in the economy, including the medium of exchange. Although no

---

[1]The material that follows owes much to the treatment given Say's Principle in Robert W. Clower and Axel Leijonhufvud, "Say's Principle, What it Means and What it Doesn't Mean," *Intermountain Economic Review*, 1974, pp. 1–16. A lucid exposition of the idea is found in Charles W. Baird and Alexander E. Cassuto, *Macroeconomics*, 2nd edition (Chicago: Science Research Associate, 1981), Chapter 3. Say's Principle is a variation and extension of the classical idea, Say's Law, discussed in Section 1.2 of this book.

individual could possibly buy or sell all of these goods (there are millions in the real world), it is convenient to describe each trader's budget constraint as follows:

$$p_1 d_1 + p_2 d_2 + \cdots + p_n d_n = p_1 s_1 + p_2 s_2 + \cdots + p_n s_n \qquad (11.1)$$

where p represents the money prices of a good, d is the quantity demanded, s is the quantity supplied and the numbers 1 through n identify each good. It is also convenient to let the nth good be the medium of exchange. (Since a dollar always exchanges for a dollar, we can immediately say that $p_n = 1$.)

The left-hand side of Equation (11.1) is the sum of the money values of all planned acquisitions of goods. It represents the dollar value of the goods, including money holdings, that the individual trader plans to acquire if he succeeds in carrying out his plans. Of course, in order to succeed, he must also succeed in carrying out his planned sales.

Now, subtract the right-hand side of Equation (11.1) from both sides of the equation. With a little manipulation it will read

$$p_1(d_1 - s_1) + p_2(d_1 - s_2) + \cdots + p_n(d_n - s_n) = 0 \qquad (11.2)$$

Each term $(d - s)$ is an individual trader's excess demand for a good. And, since the market value of each excess demand term is $p(d-s)$, we can infer from Equation (11.2) that the total market value of his excess demands must equal zero. Of course, d and s are automatically zero for goods the transactor plans neither to buy nor to sell. But if some of the $(d - s)$ terms are positive, that must mean that others are negative—in other words, that the individual has an excess supply of some goods in order to exert an excess demand for others. For many goods this will be automatically true, since in an exchange economy with specialization of labor most individuals buy a much larger variety of goods than they sell. But even for individuals with many different productive skills, market exchange requires a balancing of excess demands for goods with an equal and offsetting market excess supply of some other good or goods. If their planned sales of nonmonetary goods are insufficient to purchase all the goods they want, then they must plan to give up some of their money holdings in order to balance their expected outlays.

Equation (11.1) is no more than a symbolic expression of Say's Principle that the net value of all planned trades of an individual transactor must equal zero. Yet it permits us to make two further points. The first is that any economic good planned for purchase or sale in a market must be included in the transactor's budget constraint. Thus a d or an s can stand for a tangible commodity, a service, a unit of money, or a bond. We shall make use of this characteristic of Say's Principle in Chapter 13, when we develop the theory of interest.

The second point is that when an individual transactor plans to spend less than his planned receipts on nonmonetary goods or services, he is evidently planning to accumulate money holdings. Conversely, when he plans to spend more than his planned receipts, he is planning to reduce his money holdings. Thus d_n represents an individual's planned increase of cash assets, and s_n represents a planned reduction of cash assets. Moreover, since an individual cannot at the same time plan both to increase or decrease money holdings during the same period, s_n must be zero when d_n is positive, and d_n must be zero when s_n is positive.

11.2.2
Say's Principle at the aggregate level

Say's Principle also holds for the planned trades of all transactors. That is, the net value of all planned trades of all transactors, taken together, must equal zero. This being true, we can also say that in an exchange economy the sum of the market values of all excess demands for non-monetary goods and money must equal zero. Our task in this section is to prove this proposition.

To do so, we write out the budgetary plan of all traders in the economy. With k different traders exchanging n different goods, including money, we can list a series of excess demand equations as shown in Table 11.1. The sum of the net values of planned trades of each individual transactor is displayed in each row of Table 11.1. The sum of the market values of the excess demand for each good is shown in each column.

Although each row must sum to zero, the same need not be true for each column. After all, the sum of each column is the aggregate market value of the excess demand for each good.

The market value of the excess demand for any good is zero only if the total of all transactor demands (D) for the good equals the total of all transactor supplies (S) of the good. In that event the market in question

Table 11.1 *Derivation of the Aggregate Version of Say's Principle*

Transactor	Good 1	Good 2		Good n (money)
1	$p_1 (d_1 - s_1)_1$ +	$p_2 (d_2 - s_2)_1$	$+ \cdots +$	$(d_n - s_n)_1 = 0$
2	$p_1 (d_1 - s_1)_2$ +	$p_2 (d_2 - s_2)_2$	$+ \cdots +$	$(d_n - s_n)_2 = 0$
$\vdots$	$\vdots$	$\vdots$		$\vdots$
k	$p_1 (d_1 - s_1)_k$ +	$p_2 (d_2 - s_2)_k$	$+ \cdots +$	$(d_n - s_n)_k = 0$
Market excess demands	$p_1 (D_1 - S_1)$ +	$p_2 (D_2 - S_2)$	$+ \cdots +$	$(D_n - S_n) = 0$

is in equilibrium. But, as discussed earlier, equilibrium in any market is an unusual event; it occurs only when the planned and realized transactions of buyers and sellers are equal.

Even if zero excess demand in individual markets is an unusual event, it still remains that the aggregate value of the excess demand for all goods taken together must equal zero. For example, if the aggregate value of the excess demands for goods $1, 2, 3, \ldots, 1,000$ is positive, then the aggregate value of the excess demands for goods $1,001$, $1,002$, $1,003, \ldots, n$ must be negative and of equal value to the goods in excess demand. If the first 1,000 goods are farm goods, then the excess demand for farm goods must be accompanied by an aggregate excess supply of nonfarm goods or money. Similarly, if the first 1,000 items are the different types of labor services, then the excess demand for labor must be accompanied by an excess supply of nonlabor items or money. Finally, if the first $n - 1$ goods are nonmonetary goods and services, then the excess demand for these items must be offset by an excess supply of the nth good—money. In other words, the proposition that the market value of the aggregate excess demand for goods must sum to zero holds for any combination of goods, services, or money.

11.2.3
Some implications of the aggregate version of Say's Principle

What we just enunciated is Say's Principle at the aggregate level; that is, that the sum of the market values of planned market excess demands over all exchangeable goods must equal zero. This proposition, which amounts to little more than a truism, is the foundation of all monetary theory. But before we discuss its connection with monetary theory, we must, in the words of Clower and Leijonhufvud (footnote 1) say something about "what it means and what it doesn't mean."

First, Say's Principle does not imply equilibrium in each and every market. Equilibrium in every market implies that the price of each good is such that traders in each market plan to buy and sell the same amount of the good. Economists call such a situation *general equilibrium*. Although general equilibrium is consistent with Say's Principle, general equilibrium is neither necessary nor sufficient for the principle to be correct. Say's Principle holds no matter what prices prevail in the various markets. However, it does require that if some prices exceed the levels necessary for equilibrium in some of the markets, then prices in some of the rest of the markets must be below the levels required for equilibrium. In that way, the excess supplies of goods produced by above-equilibrium prices will be offset by the excess demands created by below-equilibrium prices.

Second, Say's Principle does not imply inevitability of movement of markets toward general equilibrium. Although absence of general equilibrium implies widespread disappointments by traders regarding realization of planned sales or purchases, it is not an implication of Say's Principle that prices in the various markets will move in the direction of an equilibrium set. To be sure, economists frequently assume that, in the absence of changes in tastes, production opportunities, and other factors, such a movement will in fact occur (above-equilibrium prices will fall and below-equilibrium prices will rise). But that assumption is based upon a separate set of propositions concerning the ways in which traders seek out and exploit market information. These propositions, and their validity, are independent of Say's Principle.

Third, since Say's Principle is only about *planned* excess demands, it says nothing about *effective or actual demands*. Effective or actual demands cannot be exercised without purchasing power. Transactors may fail to complete their planned purchases of some goods because, for reasons beyond their control, they have failed to bring off their planned sales of some goods. When that happens, their actual or effective excess demand for the goods may fall short of their planned excess demands, particularly if their purchasing power is limited to receipts from items from planned sales.

Fourth, although Say's Principle is derived from Say's Law, it has only limited application to the idea, frequently attributed to Say's Law, that "supply creates its own demand." Say's Principle simply states that in planning to sell a good an individual trader in an exchange economy must necessarily be planning to acquire another good, where goods are defined to include commodities, services, bonds, and the medium of exchange. But Say's Principle (and, to tell the truth, Say's Law) was never meant to imply that the act of offering a particular good simultaneously creates a demand for the same good. Nor was it ever meant to imply (as Say's Law did not imply) that planned supplies of goods necessarily result in the actual purchases of other goods. After all, it takes more than a plan for an act to be carried out. If traders cannot fulfill their planned sales, they cannot realize their planned purchases.

11.3
Monetary equilibrium and disequilibrium

Say's Principle has an important implication for a money economy. In a barter economy, exchange is direct; "goods buy goods." But in a money economy, exchange is indirect; traders sell goods for money and use the money so acquired to buy other goods. Hence, if traders hold instead of spend the money they acquire, the money value of their current nonmonetary goods purchases falls short of the money value of their current nonmonetary goods sales, and the excess demands for at least some of the goods in the economy turn negative. If sellers of these nonmonetary goods are surprised by the turn of events, they will find themselves either accumulating surplus inventories of unsold goods or being forced to drop prices below the ones anticipated when making plans to produce the goods they are offering to the market. In addition, failing to carry out their planned sales at expected prices, they will be forced to reduce their own effective demand for goods and services, thus compounding the problem of excess supplies of nonmonetary goods or services throughout the economy.

The desire to hold instead of spend money is an aspect of the demand for money. Economists define the demand for money as the desire at any moment of transactors to hold a certain number of dollars. The supply or stock of money is the number of dollars made available at the same point in time by the monetary authorities and the banking system. As the above paragraph states, the effect of a change in the desire to hold instead of to spend money may induce a downturn in the output or prices of nonmonetary goods or services. The main contention of this section will be that an economy-wide excess demand for money creates an aggregate excess supply of nonmonetary goods and services, and that an aggregate excess supply of money creates an aggregate excess demand for nonmonetary goods and services. Since an economy usually slumps when nonmonetary goods and services are in excess supply, and booms when the excess demand for goods and services is positive, the implication of the contention is that monetary disequilibrium is a source of fluctuations in the economy as a whole.

This implication will receive increasing emphasis throughout the rest of this book. In the meantime, however, we must give a more detailed discussion of concepts of monetary equilibrium and their connection with equilibrium and disequilibrium in the market for nonmonetary goods and services.

11.3.1
Monetary equilibrium: individual and aggregate

We begin discussion of monetary equilibrium by defining the excess supply or demand for money at the level of the individual transactor. The last term in each row of Table 11.1 shows the planned increases (d_n) or decreases (s_n) of money holdings by each transactor in the economy. Planned increases of money holdings imply that transactors want to hold more dollars than they already possess; planned decreases imply that they desire to hold fewer dollars than they own.

These definitions allow us to define for each transactor the excess demand for money. In studying the definition, recall that an excess supply of money is nothing more than a negative excess demand. So, letting M_i^d be the ith transactor's demand for money, and M_i^s the actual stock of balances on hand when he makes his plans, we have

$$M_i^d - M_i^s = d_{ni} \qquad (11.3)$$

When the individual's demand is greater than his cash holdings, d_{ni} is positive, and negative $(=s_{ni})$ when his demand for money is less than his holdings. Moving to the level of the aggregate demand for and supply of money (M^d and M^s) and the aggregate *excess demands* for and supplies of money we simply sum the terms, so that the aggregates for all (k) individuals are

$$M^d = M_1^d + M_2^d + \cdots + M_k^d \qquad (11.4)$$

$$M^s = M_1^s + M_2^s + \cdots + M_k^s \qquad (11.5)$$

$$D_n - S_n = (d_{n1} - s_{n1}) + (d_{n2} - s_{n2}) + \cdots + (d_{nk} - s_{nk}) \qquad (11.6)$$

In studying Equation (11.6) it is important to recall that s_{ni} is zero for transactors with a positive d_{ni} and positive for transactors with a zero d_{ni}, because no individual can both accumulate and reduce money holdings at the same time.

The relationship between demand for and supply of money in the aggregate and planned increases or decreases in money holdings is illustrated in Table 11.2 for an economy with three traders. As is evident from Table 11.2, there is an intimate relationship between the aggregate excess demand and supply of money and attempts of various transactors to accumulate or dispose of cash. The relationship is given by

$$M^d - M^s = D_n - S_n \qquad (11.7)$$

Equation (11.7) clearly defines the aggregate excess demand for money ($M^d - M^s$) as the net value of the aggregate planned accumulations of money ($D_n - S_n$). This aggregate difference can be positive, negative, or zero, depending on whether and how much different traders are planning to hold, add to, or subtract from their existing cash balances. Total existing balances are determined by the policies of the monetary authorities. The aggregate excess demand for money is positive if trans-

Table 11.2 *Relation between the Excess Demand (Supply) of Money and Planned Increases or Decreases in Money Holdings*

Transactor	M_i^d	$-$	M_i^s	$=$	d_{ni} (or s_{ni})
1	$1,100	$-$	$1,000	$=$	$100
2	2,200	$-$	2,400	$=$	$-$ 200
3	1,000	$-$	1,000	$=$	0
Aggregate (sum of rows)	$4,300	$-$	$4,400	$=$	$-$$100
	(M^d)	$-$	(M^s)	$=$	($D_n - S_n$)

actors on balance are trying to acquire more cash; if it is negative, they are trying on balance to get rid of cash. A zero excess demand for cash implies that, taken together, transactors do not wish to change their cash balances.

Monetary equilibrium is a situation in which the aggregate excess demand for money is zero. Such a situation arises in two ways: (1) when each transactor possesses the cash he or she wants to hold and (2) when planned cash accumulations among one set of transactors is offset by equal planned reductions in cash holdings by other transactors in the economy. The first case is clearly an unusual one; monetary equilibrium, if it should ever occur, is more likely to come about in the second way.

Monetary equilibrium cannot come about unless people actually realize their plans. For that reason, equality between planned additions and reductions of cash holdings by various transactors is insufficient to define a condition of aggregate monetary equilibrium. Individual transactors must be able successfully to carry out their planned changes in money balances. If they cannot, they will be forced to change their plans during the next period, in which case they will upset the previous equality between the aggregate demand for and existing stock of money. Thus, when later in this chapter and book we relate the idea of monetary equilibrium to a zero aggregate excess demand for money, we must remember that we are dealing with only one condition for equilibrium; the other is that, on the whole, people must achieve their planned changes in money balances.

11.3.2
Monetary equilibrium and equilibrium in the market for nonmonetary goods and services

An implication of aggregate monetary equilibrium is that it is accompanied by a particular kind of equilibrium in the market for nonmonetary goods and services. This point is easily understood if we reproduce the equation on the bottom of Table 11.1, and substitute from Equation (11.7):

$$p_1(D_1 - S_1) + p_2(D_2 - S_2) + \cdots + p_{n-1}(D_{n-1} - S_{n-1}) = S_n - D_n \quad (11.8)$$

or, since, by Equation (11.7), $S_n - D_n = M^s - M^d$, we get

$$p_1(D_1 - S_1) + p_2(D_2 - S_2) + \cdots + p_{n-1}(D_{n-1} - S_{n-1}) = M^s - M^d \quad (11.9)$$

This equation, derived from Say's Principle, tells us that the presence of aggregate excess demand for nonmonetary goods and services (left-hand side) requires the presence of an aggregate excess supply of money. Conversely, the presence of an aggregate excess supply of nonmonetary goods and services must be accompanied by an aggregate excess demand for money.

Do not underestimate the importance of Equation (11.9). It provides the theoretical underpinning for economists who believe that the ups and downs of business activity over the business cycle are primarily motivated by overall changes of excess demand and excess supply of goods and services. If this is so, the equation tells us that underlying such changes are monetary forces. These forces take the shape of changes in the supply of money, motivated by the policies of the monetary authorities, or changes in the demand for money, determined primarily by the behavior of private transactors who, in the aggregate, attempt to make changes in their desired money holdings.

Equation (11.9) also informs us of the consequences of monetary equilibrium. When planned and realized aggregate holdings of money are equal, the aggregate net value of planned trades by transactors is equal to zero. A zero net value of planned trades implies either general equilibrium, or that disappointments by transactors underrealizing their plans are offset by the good luck of other transactors more than realizing their plans. Thus, disappointments by some are accompanied by pleasant surprises by others; on balance, transactors are neither pleased nor sorry at the results of their plans. When this happens, we say that aggregate equilibrium exists in the market for nonmonetary goods and services. Since not every market is necessarily in equilibrium, the aggregate equilibrium is not necessarily a general equilibrium; nonetheless, it is not a situation that, on balance, is likely to lead to a generalized surge of prices or production in one direction or another. In that sense, we can say that it is neutral respecting the business cycle. That is, when monetary equilibrium brings forth an aggregative equilibrium, the economy is unlikely either to boom or slump.

11.4
Income equilibrium and monetary equilibrium

We must now connect the ideas of Say's Principle and of monetary and aggregate equilibrium with the concept of equilibrium money income. The discussion will place us in a position to develop the quantity theory of money.

11.4.1
Money income

Monetary theory is a branch of macroeconomic theory. A central notion in macroeconomic theory is (aggregate) money income. Gross national product is a familiar measure of money income. So is national income, which is gross national product adjusted for depreciation of the aggregate capital stock and indirect (sales and excise) taxes. In this book we shall use both terms.

People receive income in the form of transfers and earnings. Transfers are unilateral payments from one person to another, often through the agency of government—social security pensions are examples. Thus transfers do not emerge from an exchange relationship; the people who get them do not work for them, and they give nothing in return for them.

Income arising from earnings is different. People earn income when they work, lend money at interest, or rent property. The money receipts they or their employers obtain from the use of their labor or property provide the money payments that constitute their earnings.

Thus, a nation's money income arises from earnings founded upon productive activity. Transfer incomes, which do not arise from earnings, do not count in the income total. As a result, the value of a nation's production may be measured by the money income of its residents. Gross national product, for example, is measured by gross business profits (before depreciation and indirect taxes) plus wage and salary income, rental income, and interest income. National product is measured by national income before payment of income taxes.

In measuring national product, it is important to avoid double counting. For example, an automobile sold by a manufacturer to a household is fabricated from a variety of raw and semifinished materials and parts bought by the manufacturer from other firms. Thus the sales price of the automobile reflects these inputs, as well as the inputs of the firm's own resources and of its employees. If we include in national product the value of the output of the other firms, we should exclude it from the earnings of the automobile company when counting its production as part of national product. That is, we should consider the company's contribution to be the *value added* by its own production. A similar statement holds for every firm doing business in the country.

Thus, national product is the sum of all the values added by each producer in the economy. Although value added by production can be measured by the income earned by employees and by owners of the capital employed in each firm in the economy, it can also be found by calculating the money value of all *final goods and services* produced within a period of time. Final goods and services are products sold to *final buyers*. Final buyers either consume or hold these products without using them currently to produce goods and services to be sold to other buyers. They include consumer goods and services, physical capital goods, and unsold inventories, finished goods, and raw materials held by firms. The prices of final goods reflect the income payments made to their own fabricators plus the incomes earned by the employees and property owners of all firms producing the raw and semifinished materials and parts that enter into their production. For that reason, the total value of the final goods and services sold in a year is identical to the value added by production of all producers, and each is identical to national money income.

Final buyers of final products consist of (1) households, (2) business firms, and (3) government. Foreigners also purchase final products, but we shall for the present ignore them. Final products demanded by households is *consumption demand* (*C*), by business is *investment demand* (*I*), and by government is *government demand* (*G*). If we add these three sources of demand together, we get total planned expenditure on final product, Y^d. That is,

$$C + I + G = Y^d \qquad (11.10)$$

11.4.2
Say's Principle and equilibrium money income

We can now move from the discussion of Say's Principle to its application in macroeconomic theory. It is customary to confine introductory treatments of that theory to markets in final goods and services and to the supply and demand for money. Following that tradition, we shall define all planned outlays on nonmonetary commodities to be outlays on final goods and services. Similarly, we shall treat all planned sales of goods and services as if they were sales of final products.

Now, we rewrite Equation (11.9) as follows. Let each *D* in that equation refer to planned purchases of a final product and each *S* refer to planned sales of a final product. The value of demand for each final good is $p \times D$: the value of supply is $p \times S$. Thus, if we sum the values of demand and supply of all final goods we get

$$p_1 D_1 + p_2 D_2 + \cdots + p_{n-1} D_{n-1} = Y^d$$
$$p_1 S_1 + p_2 S_2 + \cdots + p_{n-1} S_{n-1} = Y^s$$

From this it follows that

$$p_1(D_1 - S_1) + p_2(D_2 - S_2) + \cdots + p_{n-1}(D_{n-1} - S_{n-1}) = Y^d - Y^s$$

This equation, in combination with Equations (11.9) and (11.10) gives us the following:

$$Y^d - Y^s = M^s - M^d \gtreqless 0 \qquad (11.11)$$

or

$$C + I + G - Y^s = M^s - M^d \gtreqless 0 \qquad (11.12)$$

Equation (11.11) and its counterpart (11.12) state that the excess nominal demand for final goods and services by households, business, and government must be matched by an identical excess supply of money. Conversely, an excess nominal supply of final products—that is, plans to produce and sell more than people plan to buy—must be associated with an equal excess demand for money.

And what of equilibrium? Equality does not imply equilibrium. Nevertheless, our algebra does tell us this: If both planned (demanded) and realized holdings of money balances are equal in the aggregate, there will be aggregative monetary equilibrium. And, as Equations (11.11) and (11.12) show, the same thing will be true of income. Equality between planned and realized aggregate money holdings will force an equality between the aggregate value of planned and realized purchases and sales of final goods and services. That being the case, there will be aggregative *money income equilibrium.* This equilibrium, which is similar to the aggregative equilibrium discussed in Section 11.3.2, will last as long as the aggregate monetary equilibrium lasts.

11.5
Equilibrium income and full
employment

General equilibrium implies a state of full employment for the economy. That is because planned and realized transactions are equal in each and every market, including the labor market. The structure of wages and prices are such that both product and labor markets clear with zero excess demand or supply in all markets. Thus there are no pleasant or unpleasant surprises. Both workers and employers are getting what they planned and bargained for.

In the unlikely event that it would occur, general equilibrium would not guarantee wealth and well-being for everyone. Moreover, it is subject to change when there are changes in tastes and preferences in technology or in the state of nature. Even so, if the economy is flexible, if there is enough competition in labor and product markets, a disrupted general equilibrium could settle into a new one if enough time were allowed to elapse before new changes arise in tastes, technology, or nature.

But neither people nor nature permit an economy to settle into a state of general equilibrium. People frequently alter their plans in response to new information, shifts in their tastes and preferences, changes in the weather, political events, and so forth. Changed plans shift demand and supply curves in the various markets. Excess demands emerge in some markets, excess supplies in others. In some industries firms fail to sell all they produce; in others production falls short of sales. In the former, unplanned and undesired stocks of unsold goods (inventories) accumulate; in others stocks fall below planned levels. As a result, some employers deplete cash balances because they receive too little money from sales to cover payments to workers and suppliers, while other employers unexpectedly accumulate cash balances because they sell more products than they produce. Unsuccessful firms lay off workers, while successful firms hire additional ones.

If the economy is in a state of aggregative income equilibrium, the stocks of goods accumulating in the warehouses of firms not realizing planned sales are offset by the running down of inventories in firms selling more than they had planned. Even so, workers laid off by unsuccessful firms are not necessarily hired by successful firms. The laid off workers may not have the right set of skills, they may live in the wrong part of the country, or their wage demands may be too high. In addition, successful firms may be cautiously awaiting further signs that their good fortune is permanent; they may not wish to commit themselves to an expanded work force.

Thus constantly shifting demands and supplies of goods and services plus sluggish responses of workers and employers to new situations may prevent adaptation of the labor force to new situations. In that event, there may also be present a certain amount of unemployment of labor during times in which money income is in equilibrium. Full employment, in the sense that at prevailing wage rates and prices employers in the aggregate are offering workers the jobs they want, is not a necessary accompaniment of income equilibrium.

SUMMARY

Inflation and fluctuations of money income frequently originate in differences between planned and realized aggregate supplies and demands for nonmonetary commodities. In a barter economy goods and services constitute the means of payment for other goods and services. Every increase or decrease in commodities offered for sale simultaneously increases or decreases the demand for other commodities. Thus, in a barter economy, excess aggregate demand or aggregate supply is an impossibility.

In a money economy, goods and services buy money, and money is used to buy goods and services. If people choose to hold sales proceeds in the form of money, a gap can open up between aggregate demand and aggregate supply. Similarly, aggregate demand may be financed with increases in the money supply or with reductions in existing cash balances, instead of with proceeds of current sales. Thus, the existence of money permits the emergence of an excess of planned aggregate supply or demand for nonmonetary commodities.

Equality between planned and realized supplies and demands signify equilibrium in the markets for money and for nonmonetary commodities. General equilibrium is characterized by equilibrium in every market. Aggregative equilibrium is characterized by equality between planned and realized *aggregate* demands and supplies—markets in which realized demand falls short of planned supplies are offset by markets in which realized demand is greater than planned supplies.

Say's Principle states that the net value of all planned trades must equal zero. Thus an excess demand for nonmonetary commodities must be accompanied by an excess supply of money, and an excess supply of nonmonetary commodities must be accompanied by an excess demand for money. Aggregative equilibrium implies a zero planned and realized excess aggregate demand for money.

Money income consists of the money earnings of workers and property owners. It equals value added by production as measured by the value of final products produced in an economy in a given period of time. Using money income as the central concept in macroeconomics, we can say that equilibrium money income implies equilibrium between the planned and realized aggregate demand and supply of money. Equilibrium income is an aggregative equilibrium. As such, it is unlike general equilibrium and does not imply full employment.

We are now ready to discuss the theory of money.

DISCUSSION QUESTIONS

1. What are the conditions for equilibrium in the market for a particular good?

2. Does Say's Principle imply that an individual trader is always in an equilibrium position respecting his purchase and sale of goods and services?

3. Does Say's Principle applied to the economy as a whole imply the inevitability of general equilibrium?

4. Why does the excess demand for or supply of money imply the presence of an excess aggregate supply of or demand for nonmonetary goods and services in the economy?

5. Does Say's Principle imply the absence of lending or borrowing?

6. Distinguish between aggregate equilibrium and general equilibrium.

IMPORTANT TERMS AND CONCEPTS

☐ aggregate income

☐ aggregate income equilibrium

☐ excess demand for (and supply of) a good

☐ general equilibrium

☐ market equilibrium

☐ monetary equilibrium

☐ Say's Principle

A somewhat more technical introductory treatment of Say's Law and Say's Principle is in Charles Baird, *Elements of Macroeconomics* (New York: West Publishing, 1977), Chapter 3. More advanced is Robert Clower and Axel Leijonhufvud, "Say's Principle: What It Means and Doesn't Mean: Part I," *Intermountain Economic Review,* 1974, pp. 1–16. An interesting and unusual discussion is in W. H. Hutt, *A Rehabilitation of Say's Law* (Athens, Ohio: Ohio University Press, 1974).

Money and the Theory of Money Income

O U T L I N E

The Quantity Theory of Money
The Fundamental Proposition of Monetary Theory
Nominal versus Real Money Balances
Elementary Theory of the Price Level
The Demand for Money
The Cambridge Equation
Interest Rates and the Transactions Demand for Money
Asset Demand for Money
Summary of Factors Affecting Demand for Money
A Monetary Theory of Money Income
Monetary Equilibrium and Income Equilibrium
Interpretation of Money Income Equilibrium
Changes in the Equilibrium Level of Income
The Equation of Exchange and the Theory of Money Income
The Keynesian Cross and the Monetary Theory of Income
The Importance of Interest Rates to the Theory of Income

It is frequently said that "inflation is caused by too much money chasing too few goods." It could also be stated that "deflation is caused by too little money chasing too many goods." Both statements contain elements of truth. But our discussion in Chapter 11 shows we can use more precise language. Inflation and booming economic conditions are usually accompanied by excess supplies of money; economic slumps, some of which in the past had deflation of prices, are usually associated with excess demands for money. Thus the element of truth in the statements is that excess demands for or supplies of nonmonetary goods and services are usually associated with excess supplies of or demands for money.

Since variations in prices and production are reflected in fluctuations in money income, changes in monetary conditions that disrupt prices and production disturb the level of money income. To explain these disturbances we must elaborate and connect a theory of money with a theory of money income. The purpose of this chapter is to do just that—to explain in some detail how the level and movements of the supply of and demand for money affect the level and movements of money income.

12.1
The quantity theory of money

The quantity theory of money was originally an explanation of the average price level of nonmonetary goods and services. In recent years, economists have broadened it to explain the level of national money income. In this section, we will concentrate upon the earlier usage. Later in the chapter we will convert the quantity theory of money into a monetary theory of income.

12.1.1
The fundamental proposition of monetary theory

Before discussing the quantity theory, we must lay down a proposition that monetary writers, including such diverse thinkers as J. M. Keynes and Milton Friedman, refer to as the *fundamental proposition of monetary theory*.[1] Friedman's version is as follows:

> Broadly speaking, the public as a whole cannot by itself affect the total number of dollars to be held—this is determined primarily by the monetary institutions. To each individual separately, it

---

[1] J. M. Keynes, *General Theory of Employment, Interest, and Money* (New York: Harcourt and Brace, 1936), pp. 84–86, and Milton Friedman, *The Optimum Quantity of Money and Other Essays* (Chicago: Aldine Publishing, 1969), p. 175. See also Leland B. Yeager, "Essential Properties of the Medium of Exchange," *Kyklos*, Vol. 21, No. 1, 1968, pp. 45–68.

appears that he can do so; in fact an individual can reduce or increase his cash balances in general only through another individual's increasing or reducing his. If individuals as a whole, for example, try to reduce the number of dollars they hold, they cannot as an aggregate do so. In trying to do so, however, they will raise the flow of expenditures and hence of money income and in this way will reduce the ratio of their cash balances to their income; since prices will tend to rise in the process, they will thereby reduce the real value of their cash balances, that is, the quantity of goods and services that the cash balance will command; and the process will continue until this ratio or real value is in accord with their desires.

Compare this with the similar conclusion of Keynes:

Thus incomes and such prices necessarily change until the aggregate of the amounts of money which individuals choose to hold at the new level of incomes and prices . . . has come into equality with the amount of money created by the banking system. This, indeed, is the fundamental proposition of monetary theory.

The world's most famous monetarist and its most famous Keynesian agree: If individuals are free to choose the amount of money they wish to hold, and if all they hold must add up to the total independently determined by the banking system and the authorities, then prices and money incomes must change until the aggregate amount of money people *wish to hold* equals the aggregate amount they *must hold*. Thus, prices and incomes change as people buy or sell nonmonetary commodities and services in an attempt to bring their money holdings into line with their desires. Once they have done so, their planned and realized money holdings are equal. In the language of Chapter 11, monetary equilibrium prevails. And, as implied by the statements of Keynes and Friedman, there is also an equilibrium level of money income. The key to the equilibrium is that the demand for money adjusts in response to changes in income and prices brought about by excess demands or supplies of money. Once these changes bring the demand for money into equality with the stock made available by the banking system and the monetary authorities, equilibrium of both money and money income is attained.

These matters will be further clarified in the rest of this chapter. But we must first discuss the differences between real and nominal money balances.

12.1.2
Nominal versus real money balances

The nominal money stock is simply the total number of units of money made available by the authorities and the banking system. For example, the nominal value of M-1B is the dollar value of currency in circulation and privately owned transaction accounts.

In contrast, *real cash (money) balances* are dollars adjusted for their purchasing power. The purchasing power of a single dollar is $1/P$, where P refers to some price index. A price index measures the average price of some bundle of nonmonetary commodities as a percentage of prices in some base year. An example is the consumer price index (CPI), which measures the changing cost of a fixed basket of consumer goods. In September 1979, the CPI in the United States stood at 200, meaning that the average price of the basket rose by 100 percent from 1967 to that date. As a result, the dollar in September 1979 could purchase only one-half of what it could purchase of that basket in 1967—i.e., $1/P = 1/2$.

Let uppercase M represent nominal money balances and lowercase m represent real money balances. The relationship between nominal and real cash balances is given by

$$M = mP \tag{12.1}$$

or

$$\frac{M}{P} = m \tag{12.2}$$

These formulas show that changes in nominal and real cash balances are not necessarily the same. Real balances do not change if changes in nominal balances are offset by equal percentage changes in the price level. Whether such offsets do or do not exist cannot be told from the formulas. To study how price levels change, we must study the basic postulates of the quantity theory.

12.1.3
Elementary theory of the price level

Let P be a price index that measures the average price of final goods and services included in money income. Interpreted in this manner, P is similar to what statisticians call the "implicit GNP deflator." For present purposes our language need not be that fancy. We can accomplish our task with a simple reference to the "price level."

The basic hypothesis of the quantity theory of money is that the price level is determined by an interaction between the supply of nominal money balances and the demand for real money balances. As we have said, the supply of nominal balances depends upon the policies of the monetary authorities and the banking system. But the demand for real cash balances depends upon the behavior of the public.

Expressing the demand for money in real terms is essential to the quantity theory. The older versions of the theory assumed that people want money only as a medium of exchange. If true, people are concerned with their money holdings only as they affect their ability to buy nonmonetary commodities. If it is their desire to buy a certain number and type of these commodities, then their demand for nominal balances will change in proportion to the price level of the commodities. Double the price level and you double the demand for nominal balances. Cut the price level in half, and you halve the demand for nominal balances. In other words, if demand for money as a medium of exchange is given by plans to buy a certain basket of goods, then the demand for real balances is given.

Let M^d be the demand for nominal balances and m^d be the demand for real balances. The connection between the two is given by

$$M^d = Pm^d \qquad (12.3)$$

As we have seen, monetary equilibrium requires equality between the supply (M^s) and demand for nominal cash balances. Using Equation (12.3) with this principle, we can write the following equations:

$$M^s = M^d \qquad \text{(equilibrium condition)} \qquad (12.4)$$

$$M^s = Pm^d \qquad \text{(restatement of equilibrium condition)} \qquad (12.5)$$

or

$$P = \frac{M^s}{m^d} \qquad \text{(quantity theory)} \qquad (12.6)$$

Equation (12.6) is exceedingly important. It says that the equilibrium price level is determined by the ratio of the nominal money supply, a variable determined by the authorities and the banking system, and the demand for real cash balances, a variable determined by the free choices of the nonbank private sector. Thus the price level is not something given to the economy. It is not determined by independent forces such as the oil cartel OPEC or by union and employer wage bargains. Instead, it depends upon the judgements and decisions of officials who operate the central bank and the private banking system and of each and every person who makes a decision to add to or subtract from his or her real cash balances. OPEC, unions, and other forces influence the price level only as they influence decisions affecting the supply of nominal money balances and the private sector's demand for real cash balances.

To see how the theory works imagine an *initial* situation in which $P > M^s/m^d$ and m^d is fixed. In this situation, the aggregate demand for nominal balances—$Pm^d = M^d$—exceeds the supply of nominal balances, M^s, as made available by the authorities and the banking system. What can people do? Assuming M^s and m^d are fixed, they have no other choice than to try to increase their money balances by reducing their demands for (or increasing their supplies of) nonmonetary commodities. In the process, they will create an excess supply of such commodities and drive down their prices. As this happens, the aggregate demand for nominal balances, Pm^d, will fall towards equality with the existing stock of nominal balances.

If, initially, $P<M^s/m^d$, there is an excess supply of nominal cash balances. The situation is then reversed. In attempting to reduce their money holdings, people will raise their demands for nonmonetary commodities and reduce their supplies. An excess aggregate demand for these commodities will appear, and prices will be driven up. As that happens, the demand for nominal money balances will rise towards equality with the existing stock of money.

$P=M^s/m^d$ describes an equilibrium price level because any other price level would set in motion forces to bring it back to the one described by the equation. Equally important, however, is that the variables M^s and m^d must, at least to some degree, be independent of the price level. If they are not, changes in the price level may alter their values so as to preclude equilibrium from ever appearing. In that event, we would be living in a world described by the commercial loan theory discussed in Section 10.2.2. Instead of determining the price level, the money supply would be determined by it. We would have no means of controlling either the rate of inflation or deflation. Monetary equilibrium and, as we shall see, money income equilibrium, would be impossible to attain.

The association between the nominal money supply and the price level is documented in Figure 12.1. The graph shows the rate of change of the implicit GNP consumption deflator is roughly tracked by a time series measuring the average rate of change of M-1B. Each point on the deflator line measures the rate of inflation for a given year. Each point on the M-1B line measures average money growth that took place during the previous eight quarters.

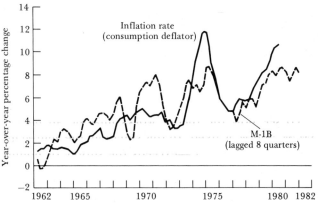

Figure 12.1 *Inflation and money (M-1B) growth rates, 1962–1980. (Source: Adrian W. Throop,* Money in the Economy *(Federal Reserve Bank of San Francisco, August 1980).)*

The failure of the eight-quarter lagged M-1B growth line to provide an exact tracking of the inflation rate is to be expected. M-1B and the consumption deflator are not perfect measures of the money supply and price level—perfect measures do not exist. Also, although it is reasonable to expect changes in the money growth rate to affect prices with a lag, the lag itself need not be constant over time. The duration of the lag depends heavily upon the speed with which people discover and spend excess money balances and upon inflationary expectations. If monetary increases raise inflationary expectations, the lag can shorten considerably over time. Finally, it must be recalled that the rate of inflation in 1972–1973 was artificially slowed down by price controls imposed by President Nixon in August of 1971 and temporarily speeded up in 1975 and 1979 by extraordinary increases in the price of oil, imposed by OPEC. These events and the deficiencies in our measures of money growth and inflation clearly disturbed the correlation between inflation and money growth as measured in Figure 12.1. Even so, the remaining correlation shows a remarkable consistency between the data and the elementary quantity theory.

12.2
The demand for money

Milton Friedman once remarked that the quantity theory is in the first instance a theory of the *demand* for money.[2] By that he meant that we cannot develop a quantity theory of prices or money income without first having a theory that explains why people hold money.

Much of the money supply is devoid of interest earnings or other forms of explicit return. People wishing to maximize their money incomes would hold all of their assets in interest bearing financial assets or in the form of real business capital goods. Their failure to do so implies that they prize the extra liquidity that money holdings impart to their balance sheet positions. How and why this desire for extra liquidity gives rise to a demand for money is the subject of this section.

12.2.1
The Cambridge equation

A widely held theory of the demand for money was developed by Alfred Marshall, A. C. Pigou, D. H. Robertson, J. M. Keynes (when young), and other members of what is known as the Cambridge (University) school of

---

[2]Milton Friedman, "The Quantity Theory of Money: A Restatement," *The Optimum Quantity of Money* (Chicago: Aldine, 1969), p. 52.

monetary theorists. That school of thought flourished from the late nine-teenth century to the early 1930s. Its ideas have since been absorbed into the modern Keynesian theory of money and the work of Freidman and other modern monetarists.

A notable and enduring idea of the Cambridge monetary theory is that money is an asset that yields utility to its holders. Most other quantity theorists had insisted that money has no inherent utility, that its value is derived solely from the value of goods and services it can buy. In con-trast, the Cambridge theorists asserted that money has value because of its superior liquidity. No other asset, they said, is universally acceptable in exchange for goods and services. Unlike other assets, money need not first be sold to be used in exchange for other goods. Moreover, it is easily stored and, compared to other goods, easy to protect against loss or dam-age. Thus the Cambridge writers said that the utility of money arises from the "convenience and security" it provides its holder.

A major motive for holding money is to bridge the gap between re-ceipt of income and planned expenditures—what Keynes later called the *transactions motive*. The Cambridge theorists thought it important to relate the demand for money to expected outlays on goods and services in the near future. The outlays may conveniently be indexed by a person's real income since the bulk of expenditures are financed out of income. From such considerations there grew up the well-known *Cambridge equation:*

$$m^d = ky \qquad (12.7)$$

where y is Y/P, real or constant dollar income—money income divided by the price index—and k is the *fraction* of income people wish to hold in the form of money. Thus, suppose real annual income is $12,000 per year paid in $1,000 monthly installments. If an individual receives income at the start of each month and spends it evenly over the month, her average daily holdings of real balances will be $500, which is 1/24 of the $12,000 annual real income. For this individual, $k = 1/24$. Another individual with the same annual real income, but paid every two months, would have an average daily holding of $1,000 and a $k = 1/12$. Using M-1B, in 1979 the Cambridge k in the United States was about .16, approximately 1/6.

The economy-wide k is a weighted average of the individual k's of all money holders. The weights are the proportion of total money balances held by each individual. The size of each k is determined in part by the frequency of income receipts of the various individuals. People paid weekly tend to carry smaller cash balances than people paid monthly, and people paid monthly usually hold less money than those paid bimonthly.

The economy-wide k is also affected by the level of transactions in intermediate goods and services—raw and semifinished materials that firms sell to each other, but not to final buyers—and in existing assets—houses, used cars, stocks, bonds, and so forth. Letting t be the measure of the real value of all transactions—final products, intermediate goods and services, and existing assets—the Cambridge k decomposes into the ratios of money to transactions and of transactions to real income:

$$k = \frac{m^d}{t} \frac{t}{y} \tag{12.8}$$

Thus, as t rises and falls in relation to y, so does the Cambridge k, provided the "transactions k"—m^d/t—does not change at the same time.

Another important institutional influence on k is the of degree vertical integration of industry. When a business buyer merges with one of its business suppliers, the transactions between the two units may no longer require money—only bookkeeping entries. Thus, an industrial trend that reduces the number of independent firms is a force that tends over time to lower k.

The Cambridge equation asserts a proportionality between the demand for real balances and the level of real income. Proportionality implies that a 10 percent increase in real income increases the demand for real cash balances by 10 percent. Theoretical and statistical studies indicate that strict proportionality between money demand and income may not hold. As individuals' wealth and income increase, some are prone to hold less money per unit of income. That is, apart from changes in the ratio of transactions to income and the merging of firms as economic growth takes place, there may also be significant economies of scale in cash holdings. The reason is that people and business firms with high incomes are positioned to hold transactions balances in the form of short-term interest bearing securities instead of in the form of money.

This brings us to the role of interest rates in money demand.

12.2.2
Interest rates and the transactions
demand for money

Although many people can and do hold transactions balances in the form of short-term securities or interest bearing deposits, many do not. Instead, they hold idle cash. Why?

One answer is that it may not be profitable to hold securities. The decision depends upon (a) the cost of transfering out of money into securities, then back, and (b) the interest earnings obtained from holding the securities. Items under (a) are frequently called *transactions costs*—the efforts expended in finding and arranging to buy and then resell securities, and the brokerage and other fees that might be necessary to arrange for the transactions. Interest earnings, (b), vary with the height of interest rates and the size and duration of the holdings. If there are lump sum transactions costs, there must be a certain minimum size and/or time duration of transactions balances before it is profitable to invest them. The higher the interest rate, the smaller is the minimum size and duration, and vice versa.

Thus, we would expect rich people and large business firms to keep to a minimum holdings of transactions balances in the form of money. After all, it is they who are best positioned to invest profitably their liquid assets in short-term bonds. Even so, as economic conditions change, we might expect others also to switch into securities. Included in these conditions are rising per capita incomes and expenditures, and rising interest rates.

Table 12.1 shows the drift of the Cambridge k in the United States during 1950–1979. Measured as the ratio between old M-1 and GNP, k_1 drifted steadily down for the whole period. Measured as the ratio between old M-2 and GNP, k_2 fell during the 1950s, but leveled off at about .40 from 1960 to 1979. The drop in k_1 was probably caused in part by economies of scale in transactions balances, but as shown by the time series of the Treasury bill rate, people may also have responded to the profit incentives provided by rising interest rates. The incentive was clearly less in the case of M-2, because after 1960, interest rates on bank time and savings deposits rose along with (but not always to the same extent as) market rates on Treasury bills and other short-term securities. Thus, to a large extent, people shifted out of M-1 into time and savings deposits, preventing k_2 from having a downward trend during the years after 1960.

The development of NOW accounts and other checking privileges at nonbank intermediaries, plus repurchase agreements, is a force that hastened the downward course of k_1 and caused it to resume its falling trend of the 1950s. Evidence in favor of this view is given by Figure 12.2, which shows a growing shortfall between the actual (old) M-1 money supply and the demand for money estimated econometrically from standard equations using pre-1975 data. The errors have almost a mirror image in the growing volume of new types of deposits and liquid nondeposit assets that are close money substitutes.

Table 12.1 *Cambridge k and U.S. Treasury Bill Rates, Selected Years, 1950–1979**

Year	k_1	k_2	T-bill Rate (%)
1950	.40	.53	1.2
1955	.34	.46	1.8
1960	.28	.42	2.9
1965	.24	.42	4.0
1970	.22	.41	6.5
1975	.19	.42	5.8
1979	.16	.39	9.1

*k_1 and k_2 are ratios of old M-1 and old M-2 to GNP.

Source: Based on data from Federal Reserve System.

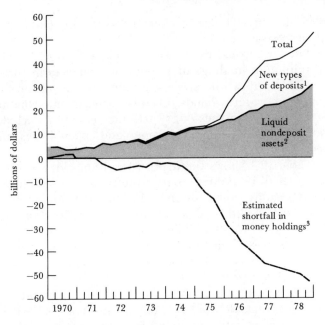

[1]Sum of corporate and state and local government savings deposits. NOW accounts, savings subject to automatic transfers, credit union share drafts, and demand deposits at thrift institutions.

[2]Sum of repurchase agreements (RPs) at nonbank government securities dealers with nonfinancial corporations. RPs at 46 large commercial banks, and assets of money market mutual funds.

[3]Post-1969 errors from an estimated money demand equation using the old definition of M-1.

Figure 12.2 *The growth of close money substitutes has mirrored the shortfall in money demand. (Source: John Wenniger and Charles Sevesind, "Defining Monetary Aggregates for a Changing Financial System,"* Federal Reserve Bank of New York Quarterly Review, *Spring 1978, p. 8.)*

The most basic principle of economic science, the law of demand, states that the more expensive a good, the less people will take of it. The major costs of holding transactions balances in the form of money are the short-term interest rates that can be earned from Treasury bills and other short-term instruments. For that reason, economists believe that the transactions demand for money is sensitive to short-term interest rates. Other things being equal, the higher the rates, the less likely people are to hold transactions balances in the form of money, and vice versa.

12.2.3
Asset demand for money

The demand for money goes well beyond transactions demand. As indicated in Section 1.1.4, people appear to hold far more money than required for current transactions needs. For this reason, economists of varying persuasions assert the existence of an independent *asset demand for money*.

In this view, money is but one of a series of items on the asset side of the balance sheet. For a household, it stands beside stocks, bonds, the family home, the family car, furniture, and other consumer durables. For a business firm, its stands beside inventories, machinery, and other producer durables. The asset view maintains that money holdings yield an implicit stream of returns in the form of liquidity services. Although other assets possess some degree of liquidity, their primary virtues lie in other directions—money interest from securities, housing services from the family home, transportation services from the car, and so forth. Thus, all assets worth holding yield returns in kind or in the form of interest. In this respect, money balances are like other assets.

The net worth of a household or a firm defines its total wealth and limits holdings of assets in any form. The allocation of wealth between money, bonds, stocks, and various kinds of physical assets depends upon the tastes and preferences of the household or firm and the rates of return in kind or in interest yielded by each asset. Other things being equal, the higher the returns on nonmonetary assets, the less money people will wish to hold, and the more of their wealth they will allocate to the other assets, and vice versa. Since other assets may be long-term bonds, a rise (fall) in long-term interest rates is an inducement for people to reduce (increase) their money holdings. Thus long-term interest rates, like short-term interest rates, are a factor affecting the demand for money.

The asset view also implies that the demand for money is affected by inflationary expectations. Inflation is the steady deterioration in the power of money to buy nonfinancial commodities. If the price index is rising by 10 percent a year, the purchasing power of the dollar is declining at the same rate. The process of decline is likely to induce people to reduce money holdings in favor of nonfinancial commodities. Households expecting inflation will purchase extra canned goods, buy more clothes, switch from rental units to their own homes, and so forth. Business firms will increase stocks of finished and unfinished goods and add to their plant and equipment. Since the purchasing power of bonds also falls with inflation, people will demand higher nominal interest rates to hold them. As nominal interest rates rise to reflect anticipated inflation, people will further reduce their money holdings. Thus, the demand for money is negatively related to the expected rate of inflation. As expected inflation increases, desired money holdings fall, and vice versa.

Modern monetarists maintain that it is impossible objectively to identify separate motives in money holdings. They disparage attempts to segregate transactions motives from those relating to the asset demand. Nonetheless, many economists still find it useful to point to special types of asset demands called the *precautionary* and the *speculative demands for money*.

The precautionary demand for money is a "rainy day" demand. It is connected with the uncertainty of timing of receipts and outlays. Income may not come in time to provide for payment of debts; unexpected purchasing opportunities may present themselves before income arrives to take advantage of them. Since lost opportunities and nonpayment of debts produce costs and embarrassments, or even lawsuits, people frequently build cash reserves to minimize the risk of incurring them. Balances held for this purpose appear on the balance sheets, but they are objectively indistinguishable from money held for other purposes.

The speculative motive for holding money is a Keynesian idea, discussed principally in his well-known *General Theory of Employment, Interest and Money*, Chapter 15. Keynes postulated that the demand for money partly represents asset holders' attempts to prevent losses originating in fluctuations of bond prices. People expecting interest earnings on bonds to be insufficient to cover losses from declining bond prices prefer to hold money instead of bonds. The aggregate magnitude of this *liquidity preference*, as Keynes called it, depends upon the dispersion of expectations regarding long-term interest rate changes. People expecting large jumps in the long-term interest rate will want to get out or stay out of long-term bonds and instead hold money. In so doing, they can prevent the deterioration in the value of their assets that comes with a fall in bond prices. Conversely, people expecting long-term interest rates to fall will want to earn the expected capital gains by moving out of money into bonds.

Keynes' liquidity preference hypothesis is consistent with other theories that assert the demand for money to be inversely related to the long-term interest rate. The hypothesis states that, at any moment in time, recent interest rate history influences the state of expectations about near-term future interest rates. Therefore, if the current long-term rate should jump to a very high level, most people would probably expect it to come down; acting in accordance with that expectation, they would move to hold bonds instead of money. Conversely, a temporarily low interest rate would induce many asset holders to choose money instead of bonds. Thus, a curve describing the speculative demand for money would show increased quantities of monies demanded at lower long-term interest rates, and vice versa (see Figure 12.3 in Section 12.2.4).

Keynes' liquidity preference theory is frequently criticized because it postulates an all-or-nothing choice between money and bonds. In fact, people are observed usually to hold *both* money and bonds. But, since many people hold bonds as income earning investments, and in so doing expect to hold them to maturity, it is not surprising to make such observations. Hence this criticism of Keynes' theory is not particularly conclusive. A more important criticism is that concern over fluctuations in the prices of long-term securities would lead people to substitute not money but short-term bonds for long-term securities. Since short-term securities prices fluctuate little in response to interest rate movements, such a substitution would help preserve the value of their assets in times of rapidly rising interest rates.

But Keynes' contribution should not be ignored. There may be no such thing as a generalized liquidity preference that leads asset holders to prefer money over any other asset. In bad times, however, falling real asset prices and fear of debtor defaults on bonds may give rise to a widespread temporary liquidity preference. If so, the demand for money during such periods could rapidly increase. Unless the thirst for additional liquidity is satisfied with new issues of money by the authorities controlling its supply, the jump in demand can lead to a large excess supply of goods and services and even to a recession or depression. The Great Depression of the 1930s in the United States was probably helped along by such a process.

12.2.4
Summary of factors affecting demand for money

The demand for real money balances is the demand to *hold* dollars of constant purchasing power. It is an asset holding decision affected by people's tastes and preferences, real income, institutional factors such as industrial mergers, money substitutes, interest rates on short-term and long-term securities, the expected rate of inflation, and real wealth. If the definition of money includes time and savings deposits, or other interest bearing short-term assets, then the return on those deposits and assets would also be a (positive) factor affecting the demand for money. Thus, in its most general form, we can write the demand for money as

$$m^d = f(\bar{r}_s, \bar{r}_l, \overset{+}{r}_m, \overset{\bar{-}}{\dot{P}}_e, \overset{+}{y}, \overset{+}{w}, u) \tag{12.9}$$

where r_s, r_l, and r_m refer to the nominal interest rates on short-term bonds, long-term bonds and money; $\dot{P}_e$ is the expected rate of inflation (the percentage growth rate of the price level); y is real income, w is real wealth, and u is a general symbol for institutional factors. The plus and minus signs over the variables show the direction of change in money demand as each variable increases.

Hundreds of econometric studies in this and other countries support this generalized theory of money demand. The studies differ as to the relative importance of the variables, but in virtually all of them there is evidence that one or another interest rate, and income or wealth, are important influences on the demand for real balances.

Figure 12.3 shows the general shape of the demand for money function. Movements along each curve describe changing amounts of real balances demanded as interest rates rise or fall. Shifts—for example, from m^d to $m^{d'}$—in the curve come from changes in income, changes in

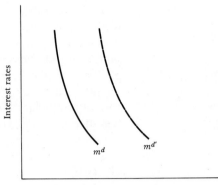

Figure 12.3 *The demand for money.*

Real money balances

wealth, changes in expectations concerning real and financial nonmonetary asset prices, changes in asset holders' tastes and preferences, and institutional developments. We describe upward and rightward shifts in the demand functions as "increases in the demand for money;" downward and leftward shifts are "decreases in the demand for money."

12.3
A monetary theory of money income

We now combine the material of this chapter with that of Chapter 11 to formulate a monetary theory of income. To bring out the essential features of the theory, we at first use the Cambridge equation. Later, we will bring in the role of interest rates and other variables as they affect the demand for money and, through it, the level of money income.

12.3.1
Monetary equilibrium and income equilibrium

Recall from Chapter 11 that the relationship between the value of excess demand for final goods and services and the excess supply of money is given by

$$Y^d - Y^s = M^s - M^d \qquad (11.11)$$

where Y represents *money income (Py)*, and M^s and M^d stand for the supply of and demand for nominal money balances. Equation (11.11) is simply an application of Say's Principle to the aggregate value of the excess demand for final products and money.

Equilibrium of nominal income requires $M^s - M^d = 0$. That is, if conditions are such that aggregate planned and realized excess demands for money are zero, so too will be the nominal value of the aggregate planned and realized excess demands for final goods and services. Thus, if

$$M^s = M^d \qquad \text{(monetary income equilibrium)} \qquad (12.10)$$

then

$$Y^d = Y^s \qquad \text{(money income equilibrium)}$$

The next step uses the relationship between real and nominal money demand and the Cambridge equation. Recall that $M^d = m^d P$ and $m^d = ky$. Substituting these equations into the monetary equilibrium condition in Equation (12.10) we get

$$M^s = m^d P \qquad (12.11)$$

$$M^s = kyP \qquad (12.12)$$

$$M^s = kY \qquad (12.13)$$

where $yP = Y$ is the nominal or money value of equilibrium income. It is equilibrium income because monetary equilibrium has forced Y^d and Y^s into equality.

12.3.2
Interpretation of money income equilibrium

Money income equals real income times the price level. As a result, the equilibrium value of Y can be compounded of many different price and real income levels. Nothing we have said argues for one compound versus another. Under full employment, real income in the short run is determined by the optimal relationship between the labor force and the capital stock; that is, aggregate full employment output is independent of the current aggregate demand for real output. Thus, under full employment, Equation (12.12) converts to

$$M^s = ky_f P \qquad (12.14)$$

or

$$P = \frac{M^s}{ky_f} = \frac{M^s}{m^d} \qquad (12.15)$$

where y_f is full employment real national income. In this form, the equation is equivalent to the quantity theory of money applied to the price level, described in Section 12.1.3. Because both M^s and y_f are assumed to be independent of the demand for money, the equation contains only one dependent variable, P.

In a world where prices are fixed, the monetary equilibrium equation determines the level of real income. Assume $P = P^*$, where the asterisk denotes fixity. We then have

$$M^s = kyP^*$$ (12.16)

or

$$y = \frac{M^s}{kP^*}$$ (12.17)

In this form, the equation shows the dependent variable to be the level of real income, y. When the Cambridge k and the price level are fixed, real income will vary directly with changes in the quantity of money.

In the real world, changes in the money supply alter both real output and the price level. Prices are usually sticky or semirigid in the short run, partly because they are based upon wages emerging from collective bargaining agreements or from informal contracts between workers and employers, and partly because business people are uncertain about market clearing prices in their respective markets. Thus, when money supply changes occur, the first thing to change in the economy is output. If the new monetary conditions persist, the price level, too, eventually changes. Consequently, to a degree that is difficult to determine, money income changes brought about by variation in the money supply become compounds of both output and price level movements.

Equation (12.15) helps explain how costly *real* shocks, such as the OPEC oil price increases, raise the whole price level. The shocks raise the marginal and average costs of production for some final goods and services. As a result, they lower the full employment level of real output. By lowering y_f, they also reduce the demand for real cash balances, $m^d = ky_f$. As equation (12.15) shows, this has the effect of raising the equilibrium price level for any given nominal money stock, M^s. Thus the jump in prices shown in Figure 12.1 for the year 1974 is to a large extent the result of the once-and-for-all displacement of the price level originating in the 1974 OPEC decision to quadruple oil prices. After this shock was absorbed by the economy, the inflation rate reverted to a level tracked by the rate of growth of the money supply.

As indicated in Section 12.1.1, the fundamental proposition of monetary theory states that income and prices adjust so as to bring the demand for money into equality with the stock of money made available by the authorities and the banking system. The reason, as we shall now demonstrate, is that excess supplies of money are connected with excess demands for nominal income, and vice versa.

Figure 12.4 portrays the demand and supply of nominal cash balances against nominal income. As it illustrates, M^d rises and falls with in-

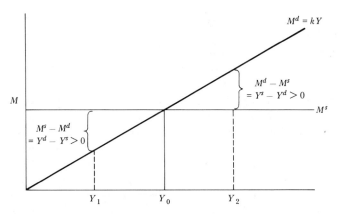

Figure 12.4 *Equilibrium nominal income.*

come, but M^s, determined by the authorities and banks, is independent of income.

Suppose that in a given monetary environment, in which M^s and k are fixed, the business sector tries to produce a money income equal to Y_1. Given the information in Figure 12.4, Y_1 cannot be an equilibrium money income. At that level of income the supply of nominal money balances is greater than the public wishes to hold, and there is an aggregate planned excess demand for goods and services. This being so, firms will be stimulated to increase prices and production. As they do so, money income will rise. As money income rises, the demand for nominal money balances will rise toward equality with the existing stock of money.

If all firms in the business sector try to produce output in value to Y_2, results opposite to the above ensue. At Y_2, there is an excess demand for money and the value of goods and services supplied exceeds that of those in demand. Failing to sell all they produce, firms will reduce output and perhaps prices, lowering the earned incomes of their workers and owners. The drop in incomes will cause the quantity of nominal balances demanded to fall towards equality with the existing stock of money.

Thus, when M^s and k are given, incomes above or below Y_0 cannot be sustained; Y_0 is the only level of money income capable of bringing the aggregate demand for nominal cash balances into equality with the existing supply. Any other income creates an excess demand or excess supply of money. And, as stated by the fundamental proposition of monetary theory, when the money people in the aggregate *wish* to hold differs from the amount the authorities and banks dictate that they *must* hold, output and prices (money income) must change until desired money holdings come into equality with the existing money stock.

12.3.3
Changes in the equilibrium level of income

Our theory reveals two forces generating movement of money income. The first is the temporary excess demand and excess supply of money created by departures of money income from its equilibrium level. The second is the change of the excess demand for money brought about by shifts in the demand for money or changes in its supply. The second force leads to changes in the equilibrium level of money income.

Changes in equilibrium money income brought about by monetary changes are shown in Figure 12.5. The figure shows that equivalent changes in money income, as from Y to Y', can result from increases in the money supply (from M^s to $M^{s'}$) or from shifts in the demand function brought on by reductions in the Cambridge k (from k to k').

Figure 12.5 also shows that increases or decreases in the money supply offset by equal shifts in the demand for money—for example, M^s to $M^{s'}$ accompanied by a shift of $M^{d'}$ to M^d—leave equilibrium money income unchanged—at Y'.

Historically, changes in money income have been provoked by shifts in both the demand and supply of money. Some of the older quantity theorists thought that, except for a trend brought about by institutional changes of various sorts, k tends to be relatively constant. Others admitted that k varies with the business cycle—falling during booms and rising during slumps. Modern monetarists agree, but they argue that the variations are not very large. They also say that some of the variations, observed through measurements of the ratio M/GNP, are in part caused by the cyclical divergencies of short-run income from its long-run growth path. Adjusting for the errors introduced into our measurements of k by these divergencies, they say, makes most of the remaining variations in k pre-

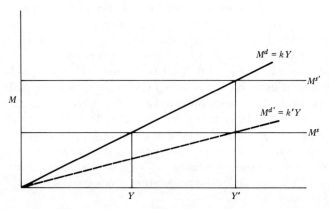

Figure 12.5 *Changes in equilibrium nominal income.*

dictable from what we know of its relationship with interest rates, wealth, and institutional changes. In short, they argue that the demand for money is a relatively stable and, therefore, predictable function of the variables indicated in Equation (12.9). If so, variations in equilibrium nominal income are dominated by changes in the money supply brought about by the policies of the monetary authorities.

We must now point out that it is improper to argue that the money supply is a critical variable in the determination of the level of full employment *real income*. Full employment real income depends upon the size and quality of the nation's capital stock, its political and social institutions, and so forth. In the long run, the real income growth path of the economy is influenced far more by these things than it is by the growth of the money supply. In the short run, of course, changes in the money supply can and do have profound effects upon the level of real income. But these effects originate in the stickiness or rigidity of money prices and wage rates. In the long run, prices and wages are more flexible; hence, most shifts in monetary growth that first change real income eventually change prices and money wages and leave few traces upon the output of final goods and services. Of course, wild variations in money growth are another matter; the random shocks they impose on the economy and polity may be so disruptive that the growth path of real income may be permanently lowered.

12.3.4
The equation of exchange and the theory of money income

Many economists prefer to state the theory of money income in terms of the *equation of exchange*. The equation, made popular by the late Irving Fisher[3], makes use of the fact that in a given period the value of all goods sold must equal the value of all goods bought. Applied to money income, the value of sales is $Py = Y$; the value of purchases equals the quantity of money, M, times V, velocity, or MV. Thus the equation of exchange may be stated as

$$MV = Py = Y \qquad (12.18)$$

Comparison with Equation (12.13) shows that V in the equation of exchange is simply the reciprocal of k, or $V = 1/k$. The reason is as follows: The Cambridge k measures the ratio of average money holdings to income. If annual income is used in the ratio, k measures the fraction of a year the average dollar is held. If $k = 1/5$, the money holdings equal

[3]Irving Fisher, *The Purchasing Power of Money* (New York: Augustus M. Kelly, 1963).

about one-fifth of annual income, about 10 weeks of income, 10 weeks being approximately one-fifth of a year. Thus, in purchasing final goods and services, the average dollar turns over at a rate of five times per year—its velocity, V, is 5.

Since V is the reciprocal of k, the factors affecting k also affect V. Changes in tastes and preferences and other factors that increase the demand for money are the same factors that slow the velocity of money, and vice versa. If k declines with a rise in interest rates, V increases; if people rush to hold money instead of bonds or real assets, V declines, and if inflationary expectations move people to abandon money holdings, V increases.

Although the equation of exchange is formally equivalent to the theory of nominal income described with the Cambridge k, we will not often employ it in this book. The concept of velocity conjures up a vision of dollars chasing around from holder to holder. But human volition motivates the income generating process; a concept like the Cambridge k, which focuses upon the factors affecting individual decisions to hold or not to hold money, is preferable to the more mechanistic idea of velocity.

12.3.5
The Keynesian cross and the monetary theory of income

An alternative approach to income determination is based upon the famous identity between consumption plus investment expenditures and the level of income—the so-called income–expenditure approach. How does this approach compare to the one discussed in Sections 12.3.1–12.3.4?

To answer this question, consider first the foundations of the income–expenditure model: (1) It is a theory of real, not money income; and (2) It relies on differences in spending behavior between consumers and business. Consumers are said to spend according to a relationship called the consumption function, which relates real consumption spending to real income earned in the process of production. Business investment spending, in contrast, is mainly determined by the profitability of capital outlays in comparison to the real rate of interest. Given the level of investment spending, the income–expenditure model states that variations of real output (income) will continue until consumption plus investment spending equals real income. At that point, equilibrium will prevail.

An algebraic version of the model is given by

$$c^d + i^d = y^s, \quad \text{or} \quad y^d = y^s = y \quad \text{(in equilibrium)} \quad (12.19a)$$

$$c^d = a + by^s, \quad a > 0, 0 < b < 1 \quad (12.19b)$$

$$i^d = i^* \quad (12.19c)$$

This model is graphed in Figure 12.6a, the so-called Keynesian cross diagram. The 45° line shoos all possible points of equilibrium between the real aggregate demand for and supply of output. The horizontal axis measures real supply, y^s, and the vertical axis measures real demand, y^d. Total demand is the sum of real consumption demand, c^d, and real investment demand, i^d, the former varying with income, the latter assumed to be fixed at i^*.

Given Equations (12.19), equilibrium income is y_0, the only value of income and output at which planned consumption plus planned investment can equal planned production. Consider a drop in output below y_0

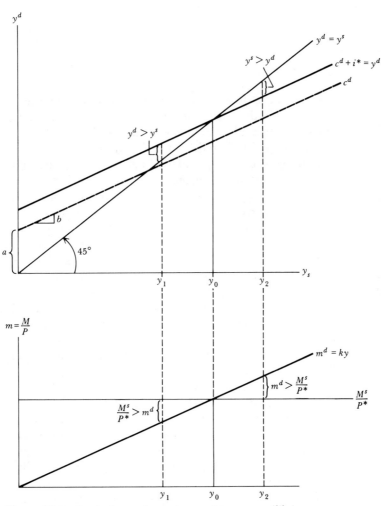

Figure 12.6 *Equivalence of monetary and income equilibrium.*

to y_1. At that output, $y^d > y^s$; hence, planned purchases exceed planned output and employers will experience unanticipated sales and declines in inventories. This will induce them to increase production, which raises income, consumption demand, and hence total demand. Since consumption grows less rapidly than does income (because b is a fraction of income), real income moves toward an equilibrium position.

In the opposite case, a rise of income *above* y_0 will cause y^d to fall short of y^s, which leads to an excess supply of final output, an incentive for firms to reduce production and real income, a force that lowers consumption demand. Consumption will fall until income reaches y_0, at which point y^d again equals y^s.

If all this sounds vaguely familiar, it is because we have already been through it with the monetary theory of income. Assume a fixed price level; the Cambridge equation model of Equation (12.17) emerges

$$\frac{M^s}{kP^*} = y \qquad (12.20)$$

where y is the dependent variable determined by the equation. As Figure 12.6b shows, the y_0 that brings consumption plus investment demand into equality with real income is the same y_0 that the fundamental proposition of monetary theory tells us must bring the demand for real balances into equality with the supply of real balances made available by the monetary authorities and banks at the fixed price level.

The correspondence between the results of the two theories should not be surprising. The excess demand for final products produced by income below y_0 must be generated by an excess supply of real money balances; conversely, an excess supply of goods and services produced by incomes above y_0 must be generated by an excess demand for real balances. Hence, in both cases, real income must adjust until the excess demand or excess supply of real money is zero.

Thus, the income equilibrium shown in Figure 12.6a is, at base, a monetary equilibrium. Without monetary equilibrium, income equilibrium is meaningless. For, suppose there is no such thing as monetary equilibrium. That is, suppose the authorities act to make the supply and demand for real money balance equal at every level of real income. In such a world, the money supply line would overlay and be identical to the money demand line. Each increase or decrease of real income would generate equal changes in real money demand and the real money supply. With a fixed price level, the authorities, in a fashion described by the commercial loan theory, would be allowing the money supply to adjust according to the "needs of trade." Say's Principle tells us that continuous equality between the demand and supply of money implies continuous equality, but not necessarily equilibrium, between planned purchases and sales of real output at every level of income. Thus, in the present instance, the aggregate demand line y^d would overlay the 45° line that plots $y^d = y^s$ at every point.

In brief, a policy that seeks constant equality between the real supply and demand for money cannot produce a unique equilibrium value for y. Instead, it produces a situation in which every point on the aggregate demand line is a point of equality between y^d and y^s. Departure of real output from any point along the line would not, and could not, generate forces to bring the economy back to the original point. Planned and realized supplies and demands for nonmonetary commodities would always be equal regardless of the level of real income. In effect, we would be in a world described by Say's Law for a barter economy.

Hence, independence between the forces affecting the demand for and supply of money is critical to the concept of both monetary and income equilibrium. Moreover, the level of income is not directly connected with the division of spending between consumption and investment. Consider the two equations, $c^d + i^d = y$ and $y = M^s/P^*k$. Since two things equal to the same thing are equal to each other, we have

$$c^d + i^d = \frac{M^s}{P^*k} = y \tag{12.21}$$

Equation (12.21) demonstrates that, if M^s and k are independent of shifts in investment or consumption demand, the level of real income is fully determined by the supply of real money balances and the fraction of real income the public chooses to hold in the form of money. Under such conditions, aggregate investment and consumption demand must be inversely related, because, in equilibrium, their sum must equal the level of income as determined by M^s/P^*k. Hence, a rise in i^d must be followed by an equivalent fall in c^d, and vice versa. In more technical terms, investment and consumption spending are gross substitutes, not complements, as implied by the income–expenditure model.

In reality, equilibrium income is to some extent affected by shifts in i^d or c^d. The shifts can cause changes in interest rates, and variations in interest rates can affect k and, under certain monetary policy procedures, also the quantity of money. To the extent that the changes in k or the money supply are significant, changes in the equilibrium level of real income might originate with shifts in the consumption function or investment demand.

Even so, we must remember the fundamental proposition of monetary theory: Short-run variations in income, real or nominal, are usually connected with attempts by the public to adjust their demand for money to the existing supply. Changes in equilibrium are brought about by changes in the supply of money or shifts in its demand. Upward or downward movements of the total demand line, $y^d = c^d + i^d$, are ordinarily associated with underlying monetary changes.

*The importance of interest rates to
the theory of income*

We close this chapter with a loose end. Until we develop a theory of interest determination, our theory of income will be incomplete. The proof is as follows: Let the Cambridge k now be a function of the interest rate, as shown in Figure 12.3. Writing this function as $k(r)$ converts the equation describing the nominal income level to

$$M^s = k(\bar{r})Y \tag{12.22}$$

where the minus sign over r reminds us that k is inversely related to the rate of interest.

Since r and Y are dependent variables, the single equation (12.22) cannot solve for either one without the other having been previously determined. At best the equation describes a series of *pairs* of r and Y that maintain equilibrium between the demand for money, $k(r)Y$, and the existing nominal supply M^s. Suppose Y rises to create an excess demand for money—$M^s < k(r)Y$. Restoration of equilibrium at the higher income level requires a shrinkage of k; a rise in r would do the job. A sufficient drop in k would, when multiplied by the larger Y, restore the equality $M^s = k(r)Y$. By similar reasoning, a decline in Y requires a drop in r to restore the equality.

We can, therefore, list pairs of values for r and Y that maintain equilibrium between the demand and supply of money. The pairs can be shown by the *MM* (money market) equilibrium curve in Figure 12.7a, which is derived from the data in Figure 12.7b. Note that each money demand function in the latter is connected with a different interest rate. For a given money supply, M^s, the rising interest rate produces a higher income level, and vice versa. An increase in the money supply would shift the *MM* curve in Figure 12.7a to the right, to $M'M'$, and a decrease would shift it to the left (not shown). A decrease in the demand for money originating in other factors, such as a growth of money substitutes, or a decrease in liquidity preference, would also shift the equilibrium curve to the right. Factors causing the demand for money to increase, would shift it to the left.

Thus, income is indeterminate without knowledge of the rate of interest. For that, we turn to the loanable funds theory in Chapter 13.

SUMMARY

The fundamental proposition of monetary theory is that nominal income must adjust until it reaches a value at which the demand for nominal cash balances equals the stock of money made available by the authorities and banks. If the real demand for money is fixed, and real output is given,

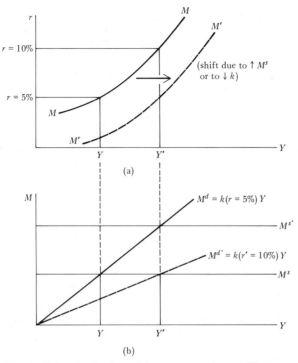

Figure 12.7 *Derivation of the money market equilibrium curve, MM.*

then the adjustment of money income to an equilibrium level is brought about by changes in prices, the equilibrium level of which must equal the ratio of the nominal money supply to the demand for real cash balances. Under these conditions, changes in the money supply cause proportional changes in the equilibrium price level and in nominal income.

The demand for real cash balances is affected by real income, interest rates, institutional factors, and real wealth. The Cambridge k, which is inversely related to the rate of interest, summarizes the relationship between real money demand and the level of real income. Integrated into an equilibrium condition for the money market, it produces a model of nominal income expressed by the equation $M^s = k(r)Y$. When $k(r)$ is a constant, the model shows that equilibrium nominal income is primarily a function of the money supply made available by the authorities.

Comparison of the monetary theory of income with the income–expenditure model shows that equilibrium in the latter is based upon equilibrium in the former. In both theories equilibrium requires a stable money demand function and a given stock of money. Shifts in investment or consumption demand cannot affect equilibrium income unless the shifts lead to changes in k or in the money supply. Since changes in interest rates can and do result from changes in consumption and investment demand, it is necessary to modify the model describing the monetary theory of income to allow for the effects of interest rates. This leaves us with a hole in the theory that Chapter 13 is designed to fill.

DISCUSSION QUESTIONS

1. What would be the effect upon the explanatory power of monetary theory if people were indifferent to the amount of money they hold? (*Hint*: Reread the section on the fundamental proposition of monetary theory.)

2. What would be the effect on the economy if the monetary authorities always adjusted the supply of money to the amount that people wished to hold?

3. Why can it be said that the quantity theory of money gives us an explanation for the determination of an *equilibrium* level of prices?

4. High taxes, high interest rates, high wages, and low productivity are frequently blamed for high prices. What would a quantity theorist say about these theories?

5. Compare the Cambridge equation to Fisher's equation of exchange. Is there any reason to choose one over the other as a basis for analyzing monetary affairs?

6. What is the basis for the transactions motive for holding money? How would the following events affect the transactions demand for money?
(a) An increase in short-term interest rates; in long-term interest rates
(b) A reduction on taxes paid on interest income
(c) A general reduction of personal and business income taxes
(d) An increase in the frequency of wage payments in the country

7. How do inflationary expectations affect the demand for money?

8. Distinguish between the asset demand and transactions demand for money.

9. Chapter 3 contained a distinction between default or credit risk and market or interest rate risk. Would either of these risks affect the demand for money? What sort of risks are connected with the precautionary demand for money?

10. What is the connection between monetary equilibrium and income equilibrium? (*Hint*: Use the Fundamental Proposition of Monetary Theory and Say's Principle.)

11. Compare the income–expenditure theory of real income with the monetary theory of real income.

12. Would the concept of equilibrium income have any meaning in a barter economy?

13. Assume that the ratio between the real money supply and the Cambridge *k* is constant. What would be the effect on the economy of an increase in investment spending? A shift in the consumption function?

14. Define and discuss the derivation of the *MM* curve. Is it true that an increase in the quantity of money or a reduction in the demand for money (i.e., a reduction in the Cambridge *k*) would shift the curve to the right? Why? What would shift it to the left?

IMPORTANT TERMS AND CONCEPTS

- ☐ asset demand for money
- ☐ Cambridge equation
- ☐ equation of exchange
- ☐ fundamental proposition of monetary theory
- ☐ income–expenditure model
- ☐ Keynesian cross
- ☐ monetary theory of nominal income
- ☐ money market (*MM*) equilibrium curve

- ☐ nominal money supply
- ☐ precautionary demand for money
- ☐ quantity theory of money
- ☐ real money balances
- ☐ speculative demand for money
- ☐ transactions demand for money
- ☐ utility of money
- ☐ velocity of money

ADDITIONAL READINGS

A useful summary of the Cambridge School approach to the quantity theory is in J.M. Keynes, *A Treatise on Money, I, The Pure Theory of Money* (London: Macmillan Press for the Royal Economic Society's Collected Works of John Maynard Keynes, 1973, originally published by Macmillan in 1930), Chapter 14. See also Eprime Eshag, *From Marshall to Keynes, An Essay On the Monetary Theory of the Cambridge School* (Oxford: Basil Blackwell, 1963).

Friedman's monetarist views are given in his well-known, but somewhat forbidding, "Restatement of the Quantity Theory of Money" in Milton Friedman (editor), *Studies in the Quantity Theory of Money* (Chicago: University of Chicago Press, 1956, reprinted in Milton Friedman, *The Optimum Quantity of Money* (Chicago: Aldine, 1969), pp. 51–67. A good overall introduction to monetarist economics is William Poole, *Money and the Economy: A Monetarist View* (Reading, Massachusetts: Addision–Wesley

Publishing, 1978). Also recommended is Charles E. Baird, *Elements of Macroeconomics* (St. Paul: West Publishing, 1977), Chapter 9.

There are numerous surveys of the literature on the demand for money. The most well-known is David Laidler, *The Demand for Money: Theories and Evidence*, 2nd edition (New York: Dun–Donnelly Publishing, 1977). Also useful, but more technical, is John T. Boorman "The Evidence on the Demand for Money: Theoretical Formulations and Empirical Results," in Thomas M. Havrilesky and John T. Boorman, *Current Issues in Monetary Theory and Policy*, 2nd edition (Arlington Heights, Illinois: AHM Publishing, 1980).

The Rate of Interest and the Theory of Income

13

O U T L I N E

Say's Principle and the Bond Market
Expansion of Say's Principle to Include Bonds
Bond Supplies and Demands as Stocks and Flows
The Theory of Interest
Private Nonbank Supply and Demand for Bonds
Changes in Equilibrium Interest Rates Due to Changes in Income
Cyclical Movements of Interest Rates
Effects of Monetary Policy on Bond Demand
Monetary Policy and Interest Rates; Income and Fisher Effects
Effects of Government Deficits on Interest Rates
Summary of the Theory of Interest
A Monetary Theory of Income
Diagrammatic Exposition of the Theory
Appendix: The Term Structure of Interest Rates

A loan is a transfer of purchasing power from a lender to a borrower. The interest a borrower agrees to pay the lender is the price of the loan. Thus market interest rates, which emerge from transactions of millions of borrowers and lenders, working indirectly through financial intermediaries or directly in security markets, are prices in the same sense that money prices of goods and services are prices.

Like all goods and services, purchasing power is a scarce commodity. When lenders surrender it to borrowers they give up the chance to use it for current consumption, to buy consumer durables, or simply to hold it in the form of money as a store of value. These valued alternative uses for purchasing power lead lenders to demand a price—interest—for giving it up. The higher the price, the more they are willing to lend.

Borrowers also value purchasing power. They too wish to use it for current consumption or for the purchase of durable goods. Borrowers include households, business firms, federal, state, and local governments. Their willingness to pay interest signifies that they value present use of purchasing power more than they value the interest. However, as interest rates rise, they tend to curtail their demands for loanable funds.

Thus, variations in interest rates regulate the supply and demand for loanable funds. Rising interest rates signify increased scarcity of these funds, leading people to economize upon their use. Conversely, falling interest rates indicate diminishing scarcity of loan money, encouraging people to use more of it. For this reason, interest rates perform the important function of allocating resources between present and future use. The lower the rate of interest, the more people are likely to purchase durable assets such as furniture, washing machines, homes, business equipment, and the like. Such assets carry with them durable streams of services and, as a result, increase the real wealth of their owners. High interest rates discourage the purchase of real assets and slow the accumulation of real wealth.

By varying the rate at which business accumulates capital, changes in interest rates indirectly affect the capacity of the economy to produce. Thus, interest rates are a key factor in the determination of the level and rate of growth of potential real aggregate income. At the same time, however, they are also a factor that affects the level of income actually realized in any period of time. As shown in Section 12.3.6, variations in market interest rates raise or lower the quantity of money demanded. In so doing, they can, depending on the posture of monetary policy, indirectly contribute to the creation of an excess demand or excess supply of money. Since monetary disequilibria communicate disequilibria to the markets for nonmonetary commodities, creating excess supplies or demands for goods and services, they also contribute to fluctuations of national income around its long-term growth path.

Thus a money-using market economy is greatly affected by interest rates. A theory of income would be incomplete without a discussion of how interest rates are determined and of how they affect the level of income. Fortunately, the materials necessary to develop a theory of interest are already in hand. We need only to amplify the ideas presented in the previous chapters of this book. We start with an expansion of the equation describing Say's Principle.

13.1
Say's Principle and the bond market

Recall that Say's Principle asserts that the aggregate net value of planned trades of all commodities—monetary and nonmonetary—must equal zero. Put differently, it states that the market value of the sum of excess demands for all goods and services, including money, must equal zero. In a simple money economy, all nonmonetary commodities are tangible goods or services. In our more complex money–credit world, however, the category of nonmonetary commodities encompasses stocks and bonds. Like other commodities, stocks and bonds are bought and sold in active (money and capital) markets; their prices are set by the forces of supply and demand. Moreover, in deciding to reduce or add dollars to their cash balances, people take into account the attractiveness of buying or selling securities as well as goods and services.

Thus, in using the equation describing Say's Principle as a framework for analyzing a money–credit economy, we must add supplies and demands for stocks and bonds to other nonmonetary commodities. As we shall see, this addition makes possible a more complete monetary theory of nominal income.

13.1.1
Expansion of Say's Principle to include bonds

To keep things simple, call all financial securities bonds. Thus the word "bond" implicitly refers to common stocks, preferred stocks, and actual bonds. Securities are marketed directly in security markets and indirectly through various financial intermediaries. (Refresh your memory on the matter with the discussions in Sections 3.1 and 3.4) Their prices, and implicitly market interest rates, are set by forces of supply and demand in their respective markets. But, since our purpose here is to describe the impact of interest rates generally on the economy, it is convenient to aggregate all securities into one category and treat them as a whole. We shall, therefore, speak of the various security markets as "the bond market."

Consider the following form of the definition of Say's Principle:

$$\sum_{i=1}^{n} P_i(D_i - S_i) + \sum_{j=1}^{m} P_j(B_j^d - B_j^s) \equiv M^s - M^d \tag{13.1}$$

where D_i and S_i refer to demands and supplies of individual final goods and services, B_j^d and B_j^s are demands and supplies of different bonds, and P_i and P_j refer to prices of final products and bonds, respectively.

Equation (13.1) states that at the beginning of any period people plan to enter the market to buy or sell final products and bonds and to either add to or subtract from their money balances. If, on average, people have more money than they want to hold, the aggregate demand for money will fall short of the existing stock of money—$M^s - M^d > 0$—and traders will be planning to reduce their cash balances. As Equation (13.1) shows, widespread attempts to reduce cash balances spill over into excess demands for bonds or for goods and services. That is, an excess supply of money carries with it the power to create an excess demand for both products and bonds. As such, it will drive up their prices or stimulate additions to their supply.

Similarly, an excess demand for money can create an excess supply of both bonds and nonfinancial commodities. When $M^d - M^s > 0$, people in the aggregate are attempting to acquire more cash. To do so, they increase their sales of bonds and goods and services and reduce their purchases. This has the effect of reducing the D_i and B_j^d and increasing the S_i and B_j^s, causing the left-hand side of Equation (13.1) to become negative, signifying a weakening of the economy. Thus, rewriting Say's Principle to include the bond market does not change the basic proposition that on balance an excess supply of money is expansionary and an excess demand for money is contractionary for the economy in general.

Now we rewrite Equation (13.1) in the aggregative style of Equation (11.11) where Y^d and Y^s refer to the aggregate values of final goods and services demanded and supplied, B^d, and B^s to the aggregate number of bonds demanded and supplied, and P_B to the average price of bonds:

$$(Y^d - Y^s) + P_B(B^d - B^s) \equiv M^s - M^d \tag{13.2}$$

Expressing Say's Principle in this form permits us to incorporate the events of the bond market into the theory of income.

13.1.2
Bond supplies and demands as stocks and flows

We need to say a few words about the supply and demand concepts as applied to bonds. First, to make things simple we are assuming the existence of a standardized bond with, say, a duration of one year to maturity. Since our present concern is with the effects of interest on the level of money income and not with the relative prices of different securities, this is a legitimate simplification. That is not to say that differences in bond maturity and differences in default risk attached to bonds are unimportant. But consideration of these dimensions of bond instruments are best taken into account later in the analysis, after we have outlined the basic theory of income determination.

Second, recall that the price of a bond is simply the discounted present value of its future stream of earnings. Thus, if the payoff at the end of one year of a standardized bond is $1.00, its price multiplied by $(1+r)$ must equal $1.00. It follows that the price of the bond varies inversely with the rate of interest according to the formula:

$$P_B = \frac{1}{1+r}$$

If this formula confuses you, reread Section 3.4.4.

Third, in this book we shall emphasize *flow supplies and demands for bonds*. Bonds are both assets and liabilities. As such, they yield streams of interest income to their holders and interest costs to their issuers. These income and cost streams are important in the portfolio decisions of firms and households, helping them to decide the overall number of bonds they wish to have alongside the other items on their balance sheets. The number of bonds they wish to have on the asset side of their balance sheets is frequently called the *stock demand for bonds*. The stock supplies of bonds are simply the number of bonds outstanding in the economy at any moment of time, recorded on the liability side of the balance sheets.

In contrast, flow demands and supplies of bonds are the additions or replacements people decide to make to the number of bonds they hold as assets or have outstanding as liabilities. These decisions are made in the light of the bonds already recorded on the asset or liability side of their existing balance sheets. If the stock demand for bonds exceeds the stock supply, people will wish to add to their bond holdings, and the flow demand for bonds will be positive. Similarly, if people or firms that already have bonds outstanding wish to increase their debts, the flow supply of securities will be positive.

Decisions to replace maturing bonds also affect aggregate flow demand and supply in the bond market. When existing bonds mature, debtors transfer money to lenders. The latter must decide whether to purchase new bonds or to use the money for something else. Similarly, the debtors must decide whether to renew borrowing or to live with smaller asset totals. If borrowers and lenders both decide to replace the maturing bonds with new ones, an equal amount of flow demand and supply will come into being. In the more usual case, however, borrowers and lenders decide to replace unequal amounts of maturing debts, causing replacement of debt to bring forth unequal flow supplies and demands for bonds.

The upshot of the above analysis is that the excess demand for bonds $(B^d - B^s)$ equals the sum of the excess demands for new bonds plus the excess demand for replacement bonds. This is shown by the following identities, in which the N and R subscripts on the bond terms stand for "new" and "replacement":

$$B^d = B_N^d + B_R^d \qquad (13.3a)$$

$$B^s = B_N^s + B_R^s \qquad (13.3b)$$

and, subtracting Equation (13.3b) from Equation (13.3a), we get

$$B^d - B^s = (B_N^d - B_N^s) + (B_R^d - B_R^s) \qquad (13.4)$$

Equality between replacement bond demand and supply—$B_R^d = B_R^s$—implies that the excess flow demand for bonds is made up solely of the excess demand for new bonds. Inequality of replacement demand and supply implies that the excess demand for bonds is increased or decreased from the level of excess demand established by people's plans to buy or sell new bonds.

13.2
The theory of interest

Interest rates are like other prices. In competitive markets prices are determined by the forces of supply and demand. The market for bonds is highly competitive. Millions of borrowers and lenders come together in markets provided by security exchanges and financial intermediaries. Interest rates set in these markets are communicated throughout the country and the world. The basic commodities traded in security markets are stocks and bonds—the things we have agreed to represent with the word "bond." The task of this section is to provide an understanding of the forces that affect the supply and demand for bonds and to show how their interaction determines the rate of interest.

13.2.1
Private nonbank supply and demand
for bonds

Many buyers and sellers of bonds are found outside banks, in the household and business sectors of the economy. Households and businesses transact their loan business directly through security markets and indirectly through financial intermediaries.

Figure 13.1 depicts the supply and demand curves for bonds as they relate to the price of bonds and the market rate of interest. As B^d and B^s in Figure 13.1a show, a rise in the price of bonds reduces the number of bonds demanded and raises the number supplied. Thus bond supply and

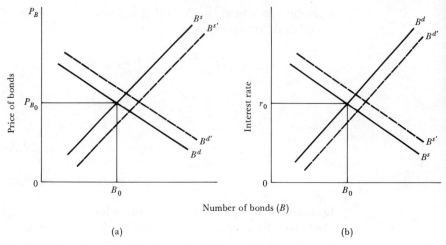

Figure 13.1 *Private nonbank supply and demand for bonds.*

demand respond to bond prices the same way that the supply and demand for any other commodity responds to its own price.

Since our purpose is to set forth a theory of interest rate determination, Figure 13.1b, showing the variation of the supply and demand for bonds against the rate of interest, is more pertinent to our discussion. To relate the two diagrams to one another, just recall that the price of bonds varies inversely with the rate of interest; that is, in the case of a one-year bond, $P_B = 1/(1+r)$. Consequently, the number of bonds demanded rises with increases in the rate of interest, and the number of bonds supplied falls—just the reverse of the directions in Figure 13.1a, which depicts the price–quantity relationships for bond demand and bond supply.

The level and slope of the bond demand curves reflect decisions by lenders to purchase bonds. Lenders are households and business firms that wish to delay use of current income for the purchase of goods and services or to convert cash holdings into bonds. They buy bonds because accumulation of interest increases the value of delayed spending power. The higher the interest rate, the larger the accumulation of purchasing power when the time comes to use it.

Thus lenders' demands for bonds are affected by the rate of interest and the level of income. Higher interest rates tempt lenders to put more income and cash into bonds. Lower interest rates cause them to buy fewer bonds and to hold more cash. Variations in income affect the demand for bonds by varying the purchasing power available to spend now or in the future. Higher incomes raise demand for bonds as well as the present demand for goods and services. Lower incomes do the opposite.

Another important factor affecting bond demand is the age profile of the public. Middle-aged people invest more than do the young and the old. The young tend to borrow, not lend. The old frequently dissipate their savings.

An increase in the demand for bonds is shown in Figure 13.1a and 13.1b as rightward shifts of the demand curves—the dashed B^d *curves*. A decrease in bond demand would shift the B^d curves to the left.

Interest on borrowed money is a cost that people must face in making decisions to borrow. The higher the interest rate the more expensive are the goods and services they buy with borrowed money. The appetites of some households for goods are so strong that it takes very high interest rates to deter them from borrowing, but others are more sensitive to interest costs. Similarly, although many business firms can absorb high interest costs to finance investments in plant, equipment, or new inventory, firms with poor investment opportunities must reduce their demands for loanable funds. Also, high interest rates discourage firms that had earlier borrowed at low interest rates from refinancing their debts with new bond issues.

Thus, the supply of bonds tends to vary inversely with changes in the rate of interest. As shown in Figure 13.1b, the number of bonds issued tends to decrease as the interest rate rises, and tends to increase as the interest rate falls.

The volume of bond supply tends to vary directly with the level of income. Households that interpret increases in their current incomes as signs of larger future incomes may be encouraged to indulge in deficit spending. In addition, since higher levels of national income represent enlarged flows of production or higher prices and costs, business firms will require more credit to finance payrolls, inventories, and the additional capital equipment needed to sustain the larger volume of business. Thus, an increase in national income typically increases the demand for loanable funds, swelling the supply of bonds and shifting B^s in Figure 13.1 to the right. Similarly, a decrease in income typically lowers the demand for loanable funds and reduces the supply of bonds, shifting B^s to the left. The dashed $B^{s\prime}$ lines in the figure illustrate the shifts for the case of an increase in income.

13.2.2
Changes in equilibrium interest rates due to changes in income

We can summarize the theory of private nonbank bond supply and bond demand as they affect the interest rate with equations relating bond demand and supply to the rate of interest and the level of money income:

$$B^d = H(\overset{+}{r}, \overset{+}{Y}) \qquad \text{(bond demand)} \qquad (13.5)$$

$$B^s = J(\overset{-}{r}, \overset{+}{Y}) \qquad \text{(bond supply)} \qquad (13.6)$$

$$B^d = B^s \qquad \text{(equilibrium condition)} \qquad (13.7)$$

The plus and minus signs over interest and income indicate the direction of effect of changes in these variables on the number of bonds demanded and supplied. An increase in income raises both bond demand and bond supply, but a rise in the interest rate lowers the number of bonds supplied while it raises the number demanded. Given the level of income, and assuming that the bond market is competitive, excess demands and supplies of bonds should lower or raise the rate of interest until supply and demand come into equality. When that occurs, there is equilibrium in the bond market and an equilibrium interest rate.

The equilibrium will persist so long as income, tastes and preferences of the public, and opportunities facing firms and households do not change. When they do change, however, the curves shift, and market activity forces the rate of interest to travel to a new equilibrium level. Thus the persistent fluctuation of interest rates in the real world should be interpreted as responses to conditions that shift the supply and demand curves for bonds.

The effect of income changes upon the equilibrium rate of interest is ambiguous. Theory tells us that both bond demand and bond supply vary directly with income; increases in income shift both curves to the right, and vice versa. Unfortunately, we cannot predict which curve shifts the most when income changes. Thus the equilibrium interest rate can rise, fall, or remain unchanged when money income changes.

This point is illustrated in Figure 13.2, which depicts the *excess demand for bonds* (EB^d). Each EB^d curve is derived by subtracting bond supply from bond demand at each interest rate for a given set of curves. Thus, at r_0 in Figure 13.1 b, bond demand and supply are equal along EB^d, making the *excess* demand for bonds zero, so that EB^d in Figure 13.2 crosses the vertical axis at r_0. As interest rates rise above r_0, the difference $B^d - B^s$ increases the excess demand (planned lending exceeds planned borrowing). Conversely, interest rates below r_0 generate an excess supply of bonds (planned borrowing exceeds planned lending). Hence, Figure 13.2 shows negative excess demands of bonds below r_0, and positive excess demands above r_0; the EB^d curve has a positive slope.[1] The other EB^d curves are similarly derived.

---

[1] A more detailed explanation of the derivation of EB^d may help. Consider figures (a) and (b):

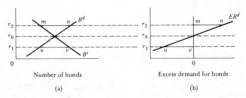

Number of bonds   Excess demand for bonds

(a)   (b)

At r_0, $B^d = B^s$, hence $EB^d = 0$, as shown in (b). At r_1, $B^d - B^s = uv$ in both figures; EB^d is negative. At r_2, $B^d - B^s = mn$, or a positive EB^d. Clearly a shift of B^d to the right lowers EB^d, and a shift of B^s to the right raises it. Equal shifts of B^d and B^s leave EB^d unchanged.

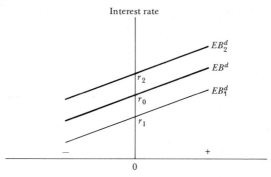

Figure 13.2 *Effects of income change on interest rates.*

EB^d in Figure 13.2 represents the excess demand curve for bonds *for a given level of income.* The equilibrium interest rate generated by the curve is r_0. Now, let income rise. If the rise in income shifts the bond demand function more than it shifts bond supply, the equilibrium rate of interest will fall to r_1. That is because the number of bonds people want to buy at the interest rate r_0 now exceeds the number borrowers want to sell; a new curve, EB_1^d now represents the true state of excess demand in the bond market. Under these new conditions, competitive forces are set in motion to drive the interest rate down to r_1.

A rise in income that increases bond supply more than bond demand raises the rate of interest, as indicated by the B_2^d curve intersection with the vertical axis at r_2. The reason is that at the old equilibrium rate, r_0, the volume of planned bond sales now exceeds the volume of planned purchases, driving down the prices of bonds and raising the interest rate.

Thus a rise in income fails to affect the rate of interest only if it leads people to shift demand and supply curves by equal amounts. This may occasionally be the case, but, in general, it probably is not. The reason is that over the business cycle, changes in money income can have very different impacts upon borrowers and lenders.

13.2.3
Cyclical movements of interest rates

Indirect evidence of the differential responses of lenders and borrowers to income changes is presented in Figure 13.3, which traces broad movements since 1910 of long-term corporate bond rates and the commercial paper rate. Over the whole period, the level of interest rates first moved from moderate to low levels in the 1930s and 1940s, then to very high levels in the 1970s. Nevertheless, the general pattern over the business cycle is reasonably stable. Interest rates usually peak at, or just after, the peak in business activity, when national income is cyclically high. The

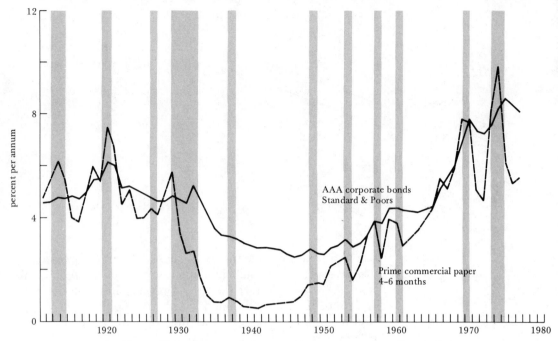

Figure 13.3 *Long- and short-term interest rates, annually. Shaded areas represent recessions and depressions. (Source: Federal Reserve System,* Historical Chart Book, *1978, p. 96.)*

trough in rates typically occurs at the same time or after the upturn in business activity (the right-hand edge of the shaded areas), almost never before.

Our theory would explain this pattern as follows: Rising interest rates during the expansion phase of the business cycle (the nonshaded areas just to the left of the shaded ones) reflect increasing excess demands for loanable funds—bond supplies increasing more rapidly than bond demands. Bond supplies are expanded by business borrowing to finance investments in fixed capital goods and in new inventories of raw materials and finished and semifinished goods. Consumers, encouraged by their higher incomes, are borrowing to add to their stocks of furniture, appliances, and automobiles. Simultaneously, rising incomes are increasing the financial savings of households; but the savings, which are invested directly in stocks and bonds or indirectly through financial intermediaries, do not increase the flow of bond demands at a pace equal to the rising flow of bond supplies. The result is a rise in interest rates.

Interest rates peak when a contraction of income sets in. The decline of income depresses the flow of bond supplies as businesses reduce their purchases of capital goods and stop adding to their inventories; consumers grow more cautious and borrow less. Also, business firms and households refrain from replacing their maturing debts with fresh bond issues. Thus, even though receding incomes may be decreasing the demand for bonds, they are also causing such substantial reductions in the supply of bonds that bond prices are pushed up and interest rates are pushed down.

Upturns in interest rates usually coincide with, or lag, the general upturn in the economy. The increase in rates signals the differential effects of rising economic activity upon bond supplies and bond demands. Lags in the upturn of interest rates may reflect accelerated bond purchases by households attempting to restore financial assets depleted during periods of enforced unemployment. For that reason, bond demands may at first increase faster than bond supplies, causing interest rates to fall for a period rather than to rise. An example is the continued decline of interest rates after the Great Depression ended in 1933. Generally speaking, however, an expansion period following the recovery eventually increases bond supplies faster than bond demands and carries interest rates in an upward direction.

Our theory of interest rate fluctuations ignores the influence of government deficit financing, the activities of the monetary authorities and the banking system, and the effects on interest rates of inflation. (We treat these topics in Sections 13.2.4 and 13.2.5). Thus it is unwise to use it to explain each of the cyclical movements of interest rates displayed in Figure 13.3. Even so, the theory has some degree of plausibility. Procyclical interest rate movements must in large measure come from procyclical fluctuations in the excess demand for bonds. Over the business cycle, the shifts of bond supply curves must be larger than the shifts of bond demand curves—that is, the demand for loanable funds must fluctuate more than its supply. To argue otherwise would be to put forth the odd notion that the demand for and supply of bonds vary inversely with changes in income, and that changes in income produce larger changes in bond demand than in bond supply. Evidence for such a view would be that credit flows slow down during booms and then speed up during slumps. As we know, however, the opposite is true. Credit flows speed up during booms and slow down during slumps. The evidence is given in Figure 13.4.

13.2.4
Effects of monetary policy on bond demand

An important addition to the supply of loanable funds comes from variations in the money supply. As discussed in Section 4.1.5 and elsewhere, excess reserves in the private banking system stimulate supplies of bank credit—that is, bank demands for bonds. Similarly, deficient reserves force banks to reduce credit supplies and decrease their demand for bonds. Swings in excess reserves frequently emerge from shifts in cur-

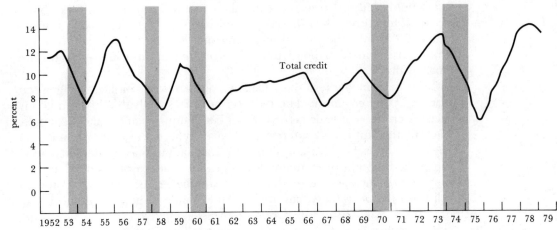

Figure 13.4 *Growth of total credit. Total credit is the percent change from four quarters earlier of credit extended to domestic nonfinancial sectors other than the federal government. Shaded areas are recessions. (Source: Richard G. Davis, "Broad Credit Measures as Targets for Monetary Policy,"* Federal Reserve Bank of New York Quarterly Review, *Summer 1979, p. 16.)*

rency holdings by the public, but the behavior of the Federal Reserve System is more important. The Fed's power to regulate the growth of the monetary base gives it ultimate power to control growth of reserves. This power, in turn, gives the Fed a direct influence upon the banking system's demand for bonds.

The Fed's role in the bond market is primarily implemented with open market operations. Each dollar it injects into the economy represents an increase in the monetary base and an increase in the market demand for bonds. Conversely, each dollar it absorbs represents a decrease in the monetary base and an increase in the supply of bonds. Thus, expansive open market operations increase both the monetary base and the excess demand for bonds, and restrictive operations decrease the monetary base and reduce the excess demand for bonds.

Changes in reserve requirements release or absorb excess reserves and cause commercial banks' demands for bonds to rise or fall. Similarly, a drop in the discount rate encourages (and a rise in the rate discourages) member bank borrowing from the Fed, indirectly influencing banks to expand (or contract) their demand for bonds. Thus, in using any of its major policy instruments, the Fed influences the rate of growth of the money supply and the overall excess demand for bonds. As a result, Federal Reserve actions to change the money supply also change the market interest rates.

13.2.5
Monetary policy and interest rates;
income and Fisher effects

The interconnections between monetary changes, the excess demand for bonds, and the rate of interest are shown in Figure 13.5a, which shows that the demand for bonds shifts directly with changes in the money supply. The resulting changes in the excess demand for bonds (Figure 13.5b) cause the rate of interest to fall when the money supply increases, or to rise when the money supply decreases.

Before leaving this topic, two comments are in order. First, note that it is *changes* in the money supply, and not the absolute *size* of the money supply that affects the excess demand for bonds. If banks are fully lent up, and if the Fed acts to maintain bank reserves at a given level, the banking system's demand for bonds is reduced to a replacement demand for securities maturing in bank portfolios. This replacement demand, when added to nonbank demand for bonds, may or may not produce an economy-wide excess demand for bonds. But even if it does, the excess demand for bonds is not being stimulated by additions to the money supply. Hence the interest variations it produces are independent of the actions of the monetary authorities.

Second, it is unlikely that the interest rate arising from monetary policy will persist. Three reasons can be given: (1) If the Fed changes the growth rate of the money supply, the excess demand for bonds will also change, leading the rate of interest to a new level (should the monetary growth rate be reduced to zero, for example, the interest rate would revert to a level determined solely by nonbank demands for and supplies of bonds); (2) Changes in the money supply change money income and

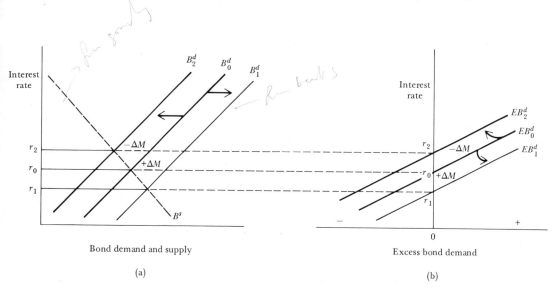

Bond demand and supply	Excess bond demand
(a)	(b)

Figure 13.5 *Effects of an increase or decrease in the money supply on the rate of interest.*

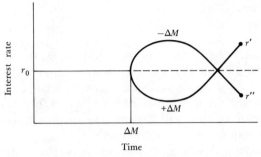

Figure 13.6 *Dynamic effects of money on interest rates.*

thereby set up a force that may further change the rate of interest; and (3) If monetary changes lead to inflation or deflation of prices, nominal interest rates may diverge from real rates.

Points (2) and (3) need further elaboration. Consider point (2): An increase in the money supply lowers the rate of interest and increases money income. But an increase in money income usually increases bond supplies more than bond demands. If so, the initial drop in rates is reversed. Conversely, a reduction in the money supply raises interest rates, but the drop in income may reduce bond supplies more than it reduces bond demands, reversing the rise in interest rates.

The point is illustrated in Figure 13.6, which plots movements in the interest rate from an initial equilibrium level, r_0. Assume that an initial drop of interest below r_0 is brought on by a one-time increase in the money supply. The one-time increase in money permanently raises income. If the rise in income raises bond demand and bond supply curves equally, the rate of interest returns to r_0 after an initial drop; but, in the likely event that it raises bond supply more than it increases bond demand, the rate of interest will rise above r_0, as to r'.

A one-time drop in the money supply may produce opposite results. Interest rates would initially rise above r_0 and then fall as a result of changes in income. The fall in interest would be back to r_0 or below (as to r''), depending upon the differential effects of the fall of income upon the supply and demand for bonds.

Point (3) has to do with a concept variously identified as the *price expectations effect* or, in honor of its best known proponent, the (Irving) *Fisher effect*.[2] Fisher was one of the leading American economists of this century. His research indicated that market interest rates are *nominal interest rates*. As such, they contain a component that reflects the inflationary expectations of borrowers and lenders as well as the *real rate of interest*. The real rate of interest is the rate that would be established in the bond

---

[2]Irving Fisher, *The Theory of Interest* (New York: Kelley, 1961. Original edition, 1930), Chapter XIX.

market if neither bond buyers nor bond sellers anticipated inflation. However, if bond buyers expect inflation, they are likely to demand compensation for the loss of purchasing power of the dollars they plan to lend. The compensation is a higher interest rate. So the bond demand curve shifts up and to the left when lenders expect inflation.

Since inflation lowers the purchasing power of the dollars borrowers must pay back to the lenders, bond sellers receive a bonus from rising prices. As a result, if they expect inflation, they will, if necessary, usually be willing to pay the higher interest rates demanded by the lenders. Thus the bond supply curve will shift up and to the right.

Assuming that both borrowers and lenders have the same inflationary expectations, the nominal rate of interest (r) will rise to a point at which it equals the real rate (rr) plus the expected rate of inflation $(\dot{p}^e)$:

$$r = rr + \dot{p}^e \tag{13.8}$$

Thus, a real rate of 5 percent plus an expected inflation rate of 5 percent will produce a nominal interest rate of 10 percent.

The nominal rate may be above or below the real rate of interest. It is above when inflationary expectations are positive, and below when the expectations are negative. Inflationary expectations are themselves related to the actual rate of inflation experienced in the past. In addition, they reflect the public's opinions about the future course of monetary and fiscal policy. For this reason, monetary impulses (positive or negative) thought to be inflationary or deflationary may be one of the causes of divergence of the nominal rate of interest from the real rate. The Fisher effect can, therefore, be added to the effect of income changes as a force that reverses the initial impact of monetary changes on the market rate of interest.

To summarize, changes in the money supply initially move market rates of interest in the opposite direction—that is, the *liquidity effect* of ΔM^s on r is negative. Once the monetary impulse is removed, interest rates would move back to their original level were it not for the changes in income or price expectations the monetary impulse provides. The changes in income frequently push interest rates up or down in a direction opposite to the direction provided by the monetary changes. The Fisher effect does the same thing—that is, the *income effect* and the *price expectations effect* are positive. Thus, as shown in Figure 13.6, the interest rate may ultimately settle above or below the level prevailing prior to the monetary change.

The graphs in Figure 13.7 provide a good deal of real-world evidence in support of this theory. Figure 13.7a shows the correlation over time between inflation and the nominal Treasury bill rate in the United States. Figure 13.7b shows a similar correlation across 10 major countries during the 1973–1978 period. These correlations are due in part to the fact that inflation raises nominal income and that, in so doing, it usually

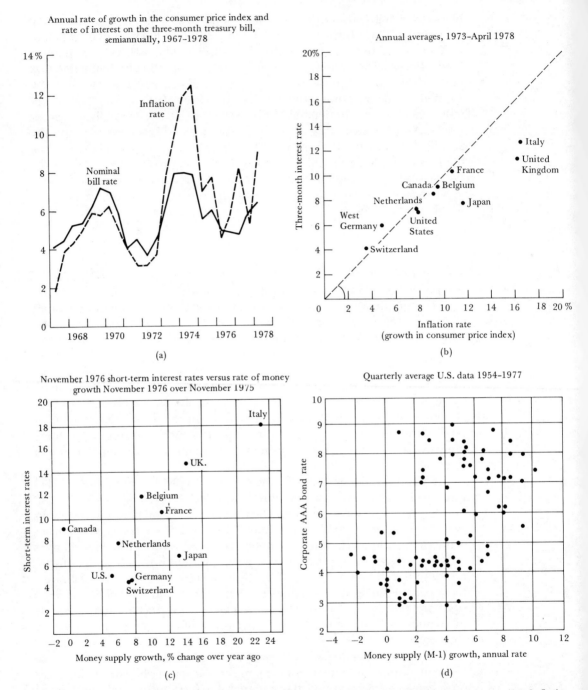

Figure 13.7 *Association of inflation and money growth with interest rates. (a) Inflation and interest rates. (b) Inflation rates and interest rates in ten major countries. (c) Interest rate versus money growth for OECD countries. (d) Interest rate versus money growth. (Source: Federal Reserve Bank of Minneapolis.)*

raises business and household demand for credit faster than it raises the supply of credit originating in enlarged household savings. In addition, persistent inflation during the 1970s probably also affected the public's expectations of inflation, so that the observed correlations may also be due to the operation of the Fisher effect. The income effect and the Fisher effect help explain the observations in Figure 13.7 (c and d). Without the presence of one or both of the effects, the correlation between money growth and interest rates internationally, or over time in the United States, would have been negative. But the negative liquidity effect of increases in money on interest rates was frequently overcome by the positive effects on interest rates of rising money incomes and of high inflationary expectations.

13.2.6
Effects of government deficits on interest rates

Every level of government at one time or another runs a deficit. State and local governments are ordinarily required by law to balance their operating budgets, but they frequently borrow to make capital improvements. Some even borrow to finance current outlays—recall New York City's recurring difficulties. At other times, these governments run fairly large surpluses—California's large accumulated surplus in 1978 invited the famous tax revolt embodied in Proposition 13.

Federal government budget surpluses are rare. Since World War II, there have been only eight surplus years; the last was in 1969. Budget surpluses are usually small. Deficits are another matter; in recent years they have frequently exceeded $30 billion.

Because of the federal government's special position in security and money markets, we must examine the impact of its deficits on security markets. In so doing, it helps to consolidate the accounts of the Treasury and the Federal Reserve. We can then define the federal government's deficit as

$$G - T = P_B B_G^S + \Delta Ba$$

where G is government spending on final products and T is tax revenue net of transfer payments. The current deficit $(G - T)$ represents expenditures net of taxes that must be made up by an equivalent amount of borrowing from the public or from purchases of government bonds by the Federal Reserve System. The number of new bonds offered the public by the government times the price of the bonds $(P_B \times B_G^S)$ is the portion of the deficit financed by the public. The portion financed by the Fed is the increase in the monetary base (ΔBa). Since the budget equation consolidates the accounts of the Fed and the Treasury, the bonds bought by the

Fed are shown as the increase in the monetary base; to enter them separately into the equation would be double counting.

Federal government surpluses—T larger than G—are usually accompanied by a retirement of government debt. With debt retirement, the government joins the private sector as a source of demand for bonds, since it buys back its own debt. However, to keep things simple, we will treat this case as one in which the government's supply of bonds is negative.

The peculiarities of federal government finance are illustrated in Figure 13.8. Suppose the government starts with a balanced budget. In that event, the excess demand curve labeled EB^d crosses the interest rate axis at an equilibrium rate of r_0. Now, let the government increase its spending and begin to run a deficit. If it finances its deficit by selling bonds to the nonbank public, the Treasury must issue new bonds for sale in the security markets. The new bonds add to the existing supply of privately issued bonds and create an overall excess supply of bonds (equal to the distance qr_0. In other words, the effect of the Treasury decision to borrow from the public is to shift the excess bond demand curve up and to the left. In the new circumstances, the excess supply of bonds cannot be eliminated unless the equilibrium interest rate rises to r_1, which is the rate at which the demand for bonds equals the total supply of bonds being issued by the Treasury and the other sectors of the economy.

A decision by the Fed to finance the Treasury's deficit would cause an initial drop (not rise) in the rate of interest. Recall from Chapter 9 that the Fed rarely directly finances federal government deficits. Instead, it "even keels" by purchasing on the open market privately held government bonds at the same time the Treasury is issuing its new bonds for the

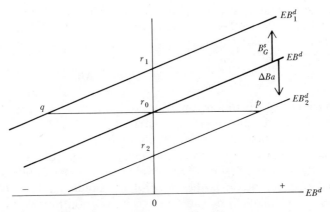

Figure 13.8 *Effects of government deficits on interest rates.*

open market. Thus, the new Treasury bonds hitting the market find an equivalent new demand in the market equal to the injections of new monetary base by the Fed. But dealers and others who have sold their holdings of government bonds to the Fed now find themselves with extra deposits in the banking system. And the banks find themselves with excess reserves. Thus the new monetary base provides both the banks and the nonbank public with the means to increase their demand for bonds. As a result, the overall excess demand for bonds should rise (say to EB^d in Figure 13.8), lowering the equilibrium market rate of interest to r_2 from the balanced budget rate, r_0.

Thus the initial effect of the government financing a deficit with funds drawn from the Fed, instead of from the nonbank public, is to lower, not raise the market rate of interest. But, because the Federal Reserve's purchases involve increases in the money supply, we cannot avoid discussing the further repercussions of the decision. The increase of the money supply will raise the equilibrium level of national income. In so doing, it will set in motion forces that may reverse the drop in interest rates brought about by the use of Federal Reserve resources to finance the budgetary deficit. As discussed above, these forces include stimulation of an excess demand for credit by business and households (which would raise the real rate of interest) and the enhancement of inflationary expectations (which would raise the nominal rate of interest). These secondary forces are stronger the larger is the deficit that is being financed with increases in the monetary base. In some cases, the forces may be strong enough not only to reverse the initial drop in interest rates, but to also raise interest rates above their previous level.

Contrary to deficits, government surpluses tend to lower interest rates. For example, when the Treasury uses moneys acquired from the public with a surplus to retire privately held government debt, it adds its own demand for bonds to that of the public. The increase in market demand for bonds raises bond prices and lowers the market rate of interest. In the case where the Treasury uses surplus tax moneys collected from the public to buy bonds held by the Federal Reserve System, there are further effects. The first is a reduction of the monetary base and the overall money supply, since the private sector's moneys are transferred from private banks to the Fed, in which case both demand deposits and bank reserves decline. The second effect is a reduction of income, induced by a reduction in the money supply. The drop in income will in most cases put downward pressure on market interest rates. Thus, although the reduction in the money supply accompanying retirement of Treasury debt held by the Fed may at first cause a rise in interest rates, the secondary effects operating through reductions in income can reverse the rise and perhaps even cause interest rates to fall below levels prior to the development of the surplus.

Our discussion shows that the economic effects of fiscal policy cannot be assessed without making a distinction between a *pure fiscal policy* and a policy implemented through the agency of monetary policy. Fiscal policy is the manipulation of government expenditures or tax revenues for the purpose of affecting aggregate demand. Except for policies designed to maintain balanced budgets, all fiscal policies change the size of the government's surplus or deficit. Pure fiscal policies involve budgetary changes that increase or decrease the private sector's holdings of government bonds. For that reason, deficits tend to drive interest rates up, and surpluses to drive them down. But fiscal policies implemented with changes in the monetary base have more complex impacts. Such deficits initially drive interest rates down, not up; surpluses drive interest rates up, not down. More important, however, the monetary changes lead to substantial movements in national income. The latter are not only important in themselves, but they eventually set in motion forces that may reverse the initial changes in the rate of interest.

13.2.7
Summary of the theory of interest

We are now in a position to provide a summary of the theory of interest. Recall that the private nonbank demand for bonds is expressed by an equation, $B^d = H(r,Y)$, while the supply of privately issued bonds is denoted by $B^s = J(r,Y)$. Combining these expressions with the behavior of the monetary authorities, banks, and the Treasury we can express the market for bonds with the following equations:

$$P_B B^d = P_B H(\overset{+}{r},\overset{+}{Y}) + \Delta M \tag{13.9a}$$

$$P_B B^s = P_B J(\overset{-}{r},\overset{+}{Y}) + P_B B_G^s \tag{13.9b}$$

Subtracting Equation (13.9b) from (13.9a), dividing through by P_B, and rearranging the terms we get

$$EB^d = HJ(\overset{+}{r},\overset{?}{Y}) + \left(\frac{\Delta M}{P_B} - B_G^s \right) \tag{13.10}$$

Equation (13.10) divides the excess demand for bonds into two parts. The first, $HJ(r,Y)$, is the private nonbank excess demand for privately issued bonds—$H(r,Y) - J(r,Y)$. As indicated in Figure 13.2 and elsewhere, this portion of the excess demand for bonds is positively related to the rate of interest. But, since changes in income may variously alter bond demands and supplies, the excess demand for bonds can shift up, shift down, or remain the same as income increases or decreases.

The second element of excess demand—$(\Delta M/P_B) - B_G^s$—is the difference between the number of bonds current changes in the money supply permit banks and money authorities to buy and the number of bonds being issued by the Treasury. ($1/P_B$ is the number of bonds $1.00 can purchase, hence $\Delta M/P_B$ is the number of bonds the change in the money supply can buy.) Since the second element combines the actions of the monetary and fiscal authorities, it is a joint policy variable. When $B_G^s = 0$, the variable describes the effects of monetary policy operating alone upon the rate of interest. When $\Delta M = 0$, it describes the effect of a pure fiscal policy. When $\Delta M/P_B = B_G^s = 0$, neither policy has influence.[3]

Thus, the private plus the public excess demand for bonds in the first instance determines the rate of interest. However, this determination can be upset by changes in the level of income. That being the case, the theory is insufficient to fully determine the rate of interest. The reason is that Equation (13.10) cannot determine both interest and income—one equation cannot determine two unknowns. To complete the theory, we need another equation. It will come as no surprise to learn that the other equation is the Cambridge equation.

13.3
A monetary theory of income

To place the theory of income in perspective, recall Equation (13.2), which restates Say's Principle for an economy possessing bonds. Setting that equation equal to zero, we get an expression for monetary equilibrium:

$$Y^d - Y^s + P_B(B^d - B^s) = M^s - M^d = 0 \qquad (13.11)$$

Clearly, monetary equilibrium in this equation does not necessarily imply income equilibrium. For that to occur, there must also be equilibrium in the bond market. That is, an aggregative equilibrium in the market for goods and services is assured if (1) the demand for money adjusts to equality with the existing supply, *and* (2) market forces bring the demand and supply of bonds into equality.

Now, adjustments of money demand and the excess demand for bonds are related to variations in the rate of interest and the level of income. Hence we can replace $P_B(B^d - B^s)$ and $(M^s - M^d)$ in Equation

---

[3] When $\Delta M/P_B$ and $B_G^s \neq 0$, the situation can be quite complex, depending upon their relative sizes and signs. The complexity arises from the indirect influence of money upon interest via its effect on income. For example, let $\Delta M/P_B = B_G^s$. In this case, the bonds being sold by the Treasury are being bought up by the Fed and the banks. Even so, the change in the money supply is likely to affect interest by affecting income, which reacts back upon the bond market by changing $HJ(r,Y)$. To test your understanding of the theory, experiment with the effects of other combinations of monetary and fiscal policy.

(13.11) with

$$P_B(B^d - B^s) = P_B HJ(\overset{?}{\overline{r}}, Y) - B_G^s)$$ (13.12a)

$$M^s - M^d = M^s - k(\overline{r})Y$$ (13.12b)

where $k(r)Y$ is the demand for money function discussed in Section 12.3.6, $HJ(r,Y)$ is the private nonbank excess demand for privately issued bonds, and B_G^s is the federal deficit financed by sales of bonds to the non-bank public.

When the Federal Reserve is maintaining the money supply at a given level, the two equations are sufficient to determine both monetary equilibrium and income equilibrium. That is to say, if income and the rate of interest are such as to bring the bond and money markets into equilibrium, by Say's Principle the market for goods and services will also be in equilibrium—that is, if

$$\left. \begin{array}{c} HJ(r,Y) - B_G^s = 0 \\ M^s - k(r)Y = 0 \end{array} \right\} \quad \text{monetary theory of income} \quad (13.13a)$$

then

$$Y^d - Y^s = 0 \qquad (13.13b)$$

Equation system (13.13) provides a complete theory of nominal income in the sense that it focuses two equations upon two unknowns, r and Y. Equation (13.13b) can be thought of as a quantity of money theory of nominal income. But, since rate of interest helps determine the demand for money, it is an incomplete theory. Similarly, Equation (13.13a) can be described as a loanable funds theory of interest. But the level of income affects the excess demand for bonds, requiring us to bring in a theory of income. Thus both equations are necessary to determine interest and income. And, once they do, the market for goods and services will be in equilibrium.

13.3.1
Diagrammatic exposition of the theory

To understand the monetary theory of income, it helps to study its workings with diagrams illustrating the relationships between the bond market and the money market. Figure 13.9 describes the bond market with a series of excess demand curves for bonds (on the left). It illustrates the money market with the two diagrams on the right (drawn from Figure 12.7 in Section 12.3.6).

Each curve in the upper right-hand side of Figure 13.9 describes

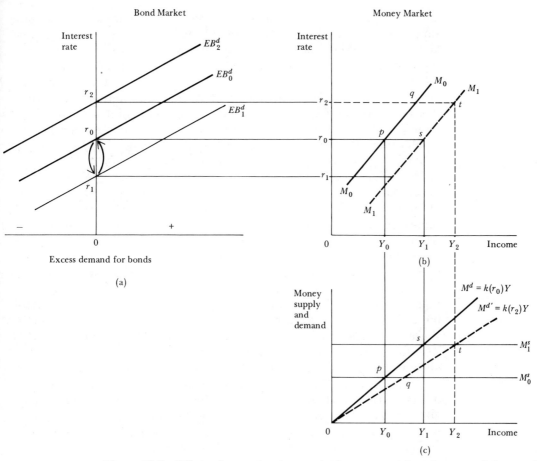

Bond Market

Money Market

(a)

Excess demand for bonds

(b)

(c)

Figure 13.9 *Effects of a one-time increase in the money supply on income and the rate of interest.*

combinations of interest and income that bring the demand for money into equality with a given stock of money. For example, the money market equilibrium curve labeled $M_0 M_0$ assumes a fixed money stock, M_0^s. As shown in Figure 13.9c, income must be Y_0 if the demand for money set by the interest rate r_0 is to come into equality at point p with M_0^s. If income were higher (lower) than Y_0, then the demand for money would exceed (fall short of) M_0^s, and the money market would not be in equilibrium. Provided that the bond market is in equilibrium (as it is for r_0 when the excess demand curve for bonds EB_0^d prevails), the equilibrium in the money market assures us that Y_0 is also an equilibrium quantity. Check this point with Equations (13.13).

A movement along $M_0 M_0$ yields different combinations of interest and income that bring equilibrium to the money market. For example, suppose the excess demand for bonds shifts to EB_2^d. The equilibrium market rate of interest would rise to r_2. The higher interest rate would shift the demand for money function in the lower right-hand figure to $M^{d'}$, and a new monetary equilibrium would be established at an income level between Y_0 and Y_1. The combination of income and interest that produces this new monetary equilibrium is also shown by point q on the M_0M_0 money market equilibrium curve. Of course, since the bond market is in equilibrium at r_2, the money market equilibrium also carries with it an equilibrium level of national income (Say's Principle).

Assuming the rate of interest is back at r_0, let us imagine an increase in the money supply to M_1^s. Suppose, also, that for some reason, the rate of interest were to remain at r_0. This combination of circumstances would signify an excess supply of money at the income level Y_0. The excess supply of money would create an excess demand for goods and services; income would start to rise. Assuming nothing that would disturb the rate of interest or the underlying determinants of the demand for money line M^d, the rise of income would continue until it would stop at Y_1, at which point the demand for money would again equal the money supply. Looking at Figure 13.9b, we note that the increase in the money supply has shifted the money market equilibrium curve to M_1M_1. Point s on M_1M_1 describes the interest rate–income combination (r_0, Y_1) that maintains equilibrium in the money market under the new monetary conditions.

We can now discuss a few of the details of the monetary theory of income. We must first trace through the effects on the level of income and the rate of interest of an increase in the money supply. In so doing, imagine that in each of the following cases we begin with an equilibrium combination of interest and income of little r_0 and Y_0. Then, we introduce a one-time change in the money supply equal to $M_1^s - M_0^s$, and trace through its effects under different assumptions.

Assumption 1. *An increase in nominal income raises the demand for and supply of bonds equally.* Under this assumption, any change in nominal income leaves the excess demand curve for bonds unchanged at EB_0^d. However, the increase in the money supply temporarily increases the excess demand for bonds and displaces the curve to EB_1^d, which temporarily reduces the rate of interest to r_1. But once the money supply ceases to change, the excess demand curve for bonds reverts to EB_0^d, and the rate of interest returns to r_0 as shown by the arrow. In the meantime, however, the extra money stock has created an excess supply of money at Y_0 forcing income to rise until it reaches Y_1. So the new equilibrium combination of interest and income (r_0, Y_1) is at point s on the new money market equilibrium curve M_1M_1.

Assumption 2. *An increase in income increases the supply of bonds more than it increases the demand for bonds.* Under this assumption, the increase in income stimulated by the increase in the money supply shifts the excess demand curve for bonds to EB_2^d. The equilibrium rate of interest rises to r_2; hence, even though the new money market equilibrium curve is M_1M_1, the point of equilibrium is t, (r_2,Y_2). Income is higher than in the previous case because the rise in the interest rate has shifted the demand for money line in the lower figure to $M^{d'}$. To bring the demand for money into equality with the new supply, M_1^s, it is necessary for income to rise above Y_1.

Assumption 3. *The increase in money causes an increase in inflationary expectations.* In this case, the nominal interest rate rises because bond buyers demand compensation for the expected loss of purchasing power of the money they are lending. Borrowers agree, since the money they must repay is worth less than the money they borrowed. Thus, the excess demand curve shifts to EB_2^d, and the rate of interest rises to r_2. Instead of settling at Y_1, income settles into a new equilibrium at Y_2—point t on M_1M_1.

The effects of a decrease in the money supply on income and the rate of interest can be analyzed exactly as we have analyzed the effects of an increase in the money supply. But we leave the analysis to the reader as an exercise. In the meantime, we show a case in which income can change without changes in the money supply or prior shifts in the demand for money. This is the case of a pure fiscal policy: Let the Treasury finance a new budgetary deficit with an issue of bonds to the private nonbank sector. As discussed in Section 13.2.5, such a policy would shift the excess demand curve for bonds to EB_2^d from EB_0^d. The rise in the interest rate to r_2 would shift the demand for money curve down from M^d to $M^{d'}$. Assuming the money supply is M_0^s, the new point of monetary equilibrium on M_0M_0 would be at q instead of p. So income would rise from its initial equilibrium level of Y_0 to a higher one, just below Y_1.

SUMMARY

Say's Principle tells us that the aggregate money value of all planned trades must be zero. Included in the planned trades are the flow demands and supplies of bonds. The bond market determines the rate of interest. Bond demands are affected by the rate of interest, the level of income, and inflationary expectations. Bond supplies are affected by the same variables. Given income and inflationary expectations, an interest rate, r_0, is determined by the interaction of bond demands and supplies.

Logically, an increase in income can raise, lower, or leave unchanged the interest rate. Over the business cycle, however, bond supplies fluctuate more than bond demand, causing interest rates to rise above and fall below r_0. Changes in inflationary expectations over the cycle reinforce the fluctuations of interest rates.

Government borrowing raises the rate of interest when pure fiscal policy is in force. A fiscal policy backed by the monetary authorities temporarily lowers the interest rate; but, since income and (perhaps) inflationary expectations are stimulated by the increase in the money supply, the nominal interest rate may eventually rise above the initial level.

Increases in the money supply initially lower the rate of interest because they create temporary excess demands for bonds, raising their prices. Once money supply increases are halted, the rate of interest rises back to its previous level, unless further boosted by the effects of higher incomes upon the excess demand for bonds and by inflationary expectations upon the nominal rate of interest.

All of these effects are consistent with a theory that integrates the supply and demand for bonds and the Cambridge equation in a comprehensive model. The remaining task is to fill out the model and to explore its ability to explain movements in income, prices, and interest rates in the real world.

APPENDIX
THE TERM STRUCTURE OF
INTEREST RATES

There is no single interest rate in the security markets. Instead, there is a whole structure of rates that rises and falls over time. Rates on various securities reflect different degrees of credit or default risk and differences in such features as call provisions, taxability, timing of coupons, convertibility into other securities (under certain conditions some bonds are convertible into stocks), marketability, and term to maturity. In this appendix, we shall discuss differences in yields between short-term and long-term bonds.

Figure 13.A.1 shows a series of *yield curves* relating the market yields on U.S. Treasury bonds to their terms to maturity. At the short end stand Treasury bills and notes; the upper end refers to long-term Treasury bonds. Credit risk does not enter into the determination of interest rates on U.S. government bonds, hence the term structure of interest rates on these bonds is primarily related to the months or years remaining to maturity.

Rising yield curves are typical of periods of slack or of recovery. As the economy moves to its expansion phase, and then to a cyclical peak, short rates rise faster than long rates, ultimately resulting in a downward sloping curve, perhaps with a little hump, as shown in the figure for March 1979. Students of the yield curve have shown that yield curves averaged over the business cycle have upward slopes, at least up to a point, after which they flatten out for long-term or very long-term bonds.

There is more than one theory for the variations in the term structure of interest rates. One prominent explanation is the *market segmentation theory*. The basic idea underlying this theory is that long-term bonds and short-term bonds are imperfect substitutes, so that under most market conditions they are likely to carry different prices. In particular, long-

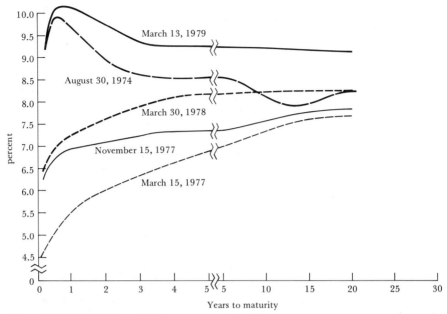

Figure 13.A.1 *Yields on U.S. government securities. (Source: Federal Reserve Bank of St. Louis, released March 30, 1979.)*

term bonds are likely to carry lower prices than short-term bonds. The reason is that changes in interest rates cause more extreme price fluctuations in long-term bonds than they do in short-term bonds. Hence, the longer the term to maturity the larger the market or capital risk to bond holders. The greater risk forces borrowers to pay lenders *risk premiums* in the form of higher interest rates.

Insurance companies, pension funds, and many other lenders are able to hold long-term bonds to maturity. As a result, they do not demand a risk premium. But, if the supply of long-term bonds issued by borrowers exceeds the demand for such bonds by long-term lenders, then many of the bonds must be bought by institutions, such as banks, and individuals who prefer medium- or short-term securities. These groups will not buy long-term bonds unless their prices (interest rates) are more attractive than those attached to short- and medium-term bonds.

According to the segmentation theory, the basic tendency for yield curves to slope upward can be explained by a "constitutional weakness" in the market for loanable funds. If it exists, this weakness is related to the fact that, on balance, institutions of the money and capital markets prefer short-term to long-term assets.

The segmentation theory explains downward sloping yield curves as a special feature of business booms. During such booms, great pressure is put on banks and other lenders for short-term inventory loans and dealer loans to stock brokers and other spectators. These pressures, together with tight monetary policy measures, accelerate the rise in short-term interest rates as compared to more slowly rising long-term rates.

Although there is some evidence supporting the segmentation hypothesis, most economists hold to another theory—the *expectations hypothesis*. According to this theory, long-term interest rates observed in the market are averages of current prevailing short rates and *expected future short rates*.

The theory is illustrated by the following ideas:

1. Any bond that matures in n years carries an interest rate R_n that, compounded, makes a dollar invested in the bond worth $(1+R_n)^n$ after n years.
2. Short-term investments in a series of one-year bonds yields a return of $(1+r_1)(1+r_2) \cdots (1+r_n)$ for each dollar invested. In this alternative, r_1 is the current rate on one-year bonds and $r_2, r_3, \ldots, r_n$ are expected one-year rates on one-year bonds in each future year.
3. Thus, an investor who wishes to lend for a period of n years has the alternative of buying an n-year bond carrying an interest rate of R_n, or of buying a one-year bond carrying an interest rate of r_1 and accumulating the proceeds of the bond for a series of $n-1$ years in a series of future reinvestments in one-year bonds earning *expected* (not actual) interest rates of $r_2, r_3, \ldots, r_n$.

Assuming the investor has great confidence in his expectations, he will be indifferent when

$$(1+R_n)^n = (1+r_1)(1+r_2)(1+r_3) \cdots (1+r_n)$$

Thus, one plus the long-term bond rate on any n-period bond is nothing more than the nth root of one plus the individual single rates expected to prevail over n periods.

To see how the theory works, assume that traders expect future rates to equal the current rate (r_1). The n-year rate (R_n) would then equal r_1. So too would R_{n-1}, R_{n-2}, and so forth. Now suppose investors expect future one-year rates to rise above the current rate. The right-hand side of the equation would then be larger than the left-hand side, hence investors would prefer a series of short-term investments to a long-term bond. Consequently, they would reduce their demands for long-term bonds and increase their demands for one-year bonds, which would have the effect of driving the long rate up and the short rate down. The tendency would be reinforced if borrowers have the same expectations as lenders. Expecting rising future rates, they would try to borrow long- and reduce short-term loans. As a result, long-term bond supplies would increase and short-term bond supplies would decrease, causing the long-term interest rate to rise higher and the short-term rate to fall even lower. The movements would stop once the terms on both sides of the equation are again equal.

The expectation hypothesis explains falling yield curves by the opposite reasoning. If traders expect a fall in future rates, lenders will prefer to lend long and borrowers will prefer to borrow short. Thus long rates will fall and short rates will rise until there is no longer any advantage of a series of short-term loans over a single long-term loan for the same period—that is, until the two sides of the equation are equal.

The expectations hypothesis has been criticized because it assumes that bond traders have expectations of future rates over long periods of time. Although there is some merit to this point, much empirical evidence is consistent with the hypothesis. For example, the changing shape of the curve over the business cycle is consistent with changing expectations of interest rates. That is, at the peak, people naturally expect falling future rates, and at the trough they naturally expect rising future rates. Nevertheless, the theory does not explain well the tendency for yield curves to have an upward slope as an average over the cycle. The segmentation hypothesis, with its stress upon risk premiums attached to long-term bonds, therefore, appears to be a useful supplement to the expectations theory.

DISCUSSION QUESTIONS

1. Some economists argue that interest is the price of money; others that it is the price of credit. Comment.

2. Monetary equilibrium and income equilibrium imply equilibrium in the market for bonds. Why?

3. Distinguish between the stock demand and supply of bonds and the flow demand and supply of bonds. Are they related?

4. Draw an excess bond demand curve using bond prices on the vertical axis. Draw another using the rate of interest on the vertical axis. How do they differ? Why?

5. Under what condition will an increase of nominal income cause the rate of interest to rise? To fall? To remain unchanged?

6. Procyclical movements in the rate of interest are evidence that the supply of bonds shifts more over the business cycle than does the demand for bonds. Why?

7. What are the short- and long-run impacts of changes in the money supply on the market rate of interest? Explain.

8. Compare the effect on the market rate of interest of a government deficit carried out under a pure fiscal policy with another carried out with the aid of an expansionary monetary policy.

9. Using the theory of interest and the quantity theory, describe the impact of a reduction of the money supply upon the level of nominal income and the rate of interest.

10. Figure 13.A.1 in the appendix shows yield curves for U.S. Treasury securities that both rise and fall. What explains these different shapes?

IMPORTANT TERMS AND CONCEPTS

- [ ] excess flow demand for bonds
- [ ] excess stock demand for bonds
- [ ] expectations hypothesis
- [ ] fiscal policy
- [ ] Fisher effect
- [ ] flow demand for (supply of) bonds
- [ ] government budget deficit
- [ ] income effect on interest rate
- [ ] liquidity effect on interest rate
- [ ] market segmentation theory

- [ ] monetary theory of income
- [ ] nominal rate of interest
- [ ] price expectations effect
- [ ] pure fiscal policy
- [ ] real rate of interest
- [ ] risk premiums
- [ ] stock demand for (supply of) bonds
- [ ] term structure of interest rates
- [ ] yield curve

ADDITIONAL READINGS

A number of the topics touched upon in this chapter are also discussed in William Poole, *Money and the Economy: A Monetarist View* (Reading, Massachusetts: Addison-Wesley, 1978). Also see, J. Huston McCulloch, *Money and Inflation* (New York: Academic Press, 1975). A dynamic version of the loanable funds–Cambridge equation approach to the theory of income and interest is in Michael Darby, *Intermediate Macroeconomics* (New York: McGraw-Hill, 1979). An incomplete version of the model (because it does not contain a loanable funds theory) is in Milton Friedman, "A Monetary Theory of Nominal Income," *Journal of Political Economy*, Vol. 79, No. 2, March/April 1971, pp. 323–337. Finally, a rather comprehensive loanable funds approach to financial markets and interest rates is in Murray Polakoff *et at., Financial Institutions and Markets,* 2nd edition (Boston: Houghton Mifflin, 1981). Inspiration for the overall model comes from D.H. Robertson, "Mr. Keynes and the Rate of Interest," *Economic Journal,* 1938, reprinted in Sir Dennis H. Robertson, *Essays in Monetary Theory* (London: Staples Press, 1956).

Well-known works on term structure theory (Appendix) include Reuben Kessell, *The Cylical Behavior of the Term Structure of Interest Rates* (New

York: National Bureau of Economic Research, 1965); Burton Malkiel, *The Term Structure of Interest Rates* (Princeton: Princeton University Press, 1966); and Burton Malkiel, *The Term Structure of Interest Rates, Empirical Evidence and Applications* (New York: McCaleb-Seiler, 1970). A good textbook treatment of the overall risk–term structure problem is in George G. Kaufman, *Money, The Financial System and the Economy,* 2nd edition (Chicago: Rand McNally College Publishing, 1977), Chapter 9.

14

The Federal Budget and the Economy

OUTLINE

Methods of Financing Government Spending
Methods that Don't Change the Money Supply
Methods that Change the Money Supply
Effects of a Pure Fiscal Policy on Money Income
Concept of Private Income
Adding Government to the Theory of Money Income
Effects of Changes in Government Spending (Taxes held Constant) on Income—
The Crowding Out Effect
Effects of Tax Changes on Income—Supply-side Theory
Tax Changes in a Money Economy
Transfer Payments and Money Income
Balanced-budget Changes in Taxes and Government Spending
Fiscal Policy Financed with Changes in the Money Supply
Financing an Increase in Government Spending with Money and Debt
Financing Tax Cuts with Increases in the Money Supply
Empirical Evidence on Fiscal Policy

Completion of our theory requires discussion of the impact of the federal government's budget upon the level of income. Federal finances are notoriously complicated, and it takes considerable expertise to unravel from budgetary data the precise impact of government spending and taxing upon the U.S. economy. But we cannot shirk this task. Federal government spending, inclusive of transfer payments, represents about one-fourth of gross national product. In addition, it is financed in ways that can have profound impacts upon the rate of growth of private incomes, interest rates, and the rate of inflation.

This chapter discusses the economics of federal budgets from several points of view. Section 14.1 takes up the various methods available to the Treasury for financing federal expenditures. Some of these methods are neutral respecting changes in the money supply, and some are not. Accordingly, different methods of financing the same level of spending are more or less disruptive of the level of income established by the private market forces.

Sections 14.2 and 14.3 modify the monetary theory of income discussed in Chapter 13 to include the effects of government spending and taxation upon the level of income and the rate of interest. We can use the modified model to explore the effects of pure fiscal policy—that is, variations in government spending and taxes financed without changes in the money supply—upon the economy. Section 14.4 discusses fiscal policy in the presence of a cooperating monetary policy.

14.1
Methods of financing government spending

Government expenditures consist of (1) purchases of goods and services, (2) transfer payments, and (3) so-called off-budget expenditures, such as government loans to farmers and homeowners (see Section 3.3). Transfer payments consist of items like social security pensions, welfare payments (for example, food stamps), and interest on the federal debt. Expenditures on goods and services include payments to federal employees and purchases of goods and services from the private sector.

The federal government's budget equation (14.1) provides an important clue as to the significance of the various ways in which its outlays may be financed:

$$G - T = B_G^s + \Delta Ba \tag{14.1}$$

$$B_G^s = B_G^{db} + B_G^{dp} + B_G^{df} \tag{14.2}$$

Government expenditures *(G)* financed with taxes *(T)* reduce its potential deficit. Hence, aside from the various (and important) allocational effects such expenditures and taxes may have upon the private economy, this method of financing spending is likely to have the least effect upon the level of money income. All other methods of financing outlays involve deficit spending. Deficits involve increases in the monetary base (ΔBa) or purchases of additional supplies of government bonds by commercial banks (B_G^{db}), nonbank domestic investors (B_G^{dp}) or foreigners (B_G^{df}).

Deficits financed with increases in the monetary base (ΔBa) raise the money supply both directly and indirectly—via creation of excess reserves and further deposit expansion. But deficits financed with sales of bonds to the private sector or to foreigners may or may not increase the money supply. Thus the inflationary impact of deficits depends upon who buys new issues of government bonds and how they pay for them.

14.1.1
Methods that don't change the money supply

Government expenditures constitute a flow of dollars to the public in the form of purchases of goods and services, transfer payments, and loans. Tax revenues consist of a flow of dollars from the public to the government. When these two flows are equal, the government is running a balanced budget; the monetary impact of the budget is nil.

When tax revenues fall short of expenditures, the deficit is positive and the government's budget has potential implications for the money stock. But this potential is unrealized if the government finances its expenditures with bond sales to (a) nonbank private investors or (b) banks that have no excess reserves.

Case (a) needs little explanation. Private individuals and nonbank businesses are powerless to create money, hence to buy government bonds they must reduce their expenditures upon privately produced goods and services and privately issued bonds. In effect, they transfer part of the existing money stock to the government, which, in making its outlays, returns it to the private sector, leaving the total money supply unchanged.

Case (b) is a bit more subtle. To be sure, bank credit expansion creates money. But to create money the banking system needs excess reserves. We already know that banks' hunger for profits plus an efficient federal funds market usually keeps system-wide excess reserves to a minimum. Thus the new Treasury bonds usually hit the market at a time banks possess little or no excess reserves; hence the government's deficit is unlikely to have much of a monetary impact.

Sales of government bonds to foreigners may or may not affect the money supply. Private foreign individuals or businesses that buy U.S. government bonds generally use existing dollars, as in case (a) described above. But the situation with foreign commercial banks and agencies is different. Current definitions of the U.S. money supply exclude commercial bank deposits owned by such entities. Thus U.S. government expenditures financed with commercial bank deposits acquired from bond sales to foreign commercial banks and to official foreign agencies increase the officially recorded money supply, because transfer of the deposits to the account of the Treasury (which disburses them to the private sector) results in an increase in privately held deposits.

14.1.2
Methods that change the money supply

Methods of financing deficits that increase the money supply divide into two subgroups: (1) methods that increase the monetary base and (2) methods that increase private bank deposits but that do not change the base. Clearly, methods that increase the monetary base have potential for a much greater monetary impact than methods that do not.

Methods that increase the monetary base include (a) Federal Reserve purchases of new government debt through direct purchases (which are rare) or indirect purchases through "even keeling," (b) Treasury expenditures of previously accumulated cash balances on deposit with the Fed, and (c) foreign central bank purchases of Treasury debt with funds on deposit at the Fed. In all of these cases, disbursement of funds borrowed or activated by the Treasury puts into the hands of people in the private sector checks that are deposited with private banks. The banks in turn send the checks to the Fed, which credits banks' reserve accounts. The result is an increase in bank reserves and the monetary base. Further expansion of the money supply arises from increases in the base.

Methods of financing the deficit that result in increases in the money supply without increasing the monetary base include (1) sales of bonds to commercial banks with excess reserves, (2) use of the Treasury's tax and loan accounts in private commercial banks, and (3) the already discussed sale of bonds to foreign commercial banks and official bodies. Method (1) is self explanatory and, in view of the limited amount of excess reserves in the banking system, is usually unimportant.

Method (2) used to be more important, but is now less so, since the Treasury keeps most of its idle balances in the Fed. However, to be complete, we should explain how it works. When the Treasury draws down its commercial bank deposits, it puts them into its deposit at the Fed. If the funds are for immediate disbursal, checks are written and placed in private hands. The recipients of the checks put them into their banks, and the latter send them on to the Fed. Thus bank reserves are unaffected by the Treasury's decision to spend funds on deposit at commercial banks. Even so, the money supply is increased. Treasury deposits at commercial banks are not part of the money supply. Private deposits are. Thus the transfer of Treasury commercial bank deposits to the public increases the money supply, even though it does not change the monetary base.

14.2
Effects of a pure fiscal policy on money income

Under a pure fiscal policy the federal government manipulates its spending or taxing policies so as to avoid changes in the money supply. That is, the Fed manages monetary policy so that deficits are financed by bond sales to the private sector, without an accompanying even keel policy.

Although a pure fiscal policy is a rarity, we cannot hope to understand the impact of the federal budget upon the economy without analytically separating monetary policy from fiscal policy. Imagining a pure fiscal policy is the best way to proceed. Later, we can discuss the consequences of combining fiscal policy with monetary policy.

14.2.1
Concept of private income

It is customary to measure the results of the behavior of the economy with concepts like gross national product or net national product. Although these concepts are important, to discuss the role of fiscal policy in shaping money income we need another concept, *private income.*

Total income (gross or net national income) includes income earned as a result of goods produced for sale to the household, the business, and the government sectors. But the income actually accruing to the private sector consists of (a) earnings net of tax payments and (b) government transfer payments. We shall call *this* income, private income (Y_N); we shall define it as

$$Y_N = Y - T \qquad (14.3)$$

where T equals *net taxes* collected by the government—tax revenues minus transfer payments.

Do not confuse private income with disposable income. Disposable income is an important concept for studies of the relationship between consumer outlays and household after-tax income. For that purpose, disposable income is defined as personal (household) income minus personal taxes. In contrast, private income includes disposable income, undistri-

Table 14.1 *Correlation* of Rates of Change of Three Measures of Real Income, 1947–1975*

	Annual			Quarterly		
	GNP	NNP	NI	GNP	NNP	NI
Net national product	.999			.996		
National income	.982	.981		.956	.967	
Private income	.842	.845	.844	.680	.681	.623

*The numbers in the table explain the percent of variations in one variable explained by variations in the other. Thus, 99.6 percent of the quarterly variations in net national product are explained by variations in GNP, while only 68 percent of quarterly changes in private income are so explained.

Source: Robert D. Auerbach and Jack L. Rutner, "The Concept of Private Income," *Federal Reserve Bank of Kansas Monthly Review,* November 1976, pp. 11–20.

buted corporate profits, and increases in the values of business inventories. It is larger than disposable income.[1]

Total income and private income need not change equally. Increases in transfer payments, or cuts in taxes, can raise private income relative to total income. Decreased transfers and increased taxes can cause private income to fall relative to total income. Thus, government tax and (transfer) expenditure policies can widen or narrow the gap between the two income measures.

The overall correlation between total income and private income is illustrated in Table 14.1, which is drawn from a study by the Federal Reserve Bank of Kansas.

14.2.2
Adding government to the theory of money income

The concept of private income permits us to incorporate government spending and taxing into the income model discussed in Section 13.3 and expressed in Equations (13.13a) and (13.13b). Simply replace total nominal income *(Y)* with private nominal income *(Y − T)* and add new issues of government bonds *(B_G^s)* to the bond equation:

$$HJ(r, Y - T) - B_G^s = 0 \qquad (14.4a)$$
$$M^s - k(r)(Y - T) = 0 \qquad (14.4b)$$

$$\text{Theory of Income}$$

$$C + I + G = Y \qquad (14.4c)$$

---

[1]Disposable income is about 60 percent of GNP; in contrast, private income is about 80 percent of GNP.

$$Y - T = Y_N \qquad\qquad (14.4d)$$

$$\frac{G - T}{P_B} = B_G^s \qquad\qquad (14.4e)$$

Equation (14.4a) states that the private excess demand for bonds—$HJ(r, Y - T)$—depends upon the rate of interest and private income. The logic of this formulation is similar to the logic in Section 13.2. Increases in private income permit both households and businesses to purchase more goods and services and more securities. Additional sales of goods and services, in turn, frequently stimulate firms to borrow more, and higher incomes often encourage households to take on more debt. Thus, increases in private income stimulate both bond supply and bond demand. Conversely, reductions in private income reduce private bond demands and supplies. However, as argued earlier, our theory cannot tell us whether the *excess demand* for bonds will rise or fall with changes in private income—that is, whether borrowers or lenders will be more affected by changes in their after-tax incomes.

When the government's budget (measured in terms of the price of bonds, P_B) is balanced, it has no need to issue bonds. Therefore, $(P_B)(B_G^s)/P_B = B_G^s = 0$ when the budget is in balance—$(G - T)/P_B = 0$. A deficit occurs when $(G - T)/P_B > 0$, and a surplus occurs when $(G - T)/P_B < 0$. Deficits imply positive values for B_G^s, and surpluses imply that B_G^s is negative. Thus, the number of new bonds issued by the Treasury (B_G^s) varies with its deficit (or surplus).

Equation (14.4b) states that the demand for money— $k(r)(Y - T)$—depends upon private income. The version of this relationship in Equation (13.13) of Chapter 13 made the demand for money a function of total income. Introduction of government requires us to shift to private income. It is private income, not total income, which measures expenditure plans of households and businesses. Hence, a change in government spending, or a shift in taxes, affects the demand for money through its effects on private income.

Assuming the government's budget is given by policy, the level of total money income and the rate of interest are determined by Equations (14.4a) and (14.4b). That is because G and T are policy variables and, as such, are not determined by the economic behavior of the public. That leaves the rate of interest, r (or its shadow, P_B), and total income, Y, to be determined by the two equations. When the values of r and Y are such that (1) the bond market is in equilibrium and (2) the supply and demand for money are equal, the whole system will be in equilibrium—that is, r and Y will be determined.[2]

---

[2]As formulated, the model fails to recognize the dependency of taxes upon the level of total income. This failing is easily remedied by inserting $Y_N = Y(1 - t)$ into the model. The symbol t represents net taxes as a fraction of total income. The new system would look like this:

14.2.3
*Effects of changes in government
spending (taxes held constant) on
income—the crowding out effect*

We are now well-positioned to discuss the effects on nominal income of changes in government purchases of final goods and services. Before we do so, however, we need a little perspective.

Before the Great Depression of the 1930s, federal government expenditures represented a tiny fraction of total spending—1.3 percent in 1929. Fifty years later, in 1979, federal government purchases of final products amounted to about 7 percent of gross national product—an increase of 530 percent.

Even so, opportunities for using variations in federal government spending to stimulate or retard national income may be quite limited. A 10 percent shift in the federal government final product expenditures in a brief period would be unusually large. But it would represent a change of only .7 percent in total national expenditure—10 percent of 7 percent is .7 percent. So, if Congress wishes to manipulate federal spending for the purpose of affecting total income, it must either make relatively large changes in its expenditures or hope that the changes it does authorize will have some sort of powerful multiplier effect on total spending.

We should also consider the nature of federal expenditures. Spending on hydroelectric dams, roads, school lunches, and other items may simply replace private or state and local government expenditures on similar items, leaving total expenditure unchanged. Another example is federally financed public housing. To be sure, there is not always direct competition between federal programs and those of the private and state and local government sectors. We have no private armies in this country. Moreover, there are many complementarities between nonfederal pro-

$$HJ[r,Y(1-t)] - \frac{G-tY}{P_B} = 0 \qquad (14.4a')$$

$$M^s - k(r)Y(1-t) = 0 \qquad (14.4b')$$

$$C + I + G = Y \qquad (14.4c')$$

$$Y(1-t) = Y_N \qquad (14.4d')$$

$$B_G^s = \frac{G-tY}{P_B} \qquad (14.4e')$$

This reformulation clearly does not change the qualitative conclusions of the theory. Equations (14.4a′) and (14.4b′) still determine the rate of interest and the level of income. (Recall that the price of bonds is inversely related to the rate of interest; hence, P_B is not a new variable.) The major consequence of recognizing the dependency of tax revenues upon income is the conversion of the government's deficit (hence, bond supply) into a (partly) dependent variable. Thus, assuming no change in G, an increase in total income raises tax revenues and lowers the deficit, and a fall of income reduces revenues and raises the deficit.

grams and those of the federal government. For example, state and local government road outlays are stimulated by matching federal grants. Even so, we must not assume that total spending on final products automatically increases equally with increases in federal government outlays.

Another consideration is the effect of expenditures on the market for loanable funds. Expenditures financed out of deficits must be financed by federal borrowing or with increases in the money supply. In the case of a pure fiscal policy, the Treasury finances its deficits with sales of new securities to the private sector or to banks and foreigners in a manner that does not change the money supply. As indicated by B_G^s in Equation (14.4a), such sales raise the market rate of interest. The result of such a rise must be a reduction of the excess supply of securities issued by the private and state and local government sectors. For, as interest rates rise, both private individuals and businesses and state and local governments have less incentive to use borrowed money. The effect of this reduction in borrowing is to reduce spending by these sectors.

The reduction in private and state and local government spending that follows upon an increase in federal government deficit spending is called the *crowding out effect*. The crowding out effect operates mainly through the discouragement of private and nonfederal government borrowing by the rise in interest rates that follows a rise in federal borrowing.

Another perspective on the crowding out effect is gained by considering the effects of an increase in government spending upon demand for money. The rise in spending initially raises both total and private income—see Equations (14.4c) and (14.4d). But the rise in private income increases the number of dollars demanded by the private sector—Equation (14.4b). Since a pure fiscal policy keeps the money supply at its previous level, the rise in money demand creates an excess demand for money. Thus, the indirect effect of the increase in government spending is to cause disequilibrium between the supply and demand for money.

The monetary disequilibrium is resolved in two ways. The first entails declines in private and state and local government spending. As discussed earlier, the decreases in these expenditures come from the direct substitutability of federal projects for projects in other sectors and from discouragement of private and nonfederal government borrowing—from, crowding out. The reductions in private and state and local government spending offset the increase in federal spending. As a result, total income and private income fall back below the levels initially established by the increases in federal spending.

The second way in which monetary disequilibrium is resolved is through the rise in interest rates brought about by the increased federal borrowing. The rise in interest rates reduces the number of dollars demanded by the private sector. These dollars then become available for purchases of bonds (thus, in part relieving the pressure on private and state and local government borrowers) and for purchases of goods and services. Thus, by reducing the number of dollars demanded at given levels of income, the rise in interest rates offsets part of the excess demand for money brought about by the increase in income initiated by the increase in government spending.

The ultimate effect of a reduction in the excess demand for money brought on by the rise in the interest rates is to offset the depressive effects of crowding out on private and state and local government spending. As a result, the rise in federal government spending can have a net stimulative effect upon total income. But the degree of stimulation depends upon the sharpness of the increase in market interest rates resulting from the increase in federal borrowing, and upon the interest-sensitivity of the demand for money. Crowding out is least likely when interest rates rise very sharply and when the demand for money is highly sensitive to changes in their level. However, if interest rates respond sluggishly to changes in federal borrowing, or if the demand for money is unaffected by changes in their level, then crowding out is most likely.

The analysis of the crowding out effect of an increase in government spending is illustrated in Figure 14.1, which is similar to Figure 13.9 in Chapter 13. Suppose that the equilibrium total income is initially $Y_0 = C_0 + I_0 + G_0$. Now, let government spending rise to a new level, say G_1. The first effect of the increase in government spending will be to raise total income to $Y_1 = C_0 + I_0 + G_1$. In Figure 14.1b, the level of income now stands above the initial equilibrium income. But at an interest rate r_0, Y_1 is off the money market equilibrium curve. A larger income at a given interest rate raises the demand for money, so that, at point b, there is an excess demand for money. This excess demand for money should create

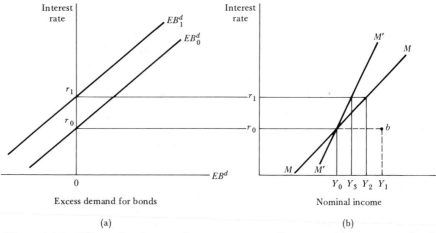

Figure 14.1 *Effects of an increase in government spending on total income—pure fiscal policy case.*

a desire on the part of consumers and business to decrease spending; consumption and investment spending should start to decline below their initial levels of C_0 and I_0.

The decline in private spending will be reinforced by the crowding out effects of a rise in the rate of interest, which raises the cost of borrowing. The rise in interest occurs because the increase in government spending enlarges the federal deficit; and, since we are assuming no change in the money supply, the deficit must be financed by a sale of bonds to the private sector. The new bonds offered for sale by the government create an excess supply of bonds at the old interest rate, r_0, and shifts the excess demand curve for bonds to EB_1^d.

The rise in the interest rate to r_1 reduces the excess demand for money, and hence relieves the downward pressure on private spending. When the money market and the bond market are each in equilibrium at r_1, the market for goods and services also comes into equilibrium at Y_2 (as dictated by Say's Principle). Notice that Y_2 is larger than Y_0, the level of income prior to the increase in government spending. The increase in government spending did not fully crowd out private spending; the money holdings released by the higher interest rate were sufficient to boost total spending to a permanently higher level.

Two conditions would affect the rise in income: (1) A steeper MM curve (for example, $M'M'$) would limit the rise of income to Y_3, which is lower than Y_2. The steeper MM curve would reflect a demand for money function that is less sensitive to changes in the interest rate. (2) A steeper EB^d curve[3] would produce a sharper increase in the rate of interest and thus stimulate a larger increase in income. Imagine a steeper EB^d curve. Now let it shift to the left by an amount equal to the horizontal leftward shift from EB_0^d to EB_1^d in Figure 14.1a. Clearly, the rate of interest would rise above r_1. As a result, money income would settle at a level higher than Y_2 (along MM) or than Y_3 (along $M'M'$).

---

[3]The steepness of the EB^d curve is related to the steepness of the bond supply and bond demand curves. In (a), the dashed curves are steeper than the solid ones. Thus the dashed excess demand curve derived from them is steeper than the solid excess demand curve derived from the solid bond demand and supply curves.

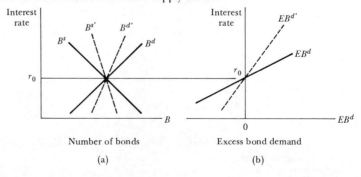

(a)   (b)

Thus, the steepness of the MM curve and the steepness of the EB^d curves compete in establishing the overall stimulus to income resulting from a rise in federal spending on final goods and services. A perfectly vertical MM curve (complete lack of interest-sensitivity of the demand for money) would completely negate the effectiveness of federal government spending changes on the level of income. So too would a perfectly flat EB^d curve (which would signify reductions in private or nonfederal government borrowing equal to increases in federal borrowing). But the real world is likely to fall between these two extreme cases. Federal borrowing is not likely to crowd out all other borrowing, and the demand for money is likely to have at least some sensitivity to the rate of interest.

14.2.4
Effects of tax changes on income—
  supply-side theory

Tax cuts and tax increases are favorite instruments of fiscal policy advocates. The standard doctrine is that tax cuts stimulate, and that tax increases depress, the level of income. In Section 14.2.5 we shall see that these predictions of the standard doctrine are not necessarily correct.

To aid our understanding of this issue, let's go back to the barter world of Say's Law. In such a world, government activities are financed by taxation-in-kind. Instead of collecting taxes in the form of money, the government sends its agents into homes and businesses to extract taxes in the form of chickens, apples, overcoats, and the like. It then pays out these commodities (perhaps after trading with the private sector for a better collection) to its employees.

In a barter world, the government finances its deficits by drawing down stores of commodities collected in previous times or by borrowing against future taxes. It cannot finance them with issues of new money.

Now, suppose the government decides to cut tax rates—for example, it instructs its agents to snatch one less chicken out of each ten chickens grown by the private sector. With more chickens in every pot, private income increases. The increase enables each household to (a) increase its consumption of chickens, (b) trade its surplus chickens for some other commodity, (c) save more chickens for future use, or (d) lend chickens to someone else for future repayment. All of these choices involve an increase in the demand for present or future consumption of commodities. Say's Law thus guarantees that the resources released by the tax cut will either be consumed or be used as trading commodities for expressing increased effective demand for other goods.

The tax cut also increases the incentives to produce. After all, if the government reduces taxes on chicken production, chicken producers will have an incentive to put more hours into raising chickens, and fewer hours into leisure or into producing other things. An across-the-board tax cut on all commodities will stimulate even more production, since people will have an incentive to reduce hours devoted to leisure and increase hours devoted to work of all kinds.

Thus, what many economists now call the *supply-side effects* of a tax cut are positive. A reduction in tax rates stimulates production. Moreover, in the world of Say's Law, the increase in production automatically increases the demand for commodities, either because people demand more of their own produce or because they will seek to trade their extra production for other commodities.

If the government has no stocks of commodities, and if it cannot borrow from its citizens, the reduction of revenues originating from the tax cut will force it to lay off government workers. But, since the tax cut promotes increased private demand for commodities, most of the former government workers should be able to find work in the private sector.

Suppose, however, that the government refuses to curtail its activities. How will it continue to pay its workers? Assuming it has few stocks to draw down, one answer is that the increased production stimulated by the cut in *tax rates* will partly offset the fall in *tax revenues*. So, even though tax rates are lower, the increase in private output permits some recovery of tax revenues at the lower rates.[4] Another answer is that the government can borrow commodities from the private sector. So long as people trust the government to pay back its debts, borrowing from the private sector can be a good solution. Along with this solution, however, is the consequence that the sustained level of government activity is retaining workers in the government sector and retarding the expansion of production in the private sector, where they would have been employed in industries experiencing increases in demand stimulated by the tax cut.

In sum, a tax cut in a barter world probably raises income. The strength of the rise depends upon the government's decision to maintain or reduce its own expenditures. If it reduces its expenditures, it frees labor and other resources for use in the expanding private sector. However, if it maintains its outlays, it bottles up these resources in public uses, in which case expansion of private production occurs only to the extent that people are willing to invest more or to reduce leisure. To be sure, the cut in tax rates on income earned from capital or labor encourages such a development. But the increase in production resulting from the

---

[4]The so-called *Laffer Curve* is based upon this idea. Expanding upon an idea presented by the fourteenth century Arab philosopher, Ibn Khaldun, Professor Arthur Laffer of the University of Southern California has argued that a cut in tax rates in our present society will so stimulate private production that it will produce tax revenues sufficient to restore most if not all of the loss in tax revenues. For comments on the Khaldun–Laffer Curve, see Barry N. Siegel, *Thoughts on the Tax Revolt* (International Institute for Economic Research, Original Paper 21, June 1979) and the collection of essays analyzing the curve in Arthur Laffer and Jan P. Seymours, editors, *The Economics of the Tax Revolt* (New York: Harcourt Brace Jovanovich, 1979).

cut would be much larger if at the same time the government reduced its own activities.[5]

14.2.5
Tax changes in a money economy

We are now in a position to discuss the effects of tax changes in a money economy. To isolate the effects we shall assume that the government is (a) pursuing a pure fiscal policy (hence not changing the money supply) and (b) maintaining its expenditures on final output.

Say's Principle greatly aids the analysis. Assume that the Federal government reduces income tax rates. Since income is earned in the form of wages and in the form of profits or interest on capital, the first effect of the tax cut is to raise private income as a proportion of any given level of total income.

The rise in private income puts more purchasing power into the hands of households and business firms. Although we cannot predict the exact manner in which the increase in purchasing power is distributed, we can safely assume that it is put to use in three possible ways—an increased demand for goods and services, an increased demand for bonds, and an increased demand for money. Moreover, since the tax cut creates incentives for additional work effort and investment, it may stimulate additional production, which, in turn, raises total income and (in line with Say's Principle) further increases the three kinds of demand.

The next step is to consider the initial effects of the tax cut on the *excess demands* for goods and services, for bonds, and for money. Consider first the excess demand for bonds. Since the government is pursuing a pure fiscal policy, the increase in its deficit is matched by an increase in its supply of bonds. But bond demand will increase by less than bond supply. The increase in private income resulting from the tax cut is only partially devoted to an increase in the private sector's demand for bonds; it may even raise private bond supply more than it raises private bond demand. Thus, it is almost a sure thing that the tax cut will give rise to an excess supply of bonds.[6]

---

[5] One caveat: Productive efficiency in the private sector to some extent depends upon government services such as police, fire fighters, courts, schools, and the like. Reduction of these activities might retard increases in private production. On the other hand, military spending and other activities (for example, Regulation Q) might impose deadweight losses on the economy. Reduction of these activities may actually enhance productivity. An example of the cost of these activities is the estimate, made by Professor Murray Weidenbaum of Washington University in St. Louis, that the cost to business in 1979 of complying with federal regulations was about $100 billion. See Siegel, *Thoughts on the Tax Revolt*, pp. 3–4.

[6] The rise in total income from the new production stimulated by the tax cut may increase tax revenues somewhat, thus reducing the deficit and the corresponding excess supply of bonds. But it is highly unlikely that it will eliminate the excess supply.

Now consider the excess demand for money. The demand for money rises and falls with increases and decreases in private income. Thus the tax cut—which raises private income as a proportion of total income and which stimulates total production and income—is sure to increase the demand for money. Moreover, the presence of a constant money supply guarantees that the increase in the demand for money will be matched by an equal increase in the *excess demand* for money.

So, we are sure of two things: The tax cut will directly or indirectly cause an excess demand for money and an excess supply of bonds. What will it do to conditions in the goods market? Unfortunately, we cannot really say. Although the tax cut initially raises the private demand for goods (government demand is unchanged by assumption), we cannot be sure that it similarly raises the private *excess demand* for goods. That is because the extra production and income stimulated by the tax cut is only partially devoted to an increase in the demand for goods. Much of the rest goes to strengthen the excess demand for money. Hence, even though the initial consequence of a tax cut would be to cause an excess demand for goods, it is within the realm of possibility that its ultimate effect (after stimulating more production) will be an excess supply of goods and services.[7]

The next question concerns the mechanism that restores equilibrium to the various markets. The answer depends upon the interaction between interest rates and the quantity of money demanded by the private sector. The excess supply of bonds exerts an upward pressure upon the rate of interest. As the rate of interest rises, it brings the bond market into equilibrium and reduces the excess demand for money. Suppose that the market for bonds comes into equilibrium before the excess demand for money is eliminated. Say's Principle tells us that, in this event, the excess demand for money will be matched by an excess supply of goods and services. The latter will cause production and/or prices to fall, dragging down money income. The drop in income will continue until the demand for money comes into equality with the existing stock of money as made available by the monetary authorities and the banking system. *In this case, the outcome of a tax cut will be a decline in nominal income.*

Now, suppose that the rise in interest rates brings the money market into equilibrium *before* it brings the market for bonds into equilibrium. In this case, there will still be an excess supply of bonds, even though there is zero excess demand for money. As a result, Say's Principle tells us, there will be an excess demand for goods. Thus, contrary to the previous case, income will rise. The rise will persist until a new equilibrium is

---

[7]So, in line with Say's Principle, we have either (1) an excess demand for money offset by an excess supply of bonds and an excess demand for goods and services equal to the difference between the excess supply of bonds and the excess demand for money, or (2) an excess demand for money offset by excess supplies in both the bond market and the market for goods and services.

achieved. The new equilibrium will be characterized by a higher level of nominal income than the one prevailing before the tax cut and by a higher rate of interest. *Thus, in this case, contrary to the previous one, the tax cut will produce a rise in nominal income.*

The ambiguous results of a tax cut originate in the conditions of the bond market and the interest-sensitivity of the demand for money (sound familiar?). To see this point, consider Figure 14.2, which is designed to illustrate the macroeconomics of tax change.

The tax cut raises the government's deficit and shifts the excess bond demand curve up and to the left to EB_1^d. The steeper the excess demand curve for bonds, the sharper will be the increase in the rate of interest. The second effect of the tax cut is a leftward shift of the money equilibrium curve from M_0M_0 to M_1M_1 (solid lines in Figure 14.2b). The leftward shift occurs because the tax cut raises private income relative to total income; as a result, the quantity of money demanded at each level of total income increases. The higher interest rate (r_1) intersects the new MM curve at a point (a), where the new equilibrium income level (Y_1) is below the old (Y_0).

Had the excess demand curve for bonds been much steeper than the one portrayed in Figure 14.2, it is possible that the rate of interest would have risen to a point high enough to intersect M_1M_1 at a point where the level of income exceeds Y_0. In that event, the tax cut would have raised rather than lowered nominal income. Another case in which tax cuts raise nominal income is depicted with the dashed MM curves. These curves are derived from a model in which the interest-sensitivity of the demand for money is quite high. Thus, although the tax cut increases the demand for money, the rise in interest rates so reduces the number of dollars de-

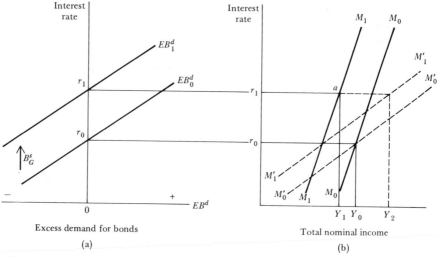

Figure 14.2   *Effects of a tax cut on nominal income and the rate of interest.*

manded by the public that the net result is an excess supply of money at the higher interest rate (r_1). The excess supply of money then creates an excess demand for goods and services—note that at r_1 the excess demand for bonds is zero, hence by Say's Principle, the excess supply of money is matched by an excess demand for goods and services. Thus, money income rises until it reaches Y_2, at which point equilibrium is restored to the money market and (by implication) the market for goods and services.

We may summarize the discussion of tax cuts as follows: A (pure) tax cut raises private income and increases the bond-financed deficit of the government. Increased bond sales by the Treasury create an excess supply of bonds. The rise in private income (supplemented, perhaps, by more private production stimulated by the tax cut), brings into being an excess demand for money. The disequilibria in money, bond, and commodity markets brought on by the tax cut are resolved by changes in the rate of interest and changes in total income. If the rise in the rate of interest is insufficient to offset the increased demand for money, total nominal income must fall until the demand for money is brought into equality with the (unchanged) money supply. Conversely, if the rise in the interest rate substantially reduces the quantity of money demanded, then the total nominal income may actually rise.

The effects of a *tax increase* are opposite to those of a tax cut. An analysis similar to the one above will show that a tax increase will decrease the interest rate, but, depending upon conditions in the bond market and the interest-sensitivity of money demand, it will either raise or lower money income.

14.2.6
Transfer payments and money
income

The analysis of Section 14.2.5 sets the stage for a discussion of the effects on total income of changes in federal government transfer payments. Suppose the government substantially increases welfare payments without changing its other expenditures or the quantity of money. The first impacts of such an act would be a rise in private income and a rise in the excess supply of bonds. What would be the ultimate effects upon total nominal income?

In most respects, an increase in transfer payments acts like a tax cut. That is, it changes demand and total income in substantially the same way—if conditions are such that a tax cut would stimulate total demand and nominal income, so would a rise in transfer payments. Similarly, if a tax cut would lower demand and total nominal income, so would an increase in transfer payments. By-and-large, the demand analyses of the two problems are the same. That is, the effects upon demand and income are uncertain for both.

But there is a difference. A tax cut creates incentives for increased work and investment. These supply-side effects should raise total income. But an increase in transfer payments has the opposite effect. It lowers work incentives and leads to a withdrawal of people from the labor force. To this extent it retards rather than stimulates total income. As a result, the net effect of a rise in transfer payments may be weaker than that of an equivalent tax cut.

14.2.7
Balanced-budget changes in taxes and government spending

A popular political theme in recent years—the centerpiece of President Reagan's 1981 economic recovery plan—is the demand for reduction of the size and budget of government. Reduction of government activity must bring with it a reduction both in its spending and in its revenues. So, let's use our theoretical apparatus to study the impact on total income of a balanced-budget reduction in government spending.

Suppose the federal budget is reduced by $10 billion and that the government simultaneously manages to reduce tax revenues by an equal amount. At first the reductions would leave private income and the government's deficit unchanged. Thus there are none of the bond market and money market repercussions discussed above.[8] However, there is still a question as to whether this situation will remain. After all, people employed producing $10 billion worth of goods and services for government have been thrown out of work. Will they be reemployed in the private sector?

Provided markets work smoothly, they probably will. The cut in taxes maintains the purchasing power of the private sector. Other things being equal, households and businesses should increase their outlays on privately produced goods and services as a replacement for government produced services. Thus, except for a period in which government workers are searching for jobs appropriate to their preferences and skills, there should be no permanent reduction in employment.

Actually, employment may increase. As we have seen, larger after-tax incomes provide incentives for increased work and investment activity. Other things being equal, more work and more investment raise total goods and services supplied to the economy. The increase in output should give rise to an equivalent increase in effective demand (Say's Principle, again). Thus, far from retarding income growth, the balanced-

---

[8]Since $Y_N = C + I + G - T$, an equal reduction in taxes and government spending leaves $M^d = k(r)(Y_N)$ and $EB^d = HJ(r, Y_N)$ unchanged.

budget reduction in government spending ought to stimulate growth of both total income and the level of employment.[9]

Similar reasoning applies to the case of a balanced-budget increase in taxes and government spending on final products. The increases initially leave private income unaffected, and private demand for money and the excess demand for bonds should also remain unaffected. So too should the excess demand for goods and services. But the increase in taxes inhibits private production and encourages people to leave the labor force or to reduce work hours. These negative supply-side effects reduce output.

14.3
Fiscal policy financed with changes in the money supply

Federal deficits are almost never financed through the "pure" method of selling bonds to the nonbank sector. Most of the time part or all of the deficits are financed with increases in the money supply. The Fed, through even keeling, frequently supports the prices of new government bond issues. In so doing it not only directly increases the money supply, but it also provides banks with excess reserves they can use to purchase government debt.

To analyze the case of fiscal policy supplemented by monetary policy, we remodel the excess demand for bonds equation along the lines of Equation (13.10) in Chapter 13 and put it together with Equations (14.4b)–(14.4e)—Equations (14.4b) and (14.4e) being modified to include changes in the money supply as a source of finance for government bonds:

$$HJ(r,Y_N) + \left(\frac{\Delta M^s}{P_B} - B_G^s \right) = 0 \tag{14.5a}$$

$$M^s + \Delta M^s - k(r)Y_N \neq 0 \tag{14.5b}$$

$$C + I + G = Y \tag{14.5c}$$

$$Y_N = Y - T \tag{14.5d}$$

$$G - T = (P_B)(B_G^s) + \Delta M \tag{14.5e}$$

Before we use these equations, note their meaning. Equation (14.5a) states that the excess private demand for bonds is offset by bonds being issued by the government and is supplemented by increases in the money

---

[9]Again, we are assuming government is not cutting back on essential services, so that its reduced activity leaves efficiency unimpaired in the private sector.

supply. If one-half of the deficit is financed with new money and one-half is financed with sales to the nonbank public, then $\Delta M^s/P_B = B_G^s$, and no immediate pressure of excess demand or supply is exerted in the bond market. However, if changes in the money supply (measured in terms of bond prices) exceed sales of new Treasury bond issues, then an overall excess demand for bonds will emerge, and the interest rate will tend to fall. Conversely, when Treasury bond supply exceeds the rate of monetary growth (again measured in terms of bond prices), there is an overall excess supply of bonds, and interest rates will tend to rise. Thus, with increases in the money supply only partially financing the federal deficit, the initial impact of the deficit may be to lower, raise, or leave unchanged the rate of interest. The ultimate effect, as we shall see, depends upon the impact of monetary changes on the level of income.

Equation (14.5b) is not actually an equation; instead, it is an inequality. There can be no equilibrium while the money supply is changing. If the deficit is partially or wholly financed with increases in the money supply, the latter will set in motion continuous increases in money income. The latter will react back upon the market for loanable funds, changing the rate of interest. The interest rate change, in turn, will alter the number of dollars demanded and, hence, change the excess demand for money. Since changes in the excess demand for money further change the level of income, we should expect further repercussions on the bond market, interest rates, and so forth.

14.3.1
Financing an increase in government spending with money and debt

Figure 14.3 portrays the effects of an increase in federal government spending financed partly by a bond issue bought up by the nonbank private sector and partly by an increase financed with a one-time change in the monetary base and in newly created bank deposits.

The excess bond demand curve labeled EB_0^d portrays a situation in which the deficit is financed equally with increases in the money supply and sales of bonds to the nonbank sector. As shown by Equation (14.5a), such a financing method leaves the excess demand curve for bonds unaffected; hence, EB_0^d doesn't shift and the rate of interest at first remains at its original level, r_0. But the same cannot be said for the MM curve. The increase in the money supply creates an excess supply of money at the original income level Y_0. Thus, income must rise until equilibrium between the supply and demand for money is regained. With interest remaining at r_0, the new equilibrium is found when income is Y_2, so the new money equilibrium curve, $M'M'$, goes through point b, which is the coordinate of r_0 and Y_2.

If future deficits are also financed with changes in the money supply,

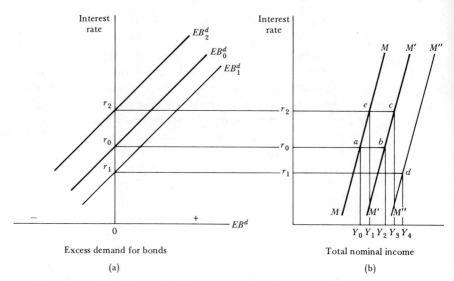

Figure 14.3 *Effects of financing increases in government spending with different combinations of bond sales and monetary changes.*

the *MM* curve would continue to shift to the right, causing further increases in nominal income. However, because we are discussing a one-time increase in the money supply, we can continue our analysis with the diagram depicting a single shift in the money equilibrium curve. The rise of income to Y_2 may stimulate private bond supply and demand. If the stimulus shifts the bond supply curve by more than the bond demand curve, the excess bond demand curve will shift up and to the left, perhaps to EB_2^d, raising the interest rate to r_2. In that event, income will rise further, to Y_3. As before, however, the degree of this additional increase in income depends upon the steepness of the excess bond demand curve and the steepness of the *MM* curve. The steeper the latter, and the less steep the former, the less the additional rise of income.

The excess bond demand curve labeled EB_1^d depicts a deficit financed with a proportionately larger increase in the money supply than in the above case. In this event, $\Delta M/P_B > B_G^s$, so the excess demand curve shifts to the right in comparison with its initial position at EB_0^d. At the same time, the *MM* curve shifts further than $M'M'$, that is, to $M''M''$. Provided there are no induced shifts in the new EB_1^d curve, income settles at Y_4 and the rate of interest becomes r_1. However, as before, the EB^d curve may shift up and to the left as a result of a more rapid increase of bond supply than bond demand. In that event, the rate of interest and the level of income would both rise above the values depicted by point *d* on $M''M''$.

We shall not explicitly deal with the case in which the deficit is being financed more with bond sales to the nonbank public than with increases in the money supply. However, the extreme case of zero monetary increase is shown by point *e*. In this event, the excess bond demand curve shifts to EB_2^d, the rate of interest rises to r_2, and the level of income rises to Y_1 from its initial level of Y_0. Since the absence of monetary change leaves the money equilibrium curve at MM, the rise in income is determined solely by the increase in the rate of interest. Note that this is the least stimulative method of financing the government's deficit. The most stimulative, which is not shown on Figure 14.3, would be one in which all of the deficit is financed with new money.

14.3.2
Financing tax cuts with increases in the money supply

It would be tedious and unnecessary to reproduce the analysis of a tax cut financed with different mixes of bond sales and monetary increases. Much of what we have said already applies. Under a pure fiscal policy, a tax cut raises the deficit. It therefore shifts the excess bond demand curve to the left. Moreover, because it increases private income, it also increases the demand for money, which shifts the MM curve to the left. These shifts can undermine any initial level of income. However, if part or all of the deficit is financed with increases in the money supply, the leftward shifts of the EB^d and the MM curves are retarded. At the extreme, with the whole deficit being financed by an increase in the money supply, the MM curve shifts to the right, and the EB^d curve shifts below its original level. Thus the rate of interest falls and the level of nominal income rises above the levels prevailing before the tax cut.

Summarizing these results and those of Section 14.3.1, fiscal policy is unambiguously expansionary when accompanied by a stimulative monetary policy. Similarly, a fiscal policy designed to slow the economy cannot be expected to do much without an accompanying tight money policy. These statements are particularly relevant to the case of tax changes, which tend to raise or lower the demand for money in a manner that retards or stimulates income in a direction opposite to that intended by the policies. Although the same charge cannot be levied against changes in government spending, the effectiveness of these methods of changing money income depends heavily upon the absence of crowding out and the direct substitution of private for public spending. Variations in public spending do best when these effects are weak. However, their effectiveness is also compromised by the interest-sensitivity of the demand for money. If such sensitivity is small, income will change very little in response to changes in spending.

Finally, it is important to emphasize that the analyses in this section assume one-time changes in the money supply. Although these changes permanently alter the level of money income, they may not permanently change the position of the excess bond demand curve. When the authorities cease changing the money supply, the excess bond demand curve returns to a level dominated by private excess bond demand and the new bond issues from the Treasury. The rate of interest therefore settles at a level that equates excess private demand with Treasury bond supply—that is, $HJ(r,Y_N) = B_G^s$. This interest rate is likely to be higher than the rate that would prevail in the absence of a government deficit.

14.4
Empirical evidence on fiscal policy

One of the ornaments of the Keynesian Revolution was the theory of fiscal policy. According to that theory, shifts in government spending or tax changes are major policy instruments. For example, an increase in government spending on final goods and services raises private incomes, and the latter raises private consumption, so the total spending in the economy may rise by more than the initial increase in government spending. Similarly, a tax cut that raises private income is expected to increase consumption and total spending by a significant amount.

The theory outlined in this chapter questions the effectiveness of fiscal policies—particularly pure fiscal policies. When deficits are unaccompanied by changes in the money supply, crowding out effects may offset the effects on total income of changes in government spending. In the case of tax cuts, increases in the demand for money supplement the negative crowding out effects. Thus, fiscal policies are unlikely to be effective unless they are accompanied by an accommodative monetary policy.

Empirical evidence suggests that fiscal policy does have some of the expected effects on total income, but its power does not seem to be strong when unaccompanied by supporting monetary changes. A variety of studies, using a number of different techniques, have arrived at roughly similar conclusions on the magnitude and timing of the effects of fiscal policy.[10] For example, an increase in government spending appears to raise income for a period of six months to a year by $.60 to $1.50 per dollar of the increase in government spending. Thus, in this early period, there may be some multiplier effects, though there is evidence in some studies of crowding out. After a year or so, however, the effects of increased gov-

---

[10]Federal Reserve Bank of St. Louis economists are among the first to have tested the effects of fiscal policy on nominal income. See Leonall C. Andersen and Jerry L. Jordan, "Monetary and Fiscal Actions, a Test of Their Relative Importance in Economic Stabilization," *Federal Reserve Bank of St. Louis Review,* Vol. 50, No. 11, November 1968, pp. 11–24. This study has had a number of critics, the most recent being Benjamin M. Friedman, "Even the St. Louis Model Now Believes in Fiscal Policy," *Journal of Money, Credit and Banking,* Vol. IX, No. 2, May 1977, pp. 365–367. Andersen answered Friedman in "Does the St. Louis Equation Now Believe in Fiscal Policy?" *Federal Reserve Bank of St. Louis Review,* Vol. 60, No. 2, February 1978, pp. 13–19. For a number of additional citations to this literature, see Michael Darby, *Intermediate Macroeconomics* (New York: McGraw-Hill, 1979), p. 226. Comments in this section are based upon Darby.

ernment spending apparently wear off, and by the end of two years little total effect remains.

Evidence upon the effects of tax changes indicates even weaker effects. Most economists agree that temporary tax changes are unlikely to have permanent effects on total income. But studies have not picked up systematic effects of tax changes of any kind. After reviewing some of the evidence, Professor Robert J. Gordon concluded that "inefficiency is the fundamental limitation of changes in tax rates as a tool of discretionary fiscal policy." Michael Darby states that, "There is much to be said for an agnostic position—aware of the arguments and awaiting more empirical evidence to decide on the effectiveness of tax changes. . . . But even a 10 percent reduction in net federal taxes would increase nominal and real income by no more than 1 percent at the peak and probably less."[11]

SUMMARY

Changes in federal government spending or taxes frequently lead to changes in nominal income. But the degree of change varies with the means of financing the government's activities. If federal expenditures are covered by taxes, their impact upon income will be minimal, mainly confined to supply-side effects. However, changes in spending financed with deficits are likely to alter total demand and total income, more so if accompanied by changes in the money supply than if not.

Federal deficits financed with bond sales to the nonbank private sector, to a banking system that is lent up, and to nonbank private investors leave the money supply unchanged. But other methods of financing the deficit alter the money stock. Treasury expenditures financed with debt bought up by the Fed, with Treasury deposits at the Fed, or with sales of bonds to foreign central banks increase the monetary base as well as the money supply. Expenditures financed with sales of bonds to banks with excess reserves or with Treasury tax and loan accounts increase the money supply without increasing the monetary base.

The effects on total income of changes in the government's budget are best analyzed in the context of a pure fiscal policy—that is, changes in the deficit financed without changes in the money supply. A rise in federal spending, for example, at first changes total income by an equal amount. However, private spending may be forced down by the direct substitution of government spending for private spending and because the rise in interest rates induced by increased federal borrowing discourages private borrowing and spending—that is, private spending is crowded out. As a result, private income (total income minus net taxes) may not rise as much as total income. However, the rise in interest rates

---

[11]Darby, ibid., p. 234. See also, Gordon, *Macroeconomics* (Boston: Little Brown, 1978), pp. 517–518. We return to this issue in Chapter 20.

also reduces the number of dollars demanded by the private sector, creating an excess supply of money. Total income can therefore rise until the excess supply of money is wiped out. But the degree of rise is limited by (a) the sharpness of the rise in interest rates induced by additional federal borrowing, and (b) the interest-sensitivity of the demand for money. If neither is large, the increase in government spending has little effect on total income.

Tax changes have unpredictable effects on total income. For example, a tax cut has the supply-side effects of raising labor supply and increasing investment. But its effects on total demand are ambiguous—increases in government borrowing raise interest rates and reduce the number of dollars demanded; however, the tax cut also raises private income and the demand for money. Thus the net effect of a tax cut on the excess demand for money is uncertain. If it is positive, a tax cut can actually lower total income. If it is negative, total income will rise.

In all cases, deficits financed partly or wholly with changes in the money supply are expansionary. Thus, in theory, fiscal policies designed to stimulate total income should be accompanied by increases in the growth rate of the money supply. Similarly, fiscal policies designed to slow the increase in income should be accompanied by slowdowns in the rate of monetary growth.

Evidence on the effects of fiscal policy on income is mixed. Changes in government spending appear to have near-term positive effects, followed by a reversal, so that after about two years the total effect is nil. In addition, there is little evidence that changes in taxes have a predictable effect upon income.

DISCUSSION QUESTIONS

1. Enumerate the ways of financing the government's budgetary deficit that would increase the money supply. Under what conditions would a budgetary surplus decrease the money supply?

2. Compare private income with disposable income. Why is private income more appropriate than disposable income to use as a variable affecting the excess demand for bonds and the demand for money?

3. Under what conditions does a rise in government spending crowd out private spending?

4. Why is it unclear that a tax cut will stimulate aggregate demand?

5. Compare the effects on aggregate nominal income of a tax cut with those of an increase in transfer payments.

6. What would be the effect upon aggregate nominal income of an attempt to stimulate the economy by means of an equal increase in government spending and taxes?

IMPORTANT TERMS
AND CONCEPTS

☐ crowding out effect   ☐ net taxes

☐ disposable income   ☐ private income

☐ government transfer payments   ☐ supply-side theory

☐ Laffer Curve

ADDITIONAL
READINGS

The literature on fiscal policy is huge. Most of it deals with Keynesian theories, which became prominent in the 1940s, 1950s, and 1960s. This chapter represents a minority view, expounded originally by pre-Keynesian classical economists and most recently by monetarists of various shades. However, even Keynesians now appear to admit the critical nature of monetary policy as a supplement to fiscal policy. For some relatively modern textbook discussions, see Robert J. Gordon, *Macroeconomics* (Boston: Little Brown, 1978), Chapters 5, 17, and 18, and Michael Darby, *Intermediate Macroeconomics* (New York: McGraw-Hill, 1979), Chapters 8 and 13. An interesting review of fiscal policy in the context of the crowding out effect is in Keith M. Carlson and Roger W. Spencer, "Crowding Out and Its Critics," *Federal Reserve Bank of St. Louis Review,* December 1975. A good history of fiscal policy is Herbert Stein's *Fiscal Revolution in America* (Chicago: University of Chicago Press, 1969). Section 20.1 of this book discusses additional evidence on the effectiveness of fiscal policies.

Transmission Mechanism of Monetary Influences on Income

O U T L I N E

How Monetary Shocks Affect Nominal Income
The Shock Absorber Function of Money
A Dynamic Interpretation of Monetary Shocks
Direct and Indirect Effects of Monetary Shocks on Spending
The Effects of Monetary Shocks on Output and Prices
Flexprice and Fixprice Markets
Price Setting in Fixprice Markets
Lags in Inflationary Expectations
Diagrammatic Treatment of Price Lags

The essence of the quantity theory of money is expressed by Say's Principle and the Fundamental Proposition of Monetary Theory. Say's Principle calls attention to the obvious but important fact that when the existing money holdings of all individuals add up to an amount greater than the individuals wish to hold, there will be an economy-wide excess supply of money and a general condition of excess demand for goods and services or for stocks and bonds. Conversely, an overall excess demand for money will be mirrored by an overall excess supply of goods and services or stocks and bonds. The Fundamental Proposition asserts that the excess demands or supplies of goods, services, and securities will cause prices, outputs, interest rates, and hence nominal income, to change until the number of dollars people wish to hold comes into equality with the number of dollars made available by the Federal Reserve and the banking system. Thus, taken together, the two concepts provide the foundations for predictions about the effects of shifts in the supply and demand for money on the direction and perhaps degree of change in nominal income.

Unfortunately, neither of these basic ideas helps us understand the details of the impact of monetary changes on the economy. Both are silent upon such important matters as the length of time it takes for monetary changes to affect prices and outputs, the market channels through which monetary impulses travel to work their effects upon prices and output, and whether the main effect of monetary shifts is on output or on prices.

Thus, to some extent, basic monetary theory is a "black box." We know what goes into the box (monetary impulses), and we know what comes out (changes in nominal income), but the theory provides us with little more than hints as to the nature of the processes that produce the transformations within the box.

A black box is a challenge to the human mind. And it should not surprise us that economists have exerted considerable effort to find out what goes on inside. In recent years, they have learned a great deal. Although much is still unknown, it is now possible to sketch out several of the important ways in which monetary changes make themselves felt upon economic behavior.

A number of things go on simultaneously within the black box. But it is impossible to talk about them all at once. So we shall divide our discussion into two parts. The first part will deal with the ways in which monetary shocks (defined below) affect nominal income. Included in the discussion will be comments upon the channels, direct and indirect, through which the shocks are communicated to the demand side of commodities markets and upon the time it takes for shocks to make themselves felt. The second part will deal with how the changes in nominal income divide into changes in price levels and changes in output.

15.1
How monetary shocks affect
nominal income

A monetary shock is an *unanticipated change* in the nominal money supply. Suppose (for convenience) we start with a monetary equilibrium. Recall from Section 11.2.2 that monetary equilibrium is defined as equality between planned or desired holdings of money and the money balances people actually possess. When the monetary authorities unexpectedly feed too much or too little money into the economy, they upset the equilibrium between the public's actual and desired cash holdings. In attempting to bring actual cash holdings into equality with desired cash balances, people begin to buy or sell goods and services or securities. They continue until monetary equilibrium is restored. At that point, they again hold the cash they want to hold.

Restoration of equilibrium after a monetary shock takes time. Moreover, since different people are likely to be differently affected by the shock, they will usually adjust their behaviors in different ways. Some will seek to adjust their money balances in the various markets for goods and services, and some will go to the market for stocks and bonds. Disturbances in these markets will set up disturbances in others, so that in the end the monetary shock affects virtually the whole range of items that are bought and sold in the economy.

15.1.1
The shock absorber function of
money

In discussing the transactions demand for money, Cambridge monetary theorists (see Section 12.2.1) frequently stressed the role that it plays in filling the gaps that are likely to develop between individuals' receipts and outlays. Most of us prefer our affairs to proceed smoothly and easily. We are upset if we cannot pay our bills on time or take advantage of good buys for lack of funds. But, should expected income or other money receipts fail to appear, that is exactly what might happen. For that reason, we like to keep by our sides a certain amount of cash as a liquid reserve. Although such a reserve is costly in terms of foregone interest earnings, it is worth having if it helps us smooth over the gaps between receipts and expenditures that bring annoyance and perhaps worry into our lives.

This role of money reserves is well described by the function of a shock absorber.[1] Shock absorbers on an automobile cushion the shocks it receives on rough roads and permit its passengers to ride in comfort. They do so by stretching when the wheels dip into holes and compressing

---

[1] The shock-absorber analogy is discussed in detail in Michael Darby, *Intermediate Macroeconomics* (New York: McGraw-Hill, 1979), pp. 149–156.

when they strike bumps. The body of the automobile rides more smoothly than do the wheels.

Money balances also act as shock absorbers. Between pay days, most people try to maintain a pattern of money holdings that relates to their spending plans. Cash balances held at the beginning of the period typically exceed those held at the end; but, over the period, there is some average level of holdings that permits people to carry out their expenditure plans. Random events that unexpectedly increase or decrease nominal cash holdings do not usually interrupt spending plans. When extra cash flows in, people simply let money balances rise above normal, and when unexpected outlays must be made, they draw down their balances below normal.

If some of the events that affect money balances are random, cash build-ups above normal are sooner or later followed by offsetting cash depletions. Understanding this, individuals do not immediately spend extra cash; nor do they withhold outlays when their cash balances decline. However, if cash build-ups or depletions persist, individuals will eventually decide to bring them into line with normal holdings. As a result, they will either change their outlays on goods and services or make adjustments in their holdings of nonmonetary financial assets.

A nonrandom monetary shock imposes unexpected changes upon average cash balances. For example, when the Federal Reserve System makes an unusually large purchase of government bonds, it usually raises their prices. People who had planned to hold the securities, but sold them because of the unusually good price, now have extra cash holdings and fewer bonds. In addition, banks have new excess reserves that they use to purchase bonds on the open market and to make loans to individuals and businesses on better terms than were previously available. The borrowers use the newly created funds to purchase goods and services or even to pay off debts ahead of time. Thus, the effect of the monetary shock is to put unexpected money receipts into a variety of hands and to cause a persistent and widespread build-up of cash balances. The build-up is widespread because each purchase puts money into the hands of a seller, and the sellers, like buyers, will eventually try to get rid of surplus cash balances.

Gradually, people's conceptions of normal money balances will change. The spending of extra cash balances eventually raises the prices and outputs of goods and services and changes the level of interest rates. These events, in turn, raise nominal income. The rise in nominal income gradually increases the level of money balances people regard as normal and desirable. At some point, the monetary shock will work itself out; unless a new shock appears, the economy will approach a new aggregative monetary and income equilibrium.

Negative monetary shocks have effects opposite to those described above. They force people to sell off assets and to reduce the demand for goods and services. In addition, they diminish bank reserves and decrease the loans and investments of the banking system, which further reduces spending. In that event, prices and outputs begin to fall and nominal income turns down. The fall in income persists until people perceive that the smaller money balances they hold are sufficient to carry out their (now reduced) expenditure plans without annoying and costly interruptions.

15.1.2
A dynamic interpretation of monetary shocks[2]

To further our understanding of the implications of monetary shocks, it helps to discuss them in the context of a dynamic world. After all, that is the world in which we live. In the real world, the money stock, nominal income, and even the Cambridge k are constantly changing. Some of these changes are random, but most appear to be composed of movements around trends that reflect the operation of forces described by the shock absorber theory of Section 15.1.1. We shall now try to use the theory to explain some of the fluctuations of nominal income.

We start by imagining a time path for nominal income that would be traced out if income equilibrium always prevailed. In such a situation, there would always be monetary equilibrium. People's actual money holdings would always equal their desired money holdings; all additions to the money supply would be just sufficient to finance the level of transactions balances people normally require to finance expenditures out of their expected income. Expected income would be growing at the same rate as actual income.

Using the relation $M_t^s = k_t^d Y_t^e$, we can express the time path of equilibrium nominal income by taking logarithms of both sides of the equation and solving for $\log Y_t^e$:

$$\log Y_t^e = \log M_t^s - \log k_t^d \qquad (15.1)[3]$$

The symbol t denotes a point in time; M^s is a policy variable, determined by the monetary authorities, and k^d is the fraction of income the public desires to hold in cash. Y^e is equilibrium income.

Figure 15.1 displays the relationship between the logarithms of the variables over time. It assumes that $\log k^d$ has a downward trend (see Table 12.1, especially for the ratio of M-1 to GNP). If the economy were

---

[2]Section 15.1.2 and 15.1.3 owe much to Michael Darby, *Intermediate Macroeconomics*, Chapters 6 and 7.

[3]Recall from high school algebra that $\log ab = \log a + \log b$. Also recall that the logarithm of a fractional number is negative. Since k is a fraction, $\log k$ is negative. Conversion of the Cambridge equation to logarithmic form facilitates graphical analysis, as will be demonstrated in this section.

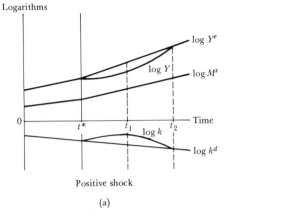

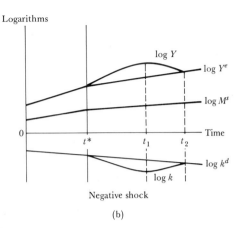

Figure 15.1 *Reactions to monetary shocks.*

always in equilibrium, income would be traveling along the path denoted by the straight line(s) labeled log Y^e. The vertical distance of log Y^e from the horizontal axis equals the absolute value of the sum of the vertical distances of log M^s and log k^d (remember, since k is a fraction, log k^d is a negative number; hence a minus in front of log k^d turns it into a positive number).

Now, imagine that the economy grows steadily until t^*, at which point the authorities unexpectedly change the growth rate of the money supply. This unexpected act is an example of a monetary shock.

Figure 15.1a displays a positive monetary shock—an unexpected increase in the monetary growth rate—as an upward tilting of the growth path, log M^s. Assuming the public is at first unaware of the change in policy, it treats its rising cash balances as random increases; instead of immediately spending the money, it lets its cash holdings build above normal. Thus, aggregate demand and nominal income continue to rise at the same rate they rose during the period prior to the monetary shock.

Sooner or later, however, the public becomes aware of the unusual growth in cash balances. The ratio of its cash holdings to income (the actual level of k) rises above the desired level, k^d. But, at some point, the growing discrepancy between actual and desired cash balances triggers an increase in the public's rate of spending. As spending accelerates, the rate of growth of income (the slope of log Y) rises above its old rate of growth. For a time, it even exceeds the rate of growth appropriate to the new equilibrium growth path shown by the slope of log Y^e_t to the right of t^*. Eventually (at t_2), however, the public reduces k to its desired level; in the absence of further monetary shocks, income will grow along the path indicated by log Y^e.

The failure of income to respond immediately to the monetary shock has an interesting implication. Between time t^* and t_1, income grows more slowly than the rate indicated by the new equilibrium growth path. After

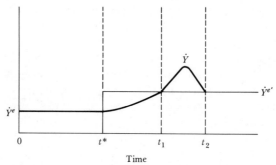

Figure 15.2 *Fluctuations of growth rate of income following a positive monetary shock.*

time t_1, however, it starts to grow more rapidly than the rate indicated by the path. That is to say, the actual growth rate of nominal income *over-shoots* the new equilibrium growth rate. But, since the actual growth rate must equal the equilibrium growth rate once k comes into equality with k^d, the growth rate of income eventually levels off until, at time t_2, it matches the new equilibrium growth rate.

A plot of the fluctuations of the growth rate of income is illustrated in Figure 15.2 ($\dot{Y}$ symbolizes the percentage rate of growth of income, also measured by the slope of log Y in Figure 15.1[4]).

The failure of income to respond immediately to a monetary shock is explained by the public's delay in adapting its actual money balances to the balances it desires to hold. If the public were able to predict the new equilibrium growth path of income, and if it were fully informed about the new growth path of the money stock, it would be in a position immediately to bring the actual level of k into conformity with the desired level. In the final analysis, therefore, the fluctuations in the growth rate of income that follow a monetary shock are explained by the public's lack of information and by its inability to predict the consequences of current

---

[4]Consider the following table:

t	a	Log a
1	10	1.000
2	20	1.301
3	40	1.602
4	80	1.903

Over time, the variable a is growing at a constant rate of 100 percent; however, log a is growing at a constant rate of .301. Thus the slope of log $a = f(t)$ would equal .301. If log $a = f(t)$ is nonlinear, its slope will measure varying growth rates.

changes in the monetary environment. If the public were fully informed, it is unlikely that shifts in the monetary growth rate would be followed by fluctuations in the growth rate of nominal income.

The consequences of a negative monetary shock are illustrated in Figure 15.1b. Note that the equilibrium growth path of income has a smaller slope after t^*. For a time, however, income continues to grow at the pre-shock rate. Initially, the public is unaware that the fall in k represents a nonrandom event. As a result, people continue to spend at the old rate. At some point, however, cash balances get too low relative to income, and the public decides to retrench; in so doing, it reduces outlays on goods and services and buys fewer securities, which reduces the ability of borrowers to purchase goods and services. Retrenchment means that nominal income must grow more slowly than in the past. In fact, the rate of growth for a time falls below the new equilibrium growth path to the right of t^*. Eventually, however, the public succeeds in its attempts to bring actual money holdings into equality with desired holdings, so that $\log k$ equals $\log k^d$. At that point, income begins to grow along the path indicated by $\log Y^e$.

A negative monetary shock also produces a fluctuation of the growth rate of nominal income, but opposite to the one produced by a positive shock. As shown in Figure 15.1b, the slope of the growth path of $\log Y$ between t^* and t_1 gradually decreases until, at t_1, it matches the equilibrium growth rate measured by the slope of $\log Y^e$. But t_1 is the point at which the shortfall of k below k^d is at a maximum. Thereafter, the public's attempt to increase its cash balances reduces the growth rate of Y, so that between t_1 and t_2, it is actually below the growth rate of Y^e. Finally (at t_2) k catches up with k^d and income begins to grow along the path described by $\log Y^e$. Figure 15.3 graphs the fluctuation of the growth rate of income.

The reverberations produced by monetary shocks are actually more complicated than the ones described in this section. The shocks generally cause fluctuations in the nominal rate of interest, in which case desired money holdings will also shift about. In the case of a positive monetary shock, for example, interest rates may at first fall; then, as nominal income growth speeds up, excess supplies of bonds increase and the fall is

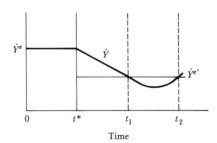

Figure 15.3 *Fluctuations of growth rate of income following a negative monetary shock.*

reversed; interest rates rise. If the shock eventually produces a permanent rise in the rate of inflation, nominal interest rates may actually rise above the level prevailing before the shock. If that happens, the public may reduce k^d, in which case the growth path log k^d may be permanently reduced, and instead of traveling along the line traced by log Y^e in Figure 15.1a, income may instead eventually travel along a somewhat higher path. But, before it does, the intermediate fluctuations of the growth rate of nominal income will be greatly complicated by the fluctuations in k^d brought about by the variations in the rate of interest.

15.1.3
Direct and indirect effects of
monetary shocks on spending

Monetary shocks cannot change the level and growth rate of nominal income without affecting level and rate of growth of aggregate demand. Aggregate demand consists of expenditures by households, businesses, and government. Thus, to influence total expenditure upon final goods and services, monetary shocks must alter the spending totals of one or more of these different economic sectors.

Monetary theorists frequently identify two channels through which monetary shocks work their effects upon spenders. The first channel involves the so-called *direct effect*. Money is an asset; it is held in portfolios along with stocks, bonds, and physical assets. The direct effect of a monetary shock concerns the substitutability of money for physical assets. For example, an unexpected build-up of money holdings that follows a positive monetary shock increases the proportion of money to physical assets in the portfolios of households and businesses. The extra money holdings carry with them extra money services—that is, more liquidity. If firms and households value the extra liquidity less than they value the services of extra physical assets, they will reduce their holdings of money in favor of increased holdings of goods. Households will therefore purchase new appliances, clothing, automobiles, and so forth; firms will add to inventories and perhaps buy additional durable capital assets. In this manner, the monetary shock translates directly into increased expenditures.

The second channel involves *indirect effects*; it works through interest rates and yields on financial and physical assets. Most new money is pumped into the economy via open market bond purchases by the Federal Reserve System. The purchases tend to raise the prices of securities held by the public and to add directly to its money holdings. In addition, they swell the excess reserves of the banking system, which then has the incentive to increase loans and securities investments. Thus, a positive monetary shock, initiated and sustained by the Federal Reserve System, provides a powerful force to lower interest rates in all credit markets. The fall in interest rates, in turn, stimulates durable goods purchases and housing demand by households and investments in inventories and new fixed capital goods by firms. State and local governments are also induced to borrow more money for road construction and other capital projects.

Another way of describing the indirect effect is through a comparison of the yields on financial and physical assets. Household durables and business capital goods yield their returns in kind in the form of services and products. Business firms can measure the money value of these returns by the dollars they earn in selling their products. But households must value the returns they get from their homes, washing machines, and automobiles by reference to the cost of such services if bought directly in the market place. In both cases, however, it is possible to imagine an "internal rate of return," comparable to an interest rate, which measures the value of the annual yield of a physical asset per dollar of investment in the assets. This rate of return, compared to the return on financial assets, provides a basis for the decision of a household or a firm to substitute physical for financial assets, or vice versa.

The indirect effect of a monetary shock can thus be described by its impact upon portfolio decisions of households and firms. The shock initially lowers rates on financial assets below those on durables and capital goods. This leads people to shift into physical assets out of financial assets. The prices of existing physical assets begin to rise. The rise in prices has two effects. The first is to stimulate production of new durables and capital goods, which has the effect of raising incomes of workers and owners of business firms. The increase in income raises household consumption spending. The second is to raise the cost of the services rendered by durables and capital goods. This rise in cost should lead households and firms to switch part of their demand for such assets into direct purchases of similar services of workers (for example, a laundress may be hired to replace an expensive washing machine). As a result, workers' incomes and expenditures are enhanced. Thus, the monetary shocks spread from the bond market to the market for existing physical assets, and then to the market for currently produced goods and services.

The description of the channels through which a monetary shock travels on its way to changing aggregate demand is nothing more than an attempt to work out the implications of Say's Principle. An excess supply of money must impose upon the economy an excess demand for goods or for securities. If it imposes an excess demand for goods and services, the impact upon aggregate demand will be direct. But, if the shock is first felt in the bond market, the effect upon aggregate demand will be indirect. Since monetary policy more often than not is implemented with open market operations and the manipulation of other Federal Reserve instruments, the indirect channels of effect of monetary changes are likely to be highly important. If so, this is another reason why there may be substantial lags in the effect of monetary policy upon the level and rate of growth of nominal income.

15.2
The effects of monetary shocks on
output and prices

The basic growth path of nominal income is dictated by the growth rate of the money supply and the time-trend of desired cash holdings as a fraction of income. The frequent departures of nominal income growth from its growth path are characterized by discrepancies between actual and desired cash holdings. Monetary shocks do not work themselves out until people adjust their money holding behaviors to the new realities imposed by the changes in money growth rates.

But the story does not end there. Fluctuations in growth rates of nominal income are compounded of changes in the rate of growth of output and changes in the rate of growth of the price level. These two elements of income change are differently affected by monetary shocks. In most cases, the rate of growth of real output is the first thing to change. Later, the shocks spread to the price level. In the long run, the rate of change in the price level swallows up most of the impact of the shocks; the rate of growth of output falls back to the pace dictated by such factors as the rate of growth of the labor force, the change of technology, the rate of growth of the capital stock, and other factors that bear upon the supply side of the economy.

This general pattern of output and price responses to monetary shocks is well documented.[5] In fact, it was known over 200 years ago to David Hume, the noted British philosopher, who wrote in his famous essay, *Of Money*:

> Though the high price of commodities be a necessary consequence of the increase of gold and silver; yet it follows not immediately upon that increase; but some time is required before the money circulates through the whole state. . . . At first, no alteration is perceived; by degrees the price rises, first of one commodity, then of another; till the whole at last reaches a just proportion with the new quantity of specie. . . . In my opinion, it is only in this interval or intermediate situation, between the acquisition of money and the rise in prices, that the increasing quantity of gold and silver is favorable to industry. . . . There is always an interval before matters can be adjusted to their new situation; and this interval is as pernicious to industry, when gold and silver are diminishing, as it is advantageous when these metals are increasing.

Milton Friedman, who perhaps more than any other modern economist has studied the lags in effect of monetary changes, argues that the

---

[5]Phillip Cagan, *The Hydra-Headed Monster, The Problem of Inflation in the United States* (Washington D.C.: The American Enterprise Institute, 1974). Milton Friedman, *The Optimum Quantity of Money* (Chicago: Aldine, 1969).

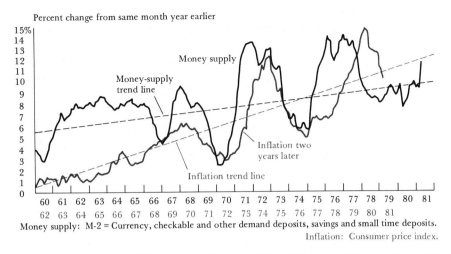

Percent change from same month year earlier

Money supply

Money-supply
trend line

Inflation two
years later

Inflation trend line

Money supply: M-2 = Currency, checkable and other demand deposits, savings and small time deposits.
Inflation: Consumer price index.

Figure 15.4 *Inflation follows money. (Source: Milton Friedman, "Monetary Instability,"* Newsweek, *Vol. XCVII, No. 24, June 15, 1981, p.80.)*

full impacts of money accelerations are typically (on the average) spread over two-year periods. Within 6 to 9 months after the shock, output starts to rise; although prices also begin to move, it takes another 18 months or so for the full impact of the positive monetary shocks to be felt upon prices, at which time the effects upon output will have petered out and the main effects will have shifted to the rate of inflation. Figure 15.4 gives some evidence for his argument.[6]

To explain the behavior of prices following a monetary shock we must look into the structure of markets for different kinds of goods and services and into the way people perceive and react to the price movements that actually occur. Prices are not created out of thin air; instead, they are made in markets. Prices reflect people's preferences, anticipations, and the opportunities and information they have at the time they decide to buy or sell goods and services.

15.2.1
Flexprice and fixprice markets

Economists are adept at describing the nature of an equilibrium. Markets in equilibrium display equality between supply and demand at prices sellers and buyers anticipated when they decided to exchange goods or

---

[6] See Friedman's discussion in the *American Economic Review*, May 1975, pp. 176–179. The timing relations between money, output, and prices are average, based upon past U.S. experience; they do not necessarily hold for each monetary shock nor for future shocks. Moreover, they do not necessarily hold for *negative* monetary shocks, which may take much longer to reduce inflation rates than positive shocks take to increase them. Incidentally, the Hume quotation is taken from this Friedman piece.

money. Inequality between demand and supply at the prevailing prices means that the plans of buyers and sellers do not mesh, that the prices have not brought forth equality between the quantity of goods offered for sale and the quantity buyers are willing to take off the market. Disequilibrium requires revision of plans; the revisions include changes in market prices and changes in the quantities of goods demanded and supplied.

Markets are rarely in equilibrium; frequent changes in demand and supply conditions are a fact of life. Some of the changes are random and therefore transitory in nature. Others are more permanent; they arise from fundamental shifts in individuals' tastes and preferences, from technological changes, government policy shifts, and so forth. The problem for the economist is to describe what happens when markets are out of equilibrium.

In modern economies there are two basic types of markets: "flexprice" markets and "fixprice" markets.[7] Examples of flexprice markets are the stock exchanges, the markets for Treasury bonds, spot and futures markets for commodities such as grain, metals, and other raw materials, and so forth. These markets are characterized by many sellers and buyers; professional traders that act as dealers and brokers, and organized exchanges such as the New York Stock Exchange and the commodities exchanges in New York, Chicago, London, and other cities. Trading in these markets is continuous and information about prices and other conditions is widely held and relatively cheap to acquire. For these reasons, the prices of goods traded in flexprice markets are highly sensitive to shifts in supply and demand conditions; convergence to equilibrium (if only temporary) is likely to occur very rapidly.

An economy dominated by flexprice markets would be relatively immune to the output effects of monetary shocks. Prices and costs would adjust rapidly to changes in aggregate demand, and aggregate output would fluctuate little in response to permanent changes in the growth rate of the money supply. But we do not live in a world dominated by flexprice markets. The prices of most products are sticky; they respond slowly to shifts in supply or demand conditions. The same is true of the markets for most types of labor. Money wages do not jump around like the price of gold when the supply and demand for labor change.

We shall use the term *fixprice markets* to describe markets in which prices move slowly in response to changes in supply and demand. As we shall see, there are varying degrees of stickiness in prices, so the concept of fixprice is not exactly descriptive of the real world. Nevertheless, it is useful to have a term that distinguishes one kind of market behavior

---

[7]The distinction is due to J. R. Hicks. See his *Capital and Growth* (New York: Oxford University Press, 1965), Chapter 7. See also his *Crisis in Keynesian Economics* (New York: Basic Books, 1974), p. 23 ff.

from another. The real world contains all kinds of markets, and price behavior varies in a spectrum from extreme flexibility to extreme stickiness.
Fixprice markets are those on the sticky side of the spectrum; flexprice
markets are the ones on the flexible side.

15.2.2
Price setting in fixprice markets

Stickiness of prices in fixprice markets frequently arises from institutional
and sellers' practices that make prices relatively unresponsive to *short-run*
shifts in demand. These practices include long-term contracts that fix
prices and wages for substantial periods of time. Some exployer–labor
union contracts, for example, run for three years. In other cases, prices
are regulated by public authorities, such as public utility commissions and
the Interstate Commerce Commission (railroad and trucking rates). Additional restrictions include legal rent controls, minimum wage laws, oil
price ceilings, interest rate ceilings, and so forth. Moreover, wage and salary levels of federal, state, and local government employees (which may
influence private sector wages and salaries) are frequently set for one-
and two-year periods by Congress and state and local legislative bodies.

Long-term labor contracts frequently produce divergencies between
wage and price movements. Negotiators may fail to anticipate the
strength of future inflation, so during the life of the contracts the real
wages of workers may decline. New contracts, recognizing past errors,
may come at a time when general inflation is slowing down; but the settlements may be such as to cause money wages to rise at rates that out-
strip increases in the price level. Eventually, employers may be forced to
pass on the wage increases to their customers, even though demand for
their products may be depressed.

Prices of products sold by large-scale manufacturing firms frequently
move more slowly than prices in general. To understand this, it is important to note that these firms do not operate in auction markets that force
them to submit to the market prices as set daily by supply and demand
conditions. They are not price takers; they are price makers. Price makers
are firms that set prices that think are best for long-run profitability. The
firms ignore temporary shifts in market demand and short-run variations
in costs. They change prices only when in their opinion basic market conditions have changed sufficiently to affect long-run profits.

Inflexibility of prices amongst large manufacturing firms[8] arises in
several ways. First, for many firms, particularly those with many different
products and many buyers, there are heavy costs attached to changing

---

[8]For documentation of such behavior, see Cagan, *The Hydra-Headed Monster* and the references therein.

prices. Decisions must be made; catalogs and price lists must be changed; sales personnel must be reeducated, and the prices of competitors must be scrutinized. Frequent changes in prices to reflect short-run changes in demand and supply conditions may simply be too costly to undertake.

Second, firms in highly concentrated industries must keep wary eyes upon their competitors. If they raise prices before their competitors do, they may lose large chunks of their markets to the other firms. On the other hand, if the firms cut prices, the other firms may interpret the action as a raid upon *their* market shares, and their response may be such as to precipitate price wars. For this reason, firms in oligopolistic industries seek ways to coordinate their price changes. The devices may include covert agreements among firms to follow the leadership of one or two particular firms in the industry, or to change prices only when some basic costs common to all firms change.

Perhaps the most widely used mechanism for coordinating price policies is for each firm in an industry to base its prices upon unit labor and raw materials cost plus some constant percentage markup. The unit cost is calculated for some standard level of plant operation or capacity utilization. The markup is set to provide a fixed target rate of return on equity. Since changes in labor and raw materials costs are roughly the same to all firms in an industry, the unit cost pricing method leads all firms in the industry to change prices at the same time in roughly the same degree.

The unit cost-markup method also assures that prices do not respond sensitively to short-run changes in demand. From the industry's point of view, prices are cost-determined, hence unless and until there are pervasive changes in unit costs—perhaps after renegotiation of wage contracts with unions—prices will change slowly, perhaps only as a response to changes in raw materials prices, many of which are determined in flex-price markets. Eventually, however, persistent changes in demand will show up in the pricing policies of the firms. For example, in the face of continuing expansions in demand, firms will find it necessary to compete for additional labor. This competition may eventually raise wage rates throughout the industry by softening firms' bargaining positions with the unions or by simply increasing the demand prices firms are willing to pay unorganized workers. The increases in wage rates are then passed along to customers in the form of increased product prices.

A final explanation of the sluggishness of prices in fixprice markets is the difficulty firms have in distinguishing between shifts in demand specific to their industries and shifts in aggregate demand that hit all industries. Changes in demand that affect particular industries are usually associated with opposite changes in demands in other industries. For that reason, changes in the composition of demand in the economy are unlikely to generate significant overall cost pressures. But changes in aggregate demand put pressure on input prices everywhere. If a firm believes it is sharing in an economy-wide increase in demand, it will raise its prices with confidence. But, if it believes that the increase in demand is peculiar to itself or its industry, it is unlikely to raise its prices; instead, it will simply expand its production and sales to meet the increase in demand. If the firm turns out to be wrong, it will discover its mistake from increases in its wage and raw materials costs. At that point it will raise its prices.

The long delays in the adjustment of many prices to changes in demand make it difficult for observers to separate the different factors in the inflationary process. Essentially, most inflation is ultimately caused by shifts in aggregate demand. Nonetheless, it is wages and other costs that frequently move first. Moreover, when wages and prices in concentrated industries are moving up during periods of general economic slack, it may appear that the combination of union and industry monopoly power is pushing up the general price level. But the increases in wages and prices may simply be delayed responses to prior increases in aggregate demand. Generally speaking, there is little evidence that big unions and big firms are inflation starters. They do play an important role in the transmission of inflationary pressures; they frequently *prolong* the process of price and wage increases when the original pressures have subsided. But to argue that their actions are responsible for the double-digit inflation experienced in recent years in the United States is to go well beyond the evidence.[9] After all, unions and concentrated industries existed in the pre-1965 years; but, except for the years immediately following World War II and for the Korean War period, the rate of inflation rarely rose above 3 percent per year. During the first half of the 1960s, prices rose by less than 2 percent per year.

15.2.3
Lags in inflationary expectations

If people could forecast the future course of wages and prices, current price changes would immediately reflect people's expectations. But people have imperfect foresight. Wage settlements that emerge from collective bargaining negotiations usually reflect inaccurate predictions of changing consumer prices or product prices of the firms with whom the unions are bargaining. Similarly, the prices firms write into contracts with customers often reflect expected future changes in raw materials costs. As a result, when actual inflation rates differ from expected inflation rates, unions and firms are moved to renegotiate labor and other contracts to reflect the new situation.

---

[9] For a similar view, see Thomas M. Humphrey, "The Persistence of Inflation," in *Essays on Inflation*, 2nd edition (Richmond: Federal Reserve Bank of Richmond, 1980), pp. 49–61. This section owes much to Humphrey's article.

To some extent, the need for renegotiations is reduced by the presence of cost-of-living provisions in labor contracts with employers or similar provisions in firms' contracts with customers. In addition, unions may demand shorter term contracts with the employers, and firms may require the same with their customers. Nonetheless, these practices are not universal, and since such provisions throw much of the inflationary risk onto employers and business customers, most contracts are not negotiated to fully protect workers or firms from unanticipated inflation.

Wage and price settlements and decisions, therefore, reflect a *catch-up element* to take into account past forecasting errors and a *forecasting element* to take into account future inflation. The latter is often based upon past inflationary trends, with heavier weights given to the recent past than to more remote years. Deviations of current inflation rates from those of the past eventually change inflationary expectations in the direction of the deviations. Thus, if this year's inflation rate is 10 percent per year, as opposed to an average inflation rate of 6 percent per year in the past 2 or 3 years, people's expectations of future inflation may be raised to, say, 8 percent for the next year. Persistence of the 10 percent inflation rate may finally lead people to expect a permanent 10 percent rate for future years. Similarly, a reduction of actual inflation back to 6 percent per year may eventually lead people to expect a 6 percent rate for future years.

Thus, the way in which people form their expectations has an effect upon the pace of inflation. If people form their expectations *adaptively*, as described above, then changes in the inflation rate may only slowly insinuate themselves into inflationary expectations. The lags in expectations, in turn, will slow the wage and price increases being currently negotiated. On the other hand, persistent experience with inflation may speed the adaptations of expected to actual price changes and hence shorten the lags. Indeed, there is a school of economists who believe that many people change their inflationary expectations *rationally* rather than adaptively. That is, they think people form their expectations by looking at the policies that produce inflation rather than at inflation itself. Thus, if during a recession the public expects the Federal Reserve System to engage in policies that will eventually accelerate the rate of inflation, people may increase their inflationary expectations before the price rises actually occur. To the extent such expectations become embodied in current contracts, the lag of prices behind changes in aggregate demand will be negative!

Although there is evidence that the lag of inflation rates behind changes in aggregate demand is shortening, few economists believe that it has been reduced to zero or has become negative. Thus the first impact of changes in aggregate demand is likely to be upon the rate of growth of real output rather than upon the rate of inflation. Eventually, however, the combined effect of rising costs and changing expectations will cause the price level to rise. At some point, most of the increase in the growth rate of nominal income will be absorbed by the changed rate of inflation; the output growth rate, at that point, will approximate its old level. The process is sketched out in Figure 15.5, which follows the inflationary process from its origin in the excess demand for goods, to increases in output and reductions in inventories, to increases in the demand for labor and other inputs that raise costs and product prices. The figure also incorporates an "expectations loop" that reinforces and prolongs the inflationary process by putting more pressure on prices either directly or indirectly through pushing up factor prices and costs. Prolonged experience with inflation can, of course, set in motion the expectations loop before excess demand raises output and demand for factors.

15.2.4
Diagrammatic treatment of price lags

The lag of adjustment of inflation rates to monetary shocks produces a cyclical change in the rate of growth of output. In the long run, the trend of output growth is dictated by the growth rates of the labor force, the stock of capital, and the trend of technological changes. Also important are the changes in the educational level and health of the population and the pace of discovery of new sources of raw materials and energy. But a positive monetary shock initially pushes output to grow faster than the long-run trend; as a result, when prices ultimately begin to rise at a faster rate, output growth must fall to a pace that is below the long-run trend. Eventually, it recovers to match the trend rate of growth; but, in the meantime, it will have undergone a cyclical fluctuation.

To show this, consider the following somewhat formal development. Let $Y = Py$, where P is a price index and y is real income. Making use of the fact that $\log Y = \log P + \log y$, and substituting this into Equation (15.1), repeated here, we have the following:

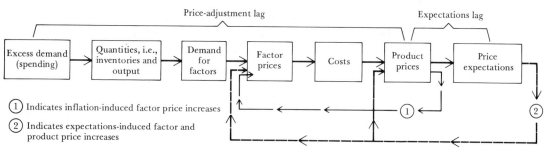

Figure 15.5 *The inflationary transmission mechanism. (Source: Thomas M. Humphrey, "The Persistence of Inflation," in* Essays on Inflation, *2nd edition (Federal Reserve Bank of Richmond, 1980) p. 51.)*

$$\log M_t^s = \log k_t^d + \log Y_t^e \tag{15.1}$$

$$\log M_t^s - \log k_t^d = \log P_t^e + \log y_t^e \tag{15.2}$$

where as before, the symbol e represents equilibrium values and d represents desired value for k.

Now make use of the fact that the proportionate (or percentage) rate of growth of a variable is measured by the change in its logarithm per unit of time. That leads us to the following equation, where dots over the letters represent the proportionate growth rates of the variables in Equations (15.1) and (15.2):[10]

$$\dot{M}^s - \dot{k}^d = \dot{P}^e + \dot{y}^e = \dot{Y}^e \tag{15.3}$$

This representation allows us to construct Figure 15.6.

Figure 15.6 represents the results of a hypothetical single monetary shock. (In the real world, of course, monetary shocks may succeed each other before the adjustment processes portrayed in the figure work themselves out.) Figure 15.6a shows that any given nominal income growth rate ($\dot{Y}^e$ or $\dot{Y}^{e\prime}$) may be divided between the inflation rate and the rate of growth of real output. Let the economy initially be on its trend rate of real output, $\dot{y}^e$. Now, at time t^*, let a positive monetary shock raise the nominal income growth rate to $\dot{Y}^{e\prime}$. As a result, the equilibrium inflation rate rises from $\dot{P}^e$ to $\dot{P}^{e\prime}$. However, as argued above, the new equilibrium inflation rate is not reached immediately. As a result, there occurs a series of output adjustments.

Because of the price lag, the monetary shock initially raises output growth above its trend rate, $\dot{y}^e$. This continues until t_1, at which time the rising rate of inflation begins to eat away at the increased rate of output growth. Thereafter, the rate of output growth starts to fall as the inflation rate accelerates to its peak at t_2. At some point, say t_3, the output growth rate hits bottom and then rises back to its trend rate $\dot{y}^e$. At this point, the inflation rate has adjusted to its new equilibrium level, $\dot{P}^{e\prime}$. Figure 15.6b traces the timing relationships between $\dot{P}$ and $\dot{y}$.

In studying the figure, note that during the adjustment process between the two equilibrium growth situations, nominal income growth is at first below and then above its new equilibrium rate. That is to say, along the curved adjustment path in Figure 15.6a, combinations of $\dot{p}$ and $\dot{y}$ are both below and above points on $\dot{Y}^{e\prime}$. The reason was given earlier in the chapter. A positive monetary shock raises the growth rate of the money supply. Instead of immediately spending the new cash, people build their

---

[10]For Example, $(\Delta \log M^s / \Delta t = \dot{M}^s$, where $t = 1$ year. Thus $\dot{M}^s$ is the annual percentage rate of growth of the money supply. Similar interpretations hold for $\dot{k}^d$, $\dot{y}$, $\dot{P}$, and $\dot{Y}$.

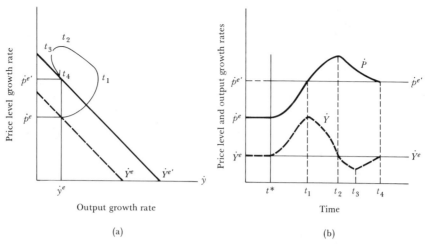

Figure 15.6 *Dynamics of price–output interactions resulting from a positive monetary shock.*

money balances; later, after they have discovered they have built them up too much, they begin to accelerate their outlays. Thus, money income first grows more slowly than its new equilibrium rate. Later, as people start to unload their excess cash balances, money income grows more rapidly than the equilibrium rate. Once cash balances are in line with the desired ratio to income, the new equilibrium growth rate (as at t_4 in Figure 15.6) is reached.

A negative monetary shock shifts the $\dot{Y}^e$ line down and produces declines in real output growth followed by declines in the inflation rate. Eventually, output growth should rise back to its trend rate, and the inflation rate should assume a lower level consistent with the lowered rate of growth of nominal income. As an exercise, try to trace out the time path of adjustment.

In the real world, we do not expect to observe patterns of inflation and real growth rates precisely as indicated in Figure 15.6 (or a similar graph portraying a negative monetary shock). As indicated above, single monetary shocks rarely occur. At times, political and other considerations lead the monetary authorities to impose a *series* of positive monetary shocks upon the economy. As the effects of each new shock wear off, and output growth rates begin to fall (and unemployment rates begin to rise), the authorities may accelerate the growth of the money supply in an attempt to restore higher output growth rates and higher levels of employment. Although they may at times achieve their objectives, the analysis given in this section and in Section 15.2.2 indicates that overly stimulative policies carry the danger of acceleration of the rate of inflation. Indeed, if the public discovers the game the authorities are playing, price adjustment lags and expectations lags may shorten considerably, in which case each new monetary shock will stimulate output growth less than the one before. At some point, further monetary shocks might be immediately followed by equivalent jumps in the equilibrium inflation rate.

In reality, the monetary authorities rarely carry inflationary policies to their limit (although in the past, as during the hyperinflation of Germany after World War II, they did). At some point, before the efforts of previous policies have worked themselves out, they may reverse themselves and reduce the rate of growth of the money supply. The October 6, 1979 actions of the Federal Reserve System, discussed in Chapter 10, are a case in point. In that event, the pattern of price and output interactions may look quite different than the one illustrated by Figure 15.6.

SUMMARY

This chapter discussed the details of the process by which monetary shocks are transmitted through the economy. Monetary shocks are unexpected changes in the growth rate of the money supply. Since they are unexpected, the public is likely to delay reacting to them. The cash balances people hold fulfill a shock-absorber function. Hence, people at first ignore random increases and decreases in their cash holdings. But once they realize that the changes imposed by the authorities are permanent, they will attempt to bring their cash holdings into line with amounts they want to have. Thus, the public will change the rate at which it purchases goods and services or securities. The result is a change in the growth rate of nominal income. In the case of a positive monetary shock, the income growth rate accelerates until it hits a new equilibrium rate. A negative shock leads to a deceleration of the income growth rate.

Monetary shocks have direct and indirect effects upon aggregate demand. The direct effects occur when the public exchanges excess money for goods and services. Indirect effects occur when the monetary shocks cause banks and the public to alter their supplies and demands for securities. The resulting changes in interest rates lead to changes in asset prices and to changes in the demand for durable physical assets. The shifts in the demand for durable assets stimulates changes in production and shifts in the demands for labor and other factors of production. Changed factor earnings promote additional shifts in the demands for goods and services, spreading the effects of the monetary shocks to other parts of the economy.

Changes in aggregate demand at first primarily fall upon the rate of growth of output of goods and services. Significant changes in the rate of inflation follow. Although there are some flexprice (auction type) markets, most goods and services are sold through fixprice (nonauction) markets in which wages and prices are somewhat inflexible. The reasons for wage–price stickiness include delays in adjustments of contacts, high costs of changing prices, and coordination of price changes in concentrated industries using price leaders or common unit cost-plus-markup rules. In addition, sellers are often unable to distinguish between interindustry demand shifts and changes in aggregate demand. These factors, together with the lag of inflationary expectations behind past changes in the inflation rate, combine to delay increases in the actual rate of inflation when the growth rate of aggregate demand accelerates.

The delayed impact on prices causes monetary shocks to first change the rate of growth of output. Eventually, however, the movement of prices will cause the output effects of the monetary changes to peter out, after which the growth rate of real income should again approximate the path dictated by supply-side factors such as the growth rate of the labor force, capital stock accumulation, and technological change. Once this state is reached, the primary force of the monetary shock will be absorbed by permanent changes in the rate of growth of the price level.

Monetary shocks in the same or opposite directions frequently occur before the effects of the previous shocks have worked themselves out. For that reason, the idealized pattern of changes in the growth rates of output and prices discussed in this chapter are not always observable in the real world. Nonetheless, there is considerable evidence that cyclical changes in the growth rate of nominal income and its division between changes in the rate of growth of output and prices are at least correlated with the change in the growth rate of the money supply. We shall review some of this evidence in the next chapter.

DISCUSSION QUESTIONS

1. What would be the effects on the economy if people completely ignored the impact of monetary shocks on their cash balances?

2. What would be the effects on the economy of complete predictability of monetary changes, assuming they are not ignored by the public?

3. Why do monetary changes lead to changes in nominal aggregate income?

4. Under what conditions would monetary shocks change the price level without changing output? Why do they normally change output before they change the price level?

5. Let output growth be 3 percent a year and the growth of the Cambridge k be 2 percent a year. What must the rate of growth of the money supply be to have a constant price level?

6. Monetarists frequently argue that monetary changes affect "real variables" (eg., real interest rates, real output, and relative product and factor prices) in the short run, but only the price level in the long run.

Using the materials of this chapter and those of Chapter 13, discuss this proposition.

7. Trace through the effects on output growth and price level growth of a negative monetary shock.

IMPORTANT TERMS AND CONCEPTS

- [ ] channels of monetary policy
- [ ] direct effects of a monetary shock
- [ ] fixprice markets
- [ ] flexprice markets
- [ ] indirect effects of monetary shock
- [ ] lags in effect of monetary changes
- [ ] monetary shock
- [ ] overshoots
- [ ] price makers
- [ ] price takers
- [ ] shock absorber function of money

ADDITIONAL READINGS

A good textbook treatment of the timing relations between monetary shocks and changes in the growth rates of nominal income, output, and prices is in Michael Darby, *Intermediate Macroeconomics* (New York: Mc-Graw-Hill, 1979), Chapters 6 and 7. Darby's work is in the tradition of Milton Friedman and Anna J. Schwartz, "Money and Business Cycles," *Review of Economics and Statistics*, February 1963 (supplement). See also Friedman's *A Theoretical Framework for Monetary Analysis* (New York: National Bureau of Economic Research, 1971), pp. 1–48 and his earlier piece, "The Lag in Effect of Monetary Policy," *Journal of Political Economy*, October, 1961. Earlier discussions of this matter are in Irving Fisher, *The Purchasing Power of Money* (New York: Augustus M. Kelley, 1963, reprint of the 1922 revised edition), Chapter 4 and, in a somewhat different tradition, in Friedrich A. Hayek, *Monetary Theory and Trade Cycle* (New York: Augustus M. Kelley, 1975, reprint of the 1933 English translation). An interesting recent discussion is in Robert Lucas, Jr., "Understanding Business Cycles," in K. Brunner and A. Meltzer (editors) *Carnegie–Rochester Conference Series on Public Policy*, Volume 5, 1977. Much relevant discussion on the problems also appears in Volume 8 (1978) of the Carnegie–Rochester Conference Series, the title of which is *The Problem of Inflation*. The distinction between the direct and indirect effects of monetary policy is criticized in Thomas Mayer, *The Structure of Monetarism* (New York: Norton, 1979). Finally, an excellent outline of the current theory of price formation during inflationary times is in Thomas M. Humphrey, "The Persistence of Inflation," in *Essays on Inflation*, 2nd edition (Federal Reserve Bank of Richmond), 1980, pp. 49–61. For a more advanced treatment, see Robert J. Gordon, "Output Fluctuations and Gradual Price Adjustment," *Journal of Economic Literature*, Vol. XIX, No. 2, June 1981, pp. 493–530. A book-length treatment of the subject is given by the late Arthur M. Okun in *Prices and Quantities* (Washington, D.C.: The Brookings Institution, 1981).

16

Money and Business Cycles: The U.S. Experience

O U T L I N E

Monetary and Nonmonetary Theories of the Business Cycle
Definition of a Business Cycle
Supply-side Cycles
Demand-side Cycles
Behavior of Money Supply over the Business Cycle
Evidence on the Cyclical Behavior of Money
Causation between Money and Business Cycles
Cyclical Changes in the Cambridge *k* (or the Income Velocity of Money)
Long-term Changes in Income Velocity
Cyclical Movements in Velocity
A "Neoclassical" Supply-side Monetary Model

Recurrent cycles of boom and bust are common in modern economies. Economists have explained the cycles in a variety of ways. In recent years, monetary theories have become popular. The approach represents a distinct shift away from the ideas of the dominant Keynesian school of thought. The dynamic money model of Chapter 15, which stresses people's adjustments to unexpected changes in the growth rate of the money supply, is an example of the monetary approach to business cycle theory.

The question before us is whether the real world contains evidence in support of the monetary approach. In this chapter we will survey evidence gathered from the behavior of the United States economy over the last century. As we shall see, the evidence lends considerable, but not conclusive, support for the monetary theory of business cycles.

16.1
Monetary and nonmonetary theories of the business cycle[1]

Before discussing the evidence, we must first define the term *business cycle* and make some preliminary distinctions between monetary and nonmonetary theories.

16.1.1
Definition of a business cycle

The term business cycle refers to *general* fluctuations around the trend rates of change of aggregate output, employment, and the rate of inflation. General fluctuations must be distinguished from shifts in the composition of output and employment or changes in the pattern of relative prices. The latter do not describe cyclical behavior as discussed by most students of the subject.

The word cycle is misleading. Economic fluctuations are not necessarily regular. The economic growth of the United States in the period 1854–1975 was interrupted by 28 business cycles. The average peak-to-peak period of these cycles was 52 months. Yet the length of the cyclical periods varied a great deal. For example, the fluctuation that took place between the cycle peaks of August 1918 and January 1920 lasted only 17 months, while the one that happened between April 1960 and December 1969 lasted a full 116 months. The standard deviation of the durations of the 28 cycles was 23.6 months, which is slightly greater than one-half of their mean value.[2]

---

[1]A classic general survey of business cycle theories is Gottfried Haberler, *Prosperity and Depression,* 3rd edition (League of Nations, 1941).

[2]The cycles are dated by the National Bureau of Economic Research. The U.S. Department of Commerce, *Business Conditions Digest,* February 1977, Appendix, p. 105, contains the dates of the peaks and troughs of all the cycles from 1854 to 1975.

Cycles have two phases. The *expansion phase* is the movement from the lower turning point, or *trough* of the cycle, to the upper turning point, or *peak* of the cycle. The *contraction phase* is the movement from peak to trough. As might be suspected, the length of the phases varies greatly among cycles. The 28 expansions ranged from 10 to 106 months, with an average of 33 months. The contractions varied from 7 to 63 months, with an average of 19 months. Thus expansions are usually longer than contractions.

16.1.2
Supply-side cycles

Since business cycles are economy-wide phenomena, they cannot be easily explained by events taking place in individual markets. For example, a sudden collapse of demand in one industry may simply reflect a sudden increase in demand for the products of another. And, although sudden changes in the channels of trade (as the nineteenth century economist David Ricardo called them) do injure profits and cause unemployment, they do not necessarily lead to overall rises in unemployment or drops in the economy-wide rate of growth. If the labor market is functioning properly, the displaced workers can find jobs in the expanding industry, or with companies that have lost workers to the expanding industry.

The collapse in the demand for the products of a single industry is a sign of general decline only if it is part of a force that also hits other sectors of the economy. Our discussions in Chapters 11–15 indicated that such a force can originate on either the demand side or the supply side of the economy.

Serious supply-side shocks are not common. An exception to the rule is the rise of the OPEC cartel and the spectacular increase of energy prices it imposed on the world. The 1973–1974 embargo of oil exports following the Yom Kippur War between Israel and the Arabs and the subsequent quadrupling of oil prices deepened a recession that began in the fall of 1973. The 1980 recession was probably influenced by a surge in oil prices in 1979.

These supply-side shocks took place at the same time the growth rate of the money supply was slowing down, so demand-side factors were also at work. Nevertheless, the experience can and should be put into the context of Say's Law. Economy-wide increases in real energy costs reduce a country's productive capacity. Say's Law implies that reciprocal effects of reduced aggregate supply include reductions in real aggregate demand. The consequences of such reductions include dislocations of labor and other resources and an increase in the overall unemployment rate. Some time must lapse before workers and capital owners find new employments for their services, so the economy cannot immediately adjust to the lower growth path implied by its reduced productive capacity. Before it does, it operates below its potential. But when workers and capital find new employments, aggregate output rises to the new growth path. Unless the economy suffers further shocks, it will continue to rise along that path.

16.1.3
Demand-side cycles

Economists have traditionally argued that business cycles originate with fluctuations in aggregate demand. The Keynesian view, which is embodied in the income–expenditure models widely taught in colleges and universities, stresses fluctuations in *autonomous expenditures*—business investment, residential construction and government outlays.

Keynesians believe that recessions originate in reductions in one or more of these expenditures and are magnified by a multiplier process that depends upon interactions between autonomous spending and consumer outlays. Consumption spending mainly depends upon household income. If reductions in investment or government expenditures impose a net loss of sales upon business firms, the firms will reduce output or accept losses by lowering prices. But, since wages, and hence prices, are likely to be sticky in the short run, the main casualty will be output.

Cutbacks in output cause layoffs and reduced incomes for workers. So workers reduce their consumption spending. Reduced consumption demand causes reductions of output, employment, and income in consumer goods industries, which lead to further drops in consumption spending. Thus the original slump in autonomous spending snowballs into a series of reductions in consumption spending that magnify the original decline in total output.

Keynesians explain revivals and upward movements of the economy by means of upward shifts in autonomous expenditures that, together with induced increases in consumption spending, carry the economy through its expansion phase.

Without necessarily disputing every element of the Keynesian view, adherents of the monetary approach to business cycles frequently point to the special assumptions required by the Keynesian theory. An expansionary situation powered by an excess demand for goods and services must be accompanied by an excess supply of money, and a contractionary situation must be driven by an excess demand for money. So monetary theorists argue that Keynesian theory is not acceptable unless it can be shown that autonomous shifts in expenditures produce reinforcing changes in the excess supply or demand for money.

An excess supply or demand for money may arise from wholesale shifts in the demand schedule for money, changes in interest rates and yields on nonmonetary assets that alter the quantity of money demanded along a given schedule, and changes in the supply of money.

In his own writing, Keynes frequently cited shifts in the demand for money (which he called liquidity preference) as a source of economic disturbance. Indeed, he *stressed* the idea, arguing that when people become frightened and uncertain about the future, their natural instinct is to get out of capital goods and into money. Conversely, when their confidence returns, the extra demand for money subsides, and they develop an appetite for capital goods.[3]

Modern writers acknowledge Keynes's theory, but they do have reservations. People cope with uncertainty in a variety of ways, including diversifying their assets into government bonds, insured time and savings deposits, short-term securities, and mutual investment funds. Thus, unless cataclysmic changes are in the offing, uncertainty need not breed shifts in the demand for money.

Changes in the excess demand for money arising from movements along given demand schedules for money may arise from a linkage between changes in autonomous spending and shifts in the demand for loanable funds. Much business capital and inventory spending is financed with borrowed money and with sales of corporate stocks. Almost all housing investments are made with funds borrowed in the mortgage markets. Thus when either (or both) of these categories of autonomous expenditures change, so too does the demand for loanable funds. As a result, interest rates and yields on common stocks also change, leading people to alter the amount of money they wish to hold.

Thus, by altering interest rates and stock yields, changes in autonomous expenditures financed with borrowed money can indirectly change the excess demand for money. But the size of this effect depends critically upon the sensitivity of the demand for money to changes in the rate of interest. If the sensitivity is great, small changes in interest rates give rise to large changes in the excess demand for money. If the sensitivity is small, large changes in interest rates are required to evoke large changes in the excess demand for money.

A number of empirical studies have indicated that the quantity of money demanded responds little to changes in the rate of interest. Most studies put the interest-elasticity of the demand for money in the $-.1$ to $-.2$ range, which means that a 10 percent increase in short-term interest rates reduces the demand for money by only 1–2 percent. Thus, although cash hoards can be attracted into the expenditure stream by movements of autonomous expenditures that increase interest rates, it usually takes

[3]Keynes's position is best spelled out in his article, "The General Theory of Unemployment," *Quarterly Journal of Economics*, Vol. 51, No. 1, February 1937, pp. 209–223, reprinted in Donald Muggridge, editor, *The Collected Writings of John Maynard Keynes, Volume XIV, The General Theory and After, Part II, Defense and Development* (London: Macmillan, for the Royal Economic Society, 1973), pp. 109–123.

increases in the supply of money to finance large and sustained movements in aggregate demand.

Since the supply of money is largely controlled by the Federal Reserve System, it is not necessarily correlated with changes in autonomous expenditures. In the past, however, the Federal Reserve System has followed policies that may have created such a correlation. As discussed in Chapter 10, acceptance of the commercial loan theory can lead to policies that cause bank reserves and the money supply to rise and fall strictly in relation to the so-called needs of trade. Similar results follow if the monetary authorities adopt and hold to an interest rate target. But in such cases it is difficult to assign responsibility for cyclical movements in the economy. Policies are not acts of nature. When authorities possess but do not use the power to prevent a reduction in autonomous expenditures from spilling over into a reduction in the quantity of money, it cannot be said with conviction that the shift in autonomous expenditures actually causes the following recession. To so argue would be analogous to asserting that a certain virus causes the flu, even though people contracting the flu refuse to accept a fail-safe vaccination.

Although some changes in the money supply do reflect Federal Reserve adherence to interest rate and other targets, many do not. Instead, they represent shifts in policies that originate in authorities' concerns over inflation, the balance of payments, the international value of the dollar, the level of unemployment, and other goals. Thus, shifting policy goals, as distinct from misplaced adherence to certain intermediate policy targets (see Section 10.1 for the distinction between policy goals and policy targets), may explain a number of past monetary shocks. If so, it cannot be said that changes in the money supply are a link in a chain of causation that begins with shifts in autonomous expenditure and ends in a change in the excess demand for money. Indeed, the reverse would be true: Changes in the money supply would be the cause of changes in the excess demand for money that ultimately cause shifts in the excess demand for goods, of which the level of autonomous expenditures is but a part.

To summarize: Monetary theory admits that some of the movements in aggregate demand associated with business cycles can come from changes in the demand for money that originate with fluctuations in autonomous expenditures. It also admits that pursuit of interest rate or other policy targets may lead the Federal Reserve System to actions that cause the money supply to change in directions that reflect shifts in autonomous expenditures. In that event, the issue of what causes the business cycle—money or autonomous expenditures—is somewhat obscure. But when the Federal Reserve System changes the money supply or its growth rate in response to shifts in its policy goals, the issue is more clear; the line of causation runs from money to spending rather than from spending to money.

Behavior of money supply over the business cycle

Modern monetarists believe that the demand for money is a relatively stable function of interest rates, income, and wealth. If that is true, the amount of money people wish to hold will grow along a line determined by trends in real income, real wealth, the price level, and nominal interest rates. So long as the money supply grows apace with the demand for money, few cyclical movements should disturb the economy. Those that do will be associated with random shifts in the factors that determine the demand for or supply of money. But should the authorities for some reason impose a monetary shock on the economy, a growing gap would emerge between the demand for and supply of money. As discussed in Chapter 15, such a gap would create a threat of cyclical movements in the economy.

Monetarists contend that most cyclical movements in the economy start not with shifts in the trend rate of growth of the demand for money, but instead with monetary shocks imposed by the authorities. Sometimes the shocks are deliberately engineered; sometimes they are by-products of shifts in policy goals or of inappropriate or incomplete monetary policy strategies. But, whatever the reason for the authorities' decisions, the monetarists claim that the resulting monetary shocks are the main source of cyclical movements in the economy.

The monetary interpretation of the business cycle predicts that growth rates of the money supply will rise during the expansion phase and fall during the contraction phase of the business cycle. In addition, because of the lags in effect of monetary shocks, growth rates of the money supply should be observed to decrease prior to cyclical peaks and to increase before cyclical troughs. As we shall see, such cyclical behavior of money can, in fact, be observed for the U.S. economy. But, as we shall argue, the behavior is not conclusive evidence for the monetarists' theory of the business cycle. Mere statistical association is insufficient to prove causation. What is needed is a demonstration that changes in money supply growth rates are not themselves the result of prior changes in the level of business activity.

16.2.1
Evidence on the cyclical behavior of money

Evidence of money supply movements over the business cycle exists for a period of more than 100 years. Milton Friedman, and Anna J. Schwartz discussed the evidence in a famous article published in 1963.[4] In their

---

[4]M. Friedman and A. J. Schwartz, "Money and Business Cycles," *Review of Economics and Statistics,* Supplement, February 1963.

discussion, they displayed a chart showing the average reference-cycle patterns for the growth rate of the (old) M-2 money supply for the period 1867–1961. They used the M-2 money supply because continuous M-1 data do not exist for the whole period. The chart, reproduced in Figure 16.1, records the relative rates of growth of the money supply at various points before and after cyclical peaks. The rate of growth of money is measured as a ratio to the average rates of growth of money during the individual cycles making up the average.

Evidence recorded on the chart is clear: (1) the growth rate of the money supply typically peaks and begins its decline relative to its cycle average *before* general economic activity reaches a peak; (2) deep depression cycles have been accompanied by wider fluctuations in the growth rate of money than have the mild depression cycles; but (3) the same general pattern of money change has accompanied both deep and mild contractions in the economy. The same comments hold for the 1908–1961 period and the 1867–1908 period. So, although the Federal Reserve System was established in 1913, its policies do not seem to have affected these patterns.

An important difference between the deep and mild depression cycles is that the absolute level of the money supply dropped during major depressions, but continued to rise during most mild cycles. Friedman

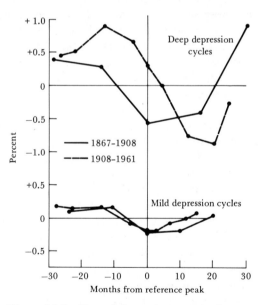

Figure 16.1 *Rate of change in money stock: average reference-cycle patterns for mild and deep depression cycles, 1867–1961. Note: War cycles, not shown, are 1914–1919 and 1938–1945. Deep depression cycles are 1870–1879, 1891–1894, 1904–1908, 1919–1921, 1927–1933, and 1933–1938. All others are mild depression cycles. (Source: Friedman and Schwartz, "Money and Business Cycles.")*

Table 16.1 *Money Supply Reductions, Deep Depression Cycles, 1867–1960*

Period	Percentage Reduction of M-2
1873–1879	4.9
1892–1894	5.8
1897–1908	3.7
1920–1921	5.1
1929–1933	35.2
1937–1938	2.4

Source: Friedman and Schwartz, "Money and Business Cycles."

and Schwartz give the figures in Table 16.1 for the decline in M-2 during deep depression cycles.

Only two mild depression cycles during the period (not shown in Table 16.1) were accompanied by reductions of the money stock—1948–1949 (1.4 percent) and 1959–1960 (1.1 percent). According to Friedman and Schwartz, these were the two most severe mild depression cycles in the period.

Although changes in the growth rate of the money supply typically precede business cycle peaks and troughs, the timing of the leads varied greatly. Using a method that identifies sudden shifts in levels of money growth, Friedman and Schwartz calculated an average lead of 7 months for cyclical peaks and 4 months for cyclical troughs. But the standard deviation of the lead was 7.9 months for peaks and 5.6 months for troughs. Thus, the variability of the lead exceeded the average lead for both peaks and troughs. This variability greatly reduces the usefulness of money supply growth rates as a device for predicting the timing of turns in the business cycle.

Most of the Friedman–Schwartz evidence is from the period before World War II. But, as shown in Figures 16.2 and 16.3, postwar evidence also backs up their findings. Figure 16.2 compares the average cyclical pattern of (old) M-2 growth for two periods in the 1867–1951 period with the pattern for the 1952–1978 period. There were five business cycle peaks during 1952–1978. The behavior of M-2 growth in the vicinity of those peaks was similar to its behavior in the two earlier periods. The main difference is that money growth accelerated before, rather than after, the onset of a recession. The relative mildness of the post-1951 recessions may be due to the early reversal of declining monetary growth rates and to the reduced amplitude of monetary growth over the cycle.[5]

Figure 16.3 shows the 1952–1978 experience in a somewhat different

---

[5]Byron Higgins, "Monetary Growth and Business Cycles, Part I: The Theoretical and Historical Perspective," *Federal Reserve Bank of Kansas Economic Review,* April 1979, p. 5.

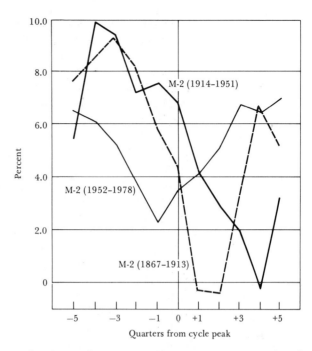

Figure 16.2 *Cyclical pattern of M-2 growth. (Source: Higgins, "Monetary Growth and Business Cycles, Part 1.")*

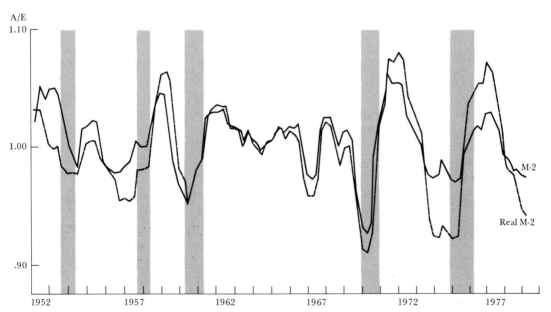

Figure 16.3 *A/E ratios for real and nominal M-2, 1952–1978. (Source: Higgins, "Monetary Growth and Business Cycles, Part 11.")*

light. Instead of measuring the rate of growth of the money supply, it tracks the ratio of the actual level of money *(A)* to the level that would have resulted if money growth had continued along an extrapolated trend established two years earlier *(E)*. Thus the ratio *A/E* is a measure of monetary accelerations and decelerations. When the ratio is unity, money growth is not changing. But when it exceeds or falls short of unity, money growth is accelerating or decelerating.

For the most part, expansions and contractions in the economy during 1952–1978 were linked with monetary accelerations and decelerations. Yet not every deceleration was accompanied by a measured recession. The 1966–1967 experience is a case in point; although many observers agree that there was a mini-recession in that period, it has not gone down in recorded history as a full-fledged contraction. Similarly, the 1978 deceleration was not accompanied or followed by a recession in 1979. Monetary economists are somewhat puzzled by this period, but the absence of a correlation between monetary deceleration and recession in that period may in part arise from what many analysts regard as a growing inadequacy of the older conventional measures of money. It may also arise from a shift in the trend rate of growth of the Cambridge *k*.[6] In any event, a recession hit the economy in January 1980, preceded and accompanied by a reduced rate of growth of M-1B and new M-2.

In summary, most of the evidence of over 100 years of monetary history supports the hypothesis that money and business cycles are correlated. Typically, monetary growth drops before or during economic contractions and rises before or during expansion periods. Not all movements of money growth are associated with cyclical movements in the economy; but most *sharp* changes in monetary growth rates do seem to precede or accompany upward and downward movements in the economy. Finally, even though fluctuations in money growth have occurred without fluctuations in the economy, there does not appear to be a case in which cyclical movements in the economy have taken place without fluctuations in monetary growth.

16.2.2
Causation between money and business cycles

The causal role of money in business cycles cannot be established by charts such as Figures 16.1, 16.2, and 16.3. Fluctuations in the money supply—even those that take place before cyclical peaks and troughs—may be due to factors that cause nominal income to fluctuate independently of money. For example, shifts in investment demand may lead to variations in interest rates that the Federal Reserve System will not toler-

---

[6]The Cambridge *k* (measured with the old M-2) fell in the last three quarters of 1979. It had been rising since the first quarter of 1977.

ate, in which case the monetary authorities may passively expand or contract the monetary base in order to stabilize interest rates. In so doing, they would cause the growth of the money supply to go up and down with the cycle.

Even so, although the authorities may have occasionally acted this way, there are episodes in which it seems fairly clear that fluctuations in the money supply resulted from policy shifts.

Friedman and Schwartz[7] have identified a number of such instances for major economic fluctuations during the 1867–1940 period. For example, the 1875–1878 depression was preceded by a decline in the monetary base brought on by political pressure to go back on the gold standard. A subsequent rash of bank failures was accomplished by withdrawals of currency from banks and strong defensive increases in bank reserve–deposit ratios. The 1920–1921 contraction was preceded by sharp increases in Federal Reserve discount rates that led to a decline in the monetary base and to a reduction in the stock of money. The 1929–1933 Great Depression was preceded by a period of zero monetary growth, due in large measure to the Federal Reserve's attempt to fight stock market speculation with tight monetary policies. Over the period, the money supply fell by 34 percent, largely because the Federal Reserve failed to maintain the monetary base, but also because a series of bank failures led to sharp increases in the public's currency holdings and to jumps in banks' desired reserve–deposit ratios. Finally, the 1937–1938 business contraction was preceded by a decision of the Federal Reserve to double legal reserve requirements. The Treasury at the same time halted the growth of the monetary base by offsetting gold inflows into the country with build-ups of its cash balance at the Federal Reserve. As a result, the money supply fell during the contraction.

Not all monetary events are attributable to policy decisions. For example, the 1907–1908 depression was preceded by a gold outflow that led to the failure of the Knickerbocker Trust Company. The resulting financial panic was accompanied by sharp increases in the public's currency–deposit ratios and in banks' reserve–deposit ratios. The resulting drop in the money supply cannot be attributed to the monetary authorities since the Federal Reserve did not begin operation until 1913. Even so, the event is a good example of a major economic contraction triggered by monetary events.

The evidence discussed by Friedman and Schwartz does not conclusively demonstrate that all business cycles must be caused by independent monetary movements. But, it does show that in a number of the serious contractions during a period of 100 years, major changes in the money stock were attributable to factors other than contemporary or prior changes in business conditions—that is, that monetary changes did not

---

[7]In "Money and Business Cycles."

develop from a one-to-one relation with prior or current nonmonetary economic forces. Thus, a strong (but, of course, not conclusive) case can be made for the proposition that appreciable changes in the rate of growth of the stock of money were the major cause of those fluctuations. We should refrain, however, from the much stronger assertion, sometimes made by proponents of the monetary view, that "appreciable changes in the rate of growth of money are a necessary and sufficient condition for appreciable changes in the rate of growth of money income."[8]

As a logical matter, sharp changes in the demand for money can also trigger movements in money income. Moreover, as we have recently rediscovered from our experience with the OPEC-imposed oil price shocks, supply-side factors are also capable of producing changes in the growth rate of income.

Friedman and Schwartz admit that the case for money supply changes as the major source of business cycle movements is weaker for minor than for major economic fluctuations. They admit that nonmonetary factors also affect the course of business or account for the quasi-rhythmical character of business fluctuations. But, when put together with the evidence of major fluctuations, they believe that the probablity is less than 50 percent that nonmonetary events were the major cause of past business fluctuations. Instead, they say that minor business cycles are merely less virulent members of the same general species as are the major cycles, and that the absence of well-tested alternative explanations strengthens the monetary explanation.

The monetary explanation is difficult to test because over the business cycle some of the monetary changes are feedbacks from business to money, rather than the other way around. We have seen this in the sharp changes in currency–deposit ratios and bank reserve–deposit ratios during major contractions described above. In fact, Phillip Cagan,[9] in an exhaustive study of the 18 cycles from 1877 to 1954, found that variations in the public's ratio of currency to deposits on the average accounted for 50 percent of the cyclical variations in the money supply. Changes in bankers' reserve–deposit ratios account for 25 percent of the variation, and changes in the monetary base accounted for the other 25 percent. These findings contrast sharply with his other finding that, for the period as a whole, changes in the monetary base explained 90 percent of the trend growth in the money supply.

The details of the cyclical movements of the money supply components are interesting. The growth rate of the base was strongest during

---

[8]Friedman and Schwartz, "Money and Business Cycles."

[9]P. Cagan, *Determinants and Effects of Changes in the Stock of Money, 1875–1960* (New York, Columbia University Press, 1965).

the early part of the expansion phase, but it usually weakened as the expansion progressed. The slowdown probably reflected the Federal Reserve's policy of "leaning against the wind" in times of boom. The reserve–deposit ratio fell during the expansion phase, but tended to level off before the peak. During contractions, the ratio tended to rise. These fluctuations probably reflected bankers' desires to reduce excess reserves when loan demands were high and to increase them when loan demands were low.

The least well understood phenomenon is the cyclical movement of the public's desired ratio of currency to deposits. Midway in a business cycle expansion the ratio typically began to rise, which had the effect of slowing the growth rate of the money supply. The rise of the ratio usually continued until midway in the contraction phase in the business cycle, at which time it began to fall. The behavior of the currency–deposit ratio may be explained by shifts in money holdings between businesses and households. During the early part of a boom, much of the money supply rests in deposits owned by businesses and financial institutions that have borrowed money or sold bonds to the banks. As this money flows into the financing of new production, it finds its way into the hands of workers and other householders. Since households have higher ratios of currency to deposits than business firms, the aggregate currency–deposit ratio begins to rise. The rise continues until it is reversed by reductions in income that accompany the growing unemployment during the contraction phase of the business cycle.

Thus, the behavior of the money stock is conditioned by the movements in the nonmonetary variables that fluctuate over the business cycle. A realistic explanation of the cycle must, therefore, take into account the effects of business activity upon money as well as the effects of money on business. A monetary theory of the business cycle that rests solely upon independent changes in the growth rate of the money supply is too simplistic. But so, too, is a theory that either ignores monetary changes or that rests its case upon the assumption that monetary changes are always dominated by prior changes in income or variables connected with income. There is, as Friedman and Schwartz have shown, too much evidence to the contrary.

16.3
Cyclical changes in the Cambridge
k (or the income velocity of
money)

Study of the cyclical movements of the Cambridge k (or its reciprocal, V, the income velocity of money) falls within the general subject of studies of the demand for money. This is a highly complex subject that we cannot examine in detail. Nonetheless, we can provide some basic information that shows that $V = (1/k)$—see Section 10.3.4—has a typical pattern of change over the business cycle.

16.3.1
Long-term changes in income velocity

Figure 16.4, which is drawn from the Federal Reserve's 1978 *Historical Chartbook,* shows annual and quarterly movements in the income velocity of money for the years 1910–1977. The chart reports income velocity as the ratio of GNP to three different measures of the money stock—old M-1, M-2, and M-3.

Up to the mid-1940s it makes little difference which measure is used. Both M-1 and M-2-velocity had similar declining trends, and they both usually fluctuated together around their trends. But after World War II some differences emerged. Although both measures reversed their downward trends, and instead began to rise, M-2 steadied in the 1960s and ceased its upward drift; M-1 continued to rise. M-3, however, had a slight downward trend. These divergent postwar movements can largely be explained by the substantial rise in interest rates that have spread to rates on savings and time deposits, making them much more attractive than demand deposits or currency as vehicles for holding financial wealth.

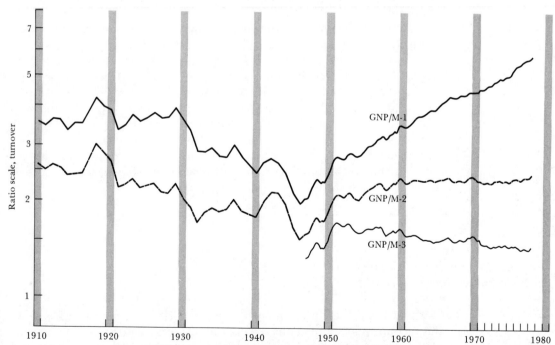

Figure 16.4 *Income velocity of money: annually, 1910–1946; seasonally adjusted, quarterly, 1947 on. (Source:* Federal Reserve Chartbook, *1978.)*

Despite the divergent postwar trends in the three definitions of income velocity, their fluctuations around trend appear to be similar. In that respect, they record the same behavior as the prewar measures. Clearly, income velocity (or the Cambridge k) is not a constant. Moreover, a closer inspection of Figure 16.4 would reveal that the years in which it rose and fell about the trend movements were not a random set. The periods in which velocity exceeded the trend were typically years containing business cycle expansions, and the periods in which velocity changed less than trend were usually years containing business cycle contractions.

16.3.2
Cyclical movements in velocity

More detailed evidence on the cyclical movements of the velocity of money is contained in Figure 16.5 and in Table 16.2. Figure 16.5 reproduces a chart published by Friedman and Schwartz showing the average behavior of old M-2-velocity for deep and mild depression cycles (excluding wars) during the period 1870-1958. Table 16.2 reports velocity movements for contraction and expansion phases of cycles during the period 1960-1979.

Both sets of data show the same basic pattern: Velocity rises during expansion phases of the cycles and falls during the contraction phases. In so doing, it reinforces the monetary growth fluctuations that so frequently provide the shocks that initiate the business cycle.

Economists do not altogether understand the reasons for the cyclical

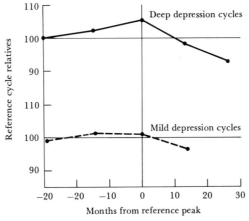

Figure 16.5 *Income velocity: average reference-cycle patterns for mild and deep depression cycles, 1870–1958.* Note: *War cycles, not shown, are 1914–1919 and 1938–1945. Deep depression cycles are 1870–1878, 1891–1904, 1904–1908, 1919–1921, 1927–1932, and 1932–1938. All others are mild depression cycles.* (Source: Friedman and Schwartz, "Money and Business Cycles.")

Table 16.2 *Cyclical Behavior of Velocities, 1960–1979 (average annual rates of growth in percent)*

Period	Old M-1	Old M-2	New M-1B	New M-2
Peak to trough				
1960 Q2–1961 Q1	−1.7	−5.3	−1.7	−6.3
1969 Q4–1970 Q4	−.3	−2.6	−.3	−1.2
1973 Q4–1975 Q1	1.3	−1.5	1.4	−.5
Trough to peak				
1961 Q1–1969 Q4	3.1	.6	3.1	.1
1970 Q4–1973 Q4	3.5	.3	3.5	−.4
1975 Q1–1979 Q4*	4.9	2.1	4.1	.6

*Quarter was not a cyclical peak; the peak occurred in January 1980.

Source: Thomas D. Simpson, "The Redefined Monetary Aggregates," *Federal Reserve Bulletin*, February 1980, p. 105.

variations of velocity. Even so, the variations are consistent with some of the theories already discussed in this book. As shown in Chapter 13, interest rates generally rise and fall with cyclical expansions and contractions. Since the demand for money, expressed as the Cambridge k, usually falls with rising interest rates and rises with falling interest rates, at least part of the cyclical fluctuation of velocity must be due to the cyclical movements of interest rates.

The monetary theory of business cycles discussed in Chapter 15 also helps to explain velocity movements. Recall that the shock-absorber function of money holdings produces a lag in the adjustment people make of actual to desired money holdings. For that reason, a negative monetary shock that lowers the growth rate of money supply is at first ignored by holders of cash balances. As a result, they continue to spend at the pre-shock rate, which reduces cash balances below desired levels. The combination of reduced growth of the money stock and continued spending produces the statistical artifact of an acceleration of the growth rate of the ratio of nominal income to the money supply—that is, an acceleration of the growth rate of the measured income velocity of money. Subsequently, when people decide their money holdings are too small, they will reduce their spending, which causes a slowing of income growth. If the money supply growth rate is not increased to accommodate the public's desire to restore its equilibrium cash holdings, the slower growth of income will produce a slowdown in the rate of growth of measured velocity. Actually, the monetary authorities usually increase the money growth rate during contractions. Since the public does not immediately spend the new money, measured velocity declines even further. The decline stops when people are convinced they have too much money. At that point, they will begin to spend or invest the extra cash. The growth rate of nominal income will then accelerate. If the acceleration exceeds the growth rate of the money supply as determined by the authorities, the growth rate of income velocity will also accelerate.

Thus two forces—variations of interest rates and lags in adjustment of actual to desired cash balances—contribute to the pro-cyclical fluctuation of the growth rate of income velocity. A third force, originally discussed by Milton Friedman,[10] is also plausible. Friedman argues that the demand for money is more closely related to wealth than it is to current money income. But wealth, which at any point in time is the lifetime accumulation of assets plus the inheritance from past generations, fluctuates less over the business cycle than does the level of money income. The velocity of money as normally measured is the ratio of money income to money holdings, not the ratio of wealth to money holdings. Thus, if desired money holdings are more closely linked to wealth than to income, the ratio of income to money will fluctuate more widely over the business cycle than will the ratio of wealth to income.

If the demand for money were more closely linked to current income than to wealth, Friedman's theory would not hold. But numerous studies have shown that wealth (or permanent income, a proxy for wealth developed by Friedman[11]) is at least as good a contender for explaining the demand for money as is income. In fact, a number of studies imply that it is more important. Thus Friedman's theory of the cyclical movements of velocity has some merit. Its major drawback is that it assumes that people are always on their demand curves for desired cash balances. As we have seen, such behavior is unlikely because it requires people to react immediately to changes in the growth rate of their cash balances. Since instant reactions to changes in money positions are unlikely, Friedman's theory must be viewed as only one of several not necessarily conflicting explanations of the cyclical behavior of the velocity of money.

16.4
A "neoclassical" supply-side monetary model

Recently, a number of economists have explored the use of econometric models to explain the effects of monetary shocks on the inflation rate and the cyclical behavior of real income. One such model was built by D. Evans Vanderford and applied to experience in the United States and five

---

[10]"The Demand for Money: Some Theoretical and Empirical Results," 1 Vol. 67, No. 4, *Journal of Political Economy,* August 1959, pp. 327–351.

[11]Ibid. Permanent income is measured as a weighted average of past incomes, where the weights are geometrically declining coefficients whose sum adds to unity.

other major economies. We shall report his findings for the United States.[12]

Vanderford's model is founded on ideas similar to those we used for the dynamic monetary shock model in Chapter 15. His model recognizes the lags that occur between unexpected changes in the growth rate of the money supply and subsequent changes in the rate of growth of real income and the rate of inflation. It also assumes that once a change in the money supply growth rate has been permanently incorporated into people's desired money holdings, its ultimate effects will be a permanent shift in the inflation rate and a settling back of the growth rate of real output into a time path dictated by changes in the labor supply, the capital stock, and other supply-side factors.

The key to Vanderford's model is the hypothesis that the economy's inflation rate equals the public's anticipated inflation rate plus a random error. The error is produced by supply-side shocks such as the OPEC oil price actions, crop failures, natural disasters, and so forth. Except for these shocks, the economy would grow along a path set by changes in the factors of production and technological developments.

The anticipated inflation rate equals the rate of growth of permanent cash balances plus a term that captures the forces that determine the growth of the economy's long-term demand for money. Permanent cash balances represent the public's perceptions of money balances that are "permanently codified" in monetary policy; as such, they do not change unless the public perceives a change in behavior by the monetary authorities. Since it takes time for a permanent change in the Federal Reserve's behavior to penetrate the public's perceptions, permanent cash balances lag behind actual cash balances when the authorities change their policies.

The lag between a monetary shock and the subsequent revision of the public's perceptions of changes in the rate of growth of permanent cash balances explains why monetary changes do not at first cause a change in the inflation rate. Instead, most of the shock is initially absorbed by deviation of real output from its long-term growth path. But, as explained earlier, output settles back to its growth path once permanent and actual rates of growth of money come into equality.

The details of Vanderford's model appear in the article cited in footnote 12. But the major results of his studies can be studied with the aid of Figures 16.6 and 16.7. The model does not explain all changes in the rate of inflation and the rate of growth of real GNP; but it does explain most. Predicted and actual fluctuations in the growth of real output are highly correlated; and, except for the Nixon price control period of 1971–1973 and the 1974–1975 oil shock, predicted and actual inflation rates also move together.

---

[12]D. Evans Vanderford, "Building a Supply-Side Model: The Permanent Money Balances Hypothesis," *Taxing and Spending*, Vol. 111, No. 1, Winter 1980, pp. 21–42.

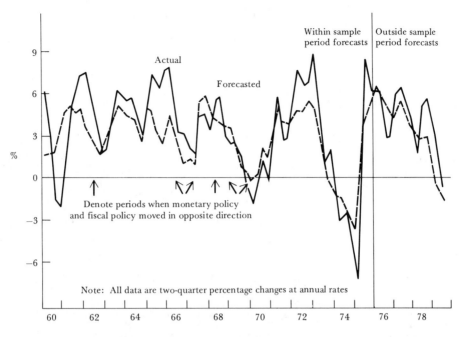

Figure 16.6 *Actual and forecasted values for the growth of real GNP. (Source: Vanderford, "Building a Supply Side Model." Reprinted with permission of the author from Tax-ing and Spending (Winter 1980), p. 32. © 1980 by the Institute for Contemporary Studies.)*

Vanderford's model was constructed with quarterly data from the first quarter of 1955 through the last quarter of 1974. Thus, a good test of the study is its predictive power for later periods. As the chart shows, it does a good job of tracking the growth rates of both prices and output during 1976–1979.

Finally, it should be noted that Vanderford ignored fiscal shocks in constructing his model. As discussed in Chapter 14, such an omission is not necessarily damaging to a monetarist model of the business cycle. It seems not to have been so in the present case.

SUMMARY

Business cycles are broad and general fluctuations of output, employment, and the rate of inflation around the general trends of these variables. The cycles vary greatly in length and severity during their expansion and contraction phases and over their total durations.

Occasionally, supply-side shocks are the source, but demand-side shocks appear to be the cause of most cycles. Both Keynesian and mone-

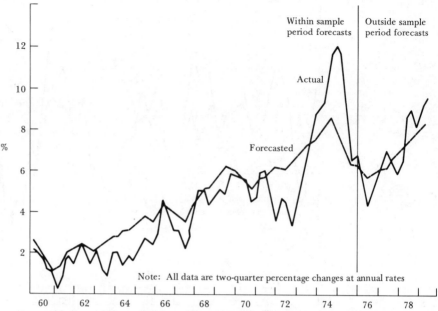

Figure 16.7 *Actual and forecasted values for percentage changes in the GNP price deflator. (Source: Vanderford, "Building a Supply Side Model." Reprinted with permission of the author from* Taxing and Spending *(Winter 1980), p. 32. © 1980 by the Institute for Contemporary Studies.)*

tary theories stress demand-side factors. Keynesian theories emphasize shocks to the economy originating in shifts of autonomous spending. Monetary theories stress shifts in the growth rate of the money supply that produce sudden and unexpected changes in the excess demand for or supply of money.

Both types of theories seek to explain business cycles in terms of the emergence of general gluts—economy-wide excess supplies of goods and services. But Say's Principle implies that an excess supply of goods implies an excess demand for money. Thus, even the Keynesian approach must somehow show that a drop in autonomous expenditures produces a rise in the excess demand for money.

An excess demand for money originates variously with (1) an upward shift in the demand for money, (2) a fall in interest rates that encourages the public to hold more money, or (3) a decrease in the quantity of money supplied by the banking system. Keynes stressed sudden shifts in liquidity preferences as the force that raises the demand for money during economic contractions. Modern Keynesians underplay this argument, believing instead that declines in autonomous spending either raise the quantity of money demanded as a result of the downward pressure on interest rates arising from fewer demands for loanable funds, or because the Federal Reserve System follows policies that reduce the supply of money when faced with declining demands for loanable funds.

Monetarists believe that the demand curve for money is a stable function of interest rates, income, and wealth, and that it is not the major source of economic fluctuations. Instead, they emphasize shifts in the growth rate of the money supply and say that these shifts usually arise from monetary policy decisions or other forces independent of changes in the demand or supply of goods and services. Thus, contrary to the Keynesians, they believe that economic fluctuations are a symptom that the economy is adapting to money supply shocks, rather than the other way around.

Almost all business contractions over the last 125 years have been preceded by reductions in growth rate of the money supply. Recoveries are ordinarily preceded by increases in the money growth rate. Severe depressions have been associated with decreases—negative growth rates—in the total stock of money. During the Great Depression, 1929–1933, the money stock fell by more than one-third.

Association of changes in the money growth rate and economic fluctuations do not prove that money causes business cycles. The real direction of causation could be from business to money; alternatively, business and money may both be affected by some third force. Friedman and Schwartz tried to show that in the case of major depression cycles monetary shocks have generally originated with policy decisions or with reactions to some foreign element, such as a gold outflow. Nevertheless, over the business cycle, at least some of the variation of the money stock is explained by the effects of business activity on loan–deposit ratios and the currency–deposit ratio. Also, by following fixed interest rate targets, or a variant of the commercial loan theory, the Federal Reserve probably permitted some of the business fluctuations to spill over into variations of the money supply.

Cyclical movements of the economy are widened by pro-cyclical changes in the velocity of money. These changes arise from pro-cyclical movements in the rate of interest and lags in the adjustment of actual to desired public holdings of cash balances. They may also arise from the failure of wealth to change as rapidly as does income over the cycle. If the demand for money is linked more closely to wealth than it is to income, then the lag of wealth behind income will produce the statistical artifact of pro-cyclical movements in velocity.

Finally, the dynamic monetary theory of Chapter 15 receives support from some of the newer supply-side econometric models, such as the one devised by D. Evans Vanderford. Without using fiscal policy and such concepts as shifts in autonomous expenditure, he was able to use monetary shocks to account for most major fluctuations in real output and the inflation rate during the 1960–1975 period. Vanderford's major errors in estimation of the inflation rate came in 1972–1974, the period encompassing the Nixon price and wage controls and the OPEC oil price shock.

1. Does a drop in the demand for and production of automobiles necessarily signify that the economy is in a recession?

2. Assuming that prices are not completely flexible, but that they eventually adjust to new supply–demand conditions, describe the effects of a negative supply-side shock on the economy. Would it produce a business cycle?

3. Why is it difficult to conclude from the data on monetary changes over the business cycle that changes in the money supply cause, rather than are caused by, the business cycle?

5. Assume that money grows at a constant rate over time, but that the economy exhibits a cyclical pattern. Aside from supply-side shocks, how could you explain such an observation?

6. How can you explain the finding that the income velocity of money typically rises during business cycle expansions, and falls during business cycle contractions?

IMPORTANT TERMS AND CONCEPTS

- ☐ autonomous spending
- ☐ business cycle
- ☐ contraction phase of a business cycle
- ☐ demand-side business cycles
- ☐ expansion phase of a business cycle
- ☐ income velocity of money
- ☐ monetary theory of the business cycle
- ☐ permanent income
- ☐ supply-side business cycle

ADDITIONAL READINGS

The footnotes in this chapter provide some of the basic sources for readings on money and business cycles. A relatively ancient, but still useful, article is Irving Fisher, "The Business Cycle Largely a Dance of the Dollar," *Journal of the American Statistical Association,* Vol. xviii, December 1923. A monetarist view by a well-known commercial bank economist (and Undersecretary of the Treasury for Monetary Affairs in the Reagan Administration) is Beryl Sprinkle, *Money and Markets: a Monetarist View* (Homewood, Illinois: R.D. Irwin, 1971). An important article stressing the details of the cyclical process following monetary shocks is Robert E. Lucas, "Understanding Business Cycles," in Karl Brunner and Allen

Meltzer (editors), *Stabilization of Domestic and the International Economy* (Amsterdam and New York: North Holland, 1977). A pioneering empirical study of the effects of unexpected monetary shocks is Robert Barro, "Unanticipated Money Growth and Employment in the United States," *American Economic Review*, Vol. 67, No. 2, March 1977, pp. 101–115.

Critics of Friedman's theory of money causation in business cycles are James Tobin, "Money and Income: Post Hoc Ergo Propter Hoc?" *Quarterly Journal of Economics*, Vol. XXXIV, No. 2, May 1970, pp. 301–317; James Tobin, "The Monetary Interpretation of History (A Review Article)," *American Economic Review*, Vol. LV, No. 3, June 1965, pp. 464–485; and articles by Hyman Minsky and Arthur Okun in the symposium on monetary economics in the *Review of Economics and Statistics*, Supplement, Vol. XLV, No. 1, Part 2, February 1963, pp. 64–77, following the Friedman and Schwartz article, "Money and Business Cycles." Statistical investigations of the causal role of money are legion. Two recent investigations that come to opposite conclusions are Christopher A. Sims, "Comparison of Interwar and Postwar Business Cycles: Monetarism Reconsidered," *American Economic Review*, Vol. 70, No. 2, May 1980, pp. 250–257, and R. W. Hafer, "Selecting a Monetary Indicator: A Test of the New Monetary Aggregates," *Federal Reserve Bank of St. Louis Review*, Vol. 63, No. 2, February 1981, pp. 12–18.

Finally, on the monetary causes of the Great Depression of the 1930s, see Karl Brunner, editor, *The Great Depression Revisited* (Boston: Martinus Nijhoff, Rochester Studies in Economics and Policy Issues, Vol. 2, 1981), especially Chapters 1–8 and 17.

Inflation: Cause and Effects

O U T L I N E

The Problem and Its Causes
Definition of Inflation
Inflation Theory—The Monetary Approach
Nonmonetary Causes of Inflation
Politics and Inflation
Some Myths of Inflation
Consumers Cause Inflation—Myth 1
Inflation is Caused by Abnormal Price Increases in Particular Markets—Myth 2
High Interest Rates Cause Inflation—Myth 3
Inflation Directly Lowers Real Income—Myth 4
Inflation and Productivity—Myth 5
Effects of Inflation on Households and Business
Inflation, Personal Income, and Real Income
Inflation, Taxes, and Capital Income
Inflation, Capital Gains, and Taxes
Inflationary Redistributions of Wealth and Income
Inflationary Redistributions between Borrowers and Lenders
Effects of Inflation on Income Distribution
Inflation Tax on Cash Balances
Effects of Inflation on Resource Allocation

Inflation is high on the list of our economic problems. The U.S. price level as measured by the consumer price index more than doubled during 1967–1979. In many foreign countries inflation has been as bad or worse. In the 11-year period 1967–1978, prices rose by 150 percent in Australia, 180 percent in Denmark, 170 percent in Greece, 227 percent in Ireland, 190 percent in Italy, and 216 percent in Great Britain. Even the so-called stable countries have suffered. Prices rose by 60 percent in West Germany and by 65 percent in Switzerland during 1967–1978.[1]

The silver lining of recessions and depressions used to be falling prices. No longer. The trend of the *lows* in the inflation rate has been rising for the last 30 years (Figure 17.1). Beginning with the 1954 recession, and in each of the following recessions, the inflation rate at and after the cycle trough was higher than the rate after the bottom of the previous recession. The simultaneous occurrence of inflation and unemployment has even acquired an unlovely name—stagflation.

Our task in this chapter is to define inflation, to present theories of the inflation process, and to discuss its effects. In Chapter 18 we shall try to identify the causes of the especially vexing problem of stagflation. When we are through we should be well positioned to discuss a few of the policy implications of our present state of knowledge.

17.1
The problem and its causes

We cannot hope to eliminate inflation without agreeing upon what it is and on what causes it. Moreover, a correct view of inflation and its causes helps us attack many of the fallacious inflation theories that confuse public discussion of the problem.

We start by defining inflation.

17.1.1
Definition of inflation

Inflation is defined by most economists as a continuing rise in the price level. This definition is commonly accepted by the general public, by members of the press and the broadcasting media, and by politicians. Its virtue is that it stresses that inflation involves *rising prices*, not just *high prices*, and that, on the average, prices in general, not just a few prices, must be rising. The definition also emphasizes a continuing rise in prices.

---

[1]International inflation estimates are from the *Statistical Abstract of the United States* (Washington D.C.: U.S. Department of Commerce, Bureau of the Census, 1979), p. 900.

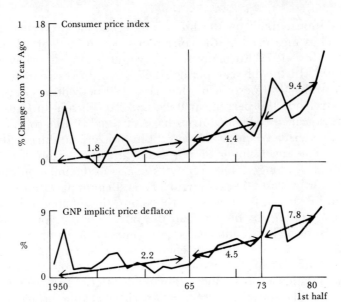

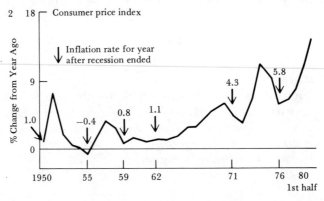

Figure 17.1 *Inflation is accelerating . . . and starts higher after each recession. (Source: Federal Reserve Bank of Atlanta Economic Review, Vol. LXV, No. 5, September/October 1980, p. 17.)*

A temporary rise followed by a leveling-off or a drop in prices poses no threat to the economy.

Some economists object to the above inflation definition. They complain that it is incomplete because it fails to define the price level and because it excludes situations in which government price and wage controls keep inflationary forces from raising prices.

Discussions of inflation usually focus upon several indexes designed to capture increases in the price level. The most commonly cited indexes are the CPI (the consumer price index), the wholesale price index (now called the producer price index), and the GNP deflator. These indexes average price movements of somewhat different collections of goods, and the weights they apply to the prices of the individual goods before computing the averages are not the same. Thus, the inflation rates reported in the press are heavily dependent upon the indexes used to measure them. If prices of goods excluded from the indexes are rising more or less rapidly than the prices in the indexes, their contributions to overall inflation will not be noted.

Actually, inflation is a very personal thing. A rise in prices lowers the purchasing power of dollars and fixed dollar assets that people own. For example, a doubling of the price of food cuts in half the amount of food you can buy with the dollars you have in your pocket or bank account and the dollars you may have invested in government or privately issued bonds. But all prices do not rise by the same amount (Figure 17.2). Some prices may actually fall while others are rising. Thus, a price index cannot capture the highly variable rates of change of different prices. Moreover, since people buy different things, an index cannot capture the changing value of money and other financial assets owned by different people.

Inflation is essentially a monetary phenomenon. It would not exist in a barter economy. It arises in a money economy because the nominal money supply grows faster than the demand for real money balances—recall Equation (12.6). An excess supply of any good drives its price down relative to the prices of other goods. The same is true of money. The price of a unit of money is its exchange value—the number of units of other goods for which it can be exchanged. For example, a rise in the price of apples from 20 to 25 cents a pound, reduces from 5 to 4 pounds the purchasing power or exchange value of money in terms of apples. Thus, an alternative definition of inflation is a continuous decline in the purchasing power of money.

Some people say that price controls can stop inflation. But this is an illusion. Price controls merely *suppress* inflation; they do not stop it. Inflation arises from an excess supply of money. An excess supply of money generates excess demands for goods and services. If controls keep prices and wages from performing their market clearing functions, shortages are sure to appear. At the controlled structure of prices and wages people will want to buy more things; but the disincentives created by the controls will lead producers to curtail production. Production will be below the market clearing levels permitted under open inflation. So dollars lose their purchasing power under suppressed inflation just as they do under open inflation, because people are unable to buy goods and services their money balances would allow.

Although it retains some inevitable vagueness, the definition of inflation that stresses loss of purchasing power of money may be superior to one that emphasizes rising prices. The latter works well during periods of open inflation (no price and wage controls); but prices and wages kept down by controls frequently mislead policymakers into believing they have overcome inflation itself instead of having simply alleviated its symp-

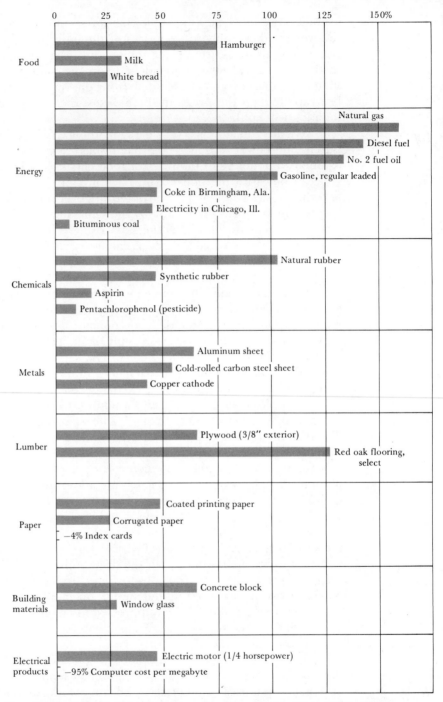

Data: Bureau of Labor Statistics, Westinghouse, International Business Machines, BW estimates

Figure 17.2 *The product prices behind the indexes: percent change of selected goods, December 1974 to December 1979. (Source:* Business Week, *No. 2623, February 11, 1980, p. 32.)*

toms. The definition of inflation that stresses loss of purchasing power of money is less likely to foster such illusions. Moreover, it contains a constant reminder that inflation is essentially a monetary phenomenon and that its cure requires appropriate monetary policies.

17.1.2
Inflation theory—the monetary approach

During open inflations rising prices and falling purchasing power of money go hand in hand. Since falling purchasing power of money originates with an excess supply of money, it may seem unnecessary to have a further explanation of inflation. "Too much money chasing too few goods" seems to capture the essence of what we want to say. Why say more?

A more elaborate discussion of inflation theory is necessary because many people think that inflation is *not* caused by an excess supply of money. Instead, they blame it on the striving of business or labor monopolies for higher wages or prices, upon deficit spending by the federal government, upon government regulation of business, upon low productivity, upon taxes, and upon outside shocks to the economy, such as OPEC oil price increases. Although there is some truth to these assertions, nonmonetary theories cannot provide independent explanations for a generalized rise in prices. They must be melded with the more basic monetary approach.

The best springboard for a discussion of inflation is the Cambridge equation. Recall that a form of the equation expresses the nominal demand for money as the real demand multiplied by a term standing for the price level. Setting the nominal demand for money (so expressed) equal to the nominal money supply, we have $M^s = m^d P$, or $M^s = kyP$, where ky equals the demand for real money balances conditioned upon the level of real income, y, M^s is the nominal money supply, and P is the price level.[2]

The static form of the Cambridge equation reports the conditions determining the price *level* when the nominal money supply, real income and the Cambridge k are given. The dynamic form of the equation, derived in Section 15.2.4, relates the *growth rate* of the price level (that is, the inflation rate) to the rate of growth of the money supply, the rate of growth of real output, and the rate of growth of the Cambridge k. The equation relating these growth rates is reproduced in Equation (17.1), where the dots over letters denote the percentage rates of change of the variables:

---

[2]Symbolic representation of the quantity theory forces us to use the price level concept, even though we admit its defects.

$$\dot{P} = \dot{M}^s - (\dot{k} + \dot{y}) \qquad (17.1)$$

In this equation, the rate of growth in the excess supply for money is expressed by the difference between the growth rate of the money supply, $\dot{M}^s$, and the *sum* of the two components of the growth rate of the demand for real money balances—the growth rate of the Cambridge k, $\dot{k}$, plus the growth rate of real income, $\dot{y}$. A convenient way to discuss inflation is to relate the rate of growth of the price level to the component parts of the growth rate of the excess supply of money.

Monetarists usually assume that the growth rate of the nominal money supply is dominated by policies of the monetary authorities. Putting this assumption together with a belief that the growth path of real income and the Cambridge k are determined by forces independent of the policies that set the growth rate of money, the monetarists conclude that variations in the growth rate of the price level are mainly due to monetary policies. True, for any given money growth rate, the rate of change of the price level will vary if the factors affecting the demand for money ($\dot{k}$ and $\dot{y}$) should vary. But policy tools give the monetary authorities the means to control the inflation rate by executing offsetting movements in the money supply growth rate.

17.1.3
Nonmonetary causes of inflation

Nonmonetary theories of inflation assert that forces other than changes in the supply of money drive up the general price level. There is some truth to this assertion, but without bringing it into the framework provided by the Cambridge equation, it can be quite misleading.

A good example of the nonmonetary approach is the argument that business and labor monopolies cause inflation. This argument must be approached with extreme care. If it is based upon the abilities of monopolies to charge higher prices than would prevail under competitive conditions, it misses the mark. *High* prices or wages are not *rising* prices or wages; by definition they are not inflationary. Moreover, the theory of monopoly speaks only to the question of relative prices; it says nothing about overall price levels in the economy. For example, consider a rise in prices sparked by the exercise of union or business monopoly power in an industry. Other things being equal, the rise in the industry's prices will reduce the demand for its products. As sales fall, workers and resources in the industry will become unemployed and seek work elsewhere. As they do, wages and prices in more competitive industries will fall as a result of the better supply conditions. The net result may well be a decline in prices sufficient to offset the rise in the price of the monopoly industry's product.

Although the mere existence of monopoly power is not sufficient to cause inflation, a growing degree of monopoly power may exert a more continuous upward push on the price level. But to show this we must prove that increasing monopolization somehow affects the growth rate of the money supply or the trend rate of change in the demand for money. There are two possibilities: (1) If monopolization forces workers and capital into less efficient uses, the growth rate of real income will diminish. As that happens, the growth of the demand for real money balances will also slow down—see Equation (17.1). Provided nothing is done to reduce the growth rate of the nominal money supply, the result will be a rise in the inflation rate. (2) The monetary authority may attempt to soften the blow of temporary unemployment resulting from increasing monopolization by raising the growth rate of the money supply. In that event, the inflation rate will accelerate above the level set by the diminished rate of growth of real income.

Another type of nonmonetary force is illustrated by the supply-side shocks administered by OPEC oil price increases. These price increases raise the price level through their negative effects on the efficiency of the economy. The increase in imported oil prices raises the prices of domestic oil and competing energy sources such as coal and natural gas. Prices in energy dependent industries are driven up, and methods of production that depend upon cheap energy are made economically less efficient. In effect, the productive capacity of the economy is lowered, retarding the growth rate of real output. As indicated in Equation (17.1), such a slowdown lowers the demand for real money balances and raises the inflation rate. But the rise is temporary; it stops once the economy resumes growing along the lower growth path imposed by the shock. Thus a one-time oil price shock raises the price level above its pre-shock level and lowers the economy's productive capacity. But, unless the monetary authorities try with a stepped-up money growth rate to offset the damage done to the economy, the shock will only temporarily raise the inflation rate.

Tax increases and government regulations of various kinds are also inflationary if they cause a slowdown in the rate of growth of real output. For example, increases in income tax rates reduce per capita private income. They also impair work incentives, causing people to increase leisure in place of working longer hours. Reductions in private income reduce the rate of saving out of total income. If the increased taxes fall upon interest earned from lending, saving incentives are further impaired. The upshot is that less money is available for capital formation and the growth rate of the economy is impaired. Of course, once firms in the economy adjust their productive techniques to an environment in which capital is relatively less abundant than labor, the economy will move along a lower growth path at its old growth rate—the one dictated by the rate of growth in its labor force. Until it does, however, real growth will be slower than before the shock; other things being equal, the inflation rate will temporarily rise above its previous level.

Government regulations do not necessarily reduce the efficiency of the economy. But when they raise production costs or foster monopolization, they reduce the output potential of the economy. A given level and structure of regulations is not necessarily inflationary; but expansion and proliferation of regulations can force the economy on to lower output paths. When that happens, the inflation rate is temporarily raised.

Welfare programs, unemployment insurance, social security pensions, and other such programs are said to be inflationary because they encourage people to drop out of the labor force, an act that lowers the productive potential of the economy. As we have seen, the basic truth in this statement is that a lowering of the productive potential of the economy entails a down-shift of its growth path. Thus, pension and welfare programs, as such, are not inflationary, but their rate of expansion can lead to rising prices. Changes in the laws and changes in the age structure and other characteristics of the population may affect this rate of expansion; to this extent, and other things being equal, they will affect the rate of inflation. But once the changes stop, the inflationary effects of the programs will subside. Moreover, it should also be noted that it is always open to the monetary authorities to make corrections in the rate of growth of the money supply to offset the inflationary impacts of these supply-side forces.

A similar point must be made respecting the argument that government deficits are inflationary. As demonstrated in Chapter 14, it is not at all clear that a pure fiscal policy executed with a tax cut is expansionary. A tax cut raises the demand for money as a fraction of total income because it raises private income as a proportion of total income. Thus, since it raises the excess demand for money at prevailing interest rates, a pure tax cut may actually be deflationary. This deflationary influence cannot be reversed unless borrowing induced by the increased deficit imposes such a steep rise in the rate of interest that the quantity of money demanded falls by enough to offset the increase in demand stimulated by the rise in private income.

A pure fiscal policy executed by an increase in government spending is unambiguously expansionary. The rise in interest rates stimulated by the enlarged deficit reduces the quantity of money demanded and raises the excess supply of money. Assuming no change in the rate of growth of real output, the price level is raised.

But we must again take care to distinguish between the temporary and permanent effects upon the rate of inflation of expansionary fiscal policies. Any *given* increase in the deficit can be expansionary, but once the effects of shifts in private income and interest rates on the demand for money have worked themselves out, no further inflationary force will operate on the price level. The price level will be higher, but its rate of increase will again be governed by the growth of the excess supply of money as determined by the monetary authorities. Only continuing fiscal shocks will keep the price level rising at a higher rate.[3]

The upshot of this discussion is that nonmonetary forces cannot permanently affect the rate of inflation unless they somehow permanently change the growth rate of the excess supply of money. None of the forces discussed in this section appears capable of imposing more than a temporary change in this growth rate. The conclusion, therefore, is that nonmonetary shocks cannot permanently change the rate of inflation unless they are continuous or somehow induce the monetary authorities to raise permanently the growth rate of the money supply.

17.1.4
Politics and inflation

The public at large and most politicians are ignorant of the causes of inflation. Their ignorance comes from lack of education in monetary theory and a bewilderment that stems from the vast array of political and economic factors that influence the price level. The *immediate cause* of inflation is an excessively high rate of growth of the money supply. Analysis of the effects of excessive monetary growth falls within the province of monetary theory. But that is just one level of analysis. Another concerns the policy process. Why do monetary authorities permit the money supply to grow excessively? Most central banks, including the Federal Reserve System, possess great power over the monetary base. Yet in country after country over the post–World War II period, the monetary authorities have let monetary growth get out of hand, producing the kind of inflation figures cited at the beginning of this chapter. We cannot understand the actual experience of inflation without probing deeply into the decision making process within the world's central banks.

Unfortunately, we cannot thoroughly discuss this topic here. Suffice it to say that monetary authorities do not work in a political vacuum. As discussed in Section 7.2, central banks frequently cave in to pressure from government administrators, legislators and even the public at large. For example, high interest rates are very unpopular; until quite recently, monetary authorities labored to keep them down; in so doing, they lost control over the monetary growth rate. Similarly, responding to demands

---

[3]This is particularly true because of the drop in the deficit resulting from income growth. As income tax revenues rise, the need to finance a given level of government spending with new bond issues declines. Declining sales of government bonds remove pressure from the loanable funds market and reduces interest rates, which has the effect of raising the quantity of money demanded and reducing the growth rate of the excess supply of money. Only a fiscal shock that permanently raises the deficit as a proportion of total income would be immune from this force.

of the public and politicians, they frequently put off attempts to moderate money growth for fear of causing recessions. Ironically, in the end they usually do it anyway. Once inflation gets out of hand, calls arise for the monetary authorities to stop or at least to slow the increase in prices. To satisfy these demands, the authorities must push down money growth, which invariably, it seems, leads to the recessions they want to avoid. The recessions, in turn, lead to calls for action on the part of the central bank to restimulate the economy. In responding to these calls, the authorities rekindle inflation.

The authorities appear to be boxed into a set of *stop–go policies*. Why is this so? Analysis of political behavior in countries with representative governments has convinced many observers that such governments systematically indulge in policies that create a bias towards inflation.

First, the Keynesian revolution of the 1930s convinced many politicians and their economic advisors that fiscal policy—manipulating taxes and government spending for the purpose of affecting the overall level of economic activity—is a legitimate and useful function of government. Since balanced budgets had previously been considered the only right way to conduct the government's fiscal affairs, this new idea, which implied the acceptance of deficit spending in recessions or in periods of less than full employment, represented a marked change in attitudes.

Second, most elected officials have now accepted the responsibility for maintaining high or "full" employment of the labor force. In the United States this acceptance was formalized in the Employment Act of 1946, which proclaimed maximum employment as a national objective, and in the Full Employment and Balanced Growth Act (Humphrey–Hawkins Bill) of 1978, which called for achievement of a 4 percent unemployment rate and a 3 percent inflation rate by 1983 (check it out!). Governments are not always able to keep their promises; nonetheless, the very existence of promises conditions the thoughts of the public and many legislators. The thoughts become dangerously inflationary when politically acceptable definitions of full employment are above the level that can be achieved without acceleration of the inflation rate. For example, in the 1970s most economists agreed that an unemployment rate of 5.5 to 6 percent could be maintained without accelerating inflation. If true, attempts to achieve quickly the 4 percent unemployment rate called for by the Humphrey–Hawkins Bill would have accelerated the already high inflation rate of the late 1970s.

A third factor creating inflationary bias in modern representative governments is the operation of interest group politics. Government is the source of subsidies or special tax treatment for business, agriculture, poor people, cities, and so forth. The benefits acquired by interest groups from government usually far exceed the tax costs to the receiving groups; instead, the costs are spread over all taxpayers, whether or not they have received the benefits. This situation creates incentives and opportunities for political entrepreneurs within the interest groups and within the government. It pays businessmen, farmers, labor leaders, and others to support and lobby congressmen to pass favorable legislation. Since the costs of the programs favored by the interest group are thinly spread over the population as a whole, little organized opposition to individual programs is likely to develop. In the meantime, legislators are tempted to support the programs of groups willing to reciprocate with money and political backing for the next election. They can also point with pride to positive accomplishments for their constituencies. Finally, with many interest groups approaching different legislators, congressmen have an incentive to logroll—to trade support for programs wanted by their constituencies.

Thus, interest group politics puts great pressure upon the spending side of the budget. By comparison, the tax side has few constituents. A legislator who favors general tax increases is an unpopular fellow. Congressmen are unlikely to vote for an increase in taxes unless they can find some special reason to justify their votes. For example, in 1979–1980 the unpopularity of the major oil companies emboldened the President to propose and Congress to pass the so-called windfall profits tax on domestic oil producers. A few years earlier Congress passed a less popular increase in social security taxes; but the prospect of a major deficit in the Social Security Trust Fund probably saved most congressmen from adverse reactions from their constituents.

But these examples are the exception; history suggests that legislators are far more willing to raise expenditures than they are to raise taxes. So budgetary deficits, even during periods of economic boom, are the rule. Budgetary surpluses appear occasionally, but they are generally small and short-lived.

A final factor creating an inflationary bias in government might be called the *shortsightedness effect*. To stay in office, politicians favor policies and programs that yield *current benefits* for their supporters. Voters may not identify distant benefits with current legislation and, worse, they may credit them to acts of future politicians. In the meantime, politicians presently in office must make a record for the next election. Programs that take effect in the short-run further that aim. To be sure, the programs may expand the federal deficit and, as a result, raise future taxes or, if funded by increases in the money supply, raise the inflation rate. But people are shortsighted; they tend to discount the value of delayed costs as against the value of current benefits, particularly when the costs are spread over many years or when they appear in the form of future inflation rather than explicit taxes. Moreover, they are unlikely to anticipate the future costs of inflation associated with current programs.

To summarize, inflation has no simple explanation. Its final causes rest with the social and political forces that motivate politicians to spend and to ignore or discount the budgetary deficits that are created by such spending. The Keynesian beliefs that deficits are a permissible tool of fiscal policy and that such policy is a useful device for maintaining full employment reinforce and legitimatize political actions to raise expenditures without commensurate increases in taxes.

Deficits put upward pressure on market rates of interest. The rise in interest rates, in turn, creates political pressure on the monetary authorities to increase the growth rate of the money supply. When monetary growth becomes excessive, acceleration of the inflation rate is inevitable. Although most of the public suffers from the higher rate of inflation, the monetary authorities are usually reluctant to severely curtail monetary growth for fear of tipping the economy into a recession. Eventually, however, accelerating inflation builds a constituency for slowing it down, in which case the authorities are emboldened to brake the growth rate of the money supply. Monetary shocks thus imposed upon the economy ordinarily produce recessions. The recessions then become the occasion for political demands to increase spending or cut taxes. The monetary authorities, in the meantime, try to aid economic recovery by restoring higher monetary growth rates. The stage is then set for another cycle of inflation and recession.

17.2
Some myths of inflation

The popular and even technical literature on inflation contains a number of myths. The myths pertain not only to the causes and effects of inflation, but also to policies that may be used to stop it. In this section we shall take a look at a few of the more prominent of these myths.

17.2.1
Consumers cause inflation[4]—myth 1

This is a favorite assertion of politicians and monetary authorities who want scapegoats for their own inflationary policies. In 1974, for example, Arthur Burns charged that American consumers were impulsive buyers—that they failed to shop for bargains and thereby let sellers get away with raising their prices. In 1978 President Carter said that his inflation program would not work unless consumers voluntarily cut back on their spending.

Consumers are no more responsible for inflation than is any other private group in the economy. They cannot stop the rise in prices by sim-

---

[4]Sections 17.2.1 and 17.2.2 owe much to James Gwartney and Richard Stroup, *Macroeconomics: Private and Public Choice*, 2nd edition (New York: Academic Press, 1980) pp. 330–331.

ply saving more and spending less. When consumers save, they usually put their money into stocks and bonds, savings and time deposits, mutual funds shares, and so forth. The savings are rechanneled into investment spending, expenditures by state and local governments, or even into federal spending. So reductions in consumer spending usually change the composition of economy-wide spending, not its total amount. Total spending drops only if savings are put into additional money holdings. During inflationary periods this is unlikely behavior. But even if consumers decided to enlarge their money hoards, the effect on inflation would be temporary. Only *continuing additions* to cash balances would permanently reduce inflation.

17.2.2
Inflation is caused by abnormal price increases in particular markets— myth 2

This widespread myth comes from the failure of some people to compare prices in particular markets to prices in other markets. It is easy to mistake an increase in a set of *relative prices* for an increase in the *price level*. Even if the excess demand for money were zero, the prices of some goods would probably be on the rise. A zero excess demand for money requires only that there be a zero excess demand for nonmonetary commodities taken as a whole. It does not require zero excess demand in each market. In a dynamic economy some prices will be below their market equilibrium and rising, while other markets' prices will be above their equilibrium levels and falling. So, even when monetary pressure of inflation is absent, certain prices will be on the rise. Ignoring the falling prices and emphasizing the rising prices could easily mislead inflation watchers.

Even when an excess supply of money is driving up the whole price level, market forces will cause some prices to rise faster than others. But an above-average increase in the prices of some commodities does not signify a rise in the overall inflation rate. To so argue would be to imply that a failure of other prices to rise as fast as the average signifies a reduction of the inflation rate. Neither statement would be true.

More fundamentally, it is circular reasoning to blame inflation on rising prices. Inflation is *defined* as a rising price level. Blaming inflation on rising prices is tantamount to saying that rising prices cause rising prices. The only way to avoid this logical error is to go behind the increases in prices in order to see whether they reflect forces that have created an excess demand for goods and services in general. For example, the huge 1974 increase in OPEC oil prices raised domestic production costs in the United States so much that it lowered the growth path of aggregate production. Insofar as the reduction of output caused an excess supply of money to emerge, the effect of the OPEC action was to increase (albeit temporarily) the inflation rate. But, in general, if there is no such special factor behind observed price increases, it is illogical to blame inflation upon the increase in any particular price or set of prices.

17.2.3
High interest rates cause inflation[5]— myth 3

This myth is particularly popular in the business community and in Congress. Members of this school—sometimes called *the interest cost-push school*—insist that high interest rates are inflationary because they raise business costs that firms must recoup by raising their product prices.

Interest cost-push theorists rarely explore the reasons for higher interest rates. They fail to note that a rise in interest rates unaccompanied by an increase in the ratio of aggregate demand to real aggregate output cannot be inflationary. As a result, they mistake a rise in a particular set of relative prices for a rise in the absolute price level.

Let us provisionally grant the interest cost-push theorists' position that firms price their products using a formula based upon interest and other costs. Now, assume that a general rise in interest rates raises the cost of borrowed money. What will happen to the price level? The answer clearly depends upon the state of aggregate supply and demand. If the rise in interest rates is unaccompanied by a change in total demand or total output, the price level will not increase. Instead, there will be a change in relative product prices and relative prices of productive inputs. Industries that depend heavily upon borrowed money will to some extent raise their prices. The rise in prices will reduce their sales, causing them to hire fewer workers and to reduce purchases of raw materials. Labor and other resources released from interest-sensitive industries will seek employment in industries that are not interest-sensitive, tending to drive down their wages and prices. These wage and price declines will offset the wage and price increases in the interest-sensitive industries and leave the overall price level unchanged.

To be sure, a rise in interest rates will not leave total demand and supply unchanged. Even assuming no change in the quantity of money, higher interest rates lower desired cash holdings of the public. In addition, the reshuffling of productive factors may reduce aggregate output due to less efficient allocation of resources. Thus, the rise in interest rates may indirectly create an excess supply of money that, in turn, raises the price level. But the interest cost-push school says nothing about changes in aggregate demand or aggregate supply; hence, indirect effects on the price level of interest rate changes do not confirm their theory.

---

[5]See Thomas M. Humphrey, "The Interest Cost-Push Controversy," in *Essays on Inflation*, 2nd edition (Richmond: Federal Reserve Bank of Richmond, 1980), pp. 92–99.

Of course, this argument improperly ignores the causes of rising interest rates. In most cases, the forces that cause interest rates to rise are also forces that simply change relative prices or that deflate rather than inflate the economy. Full consideration of the circumstances surrounding rising interest rates weakens rather than strengthens the interest cost-push theory.

Rising interest rates come from increases in the demand for loanable funds or decreases in their supply. An increase in the demand for loanable funds comes from private or public borrowers who wish to raise their current spending. By offering higher interest rates they are able to lure away additional money from lenders. Lenders include banks, households, and business firms. In most cases, extra loanable funds provided by firms or households come from reductions in current spending upon investment or consumer goods. Since these reductions in commodity demands offset the increased demands by borrowers, the larger volume of loans does not affect the overall level of demand, and no additional pressure is exerted upon the price level. Instead, the price increases of goods bought by borrowers are offset by reductions in the prices of goods bought by lenders.

A rise in interest rates that accompanies a reduction in the supply of loanable funds is usually neutral or deflationary. It is usually neutral when the reduction in lending originates in the private nonbank sector of the economy. To be sure, households or firms may reduce their lending because they want to buy more goods. But the rise in interest rates that accompanies their reduced lending makes goods more expensive for borrowers. In this event, the rise in prices of goods favored by lenders is offset by a fall in the prices of goods favored by borrowers, and no upward pressure is put on the overall price level.

In two cases a reduction in the supply of loanable funds is actually deflationary. Both cases involve an increase in the excess demand for money. The first occurs when banks reduce their overall holdings of earning assets. Since such an act decreases the supply of money, it causes an increase in the excess demand for money. In the second case the excess demand for money increases when private nonbank lenders reduce their lending because of a desire to hold more money. In both of these cases, therfore, a reduction in the supply of loanable funds puts downward pressure on the price level.

The recorded positive correlations between inflation and interest rates no doubt encourage the interest cost-push school. Nonetheless, such a correlation does little to confirm the theory. Instead, it provides support for the opposite idea that high or low interest rates are caused by, rather than are a cause of, high or low rates of change in the price level. As discussed in Section 13.2.4, a sharp reduction in the rate of growth of the money supply at first raises the interest rate. But the reduction in money growth also causes a decline in output and then the rate of inflation. These output and price level changes feed back to credit markets causing the excess demand for loanable funds to decline and to lower real interest rates. An additional drop in nominal interest rates occurs if the falling inflation rate lowers the public's expected rate of inflation.

Thus, it is not at all unusual to observe low interest rates in association with a drop in the rate of inflation. Moreover, when a rise in the growth rate of the money supply stimulates output and raises the rate of inflation, an increase in the excess demand for loanable funds and a rise in inflationary expectations will raise nominal interest rates. The mistaken view of the interest cost-push school comes from ignoring the overall monetary environment that surrounds interest rate and price level changes. They fail to see that interest rates and prices are variables that respond to larger forces. As such, they have only limited direct impact upon each other.

17.2.4
Inflation directly lowers real income—myth 4

Does inflation lower aggregate real income? Perhaps. But not in the sense reported in the press. Each month the media report the latest figures for personal income. At the same time they usually compare changes in personal income to changes in the consumer price index. If prices have risen more rapidly than personal income, they frequently conclude that inflation has directly reduced real income.

To see why such a statement is wrong, recall that aggregate real income consists of real earnings of employed workers and of other owners of productive resources. Moreover, since real income consists of the goods and services produced by productive resources, it cannot be directly affected by the level of prices. It varies only because of variations in the level and efficiency of productive inputs. In contrast, variations in nominal income (the sum of prices times real outputs) can come from variations in both prices and output. So, when nominal income is rising less rapidly than the level of prices, it is a simple arithmetic truth that real income must be falling. But an arithmetic truth implies nothing about causation. In particular, it does not prove that inflation reduces real income. Indeed, the main purpose of the arithmetic operation is to give us information, not an explanation, of what is happening to real income. The explanation of its changes rests with branches of economic theory that discuss the changes in employment and efficiency of productive resources.

The above argument should not be taken to rule out indirect effects of inflation on the level of real output. It is quite possible for inflation to discourage capital formation and to reduce work incentives of the labor force. In that sense (discussed later in Section 17.3) inflation reduces real income by reducing the level of efficiency of productive inputs. But this is a very different kind of argument than the arithmetic tautology discussed in this section.

17.2.5
Inflation and productivity—myth 5

Inflation comes from too much money chasing too few goods. This correct statement frequently misleads people into believing that inflation is best attacked by increasing the rate of growth output. Some real experts are so misled. For example, Dr. C. Jackson Grayson, chairman from 1971 to 1973 of the Federal Price Commission (administering President Nixon's price-control program) and founder and director of the American Productivity Center, was recently quoted as saying, "Unless the whole country pays attention to greater productivity in the 1980s, we simply won't survive. That's the only way we're going to get inflation down."[6]

Slow productivity growth is indeed a problem in the United States. Growth of output per worker in the private business sector dropped from 2.9 percent per year in the 1960s to under 1.6 percent per year in the 1970s. There is little question that faster productivity growth could close the gap between growth of monetary expenditure and growth of aggregate output. But that does not mean that improving productivity is the key to stopping inflation.

To see why, consider some simple arithmetic. During 1970–1979 nominal GNP (inclusive of business and government output) grew at the rate of 10.3 percent per year. In the same period, real GNP rose at an annual rate of 3.2 percent. Since the difference between nominal and real GNP is prices, the annual rate of inflation implied by these two growth rates is 7.1 percent. Now, real output growth is the sum of the rates of change in the employed labor force and labor productivity. Since employment in the 1970–1979 period grew at the rate of 2.3 percent a year, labor productivity rose at the rate of only 0.9 percent a year (which is 0.7 of a percentage point below the productivity growth of the private business sector, cited in the last paragraph). These relationships are set forth in Table 17.1.

Table 17.1 is constructed from an identity relating growth rates of nominal and real gross national product to growth rates of the labor force, productivity, and the rate of inflation (see description of the symbols in the table):

$$\dot{P} \equiv \dot{Y} - \dot{y} = \dot{Y} - (\dot{l} + \dot{y/l}); \quad \text{where } \dot{y} = \dot{l} + \dot{y/l} \tag{17.2}$$

---

[6]Alan Waldman, "The Apostle of Productivity," *Mainliner* (United Airlines), May 1980.

Table 17.1 *Average Annual Growth Rates of GNP: Prices, Employment, and Productivity, 1970–1979*

1. Nominal GNP $(\dot{Y})$	10.3%
2. Real GNP $(\dot{y})$	3.2
3. Inflation rate $(\dot{P})$*	7.1
4. Employed labor force $(\dot{l})$	2.3
5. Labor productivity (y/l)**	0.9

*Line 1 minus line 2.
**Line 2 minus line 4.

Source: Statistical Abstract of the United States and *Federal Reserve Bulletin*

To relate this identity to monetary change, we can use the Cambridge equation to express the growth of the demand for nominal GNP in terms of its monetary aspects. Since $Y = M/k$, the growth rate of nominal GNP can be stated as

$$\dot{Y} = \dot{M} - \dot{k} \tag{17.3}$$

Substitution of Equation (17.3) into (17.2) allows us to write Equation (17.4), which analyzes the inflation rate in terms of the growth rates of the old M-1 money supply, the Cambridge k, the rate of growth of the labor force, and the rate of change in labor force productivity. The numbers for 1970–1979 beneath the equation are taken from Table 17.1 and from monetary data provided by the Federal Reserve System:

$$\dot{P} = (\text{M-1}) - (\dot{k} + \dot{l} + y/l) \tag{17.4}$$
$$7.1 = 6.3 - (-4 + 2.3 + 0.9)$$

Clearly, the least important item influencing the inflation rate in 1970–1979 was the rate of growth in labor productivity. Other things being equal, a doubling of productivity growth would have reduced the inflation rate by only nine-tenths of a percentage point. Moreover, raising productivity growth through the agency of public policy is an exceedingly difficult task, particularly since economists do not completely understand why productivity growth has fallen off in recent years. At minimum, the country must raise its rate of capital formation and improve the pace of technological change. In a highly sophisticated and complex economy, where capital formation and technological innovations are done by millions of people in different situations, the proper government policies are not obvious. In the meantime, easier inflation-fighting methods are at hand.

Since, like productivity growth, the trends of the labor force growth and the Cambridge k are not directly subject to policy influences, the authorities should concentrate on reducing the monetary growth rate. Admittedly, substantial reductions in the growth rate of the money supply raise other problems. If done too quickly, reducing the monetary growth rate might provoke an unpopular and painful recession. For that reason, the authorities might best gradually impose monetary restraint. But, however it is done, it is clear that manipulating money growth is both mechanically easier and quantitatively more important for combating inflation than is a policy that seeks to accelerate the growth rate of labor productivity.

Do not misunderstand the thrust of this discussion. Improving productivity growth is clearly a desirable policy objective. But raising productivity growth fights impoverishment more than it fights inflation. Commentators like C. Jackson Grayson confuse the two policy goals. In so doing, they also implicitly confuse the cause and effect relationships between inflation and productivity. Although improving productivity growth may do little to reduce inflation, reduction of inflation may do a great deal to help the growth of productivity. Inflation so distorts and penalizes economic decision making that it may seriously hamper the efficient functioning of the economy. This problem is the subject of Sections 17.3–17.5.

17.3
Effects of inflation on households and business

Among the effects of inflation is the redistribution of wealth and income. Gainers' assets and incomes rise in value along with the rising price level. Losers' assets and incomes fail to keep pace with the inflation rate. Inflationary income and wealth redistributions are not only unfair, but they also pose a major danger for the efficient functioning of the economy. If people's normal expectations of rewards from saving and earning are frustrated by inflation, they may consume rather than save and take more leisure rather than work. By thus leading people into decisions they would otherwise not make, inflation can reduce the growth rate of capital and labor inputs into the production process and thereby lower the growth rate of the economy.

In this section we will identify some of the gainers and losers from inflation. The discussion first deals with the redistribution of income that takes place between the government and the people. It then focuses on redistributions of wealth and income between groups within the private sector.

17.3.1
Inflation, personal income, and real income

In the United States, the progressive income tax system raises taxes faster than incomes. As people move into higher income brackets, marginal tax rates associated with the higher brackets also rise. For example, in 1979 a family earning a taxable income between $24,600 and $29,900 paid the federal government a marginal tax rate of 32 percent, while a family with taxable income between $29,900 and $35,200 paid additional taxes equal to 37 percent of the last $5,300 of its income. The maximum marginal tax rate on family income earned from work was 50 percent for taxable incomes over $60,000; the marginal tax rate on incomes from interest, dividends, and other forms of wealth was 70 percent for incomes over $215,400.

In addition to raising commodity prices, inflation increases money wages, salaries, nominal interest rates, and other types of income payments. It therefore increases the real tax burden of the household sector of the economy. Even if a family's gross nominal income keeps pace with the rise in commodity prices, its after-tax real income will fall. So inflation undermines real private disposable income as it increases the real income of the government. It channels into public uses resources that would have gone into private uses.

The interaction of taxes and inflation is measured for some recent years by Table 17.2 and Figure 17.3. In 1974 and 1978 the government gained over $7 billion in extra taxes solely from the operation of inflation. Although the heaviest burden fell upon families with adjusted gross income (AGI) of $20,000 to $50,000, over the years of inflation, taxes have also injured families with median incomes—as Figure 17.3 shows, the push of inflation on income during the 1960–1979 period raised social security and income taxes by a factor of over five, while real after-tax median incomes rose by only 30 percent. Although tax rates did change somewhat during this period, there is little question that the slower rise of median real after-tax incomes came primarily from inflation pushing

Table 17.2 *Increase in Individual Income Taxes Resulting from Inflation by Adjusted Gross Income Class, Selected Years (in millions of dollars)*

AGI Class	1974	%	1976	%	1978	%
Under $5,000	$ 425	6	$ 166	3	$ 128	2
$5,000–$10,000	1,035	15	664	13	729	10
$10,000–$15,000	1,249	17	760	15	934	12
$15,000–$20,000	1,210	17	831	16	1,094	15
$20,000–$50,000	2,279	32	2,000	39	3,437	45
$50,000–$100,000	637	9	514	10	861	11
$100,000+	289	4	179	4	359	5
Total	7,124		5,114		7,542	
CPI	+12.2%		+4.8%		+6.5%	(est.)

Source: Joint Committee on Taxation; cited in Bruce Bartlett, "Why Government Will Never Stop Inflation," *The Libertarian Review,* March 1979.

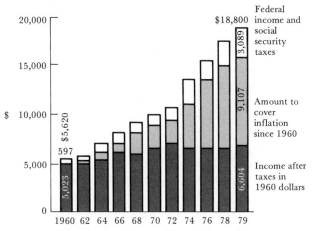

Figure 17.3 *Median family income—the bite of taxes and inflation. (Source: The Conference Board; cited in John H. Moore,* Inflation and the Burden of Taxation *(Washington, D.C.: National Federation of Independent Business, Public Policy Discussion Series, 1979).)*

families into higher income tax brackets. In addition, Congress increased the maximum income level subject to social security taxation, thus maintaining that tax as a proportion of median gross incomes.

Inflation allows the government to raise the level of taxation without passing new tax laws. This "taxation without representation" can be stopped by indexing taxes, that is, by making the width of income tax brackets proportional to changes in the consumer price index. In this way, people whose nominal incomes increase by the same percentage as the rise in the consumer price index would not be shoved into higher tax brackets, and their real after-tax incomes would be preserved. Only those whose real incomes rise by enough to carry them into the higher (adjusted) tax brackets would be subjected to the higher marginal tax rates.

Congress resisted the idea of tax indexation for a long time. It didn't want to lose the extra revenues that automatically came with increases in nominal incomes. But political pressure built for it to change its mind. Finally, in July of 1981 it passed a major tax-cut measure that authorized indexation of income taxes beginning in 1985.

17.3.2
Inflation, taxes, and capital income

Plowbacks of business profits into new capital assets is an important source of productivity growth. But interaction of inflation and the tax system raises effective tax rates on corporate income and reduces the rate of return on capital investments. Such a reduction may have caused a decline in business investment and slowed productivity growth in the 1970s.

Corporate taxes are levied upon reported corporate profits. Reported profits consist of revenues minus production and capital costs. In addition to wages and salaries, production costs include the costs of raw and semifinished materials used in the production process. In addition to interest and other finance charges, capital costs include depreciation of plant and equipment. Many companies measure the costs of raw and semifinished materials used in production at their original purchase prices instead of replacement costs. During inflationary times, this practice overstates reported profits, since to replace these inputs the firms must pay higher prices. An additional overstatement of profits comes from a rule in the law that forces firms to measure depreciation in terms of historical costs of existing plant and equipment instead of replacement costs. In times of rapid inflation, this requirement leads to a serious understatement of depreciation and overstatement of reported profits. Overstatement of profits, in turn, raises corporate taxes.

The impact of inflation on the effective corporate tax rate and the after-tax return on replacement cost of capital is shown in Figures 17.4 and 17.5. Clearly, the sharp increase of the effective tax rate on profits in

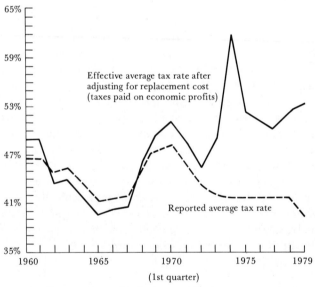

Figure 17.4 *Impact of inflation on effective corporate tax rate, 1960 to 1979. In order to take into account two inflationary effects, the following adjustments are made: (1) Before-tax profits are reduced by the increase in depreciation that would result if plant and equipment were valued at replacement cost rather than original cost (capital consumption allowance), and (2) the capital gain from the increase in inventory prices due to inflation is eliminated. (Source: U. S. Department of Commerce, Bureau of Economic Analysis; cited in* Stimulating Technological Progress *(New York: Committee for Economic Development, 1980), p. 5.)*

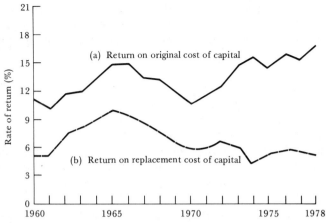

Figure 17.5 *Trend in return on total capital investment (original versus replacement cost basis) for nonfinancial corporations, 1960 to 1978. (a) After-tax profits plus interest divided by original cost of plant and equipment. (b) After-tax profits plus interest minus capital consumption allowance and inventory gains divided by replacement cost of capital. (Source: U. S. Department of Commerce, Bureau of Economic Analysis; cited in* Stimulating Technological Progress *(New York: Committee for Economic Development, 1980), p. 6.)*

1973–1975 hurt the rate of return on replacement cost of capital. In the rest of the period, the rate of return failed to recover its mid-1960s level. This failure probably contributed to the productivity slowdown of the 1970s. Inflation-imposed reductions of real after-tax returns on replacement cost of capital would disappear with an overhaul of depreciation rules in the tax law, permitting either more rapid write-offs of newly purchased equipment or adjustment of depreciation costs for changes in the price level.[7] But opponents to such changes argue that inflation reduces the real value of corporate debt and thus produces a benefit that compensates corporation owners for losses from understated depreciation.

This argument has some truth; but, according to Harvard Professor Martin Feldstein, President of the National Bureau of Economic Research, it overlooks two important points.[8] First, as inflation gets built into expectations of lenders, corporate debtors must pay higher nominal interest rates to their creditors. Higher nominal interest rates permit companies to deduct, as costs, nominal interest expenses that exceed real in-

---

[7]In July 1981, Congress enacted a tax law giving businesses substantially faster write-offs for investments in plant and equipment. The law was part of the omnibus tax cut legislation proposed to Congress by the Reagan Administration and was consistent with the supply-side objectives of using tax cuts to raise the rate of capital formation in the U.S. economy.

[8]M. Feldstein, "Adjusting Tax Rules for Inflation—Capital Gains and Capital Income," *Tax Review*, Vol. XL, No. 1, January 1979, pp. 1–4.

terest expenses and, to that extent, give them taxable profits that understate true profits. Nonetheless, it is not at all certain that this understatement of profits offsets the overstatement due to inadequate depreciation.

Second, and much more important, is the failure of the opponents of tax law revision to recognize the effect of inflation on the tax liabilities of lenders. Lenders pay taxes on nominal interest income, not on real interest income. Hence, depending on the tax bracket of the individual lender, the real after-tax interest return will fall as the rate of inflation increases. For example, suppose a lender has a marginal tax rate of 50 percent of income. With zero inflation, a 5 percent interest return on a corporate bond will give the lender a 2.5 percent real after-tax return. If an inflation rate of 5 percent raises the nominal interest rate to 10 percent, the lender's real after-tax return will fall to zero—a 50 percent tax on the nominal 10 percent return leaves a 5 percent nominal after-tax return that, adjusted for a 5 percent rate of inflation, yields a zero after-tax return.

Thus, the undertaxation of corporate stockholders from higher nominal interest rates is offset by overtaxation of corporate bondholders. If the tax rates of corporations and their lenders are equal, the debt effect is irrelevant; only the excess tax from understated depreciation remains. If corporate tax rates substantially exceed those of bond holders, the debt effect may completely offset the effect of depreciation. It is Feldstein's view, however, that tax rates imposed on corporations and their lenders are so close that the debt effect can be effectively ignored. If so, the impact of inflation on effective corporate income tax rates and after-tax returns on replacement investment are approximately as shown in Figures 17.4 and 17.5, and the case for overhaul of depreciation tax law remains.

17.3.3
Inflation, capital gains, and taxes

A capital gain (loss) is the difference between the price paid by an investor for an asset and the current market value of the asset. Realized capital gains (losses) occur when assets are sold at higher (lower) prices; when assets are kept, gains (losses) are unrealized.

Inflation causes overtaxation of realized capital gains (unrealized gains are not taxed) because taxes are levied on nominal rather than real gains. As a result, real after-tax capital gains are often cancelled or even converted into losses by the tax system. For example, assume that an asset bought and held for two years appreciates in value by an amount equal to the increase in the consumer price index. Its real value in terms of the price index will not have changed; but, if the asset is sold, the nominal capital gain will be taxed, and the realized after-tax gain will be negative.

A study of 30,000 individual 1973 income tax returns by Martin Feldstein and associates revealed that people were actually paying taxes on real losses. The stocks this group sold had risen in market value by $4.6 billion; but during the holding periods of the stocks the price level had risen by enough to convert the nominal gains into real capital losses of nearly $1 billion. Even so, the stockholders paid taxes on the $4.6 billion of nominal capital gains. The tax system actually increased their losses. Moreover, although people at all income levels paid taxes on their artificial gains, the losses were greatest for people earning less than $100,000. In fact, over 90 percent of the losses were sustained by people in adjusted gross income brackets of below $50,000.

Investments in business ventures are usually risky affairs; nevertheless, the chance to make large capital gains frequently entices people to make investments they would otherwise avoid. The present tax laws clearly discourage such risk taking. Moreover, they create incentives for people to invest in paintings, antiques, large houses, and other consumer assets instead of into business capital.

Congress has enacted modest reductions in capital gains tax rates; but in an era of inflation it could also permit inflation indexing of the gains. The U.S. Treasury and many congressmen argue that such a change in the law would severely reduce tax revenues; but a number of economists, including Professor Feldstein,[9] say that tax reform would encourage venture capital and release unrealized capital gains locked up in portfolios of tax-shy investors. Realization of the gains, in addition to more rapid turnover of new capital acquisitions through market sales, could actually increase the Treasury's revenue from the capital gains tax.

17.4
Inflationary redistributions of wealth and income

The distribution of income and wealth partly depends upon the prices transactors pay and receive. In a free economy, prices are in a constant state of flux, reflecting daily shifts of supply and demand conditions in a variety of markets. The unpredictability of these changes imparts a strong element of luck to the distribution of income and wealth. For example, in the early 1970s crop failures in the Soviet Union sent up the world price of grain and enriched American farmers. At the same time, American and other grain consumers experienced a decline in the purchasing power of their incomes.

---

[9]"Adjusting Rules for Inflation."

Inflation makes prices more unpredictable. Studies by a number of economists have demonstrated that relative prices are more variable the higher the rate of inflation. Hence, as inflation progresses, buyers and sellers find it harder to separate changes in relative prices from changes in the absolute level of prices. As a result, they frequently make unintentional self-destructive decisions. These decisions can create substantial shifts in the distribution of wealth and income between borrowers and lenders, employers and employees, and individuals at the beginning and the tail end of the inflationary process. The decisions may also lead to redistributions of wealth between the government, banks, and money holders.

17.4.1
Inflationary redistributions between borrowers and lenders

A standard argument is that inflation benefits debtors at the expense of creditors. Although this observation is generally correct, it does not follow that inflation helps all debtors or injures all creditors. In fact, under certain circumstances, inflation may hurt some debtors and help their creditors.

In order to understand the effects of inflation on lenders and borrowers we must distinguish between *anticipated inflation* and *unanticipated inflation*. Any actual inflation rate can be divided into an anticipated and an unanticipated part. Anticipated inflation is what peoples' forecasts lead them to expect. Unanticipated inflation is the difference between inflation forecasts and the actual rate of inflation. Since forecasting inflation is a costly and uncertain enterprise, most people incorrectly predict the inflation rate. Moreover, the longer the period of forecast, the more likely is an incorrect prediction. Thus any particular experience of inflation is likely to contain an unanticipated element. The element will be positive if the actual inflation rate exceeds the predicted rate, and negative if the actual rate falls short of the predicted rate.

A lender and a borrower expecting an 8 percent inflation rate during the loan period may agree upon a nominal interest rate high enough to compensate the lender for loss of purchasing power of both the principal sum lent and the interest income received during the loan period. If the 8 percent inflation forecast is correct, neither borrower nor lender will receive an inflationary gain. But an incorrect inflation forecast will result in a redistribution of real wealth and income between the lender and the borrower. If unanticipated inflation is positive, the borrower will gain at the expense of the lender, and if unanticipated inflation is negative, the lender will gain at the expense of the borrower.

The argument that inflation benefits debtors at the expense of creditors clearly depends on an empirical assumption that people generally underpredict inflation. Although direct evidence backing this assumption is unavailable, economists have found some indirect supporting evidence. Since 1947, J.A. Livingston, a journalist with the *Philadelphia Inquirer*, has conducted a semiannual survey of about 50 economists in the business and academic communities, asking, among other things, for their forecasts of the consumer price index. John A. Carlson of Purdue University has matched these forecasts against the actual CPI for the period of 1948–1974.[10] He found evidence of both positive and negative unanticipated inflation; but, in periods of pronounced jumps in the inflation rate, anticipations of inflation usually lagged far behind actual inflation. Thus, it is probably true that in the recent past positive unanticipated inflation, with redistributions of real wealth and interest income from lenders to borrowers, have been the norm.

Many lenders are also borrowers. For example, households with savings in pension plans, banks, insurance policies, or bonds frequently owe money on automobiles, appliances, furniture, and homes. Thus, only people with positive *net* financial asset positions risk loss of real net worth from unanticipated inflation. People with negative net financial positions avoid such risks. This fact drives many individuals to seek loans in order to reduce inflation risks. As they borrow, nominal interest rates rise, increasing the returns to lenders and reducing their risks of loss. In this manner, the market tends to redistribute risks of unanticipated inflation between lenders and borrowers.

Another method of protecting financial assets against inflation is the indexation of loans. Under this method, the principal sum of a loan or the interest income are adjusted upward in accordance with the change in some price index. Indexed loans are common in countries with endemic inflation, such as Israel, Brazil, and Argentina. Despite considerable inflation experience during the last 15 years, indexed loans are uncommon in the United States. Instead, lenders such as banks and savings and loan associations have opted for variable interest rate term loans. The interest rates on such loans are tied to short-term nominal interest rates (which are affected by current market expectations of inflation) and thus provide lenders with some protection against inflation risk. But the lag in expectations of inflation behind actual inflation causes nominal interest rates to lag behind inflation. As a result, variable interest rate loans provide lenders with only partial protection against inflation risk.

---

[10]Carlson's results and their implications are discussed in Donald J. Mullineaux, "Inflation Expectations in the U.S.: A Brief Anatomy," *Federal Reserve Bank of Philadelphia Business Review*, July/August 1977.

Pensioners are probably the group hardest hit by inflation. Their pension benefits are usually based on incomes earned during less inflationary years and before it was possible to anticipate the recent rapid deterioration in the value of money. Even so, not all pensioners lose from inflation. Social security pensions and retirement benefits of federal government employees are regularly adjusted to reflect changes in the consumer price index. A few state and local government and private pension plans are also partially or wholly adjusted to reflect changes in the CPI. Nevertheless, the bulk of private and nonfederal government employee pension plans are devoid of inflation protection; people under these plans suffer declines in the purchasing power of pension benefits in direct proportion to increases in the consumer price index.

It used to be thought that inflation redistributed real incomes away from workers towards employers and business owners. But evidence of such a shift on a permanent basis is lacking. Spurts of inflation may bring about temporary increases in the relative share of profits, but over the long run workers can regain their previous positions.

Temporary reductions in workers' relative income shares occur when employers make better inflation predictions than employees or their unions. Again, unanticipated inflation is the source of the problem. But continued experience with inflation causes workers to demand shorter-term contracts and extra large wage increases to compensate for the risk of surprise inflation. In addition, they ask for, and in many cases get, escalator clauses that partially or wholly link their wages to changes in the consumer price index. In 1978 more than 8.5 million of the 19.5 million workers in the union sector of the economy were covered by contracts that call for automatic wage adjustments based on changes in the cost of living. This is considerably more than the 2.5 million workers covered in 1968. Since many nonunion employers base wage increases on union wages, the effect of such indexation on the overall wage level is much larger than indicated by the 8.5 million figure.[11]

Even a large number of the poor are given cost-of-living protection. Food stamp allotments are based upon an index of food costs, and eligibility for some governmental assistance programs is based upon a poverty line geared to changes in the price level.

Automatically escalated payments have penetrated contracts in a number of areas of the economy, although the exact number is not

---

[11]See Marcelle V. Arak, "Indexation of Wages and Retirement Income in the United States," *Federal Reserve Bank of New York Quarterly Review*, Vol. 3, No. 3, Autumn 1978, p. 16.

known. Business contracts for delivery of goods and services frequently specify that payments depend on the level of certain prices; some lessors have CPI adjustments in leases, and alimony, child payments, royalty recipients, and beneficiaries of certain insurance policies are at times similarly protected. According to the Bureau of Labor Statistics, about half the U.S. population is in one way or another protected by escalator clauses.

In the long run, a steady, predictable inflation would probably have little appreciable effect on the distribution of income and wealth. However, the unpredictability of inflation creates economic distortions that upset the relative earnings of various groups in the economy. Such distortions would occur if the inflation rate were zero and accompanied by wide fluctuations of the price level around the zero trend. Unfortunately, the variability, and hence unpredictability, of prices increases as the overall inflation rate rises. As a result, continuous redistributions of income and wealth usually accompany high rates of inflation.

17.4.3
Inflation tax on cash balances

A subtle, but nevertheless real tax imposed by inflation is the loss in real value of money balances. Although people can reduce this tax burden by holding fewer dollars, they cannot avoid it altogether. They need money to facilitate transactions and to protect themselves against unforeseen contingencies. The less money they hold, the more they must keep their wealth in nonmonetary illiquid forms. The penalty for holding money is foregone interest and income on nonfinancial property. But money is the medium of exchange; the time and trouble and perhaps capital losses entailed in cashing in other assets when money is needed makes it worthwhile to hold a significant proportion of assets in the form of money itself.

Each percentage point rise in the inflation rate imposes a like cost on the holding of cash balances. This cost encourages people to convert cash into real goods. Moreover, since inflationary expectations raise interest rates, people also have an incentive to shift assets out of money balances into securities. The result of these portfolio shifts is less liquidity and an increase in transactions and perhaps storage costs (see Section 1.1.2)—impairment of money as a medium of exchange.

The inflation tax on cash balances held by the public has been somewhat reduced by the evolution of NOW accounts, automatic transfer savings accounts, credit union share drafts, and other interest bearing transactions accounts. But such devices do not represent a gain for the private sector taken as a whole. The interest paid on transactions imposes costs on financial institutions that are borne by their stockholders; in addition, it creates increased accounting costs. Thus a shift of cash balances out of noninterest bearing demand deposits into interest bearing transactions accounts leads both to a redistribution of income between owners of financial institutions and their deposit customers and to a general rise in operating costs. Higher operating costs are a deadweight burden on the economy that ties up resources that could be used elsewhere.

The government's portion of the inflation tax comes from the money it issues. That money includes currency and coin and the reserves created by the Federal Reserve System—the monetary base. Since the bank and nonbank public earns no interest on the monetary base, inflation-imposed reductions in the real value of the existing base represent a full tax. Moreover, since the base is largely under the control of the Fed, the tax cannot be escaped through voluntary reductions in holdings of the base. Thus deficit spending financed by expansion of the monetary base allows the government to compete away real resources from holders of cash balances in the private sector. In that respect, inflationary money creation is properly called a tax.

17.5
Effects of inflation on resource allocation

We end this chapter with a comment on the effects of inflation on resource allocation. Resources are the things we use to produce goods and services. In a properly functioning economy labor, capital, and raw materials should move into areas of production that are most highly valued by individuals in the economy and away from less valued uses. Efficient allocation of resources requires a properly functioning price system. If inflation interferes with the functioning of market prices, the efficiency of the economy will decline, and most people will have less real income and wealth. This process of deterioration was well described by Milton Friedman in his Nobel Lecture in 1976:

> A fundamental function of a price system, as Hayek (has) emphasized so brilliantly, is to transmit compactly, efficiently, and at low cost the information that economic agents need in order to decide what to produce and how to produce it, or how to employ owned resources. The relevant information is about *relative* prices—of one product relative to another, of the services of one factor of production relative to another, of products relative to factor services, of prices now relative to prices in the future. But the information in practice is transmitted in the form of *absolute* prices—prices in dollars or pounds or kroner. If the price level is on the average stable or changing at a steady rate, it is relatively easy to extract the signal about relative prices from the observed absolute prices. The more volatile the rate of general inflation,

the harder it becomes to extract the signal about relative prices from the absolute prices: the broadcast about relative prices is as it were being jammed by the noise coming from the inflation broadcast. At the extreme, the system of absolute prices becomes nearly useless, and economic agents resort either to an alternative currency, or to barter, with disastrous effects on productivity.

Friedman's comments are not pure theory. Experience with hyper-inflation in Germany in the 1920s and in other countries clearly shows that after a point people start avoiding money payments and instead revert to the costly process of barter. In addition, they spend money that comes into their hands as quickly as possible, preferring goods of any kind to holding cash that quickly loses its value. They end up with many items they would not otherwise have bought.

Of course, hyperinflation is not required before people revert to barter. Part of the widely publicized recent shift of economic activity into the so-called underground or subterranean economy represents a desire to barter labor. This is done through so-called labor banks. Operators of such banks arrange for people to exchange services. For example, an individual desiring the services of, say, a carpenter contacts the bank. The bank, in turn, contacts a carpenter. When the service is performed, the carpenter receives a credit in the bank, and the individual receiving the service incurs a debt that can be discharged by working for another member of the bank. Although such banks help improve the efficiency of barter, they cannot duplicate the efficiency of a money economy. In the latter, people can search the broader market for a carpenter and other labor services; they are not confined to those offered through the labor bank.

Current rates of inflation are not high enough to force a wholesale reversion to barter. Nevertheless, in the ways discussed in this chapter, they do undermine the efficiency of the economy. Moreover, by interacting with the tax system, inflation raises the burden of private and corporate income taxes and robs savers of positive real returns on savings. This interaction tends to reduce the incentives to save and invest and it might even increase the desire for leisure instead of work. Thus, although the economy is in no danger of grinding to a halt, continuation of high inflation rates will keep productivity from growing as fast as it could with more stable prices.

SUMMARY

Inflation is commonly defined as a continuous rise in the price level or a falling purchasing power of money. Since each individual spends his money differently, no single index of prices can capture the effects of inflation. Moreover, when inflation is repressed, rather than open, price indexes cannot capture the changing purchasing power of money. Thus, there is no satisfactory definition of inflation that covers all situations.

Inflation is caused by a rate of growth of the nominal money supply that exceeds the growth of the demand for real money balances. So-called nonmonetary theories of inflation frequently confuse changes in relative prices with changes in the overall level of prices. Cost push or monopolistic forces that work on the economy as a whole affect the price level indirectly by lowering the rate of growth of real income. The latter, in turn, leads to a slowing of the rate of growth of the demand for real money balances. If, in the meantime, the rate of growth of the nominal money supply has not been reduced, the result will be an increased rate of inflation.

But nonmonetary forces cannot permanently alter the rate of inflation without working in a continuous fashion. For example, a one-time increase in labor or product monopoly, or a one-time jump in OPEC oil prices, will cause a temporary bulge in the inflation rate. After the one-time forces dissipate, prices will continue to rise at the rate dictated by the excess rate of growth of the nominal money supply.

Excessive growth of money is the proximate cause of inflation. A complete theory of inflation must explain why the monetary authorities do not keep money growth on a leash. One answer is that the authorities are under constant pressure to accommodate the deficits generated by Congress and the Administration in their attempts to satisfy desires of political constituents. Another answer is that they are locked into a pattern of stop–go policies in which flip-flops in monetary policies are used first to stimulate the economy and second (having overdone it) to fight off accelerating inflation. The tight monetary policies create recessions and unemployment, conditions that create political pressures for the authorities to revert to easy monetary and fiscal policies. Since inflation is only partially moderated during the recession period, each recovery starts from a higher inflation base than did the previous recoveries. As a result, the expansion phase of the business cycle carries the price level beyond its earlier peak. The ultimate result of the pattern of stop–go policies is a secular rise in the rate of inflation.

Erroneous notions concerning inflation abound. These include such ideas as (1) overspending by consumers causes inflation; (2) high interest rates cause increases in the price level; (3) inflation is caused by abnormal price increases in particular markets; (4) inflation directly lowers real income; and (5) the best way to kill inflation is to raise productivity. Most of these fallacious ideas confuse relative price changes with changes in the price level or fail to appreciate the monetary nature of inflation.

Inflation pushes people into higher income tax brackets and raises the effective personal income tax rate on real income when tax brackets are unindexed for inflation. It also increases effective rates of taxation on business profits and thereby reduces the rate of return on capital income. Studies have also demonstrated that inflation causes taxes on real capital gains to rise, sometimes to a level of more than 100 percent. These effects of inflation on taxes can be moderated or eliminated by measures that index income tax brackets, permit accelerated depreciation on business capital, permit firms to deduct for depreciation using replacement instead of book values, and index capital gains for purposes of taxation.

Unanticipated inflation causes redistributions of real wealth between creditors and debtors, between workers and employers, and between pensioners and other members of the community. In recent years indexation of contracts, social security, food stamps, and other items have provided protection for workers, pensioners, and welfare recipients, though not everyone in these classes is protected. Moreover, inflation indexation of loans has not spread very widely; instead, the financial system appears to be moving to shorter-term loan contracts and floating interest rate loans, away from long-term fixed interest loans that were so common in noninflationary times.

Finally, inflation reduces the overall welfare of the private sector by imposing a tax on cash balances. In addition, by jamming the price signals so necessary for the efficient functioning of a market economy, it interferes with the allocation of resources and encourages a reversion to barter.

DISCUSSION QUESTIONS

1. What is wrong with defining inflation in terms of a rise in some particular price index?

2. Why do monetarists deny validity to nonmonetary theories of inflation? Can nonmonetary theories be treated as special cases of a more general model emphasizing monetary forces?

3. What is wrong with a theory that blames inflation on high spending consumers or business?

4. Since high interest rates and high inflation usually go hand-in-hand, can it be argued that inflation comes from high interest rates rather than the other way around?

5. Most trade unionists deny that unions cause inflation. Do you agree?

6. Under the present tax system, it is possible for real capital to be taxed at more than 100 percent as a result of inflation. Explain.

7. What is the significance of the distinction between anticipated and unanticipated inflation?

8. How does inflation interfere with the "price signals" that are supposed to guide an efficiently operating market economy?

9. Is there any way for people to avoid the so-called inflation tax? If so, at what price?

IMPORTANT TERMS AND CONCEPTS

- ☐ anticipated inflation
- ☐ capital gains
- ☐ Employment Act of 1946
- ☐ hyperinflation
- ☐ inflation
- ☐ inflation tax
- ☐ interest cost-push theory of inflation

- ☐ nonmonetary theories of inflation
- ☐ shortsightedness effect
- ☐ stagflation
- ☐ stop–go policies
- ☐ suppressed inflation
- ☐ tax indexation
- ☐ unanticipated inflation

ADDITIONAL READINGS

The literature on inflation is overwhelmingly large. But, fortunately, one need not read it all to understand the issue. As a starter, read *Money and Inflation: A Monetarist Approach*, by J. Huston McCulloch (New York: Academic Press, 1975). This slim paperback is similar in approach to this book, and therefore is packed with good sense. Next, go to the collection of articles edited by the Federal Reserve Bank of New York, *Federal Reserve Readings on Inflation* (1979)—the best $2.00 buy in the field—a source that gives a more eclectic approach to the causes and effects of inflation. Another good Federal Reserve source is Thomas M. Humphrey, *Essays on Inflation*, 2nd edition, (Richmond: Federal Reserve Bank of Richmond, 1980). Humphrey is a superb expositer and synthesizer of the monetary and inflation literature. His essays contain analyses of every variety of inflation theory, essays on the stagflation problem, discussions of the international aspects of inflation, studies of classical monetary thought on the subject, and discussions of price controls and indexation. Readers who would like to probe the Federal Reserve literature even more deeply can go to the most recent issue of *The Fed in Print*, an index of articles published in Federal Reserve publications. Address a card to the Librarian, Federal Reserve Bank of Philadelphia.

Don't overlook the literature on inflation written by prominent members of the Austrian school of economics. Examples are Friedrich A. Hayek, *A Tiger By the Tail: The Keynesian Legacy of Inflation* (San Francisco: Cato Institute, 1979) and Ludwig von Mises, *Human Action* (Chicago: Henry Regnery Company, 1963, 3rd revised edition), Chapter XVII.

Two other useful collections of articles are in David Heathfield, editor, *Perspectives on Inflation* (London and New York: Longmans, 1979) and Fred Hirsch and John H. Goldthorpe (editors), *The Political Economy of Inflation* (Cambridge: Harvard University Press, 1978).

Finally, for extensive technical literature, read R. J. Gordon, "Recent Developments in the Theory of Inflation and Unemployment," *Journal of Monetary Economics*, Vol. 2, No. 2, April 1976, pp. 185–220, and D. Laidler and M. Parkin, "Inflation, A Survey," *Economic Journal*, Vol. 85, No. 335, December 1975, pp. 741–809.

Inflation and Unemployment: The Stagflation Problem

18

OUTLINE

The Natural Unemployment Rate Hypothesis

The Natural Rate and Frictional–Structural Unemployment

Cyclical Unemployment

Expectations-augmented Phillips Curves and the Accelerationist Hypothesis

Why the Short-run Phillips Curve is Negatively Sloped

Adaptive Expectations

Rational Expectations

Rational versus Irrational Expectations

Policy Implications—Friedman's Money Growth Rule

Most economists used to think that inflation and unemployment were substitutes. The belief was reinforced by an influential study by A.W. Phillips, who claimed discovery of a stable long-run (100-year) relationship between changes in money wages and levels of unemployment rates in the United Kingdom.[1] Studies of the relation between prices and unemployment in the United States also produced negatively sloped Phillips curves, like the one drawn through the observations recorded for the 1950s and 1960s in Figure 18.1. These studies convinced many economists and policymakers that a choice must be made between more unemployment and more inflation. Keeping inflation down, they believed, would permanently raise the unemployment rate; but, keeping unemployment down would permanently raise the inflation rate.

Discussions of this trade-off led to many debates comparing the evils

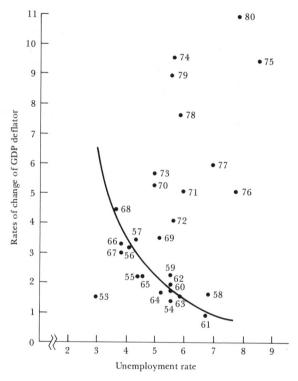

Figure 18.1 *Inflation and unemployment, 1953–1980. (Source: Based on data from the United States Government,* Economic Report of the President, 1981, *statistical appendices.)*

---

[1]A. W. Phillips, "The Relation Between Unemployment and the Rate of Change of Money Wage Rates in the United Kingdom, 1861–1957," *Economica*, Vol. 25, 1958, pp. 283–299.

of unemployment and inflation. But the debates may have unnecessarily divided economists into opposing camps. In the 1970s the apparent permanent trade-off between inflation and unemployment disappeared. The dots on the diagram began to drift in a northeasterly direction. Instead of a single Phillips curve, it now seems appropriate to draw a series of curves, one for the early 1970s and another for the middle and late 1970s. If there is a trade-off, it is no longer permanent, and it lasts only a few years. For all we know, even the temporary trade-off may vanish in the years to come. It may be that the simultaneous presence of unacceptable levels of unemployment and inflation—stagflation—will persist as the problem of our age.

18.1
The natural unemployment rate hypothesis

In the late 1960s economists were already questioning the long-run stability of the Phillips curve. In 1967 Milton Friedman and Edmund Phelps independently argued that the long-run Phillips curve is in reality a vertical line built over what Friedman called the *natural unemployment rate*. In contrast, the negatively sloped short-run Phillips curves describe temporary, shifting relationships that cross the long-run vertical curve at various points, as in Figure 18.2.

The natural unemployment rate and the shifting Phillips curve ideas are tied together in an interesting hypothesis proposed by Friedman in

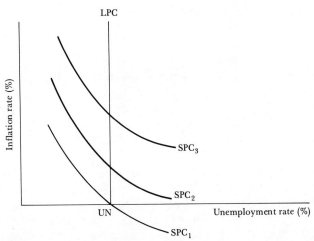

Figure 18.2 *Short-run and long-run Phillips curves. SPC = short-run Phillips curve; LPC = long-run Phillips curve; UN = natural unemployment rate.*

his 1967 Presidential address to the American Economic Association. The key idea in this theory is that departures from the natural unemployment rate occur because workers are unable to forecast accurately the rate of inflation. As a result, they accept (or reject) jobs they would refuse (or take) if they could make accurate forecasts. Thus, an unexpected increase in inflation reduces unemployment below the so-called natural rate, and an unexpected decrease in inflation raises unemployment above the natural rate. But these are temporary changes in unemployment; once inflationary expectations catch up with reality, workers take actions that restore the natural rate. It follows that the natural unemployment rate is consistent with many different inflation rates. The upward drifting short-run Phillips curves reflect the catch-up of expected with actual inflation, and the points at which they cross the vertical long-run curve describe an unemployment rate at which expected and actual inflation rates are roughly equal.

18.1.1
The natural rate and frictional–structural unemployment

The natural unemployment rate is the rate that would prevail if workers and employers were able to make accurate predictions of inflation at all times. If that were the case, workers would be taking jobs that offer present and future nominal wage rates that give them the real wages they are willing to accept in exchange for their services. At the same time, employers would also be satisfied; they would be offering current and future wages that would provide satisfactory levels of profit and that would protect them from losing money from bad inflation forecasts.

The natural rate of unemployment is closely linked to the idea of aggregate equilibrium. Recall from Section 11.1.2 that equilibrium in a particular market implies that buyers and sellers are actually experiencing the prices they expect to find when planning the qualities and quantities of goods and services they are trading in the market. Assuming no changes in underlying market conditions, the prices and quantities anticipated and realized in market exchanges should not change unpredictably. In aggregative equilibria we cannot expect this to happen in each market. But we should expect people disappointed by their market exchanges to be balanced by people pleasantly surprised by their transactions.

The natural unemployment rate is an aggregative equilibrium concept. As such, it does not assume that everyone who wants a job at current and expected real wages is currently employed. It recognizes that employment opportunities are constantly changing from shifts in demand, changes in production processes, changing skill requirements of workers, and changes in public policies that impact individual industries or the overall economy. Some of these changes are permanent, others are temporary; some are predictable, others are not. There is plenty of scope for pleasant and unpleasant surprises for workers and employers. Aggregate equilibrium in this kind of dynamic setting cannot usefully mean that in making their plans all workers and employers have guessed right about the future. Instead, it must mean that, *on balance*, expectations of inflation are correct—that on both sides of the labor market there are traders that have underpredicted or overpredicted inflation, and that the mistakes they have made offset each other so as to produce an unemployment rate that, other things being equal, is immune to variations in the *level* (as opposed to the predictability) of the inflation rate.

Economists ordinarily classify unemployment as *frictional, structural,* or *cyclical.* Frictional unemployment comes from the dynamic workings of the labor market. Shifts in the composition of product demands both destroy and create job opportunities. Workers losing jobs in declining markets or industries must search for work in growing industries. Adding to the volume of the unemployed are new workers and retired workers who have decided to rejoin the work force.

If all unemployed workers could immediately find jobs, frictional unemployment would disappear. But no automatic mechanism exists to bring employers with job openings into immediate contact with the unemployed. As a result, employers and workers must seek each other out. Jobs are advertised through the press, labor exchanges, placement services, and word of mouth. Workers hunt for jobs in their home towns, nearby communities or far away places. Experienced workers frequently find satisfactory jobs with little waste of time. Inexperienced workers have more trouble, and the jobs they find are often unsatisfactory or unsuited to their skills. As a result, they tend to have frequent and relatively long spells of unemployment.

Frictional unemployment is clearly consistent with the notion of natural unemployment. It arises from the daily shifts of demand and supply that take place in a market economy. It has relatively little to do with the inability of workers or employers to forecast correctly the overall inflation rate. It is more closely connected with the inability of employers and workers to make good predictions of *relative prices.* If workers and employers could make good predictions, they would make their labor market decisions in advance of the shifts in demand and supply conditions; there would be no frictional unemployment. Inflation affects frictional unemployment only as it leads market participants to confuse overall price level changes with changes in relative prices. If and when that is the case, the frictional unemployment rate will be positively correlated with inflation.

Structural unemployment comes from a mismatch between available jobs and the combination of skills, ages, locations, sex, union affiliation, and other characteristics of some of the unemployed. Some economists liken structural unemployment to the square-pegs-in-the-round-holes problem. The pegs are the unemployed workers; the holes are the jobs they cannot fill. But square pegs can be whittled round, and round holes can be carved square. The instrument for making such changes in a market economy is changes in relative prices. For example, relatively high wages for workers with skills in short supply encourage workers without them to train for better jobs; they also give incentives to employers to alter methods of production or to change product mixtures in order to replace some of the high paid workers with lower paid, less skilled employees.

The automatic workings of the market cannot reduce structural unemployment when minimum wage laws, union wage scales, and other impediments prevent necessary adjustments in wages, prices, and working conditions. In the absence of programs designed to remove the impediments, government must instead turn to job training, job creation, and job location programs. Macroeconomic policies that stimulate aggregate demand and force up the general price level cannot do much to lower permanently the level of structural unemployment.

Welfare systems and unemployment compensation programs may also be responsible for some structural unemployment. For example, unemployed food stamp recipients and Aid for Dependent Children recipients 16 years or older must register for work with state employment agencies, even though they may be marginally seeking employment or are marginally employable at the existing minimum wage. Kenneth Clarkson of the University of Miami and Roger Meiners of Texas A&M[2] say that in 1976 about 2 million people were counted as unemployed because of the work registration requirement for these two welfare programs. At that time, 2 million workers accounted for 2 percent of the labor force; hence, the unemployment rate exclusive of these workers in the labor force would have been 5 instead of 7 percent. Although U.S. Department of Labor economists dispute the 2 percent figure, they agree that as much as one-half of a percentage point of the unemployment rate comes from this source.

Unemployment compensation raises the natural unemployment rate in two ways. First, it greatly reduces the net or after-tax loss of income of people thrown out of work. Unemployment benefits in most states provide tax free payments equal to 50–60 percent of the average pre-tax gross earnings of the workers, which amounts to 65–75 percent of their lost net income. Benefits of this magnitude encourage unemployed workers to take vacations, repair, or renovate their cars or homes, take odd jobs with unreported income, and to be more choosy about pay and other conditions before accepting a new job. The measured duration of job search rises in such circumstances, which has the effect of raising the recorded unemployment rate.

---

[2]K. Clarkson and R. Meiners, "Government Statistics as a Guide to Economic Policy: Food Stamps and the Spurious Increase in Unemployment Rates," *Policy Review*, Vol. 2 (Summer, 1977), pp. 25–51.

Second, unemployment compensation subsidizes employers that offer seasonal or unstable jobs. Without unemployment compensation, workers attracted to such firms would demand higher wages, and employers would try to develop production methods or work rules that stabilize employment. The costs of these adjustments would be shifted to consumers of the products of the affected industries, away from the general taxpayer. In so far as they would throw marginal workers out of jobs, however, they might increase the welfare rolls and hence raise the natural unemployment rate.

Martin Feldstein and other researchers on the effects of unemployment compensation have argued that the system raises the natural unemployment rate by about 1 percentage point. Putting this number together with the estimates of the effects on unemployment of food stamp and aid to dependent children programs, the natural rate of unemployment may be 1.5 to 3.5 percentage points higher than it would be without such social programs. If so, the unemployment rate in 1979, just before the onset of the 1980 economic turndown, would have been 2.3 to 4.3 percent instead of the measured rate of 5.8 percent of the civilian labor force.

If we add together frictional and structural unemployment (including the effects on unemployment of welfare and unemployment compensation), we get a fairly good approximation of the natural unemployment rate. Economists used to think that the natural unemployment rate was 3 to 4 percent of the labor force. Because of changes in the age–sex composition of the labor force, minimum wage laws, welfare, unemployment compensation, and other factors, estimates are now in the 5.5 to 6.5 percent range. Unless Congress changes the unemployment incentives built into tax laws, welfare and unemployment compensation systems, minimum wage laws, and the like, the natural rate probably will not return to the 3 to 4 percent range.

18.1.2
Cyclical unemployment

Unemployment arising from fluctuations in aggregate output around its long-run growth path is cyclical unemployment. Business cycle contractions raise unemployment above the natural rate. If business expansions are strong, they push it below, as indicated in Figure 18.3, a chart that features estimates of the natural rate of unemployment by Robert J. Gordon of Northwestern University.

Most cyclical unemployment comes from widespread layoffs that accompany declines in aggregate demand. As a result, it strikes experienced adult workers as well as new workers and reentrants into the labor force. Much cyclical unemployment would disappear if wages and product prices were flexible. In that event, adjustments in the excess demand for

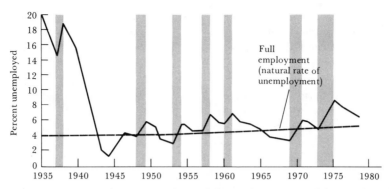

Figure 18.3 *Unemployment and instability in the aggregate labor market. Shaded areas represent periods of business recessions as defined by the National Bureau of Economic Research. (Source: James D. Gwartney and Richard Stroup,* Macroeconomics: Private and Public Choice *(New York: Academic Press, 1980), p. 137. The natural rate of unemployment is from Robert J. Gordon,* Macroeconomics *(Boston: Little, Brown, 1979).)*

real cash balances would be brought about by falling prices rather than by reductions in real income. But even if prices were to fall, rigid money wage rates would force employers to lay off workers rather than to carry on production at a loss. What tends to happen, of course, is that in many industries both prices and wages move slowly on the downside; hence, the decline in demand causes firms to reduce production and employment. If real aggregate demand stabilizes at a lower level, layoffs cease. In fact, some workers are usually rehired to restore inventories that may have fallen too low. But production and employment will not rise back to pre-recession levels unless by one means or another aggregate demand for a larger output is restored. In a noninflationary economy, this requires a drop in the price level or an increase in the money supply. In an inflationary economy, a slowing of the inflation rate relative to growth in the money supply is needed. Such a policy would prevent a recurrence of the excess demand for real money balances that might reappear at higher levels of real income.

In principle, cyclical unemployment is negative as well as positive. Negative cyclical unemployment occurs when the actual unemployment rate drops below the natural unemployment rate. It usually arises when an extraordinary increase in aggregate demand causes the inflation rate to accelerate. In that event, inflation and the unemployment rate move up and to the left along a short-run Phillips curve. Unless and until the curve begins to shift in a northeasterly direction, the negative cyclical unemployment rate can be maintained. But, as already discussed, good reasons exist for doubting the long-run stability of the Phillips curve. If the more rapid rate of inflation is maintained, changes in inflationary expectations are likely to shift the curve up and to the right.

18.2
Expectations-augmented Phillips curves and the accelerationist hypothesis

Inflationary expectations tend to converge to the actual inflation rate. If inflation is held steady for a long enough period, the short-run Phillips curve will shift until unemployment is such that the actual and expected inflation rates are equal—at the natural rate. At that point, the short-run Phillips curve crosses the vertical long-run curve built above the natural unemployment rate.

The process is illustrated in Figure 18.4. Assume that the initial actual rate of inflation is 10 percent a year and that the prevailing unemployment rate is 4 percent. This combination of inflation and unemployment a places the economy on the short-run Phillips curve SPC_1. The expected inflation rate $\dot{P}^e$ associated with SPC_1 is 8 percent. So unemployment is below the natural unemployment rate and inflationary expectations are below the rate of inflation actually being experienced. If the 10 percent rate of inflation is sustained, inflationary expectations should

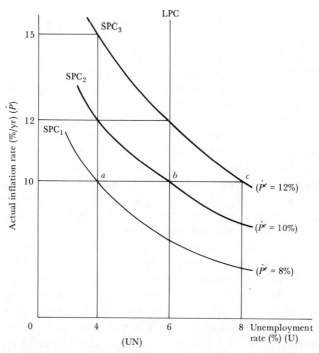

Figure 18.4 *Expectations-augmented Phillips curve and accelerationist hypothesis.* $\dot{P}^e =$ *expected inflation;* $UN =$ *natural unemployment rate.*

gradually rise. As they converge to 10 percent, unemployment will converge to 6 percent, to point b on SPC_2, the Phillips curve associated with inflationary expectations equal to 10 percent.

Assume now that the economy starts with an unemployment rate of 8 percent and an expected inflation rate of 12 percent—that is, that it is on point c of SPC_3. A sustained inflation rate of 10 percent should eventually lower inflationary expectations; once they reduce to the 10 percent rate, the Phillips curve will have shifted to SPC_2. So, whether we start with inflationary expectations higher or lower than the actual rate of inflation, the expectations-augmented Phillips curve theory argues that adjustments in inflationary expectations will bring the economy back to the natural rate of unemployment—defined, as you may recall, as an unemployment rate at which actual and expected wages and prices are equal.

The theory has two important policy implications. The first is that using inflation to stimulate the economy is eventually self-defeating, since sooner or later the expectation of inflation catches up with actual inflation. The second is that any attempt to hold unemployment below the natural rate will result in accelerating inflation. The *accelerationist hypothesis* is illustrated by Figure 18.4. An attempt to use monetary or fiscal policies to keep unemployment at 4 percent will cause the Phillips curve to shift up. If it goes to SPC_2, a 12 percent inflation rate would be required to hold unemployment at 4 percent of the labor force. A shift to SPC_3 would require a 15 percent inflation rate.

Now that we know the implications of the expectations-augmented Phillips curve, we must examine two important questions: (1) Why do the short-run Phillips curves have negative slopes? (2) How do people form inflationary expectations?

18.2.1
Why the short-run Phillips curve is negatively sloped

Most theories of the negative slope of the short-run Phillips curve emphasize temporary changes in real wage rates. Real wage rates are money wage rates corrected for changes in the purchasing power of money. When prices of goods and services outrun money wages, real wage rates fall; when prices rise more slowly than money wages, real wages rise. Falling real wages stimulate employers' demand for labor, and rising real wages lead firms to reduce offers of employment. The effect on workers, however, is the opposite. Rising real wages increase their offers to work, and falling real wages discourage their acceptance of jobs.

Economists studying the economics of job information and job search offer an interesting explanation for negatively sloped short-run Phillips curves. To illustrate their argument, we shall assume the economy is initially operating at a level consistent with the natural unemployment rate. At this point, most unemployment is frictional; its level depends upon the number of people looking for jobs and the average duration of their search. The number of people hunting for jobs depends on the number of new entrants and reentrants into the labor force and the number who have quit, been fired, or been laid off from jobs. But the time they spend searching for work depends upon a variety of factors, including their job and wage expectations and their financial resources for conducting job searches.

A worker starting the search for work usually has certain minimum standards for accepting a job. Included in these standards is a *reservation wage*. A reservation wage is a wage, other things being equal, below which a worker will refuse a job offer. Jobs offered at or above the reservation wage will be accepted. Although the reservation wage differs from worker to worker, it is easy to identify a number of factors affecting its level. These include the following: other job conditions; a worker's knowledge of wage conditions in his or her perceived labor market; the worker's financial resources, including savings, eligibility for unemployment compensation or welfare, and current earnings of the spouse or other family members; and the prices of food and other items making up the cost of living. Thus the reservation wage is a variable for each worker; it depends negatively upon the desirability of other conditions of employment and positively upon the worker's financial resources and the prices of food and other consumer goods. But knowledge about wages in the job market may increase or decrease the reservation wage, and the necessary knowledge is largely gained in the job search process.

The best strategy for unemployed workers is to adopt a reservation wage (subject to the acceptability of other job conditions) and continue to look for work until a job is found at or above that wage. Some workers are lucky enough to immediately find such jobs; but most look for some time. High reservation wages increase the average duration of job searches. Moreover, searching for work is costly. The wage (net of unemployment benefits) of each job turned down is an opportunity cost that must be assessed against the present value of the reservation wage. The reservation wage is chosen so that the expected marginal value of further search is just equated with the expected marginal cost of further search. For the average worker, the marginal cost of search is likely to increase with the value of the last job turned down, and the marginal benefit that further search may be expected to reveal is likely to fall. Thus the average duration of unemployment will be determined by the length of the job search process as determined by equality between the marginal costs and marginal benefits of further search.

Information turned up in the hunt for work may lead workers to adjust their reservation wages up or down. But the information may be unreliable; if so, workers may be misled by their job search strategies. For example, suppose an increase in aggregate demand raises the price level. Since employers are the first to experience the rise in prices, they will increase the number of job offers at prevailing wages. Workers not yet aware of the rise in prices will hold fast to existing reservation wages. At the same time, for reasons they do not understand, they will be uncovering and accepting more job opportunities at the prevailing structure of reservation wages. Thus, the average duration of job searches will shorten, and the unemployment rate will fall below the natural rate. The observing economist will note a movement up and to the left along the prevailing short-run Phillips curve.

A movement down and to the right on the short-run Phillips curve would follow an unexpected decline in the inflation rate. In that event, employers, seeing a rise in real wages, would reduce job offers and perhaps lay off workers. Unaware of the new economic environment, many unemployed workers would continue to search for jobs at prevailing reservation wages. Fewer job offers at the prevailing structure of reservation wages would increase the average duration of job searches and thus raise unemployment above the natural rate.

Eventually, changed conditions of demand would become apparent to the unemployed and alter their reservation wages. Thus the inflation-induced reductions of real wages that help push unemployment below the natural rate are eventually reversed when workers, discovering the rise in consumer prices, raise their reservation wages to fit the new conditions. Employers confronted with higher wage demands offer fewer jobs at the new structure of reservation wages. Thus, the short-run Phillips curve shifts up and unemployment converges to the natural rate. When a slowing of aggregate demand growth promotes a rise in real wages and increases in unemployment above the natural rate, the same process, in reverse, shifts the short-run Phillips curve down and to the left, for the drop in expected inflation lowers the structure of reservation wages. Employers find more job takers, and unemployment begins to revert to the natural rate.

Money wage rates tend to be sticky on the downside. Implicit and formal contracts between workers, unions, and employers ordinarily eliminate money wage cuts as a method of coping with declining demands. Contracts often commit employers to rises in wage rates over 2–3 year periods. In addition, cost-of-living clauses in contracts may keep wages rising in response to past inflation, even when current and expected inflation rates are dropping. Moreover, scheduled increases in legal minimum wages are immune to recessions. As a result, unemployment may stay above the natural rate for longer periods than would be the case if declining reservation wages of unemployed and unorganized workers dominated the supply side of the labor market.

Formal and informal contractual arrangements can, by delaying increases, reduce the flexibility of wages during periods of boom. Thus, wages are to some extent sticky on the upside as well as the down. Nevertheless, experience seems to show that for labor as a whole, wages are less flexible on the downside during recessions than they are on the upside during booms. Hence, as illustrated by Figure 18.3, cyclical unemployment below the natural unemployment rate is likely to be more short-lived than cyclical unemployment above the natural rate.

18.2.2
Adaptive expectations

Most economists now believe that short-run Phillips curves are unstable and that changes in inflationary expectations shift them up or down so as to produce a vertical long-run curve. But the eventual disappearance of a trade-off between unemployment and inflation has left unresolved the debate over macroeconomic stabilization policy. If inflationary expectations are slow to develop, stimulative policies can still produce significant dividends by pushing unemployment below (and national output above) levels dictated by the natural unemployment rate. The dividends may be worth the cost of the eventual acceleration of inflation. Also, slowly developing expectations could unacceptably increase the unemployment and output costs of a policy that seeks to lower the inflation rate. (See Section 20.1.4 for a deeper discussion of this issue.)

Both the benefits and costs of short-run macroeconomic stabilization policies are smaller when inflationary expectations change rapidly in response to changes in policy or changes in the prevailing inflation rate. Hence, the shorter the lag of expectations, the less persuasive is the case for stabilization policy. By the same token, the stronger is the case for steady-as-you-go measures that emphasize bringing inflation under control. Indeed, in the limiting case, immediate adaptation of inflationary expectations would completely destroy the case for short-run stabilization strategies, since such policies would be incapable of moving unemployment off the level dictated by the natural rate.

Economists disagree on how inflationary expectations are formed and how rapidly they respond to prevailing conditions. Until recently, most economists believed that expectations are formed adaptively. Adaptive expectations theorists say that people predict future inflation by extrapolating past inflationary trends. Since most people use past experiences as guides to the future, this theory has some intuitive appeal. Nevertheless, recent theoretical and empirical work has raised serious doubt about its validity.

Understanding these criticisms requires us to delve a bit deeper into adaptive expectations theory. Basically, the theory assumes that past inflation is *the only* information people use to formulate predictions of future inflation. Beyond that, it says little other than to assume that the weights people attach to inflation during various past periods are both stable and discoverable by econometric techniques. By implication, therefore, econometric studies should enable policy makers to assess the usefulness of short-run stabilization policies. For example, if econometric studies uncover small weights for recent inflation, and long lags, then a policy that stimulates current inflation is unlikely to disturb the short-run Phillips curve for several years. But if studies uncover large weights for recent inflation, and short lags, the stabilization policies are more likely to produce rapid shifts in the curve.

Studies using adaptive expectations worked well in the 1960s, but failed miserably in the 1970s. The studies predicted that the United States could reduce unemployment to 4 percent while sustaining an inflation rate of only 5–6 percent a year. Although there was some debate over how long this trade-off could be exploited, most economists believed that it provided a sound basis for stabilization policy. As Figure 18.1 shows, confidence in the trade-off was seriously misplaced; unemployment in the middle and late 1970s climbed well above 4 percent, and inflation rates associated with the higher unemployment rates also escalated.

18.2.3
Rational expectations

Thomas Sargent, Robert Lucas, and other members of the so-called *rational expectations school* think they know what went wrong. They point out that adaptive expectations theory is fundamentally flawed; it assumes that people use only the knowledge of past price trends to formulate predictions of future inflation. That means they make no effort to discover or use other information to revise their opinions. They therefore ignore theoretical information generated by economic research, empirical and other information released by private and public agencies through radio, television, and the press, and the stabilization policy strategies of the monetary or fiscal authorities. That is, they pay no attention to things like OPEC oil price increases, large jumps in the growth rate of the money supply, the pressures that build on the authorities for tax cuts during recessions, outbreaks of wars, and so forth. Ignoring such events is clearly irrational; it leads people into systematic forecasting errors that might have been avoided if they used information other than that contained in a string of past inflation experiences. After all, these experiences contain only limited information about the future, particularly when they include price increases that took place a number of years ago.

Systematic forecasting errors can be costly. Rational people try to improve their ability to predict the future; they invest time and money in collecting better information about the probable course of prices and other economic variables. The information includes expert opinion, the political climate, the policy strategies of the government, and so forth. Businesses and workers (through their unions) frequently hire professional economists to assist in the collection and interpretation of the data. They also study the press, which itself spends considerable effort in collecting and disseminating information and opinion about the future. Considering the large volume of information available for revising opinions on the future course of inflation, it is unlikely that economic actors confine themselves to an adaptive expectations scheme that produces systematic errors of judgement.

Rational expectations theorists assume that people use information efficiently. Efficiency is achieved by collecting information until systematic errors are reduced enough to make the acquisition of additional knowledge too expensive. Thus, people may not have the best possible predictions of the future, but they do eliminate much of the systematic error created by lack of information. What remains is a set of expectations surrounded by probability distributions largely reflecting unsystematic or random errors.

An interesting implication of this theory is that people's subjective probability distributions concerning future events are likely to resemble objective or actual probability distributions. This rather startling conclusion is an implication of the assumption of rationality. Large differences between subjective and objective probability distributions would introduce systematic errors and create incentives to seek additional information until the profits from the new learning are zero. Thus, although subjective and objective probability distributions are unlikely to match perfectly, rational economic agents will try to bring them as close together as economic incentives permit.

The short-run Phillips curve would disappear if fiscal and monetary shocks that change the rate of inflation were fully anticipated by business and labor. In that event, workers and employers would understand that the changes in demand experienced in their own labor and product markets were part of a more general rise in demand, and that wages and prices in their industries must adjust to the changes in the general price level. Hence, actual and expected inflation would more or less coincide; the aggregate demand shocks, having been anticipated, would have little effect upon the average real wage rate, relative product prices, or aggregate output and employment. Unemployment would remain at the natural rate.

In contrast, *unexpected* monetary and fiscal shocks would cause employment and output to change. Rational agents would not be able to distinguish between a rise in the demand for their services or products and a change in aggregate demand. Consequently, firms would be led to change output and prices on the assumption that the markets for their products are changing relative to the markets for other products. Workers, experiencing unexpected changes in the demand for their services, would not appreciably alter their reservation wages; hence, the changes in the demand for labor would impact directly upon the level of employment. Thus, rational expectations theory explains short-run Phillips curves by showing that they are consistent with unexpected aggregate demand shocks.

Rational expectations can rob macroeconomic stabilization policy of much of its bite. Unless policy makers can fool economic agents, they might fail to lower unemployment with stimulative monetary or fiscal shocks. But rational expectations theory implies that *systematic* attempts to fool the public are noticed by economic agents. For example, if the government typically follows up a rise in the unemployment rate with stimulative monetary policies, the agents learn to expect such policies and their inflationary consequences. In that event, workers and employers redo contracts and make other decisions that could destroy the increase in output and employment desired by the authorities. The government can, of course, change its policy strategy, but economic incentives stimulate people to collect information until the new policies are understood. In open societies like the United States, policy strategies are rarely secret; hence, the learning process probably takes little time.

The effect of rational expectations on the Phillips curve was recently illustrated in a study by Paul Anderson of the Federal Reserve Bank of Minneapolis. Using a small scale econometric model designed by the Federal Reserve Bank of St. Louis research staff, Anderson constructed two Phillips curves. Both curves assumed an initial unemployment rate of 5.8 percent and a starting inflation rate of 2 percent a year. But the first curve was built on the assumption of adaptive price expectations (assumed in the original version of the St. Louis model), while the second assumed rational expectations. Anderson then "shocked" the model by assuming a rise in money growth to 6 percent a year. The results are shown in Figure 18.5. The original version of the model (using adaptive expectations) displays a relatively flat Phillips curve, implying considerable policy leverage for reducing unemployment. In contrast, the rational expectations version throws off a steep curve, with little scope for policy to reduce unemployment.

18.2.4
Rational versus irrational expectations

Econometric studies like those reported by Anderson do not prove that economic agents actually form expectations rationally. Indeed, no study has yet done that. At best, the evidence shows that rationality cannot be rejected as an assumption of behavior. The evidence is consistent with other explanations of how expectations are formed, including so-called irrational adaptive schemes.

Criticisms of rational expectations abound. Although none has called for outright rejection of rationality, the idea has not remained untarnished.

One serious question is whether a sharp line separates systematic and unsystematic policies.[3] Modern democratic governments are probably un-

---

[3] The following ideas owe much to Gottfried Haberler, *Notes on Rational and Irrational Expectations*, American Enterprise Institute Reprint Series, 1980.

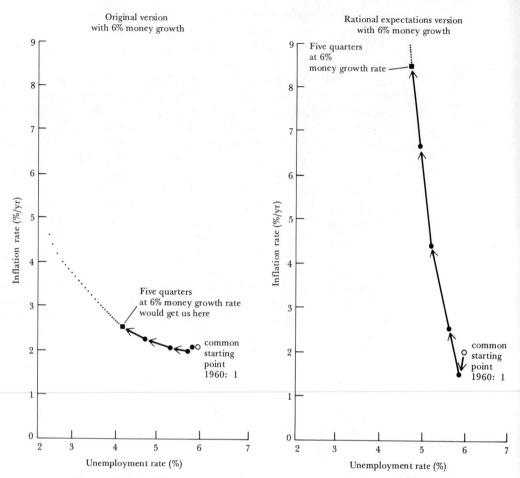

Figure 18.5 *Policy stimulation results using the St. Louis Federal Reserve Bank model. (Source:* Federal Reserve Bank of Minneapolis Annual Report, *1977.)*

able to pursue truly systematic and consistent monetary–fiscal policies. Systematic and unsystematic policies are usually intermingled in a way that defies simple division between the two categories. Moreover, multiple objectives, such as restoring full employment and guarding against deterioration of the external value of the currency, frequently conflict, so that even professional economists cannot always figure out what the authorities are doing. Government policies are usually spread out over a range; the question is one of more or less predictability, not one of either–or.

It follows that, as a matter of principle, it is impossible to demonstrate whether the business cycle is the result only of unsystematic and hence unpredicted policy shocks. Moreover, it is highly unlikely that private economic actors will interpret government policies in the same way and draw the same conclusions for the future. That would require them to hold the same economic model and that the model be an accurate description of the workings of the economy. Since professional economists are frequently divided on such matters, these assumptions are, to say the least, highly implausible.

Rational expectations theorists tend to ignore institutional rigidities, such as those found with many manufactured product prices and money wage rates. As discussed in Section 15.2.2, except in securities and basic commodities, flexprice markets are relatively rare in modern economies. Instead, informal and formal contractual arrangements and other factors make prices and wages slow to respond to shifts in demand. But rational expectations theorists heavily stress individuals' reactions to present and anticipated prices. Institutional impediments to these reactions give the authorities scope for pursuing systematic policies that exploit the lagged reactions.

These criticisms do not devastate the rational expectations theory. They simply take the edge off extreme claims. Short-run Phillips curves are likely to be the product of both unsystematic and systematic shocks. But the longer inflation lasts, the more "rational" economic actors are likely to become. For example, instead of continuing to pour time and money into fruitless attempts to improve predictions, they will demand inflation-indexed contracts. Although no price index can truly portray the price level taken as a whole, indexation of wage, credit, and other contracts adds considerable flexibility to the price structure. Insofar as it does, it takes some of the bite out of monetary–fiscal stabilization policies.

18.2.5
Policy implications—Friedman's money growth rule

The extreme form of the rational expectations theory implies that systematic monetary–fiscal policies cannot move an economy overcome by an unexpected demand or supply shock back to its long-run real growth path. The theory therefore implies that authorities should abandon short-run macroeconomic stabilization policies and, instead, pursue a steady-as-you-go policy.

An example of such a policy is the constant money growth rule proposed by Milton Friedman many years ago and still widely discussed. Friedman believes that the Federal Reserve authorities should choose and maintain a money growth rate consistent with some long-run inflation objective. For example, if the objective is a zero inflation rate, and if real output and the Cambridge k are both growing by 3 percent a year, the money growth rate would be 6 percent a year. If, on the other hand, the trend of the Cambridge k is zero, the rule would imply a 3 percent money growth rate. Different inflation objectives and growth rates of potential output and the Cambridge k would produce different growth rate rules. But the main point is that authorities should choose some particular money growth rate and stick to it, ignoring, at the same time, the temptation to fine-tune the economy in the short run.

Friedman suggested his policy rule as a method for preventing policy errors that he believes are endemic to the Federal Reserve System. The rational expectations theory does not assume incompetence among policy makers; instead, it relies upon the rationality of economic actors. Nonetheless, rational expectations theory cannot completely destroy the case for short-run stabilization policy if institutional rigidities, confusion over systematic and unsystematic policies, and other imperfections prevent economic actors from fully exploiting their capacity to learn about the future. Moreover, recent research has uncovered evidence that expectations may in fact be adaptive, although in ways that are more complicated than earlier studies assumed.[4] Although this research is incapable of rejecting rational expectations, it does indicate that expectations reported in surveys of professional economists appear to have been formulated upon the basis of past prices alone. If true of economic actors in general, the presence of such "irrationality" would support short-run stabilization policy based upon a Phillips curve trade-off.

Some economists use rational expectations to support the theory that the monetary authorities can wind down the long run inflation rate without seriously damaging the economy. Adoption of a steady money growth rule would presumably be eventually discovered and acted upon by economic agents. But market participants, including trade unions and other pressure groups are unlikely to moderate demands unless they are confident that the government will pursue its long-run policy without interruptions as soon as unemployment rises. If the monetary authorities persist in accommodating temporary inflationary surges arising out of supply shocks or extraordinary wage increases, it will lose credibility.

Thus "credibility" differs from "rationality" in an important respect. The rational expectations theory says that from studies of the policy record, the public infers systematic actions by government officials. The credibility hypothesis[5] states that the public can detect such a system only if the authorities *convince* market participants that it is behaving in a consistent fashion. That is, officials must take the guesswork out of the learning process so that people will not be confused by overlaps between systematic and nonsystematic policies. In that way, unions, for example, will learn to expect increases in unemployment for its members as a consequence of forcing employers to pay extra high wages. Similarly, businesses with monopoly power will expect to suffer loss of sales when de-

---

[4]R.L. Jacobs and R.A. Jones, "Price Expectations in the United States, 1947–1975," *American Economic Review*, Vol. 70, No. 3, June 1980, pp. 269–277.

[5]First discussed systematically by William Fellner, *Towards a Reconstruction of Macroeconomics, Problems of Theory and Policy* (Washington D.C.: American Enterprise Institute, 1976). Also discussed in Haberler, "Notes on Rational and Irrational Expectations."

manding outsized price increases for their products. Thus a *credible* policy to wind down inflation through devices such as Friedman's money growth rule may do much to lead the economy out of the stagflation trap.

SUMMARY

Disappearance of the negatively sloped long-run Phillips curve has caused economists to hypothesize the presence of a series of short-run Phillips curves, each dominated by a given state of inflationary expectations and a single, vertical long-run Phillips curve, characterized by equality between inflationary expectations and varying inflation rates. The vertical long-run curve is built over the natural unemployment rate. The natural unemployment rate is variously defined as the frictional–structural unemployment rate or as a rate such that, on the average, employers filling jobs and workers findings jobs are paying or getting the wages and prices they expect. The absence of disappointed expectations maintains the average duration of the search process and keeps unemployment at the frictional–structural level.

Cyclical variations of unemployment around the natural unemployment rate are said to develop from unanticipated aggregate demand shocks. These shocks fool both workers and employers into believing that the prices, wages, and output changes they are witnessing are special to their industries. As a result, unemployment falls or rises along given Phillips curves. But once expectations catch up with realities, the Phillips curves begin to move. So, inflationary shocks shift the curves up and to the right, while deflationary shocks move them down and to the left.

Two important policy implications of this theory are the following: (1) Policies that seek to reduce and maintain unemployment below the natural unemployment rate will lead to accelerating inflation. (2) Macroeconomic stabilization policies have temporary beneficial effects that are soon reversed by changing expectations.

The key to resolving disputes over the connection between inflation and unemployment lies in discovering how inflationary expectations are formed. Earlier theories relied upon simple adaptive expectations schemes that assume that people irrationally extrapolate past inflation into the future. Such behavior conflicts with rational economic behavior; it implies that people persistently hold to views that generate costly errors—errors that could be overcome by investing time and money in collecting information to correct them.

Such considerations have led to the rational expectations theory. The extreme form of this theory holds that people invest in information to the point that their subjective views of the probability distribution of economic events, including the actions of policymakers, are close to the actual probability distributions. This enables them to predict systematic policy actions and the consequences of the actions. As a result, there is little or no short-run trade-off between inflation and unemployment available for policymakers to exploit with systematic contracyclical stabilization policies.

The extreme form of rational expectations is unacceptable to many economists. While recognizing the contributions the theory has made to the understanding of how expectations are formed, they reject the notion that the public has the means to distinguish between systematic and unsystematic policies of the government. Moreover, they disagree that study of the economy necessarily leads people to hold the same economic model describing how policy actions affect the economy. Also, they believe that rational expectations, with its emphasis upon flexible prices, ignores institutional and other sources of wage–price rigidities. Finally, they add that winding down inflation without serious damage to the ecomony requires *credible* as well as predictable policies.

DISCUSSION QUESTIONS

1. What explains the negative slopes of short-run Phillips curves?

2. Why is the natural rate of unemployment defined by the sum of frictional and structural unemployment?

3. Why is the manner in which people form expectations of inflation critical to the successful conduct of monetary–fiscal policies to reduce cyclical unemployment?

4. What measures may be taken to reduce the natural unemployment rate? How do these measures compare with policies to reduce the cyclical unemployment rate?

5. In Chapter 15 it was argued that monetary shocks may be the basis for most past business cycles in the United States. How does this theory relate to the expectations-augmented Phillips curve theory?

6. Why does the strong form of the rational expectations hypothesis support Friedman's constant money growth rule?

IMPORTANT TERMS AND CONCEPTS

- ☐ acceleration hypothesis
- ☐ adaptive expectations
- ☐ credibility hypothesis
- ☐ cyclical unemployment
- ☐ expectations-augmented Phillips curve
- ☐ frictional unemployment
- ☐ long-run Phillips curve
- ☐ money growth rule
- ☐ natural unemployment rate
- ☐ Phillips curve
- ☐ rational expectations
- ☐ reservation wage
- ☐ short-run Phillips curve
- ☐ structural unemployment

Discussions of the unemployment–inflation trade-off appear in several of the citations at the end of Chapter 17, notably in the Gordon and Laidler-Parkin surveys of inflation theory. Additional suggestions are Milton Friedman, "The Role of Monetary Policy," *American Economic Review*, Vol. 58, No. 1, March 1968, pp. 1–17, and Edmund S. Phelps, *Inflation Policy and Unemployment* (New York: Norton, 1972). See also Thomas M. Humphrey, *Essays on Inflation,* 2nd edition (Richmond: Federal Reserve Bank of Richmond, 1980), pp. 62–82. An excellent textbook discussion of the problem is in Michael Darby, *Intermediate Macroeconomic Theory* (New York: McGraw-Hill, 1979), Chapter 14. Milton Friedman's Nobel Lecture, "Inflation and Unemployment," *Journal of Political Economy*, Vol. 85, No. 4, June 1977, carries the disturbing message that the long-run Phillips curve may actually be positively sloped, so that inflation increases the natural unemployment rate over the long run.

Discussions of the rational expectations challenge are legion. Start with Bennett T. McCallum, "The Significance of Rational Expectations Theory," *Challenge*, Vol. 22, No. 6, January/February 1980, pp. 37–43. Although a bit difficult for the normal undergraduate, a very useful follow-up piece is T. J. Sargent and N. Wallace, "Rational Expectations and the Theory of Economic Policy," *Journal of Monetary Economics*, Vol. 2, No. 2, April 1976, pp. 169–183. The Gordon survey piece in the same issue also contains a good discussion. A good survey is in Brian Kantor, "Rational Expectations and Economic Thought," *Journal of Economic Literature*, Vol. XVII, No. 4, December 1979, pp. 1422–1441. Also see Stanley Fischer (editor), *Rational Expectations and Economic Policy* (Chicago: University of Chicago Press, 1980). The extensive references cited in these pieces should satisfy the most ardent student of the subject.

Finally, a useful collection of papers by a number of economist-luminaries can be found in *After the Phillips Curve: Persistence of High Inflation and High Unemployment* (Boston: Federal Reserve Bank of Boston Conference Series No. 19, June 1978). This volume includes papers by Robert Lucas, Thomas Sargent, Franco Modigliani, Robert Solow, Benjamin Friedman, and several other participants in the policy debate.

Money, The Balance of Payments, and Exchange Rates

19

OUTLINE

Money and the Balance of Payments under Fixed Exchange Rates
The Balance of Payments between Regions of a Country
The Balance of Payments between Different Countries
The World Distribution of Money
Paper Money Standards
Restatement of the Theory
Policy Implications of the Monetary Theory of Balance of Payments
Flexible Exchange Rates and the Purchasing Power Parity Theory
Propositions of the Theory
Outline of the PPP Theory
Short-run Deviation of Exchange Rates from PPP
Empirical Tests of the PPP Theory
World Inflation

Monetary events have important influences upon the international balance of payments and exchange rates between national currencies. They often cause surpluses or deficits in a country's balance of payments, which, in turn, have further repercussions within the country. Monetary and fiscal policy is often directed to removing imbalances in the international accounts. The same is true of exchange rates, variations in which are often taken to be the source of domestic economic troubles. For these reasons, it is important to have the guidance of a theory that helps policymakers understand the causes of changes in the balance of payments and exchange rates and which comes to their aid when they seek to improve the international position of the dollar.

This chapter emphasizes the monetary approach to the balance of payments and exchange rates. It is an extension of the quantity theory of money outlined in Chapters 11–13. But in order to apply the quantity theory to the international sphere, it is best to divide it into two subjects. The first is the monetary theory of the balance of payments in a world with fixed exchange rates, such as existed much of the time in the nineteenth and twentieth centuries under the gold and gold exchange standards. The second subject is the monetary theory of exchange rates, designed to explain the effects of money on exchange rates in a world of floating or flexible exchange rates, such as has existed since 1973. This theory is frequently called the purchasing power parity theory of exchange rates. As we shall see, both theories are useful for the purpose of explaining the problem of world inflation, mentioned at the outset of Chapter 17.

19.1
Money and the balance of payments under fixed exchange rates

The balance of payments is the net result of transactions between people within a particular geographic location and people in other places. The transactions include goods, services, or securities. It is the practice of balance of payments theorists to divide transactions into two groups: (1) goods and services, that is, the current (or trade) account, and (2) securities, that is, the capital account. A current account surplus (frequently called a trade surplus) occurs when people in other locations spend more on local goods and services than the people at home spend on goods and services in other locations. A current account (trade) deficit occurs when local expenditures on outside goods and services exceed outside spending on local goods and services. A surplus (deficit) on the capital account is similarly defined as positive (negative) net sales of securities to people in other locations.

The sum of the surpluses or deficits on the current and capital accounts is called the balance of payments. Clearly, a balance of payments surplus implies a net inflow of money from the outside to local transactors; conversely, a balance of payments deficit implies an outflow of money from local transactors to people in other areas. Thus, balance of payments surpluses and deficits in a particular locality may be accompanied by local, and perhaps external, monetary shocks. These shocks, as we shall see, are a basis for adjustments within the local and outside economies, and perhaps for elimination of the balance of payments surpluses and deficits themselves. How this may come about is discussed in this section.

19.1.1
The balance of payments between regions of a country

Our principal goal in this section is to discuss the forces that eliminate balance of payments surpluses or deficits—the so-called adjustment problem. The main features of balance of payments adjustment are best introduced with an examination of interregional trade within a particular country. A country like the United States is, in effect, a common market. It has a common currency, a common language, and a common set of laws regulating interregional transactions. In addition, labor, capital, and commodities are free to move without restrictions, making it possible for people to benefit from profit opportunities throughout the country. These conditions free us to study the principles of balance of payments theory without the complications imposed by different currencies, languages, and laws that exist between nations.

A major idea connected with balance of payments theory is the *law of one price*. This "law" asserts that market forces will tend to bring about a single price for identical goods selling in different parts of a trading area. The market forces creating this tendency are based upon arbitraging activity. *Arbitrage* is an activity in which traders exploit existing price differences for particular goods in different locations. Such traders abound in market economies. They are constantly looking for profitable arbitraging opportunities. They buy up goods in low-priced areas and resell them in high-priced areas. As a result of this activity, prices in high-priced areas fall, and prices in low-priced areas rise. The process continues until, except for differences in transportation and other transactions costs, the prices of the same goods in all parts of the trading area are the same.

The law of one price applies best to standardized commodities—those for which arbitrage has the best chance of working. Commodity and financial markets are particularly good settings for the operation of the law. National markets in grain, metals, hides, Treasury bills, commercial paper, and so forth, keep prices for these goods similar throughout the country. Another setting for the operation of the law is a national market for standardized manufactured goods. These goods and their close substitutes are objects for profit-seeking arbitraging entrepreneurs.

Arbitrage does not work well in markets where there is little scope for entrepreneurial activity. Examples are the markets for various classes of labor and for risk capital. Yet, even in these markets there is a tendency for equalization of prices. The tendency is brought about by interregional movements of labor and capital instead of by arbitraging activity.

The monetary implication of the law of one price is that, except for the costs of moving goods and factors of production between regions, the purchasing power of a common currency tends to equality in all parts of a country. Thus, a dollar tends to buy roughly the same bundle of goods in all parts of the United States. The price level faced by people in each region is therefore determined by the supply and demand for money in the whole country.

The law of one price has an important bearing on interregional money flows. From a regional point of view, long-run differences between the supply and demand for money cannot be reconciled by price level adjustments within the region. Instead, adjustments must come from changing regional money holdings or regional levels of real income. It is these adjustments that cause inflows and outflows of money that alter the balance of payments of the regions.

To understand these adjustments, consider the following example (see Figure 19.1). Divide the United States into East and West. Assume that monetary equilibrium prevails in the country as a whole, but that monetary disequilibrium is present in both the East and the West. Since monetary equilibrium requires equality between the demand for and supply of existing cash balances, monetary equilibrium in the country as a whole cannot prevail without one region's excess demand for money equaling the other region's excess money supply. So, for the sake of argument, let excess demand for money in the West be offset by an equal excess supply of money in the East.

Given the common price level, people in the East and West must adjust to their respective monetary disequilibria by changing real expenditures. For example, to satisfy their desires for extra cash balances, Westerners must reduce expenditures on both domestic goods and upon imports from the East. The decrease in imports reduces money outflows to the East; the reduction of purchases of home goods releases goods for export, which brings in money from the East. In addition, the West reduces its net outflow of loanable funds, since to acquire additional cash, Westerners would tend to lend less to and borrow more from the East.

Taken together, the two components of the Wests's balance of payments would move the balance of payments as a whole into a surplus position. Indeed, it is the existence of a balance of payments surplus that enables the West to adapt to a regional excess demand for money. As

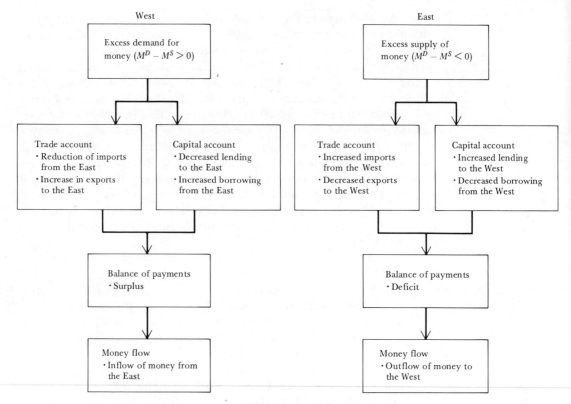

Figure 19.1 *Interregional balance of payment and money flows in a common market.*

money flows into the region, the gap between actual and desired holdings of money begins to close. In addition, some unemployment may develop from the drop in domestic expenditures on Western goods, lowering real income and Westerners' demand for money. Thus, the excess demand for money would ultimately be eliminated by monetary inflows and by a reduction in the demand for money in the West.

The balance of payments surplus in the West has its counterpart in a balance of payments deficit in the East. In adjusting to an excess regional supply of money, Easterners increase their imports of goods and spend more money on home production, which reduces goods available for export. At the same time, they lend more money to Westerners and borrow less. Thus, money flows out of the East to the Western part of the country; and the increased spending on Eastern goods raises Eastern real incomes. The rise in real incomes increases Easterners' desire to hold money, which helps close the gap between the demand for money and its excess supply.

The fall in real incomes in the West and the rise of real incomes in the East are accompanied by a West-to-East flow of labor and other productive factors. The flow maintains the level of real income in the country as a whole (except, perhaps, from some small loss in output due to somewhat higher frictional unemployment as labor and other factors search for work in unfamiliar places). As a result, the aggregate demand for money in the country as a whole need not change as a consequence of the employment changes taking place in the two regions. This being the case, the monetary flows between the regions need not disturb the aggregate monetary equilibrium for the country as a whole.

Other things being equal, the money flows between East and West should result in a balance of payments equilibrium. The equilibrium is characterized by equality in each region of the sum of payments to and from the other region for goods, services, and financial securities. But the force that secures the equilibrium is equality in each region of the demand for and supply of money. Without monetary equilibrium, one or more items in the balance of payments would be out of equilibrium, setting in motion interregional monetary flows and adjustments in regional demands for money. The flows and adjustments would continue until monetary equilibrium is achieved.

Thus, balance of payments equilibrium and monetary equilibrium are two sides of the same coin. Balance of payments equilibrium in each region requires monetary equilibrium in each region and vice versa. The reader will undoubtedly note that such a requirement is nothing more than an application of Say's Principle, discussed in Chapter 11.

19.1.2
The balance of payments between
different countries

Extending balance of payments theory to the international scene is relatively simple, though it does call for a few modifications. The first is the recognition of different currencies. Each country has its own medium of exchange and its own monetary control mechanism. Prices of goods bought at home are quoted in terms of the national medium of exchange. The exchange rates between national monies may be fixed by the authorities, or permitted to float in response to market forces. In this section we assume they are fixed.

In former times, countries fixed exchange rates by defining their currencies in terms of gold. For example, the British pound used to buy 4 times as much gold as did the American dollar. So the exchange rate of dollars for pounds was 4 to 1. In seeking to buy British goods, Americans first had to sell dollars and buy pounds. Selling too many dollars for pounds tended to raise the price of pounds above $4.00. At some point it paid for Americans to buy gold and to sell it for pounds at the official price. Shipping gold instead of dollars maintained the official exchange rate in the neighborhood of 4:1, but it also reduced the U.S. monetary base. In Britain, the monetary base was increased.

The reverse sequence occurred when the British sought American goods. They had to buy dollars with pounds. If the purchases raised the pound price of dollars above the official exchange rate, they would use their pounds to buy gold and sell the gold to Americans for dollars at the official gold price. Thus, gold would flow out of Britain into the United States, reducing the British monetary base and increasing the U.S. base.

Under the gold standard, domestic money supplies were closely linked to the domestic gold supply. The latter provided a good portion of total bank reserves. So, by expanding or contracting domestic bank reserves, international gold flows were capable of producing significant changes in domestic money supplies.

Of course, gold was not the sole determinant of the domestic money supply. The monetary base was also influenced by central bank credit and by Treasury currency issues. Moreover, in each country changes in bank reserve–deposit ratios and the public's currency–deposit ratios could alter domestic money multipliers. Nevertheless, the pledge of each country to maintain the gold price of its currency so as to produce fixed exchange rates with other currencies provided a disciplining device. The only way the pledge could be honored without endangering the domestic gold reserve was for the monetary authorities to keep rein on the amount of deposits or currency in circulation. An excessive money stock would sooner or later lead to gold purchases by citizens seeking to buy foreign goods and services or foreign securities. The gold purchases would drain the domestic gold reserve and weaken the country's ability to sustain its foreign trade. Eventually, a responsible authority would be forced into actions designed to slow internal monetary expansion.

The gold standard broke down in the 1930s. In its place emerged a gold exchange standard that lasted until 1971. Under this standard, the dollar was fixed in terms of gold, and other currencies were defined in terms of the dollar. The dollar was used alongside gold by most countries as a reserve for international payments. This peculiar arrangement came about as a result of the chaotic financial conditions of the Great Depression and World War II, during which time the United States acquired most of the world's gold. So, to solve the resulting gold shortage, countries began using the dollar in international trade. Since the U.S. Treasury promised to buy and sell gold at the price of $35.00 per ounce, the dollar was as good as gold and widely acceptable as an international reserve asset.

To study the workings of the international balance of payments system, we shall initially assume the existence of an international gold standard. This assumption, which we relax below, helps bridge the gap between interregional and international balance of payments theory.

Assuming existence of an international gold standard is tantamount to assuming a global money supply. Strictly adhered to, an international gold standard ties domestic money creation to domestic gold reserves. When these reserves expand or contract with favorable or unfavorable balances of payments, so too do domestic money supplies. Monetary authorities that do not permit international gold flows to change domestic money supplies are simply not playing the gold standard game; they stand outside the pale of our present analysis.

The global money supply is the sum total of domestic money supplies. If each currency is defined as equal to the same amount of gold, the global money supply is calculated by simple addition of the money supplies of each country. But if each currency defines itself differently in terms of gold, we must weigh each currency in terms of a common unit before adding them together. Using the dollar as the common unit, and assuming that each British pound is worth $4, we can calculate the British contribution to the world money supply by multiplying the number of pounds in circulation times four. Doing this for every other currency, and adding them all to the U.S. money stock, we arrive at the global money stock.

Parallel to the global money stock is the idea of an international price level. This price level is assumed to emerge in the long run out of the interaction of the global demand for money with the global money stock. Although unanticipated short-run variations in the world money supply may cause cyclical changes in the level of world output and employment, these variations would not necessarily cause permanent changes in the worldwide natural unemployment rate nor in the worldwide level of production connected with the natural rate. That is, once people are aware of a given change in the money supply, equality will emerge between desired and actual cash holdings and between anticipated and actual levels of money prices. Therefore, given world output and the global money supply, there should eventually emerge an equilibrium international price level applicable to every country.

The international price level applies to all tradable goods and, in more or less degree, to the substitutes for these goods. Since the range of tradable goods is rather large, so too is the range of substitutes. Hence, except for international price differences brought about by transportation costs, official trade barriers or other hindrances to the movements of goods and people, a unit of currency should have the same purchasing power wherever it is spent. That is, a British pound should buy roughly the same quantity of goods whether it is spent in Britain or, after being exchanged for dollars, it is spent in the United States. The same would be true of dollars, pesos, rubles, or any other national currency.

Thus, the law of one price should operate internationally as well as nationally. It is kept in force by two mechanisms. The first is entrepreneurial arbitraging, already discussed in Section 19.1.1. Although information is frequently less available internationally than nationally, profit opportunities from arbitraging goods or securities will eventually attract business people at home and abroad to make transactions that iron out international price differences.

The second mechanism is short-run money flows. When prices of similar goods differ between countries, people sell goods to the high-priced countries and buy goods from the low-priced countries. Thus, gold is transferred to countries with low prices away from countries with high prices. Since price levels in countries move in proportion to changes in domestic money stocks, the gold movements will force a convergence of price levels of each country to a common level—that is, to the international price level. Once this level is reached, the gold movements will stop. In effect, every country will be experiencing the price level appropriate to the given global money stock and global money demand.

The basic ingredients of an international balance of payments theory are now in place. The existing population, capital stock, and technology of each country determines its full employment level of output. Assuming that in each country the Cambridge k is fixed, the real demand for money multiplied by the world price level, adjusted by the exchange rate, equals the nominal demand for money. The nominal demand for money compared with the nominal supply of money sets in motion forces that result in a favorable or unfavorable balance of payments.

For example, if the nominal demand for money in the United States exceeds the existing money stock, Americans will attempt to increase their exports and reduce their imports of goods, services, or securities. That is, the national excess demand for money will be accompanied by a national excess supply of nonmonetary commodities. This condition will lead to a surplus in the U.S. balance of payments—an inflow of gold.

Similar reasoning implies that an excess national supply of money is accompanied by an excess demand for nonmonetary commodities from the rest of the world. As the country acquires foreign goods, services, or securities, its balance of payments turns unfavorable, and it loses gold.

19.1.3
The world distribution of money

The monetary theory of the balance of payments implies the existence of forces that, left to operate under given conditions, eventually produce a balance of payments equilibrium for each country. Assume that the existing global demand for money is in equilibrium with the global money supply, but that two or more countries are experiencing balance of payments disequilibria. Such a situation would imply that the balance of payments disequilibria are the result of a maldistribution of the world's money supply.

A maldistribution exists if the stock of money in two or more countries differs from the amount demanded in each of those countries. For example, if the excess demand for money in the United States is positive, the excess demand for money in one or more foreign countries must be negative; money must be flowing into the United States from abroad. The observing economist would find a favorable (surplus) balance of payments for the United States, and an unfavorable (deficit) balance of payments for the other countries (as a whole). But since the defining characteristic of a balance of payments disequilibrium is a gold flow, the disequilibria will eventually disappear if the overall equilibrium between the global demand for and supply of money stays undisturbed. Sooner or later, the gold flowing into the United States eliminates its aggregate excess demand for money. Once that happens, the national excess supply of nonmonetary commodities and securities disappears. At the same time, the deficit in the rest of the world's balance of payments also disappears, implying monetary equilibrium for countries outside the United States.

Since elimination of the maldistribution of money occurs once the excess demand for money in each country is zero, it follows that the equilibrium distribution of the money stock between countries cannot be affected by monetary policy. For example, suppose a government draws on nationalized gold mines to increase the country's domestic money supply. Other things being equal, this act creates an excess supply of money within the country. Part of the excess supply is spent upon imports and part on goods previously destined for export; another part is lent abroad. The ensuing balance of payments deficit scatters the new money over the rest of the world. As a result, the world money supply and the world price level rise. But the distribution of the new money ultimately depends upon the demand for money in various countries. Countries with large demands get the most; countries with small demands get the least. Once the world price level has risen in proportion to the increased global money stock, the demand for money in each country determines the equilibrium distribution of the stock.

19.1.4
Paper money standards

A world with paper currency standards instead of a gold standard would operate in much the same way as described above, provided, of course, that monetary authorities in each country limit the amount of national monies in circulation. Assuming that international agreements would fix exchange rates between countries, central banks would stand ready to buy foreign monies with domestic monies at the fixed exchange rates. Thus, currency outflows from countries with balance of payments deficits would reduce domestic money supplies in deficit countries and increase money supplies of surplus countries. The world price level, measured in terms of one of the currencies, would be determined by the global supply and demand for money. Assuming a fixed world money supply, the system would ultimately produce an equilibrium distribution of the stock of paper money.

To be sure, a worldwide monetary equilibrium with a paper currency world is something of a pipe dream. Without some sort of discipline, such as that provided by an international gold standard, governments would have a great incentive to expand domestic money supplies. The increased money would encourage citizens to expand imports and to buy goods previously destined for export. Thus, internal money creation would be a route to increasing national consumption beyond national production, at the expense of the rest of the world. Since each country would have an incentive to do the same thing, the result would be a competitive expansion in domestic and world money, with world inflation as a consequence. As we shall discuss in Section 19.1.5, something of this sort went on under the gold exchange standard that broke down in the early 1970s.

19.1.5
Restatement of the theory

Although the verbal statement of the monetary theory of the balance of payments is relatively clear, it helps to have a symbolic representation of the model. To make it simple, assume we are dealing with a system with two countries, a fixed exchange rate, and domestic money supplies under control of the monetary authorities. The authorities, in turn, are committed to play the "gold standard game"; that is, they let domestic money supplies rise and fall with expansions and contractions in their foreign exchange (perhaps gold) reserves.

We start with a statement of the global quantity theory of money. Let an asterisk refer to the foreign country and the exchange rate between home and foreign currency be designated X. The M and P refer to money stocks and price levels, respectively, the y denotes real income, the R stands for international reserves, the C is domestically created portions of the domestic money supplies, and the subscript w stands for the world:

$$P_w = P = XP^* \quad \text{(world price level and the law of one price)} \tag{19.1}$$

$$M^d = kPy \quad \text{and} \quad M^{d*} = k^*P^*y^* \quad \text{(home and foreign demand for money)} \tag{19.2}$$

$$M_w^d = kPy + k^*(P/X)y^* \quad \text{(world demand for money)} \tag{19.2a}$$

$$M = C + R \quad \text{and} \quad M^* = C^* + R^* \text{(home and foreign money supplies)} \tag{19.3}$$

$$M_w = M + XM^* \text{(world money supply)} \tag{19.4}$$

As it stands, the system is capable of determining the equilibrium world price level. Recall that the simple quantity theory states that the price level is determined by the ratio of the nominal money supply to the demand for real money balances. Putting this into a world context, we have

$$P_w = \frac{M_w}{m_w^d} \qquad (19.5)$$

where $m_w^d \, (= M_w^d/P)$ is the world demand for real balances. Now, substitute terms from Equations (19.1), (19.2), (19.2a), and (19.4) into (19.5) and scale the exchange rate so the $X = 1$. The result is

$$P_w = \frac{M + M^*}{ky + k^* y^*} \qquad (19.6)$$

So, the world price level is, in the long run, determined simply by the money supplies, production levels, and real demands for money in all the countries. Moreover, Equation (19.6) makes it clear that domestic monetary expansion in any country can raise the world price level. That is, in a fixed exchange rate world, the domestic monetary authority of any given country is capable of setting in motion a worldwide inflation. What may stop this from happening is a limited supply of international reserves. Domestic monetary expansion by an individual country exposes it to risk of reserve losses. If other countries are not also expanding their money supplies, the country will eventually run out of reserves. Long before that happens, the country will either cease internal monetary expansion or borrow from abroad. Borrowed reserves, however, reduce the ability of foreigners to buy goods; hence, from a global point of view, international borrowing is not inflationary.

An interesting and exceptional case occurs when the currency of an expanding country is used by other countries as international reserves. In that event, the reserve currency country can run continuous balance of payments deficits without fearing retribution from the rest of the world. In so doing, of course, the reserve currency country is positioned to start a worldwide inflation. The United States played such a role during the 1960s. Eventually, however, the world became overstuffed with dollars and began demanding gold from the U. S. Treasury, which promised to pay out gold at the fixed rate of $35 per ounce. U.S. gold reserves declined to a point (about $12 billion) that threatened its reserve currency position. A large run on the dollar by foreign countries could well have wiped out the whole gold reserve. At that point (August 1971), the United States went off the gold exchange standard and cancelled its promise to sell gold. Soon afterwards (1973), the whole fixed exchange rate system broke down, a victim of overexpansion of the U.S. money supply.

To carry the theoretical statement forward, we need three more sets of equations: money stock adjustment equations; balance of payments equations; and domestic expenditure equations.

To write the money stock adjustment equations, let $\dot{M}$ refer to the rate of change of money holdings per unit of time, and A represent an adjustment coefficient that expresses the speed at which money balances flow into or out of a country in response to an excess demand or supply of money:

$$\dot{M} = A(M^d - M) \quad \text{and} \quad \dot{M}^* = A^* (M^d - M^*);$$
$$A \text{ and } A^* \text{ between 0 and 1} \tag{19.7}$$

The closer A is to unity, the faster the adjustment. If it is unity, the excess demand or supply of money is gone within one period. If it is close to zero, the adjustment takes many periods.

The balance of payments equations link changes in the money supply to changes in international reserves and the payments balance Z. Thus, if domestic monetary authorities do not interfere with the impact of payments disequilibria on reserve flows and the domestic money supply, we have $Z = \dot{R} = \dot{M}$. That is, a surplus (deficit) in the balance of payments equals flows of reserves which raise (lower) the money supply. Moreover, if the world has a given amount of international reserves, we have $Z = -XZ^*$, or the home country's surplus equals the foreign country's deficit. This permits us to write a complete balance of payments equation:

$$Z = -XZ^* = \dot{M} = \dot{R} = -X\dot{M}^* = -X\dot{R}^* \tag{19.8}$$

Thus, by definition, the balance of payments surplus of one country is the balance of payments deficit of the other; the movement of reserves from one country to the other brings about this equality. The reserve flows, in turn, are driven by adjustments of domestic money supplies to domestic money demands. So, in the last analysis, the balance of payments between countries is the allocation mechanism that distributes a given global money stock across countries.

Finally, we can complete the model by stating the relationship between domestic expenditures and money inflows and outflows. Let y^d be domestic spending on both domestic and foreign commodities. If y is real income domestically produced, we can write

$$P (y^d - y) = -\dot{M} \quad \text{and} \quad P^* (y^{d*} - y^*) = -\dot{M}^* \tag{19.9}$$

Thus, if money is flowing out of the country (the national excess demand for money is negative), domestic expenditure exceeds domestic output. If money is flowing into the country (national excess demand for money is positive), domestic expenditure falls short of domestic production. It therefore follows that a global balance of payments equilibrium implies (1) income equilibrium in each country (that is, $y^d - y = y^{d*} - y^* = 0$) and (2) monetary equilibrium (that is, $\dot{M} = \dot{M}^* = 0$).[1]

Thomas M. Humphrey, from whom much of this analysis has been borrowed,[2] summarizes the monetary model of the balance of payments as follows:

1. The world stock of money determines the world price level.

2. International arbitrage brings national price levels into equality with world price levels for a given exchange rate.

3. National price levels determine national nominal demands for money.

4. National money demands in conjunction with national money supplies determine the rate of money stock adjustment.

5. Money stock adjustment determines spending, trade balances, and the direction and volume of international money flows.

6. This process continues until the equilibrium international distribution of money is achieved, and money market equilibrium is restored in each country. At this point, the system is said to be in a steady-state equilibrium.

19.1.6
Policy implications of the monetary theory of balance of payments[3]

The monetary theory of the balance of payments has some surprising policy implications. The implications are of particular relevance to small

---

[1]We have left out the securities markets; however, by Say's Principle, zero excess demands for money and commodities implies zero excess demand for foreign securities. In the short run, of course, it is possible to have balance of payments equilibrium without income equilibrium in each country, since deficits or surpluses of commodity trade balances—that is, $y^d - y \neq 0$—can be financed with foreign borrowing or lending. In the long run, however, no country would be willing to lend to another country indefinitely, and the borrowing country would be forced to pay up. Of course, political intervention may delay or indefinitely put off repayment, in which case a borrowing country may run continuous trade deficits without losing international reserves.

[2]"A Monetarist Model of World Inflation and the Balance of Payments," *Federal Reserve Bank of Richmond Economic Review*, November/December 1976. Reprinted in Humphrey's *Essays on Inflation*, 2nd edition (Richmond: Federal Reserve Bank of Richmond, 1980), pp. 100–109.

[3]This section relies heavily on Humphrey, ibid.

countries operating in a world of fixed exchange rates. Although they do not apply with equal force to large countries, or to a world with floating exchange rates, it is still instructive to discuss them.

The first implication is that policies designed to affect the balance of payments are unnecessary and, in the long run, useless. They are unnecessary because the automatic operation of the international adjustment mechanism eventually corrects balance of payments surpluses and deficits. They are useless because it is the public's demand for money, not the policies of the monetary authorities, that determines the international allocation of money and, hence, the balance of payments of each country.

For example, suppose the authorities of a country try to improve its balance of payments by devaluing its currency. Devaluing a currency means raising the domestic currency price of foreign currencies (or gold). In the short run, a devaluation raises the home currency prices of imports. But the law of one price says that prices must adjust so as to equate the purchasing power of currency in all markets. Assuming the devaluation does not affect the foreign price level, as would be the case for a small country, arbitrage eventually raises the prices of domestic goods in the same proportion as the devaluation. The higher price level, in turn, causes a temporary balance of payments surplus, because it creates an excess nominal demand for domestic money. But the favorable balance of payments disappears once monetary inflows from abroad have satisfied the excess demand for money. Thus, the long-run effect of the devaluation is to raise the domestic price level; but no permanent improvement in the balance of payments remains.

A second implication of the theory is that domestic monetary authorities in small countries cannot control the domestic money supply. This implication flows directly from the fact that internal monetary policies create excess demands for or supplies of money. Since an excess demand for money causes a balance of payments surplus, and an excess supply of money causes a balance of payments deficit, external monetary inflows and outflows offset the changes in the money supplies attempted by policy makers.

A third implication, closely related to the second, is that balance of payments deficits are usually the fault of domestic monetary authorities. There can be no balance of payments deficits without excessive domestic monetary growth. The latter comes about when domestic monetary authorities expand money supplies more rapidly in relation to money demand than do foreign authorities. Failure to keep track of, and to adapt to, foreign monetary policies can thus lead to chronic balance of payments disequilibria.

A fourth policy implication is that in a world of fixed exchange rates, small countries cannot control domestic price levels or rates of inflation. The law of one price links domestic prices to the world level, and the growth of the global money supply determines the international rate of inflation. The only way a small country can avoid importing world inflation is to force up the international value of its money. For each percentage point increase in world prices, it must lower the home currency price of foreign exchange by an equal amount. In that way, goods sold abroad continue to yield the same home currency prices and arbitragers are unable to increase domestic prices in line with the higher foreign prices.

Finally, to choose an inflation rate that differs from the world inflation rate requires a country to adopt a flexible (or floating) exchange rate. To see this, assume that a country has an initial zero payments balance and that its domestic price level is rising at the same rate as that of the world. Now, suppose the authorities decide to lower the domestic inflation rate. To do this, they must reduce the domestic monetary growth rate below that of the rest of the world. In so doing, of course, they create at home an excess demand for domestic currency. Residents adjust to the deficiency of money by buying fewer foreign goods and increasing sales abroad. In so doing, they increase the inflow of foreign exchange and decrease the outflow of home currency, causing emergence of a favorable payments balance.

In a fixed exchange rate world, a favorable balance of payments causes the money supply to rise to satisfy the excess demand for home currency. But, if exchange rates are flexible, the home currency instead simply rises in value on foreign exchange markets. The rise in value is caused by the decreased outflow of home currency and the increased inflow of foreign currency to the foreign exchange markets. Faced with a relative shortage of the home currency, foreign exchange traders let the price of the home currency rise in terms of foreign currencies, which, by raising its international value, lowers the exchange rate.

A restrictive domestic monetary policy that causes a reduction of the exchange rate will (by the law of one price) also cause a reduction in the domestic inflation rate relative to the rate in the rest of the world. At the same time, the fall in the exchange rate promotes equilibrium in the balance of payments. This comes about because the slowing of domestic inflation reduces the growth rate of the demand for nominal money balances. Once the level of money demand falls into equality with the money supply, the exchange rate will cease to fall. At that point, the monetary authorities can maintain the lower monetary growth rate without fear of losing control over the domestic inflation rate. Thus, domestic inflation can be kept below international inflation with appropriate policies.

Most of the above policy implications apply to small countries with open economies. But a large country, like the United States, has more control over its domestic money supply and price level, even in a fixed exchange rate world. The reason is quite simple. A large country makes a large contribution to the global money stock, hence a significant change in its domestic money supply can have a pronounced effect upon the world price level. In the days of the gold–dollar exchange standard, large increases in the U.S. money supply tended to raise domestic and foreign price levels rather directly. In raising domestic price levels, the increase in the money stock also raised the domestic U.S. demand for nominal dollars, which had the effect of reducing the excess supply of dollars and softening the blow to the balance of payments.

The mechanism by which increases in the U.S. money supply raised the world money supply was related to its role as a reserve currency. Dollars flowing abroad from U.S. trade deficits were bought by foreign central banks from their citizens, in order to maintain fixed exchange rates. The central banks then bought U.S. Treasury bonds to hold as international reserve assets. Thus the U.S. trade deficits were largely offset by inflows of capital from foreign central bank loans, leaving less of a deficit in the U.S. balance of payments (the sum of the trade and capital account balances) and only a minor negative impact on the U.S. money stock. In the meantime, however, foreign central bank purchases of dollars from their own banks or residents increased their domestic monetary bases, which had the effect of converting the initial U.S. dollar outflow into increases in the stocks of foreign monies. Hence, the use of dollar assets as international reserves caused central banks to set in motion forces that augmented the global money supply effects of changes in the stock of U.S. dollars.

19.2
Flexible exchange rates and the purchasing power parity theory

Although the dollar still retains some of its previous reserve currency role, it is no longer bound to other currencies by fixed exchange rates. Instead, exchange rates fluctuate in response to market forces, and central banks are to a large extent free to control the growth rates of their internal money supplies. In these circumstances, the monetary theory of the balance of payments is less useful. Instead, we need a theory that explains fluctuations in international exchange rates. Fortunately, such a theory is readily constructed with the materials provided earlier in this chapter. The monetary approach to the balance of payments combines easily with an ancient doctrine called the purchasing power parity (PPP) theory. This theory and its extensions are capable of explaining the movements of international exchange rates between national currencies over both the short and the long run.

19.2.1
Propositions of the PPP theory

In a world of flexible exchange rates, countries are free to determine their own price levels. Given internal demands for real money balances, internal price levels eventually adjust to domestic money supplies as determined by domestic monetary policies. Monetary authorities frequently choose policies that result in different price levels. But different price levels in terms of a particular currency cannot persist in a world with international trade. Currencies are valued for what they can buy; a situation will not last in which a currency can buy more or better goods in one country than in another. For example, if prices are such that a dollar can buy more or better Japanese goods than American goods, people will tend to buy Japanese goods and avoid American goods, which will lead them to sell dollars and buy yen. Thus, holders of low-valued currencies (of countries where prices are high) will seek to convert their monies into high-valued currencies (of countries where prices are low). The excess demand for high-valued currencies will drive up their exchange rates until the advantage gained from purchasing goods in those countries is eliminated. At that point, the exchange rate between the currencies will match the ratio of price levels between the countries.

The main proposition of the PPP theory is that, in the long-run, exchange rates adjust to the relative purchasing powers of different national currencies. Moreover, since internal purchasing powers of currencies are determined by relative demands and supplies of domestic currencies, exchange rates are ultimately determined by the factors that affect the demand for money (for example, real income and interest rates) and the money supply in each country. Thus the purchasing power parity theory asserts that, apart from internal monetary policies, or policies that affect long-term economic growth, authorities ultimately have little scope for manipulating exchange rates.

19.2.2
Outline of the PPP theory

The PPP theory starts with the proposition that in the long run the nominal value of exports of goods and services will tend to equal the nominal value of imports. For this to occur, the *relative* price levels of the two countries (measured in terms of a given currency) must equal the terms of trade, T. The terms of trade is a measure of the real goods given up through exports per unit of goods acquired through imports.

To see this, let Q stand for exported goods, and Q^* stand for imported goods. A country's balance of trade equilibrium would be defined as $PQ = XP^*Q^*$, where X is the rate of exchange (for example, the dollar price of pounds) that converts foreign prices, P^*, into prices expressed in terms of the domestic currency, P. This equation permits us to write the relationship between the equilibrium exchange rate and the equilibrium ratio of national price levels:

$$X = \frac{PQ}{P^*Q^*} = \frac{TP}{P^*}, \quad \text{where} \quad T = \frac{Q}{Q^*} \tag{19.10}$$

In this equation, T represents the *barter terms of trade*—if there were no money, goods would trade between countries in the ratio, T. Thus, T represents the relative scarcities of goods in different countries. If home country goods are relatively more scarce than foreign goods, residents of the home country will require more than a unit of imports per unit of exports, and T will be less than unity. Conversely, relative abundance of home country goods will force T above unity. Thus, in the final analysis, the barter terms of trade represents the real factors affecting the supply and demand for goods throughout the world.

The exchange rate between currencies reflects both the relative scarcities of home and foreign goods and relative price levels. The long-run exchange rate will differ from the terms of trade only as the ratio of the relative price level differs from unity. Thus, our next task is to set out the equations that determine the individual and relative price levels.

From Section 12.1.3, we know that equilibrium internal price levels equal the ratios of nominal money supplies to real money demands:

$$P = \frac{M}{m^d} \quad \text{and} \quad P^* = \frac{M^*}{m^{d*}} \tag{19.11}$$

Using the Cambridge equation, $m^d = ky$, and taking the ratio of domestic to foreign prices, we have

$$\frac{P}{P^*} = \frac{M}{M^*} \frac{k^*}{k} \frac{y^*}{y} \tag{19.12}$$

Thus, in the long run, the ratio of price levels is determined by the ratio of home to foreign money supplies and (given home and foreign values for the Cambridge k) the ratio of real foreign output to domestic output.

Note that Equation (19.12) defines the long-run equilibrium ratio of relative prices without reference to the exchange rate. Flexibility of the exchange rate permits each country to determine its own equilibrium price level. So, instead of determining relative price levels, the exchange rate must itself be determined by relative price levels. That is, the line of causation must run from internal real and monetary conditions to internal price levels to the exchange rate, not the other way around. Hence, combining Equation (19.12) with Equation (19.10), we have Equation (19.13), which shows that the exchange rate is determined by the terms of trade, output, and monetary demand and supply conditions in each country:

$$X = T \; \frac{M}{M^*} \; \frac{k^*}{k} \; \frac{y^*}{y} \tag{19.13}$$

19.2.3
Short-run deviation of exchange rates from PPP[4]

Equation (19.13) describes the factors determining the long-run equilibrium exchange rate. The factors are those that determine relative equilibrium price levels. Equilibrium price levels are ones under which the actual and expected purchasing power of money are the same. Given this condition, people have no reason to change the proportions of money they hold to their nominal incomes—that is, the Cambridge k is stable. In the short run, however, expected and actual price levels differ. In that event, inflationary expectations take hold and force people into actions that move exchange rates away from the equilibrium values predicted by the PPP theory.

The short-run theory of exchange rates acknowledges the significance of inflationary expectations by showing that (1) changes in nominal interest rates change the Cambridge k in various countries, (2) nominal interest rates between countries are changed when inflationary expectations change, and (3) inflationary expectations change when expected monetary policies change.

Using the notation of Equation (13.8)—in Section 13.2.4—we can set forth the relationship in home and foreign countries between the nominal interest rate, r, the real interest rate, rr, and the expected rate of inflation, $\dot{p}^e$:

$$r = rr + \dot{p}^e \quad \text{and} \quad r^* = rr^* + \dot{p}^{e*} \tag{19.14}$$

Equations (19.14) are built around the Fisher effect (Section 13.2.4), which states that nominal interest rates equal the real rate of interest and the expected inflation rate. The real rate of interest is, of course, deter-

---

[4]Much of this section follows T.M. Humphrey and T.H. Lawler, "Factors Determining Exchange Rates: A Simple Model and Empirical Tests," *Federal Reserve Bank of Richmond Economic Review*, Vol. 63, No. 3, May/June 1977, p. 10. Reprinted in Humphrey, *Essays on Inflation*, pp. 110–115.

mined by supply and demand for loanable funds in each country. But, except for differences in risks and the cost of transporting loanable funds between markets, competition for borrowing and lending on an international scale ought to equalize the real rate of interest. (This is merely a statement of the law of one price as applied to bonds.) But people do not readily lend to foreigners if they expect a high rate of inflation abroad to erode the purchasing power of the principle sum of their loans. For that reason, nominal interest rates must adjust to reflect expected inflation rates in each country. So, even though real interest rates (adjusted for differential risks and transactions costs) may be equal between countries, nominal interest rates will differ if inflationary expectations differ between countries.

International traders and lenders are particularly sensitive to domestic monetary policies. For this reason, we can, without seriously misrepresenting the truth, argue that inflationary expectations in each country are formed by traders' and lenders' expectations of excessive monetary growth. The higher the expected excess monetary growth rate, the higher will be the expected rate of inflation. If excessive monetary growth is measured by the expected rate of growth of the ratio of money to real output (l^e), we can write equations for expected inflation for home and foreign countries as

$$\dot{p}^e = l^e \quad \text{and} \quad \dot{p}^{e*} = l^{e*} \tag{19.15}$$

Combining equations (19.14) and (19.15) allows us to write.

$$r = rr + l^e \quad \text{and} \quad r^* = rr^* + l^{e*} \tag{19.16}$$

So, in the short run, and abstracting from factors relating risks and costs of lending (that is, assuming equality between real interest rates), nominal interest rates differ between countries by an amount equal to differences in expected excess growth rates of the money supply.

To finish the model, we apply Equation (19.16) to the demand for money as affected in each country by the nominal interest rate and the level of real income. That is, where $k = k(r)$ in each country, we combine Equation (19.16) with (19.13) to get

$$X = T \frac{M}{M^*} \frac{k^*(rr^* + l^{e*})}{k(rr + l^e)} \frac{y^*}{y} \tag{19.17}$$

Equation (19.17) recognizes that the exchange rate is determined by real factors, such as the terms of trade, relative preferences for money holdings, relative interest rates, and relative output levels. But it also takes into account monetary policies, as denoted by the ratio of national money supplies, and private expectations about the future of monetary policies, as denoted by expected excess monetary growth rates.

The theory predicts that a country's exchange rate will rise when its domestic money supply, adjusted for changes in its domestic demand for money, rises relative to the demand-adjusted change in the money supply abroad. Since the demand for money rises with increases in real output, the theory predicts a fall in the exchange rate when domestic output rises faster than output abroad. This particular prediction contradicts the usual notion that a rise in domestic output encourages imports and, as a result, depreciates the country's currency by weakening the balance of trade. But the quantity theory of money implies that an increase in the demand for money lowers the domestic price level. Assuming no changes in foreign money demand, the demand-induced drop in the domestic price level lowers the ratio of domestic to foreign prices, improving its currency's value by lowering the exchange rate. In brief, the theory simply extends the notion that a rise in a country's demand for money increases the value of its money stock; it does so in terms of foreign as well as domestic goods.

Expectational factors influence the exchange rate via the nominal rate of interest. Expectations of inflationary actions by domestic authorities, relative to actions of foreign authorities, raise nominal interest rates relative to those abroad. The rise in rates shrinks the domestic demand for money relative to foreign money demand, causing a rise in domestic prices relative to foreign prices. In the process, the exchange rate rises to reflect the new purchasing power parity. Again, this prediction runs counter to the commonly held view that a rise in domestic interest rates relative to those abroad improves the balance of payments and, hence, lowers the exchange rate. The conventional opinion asserts that the rise in interest rates attracts foreign capital and discourages domestic spending on imports, improving both the capital account and the trade balance, leading to an appreciation of (rise in the international value) the domestic currency. But a rise in interest rates encourages people to reduce money holdings, which speeds up the velocity of money, tending to raise, not lower, prices. Thus, a rise in nominal interest rates due to inflationary expectations tends to raise the ratio of domestic to foreign prices and to depreciate the international value of the currency.

19.2.4
Empirical tests of the PPP theory

Since 1973 flexible exchange rates have prevailed in international financial markets. Although frequent attempts by monetary authorities in the United States and abroad to stabilize exchange rates occasionally keep the rates from reflecting market forces, enough experience now exists to provide materials for testing the theory discussed in this chapter.

Broadly speaking, the empirical evidence supports the theory. Figure 19.2, for example, shows that, on the whole, the exchange rate of the dollar (measured in terms of its ability to buy foreign currencies—$1/X$ in terms of the notation used in this book), followed the changes in the ratio of foreign to domestic prices. Nevertheless, it is also clear that some of the variations in the exchange rate failed to reflect the changes in price ratios. To that extent, the data are inconsistent with the simple version of the purchasing power parity theory.

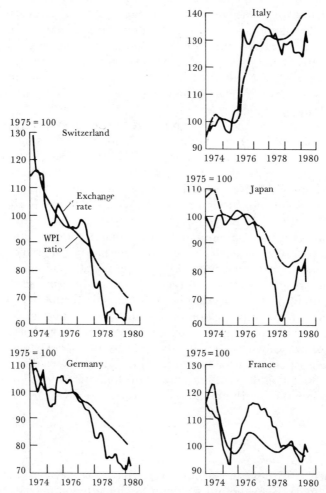

Figure 19.2 *A comparison of exchange rates and prices. Exchange rate is the foreign currency price of the dollar. WPI ratio is foreign prices divided by U.S. prices, using wholesale price indexes to measure prices. (Source: Michael Keran and Stephen Zeldes, "Effects of Monetary Disturbances on Exchange Rates, Inflation and Interest Rates," Federal Reserve Bank of San Francisco Economic Review, Spring 1980.)*

Deviations of exchange rates from purchasing power parity may be partly explained by expectations. For example, if current monetary policies create the impression that in the future domestic inflation will worsen relative to inflation abroad, commodity and capital market traders will expect a worsening of the exchange rate in the future. This expectation leads them to reduce holdings of domestic monetary and other financial assets in favor of foreign assets. As a result, the value of the domestic currency in terms of foreign currencies may drop, even though current purchasing power ratios are predicting stronger values.

Evidence consistent with this view is given in Figure 19.3. A rise in

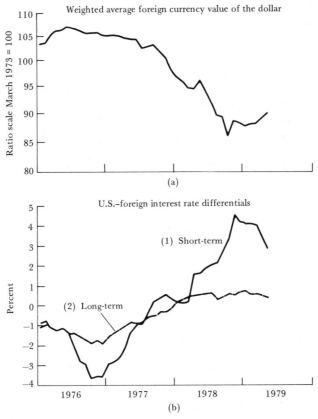

Figure 19.3 *Foreign exchange value of the U.S. dollar and interest rate differentials. (1) Secondary market rates for 90-day large certificates of deposit in the United States less the weighted average of foreign 3-month money market dates. (2) U.S. long-term government bond yields less the weighted average of foreign long-term government bond yields. Latest data plotted May 1979. (Source: Federal Reserve Statistical Release H. 13;* Federal Reserve Bulletin; *International Monetary Fund;* International Financial Statistics, *cited in D. R. Mudd, "Do Rising U.S. Interest Rates Imply a Stronger U.S. Dollar?"* Federal Reserve Bank of St. Louis Review, *June 1979.)*

inflationary expectations for the domestic economy relative to those abroad should (1) raise domestic nominal interest rates relative to those abroad and (2) lower the value of the domestic currency relative to foreign currencies, even though relative price levels are predicting a stronger value for the home currency. Figure 19.3a shows a drop of more than 15 percent of the international value of the dollar in the period mid-1976 to early 1979. At the same time, the gap between U.S. interest rates and foreign interest rates rose dramatically. The swing in the short-term interest rate gap was about 7.5 percentage points, while the long-term interest rate gap rose by almost 3 percentage points. All this movement took place against the background of a U.S. inflation rate that was actually below that of the rest of the world.[5]

Although inflationary expectations may exert a strong influence on exchange rates, expectations arising out of uncertain general economic and political conditions may provoke behaviors that move the rates away from levels predicted by purchasing power parity. The 1970s were especially chaotic. Highly variable inflation rates, uncertainties about oil and food prices, strains in international political and economic relations, and uncertainties about general economic policies create feelings of unrest among voters and economic actors. In these circumstances, the dollar and other currencies are prey to internal or external events that upset the calculations and expectations of capital holders and of companies that do business abroad. News that carries promises or threats to change the tariffs, quotas, or the underlying terms of trade between countries can upset current exchange rates by provoking capital flows from one country to another. It is quite possible, therefore, that the decline of the dollar in the late 1970s reflected, at least in part, market participants' uncertainties about the course of U.S. domestic and international economic and military policies.

Finally, it is important to note that departures of exchange rates from purchasing power parity may in fact reflect the beginnings of long-term economic, social, or political changes in the various countries. Examples of such changes are discoveries or depletions of natural resources; widespread increases in labor costs due to strong labor movements; political chaos that disrupts or corrupts productive and commercial activity; permanent changes in tariffs, quotas, or border taxes; and changes in transportation costs (such as those brought about by energy price increases). These factors can cause permanent changes in exchange rates quite apart from changes in relative price levels as determined by mone-

---

[5]For example, data from the International Monetary Fund indicate that inflation measured by consumer prices during 1972–1975 and 1975–1978 was 25 to 40 percent lower in the United States than it was in the rest of the world.

tary changes. They show themselves in the effects they have upon the terms of trade or the relative output capacities of different countries.

In the last analysis, a country's exchange rate is like a grade on a report card. The better its economic, political, and social conditions relative to other countries, the stronger will be the international standing of its currency. Bad policies, a worsening economic climate, or chaotic political conditions will sooner or later be reflected in a weakened currency. Thus, the opinions of residents and people abroad about a country's overall performance ultimately find expression in the rate of exchange between its own currency and foreign currencies.

19.3
World inflation

We end this chapter with a brief discussion of world inflation in the 1960s and 1970s. This period is especially interesting because it contains a broad range of experience relevant to the monetary theories of the balance of payments and exchange rates.

During the 1960s the world was on a dollar–gold exchange standard, with exchange rates pegged to levels determined by monetary authorities. This standard was gradually undermined by monetary and fiscal policies in the United States and some other countries, so that during the late 1960s inflation and speculative international capital outflows forced devaluations of the British pound and the currencies of a few other important trading countries. In 1971, the dollar came under attack and President Nixon stopped Treasury gold sales, an act that destroyed the gold–exchange standard. Attempts to create a substitute fixed exchange rate system failed. Since 1973, the world has been operating with a flexible exchange rate system, modified from time to time by attempts of monetary authorities to stabilize rates through official market interventions.

As we have seen, under fixed exchange rates, inflationary domestic money policies cause changes in both domestic and world price levels. Excess supplies of money spill over into other countries and force up the world price level. As a result, inflation rates between trading countries should be roughly similar. In contrast, floating exchange rates give countries a means to insulate themselves at least partially from inflationary policies originating abroad. The inflation they actually experience, therefore, is more likely to be the result of domestic policies than of policies of other countries. This being the case, the inflationary experience of the 1960s and 1970s should provide materials to test the validity of the basic monetary approach to international finance.

The data displayed in Figures 19.4 and 19.5 illustrate the kinds of materials that may be used to test the theory. The seven industrial coun-

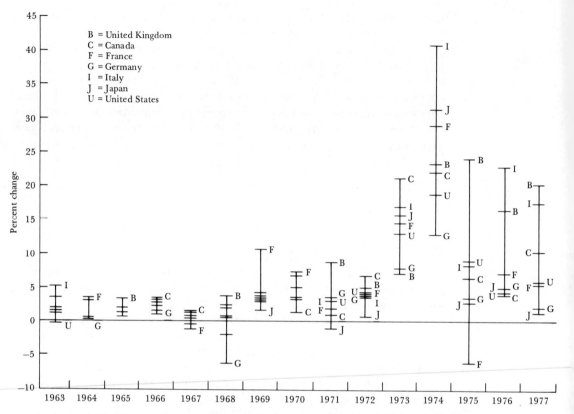

Figure 19.4 *Yearly percent change in wholesale prices for seven industrial countries, 1963–1977. (Source: Norman S. Fielke, "The International Transmission of Inflation,"* Managed Exchange-Rate Flexibility: The Recent Experience *(Federal Reserve Bank of Boston), Conference Series No. 20, October 1978.)*

tries portrayed in Figure 19.4 carry on a good deal of trade with one another and with nonindustrialized countries. During the fixed exchange rate period of the early and middle 1960s, the inflation rates of the countries were relatively close, as might be expected from the theory. Note that the price indexes used in the chart measure average rates of change in wholesale prices, so they are also more heavily weighted with internationally traded goods than would be indexes that measure consumer prices.

As might be expected, the rates of change in wholesale prices began to diverge as countries adjusted exchange rates in response to balance of payments difficulties in the late 1960s. Finally, in the 1970s, particularly after establishment of the floating rate system, the variation of wholesale price movements between countries became very large. The large variation of price changes indicates that, for reasons of their own, monetary

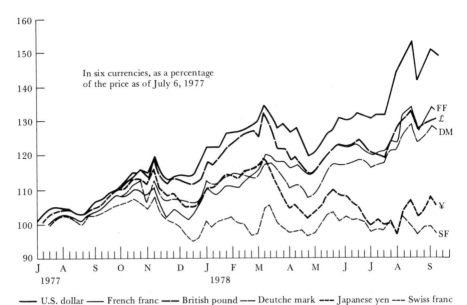

In six currencies, as a percentage
of the price as of July 6, 1977

——— U.S. dollar ——— French franc —— British pound —— Deutche mark --- Japanese yen --- Swiss franc

Figure 19.5 *The price of gold. (Source: Roy W. Jastram, "Gold and Floating Curren-cies,"* The Wall Street Journal, *November 18, 1978. Reprinted by permission of* The Wall Street Journal, © *Dow Jones & Company, Inc. 1978. All rights reserved.)*

authorities in the different countries chose very different inflation rates. Had they chosen similar inflation rates, the observed variation in inflation rates would have been much smaller.

Wholesale price indexes contain many goods that are not traded in-ternationally; hence, their short-run fluctuations reflect internal as well as external factors. Gold is perhaps the most widely traded good in the world. When exchange rates were fixed, its price moved down by the same percentage in whatever currency it was quoted. Under floating ex-change rates, however, its foreign currency price fluctuates because (1) dollar prices of gold go up and down and (2) foreign currency–dollar exchange rates fluctuate. This fact is demonstrated in Figure 19.5, which shows the changes in the price of gold in terms of six major currencies during the period July 1977–September 1978. The chart gives a convinc-ing illustration of the effects on the price of an internationally traded good when countries pursue different monetary policies under floating exchange rates.

SUMMARY

The monetary approach to balance of payments and exchange rate the-ory is an application of the quantity theory of money to the international scene. Balance of payments theory pertains to a world in which exchange rates between national currencies are fixed, either because the world is operating on a gold standard or because countries using paper currencies have agreed to maintain fixed exchange rates.

With fixed exchange rates, it is possible to calculate a global money supply expressing the value of different domestic money supplies in terms of just one of the currencies. It is also possible to define a global demand for money. Equality between global demand and supply of money is the condition for global monetary equilibrium. The world price level is determined by the ratio of the nominal global money supply to the real global demand for money (as determined by the level of real global income and the global rate of interest). The law of one price assures that in the long-run the price level and interest rate in each country will be the same as the world price level and the world interest rate.

Balance of payments disequilibria arise out of discrepancies between the demand and supply of money in various countries. Countries with excess supplies of money experience balance of payments deficits—net inflows of nonmonetary commodities and securities. Countries with excess demands for money experience balance of payments surpluses—net outflows of nonmonetary commodities and securities. Monetary outflows accompany balance of payments deficits, and monetary inflows accompany balance of payments surpluses. Hence, other things being equal, international monetary flows eventually bring about monetary and balance of payments equilibria in all countries. In the last analysis, therefore, the theory implies that basic conditions of production and national demands for money determine the international distribution of currencies. Except in large countries, domestic monetary authorities are denied the power to influence the balance of payments through manipulation of domestic money supplies or domestic interest rates. In addition, they have little power to influence domestic income, employment, or price levels.

Application of the above theory to a world of floating exchange rates produces the purchasing power parity (PPP) theory of exchange rates. The PPP theory states that, in the long-run, exchange rates must adjust to equalize the relative purchasing power of money between countries. That is to say, exchange rates must settle down to a point where, except for the terms of trade and the cost of transporting goods, they equal the ratio of price levels between goods produced and sold in the countries.

The price level of goods in each country is determined by the supply and demand for money. The demand for money, in turn, depends upon production and the nominal interest rates in each country. Nominal interest rates are the sum of real interest rates and expected inflation rates in each country. Since the law of one price states that, except for risk and the cost of borrowing and lending, real interest rates between countries tend to equality, differences in expected inflation are an important reason for divergencies of nominal interest rates between countries.

Given the terms of trade, the demand for money in each country, the nominal interest rate, and domestic output in each country, the exchange rate depends upon the ratio of national money supplies. Changes in the ratio of national money supplies change the ratio of national price levels, in which case traders have an incentive to spend money in countries with lower price levels. Their actions bid up the domestic prices of the currencies of low-priced countries and raise the exchange rates (lower the international values of the currencies) of high-price countries. Exchange rates will fall for countries whose outputs grow faster than those of other countries, and will fall for countries whose interest rates are rising relative to other countries.

Deviations from purchasing power parity frequently arise from traders' reactions to monetary policies or from domestic and world conditions that affect countries' prospective economic health. Chaotic conditions and inflationary domestic policies during the 1970s caused exchange rates to diverge in the short run from levels predicted by the PPP theory.

The theories discussed in this chapter help explain world inflation in the 1960s and 1970s. During the fixed exchange rate years of the 1960s, wholesale price movements between major trading countries were fairly close, as would be predicted by the monetary balance of payments theory. Since 1973, exchange rates have floated; consistent with the PPP theory, wholesale price index movements have varied widely between countries, as has the price of gold measured in terms of different currencies.

DISCUSSION QUESTIONS

1. The United States and other countries have frequently been accused of "exporting inflation." What evidence would be needed to evaluate such a charge? Can a country export inflation in a world with floating exchange rates?

2. As an exercise, use the monetary theory of the balance of payments to describe the impact on the balance of payments, the domestic price level and/or domestic output of (a) an increase in tariffs on foreign imports; (b) a subsidy on exports to foreign countries; and (c) imposition of a quota on imports of goods from abroad. (In your answers assume a fixed exchange rate.)

3. Use the purchasing power parity theory to describe the probable impact of OPEC oil price increases on exchange rates in the 1970s.

4. What happens to the concepts of the world money supply and the world price level under conditions of floating exchange rates?

5. Why do fixed exchange rates destroy the ability of domestic monetary authorities in small countries with open economies to control their domestic money supplies?

6. The purchasing power parity theory of exchange rates predicts a fall in the international value of a currency whose interest rates are rising relative to those abroad; yet we frequently observe the opposite, especially in the short run. Does such an observation disprove the theory?

IMPORTANT TERMS AND CONCEPTS

- [ ] arbitrage
- [ ] balance of payments
- [ ] capital account balance
- [ ] devaluation of a currency
- [ ] equilibrium world distribution of money
- [ ] fixed exchange rate
- [ ] flexible (floating) exchange rates
- [ ] global (or world) demand for money
- [ ] global money supply

- [ ] gold standard
- [ ] gold-exchange standard
- [ ] international price level
- [ ] law of one price
- [ ] monetary theory of the balance of payments
- [ ] paper standard
- [ ] purchasing power parity theory
- [ ] reserve currency
- [ ] terms of trade
- [ ] trade (current account) balance

ADDITIONAL READINGS

An enormous literature has developed over the last 10 years on balance of payments and exchange rate theories. The monetary approach, featured in this chapter, is still controversial and, as is illustrated in Sections 19.2.3 and 19.2.4, is unable to provide a comprehensive explanation for international events. Nonetheless, substantial agreement exists that the approach is essential to understanding long-term movements in international payments and exchange rates.

Beginners in this subject can gain much from the series of articles on the monetary approach written by Thomas M. Humphrey and published in his *Essays on Inflation*, 2nd edition (Richmond: Federal Reserve Bank of Richmond, 1980). A more advanced collection of papers by major figures in the field (John Bilson, Rudiger Dornbusch, Jacob Frenkel, and Michael Mussa) is in J.A. Frenkel and H.G. Johnson (editors), *The Economics of Exchange Rates* (Reading, Mass.: Addison-Wesley, 1978). Advanced students should also consult M. E. Kreinen and L. H. Officer, *The Monetary Approach to the Balance of Payments: A Survey* (Princeton: International Finance Section, Department of Economics, Princeton University, Princeton Studies in International Finance No. 43) and L. H. Officer, "The Purchasing Power Parity Theory of Exchange Rates," *International Monetary Fund Staff Papers*, March 1976.

Reviews of the experience with flexible exchange rates in the 1970s are in J. A. Frenkel, "Flexible Exchange Rates in the 1970s," *Stabilization Policies: Lessons From the 70s and Implications for the 80s* (St. Louis: Center for the Study of American Business and Federal Reserve Bank of St. Louis, April 1980), and in Rudiger Dornbusch, "Exchange Rate Economics: Where Do We Stand?" *Brookings Papers on Economic Activity*, 1:1980, pp. 143–185.

Students interested in broader historical and doctrinal issues should consult Leland Yeager, *International Monetary Relations: Theory, History, and Policy*, 2nd edition (New York: Harper and Row, 1976).

20

New Views on Stabilization Policies

O U T L I N E

Brief Review of Empirical Evidence on Policy Activism
Fiscal–Monetary Policy Multipliers
Forecasting Errors
Rules versus Activism
The Costs and Benefits of Eliminating Inflation
The Credibility Effect and Gradual Policies for Controlling Inflation
The Credibility Effect, the German Hyperinflation, and the Fed
Incomes Policies
Can Democracy Tame Inflation?
Representative Government, the Political Business Cycle, and Economic Stabilization
Breaking the Boundaries of Government Power
Restoring the Boundaries—Keeping the Budget in Line
Restoring the Boundaries—Keeping the Fed in Line

The events of the 1970s produced a remarkable change in the attitudes of many professional economists and government officials about the ability of the government to iron out short-run economic fluctuations in the economy. In the 1960s, the apparent success of the 1964 Kennedy–Johnson tax cut had convinced most important policymakers that the government can and should manage aggregate demand (with fiscal policy as the primary tool) so as to eliminate the business cycle. Perhaps moved by excessive enthusiasm, Walter Heller, President Kennedy's chief economic advisor and architect of what was called the "New Economics," wrote in 1966 that "We must now take it for granted that the government must step in to provide the essential stability at high levels of employment and growth that the market mechanism, left alone, cannot deliver."[1]

By 1980, Heller's widely accepted optimistic view had changed to a widely held pessimistic view. In a strongly worded bipartisan statement, the 1980 *Midyear Report* of the Joint Economic Committee of Congress condemned monetary–fiscal activism and, instead, called for tax and other policies that would "improve the structure and performance of the economy over the long run." The Committee's report was based upon a study of the federal government's response to six recessions since World War II. The study convinced the Committee and its staff that monetary–fiscal policies have been unreliable instruments for "fine tuning" the economy and that, in some cases, they actually damaged the economy by overstimulating economic recoveries.

With monetary–fiscal policy fine-tuning in disrepute, many observers and policymakers turned to so-called supply-side remedies for the country's economic woes. The proposed remedies included changes in business and personal income taxes and establishment of new government agencies designed to upgrade and enlarge the nation's capital stock and to improve the skills and employability of the labor force. The Reagan Administration in its first six months in office in 1981 won Congressional support for a supply-side tax cut program.

Many aspects of the new attitudes towards short-run stabilization policies were discussed in the professional economics literature of the 1960s and 1970s. Criticisms of activist monetary policies were anticipated by Milton Friedman and Anna J. Schwartz in their monumental *Monetary History of the United States* (1963). This book, along with other studies by Friedman and his followers, attempted to establish the case for a constant money growth rule (see Section 18.2.5). Similar studies by monetarists, particularly those located in the research department of the Federal Reserve Bank of St. Louis, challenged the power of fiscal policy instruments as compared to the power of monetary policy instruments. By the mid-1970s most economists agreed that monetary policy was at least as powerful as fiscal policy. But, by then, the debate had shifted to the question

---

[1]Walter Heller, *New Dimensions of Political Economy* (New York: Norton, 1966), p. 9.

of whether stabilization policy itself, no matter what policy instruments are used, can be effective. The issues here concerned the stability of the Phillips curve trade-off of inflation and unemployment, the ability of the political process to produce the right policies and the ability of policymakers to make accurate forecasts of the economy. As we have seen, it also involved the issue of whether a public, with rationally held expectations, can frustrate the best intentions of the monetary–fiscal authorities.

This chapter provides a brief summary of a number of the professional discussions of the stabilization issue. In addition, it surveys the question of where we go from here. In discussing this question, we shall touch upon a variety of proposals made by economists to ease our way out of the current unsatisfactory state of the economy into a more stable economic world.

20.1
Brief review of empirical evidence on policy activism[2]

The empirical evidence on policy activism is difficult to interpret. Nevertheless, it is useful to discuss briefly the kinds of evidence economists use to develop judgments about the effectiveness of monetary–fiscal policies as tools for stabilizing the economy. The evidence concerns (1) the size of so-called fiscal and money multipliers (that is, the degree to which dollar changes in government spending, taxes, or private bank reserves lead to changes in real gross national product); (2) the ability of policymakers to make good economic forecasts; (3) the relative merits of constant growth rate rules versus policy activism; and (4) the costs and benefits of attempting to solve inflation or unemployment with demand management policies.

20.1.1
Fiscal–monetary policy multipliers

In recent years economists have built a number of large-scale econometric models designed to study the behavior of the economy. The models reflect theoretical views on how real income, prices, interest rates, and other variables react to fiscal and monetary policies. Researchers test their theoretical views by trying to fit the various models to the economy with the

---

[2]This section draws heavily on L. Meyer and R. Rasche, "Empirical Evidence on the Effects of Stabilization Policies," Federal Reserve Bank of St. Louis and Center For the Study of American Business, *Stabilization Policies: Lessons from the 70s and Implications for the 80s* (1980), and Robert J. Gordon, "What Can Stabilization Policy Achieve?" *American Economic Review*, Vol. 68, No. 2, May 1978, pp. 335–341.

use of past data. If the fitting of a particular model survives certain statistical tests, it is assumed to be a valid description of the economy and of the way in which policy instruments affect its behavior.[3] Economists can then proceed to study the effects of policy on the economy by feeding hypothetical changes in fiscal or monetary policy variables into the computer and inspecting on computer readouts the effects of the changes on real gross national product, prices, interest rates, and other dependent variables. These so-called *simulation studies* are then reported to policy-makers, who use them along with other information to come to policy decisions.

The major products of policy simulations are fiscal and monetary policy multipliers. Fiscal policy multipliers measure the change in real gross national product that may be expected from policy-induced shifts in taxes or government spending. For example, a government expenditure multiplier measures the change in real GNP per dollar of change in real government spending on final product. Similarly, a tax multiplier measures the change in real GNP per dollar change in a legislated cut in (say) personal income taxes. Monetary policy multipliers measure the change in real GNP per dollar change in unborrowed reserves, the monetary base, or some other monetary aggregate assumed to be the operating policy target of the monetary authorities.

Meyer and Rasche studied the time pattern and size of policy multipliers from seven major econometric models. When averaged together, the government expenditure multipliers estimated from the models showed a rise from a little over 1.25 in the first quarter after a policy change to a cumulative rise of 2.25 after two years. Thereafter, a decline set in; after five years the average multiplier was just a little over 1. Unfortunately, the multipliers reported by the different models varied so much that their mean values are suspect, particularly for periods in excess of three years. One model, produced by the Federal Reserve Bank of St. Louis, reported a government expenditure multiplier of .5 for one year, followed by slightly negative cumulative values for later years, which, given the usual statistical errors, probably indicates a zero overall cumulative effect of changes in government spending on real GNP.

The tax multipliers studied by Meyer and Rasche were smaller than the government expenditure multipliers; they increased from an initial mean value of .67 to a peak value of 1.5 at the end of the second year, falling thereafter to 1.25 after four years. Again, the agreement between the models is not high; the St. Louis model, in fact, produced a zero value for the tax multiplier.

The monetary policy multipliers in the models depended for the most part on unborrowed bank reserves as the policy variable. The multipliers for early quarters were small, but built up to quite large average

---

[3]But it may not be a unique description; other models may fit as well or better.

values (6 to 7) by the end of two to four years. The multipliers from individual models departed substantially from the average; the St. Louis model, for example, showed a zero influence of money on real GNP after four years.

Our brief review of estimated policy multipliers indicates that economists know very little about the probable size and timing of policy impacts on the economy. Even if the multipliers estimated from past behavior in the economy hold true in the future, policymakers must still pick the most reliable model to use in assessing the size and timing of their fiscal or monetary policy moves. Until it can be determined which, if any, of the models is most reliable, policymakers have no basis for making such a choice.[4]

Econometric models must be kept up to date; failure to incorporate new information hampers their ability to describe the effects of legal and structural changes on the economy and weakens their use as tools for forecasting or for making policy simulations. But, even if the models are frequently reestimated, they may contain inherent defects that leave them useless for policy simulations. Professor Robert Lucas of the University of Chicago asserts that the parameters (constants) and multipliers embedded in exisitng models reflect the public's past reactions to government policies. Since these reactions depend upon the information available to the public at the time policies are proposed or undertaken, they cannot be duplicated in policy simulations, which of necessity cannot reproduce the historical conditions for the future that influenced public reactions to past policies. If correct, Lucas's criticism (which does not affect use of econometric models for making forecasts) undermines econometric policy simulations as a source of information for policy advisors.

20.1.2
Forecasting errors

Stabilization policies require authorities to make good economic forecasts. Yet, as every economist will acknowledge, economic forecasting is still a relatively primitive art. Even with the most advanced econometric techniques, every forecast depends upon a set of assumptions concerning economic and political conditions and particular policies of the government. If these conditions do not hold, forecasters will err in their predictions.

A closely related problem is that economic forecasts cannot carry probability statements. Forecasters build their models by studying the

---

[4]Michael Evans, a major participant in building the Wharton and Chase Econometrics models, now says that econometric models built around Keynesian demand theories are seriously flawed, primarily because they ignore supply-side factors. See his "Bankruptcy of Keynesian Econometric Models," *Challenge*, Vol. 22, No. 6, January/February 1980, pp. 13–19.

past behavior of the economy. The regularities they perceive are distilled out of average relationships between economic variables. But these averages conceal a good deal of unexplained variation around means or trends. As a result, it is impossible to denote the probability of a particular event occuring in the future. All the forecaster can do is to assert that if he could make the same forecast under the same conditions a very large number of times, he would be right (within a certain range) a certain percentage of the times. Recent studies[5] of the accuracy of economic forecasts have revealed that, on the whole, economists' predictions of nominal GNP one year into the future have been relatively good. But within-year predictions of quarter-to-quarter changes have not been so good; perhaps more important, forecasts of changes in real GNP and the inflation rate have been subject to large errors. Particularly unfortunate has been the failure of many forecasters to catch the upper and lower turning points of the business cycle. This is partly due to their tendency to underpredict inflation, which means that they frequently overpredict changes in real GNP. For that reason, most forecasters missed the deep recession that started in late 1973.[6]

Failure to predict business cycle turning points increases the chance of perverse reactions by the economy to stabilization policies. For example, policies undertaken to offset the effects of an expected recession may be too stimulative if the economy falls into a recession later than predicted by the economic forecasters. Similarly, stimulative policies undertaken *during* a recession may take hold too late to help an economy that has already turned up before the date anticipated by the policymakers. Indeed, the tendency of policymakers to err on the stimulative side is one of the reasons cited by the Congressional Joint Economic Committee in its 1980 *Midyear Report* that rejected the use of short-run stabilization policies.

20.1.3
Rules versus activism

Economists have been debating the question of policy rules versus policy activism for over 40 years. Generally speaking, the economists who believe in policy rules want to eliminate activist monetary–fiscal policies and instead to rely upon steady-as-you-go policies, such as Friedman's constant money growth rate rule. The debate rests upon two fundamental issues:

---

[5]Victor Arnowitz, "On the Accuracy and Properties of Recent Macroeconomic Forecasts," *American Economic Review*, Vol. 68, No. 2, May 1978, pp. 313–319.

[6]Perhaps as a reaction to this failure, economists began predicting the January 1980 recession almost two years before it happened. Since most of these predictions were for a recession to commence well before January 1980, the forecasters cannot brag about their success.

1. The inherent stability of the private sector of the economy.

2. The potentially destabilizing effects of policy.

Advocates of policy rules believe that the private sector of the economy is inherently stable. The belief implies that disturbances that push the economy away from its normal growth path cannot result in cumulative deviations from the growth path, unless accompanied by perverse government policies. That is, left to itself, in a stable and predictable monetary–fiscal environment, the private sector is quite capable of throwing off external or internal economic shocks and finding its way back to an equilibrium (full employment) growth path. In contrast, as indicated by the Heller quotation on page 483, policy activists believe that the economy requires the aid of government policies to stay on its full employment growth path.

We have already touched upon the potentially destabilizing effects of government policies. Advocates of policy rules not only question the accuracy of econometric policy evaluation and economic forecasts, but they also argue that political infighting and administrative procedures frequently delay or distort policy decisions and result in badly timed or inappropriate actions by fiscal or monetary authorities. Thus, even if economists had well-tested models available for accurate policy simulations and economic forecasts, the political process might itself create enough uncertainty to destabilize the economy.

Empirical evidence on these issues does not particularly resolve them. For example, we have no real evidence on whether the private economy is inherently stable or unstable. Major disturbances in the economy have been accompanied by policy actions, so it is impossible to distill out of actual experience evidence of the inherent stability of the private economy. Thus belief or disbelief in the proposition is largely a matter of faith that the price system, left to its own devices, can provide mechanisms to keep the economy from wandering too far from its full employment growth path.

Evidence on the relative effectiveness of active policy versus a policy of fixed rules comes mainly from simulations of econometric models. Conclusions drawn from the evidence must therefore be conditioned by the possibility that the econometric models may not be valid descriptions of the way the economy works. With that in mind, we may comment upon the result of the studies surveyed by Meyer and Rasche.

Before we do, however, we should note that the size of policy multipliers are not particularly important for comparing activism with fixed-rule approaches. More important is the time pattern of response and the predictability of the policy multipliers. That is because the critics (notably Friedman and his followers) of policy activism have emphasized the sometimes long and variable lags between the noticing of policy needs and the taking of policy actions and their impacts on the economy.

There are three possible types of activist policy strategies that may be compared with fixed rules of the Friedman type: (1) the ones actually used in the past; (2) systematic feedback rules that automatically bring policy actions into operation when economic indicators (for example, the unemployment rate) depart from some desired level or growth path; and (3) optimal control policies, which are the best policies available to policy-makers as revealed by study of the interaction of policy instruments with the structural parameters of a good econometric model, which forecast future performance based on current and past values of exogenous variables outside the control of the authorities and on the dynamic structure of the economy. (Optimal control strategies clearly do not provide convincing evidence for discretionary policy, but as Meyer and Rasche state, they do provide evidence on the *potential* for discretionary policy to improve economic performance.)

Studies that have compared fixed-rule policies with each of the alternative activist policy regimes have concluded either (1) that fixed rules don't significantly improve economic performance over that generated by activist policies, or (2) that, on the average, activist policies are clearly superior to fixed-rule policies. But more important, perhaps, is the finding of some of the optimal control studies that the relatively poor overall performance of the fixed-rule policies occurred when *all* policy rules (fixed and activist) performed badly. On the other hand, when the average performance of all policies was good, fixed rules operated about as well as discretionary policies. The interesting implication of these studies is that policymakers should refrain from frequent fine tuning of the economy, but should actively intervene when the economy is facing a major disturbance.[7]

Finally, it is important to recall the criticisms of policy activism made by rational expectations theorists (see Section 18.2.3). These theorists reject econometric models as a basis for policy evaluation and, further, they argue that systematic activist policies lose their punch as the public learns to anticipate both the policies and their likely effects on the economy. If these criticisms are correct, the exercises reported above, which use econometric models to compare activist with fixed rule policies, provide little or no information on the relative efficiency of the two policy approaches. Indeed, they leave the whole issue up in the air. Econometric studies made by rational expectations theorists have not proved that people form their price expectations rationally rather than adaptively (that is, upon a distributed lag of past inflation rates); however, their studies have indicated that the rational expectations hypotheses cannot be rejected by the evidence. Until such time as economists can produce studies that convincingly reject the rational expectations hypothesis, the case for fixed rules

---

[7]This has long been the advice of monetary theorists. D. H. Robertson, F. A. Hayek, and others preached activism in the 1930s in order to prevent what they called secondary collapses from converting minor contractions into major depressions.

as opposed to policy activism will carry support from a significant segment of the economics profession.

20.1.4
The costs and benefits of eliminating inflation

Much econometric research indicates that bringing inflation down to zero would entail large costs in the form of unemployment and lost output. Studies by Meyer and Rasche, based upon Phillips curve estimates, imply that eradication of inflation might take 8–23 years and cost 400–1800 billion 1978 dollars. Studies using the Federal Reserve Bank of St. Louis and other monetarist models show somewhat shorter periods of adjustment and smaller overall costs; however, even these approaches suggest costs large enough to deter consideration by politically sensitive policymakers.[8]

Two important criticisms of these cost studies are (1) that they do not compare the benefits of eliminating inflation with the costs, and (2) that the models they rely upon are fundamentally flawed by failure to take into account changes in expectations that a properly conceived policy would bring about.

Benefits from the elimination of inflation are hard to quantify. In the past, most economic theorists emphasized the deadweight welfare losses that come about when inflation induces people to reduce cash holdings below levels they previously believed optimal for the conduct of their business affairs. But the uncertainty generated by variable inflation and the interaction of inflation with business and personal income taxes can seriously distort and reduce incentives to work, save, and invest. Continuing inflation can therefore cause long-term economic losses for everybody by forcing the growth path of the economy below the level it would attain in a noninflationary world. The major benefit from purging the economy of inflation would be the larger annual outputs gained from restoring the economy to a higher growth path.

The major costs imposed upon the economy by a decision to eliminate inflation would occur in the immediate or near-term future. As the economy gradually adjusts to the deflationary shock, the costs would diminish and the gain, in the form of an upward shift in the growth path of real output, would gradually appear. Since it is inappropriate to compare directly costs and benefits occuring at different points in time, analysts should reduce costs and benefits to their present values. This was done in the study by Meyer and Rasche, with some interesting results.

---

[8]The studies surveyed in Meyer and Rasche, "Empirical Evidence on the Effects of Stabilization Policy." Works surveyed include papers by George Perry, Phillip Cagan, and Jerome Stein.

Since we have no way of measuring the height of the potential output growth path in the absence of inflation, it is impossible to measure directly the benefits from eradicating inflation. So, instead, Meyer and Rasche calculated the *minimum* present value of the periodic future gains that would justify eradicating a 7.5 percent inflation. They were able to do this because the Phillips curve studies of George Perry of the Brookings Institution, Phillip Cagan of Columbia University, and Jerome Stein of Brown University allowed them to estimate the present value of the transitional losses from eradicating inflation. Having estimates of the stream of transitional losses, it was a rather simple exercise to calculate the present value of the per period permanent future gain that would justify incurring the losses. The exercise produced ten estimates ranging from 13 to 73 billion 1972 dollars. Six of the ten estimates fell below $50 billion; only two (based on Perry's Phillips curve studies) were above $60 billion.

The Meyer–Rasche estimates ignore other benefits from eliminating inflation, such as elimination of the deadweight welfare costs of doing with relatively small holdings of cash, income and wealth distribution effects of uncertain inflation, and the costs of acquiring accurate economic information in a world in which prices are fluctuating widely. Even so, these items, taken together with the estimates of the minimum output gains from eradicating inflation, suggest that the case for antiinflation policies should be taken seriously.

Unfortunately, the transitional costs of trying to eliminate inflation are easily perceived; the distant potential benefits exist only in the reasonings and imaginations of economic theorists. In a world in which policymakers are judged for visible and immediate achievements, it is understandable that policies with distant potential benefits do not head their list of concerns.

20.1.5
The credibility effect and gradual policies for controlling inflation

Theorists who emphasize the rationality of expectations and the importance of credible government policies argue that econometric studies of the costs and benefits of eradicating inflation should be taken with a large grain of salt. All of these studies depend upon Phillips curve or monetarist econometric models that assume price level expectations are formed with relatively long distributed lags. Should government announcements and behavior convince the public that inflation will be brought under control, the coefficients of the econometric models describing the reaction of peoples' price expectations to past inflation rates would no longer be valid. Instead, lags in expectations would become much shorter, and the short-run Phillips curves that measure the unemployment–inflation trade-off would improve much more rapidly than predicted by econometric models. If that is true, the costs of eradicating inflation calculated with the aid of models that ignore the credibility effect may be substantially overestimated.

Professor Allan H. Meltzer of Carnegie-Mellon University has long advocated a plan of attacking inflation through a gradual reduction of the money supply. The success of his plan depends upon the ability of monetary authorities to convince the public that it means business. Mere announcement of a plan is not sufficient. The public must, through observation of policy actions, become convinced that the authorities are following through on their intentions.

Meltzer's plan for gradual reduction of the money supply is based upon an analysis of what he calls the *inference problem*.[9] Suppose the Fed announces a policy of gradual reduction of the money supply. In pursuit of that goal, it must manage bank reserves or the monetary base so as to reduce gradually the monetary growth rate. Yet, as discussed in Section 8.2.2, the Fed's day-to-day or week-to-week open operations are far from gradualistic. Variations in the float, changes in currency in the hands of the public, and shifts in Treasury balances at the Fed force it to undertake frequent defensive open market operations, sometimes of a rather substantial magnitude. It is not unusual for the Fed to be over or under its monetary growth targets for several months at a time. Hence, even though its targets remain unchanged, its activities may produce wide short-run variations in the monetary growth rate. The inference problem of the public is how to filter out of these variations changes in the permanent direction of monetary policy.

More specifically, in a given week changes in the money growth rate may be decomposed into a permanent component, based upon long-run policy, and an ephemeral or transitory component, based on short-run or defensive policies or random factors. Since weekly data released by the monetary authorities do not (and probably cannot) identify for the public the permanent and transitory components in the most recent monetary change, the public itself must somehow infer these elements from the information at hand. If people decide the change has been permanent, the change will have an effect upon their behavior respecting borrowing, lending, pricing of products, and so forth. If they decide the change is transitory, their behaviors on these matters will be relatively unaffected.

The implications of the inference problem seem clear. If the Fed allows substantial and numerous deviations from its policy targets, the public may take these deviations to indicate a permanent change in monetary growth targets and act accordingly, even though the Fed has not actually changed its policies. Hence, if it wishes to maintain its credibility with the

---

[9] The following discussion is based upon Meltzer's paper, "The Case for Gradualism in Policies to Reduce Inflation," in *Stabilization Policies: Lessons from the 70s and Implications for the 80s.*

public, the Fed must work hard to reduce the fluctuations of the monetary growth rate around its policy targets. It must not rely on interest rates as the operating target of monetary policy, since to do so causes frequent deviations of actual from targeted monetary growth rates. In addition, it should reduce the float and other factors that introduce a random element in the money supply. The smaller the variance of the transitory element in the money supply, the easier it is for the public to perceive the permanent element and the faster people are likely to react to announced changes in the monetary growth targets.

If the authorities succeed in stabilizing the monetary growth rate around announced targets, their credibility will improve and public expectations of inflation are likely to respond both favorably and relatively rapidly to policy-induced reductions of the monetary growth rate. Favorable reactions include reductions in demands for large wage increases and a slowing of price increases in the fixprice sectors of the economy. If this happens, the costs of eradicating inflation will be smaller than indicated by the studies based upon econometric models that do not take the credibility effect into account.

20.2
The credibility effect, the German hyperinflation, and the Fed

In late 1923, the German price level was rising at an annual rate of 300,000 percent. Yet, in response to strict monetary policies introduced by Dr. Hjalmer Schacht, within a short time the inflation ceased, and the damage to output and employment was relatively mild. Thomas Humphrey,[10] who studied this episode in the light of the modern theories of expectations, believes this "miracle" was due to the German government's strong reputation for credible policies.

The German hyperinflation, which was set in motion by the German government's attempt through monetary policy to paper over the burdens imposed upon the country by the reparations extracted from it by the Allies in the Versailles Treaty, was accompanied by vast quantities of newly printed money. Moreover, German government officials clearly misunderstood the sources of the inflation. Instead, they believed it their duty to make sure that each new rise in the price level was accompanied by a fresh issue of money. Reichsbank President Rudolph Havenstein even boasted of the installation of new high-speed currency printing presses that enabled the bank to keep pace with the skyrocketing prices.

Yet, through it all, the German government retained its credibility

---

[10]T. Humphrey, "Eliminating Runaway Inflation: Lessons From the German Inflation", *Federal Reserve Bank of Richmond Economic Review*, July/August 1980.

with the public. It promised the people that it would supply enough money to keep up with inflation, and it kept its promise! Everything was out in the open. The government could be trusted to carry through on its announced policies, even though the policies were bad.

Humphrey believes that the German government's reputation for credibility was the basis for its successful and relatively costless stabilization policy. When the government announced the new policy, giving Hjalmer Schacht responsibility for enforcement, it promised to carry it out with strict monetary controls. The public accepted the announcement at face value. Germans refrained from behaviors, such as outsized wage–price demands, that would have sent the country into a major and prolonged depression. Economic losses were confined to a 10 percent drop in output below the GNP potential in 1924.

The key to success in stabilizing the German hyperinflation was the absence of policy surprises. During the 1970s in the United States, policy surprises were more the rule than the exception. For example, despite numerous anti-inflationary pronouncements by Federal Reserve Chairman Arthur Burns in the early 1970s, the growth rate of the money supply accelerated from 3.8 percent a year in 1969 to 7.5 percent in 1972. Burn's successor, G. William Miller, let monetary growth rise from 5.3 percent a year in 1975 to an average of 8 percent a year in 1978–1979. To compound the problem, monetary growth rates in the last half of the 1970s were often outside the targets set by the Fed itself. Instead of forcing the money supply back within the target range, the Fed frequently redefined the targets, in effect embodying its past errors in the new targets. Such behavior was hardly likely to instill public confidence in the Fed's announced policies.

The new monetary control procedures instituted on October 6, 1979 were designed to eliminate monetary control errors. As required by the Humphrey–Hawkins Act, the Fed had set a target growth rate for the money supply for 1980—a range of 4–6.5 percent for M-1B. Yet the Fed's record in late 1979 and during the first three-quarters of 1980 was not the stuff out of which confidence and credibility are born. As shown in Figure 10.5 (Chapter 10), M-1B declined well below the target range in the first half of 1980. Beginning in late April, the authorities accelerated the growth in reserve aggregates and pushed the money supply rapidly into and above the target range. Thus, the money supply was out of the target range most of the year. In the meantime, interest rates were fluctuating wildly (Figure 10.5).

In its September 1980 *Monthly Economic Letter*, Citibank concluded that

> Financial markets, in effect, have given the Fed a vote of no confidence. One reason for the skepticism may well be the course policy took last summer (of 1979). After a period of monetary

stringency in the winter and early spring of 1979, monetary
expansion took over and continued with only minor interruption
until early this year. With the economy still in recession and
unemployment likely to rise further, the market participants
appear to be viewing the latest turn to expansion by the Fed as a
signal that the stage is being set for yet another inflationary cycle.

Evidence for Citibank's view was the sharp revival of interest rates after
their low point in June 1980.

This episode illustrates the general point made by Professor Meltzer.
Time after time Federal Reserve Chairman Paul Volcker and other officials of the System reiterated their determination to stick to their plan to
"wring inflation out of the economy over time." Indeed, in the middle of
1980 they even reduced the top end of the 1981 target range of monetary
growth by about one-half percentage point below the 1980 range. Yet the
markets refused to listen. In the face of an extraordinary rise in the
money supply during the summer, interest rates actually rose, signifying
revival of inflationary expectations. This is strong evidence that market
participants believe what they see, not what they hear. Had the Fed maintained monetary growth within its announced target range during the
first 8 months of 1980, the economic history of the period might have
been very different.

20.3
Incomes policies

Despair over slowing inflation with monetary–fiscal policies leads many
economists to advocate incomes policies. Incomes policies are designed to
slow wage and salary increases that many economists believe to be the
source of continuing inflation during recessions. These economists speak
of an underlying or basic inflation rate that is presumably determined by
the overall rise in wage costs that comes from a combination of wage rate
changes and changes in output per unit of labor input. The latter item,
which measures labor productivity, typically slows during recessions;
combined with continuing wage increases, it puts upward pressure on
prices even when demand for output is falling. So, to relieve this pressure, and to knock down the underlying inflation rate, these economists
have advanced several schemes for retarding average wage and salary increases throughout the economy.

None of these schemes involves returning to price–wage controls,
such as those imposed during the Nixon Administration during 1971–
1974. Moreover, most economists agree that the so-called voluntary wage
and price guidelines, like those used during the Johnson and Carter
Administrations, do not work well. Instead, most discussion concerns two

recently proposed plans, one advocated by Sidney Weintraub and Henry Wallich and another by Arthur Okun.[11]

The Wallich–Weintraub tax-based income plan (TIP) would stiffen the wage-increase resistance of employers by raising the income tax rate on corporations that grant wage increases above a certain norm. The additional revenue obtained would be offset by cutting some other tax, perhaps the standard corporate income tax rate, leaving overall tax collections about the same countrywide.

TIP has at least one major advantage over outright wage controls; it would allow extra wage increases in corporations that can pay them even with the additional tax. However, the tax could threaten the survival of low-profit firms that are unable to resist outsized wage demands from strong unions and weaken companies already in marginally profitable conditions. More fundamentally, perhaps, TIP would promote wage increases according to the profitability of employers, not the marginal value productivity of the workers they employ. As a result, prolonged application of the policy might seriously distort the allocation of labor. In that respect, at least, it would not differ fundamentally from wage–price controls that also produce distortions in the economy. The main advantage of TIP, therefore, is that it might require less heavy-handed bureaucratic means for slowing wage and price increases than the means required by direct controls.

Arthur Okun's proposal is for a wage insurance plan (WIP). With a number of exceptions, WIP would insure employees who are willing to limit their wage demands against an inflation rate exceeding 7 percent a year. Thus, if inflation were 9 percent instead of 7 percent a year, WIP would have Congress compensate workers for the 2 percent shortfall by subsidizing their incomes.

The danger in the Okun plan is that Congress might compensate workers by increasing budgetary deficits that are accommodated by new money created by the Federal Reserve System. The plan could thus set the stage for further departures of inflation from the 7 percent standard; unless Congress could actually guarantee an inflation rate at or under 7 percent a year, the stage could be set for accelerating inflation.

Neither TIP nor WIP attacks the monetary origins of inflation. At best, they are an aid to demand management policies that seek to slow inflation without jacking up the unemployment rate to intolerable levels. Without the backing of a proper monetary policy, neither plan would really succeed in permanently reducing the inflation rate. For that rea-

[11]H. Wallich and S. Weintraub, "A Tax-Based Incomes Policy," *Journal of Economic Issues,* Vol. 5, June 1971, pp. 1–17; A. Okun, "The Great Stagflation Swamp," *Challenge,* Vol. 20, No. 5, November/December 1977, pp. 6–13. The discussion in this section benefited from Thomas Mayer, "Innovative Income Policies: A Skeptic's View," a paper presented at a conference on "New Approaches To An Income Policy for the United States," Middlebury College, April 19–20, 1979.

son, we must now discuss the capacity of our system of democratic government to establish a long-term program for wringing inflation out of the economy.

20.4
Can democracy tame inflation?

The Federal Reserve System cannot pursue policies credible to the economic community without a certain measure of independence or insulation from political influences. Unfortunately, however, the history of monetary policy abounds with incidents of political pressure. For example, rightly or wrongly, it is believed that Federal Reserve Chairman Arthur Burns deliberately stimulated monetary growth during 1972 to help the reelection of President Nixon (a charge that Burns has denied). On October 20, 1977, the White House posted a "Notice to the Press" complaining that the Fed's efforts to restirct money growth were forcing up interest rates that, in President Carter's opinion, would damage the economy. Again, during the heat of the 1980 election campaign, at a time when the Fed was operating under a decision taken in August to raise temporarily the target monetary growth rate (presumably to bring the money supply within its long-term target range), Governor Charles Partee of the Federal Reserve Board was quoted in the widely read editorial page of the *Wall Street Journal* (September 26, 1980) as saying any move to tighten money is "pretty tough for an election year."[12]

Our purpose here is not to berate the monetary authorities for bending to political pressures; instead, we wish merely to acknowledge that no governmental institution in a democracy (or any other political system, probably) can avoid them. Despite their relative immunity from threats of direct retaliations for unpopular decisions, the Board of Governors and other policymakers in the Federal Reserve System are quite sensitive to the wishes of the President and key members of Congress. To be sure, at times they must displease other policymakers; they must frequently keep rein on the money supply even though large federal deficits are pushing up interest rates, and they must occasionally impose tight money policies

---

[12]*Business Week*, October 6, 1980 reported a belief among a significant group of money market analysts that the Fed was fueling the Carter campaign with large increases in bank reserves, partly to keep interest rates down in an attempt to honor an alleged agreement between President Carter and his chief rival during the primary elections, Senator Edward Kennedy, to keep interest rates stable or perhaps artificially low during the heaviest days of the campaign. Ironically, interest rates rose sharply during the campaign, perhaps in response to a revival of high inflationary expectations brought on by the increased monetary growth rate. The charge against the Fed was probably ill-founded (in fact, a few days later Carter actually criticized the Fed for pursuing so-called monetarist policies and permitting interest rates to rise); nevertheless, that important members of the financial community believed it illustrates how important it is for the Fed to act in a credible fashion.

even when such policies risk recession. Nevertheless, monetary policy-makers dislike being called poor team players. If political pressure is great enough, they often reverse or relax policies for short-term gains, even though such lapses may undermine long-term goals of fighting inflation and maintaining the international value of the dollar.[13]

In the final analysis, therefore, establishing credibility for monetary policy is part of the wider problem of establishing credibility for the government as a whole. This brings up the broader question of the ability of representative democracy to institute and maintain a long-term plan of action to eliminate inflation. If democratic institutions cannot formulate or adhere to such a plan, we cannot expect the public to trust the pronouncements or plans of the monetary authorities, no matter how sincerely formulated. For that reason, before commenting further on the problem of credibility, we must review the political mechanisms that generate and sustain various government policies.

20.4.1
Representative government, the political business cycle, and economic stabilization[14]

In Section 17.1.4, we identified several characteristic features of representative government that contribute to a persistent rise in government spending and an inability of policymakers to adhere to stern measures that might over time wring inflation out of the economy. The first is the play of interest group politics, which forces legislators and other elected officials to enact measures that subsidize or otherwise concentrate benefits on important constituencies, while spreading the costs thinly (and hence, unnoticed) over the population as a whole. The second is the almost obligatory shortsightedness of politicians who, in order to maximize votes in the next election, support visible policies that produce short-run results instead of obscure measures that spread benefits for the public over the long run.

These features of representative government produce a collective decision making process that frequently ignores the more remote consequences of government policies. Individuals cannot make personal expenditure decisions without considering their effects upon present or future asset positions or upon the opportunities they foreclose now or in

---

[13]Two useful discussions on this point may be found in William Poole, "Current Issues in Monetary Control," *Federal Reserve Bank of Richmond Economic Review*, Vol. 66, No. 4, July/August 1980, pp. 20–27, and Phillip Cagan, "The New Monetary Policy and Inflation," William Fellner (editor), *Contemporary Economic Problems* (Washington: American Enterpsie Institute, 1980).

[14]This and the next two sections benefited greatly from Robert Lubar, "Making Democracy Less Inflation-Prone," *Fortune*, Vol. 102, No. 6, September 22, 1980, pp. 78–86.

the future. Simple contemplation of the price of an expensive object is often sufficient to convince or compel a person to avoid an outlay. Legislators advocating expensive programs that benefit their constituents often disregard their prices, since the budgetary impacts usually fall diffusely on the constituents of other legislators. Moreover, the initial costs of programs, such as social security pensions, medicare, or a new weapons system are frequently small, and the future costs, though potentially large, are highly uncertain. And, since the costs must be dealt with by future legislators, they are likely to be less influential on current decisions.

The political realities of representative government may seriously interfere with its ability to stabilize the economy. After all, politicians earn votes by spending or by cutting taxes, not by limiting federal deficits. Pessimistic theorists, such as Yale Professor William Nordhaus (also a former member of the President's Council of Economic Advisors) have even advanced the theory that the modern business cycle is in fact a *political business cycle*. Briefly formulated, Nordhaus' position is, "Within an incumbent's term of office there is a predictable pattern of policy, starting with relative austerity in early years and ending with a potlach right before elections." After elections, austerity is presumably restored in order to fight the inflation set in motion by the pre-election spending binge.

The Nordhaus theory is controversial; nonetheless, the actions of President Nixon during his first term of office give it partial support. Nixon blamed his 1960 loss to John Kennedy in good part on the restrictive policies followed by the Republican administration of President Eisenhower. Upon attaining office in 1969, Nixon also tightened monetary and fiscal policies; but, in the election years of 1972, supported by a spurt in the monetary growth rate, he was able to pour additional stimulus on the economy.

Whether or not the political cycle theory is correct as a general theory, it is still true that politicians frequently promise or ladle out tax cuts and other benefits just prior to elections. A recent example is the 1980 election campaign in which President Carter, Ronald Reagan, and Congress vied with one another for the honor of producing the best tax cut. Quite apart from the merits of such proposals, it is clear that macroeconomic decisions taken politically are unlikely to provide optimal stabilization policies.

Overlaying cyclical instability induced by government budgetary and monetary policies is the growing incapacity of government to deal with the long-term macroeconomic consequences of particularized microeconomic policies. The overall budget is increasingly becoming hostage to many programs passed to serve important constituencies. The discretionary part of the budget is declining relative to the so-called mandatory or uncontrollable part, leaving less and less maneuvering room for using budgetary means to resist inflation. A recent study by the Office of Management and Budget classified 76 percent of the budget as relatively uncontrollable, up from 64 percent in 1970. Formal and informal inflation indexing of about three-quarters of all government outlays is a major source of the problem. For example, the huge social security and federal employee pension programs are fully protected against changes in living costs as measured by the consumer price index. Between 1965 and 1978, federal outlays rose from 18 to 23 percent of gross national product, largely due to indexation of benefits and increases in the number and size of transfer programs.[15]

The political pressure on federal budgets has provided an alarmingly persistent rise in the federal deficit, particularly in the 1970s. Unless financed by increases in the money supply, federal budgetary deficits are not very inflationary. Nonetheless, political pressures on the Federal Reserve do at times produce a rough correlation between deficits, the money supply, and inflation. Such a correlation is shown for the post-World War II period up to the mid-1970s in Figure 20.1.

20.4.2
Breaking the boundaries of government power

The United States has had a representative democracy since the inception of the Republic some 190 years ago. It is therefore puzzling that the problem of secular inflation has emerged only recently. Previous bouts with inflation, brought on mainly by excessive money created during major wars (for example, the infamous greenbacks of the civil war) seldom lasted long into peacetime. Why is it that the play of interest group politics and the myopia of politicians waited until our time to produce an intractable inflation?

A fair question; not easy to answer. Some students of the problem blame a combination of separate developments that have destroyed traditional boundaries to federal power. Examples are as follows:

1. A breakdown of the discipline of the balanced budget, which was cast aside during the 1930s under the New Deal. Keynesian theory later made a virtue of deficits as a device for buoying up aggregate demand during economic slumps and for stimulating growth. For example, Walter Heller, President Kennedy's chief economic advisor, by and large abhorred budgetary surpluses, arguing that they impose a "fiscal drag" on aggregate expenditure and hence slow economic growth.

---

[15]See "Why Federal Spending is So Hard to Control," *Business Week*, No. 2655, September 22, 1980, pp. 108–113, for an insightful discussion of this problem. A deeper discussion, which influenced the discussion here, is in Raymond E. Lombra, "Policy Advice and Policy-Making: Economic, Political, and Social Issues," Michael P. Dooley *et al.*, (editors), *The Political Economy of Policy-Making* (Beverly Hills and London: Sage Publications, 1979), pp. 13–34.

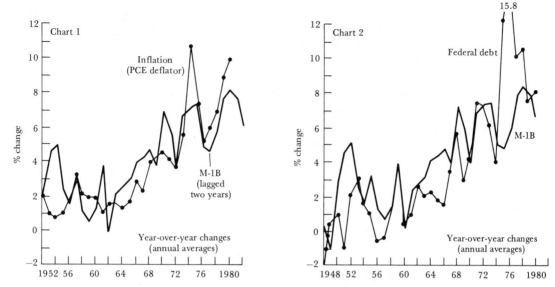

Figure 20.1 *Inflation, money growth, and changes in the federal debt. (Source: Michael W. Keran, "Reconciling Monetary and Fiscal Policy,"* Federal Reserve Bank of San Francisco Weekly Letter, *February 27, 1981.)*

2. A breakdown of the gold standard in the 1930s and the gold exchange standard in 1971. Under these standards, unfavorable balance of payments often provided officials with justification for more cautious monetary policies. Loss of gold or foreign exchange, or rapid buildups of debts to foreigners, were considered a threat to national economic well-being and signaled the need for less inflationary domestic policies. The new floating exchange rate fosters the illusion that expansionary monetary–fiscal policies do not have international repercussions.[16]

3. Gone are the days when the courts enforced strict construction of the Constitution. Judges no longer regularly declare unconstitutional acts of Congress that infringe upon states rights or go beyond the powers explicitly given to the federal government by the Constitution. This tendency, together with broad interpretations of the meaning of interstate commerce, equal protection of the law, and the due process clause of the Constitution, have enabled Congress to extend the minimum wage law and other regulations deep into the innards of the economy.

---

[16]But, as we are now learning, there are repercussions in the form of declines in the international value of the dollar.

4. A breakdown of party discipline in both major political parties and a dimunition of the power of key congressional veterans entrenched in chairmanships of important committees and in leadership positions in both houses. The congressional reform movement, carried out for the purpose of democratization has undermined the ability of the more conservative elements of Congress to block legislation that adds to the government budget.

5. The growing volume and complexity of proposed legislation, which has undermined the ability of legislators to understand (or even read) the legislation before them. The situation has led Congressmen to lean more heavily upon the advice and information of lobbyists and professional staff, now expanded greatly in number and in influence and generating legislative ideas of its own.

6. The expansion of rights or asserted rights of a large variety of minority and other groups, each with its special economic demands on the federal government. The "rights explosion" has greatly complicated the task of slowing the rise of the federal budget. At the same time, the political strength of interest groups has weakened Congress' ability to eliminate old programs to make way for the new.

20.4.3
Restoring the boundaries—keeping
the budget in line

The country is unhappy with the inflationary consequences of its public policies; like a drunkard seeking a cure, it is in the process of trying to find its way back to economic health. Congress has sensed the despair of much of the electorate and is looking for a way to discipline itself. A large majority passed the Budget Act of 1974, setting up a process that may eventually bring the budget under control. Traditionally, Congress considered each expenditure item on its own merits, without measuring its budgetary consequences. Under the new process, Congress prepares a spring version of an overall target budget to be approved in September for the beginning of the fiscal year each October 1. Legislators are aided by the Congressional Budget Office, which is required by law to cost out all pending legislation for the purpose of fitting it into the overall budget plan.

The new budgetary process was unable to avoid a string of deficits that added up to $282 billion from the inception of the Budget Act through 1980. Congress did not seriously address the task of producing a balanced budget until spring 1980. When it finally did, it forced upon a number of reluctant Congressmen and their constituents a series of budget cuts totaling about $16 billion. It was a searing experience for all concerned. Chairman Robert Giaimo of the House Budget Committee (not running for re-election) helped the budget through the Congress, but at one point declared, "I've got to tell you that the mileage around here is still to be a giveaway artist . . . . There's no mileage in talking the way I'm talking."[17] By late 1980, with the country in recession, the balanced budget was already coming apart, even before the 1981 fiscal year commenced.

The election of Ronald Reagan in November 1980 may represent a historic turning-point in the nation's fiscal affairs. Together with a Republican majority in the Senate and a working majority of conservative Democrats and Republicans in the House of Representatives, Reagan enacted a $35 billion cut in social and other programs. Although some of the programs were cut absolutely, others simply had their increases pared back. If continued into the future, these cuts may signal a permanent slowdown, if not a change in direction, of the growth of federal government spending.

Even so, observers are so pessimistic about Congress resisting interest group politics that they may still support some recently proposed constitutional amendments to put a permanent leash on growth of government spending. Major ideas include outlawing federal deficits or putting mechanical limitations on the growth of federal spending. One proposal, put forth by the National Tax Limitation Committee, would constitutionally limit the annual percentage increase in federal spending to the equivalent percentage rise in GNP, unless Congress votes by a two-thirds majority for an emergency lifting of the ceiling. Former Federal Reserve Chairman Arthur Burns and the Committee to Fight Inflation prefer prohibition of budgetary deficits, unless permitted by a 60 percent vote of Congress.

These proposals would introduce formal restraints on a government that in the past responded to informal restraints, such as the general public abhorrence of unbalanced budgets. Aside from the difficulty of guiding the measures through the political thickets that hinder embodiment of the measures in the Constitution, many observers question the wisdom of enshrining in the Constitution shaky calculations and concepts like the federal deficit and GNP. Moreover, a resourceful Congress could always find ways to escape the Constitutional limitations by passing measures that shift the budgetary impact from the federal government to state and local governments or to federal lending agencies.

These defects would be partly overcome if Congress were to adopt different voting rules. For example, Alan Greenspan, Chairman of President Ford's Council of Economic Advisors, would simply require that "every claim on federal revenues" receive an affirmative vote of 60 percent or two-thirds of each house of Congress.[18] Greenspan's definition of claims on federal revenues includes both spending bills and indirect

---

[17]Quoted in Robert Lubar, "Making Democracy Less Inflation–Prone."
[18]Quoted in Lubar, "Makiing Democracy Less Inflation-Prone."

measures such as off-budget loans and loan guarantees (like those given to New York City, Lockheed, and the Chrysler Motor Company in the 1970s).

Greenspan's voting requirement would not prevent Congress or federal government agencies from mandating state and local government or private business expenditures needed to comply with federal government regulations. Washington University Professor (and Chairman of President Reagan's Council of Economic Advisers) Murray Weidenbaum, for example, has estimated that the business sector cost of complying with federal regulations amounted to over $100 billion in 1979. Laws requiring mainstreaming of handicapped children, access of physically handicapped people to public buildings and transportation facilities, preventing or reducing environmental pollution, and other federal government measures have further increased compliance costs to both business and nonfederal governments. Although these federally imposed costs are not necessarily inflationary, they do put political pressure on Congress from private groups and state and local governments to help pay for the costs of the federally mandated programs. Accumulation of such pressures would weaken Greenspan's 60 percent or two-thirds voting rule.

20.4.4
Restoring the boundaries—keeping the Fed in line

Holding down increases in federal spending and keeping the deficit within manageable bounds are perhaps necessary steps in controlling inflation; but, as argued throughout this book, inflation cannot be conquered without eliminating excessive monetary growth. Many observers now argue that the crisis in our political constitution has been joined by a crisis in our "monetary constitution," meaning that we must somehow make sure that Federal Reserve policies be forced onto a path that leads to permanent inflation control.

Milton Friedman's proposal of a fixed monetary growth rule is one of these ideas. Given the disagreement over the proper definition of money, Friedman's rule would be difficult to implement. Nonetheless, things have come to such a pass that he now believes that some sort of steady-as-you-go growth rule must be required by a Constitutional amendment.[19]

Such a Constitutional amendment would be difficult to implement. The Fed's record in controlling the money supply has not been good; legitimate doubts exist that a mandated growth rate would improve its performance. Nonetheless, it may be worth a try, by statute if not by a Con-

---

[19]For a survey of other proposals, see John A. Davenport, "A Testing Time for Monetarism," Vol. 102, No. 8, *Fortune*, October 6, 1980.

stitutional amendment. But a number of changes in Fed procedures should be instituted along with the growth rule. One is elimination or at least substantial reduction of the float. Another is removal of lagged reserve requirements. These items, together with the installation of a penalty discount rate, would substantially reduce the slippage in Fed control over bank reserves and the monetary base. A more extreme measure, suggested long ago by the great monetary theorist Irving Fisher, would be a substantial raising of reserve requirements, perhaps to 100 percent. This radical (and probably politically unfeasible) measure would reduce the variability in the money multiplier that comes from the shifts of deposits between different banks and different deposit classes.

A totally different approach to monetary control would be to restore the discipline of the gold standard. Returning to the gold standard is not widely accepted among professional economists. Most would say that such a standard would fail to provide for domestic and international equilibrium simultaneously. The stable exchange rates of the gold standard would be kept in line by an accommodation of domestic incomes and prices to inflows and outflows of gold. Thus, the domestic economy would be hostage to international balance of payments adjustments. Even so, some economists have concluded that present-day floating exchange rates have given policymakers too much room to pursue inflationary schemes. These economists have therefore accepted the gold standard, even though it is an inferior alternative to effective money supply control by the Fed.[20]

A more exotic recommendation is the proposal of Friedrich A. Hayek[21] to eliminate the monopoly of the Federal Reserve and the Treasury over monetary control. He would, instead, authorize private banks or corporations to issue currency that would compete with money issued by the government. Since entry into the money-making industry would be free, the money issuers would compete with each other as well as with the government.

What would entice people to hold privately issued monies instead of government money? Hayek thinks banks would pay interest on their money issues and would promise to redeem the money on demand in terms of a basket of commodities, gold, silver, or other precious metals. Different banks would offer different deals, depending in part on their ability to require repayment from loan customers in similar terms. Over-issue would be avoided by the rising costs associated with each successive

---

[20]A survey of opinion is in John A. Davenport, "The New Allure of the Gold Standard," *Fortune*, Vol. 101, No. 7, April 7, 1980, pp. 86–94. See also Henry Hazlitt, "How to Return to Gold," Vol. 39, No. 9, *The Freeman*, September 1980, pp. 523–526.

[21]F. A. Hayek, *Denationalization of Money: An Analysis of the Theory and Practice of Concurrent Currencies* (London: Institute of Economic Affairs, 1976). Also see Lance Girton and Don Roper, "Substitutable Monies and the Monetary Standard," in Michael P. Dooley *et al.* (editors), *The Political Economy of Policy-Making*.

expansion of monetary liabilities and the competition of different money producers for the public's favor.

If implemented, Hayek's proposal would result in a large number of competing monies. Moreover, it would provide alternatives for people who wish to escape from holding government or privately issued monies that are unbacked by commodities or that pay no interest. Thus, inflation of these currencies would hold no threat to the public at large; only those whose faith in the government currency somehow transcends their fear of losses through inflation would maintain balances of government money. Hayek believes, however, that the presence of competitive private monies would force the government to restrain excessive monetary growth.[22]

SUMMARY

The "new views" on stabilization policies are mostly negative. Policy activism, frequently called fine tuning or demand management, is in serious disrepute with much of the economics profession and with important parts of the official community, such as the Joint Economic Committee of Congress.

Some of the pessimism about policy activism comes from econometric studies. Econometric models used in policy evaluations yield a variety of policy multipliers whose size as well as timing uncertainties of policy impacts make them poor tools for policymakers to use. In addition, the forecasting record of economists is so unimpressive that authorities now fear that policies based upon such forecasts may actually destabilize, instead of smooth out the fluctuations of the economy.

The debate over policy activism has revived the idea, long advocated by Milton Freidman, that the Federal Reserve should adopt a steady-as-you-go long-term monetary growth rule. Although studies comparing this rule to a policy using optimal control strategies favor activism, it has not been shown that a fixed policy rule performs poorly. When the average performance of all policies are good, the fixed rule does about as well as activist rules. An important implication of these studies is that policymakers should generally refrain from fine tuning, actively intervening only during serious economic slumps.

Rational expectations theorists say that econometric policy evaluation is basically flawed because the models are fitted to data containing reac-

---

[22]Henry Hazlitt, a friend and economic thinker close to Hayek, has attacked the proposal as being naive. It requires scrupulously honest private money issuers, willing to back up their promises to redeem money in commodities and to pay interest. Hazlitt's reading of the wild banking days of our early history, when banks issued millions of dollars of fraudulent currencies, leads him to doubt the realism of Hayek's idea.

tions to policy changes that in their nature cannot be reproduced for the future. Thus, studies of fixed versus activist policies with econometric models may also be basically flawed and provide no information upon the rules versus activist debate. The same criticism may be directed against studies that, using Phillips curve and monetarist econometric models assuming adaptive expectations, purport to measure the cost of eradicating inflation. Though, as Meyer and Rasche have shown, the costs may not be absurdly out of line in comparison with the benefits, the models are unable to predict the costs of a *credible* policy to wring inflation out of the economy over time. As elimination of hyperinflation in Germany in the early 1920s has shown, the cost of a credible antiinflationary policy may be much smaller than economists have estimated.

Professor Allan Meltzer has deepened our understanding of the requirements for a credible policy. His analysis of the public's inference problem shows that policymakers must reduce the frequency and size of the transitory monetary changes and increase the frequency and size of the permanent components of monetary changes. Otherwise, the public will be unable to discover if the authorities are holding to their word.

The Fed's record in the 1970s was not the kind upon which policy confidence in policy announcements is built. As a result, attempts by the authorities to wring inflation out of the economy are faced with continuing increases in prices based, to some extent, on wage increases negotiated by unions and workers who anticipate continued inflation. Since continued wage–price inflation heightens the output and employment losses from anti-inflationary stabilization policies, many writers now propose a return to incomes policies. The Wallich–Weintraub TIP plan and the Okun WIP plan are widely discussed examples of such policies.

But many observers now think the problem of policy credibility is tied up with the belief that democratic government is unable to tame inflation. Political pressures of interest groups, the myopia of elected officials, liberal court rulings enhancing the power of the federal government, breakdown of party discipline imposed by congressional leaders, and the destruction of the traditional boundaries on government (that is, the balanced budget and balance of payments taboos) have helped unleash the inherent inflationary tendencies of representative government. The persistent demands of various interest groups now put constant pressure on the federal budget, produce deficits, and provoke the Federal Reserve, itself a politically sensitive institution, into excessive monetary expansion.

Restoring the ability of government to fight inflation is not easy. Proposals abound for Constitutional amendments to balance the federal budget, limit growth in government spending, and limit growth in the money supply. Other proposals include a return to the gold standard and denationalization of money. Some observers also want special voting rules that hinder Congress when it is faced with budgetary legislation.

1. Briefly discuss the value of econometric models as guides to fiscal–monetary policy decisions.

2. Economists usually have similar training, yet they are divided on whether fiscal–monetary policies should be "activist" or given over to some sort of fixed rule or rules. What explains this division?

3. Compare the costs and benefits of policies to eliminate inflation. What can be done to reduce the costs?

4. What steps must monetary authorities take to improve their credibility?

5. Define and give examples of income policies. Upon what theory of inflation do they rest? Does the theory preclude the use of monetary policy to fight inflation?

6. Is representative government inherently inflationary? Discuss.

IMPORTANT TERMS AND CONCEPTS

☐ feedback policy rules
☐ fiscal policy multipliers
☐ incomes policies
☐ inference problem
☐ monetary policy multiplier

☐ optimal control policies
☐ political business cycle
☐ policy stimulation studies
☐ rules versus activism debate

ADDITIONAL READINGS

Some of the older literature on stabilization policies is still worth reading. For example, the case for fixed policy rules versus policy activism was first explored in sensitive detail by Henry C. Simons in "Rules versus Authorities in Monetary Policy," *Journal of Political Economy*, Vol. 44, No. 1, February 1936, pp. 1–30. Milton Friedman built on Simon's work in his widely read, "A Monetary and Fiscal Framework for Economic Stability," *American Economic Review*, Vol. 38, No. 2, June 1948, pp. 245–264. Also influential was Friedman's "The Role of Monetary Policy," *American Economic Review*, Vol. 58, No. 1, March 1948, pp. 1–17. Attacks on stabilization policy from rational expectations theorists are discussed in a variety of places. For a recent volume on these ideas, see S. Fischer (editor), *Rational Expectations and Economic Policy* (Chicago: University of Chicago Press, 1980). A defense against the criticisms of Friedman and the rational expectations school is Franco Modigliani, "The Monetary Controversy or, Should We Forsake Stabilization Policy?" *American Economic Review*, Vol. 67, No. 1, March 1977, pp. 1–19.

A good survey of developments in the theory of stabilization is John B. Taylor, "Recent Developments in the Theory of Stabilization Policy," *Stabilization Policies: Lessons From the 70s and Implications For the 80s* (St. Louis: Center For The Study of American Business, Washington University, April 1980). Also useful is the 10th anniversary issue of the *Brookings Papers on Economic Activity, 1:1980*, particularly the paper by James Tobin, "Stabilization Policy Ten Years After," pp. 19–71.

The political economy of inflation is now at the forefront of much thinking about stabilization policies. Two good introductions to this topic (which strongly influenced the material in Section 20.4) were published by *Fortune*: Robert Lubar, "Making Democracy Less Inflation-Prone," Vol. 102, No. 6, September 22, 1980, pp. 78–86, and Everett Carll Ladd, "How to Tame the Special Interest Groups," Vol. 102, No. 10, October 20, 1980, pp. 66–80. For a somewhat deeper discussion of the issues, with a good bibliography, see Raymond E. Lombra, "Policy Advice and Policy-Making: Economic, Political, and Social Issues," Michael P. Dooley *et al.*, (editors), *The Political Economy of Policy Making* (Beverly Hills and London: Sage Publications, 1979), pp. 13–34. Finally on an entirely different level, for a magisterial treatment of the problems of representative democracy, see F. A. Hayek's three-volume study, *Law, Legislation and Liberty* (Chicago: University of Chicago Press, 1973(*1*), 1976(*2*), 1979(*3*)).

Glossary

Numbers in parentheses after each definition refer to the chapter and section where the term or concept is discussed.

Acceleration hypothesis An implication of the natural unemployment rate hypothesis, the acceleration hypothesis asserts that attempts to maintain unemployment below the natural rate through aggregate demand policies will cause accelerating inflation. (18.2)

Accord between the Federal Reserve System and the Treasury 1951 agreement that freed the Fed from responsibility of pegging interest rates on government bonds and thereby freed it to conduct monetary policy through improved control over the money supply. (7.2)

Adaptive expectations Theory that people base inflation predictions solely upon past trends of the inflation rate. (18.2.2)

Aggregate income Aggregate earnings of owners of resources used in productive activity. Equals value added by production as measured by gross national product or national income. (11.4.1)

Aggregate income equilibrium Aggregate excess demand for some goods and services offset by equal and offsetting aggregate excess supply of other goods and services. Requires monetary equilibrium. (11.3)

Announcement effects Impact on market transactor's expectations of Federal Reserve policy actions. (9.1.1)

Anticipated inflation Forecasts of inflation made by market transactors. (17.4.1)

Arbitrage Purchasing a particular good at a low price and reselling it at a higher price in another part of a trading area. Arbitrage creates a tendency for the prices of identical goods selling in a market area to equalize. (19.1.1)

Asset demand for money Money held for its implicit services (or money interest) as an asset. The amount demanded depends upon asset holders' tastes and preferences and wealth and upon bond interest rates and yields on real assets that may be held instead of money. (12.2.3)

Automatic transfer from savings (ATS) accounts Deposits that are transferable from savings accounts paying interest to checking accounts as needed to cover overdrafts or to maintain a minimum balance. In effect, ATS accounts are interest bearing checking accounts. (2.1.3)

Autonomous spending Keynesian term for spending not induced by changes in, or the level of income. Examples are business investment spending, residential construction spending and government expenditures on final product. (16.1.3)

Balance of payments Net value of purchases and sales of goods and services and of securities between people in a particular geographical area and those outside the area. A balance of payments surplus occurs when the value of sales exceeds the value of purchases; a deficit occurs when purchases exceed sales. (19.1)

Balance sheet Statement containing enumeration of assets, liabilities and resulting net worth of an economic unit. Principle items on a bank's balance sheet include assets such as cash reserves, loans, and investments; liabilities such as demand deposits, savings and time deposits, and capital accounts representing net worth. (4.1.1)

Bank capital Capital stock and accumulated undistributed profits held by a bank in various capital accounts. (4.1.2)

Bank holding companies Companies that own banks in addition to nonbank enterprises. (4.2.2)

Bank Merger Act of 1960 Empowers federal regulatory authorities to approve bank mergers. (5.3.3)

Banker's acceptance A negotiable bill of exchange on which a foreign importer's bank has written "accepted." A bill of exchange is written by a creditor on a person owing him money; the bill is payable on demand or at some specified future date. (4.2.3)

Barter Direct exchange of goods or services between two people who find the exchange mutually advantageous. Requires mutual coincidence of wants. (1.1.1)

Base-multiplier formula Summarizes the factors affecting the money supply. The formula equals the monetary base times the money multiplier; the multiplier contains the currency–deposit ratio, the time deposit ratio, and various reserve–deposit ratios. (6.1.3–6.1.5)

Bills only policy Policy followed by FOMC for an 8-year period (following March 1953) of confining open market operations to short-term government securities. (9.1.2)

Board of Governors of the Federal Reserve System Chief administrative and policy board of the Federal Reserve System. The seven Board members are members of the Federal Open Market Committee. (7.1.1)

Bonds Marketable or nonmarketable fixed income securities specifying the coupon rate of interest, frequency of payments, term to maturity, and redemption (maturity or par) value. (3.4.1)

Branch banking A form of banking organization wherein a bank has more than one office providing normal banking services. (5.3.1)

Broker An agent who acts for others who wish to buy or sell stocks or bonds. (3.1.1)

Business cycle General fluctuations (not necessarily regular) of aggregate output, employment, and the rate of inflation around their trends. (16.1.1)

Cambridge equation Demand for

money equation stressing the transactions demand for real money balances as a fraction of real income, y. The so-called "Cambridge k" is this fraction. The equation is $m^d = ky$, where m^d is the demand for real money balances. (12.2.1)

Capital account Par value of a bank's outstanding stock, its surplus, undivided profits, and special reserve accounts. (4.2.2)

Capital account balance Surplus or deficit arising out of sales and purchases of securities between people of a given region or country and people on the outside. (19.1)

Capital gains Increase in the market value of an asset from date of purchase to some future date. Realized capital gains occur when the asset is sold; unrealized gains occur before the asset is sold. Capital losses occur when the price of the asset falls after the date of purchase. (17.3.3)

Capital market Financial market that deals in stocks and bonds with duration of more than one year. (3.4.4)

Cash items in process of collection (CIPC) Checks received by a bank or financial institution, written on other intermediaries, but in the process of being cleared. Deducted from total demand deposits for purposes of calculating the money supply. (2.1.1)

Central bank Official bank of a country that conducts monetary policy, issues currency, lends to private banks, regulates exchange rates with foreign currencies, and acts as the central government's fiscal agent. (7.1.2)

Certificates of deposit (CDs) Large (usually $100,000 or more) time certificates of deposit, issued to mature at a given date, and salable by original or other holders to third parties through secondary markets, much like other marketable short term bonds. (2.1.1)

Channels of monetary policy Direct and indirect channels through which monetary shocks affect expenditures on goods and services. (15.1.3)

Clearing house Institution for banks to cancel checks drawn on them, possessed by other banks, against checks in their possession, drawn on other banks. (4.1.3)

Commercial banks Depository institutions specializing in commercial lending and demand deposits, but with considerable business in lending to consumers and other borrowers and in issuing savings and time deposits. (3.2)

Commercial loan theory—individual banks Also called the *real bills doctrine*. Applied to individual banks, the theory maintains that loans made to business to finance production or commercial transactions are self-liquidating. Commercial loan theorists argue that most if not all bank loans should be confined to short-term production or commercial loans in order to assure bank liquidity. Applied to the banking system as a whole, the doctrine asserts the deposits created in the process of commercial or production loans can never be too much or too little, since they presumably are just sufficient to meet the "needs of trade." (4.1)

Commercial loan theory—monetary

policy Applied to monetary policy, indicates that the money and credit supply ought to be permitted to rise or fall in line with the so-called "needs of trade." (10.2.1)

Commercial paper Marketable short-term unsecured bonds, usually with maturities of 6 months or less, issued in large denominations of $1,000,000 or more by well-established businesses. (3.4.4)

Common stocks Sometimes called shares or equities, common stocks are variable income securities representing ownership shares in a corporation. Income from stocks comes in the form of dividends periodically declared by the board of directors of the corporation. (3.4.3)

Compensating balances Deposits required by banks of loan customers. (5.1.1)

Comptroller of the Currency Chief regulator of national banks. The office was created by the National Banking Act of 1863, which set up the national banking system. (4.1.2)

Contraction phase of a business cycle Movement of the economy from a business cycle upper turning point or peak to its trough. (16.1.1)

Correspondent banks Banks, usually large, that hold deposits of other banks, usually small. Correspondent banks also provide check clearing and other services to the smaller banks. (4.1.3)

Credibility hypothesis Hypothesis that people cannot rationally form opinions about government policy intentions unless the government, through its actions, convinces the public that it means what it says. (18.2.5)

Credit Loans made by lenders to borrowers. Examples are personal loans, bank loans, purchases of corporate, municipal or U.S. government bonds, and "trade credit," such as doctors' bills and charge accounts. (1.2.3)

Credit Control Act of 1969 Authorizes the President to invoke standby credit controls for the purpose of preventing or controlling inflation. First used on a temporary basis in the spring of 1980. (9.4.2)

Crowding-out effect Reduction in private and state and local government spending caused by an increase in the federal deficit. (14.2.3)

Currency and coin Paper and metallic money issued by the Treasury and (mainly) by the Federal Reserve System. Currency and coin held by the private and nonbank sector are part of the officially defined money supply. Currency and coin held in bank vaults or by the U.S. Treasury or Federal Reserve System is not part of the money supply. (2.1.2)

Currency–deposit ratio Ratio of the public's desired holdings of currency to its holdings of demand deposits. (6.1.2)

Currency in circulation Currency and coin held outside banks, the Federal Reserve System, and the Treasury. A factor absorbing member bank reserves and a use of the monetary base. (8.2.1)

Cyclical unemployment Unemployment arising from fluctuations of the economy around its full (natural) unemployment growth path. (18.1.2)

Dealers Firms or individuals that buy and sell stocks or bonds for the purpose of profiting from the differences between buying and selling prices. In effect, wholesalers for financial assets. (3.1.3)

Debt management Strategy of sales and purchases of bonds in different maturity ranges in order to influence the term structure of interest rates. Exemplified by Operation Twist. Occasionally practiced by both the Fed and the Treasury. (9.1.2)

Default (credit) risk Risk of losing loaned money due to inability of borrower to repay. (3.1.3)

Defensive open market operations Federal Reserve purchases and sales of securities for the purpose of offsetting predicted or unpredicted fluctuations in bank reserves that cause reserves to deviate from levels targeted by the monetary authorities. (8.2.2)

Deferred availability cash items Liability item on Fed's balance sheet representing a temporary (no more than 2-day) deferral of credits to the accounts of banks that have received checks drawn on other banks. Federal Reserve credit in the form of float is calculated by subtracting deferred availability cash items from cash items in the process of collection on Federal Reserve banks' balance sheets. (8.1.3)

Demand deposits Checkable deposits in commercial banks and other depository institutions. Similar de-

posits in savings institutions are called *share drafts* or *NOW accounts.* The latter bear interest. Checkable deposits can be cashed on written demand or transferred to third parties by written order of the depositor to the bank or savings institution. Checkable deposits owned by private (nonbank, nonfinancial institution) entities are defined as part of the money supply. See M-1A, M-1B, and other definitions of money. (1.1.4)

Demand-side business cycles Business cycles set in motion by monetary or fiscal shocks or by changes in autonomous spending. (16.1.3)

Deposit–reserve ratio Ratio of bank deposits to bank reserves. Sometimes called the "deposit multiplier." (6.1.1)

Derivative deposits Deposits created by banks in the process of lending or purchasing securities. (4.1.5)

Devaluation of a currency Policy decision to raise the foreign currency price or the gold price of the domestic currency. (19.1.6)

Direct and indirect finance Lending by surplus income units to deficit spenders either directly, via personal loans or security markets, or indirectly through banks, thrifts, or other financial intermediaries. (3.1.1)

Direct effects of a monetary shock Excess demand or supply of money offset by sales or purchases of goods and services, instead of by borrowing and lending. (15.1.3)

Discount mechanism Loan facilities at Federal Reserve banks; availability and cost of funds to banks and thrifts at the discount window are an instrument of monetary policy. (9.2)

Discount rate Interest rate charged to depository institutions borrowing money from Federal Reserve banks. (4.2.2)

Disintermediation Loss of time and savings deposits by banks and thrifts when market interest rates rise above rates financial intermediaries can offer to depositors. (4.2.1)

Disposable income Personal (household) income minus personal taxes; includes social security and other transfer payments, but excludes social security taxes. (14.2.1)

District Federal Reserve banks Twelve district Federal Reserve banks administer discount windows, administer Federal Reserve regulations, participate in the check clearing system, conduct research, and participate in the formulation of monetary policy by the FOMC. (7.1.1)

Dynamic open market operations Open market operations designed to meet monetary growth targets set by the monetary authorities. (8.2.2)

Effective demand Demand for goods backed up by purchasing power. In a barter economy, purchasing power is other goods offered in exchange; in a money economy, the medium of exchange is purchasing power. (1.2.1)

Efficient market A market in which stock or bond prices reflect the most current information available to well-informed investors. Systematic profits from speculative activity are unlikely if markets are efficient. (3.4.5)

Employment Act of 1946 Act giving the federal government and its agencies the responsibility of conducting its affairs so as to maximize employment. (17.1.4)

Equation of exchange Irving Fisher's equation summarizing the elements of the quantity theory of money: $MV = Py = Y$, where M is the nominal money supply, V its velocity, P the price level of output, and y the level of real output (income). Y is the level of nominal income. Fisher's equation is an alternative to the Cambridge equation, since $V = 1/k$. (12.3.4)

Equilibrium world distribution of money Theory that under fixed exchange rates international money flows tend to distribute the global money supply between countries in accordance with the demand for money in each country. (19.1.3)

Eurodollars Dollar denominated deposits held in banks outside of the United States—principally in foreign subsidiaries of U.S. banks. (2.1.3)

Even keel policy Federal Reserve purchases of government securities designed to offset negative impact on bond prices of exceptionally large Treasury bond sales. (9.1.3)

Excess demand for (and supply of) a good Excess of planned purchases (sales) of a good over planned sales (purchases) of the good at its prevailing price. (11.1.1)

Excess demand for (supply of) money An excess demand for money implies a desire to hold money balances in excess of balances already owned. An excess supply of money implies a desire to hold less money than the balances already owned. Say's Principle implies that an aggregate excess demand for money implies an aggregate excess supply of goods, and that an aggregate excess supply of money implies an aggregate excess demand for goods. (1.2.1)

Excess flow demand for bonds Flow demand for bonds minus flow supply of bonds, expressed as an increasing function of the rate of interest. (13.2.2)

Excess reserves Reserves held by banks or thrifts in excess of minimum reserves required by the Federal Reserve System or by state banking laws. (4.1.5)

Excess stock demand for bonds Stock demand for bonds minus existing stock of bonds. (The flow demand for bonds equals excess stock demand, provided adjustment of the stock of bonds to the desired level takes one period.) (13.1.2)

Expansion phase of a business cycle Movement of the economy from the lower turning point or trough of a cycle to its peak. (16.1.1)

Expectations hypothesis A term structure of interest rate theory that asserts that interest rates on long-term bonds are averages of current short-term rates plus averages of expected future short rates by market participants. (13.Appendix)

Expectations-augmented Phillips curve Theory that any given short-run Phillips curve is based upon a given set of expectations of inflation by market participants. Shifts in the curves are then associated with changes in expectations. (18.2)

Federal Deposit Insurance Corporation Agency created by Congress in 1934 to provide mandatory deposit insurance for depositors of national banks and for state banks that volunteer to buy it. (5.2.2)

Federal funds Surplus bank reserves on deposit with the Federal Reserve System lent to other banks, usually on an overnight basis. (3.4.4)

Federal funds market Market in immediately available reserve free funds lent and borrowed by banks; a substitute for going to the discount window for banks in need of funds to meet reserve requirements. (4.2.2)

Federal Open Market Committee (FOMC) Twelve-member committee composed of seven members from the Board of Governors and a rotating group of five district Federal Reserve bank presidents, charged with the task of formulating System policy on open market purchases and sales of government securities, the main tool of monetary policy. (7.1.1)

Federal Reserve notes Currency issued by Federal Reserve banks, the most commonly used currency in circulation. (2.1.2)

Federal Reserve System The central bank of the United States. All national banks must join the System; other depository institutions can do so if they wish. (4.1.2)

Feedback policy rules Fiscal or monetary policy rules that call for systematic responses to changes in the unemployment rate, inflation rate, or other economic variables. (20.1.3)

Financial intermediaries Financial institutions that create obligations or claims on themselves in order to collect money for relending. Major intermediaries are commercial banks, thrift institutions, mutual investment companies, pension funds, and life insurance companies. (3.1.1)

Fiscal policy Manipulation of government spending or taxes for the purpose of affecting aggregate demand. (13.2.5)

Fiscal policy multipliers Ratios of the change in real gross national product to policy-induced shifts in government spending or taxes. (20.1.1)

Fisher effect Another name for the price expectations effect on nominal interest rates. (13.2.4)

Fixed exchange rates Exchange rates between national currencies fixed by actions of the monetary authorities or by use of gold as an international and national medium of exchange, each country defining its currency in terms of a fixed quantity of gold. (19.1.2)

Fixprice markets Hick's term for oligopolistic and other markets in which prices respond sluggishly to changes in demand or factors affecting supply. (15.2.1)

Flexible (floating) exchange rates Exchange rates between domestic and foreign currencies determined by market forces instead of by decisions of monetary authorities. (19.1.6)

Flexprice markets Hick's term for competitive or auction type markets in which prices respond flexibly to shifts in demand or supply. Raw materials and securities markets are examples. (15.2.1)

Float Cash items in the process of collection minus deferred availability cash items on the balance sheets of the Federal Reserve banks. In effect, interest free loans to banks. (8.1.3)

Flow demand for (supply of) bonds Number of bonds people plan to add to the asset (liabilities) side of their balance sheets. Consists of newly added bonds plus bonds to replace those that have matured. (13.1.2)

Free (or net borrowed) reserves Excess reserves minus reserves borrowed from the Federal Reserve banks. (10.1.2)

Free reserves doctrine Use of free reserves as an operating target and as an indicator of monetary policy. (10.2.2)

Frictional unemployment New workers, labor force reentrants, or people laid off due to changes in the composition of demand, looking for jobs. (18.1.1)

Fundamental proposition of monetary theory Given the stock of money, the level of nominal income and interest rates will adjust until the stock of money that people wish to hold (i.e., the stock of money demanded) comes into equality with the existing stock of money. (12.1.1)

General equilibrium Market prices

structured so as to produce equilibrium in every market for a good or service in the economy. (11.2.3)

Global (world) demand for money Under fixed exchange rates, the sum of all national aggregate demands for money, expressed in terms of a single currency. (19.1.2)

Global money supply Sum total of all national currencies, expressed in terms of any one of them, at fixed exchange rates. (19.1.2)

Gold certificates Paper money issued by the Treasury to Federal Reserve banks and backed 100 percent by gold bullion owned by the Treasury. (8.1.1)

Gold-exchange standard Countries defining currencies in terms of a fixed amount of gold, but using currencies, such as the dollar or the pound sterling, alongside gold as international reserves. (19.1.2)

Gold standard International and national monetary arrangement in which countries defined their currencies in terms of gold and stood ready to convert them into gold at the fixed rates. (19.1.2)

Government budget deficit Government outlays on goods and services minus taxes net of transfer payments. Equals money raised by borrowing in the private sector plus bonds purchased by the Federal Reserve System. (13.2.5)

Government transfer payments Social security pensions, welfare payments in money or kind, and other payments to the private sector that are not for services rendered to the government. (14.2.1)

Humphrey–Hawkins Act 1978 Full Employment and Balanced Growth Act, requiring, among other things, reports of the Fed concerning targets for monetary growth. (7.1.2)

Hyperinflation Extremely rapid increases in the price level, usually leading to a breakdown in a currency, or to a currency reform replacing old money units with new money units. (17.5)

Illiquidity Inability of a bank to meet cash withdrawals on short notice. (5.1)

Income effect on interest rate Change in the real rate of interest due to a change in income. (13.2.4)

Income-expenditure model Theory of real income that asserts that equilibrium real income is determined by the interaction of real investment spending, as determined by interest rates and profit expectations of business, and real consumption spending, as determined by the level of real income. (12.3.5)

Income velocity of money Ratio of GNP or some other measure of aggregate income to the money supply. (16.3)

Incomes policies Wage–price guidelines or other plans devised to restrict wage and price increases to ceilings set by the federal government. Examples are the "voluntary" guidelines of the Johnson and Carter Administrations. Others are the tax-based income plan (TIP) and the wage insurance plan (WIP). (20.3)

Indexation Adjusting debts for changes in the price level, as measured by changes in the consumer price index or some other price index. The object is to recover part or all of the changes in the purchasing power of the obligation due to unanticipated inflation. (1.1.5)

Indicator of monetary policy A variable that quantifies the relative strength of policy actions on the ultimate objectives of policy. (10.1.3)

Indirect effects of monetary shock Excess demand or supply of money offset by sales or purchases of securities, thus affecting interest rates and, through interest rates, expenditures on goods and services. (15.1.3)

Indirect exchange Exchange of a desired good for another less desired good, to be traded for a good more desired than the one first given up. Exchanges involving money are an example of indirect exchange. (1.1.1)

Inference problem Problem facing the public of how to interpret policy actions of the authorities in terms of their policy pronouncements. (20.1.5)

Inflation Rising general price level; alternatively, a falling value of money. (17.1.1)

Inflation tax Reduction in the real value of cash balances owned by the public, as a result of inflation. (17.4.3)

Instruments of monetary policy Mechanisms used by Fed to pursue monetary policy objectives. General instruments include open market operations, changes in reserve requirements, and discount rate adjustments. Selective instruments include changes in stock market credit

margins, Regulation Q, and, occasionally, selective credit controls over consumer and business lending. (10)

Interest cost-push theory of inflation Theory that inflation arises from increases in interest rates that raise business costs. (17.2.3)

Intermediate policy targets Specified levels or growth rates of variables thought to be influential in affecting ultimate targets of monetary policy. Intermediate targets include monetary aggregates or long-term interest rates. (10.1.1)

International Banking Act of 1978 For the first time brought foreign banks operating in the United States under national control; previously they had operated principally under state control. (5.3.2)

International price level Global price level of tradable goods or close substitutes emerging out of international arbitrage and the operation of the law of one price. (19.1.2)

Investment bankers Firms that underwrite or otherwise market newly issued stocks and bonds for borrowing firms. (3.1.1)

Investment (mutual) companies Firms that issue shares, often marketable, for the purpose of purchasing stocks or bonds. The value of the shares reflect the value of the stocks or bonds they hold. Investment companies pay shareholders dividends that are based upon the earnings of the assets they hold minus costs of administration. (3.1.1)

Investments (bank) Bank holdings of marketable securities, mostly U.S. and state and local government bonds, but some corporate bonds as well. (4.3.1)

Keynesian cross Well-known 45° diagram that shows equilibrium income in the form of an equality between aggregate demand (planned investment and consumption, which is a function of income) and the aggregate level of output. When planned spending and output are equal, equilibrium income is shown to prevail. (12.3.5)

Keynesian school of macroeconomics Originating in the doctrines of John Maynard Keynes, as enunciated in his *General Theory of Employment, Interest and Money* (1936), this school believes that business cycles result from changes in business investment and/or government spending. As distinct from monetarists, Keynesians today frequently argue that changes in the money supply are the result, not the cause, of business cycles. (1.2)

Laffer curve Curve describing relationship between tax revenues and tax rates, an old idea revived by Arthur Laffer, who believes that cuts in taxes in the United States and perhaps elsewhere will actually raise total revenue because of the stimulus given to productive activity. (14.2.4)

Lagged reserve requirements Policy of the Fed to require reserves computed as percentages of deposits two weeks earlier than the computation week. (9.3.2)

Lags in effect of monetary changes Monetary shocks first impact upon real output, then upon the price levels, each impact with a lag. (15.2)

Law of one price Tendency for market forces (arbitrage) to bring about a single price for identical goods selling in different parts of a trading area. (19.1.1)

Lender of last resort A major function of central banks, which is to be the ultimate provider of ready cash to the economy and banks in times of crisis, such as runs on banks by depositors. (9.2.2)

Leveraging For a bank, leveraging means to increase earnings on capital by increasing deposits and other forms of borrowed money in order to increase loans and investments. (5.1.1)

Liabilities management Managing deposits and other liabilities in order to maintain a profitable portfolio of assets. Certificates of deposit, Eurodollar loans, repurchase agreements, and money market certificates are major instruments for liabilities management. (5.1.3)

Line of credit Agreement by a bank to lend a customer up to a given amount without detailed negotiations. (4.3.2)

Liquid position of banks Possession of sufficient cash or ready access to cash to meet unexpected demands for cash by depositors. (4.1)

Liquidity Speed and cost of converting an asset into money. Highly liquid assets can be converted into money rapidly with little cost. By definition, money is the most liquid of assets. (1.1.4)

Liquidity effect on interest rate Reduction (increase) in the real rate of interest due to a change in the money supply. (13.2.4)

Long-run Phillips curve Vertical line, built over the natural unemployment rate, indicating that in the long run the inflation rate is independent of the rate of unemployment, contrary to the findings of Phillips and others. (18.1)

M-1 Pre-1980 narrow definition of money. Includes net demand deposits in commercial banks plus currency and coin in circulation outside banks and federal government. Net demand deposits are total demand deposits minus deposits due to the federal government and to other commercial banks, minus cash items in process of collection. (2.1.1)

M-1A Demand deposits in commercial banks, minus deposits due to domestic commercial banks, foreign banks and the U.S. government, plus currency and coin outside banks. (2.1.3)

M-1B M-1A plus NOW accounts and ATS accounts at commercial banks, and demand deposits, NOW accounts, and credit union share drafts balances at thrift institutions. (2.1.3)

M-2 M-1B plus savings and small denomination time deposits (under $100,000) at all depository institutions, money market mutual funds shares, overnight repurchase agreements (RPs) issued by commercial banks, and some overnight Eurodollars held by U.S. residents. Pre-1980 M-2 was simple M-1 plus all small denomination time deposits at commercial banks. (2.1.3)

M-3 M-2 plus large denominated time deposits in all depository institutions and term repurchase agreements issued by commercial banks

and savings and loan associations. Pre-1980 M-3 was pre-1980 M-2 plus time and savings shares and deposits in thrift institutions. (2.1.3)

Manager of the System Account Officer at the Federal Reserve Bank of New York trading desk charged with implementing policies set forth by the Federal Open Market Committee. (9.1.2)

Margin requirements Selective instrument of policy given to the Fed by the 1934 Securities and Exchange Act, permitting the monetary authorities to set the percentage of purchase price of stocks that may be financed by credit. (9.4.1)

Market equilibrium Occurs when the market price for a good is such that planned purchases and sales of the good are equal. Equilibrium implies planned and realized purchases and sales for each transactor are equal—i.e., absence of disappointments for all traders. (11.1.2)

Market risk Risk of taking a loss on an asset at time of sale or purchase due to change in its market price. (3.1.3)

Market segmentation theory Term structure of interest rate theory which asserts that bonds with different terms to maturity are imperfect substitutes, hence they have different markets determining their prices and interest rates. (13. Appendix)

Medium of exchange Principal function of money. Objects which serve widely as instruments of indirect exchange are money, or media of exchange. (1.1.2)

Member bank reserve equation Equation stating factors that supply or absorb member bank reserves. (8.2)

Member banks Member banks of the Federal Reserve System. National banks are required to be members; state banks may join at their discretion. (7.1.1)

Monetarist school of macro-economics Headed by Milton Friedman, this school believes that the major source of fluctuations in aggregate output and prices is to be found in excessive fluctuations of the money supply. The school also attributes long-term inflation to high trend rates of growth in the money supply. (1.2)

Monetary base Currency in circulation plus bank reserves. Sometimes called "high-powered money." (6.1.1)

Monetary Control Act of 1980 Short name for Depository Deregulation and Monetary Control Act of 1980. The Act made all depository institutions subject to Federal Reserve reserve requirements, revised the structure of the requirements, and set up a process for deregulation of ceiling interest rates on time and savings deposits. (4.1.4)

Monetary control procedures Procedures followed by the FOMC and the Manager of the Open Market Account for implementing intermediate policy targets set by the FOMC. (10.3.1–10.3.2)

Monetary equilibrium Total or aggregate demand to hold money equals existing stock of money. (11)

Monetary policy multiplier Ratio of changes in real gross national product to changes in the money supply, the monetary base, unborrowed reserves, or some other reserve aggregate. (20.1.1)

Monetary shock Unanticipated change in the nominal money supply or in the growth rate of the nominal money supply that disturbs a monetary equilibrium. (15.1)

Monetary theory of income Theory describing the interaction of the money market and the bond market to determine the level of money income and the market rate of interest. (13.3)

Monetary theory of nominal income Theory which states that nominal income in an economy must adjust so as to bring the demand for money, expressed as a fraction, k, of nominal income into equality with the existing stock of money. An income level which achieves such an equality is called an equilibrium of income. (12.3)

Monetary theory of the balance of payments Interprets balance of payments surpluses as the result of excess demands for money in a region or country and balance of payments deficits as the result of excess supplies of money. The theory postulates that interregional or international money flows eliminate the surpluses or deficits and thus create balance of payments equilibrium and monetary equilibrium at the same time. (19.1)

Monetary theory of the business cycle Theory that business cycles are mainly explained by monetary shocks and the train of events they set in motion. (16.2)

Monetization of debt Creation of demand deposits for bank borrowers. The new deposits remain in the banking system unless reduced by net repayment of debt to the system by deposit holders. (4.1.5)

Money An object acting as a universally accepted medium of exchange, a unit of account, a standard for deferred payment, and a liquid store of value. Things that serve as money are discussed in Chapter 2. (1.1.2–1.1.5)

Money growth rule Proposal by Milton Friedman that monetary authorities should abandon activist discretionary policies and adopt a constant growth rate for the money supply, to be adhered to during both business cycle expansions and contractions. (18.2.5)

Money market certificates Six-month time certificates offered by banks and thrifts in minimum denominations of $10,000 at interest rates slightly higher than six-month Treasury bills; designed to reduce disintermediation during periods of high interest rates. (4.2.1)

Money market conditions Free or net borrowed reserves and short-term market interest rates thought to be close to Federal Reserve control as operating targets. Also a phrase used to indicate degree of tightness or ease in money and credit markets. (10.1.2)

Money market (MM) equilibrium curve Diagram showing the combinations of money income and interest rates that maintain equilibrium between the supply of and the demand for nominal money balances. (12.3.6)

Money markets Financial markets that deal with bonds of one year or less. Examples are the Treasury bill market, the federal funds market, and the commercial paper market. (3.4.4)

Money multiplier Ratio of the money supply to the monetary base. (6.1.3)

Money supply theory Theory describing how interaction of the banks, the nonbank private sector, and the monetary authorities create and change the money supply. Theory is summarized by the base-multiplier formula. (6.1)

Moral suasion Speeches, congressional testimony, newspaper articles, and threats by monetary authorities designed to change behavior of lenders and borrowers in ways consistent with the direction of monetary policy. Often a substitute for vigorous conduct of monetary policy with regular tools. (9.5)

Mutual savings banks State-chartered organizations that issue savings deposits, NOW accounts, and regular demand deposits and use their funds mainly to buy home mortgages and high-grade corporate securities. (3.2)

National Bank Acts of 1863 and 1864 Set up the national banking system, Comptroller of the Currency, and established a "uniform currency" of national bank notes, most of which are now retired. (5.2.1)

National bank notes Currency issued by national banks under authorization of the National Bank Acts of 1863 and 1864, now almost completely retired from circulation. (2.1.2)

Natural unemployment rate Rate of unemployment at which, on balance, workers' and employers' anticipations of inflation equal actual inflation. Sometimes defined as the rate of unemployment matching the sum of frictional and structural unemployment. (18.1)

Negotiable order of withdrawal (NOW) accounts Interest bearing deposits using negotiable orders of withdrawal similar to checks. (2.1.3)

Net taxes Tax payments to the government minus transfer payments from the government to the private sector. (14.2.1)

Net worth Assets minus liabilities equal net worth of an economic unit. Thus, net worth represents the value of the unit's own claims against its assets, as against those of its creditors should the unit be dissolved. (4.1.1)

Nominal money supply Actual number of monetary units in hands of individuals and nonbank businesses. (12.1.2)

Nominal rate of interest Rate of interest prevailing in the market, taking into account a premium for inflationary expectations. Provided borrowers and lenders have the same inflationary expectations, the nominal rate of interest equals the real rate of interest plus the expected rate of inflation. (13.2.4)

Nonborrowed reserves Total member bank reserves minus borrowed reserves. (8.3)

Nonmonetary theories of inflation Theories that stress the effects of changes in taxes, supply-side shocks, or labor and business monopoly on the inflation rate. (17.1.3)

Open market operations Federal Reserve purchases and sales of government securities for the purpose of changing bank reserves or the monetary base. (9.1)

Operating policy targets Reserve aggregates (such as nonborrowed reserves, free reserves, or the monetary base) or short-term interest rates thought to be important as means to achieving intermediate policy targets. (10.1.2)

Operation Twist Open market policy in 1961 of selling short-term securities and purchasing long-term securities in order to influence the term structure of interest rates. Operation Twist signaled the end of the bills only policy of the 1950s. (9.1.2)

Optimal control policies Best policies available to authorities as revealed by a study of the interaction of policy instruments with forecasts of exogenous variables in the context of a good econometric model. (20.1.3)

Overshoots Movements of variables such as the inflation rate or real income beyond equilibrium positions as a consequence of a monetary (or other) shock to the economy. (15.1.2)

Paper standard Domestic money supplies in each country, unbacked by and not convertible into gold, silver, or any other commodity, but with an agreement by each national authority to buy other currencies at fixed exchange rates. (19.1.4)

Penalty rate Discount rates charged to banks in excess of the rates they can earn in their own lending operations. Federal Reserve bank discount rates are not penalty rates. (9.2.3)

Permanent income Expected average lifetime income, usually measured by a weighted average of past incomes. Concept was invented by Milton Friedman who used it as a proxy for wealth in consumption and demand for money studies. (16.3.2)

Phillips curve Negative relationship between inflation rate and unemployment rate, named after A.W. Phillips, who discovered it in 1958. (18. Introduction)

Policy goals Ultimate targets of monetary policy, such as level of gross national product, rate of inflation, the balance of payments, etc. (10.1)

Policy simulation studies Feeding hypothetical policy changes into an econometric model of the economy to estimate the impact of the changes on the economy. (20.1.1)

Political business cycle Theory that government policies are formulated to produce economic conditions favorable to the reelection of the incumbent president. (20.4.1)

Portfolio For a bank, the array of cash and earning assets appearing on its balance sheet. (5.1.2)

Precautionary demand for money Money held because of uncertainty of timing between receipts and outlays. Differs from the transactions demand for money, which depends soley upon the lack of synchronization of receipts and outlays, even though there is no uncertainty about them. (12.2.3)

Present value of a bond A sum of money which, if invested at a given interest rate, will yield a given set of payments in the future, the payments to include coupon interest and redemption values. (3.4.5)

Price expectations effect Increase or decrease in the nominal rate of interest due to changes in inflationary expectations. (13.2.4)

Price makers Firms and other transactors that have power to set prices independently of current market forces. (15.2.2)

Price takers Transactors that must accept ruling market prices, having no ability to set prices of their own. (15.2.2)

Primary and secondary (indirect) securities Primary securities are issued to lenders by primary borrowers (deficit income units such as firms, households, and government). Secondary (indirect) securities are claims on financial intermediaries (e.g., bank deposits, savings and loan shares, and mutual fund shares) that are bought mainly by surplus income units (mainly households). The money acquired by the intermediaries is mostly channeled into primary securities issued by deficit income units. (3.1.1)

Primary deposits Bank deposits arising out of deposit in a bank of currency or checks drawn on other banks. New primary deposits for the banking *system* must come from currency deposits, deposits by the

Treasury, or deposits from abroad. (4.1.5)

Prime interest rate Interest rate charged to best corporate customers by major banks. (5.1.1)

Private income Total income (gross or net national income) minus net taxes. (14.2.1)

Purchasing power parity theory Theory that in a world of flexible or floating exchange rates, uninhibited market forces will bring exchange rates between currencies into line with differences in national price levels. (19.2)

Pure fiscal policy Fiscal policy conducted without supporting changes in the money supply by the monetary authorities. Deficits or surpluses generated by a pure fiscal policy change the private sector's holdings of government securities by amounts equal to the deficit or surplus. (13.2.5)

Quantity theory of money Older version stressed the central role of the stock of money in determining the level of money prices. Newer version expands the role of money to include determination of the level of money income in a country. The older version is simply stated by an equation stating that the equilibrium level of money prices is determined by the ratio of nominal money balances to the aggregate demand for real money balances. (Section 12.1.3). (12.1)

Rational expectations Theory that people base predictions on inflation on many sources of information, not just inflation trends, as assumed by the adaptive expectations school.

Rational expectations imply deliberate collection of information about price trends, monetary and fiscal policy, monetary theory, and other events in order to make inflation forecasts. Information is presumed to be collected until the marginal cost of additional information equals its marginal value to the individual decision maker. (18.2.3)

Real money balances Nominal money balances, supplied or demanded, measured in terms of their purchasing power, $1/P$, where P is some price index, such as the consumers' price index. Symbolically, real money balances are $m = M/P$ where M is the number of nominal money units (say dollars). (12.1.2)

Real rate of interest Rate of interest that would prevail in the bond market in the absence of inflationary expectations. (13.2.4)

Regulation Q Regulation under which the Fed and other regulatory authorities set maximum interest rates on time and savings deposits; presently being fazed out under the 1980 Depository Institution Deregulation and Monetary Control Act. (4.2.1)

Reluctance to borrow theory Belief that banks voluntarily limit their borrowing from Federal Reserve banks because of a reluctance to be in debt to the Fed, even though the Fed does not charge penalty discount rates. The theory is the basis for W.W. Reifler's theory of credit control (followed by the Fed in the 1920s) and the free reserves doctrine in the 1950s and 1960s. (9.2.3)

Repurchase agreements at commercial

banks (RPs) Business loans to banks secured by U.S. government securities that can be terminated at any time. (2.1.3)

Required reserves Minimum reserves computed as a fraction of various types of deposits. Reserve requirements are administered by the Federal Reserve System within limits specified in the 1980 Monetary Control Act, which replaces older legislation. (4.1.4)

Reservation wage Wage below which an unemployed worker searching for work will refuse a job offer. (18.2.1)

Reserve bank credit The sum of Federal Reserve holdings of government securities, loans to member banks, float, and miscellaneous assets. A factor supplying bank reserves and a source of the monetary base. (8.2.1)

Reserve currency Currency used as international monetary reserves by nonreserve currency countries, such as the dollar after World War II and the British pound sterling before the dollar. Reserve currencies accompanied the gold-exchange standard and were convertible into gold at a fixed rate of exchange. (19.1.5)

Reserve position of a bank Degree of debt to the Federal Reserve. (9.2.4)

Reserves Bank vault cash or deposits with the Federal Reserve banks or correspondent banks. Federal Reserve System required reserves must be held as either vault cash or as a deposit with a Federal Reserve bank. State banking laws permit state-chartered banks to hold reserves in the form of correspondent deposits or, in some states, in U.S. Treasury bonds or other high quality short-term securities. (4.1.4)

Risk premiums Theory that long-term bonds must carry higher interest rates than short-term bonds to compensate long-term bond holders for larger market risk entailed in holding long-term bonds. The risk premium is the extra interest demanded by lenders to incur the extra market risk. (13. Appendix)

Rules versus activism debate Debate over active use of monetary-fiscal policies to stabilize the economy versus fixed policy rules, such as Friedman's money-growth rule. (20.1.3)

Savings and loan associations Depository institutions that issue shares, time deposits, and NOW accounts and that specialize mainly in real estate lending. (3.2)

Savings deposits Interest-bearing bank deposits with no set maturity date; frequently called passbook savings deposits. Legally, they may not be withdrawn without 30 days notice, but are usually available on demand. (4.2.1)

Say's Law "Supply creates its own demand," in the sense that all production (supply) is designed either to satisfy the demand of the producer (e.g., subsistence farmers) or to be exchanged for other goods. In a money economy, goods are sold for money and then exchanged for other goods. If producers hold instead of spend money, goods supplied may not result in demand for other goods. Hence, while Say's Law implies an impossibility of overproduction in a barter economy, it does not do so for a money economy. (1.2.1)

Say's Principle In a money economy, the aggregate excess demand for goods, services, and money is zero. Implied is the idea that a zero excess demand for money (equilibrium in the "money market") brings with it a zero aggregate excess demand for goods and services (i.e., equilibrium in the "goods market"). For a more precise definition of Say's Principle, see Section 11.2. (1.2.1)

Secondary reserves Short-term earning assets easily cashed to pay depositors demanding cash. Not part of official reserves. (5.1)

Shock-absorber function of money Use of money balances as a reserve that absorbs unanticipated money receipts or expenditures. (15.1.1)

Short-run Phillips curve Temporary negatively sloped Phillips curve which shifts as inflationary expectations catch up to the actual inflation rate. (18.1)

Shortsightedness effect Tendency of politicians to favor legislation whose benefits occur early, but whose costs appear later. (17.1.4)

Solvency Sufficient capital for a bank to pay off depositors and creditors after selling off assets. An insolvent bank has negative net worth. (5.1)

Special drawing rights (SDRs) A type of international money issued by the International Monetary Fund and allocated to its member countries, which use them as part of their international reserves. (8.1.1)

Speculative demand for money Keynes's idea that asset holders choose to hold money instead of securities in the belief that interest rates are likely to rise and thereby cause capital losses on the securities. If, as interest rates fall, more and more asset holders entertain such fears, the aggregate amount of money demanded should increase. Thus, Keynes's theory of the speculative demand for money—frequently called his theory of liquidity preference—is a rationalization for the inverse relationship between interest rates and the demand for money balances. (12.2.3)

Stagflation Simultaneous occurrence of inflation and unusually high unemployment. (17.Introduction)

Standard for deferred payment Use of money to express debts. Thus, instead of pigs and potatoes, borrowers promise to pay lenders money or its equivalent. Money as a standard for deferred payments declines during inflations; instead, loan contracts are frequently indexed for price level changes. (1.1.5)

Standard of value See *unit of account*. (1.1.3)

Stock demand for (supply of) bonds Total number of bonds people wish to hold (already possess), given their net worth and yields on alternative assets. (13.1.2)

Stop–go policies Monetary-fiscal policies that alternatively stimulate and retard aggregate demand and thereby contribute to fluctuations in the economy. (17.1.4)

Store of value Use of an asset to hold

in order to preserve purchasing power for the future. Money is a highly liquid store of value, though in inflationary times its purchasing power erodes with rising prices. (1.1.4)

Strategy of monetary policy A plan that links the goals of monetary policy with the specification and setting of policy instruments and targets designed to achieve the goals. (10.1)

Structural unemployment Unemployment arising out of a mismatch between skills and other requirements of available jobs and the characteristics of the unemployed labor force. (18.1.1)

Supply-side business cycle Business cycle set in motion by a supply-side shock, such as an increase in OPEC oil prices, wars, or natural disasters. (16.1.2)

Supply-side theory Stimulation of economy (via increased work effort and saving) resulting from tax cuts. An alternative to the view that fiscal policy operates on the economy primarily through its effects on aggregate demand. (14.2.4)

Suppressed inflation Prices kept down by controls during a period in which monetary forces are creating an inflationary environment of excess demand for goods and services. (17.1.1)

Surplus (deficit) income units Individuals or organizations that receive more (less) money income than they spend on goods and services. Surplus (deficit) units either accumulate (reduce) cash holdings or lend (borrow) to other income units directly or through financial intermediaries. (3.1)

T-account A double entry accounting device used to describe the impact upon a bank's balance sheet of each of its transactions. (4.1.2)

Tax and loan accounts U.S. government deposits in commercial banks. They are not counted as part of the money supply. (2.1.1)

Tax indexation Adjusting income tax brackets proportionally to inflation in order to preserve marginal tax rates on real incomes. (17.3.1)

Term loans Loans made for long periods of time, sometimes for interest rates that float in order to keep pace with going market rates. (5.1.2)

Term structure of interest rates Structure of interest rates on bonds as they relate to term maturity of bonds. (13.Appendix)

Terms of trade Real rate of exchange between domestic and foreign goods. Sometimes called the barter terms of trade. (19.2.2)

Tied discount rate Discount rate tied to some open market rate, such as the federal funds rate or the Treasury bill rate. (9.2.5)

Tight money (versus easy money) High interest rates and low availability of credit (versus low interest rates and high availability of credit). (10.1.2)

Time deposit ratio Ratio of savings and time deposits to demand deposits; reflects the behavior of nonbank private depositors. (6.1.4)

Time deposits Interest-bearing deposits with defined maturity dates sold to both business and consumer customers; early encashment is penalized by partial loss of interest. (4.2.1)

Trade (current account) balance Surplus or deficit of sales over purchases of goods and services between people in a particular region or country and people outside. (19.1)

Transactions costs Costs involved in searching for desired objects or for trading partners. Also included are storage costs of goods to be traded, including warehousing, spoilage, and interest costs. (1.1.2)

Transactions demand for money Money desired to bridge the gaps that occur between receipt and expenditure of money income. (12.2.1)

Treasury bills Short-term U.S. government bonds issued for three, six, nine, or twelve month maturity periods, without coupon interest. Interest earned is the difference between the price paid and the redemption value at maturity. (3.4.1)

Treasury cash holdings Treasury currency and coins held by the Treasury itself. Absorbs bank reserves. (8.2.1)

Treasury currency outstanding Coin and currency issued by Treasury and held by public, banks, the Fed, and by the Treasury itself. A factor supplying bank reserves and a source of the monetary base. (8.2.1)

Treasury (foreign and other) deposits at Federal Reserve banks Absorb bank reserves and reduce the monetary base. (8.2.1)

Unanticipated inflation Difference between actual inflation and inflation as predicted by market participants. (17.4.1)

Unit of account Use of money as a basis for quoting prices of objects exchanged or valued for the purpose of measuring financial positions (balance sheets or income statements). Another term for this function of money is *standard of value*. (1.1.3)

Utility of money Implicit yield on money holdings that arises from the convenience and security it provides to its holders. Basis for the transactions demand for money. (12.2.1)

Velocity of money Number of times the average dollar in hands of the public turns over in the purchase of goods and services. The velocity of money, V, is the reciprocal of the Cambridge k, which measures the fraction of income held in the form of money. If income is measured annually, the Cambridge k in effect measures the average fraction of a year that the average dollar is held. (12.3.4)

Yield curve Chart showing term structure of interest rates prevailing in the market on a given date. (13.Appendix)

Index

Advisory Committee on Monetary Statistics (Bach Committee), 37, 39
Anderson, Benjamin M., 219
Anderson, Leonall C., 340n
Anderson, Paul S., 8–9, 443
Arak, Marcelle V., 420n
Armco, 124
Armco Credit Corporation, 124
Arnowitz, Victor, 487n

Bach Committee, 37, 39
Baird, Charles W., 241n
Balance of payments
  arbitrage, 452, 453
  fixed exchange rates, 451–66
    between different countries, 455–58
    between regions of country, 452–55
  flexible exchange rates, 466–75
  law of one price, 452–53
  policy implications, 463–66
  world distribution of money, 458–59
  See also Purchasing power parity theory
Balbach, Anatol, 141
Bank Holding Company Act, 1956, 92
Bank Merger Act of 1960, 122–23
Bank of America, 118n
Bank of Canada, 193
Banker's acceptance, 92–93
Banking Act of 1933, 149
Banking Act of 1935, 81, 149, 155, 187, 194
Banks
  branch banking, 118–20, 121n
  competition with other lenders, 124–25
  deposit insurance, 116–17

failures, 116–17
foreign banks, 120–22
historical background, 113–15
holding companies, 92, 123
investment bankers, 46
liability management, 111–12
mergers, 122–23
monetization of debt, 83
mutual savings banks, 53–54
portfolio management, 107–10
profit analysis, 102–06
regulation, 113–17
running a bank, 105–12
savings and loan associations, 51–53
structure of industry, 118–25
See also specific headings, e.g.: Commercial banks; Reserves
Banks for Cooperatives, 55
Barclay Group, 121
Barter economy, 3–5
  Say's Law and, 15
  taxation-in-kind, 329
Benston, George, 202
Berkman, Neil G., 38n
Blumenthal, Michael, 222
Bond, David, 58n
Bonds, 58–59
  credit risk, 58–59
  excess demand, 294
  interest rates and, 64–67, 291, 301
  marketability, 59
  monetary policy and bond demand, 297–98
  payments stream, 59
  Say's Principle, 288–91
  serial bonds, 59
  stock demand, 290
  supply and demand, 289–91
    private, 291–95
  term to maturity, 58
Brunner, Karl, 220
Budget Act of 1974, 502

Bureau of Federal Credit Unions, 54
Burns, Arthur, 404, 494, 497, 503
Business cycles, 369–87
    contraction phase, 370
    definition, 369–70
    demand-side cycles, 370–71
    expansion phase, 370
    Keynesian view, 371–72
    monetary sources, 17–18
    money supply and, 374–81
    supply-side cycles, 370–71
    theories, 369–73

Cacy, J.A., 18n
Cagan, Phillip, 345n, 357n, 380, 491, 498n
Cambridge equation, 262–64, 278, 307, 348–52, 378, 397–98, 410, 445, 458
    cyclic changes, 381–85
Cambridge school, 262–63, 346
Campbell, Colin, 30n
Campbell, Rosemary, 30n
Capital accounts, 93
Capital formation, 11–12
Capital gains, 416–17
Capital income, 413–16
Capital markets, 62–63
Carlson, John A., 419
Carter administration, 160, 193, 197, 199, 222, 404, 495, 497, 499
Cassuto, Alexander E., 241n
Certificates of deposit. See Time deposits
Chandler, Lester V., 217n
Chase Manhattan, 118n
Cheng, Hang-Sheng, 120n
Citibank, 494–95
Citicorp, 118n
Clarkson, Kenneth, 433
Clower, Robert W., 14n, 241n
Coldwell, Phillip E., 119n
Commercial banks, 73–97
    assets, 93–97
    balance sheets, 74–76
    banker's acceptance, 92–93
    borrowing funds, 89
    capital accounts, 93
    chartering a bank, 76–78
    compensating balances, 106

correspondent banks, 80
    deposit and clearing operations, 78–80
    deposit costs, 106–07
    derivative deposits, 85
    discount rate, 89
    discount window, 89
    federal funds market, 89–90, 91
    Federal Reserve System member, 77
    holding companies, 82
    illiquidity, 101–02
    insolvency, 101, 102
    investments, 94–95
    lending and deposit creation, 82–86
    leveraging, 103–04
    lines of credit, 96
    liquid position, 74
    loans as assets, 95–97
    primary deposits, 85
    prime interest rate, 105–06
    purchased funds, 111, 112
    repurchase agreements, 90, 91
    reserves, 80–82. See also Reserves
    setting up, 76–78
    time and savings deposits, 87–89
    See also Banks
Committee to Fight Inflation, 503
Commodity Credit Corporation, 56
Consumer Checking Account Equity Act of 1980, 52
Consumer price index, 259
Coupon payments, 59
Cowing, Cedric, B., 51n
Cox, Albert, 202
Cramers, J.S., 9n
Credit
    business fluctuations and, 18–21
    controls, 199–201
Credit agencies, 55–57
Credit Control Act, 1969, 199, 200
Credit unions, 54
Crowding out effect, 326–29
Currency, 27–31
Currency Act of 1863, 28

Darby, Michael, 340n, 341, 348n
Davenport, John A., 504n, 505n
Debentures, 59

Demand. *See* Money demand; Supply and demand
Demand deposits, 36
Depository Institutions Deregulation and Monetary Control Act of 1980, 80n, 161–63, 189,
  Consumer Checking Account Equity Act of 1980, 52
  definition of money, 31
  deposit insurance, 117
  elimination of Regulation Q, 88, 202
  FRS monetary controls, 149–50, 161
  float, 173
  reserve requirements, 81, 131n, 141, 142, 173n, 194–95
Discount mechanism, 187–94
  coordination of open market functions and discount rates, 190–92
  lender of last resort function, 188–89
  mechanics, 187–88
  reluctance theory, 190, 191
  signal and announcements effect, 193–94
Disintermediation, 88
Dooley, Michael P., 500n

Eastburn, David P., 217n
Edge Act, 121
Ehbar, A.F., 199n
Eisenhower administration, 499
Employment
  full employment, 252–53
  See also Unemployment
Employment Act of 1946, 402
Equilibrium. *See* Market equilibrium; Monetary equilibrium
Eurodollar deposits, 34
Evans, Michael, 486n
Even keeling, 186–87, 304, 321, 336
Exchange rates, 170

Farm Credit Administration, 55
Farm credit agencies, 55
Farmer's Home Administration, 56

Federal Deposit Insurance Corporation, 115, 116–17, 202
Federal Finance Bank, 56
Federal Home Loan Bank Board, 53, 61, 82, 202
Federal Home Loans Banks, 55, 56, 195
Federal Housing Administration, 56, 96
Federal Intermediate Credit Banks, 55
Federal Land Banks, 55
Federal National Mortgage Association, 55, 56, 61
Federal Reserve Act of 1913, 81, 115, 149
Federal Reserve bank notes, 28
Federal Reserve Bank of New York, 155, 156
Federal Reserve Bank of St. Louis, 153, 213, 226, 340n, 443, 483
Federal Reserve Bulletin, 31, 155, 173, 187, 217
Federal Reserve notes, 28
Federal Reserve Reform Act, 1977, 157
Federal Reserve System, 130–31, 149–63, 504–06
  Accord of March 1951, 159, 185
  balance sheet, 167–73
  bank holding companies, 123
  bank mergers, 122
  bills only policy, 185
  Board of Governors, 153, 154–55
  clearing house for members, 78–80
  commercial banks as members, 77
  commercial loan theory, 217–19
  creation, 14
  credit controls, 199–201
  currency issuance, 27–28, 30
  debt management, 186
  deferred availability cash items, 172–73
  definition of money, 31
  discount mechanism. *See* Discount mechanism
  district banks, 149, 151–54
  emergency credit, 189
  even keeling, 186–87, 304, 321, 336
  Exchange Equalization Fund account, 169

Federal Reserve System *(cont.)*
  Federal Advisory Council, 156
  Federal Open Market Committee,
      152, 153, 155–56, 157, 184n,
      185, 187, 192, 210–13,
      220–21, 225, 226, 228
  float, 173
  gold certificates, 167–69
  independence, 158–60
  Inter-District Settlement Fund, 80
  liabilities, 172–73
  membership, 53, 70, 150–57,
      160–61
  monetary policy, 197–205
  moral suasion, 205
  mutual savings banks as members,
      53
  new money, 47–48
  Open Market Account, 171, 173,
      213, 220, 221, 223, 226. *See
      also* Open market operations
  Operation Twist, 185–86
  organization, 27, 149–58
  Regulation Q. *See* Regulation Q
  relations with Congress, 156–58
  reluctance theory, 190, 191
  reserves. *See* Reserves
  security loans, 96–97
  Special Drawing Rights, 167,
      169–70
  structure, 150–56
Feldstein, M., 415–16, 434
Fellner, William, 446n, 498n
Financial instruments, 57–68. *See also*
      specific instruments, e.g.:
      Bonds
Financial markets
  direct and indirect finance, 44–48
  financial intermediaries, 49–51
  necessity, 48–49
  types of, 43–51
Fiscal policy
  empirical evidence, 340–41
  financed through increase in
      money supply, 336–40
  See also Government expenditures
Fisher, Irving, 219, 275
Fisher effect, 300–03, 469
Floating rate loans, 109
Ford administration, 197

Fortson, James, 38
Friedman, Benjamin M., 340n
Friedman, Milton, 263
  bank failures, 117
  base-money multiplier formula,
      146n
  definition of money, 36–37, 38
  discounting, 194
  federal deposit insurance, 194
  free reserve theory, 219
  fundamental proposition of
      monetary theory, 257–58
  inflation, 422–23
  monetary changes, 12–13, 354–55
  monetary growth rule, 445–47,
      483, 487, 489, 504, 506
  money and business cycle, 374–76,
      379–80, 381, 383, 385
  natural unemployment rate, 430
  quantity theory of money, 262
Full Employment and Balanced
      Growth Act, 1978, 157, 402,
      494

*General Theory of Employment, Interest
      and Money* (Keynes), 13n, 268
Giaimo, Robert, 502–03
Girard Trust Corn Exchange Bank,
      122
Girton, Lance, 505n
Glass, Carter, 218
Gold certificates, 167–68
Gold exchange standard, 169, 456
Gold standard, 169, 456–57
Gordon, Robert J., 341, 434, 484n
Government expenditures
  balanced-budget changes, 335–36
  changes in spending, 325–29
  crowding out effect, 326–29
  financing methods, 319–22
  interest rates and deficits, 303–06
  pure fiscal policy, 322–36
Government National Mortgage
      Association, 55, 56
Grayson, C. Jackson, 409, 411
Greenspan, Alan, 503–04
Gross national product, 13, 210–12,
      250, 485, 487
Gwartney, James, 404n

Haberler, Gottfried, 369n, 443n, 446n
Hamblen, Mary, 18n
Havenstein, Rudolph, 493
Hayek, Friedrich A., 422, 489n, 505, 506
Hazlitt, Henry, 16, 505n, 506n
Heller, Walter, 483, 500
Hicks, J.R., 356n
Higgins, Byron, 376n
Holding companies, 92, 123
Holman, Paul M., 110n
Homeowners Loan Act, 52
Hume, David, 354
Humphrey–Hawkins Act, 157, 402, 494
Humphrey, Thomas M., 11n, 359n, 406n, 463n, 469n, 493, 494
Hutt, W.H., 14n

Income
    equilibrium, 251–53
    fiscal policy and, 322–36
    inflation and
        distribution of income, 420–21
        income policies, 495–97
        real income, 408–09
    interest rates and, 287–311
    monetary shocks and nominal income, 346–53
    monetary theory, 307–11
    money income, 249–51
    private income, 322–23
    taxation and, 329–31
    transfer payments and, 334–35
Indexation, 11
Inflation, 393–423
    abnormal price increases as cause of, 405–06
    adaptive expectations, 360, 440–41
    catch-up element, 360
    consumers cause inflation, 404–05
    definition, 393–96
    effects of, 411–16
    escalator clauses, 420–21
    forecasting element, 360
    German hyperinflation, 493–94
    interest rates and, 300–03, 406–08

    lags in inflationary expectations, 359–64
    monetary growth rule, 445–47
    monetary theory, 397–98
    nonmonetary causes, 398–401
    politics and, 401–04
    productivity and, 409–11
    rational expectations, 360, 441–43
        versus irrational expectations, 443–45
    redistribution of wealth and income, 417–23
        between borrower and lender, 418–19
        cash balances, 421–22
        income redistribution, 420–21
        resource allocation, 422–23
    stabilization policies. See Stabilization policies
    world inflation, 475–77
Interest rates, 202–03, 212, 216
    cyclical movement, 295–97
    expectations hypothesis, 314–15
    government deficits and, 303–06
    income equilibrium, 280
    income theory and, 287–311
    inflation and, 300–03, 406–08
    market segmentation theory, 312–14
    monetary policy, 298–303
    nominal interest rate, 300–01
    policy targets, 223–24
    prime interest rate, 105–06
    real rate of interest, 300–01
    security prices, 64–68
    term structure, 312–15
    theory, 291–307
    transactions demand for money, 264–66
International Banking Act of 1978, 120, 121
International Monetary Fund, 167, 169
Investment bankers, 46

Jackson, President Andrew, 114
Jacobs, R.L., 446n
Johnson administration, 495

Joint Economic Committee, 157, 224, 226, 483, 487, 506
Jones, R.A., 446n
Jordan, Jerry L., 340n

Kane, Edward J., 204
Kaufman, George G., 38, 215–16, 221
Kemmerer, Edwin, 219
Kennedy, Edward, 497n
Kennedy, John, 499, 500
Keynes, John Maynard, 13n
  definition of money, 37n
  demand for money, 262
    transactions motive, 263
  fundamental proposition of monetary theory, 257, 258
  liquidity preference theory, 268–69, 371–72
Keynesian cross, 276–79
Keynesian school
  business cycles, 371–72
  fiscal policy, 402, 403–04
  income theory, 276–79
  interest rates, 212
  monetarist school contrasted, 13
Khaldun, Ibn, 330n
Khaldun–Laffer curve, 330n
Knickerbocker Trust Company, 379

Laffer, Arthur, 330n
Laffer curve, 330n
Lang, Richard W., 141n
Lawler, T.H., 469
Leijonhufvud, Axel, 14n, 241n
Lenin, 3
Leveraging, 103–04
Life insurance companies, 54
Liquidity preference, 268, 372
Livingston, J.A., 419
Lombra, Raymond E., 500n
Lubar, Robert, 498n, 503n
Lucas, Robert, 441

McCulloch, J. Huston, 4n
McFadden Act, 121, 122
Mackay, Charles, 51n
McNeill, Charles R., 82n
Malthus, 14

Market equilibrium, 239–41, 355–57
  general equilibrium, 244–45
  monetary equilibrium and, 248–49
Marshall, Alfred, 262
Marx, 14
Mayer, Martin, 124n
Mayer, Thomas, 496n
Meiners, Roger, 433
Meiselman, David, 38
Meltzer, Allan H., 220, 492
Merril, David, 184n
Meyer, L., 484n, 485, 488, 489, 490–91
Mill, James, 14
Mill, John Stuart, 14, 16
Miller, G. William, 494
Monetarist school, 13
Monetary Control Act of 1980. *See* Depository Institutions Regulation and Monetary Control Act of 1980
Monetary equilibrium
  crowding out effect, 326–29
  fiscal policy and, 326
  income equilibrium and, 249–52, 270–80
  individual and aggregate, 246–48
  interest rates and, 326–27
  market equilibrium and, 248–49
Monetary History of the United States (Friedman and Schwartz), 483
Monetary policy, 209–32
  bond demand, 297–98
  commercial loan theory, 217–19
  equation of exchange, 275–76
  free reserve theory, 220–22
  fundamental proposition, 257–58
  income, 307–11
  indicators, 215–17
  inference problem, 492
  interest rates, 222–24, 298–303
  money income, 270–80
  strategy, 209–32
  See also specific headings
Monetary shocks, 345–64
  business cycles and, 378–81
  dynamic interpretation, 348–52
  nominal income, 346–54
  output and prices, 354–64
  spending and, 352–53
  supply-side monetary model, 385–87

Money
  barter economy contrasted, 3–5
  capital formation and, 11–12
  cyclical behavior of, 374–78
  definition, 25–27, 35–39
    a priori definition, 35–37
    empirical definition, 37–39
  demand for. *See* Money demand
  economic instability and, 12–21
  functions, 3–12
  income velocity of, 381–85
  indirect exchange, 5–6
  medium of exchange, 5–6, 8, 36
  quantity theory of. *See* Quantity
      theory of money
  shock absorber function, 346–48
  standard for deferred payment,
      10–11
  standard of value, 7–8
  store of value, 8–9
  time deposits and, 138–40
  unit of account, 7–8
Money demand, 262–70
  aggregate excess demand, 16–17
  asset demand, 266–69
  effective money demand, 15
  excess demand, 16–17, 332
  general overproduction and, 16
  liquidity preference, 268, 372
  precautionary demand, 267–68
  speculative demand, 267, 268
  tax changes and, 331–34
  transactions motive, 263, 264–66
Money market certificates, 88
Money markets
  capital markets and money
      markets, 62–63
  conditions, 213
  federal funds market, 63
Money supply
  changes in, 1960–1978, 144–46
  currency behavior of public and,
      136–38
  currency component of, 27–31
  high-powered money, 129
  model of, 129–44
  monetary base, 129–32
  money multipliers, 138, 139–40,
      141
  shifts in, 142–44
Morris, Frank E., 204n
Mortgage

  bonds, 59
  loans, 55–56
  shared appreciation mortgage, 61
  variable interest rate, 61
Mote, Larry, 119n
Mudd, Douglas R., 197n
Mullineaux, Donald J., 419n
Mutual savings banks, 53–54

Nadler, Paul S., 112n
National bank notes, 28
National Banking Act of 1863, 76,
    81, 114
National Banking Act of 1864, 28,
    114
National Credit Union Central
    Liquid Facility, 82, 195
National Tax Limitation Committee,
    503
Nixon administration, 169, 495, 497,
    499
Nonmonetary economy. *See* Barter
    economy
Nordhaus, Wlliam, 499
Notes, 59
NOW (Negotiable order of
    withdrawal) accounts, 9n, 52,
    78

O'Bannon, Helen, 58n
Of Money (Hume), 346
Okun, Arthur, 496
OPEC, 17, 370, 380, 399, 405–06
Open market operations, 183–87
  discount rates, 190–92
  effects on money and credit
      markets, 183–84
  manager's operating techniques,
      185–86
  Treasury financing and, 186–87
Operation Twist, 185–86

Partee, Charles, 497
"Pass-through" securities, 56
Patman, Wright, 157
Penn Central Railroad, 189
Pension funds, 54–55
Perry, George, 491
Phelps, Edmund, 430
Philadelphia National Bank, 122
Phillips, A.W., 429

Phillips curve, 429, 430, 435, 436–45
  adaptive expectations and, 440–41,
    443–45
  rational expectations and, 441–45
  short-run Phillips curve, 437–40
Pigou, A.C., 262
Poole, William, 498n
Preferred stock, 62
Price expectations effect, 300–03
Prices
  consumer price index, 259
  fixprice markets, 356–59
  flexprice markets, 356
  lags in inflationary expectations,
    359–64
  monetary shocks and, 354–64
  quantity theory of money, 259–62
Promissory notes, 59
Proxmire, Senator William, 57
Purchasing power loan, 60
Purchasing power parity theory,
    466–75
  empirical tests, 471–75
  outline, 467–69
  propositions, 467
  short-run derivation of exchange
    rates, 469–71

Quantity theory of money, 257–62
  elementary theory of price levels,
    259–62
  nominal versus real money
    balances, 258–59

Rasche, R., 484n, 485, 488, 489,
    490–91
Reagan administration, 335, 483,
    499, 503
Rechter, Denis M., 82n
Reekers, G.M., 9n
Reluctance theory, 190, 196
Regulation Q., 88, 92, 123, 155, 189,
    198, 201–05, 331n
Repurchase agreements, 34, 90, 91,
    171, 172, 185
Reservation wage, 438
Reserve aggregates, 213

Reserves, 80–86
  commercial banks, 80–82
  deposit-reserve ratio, 132–36
  excess reserves, 143
  FRS member banks, 173–77,
    194–97
  lagged reserve requirements, 195,
    196
  mechanics, 195–96
  Monetary Control Act of 1980, 81,
    131n, 141, 142, 173n, 194–95
  policy instrument, 196–97
Resler, David H., 141
Reuss, Henry, 157
Ricardo, David, 14, 370
Riefler, Winfield W., 190
Robertson, D.H., 262, 489n7
Roos, Lawrence K., 226–228, 226n
Roper, Don, 505n
Rose, Sanford, 112n
Rural Electrification Administration,
    56

Sargent, Thomas, 441
Savings and loan associations, 51–53
Savings deposits, 37, 87–89
Say, J.B., 14
Say's Law of Markets, 14–16, 245,
    251–52, 279, 329, 370
Say's Principle, 16–17, 18, 241–52,
    278–79, 307, 310, 331, 353
  aggregate level, 243–45
  bond market and, 288–91
  income equilibrium, 249–52
  individual transaction level, 241–43
Schacht, Hjalmer, 493, 494
Schadrack, Frederick C., 38
Schwartz, Anna J., 12, 36–37, 38n,
    146n, 374–76, 379–80, 381,
    383, 483
Securities
  common stock, 61–62
  interest rates and, 64, 67
  margin requirements, 198
  "pass-through" securities, 56
Securities and Exchange Act of 1934,
    198
Serial bonds, 59

Seymours, Jan P., 330n
"Shared appreciation" mortgage, 61
Shearer, Ronald, 58n
Sinking funds, 59
Small Business Administration, 56
Smith, Warren, 193, 220
Sowell, Thomas, 14n
Special Credit Restraint Program,
    199
Special Drawing Rights, 167, 169–70
Sprague, O.M.W., 219
Stabilization policies, 483–506
    costs and benefits, 490–91
    credibility effect, 491–95
    democracy and, 497–506
    empirical evidence, 484–93
    fiscal-monetary policy multiplier,
        484–85
    forecasting error, 486–87
    incomes policy, 495–97
    rules versus activism, 487–90
Stagflation, 429–47. *See also* Inflation;
    Unemployment
Stein, Jerome, 491
Stroup, Richard, 404n
Student Loan Mortgage Association,
    56
Supply and demand, 237–39
    bond market, 289–91
        private demand, 291–93
    excess demand, 239
    excess supply, 239
    law of demand, 238
    market equilibrium and, 239–41
    planned behavior, 238
    Say's law, 14–16
    schedules, 238
Supply-side economics
    business cycles, 370–71
    monetary model, 385–87

Taggart, Robert, 204n
Tatom, John A., 141n

Taxes
    income and tax changes, 329–31
    inflation, 411–17
    money economy and tax changes,
        331–34
    politics and, 403
Tennessee Valley Authority, 56
Timberlake, Richard H., Jr., 38
Time deposits, 87–89, 111
    money supply theory and, 138–40
Tucker, James, 11n

Unemployment
    cyclical unemployment, 434–35
    frictional unemployment, 432
    inflation and, 402. *See also*
        Stagflation.
    natural unemployment rate
        hypothesis, 430–35
    Phillips curve. *See* Phillips curve
    structural unemployment. 432–34

Vanderford, D. Evans, 385–87
Variable interest rate loan, 60–61
Variable interest rate mortgage, 61
Velocity of money, 381–85
Veterans Administration, 56
Volcker, Paul, 228, 495

Wage insurance plan, 496
Waldman, Alan, 409n
Wallich, H., 496
Wallich–Weintraub tax-based income
    plan, 496
Weber, Warren, 11n
Weidenbaum, Murray, 331 n5, 504
Weintraub, S., 496
Willis, H. Parker, 218, 219
Woglom, Geoffrey, 204n

Yeager, Leland, B., 257n

A 1
B 2
C 3
D 4
E 5
F 6
G 7
H 8